Canadian Working-Class History

Canadian Working-Class History

Selected Readings

Third Edition

Edited by
Laurel Sefton MacDowell
and Ian Radforth

Canadian Scholars' Press
Toronto

Canadian Working-Class History: Selected Readings, 3rd Edition
edited by Laurel Sefton MacDowell and Ian Radforth

First published in 2006 by
Canadian Scholars' Press Inc.
180 Bloor Street West, Suite 801
Toronto, Ontario
M5S 2V6

www.cspi.org

Canadian Scholars' Press gratefully acknowledges financial support for our publishing activities from the Government of Canada through the Book Publishing Industry Development Program (BPIDP).

Library and Archives Canada Cataloguing in Publication

Canadian working class history / edited by Laurel Sefton MacDowell and Ian Radforth. -- 3rd ed.

Includes bibliographical references.
ISBN 1-55130-298-5

1. Working class--Canada--History. 2. Labor movement--Canada--History. 3. Labor unions--Canada--History. I. MacDowell, Laurel Sefton, 1947- II. Radforth, Ian Walter, 1952-

HD8104.C36 2006 305.5'62'0971 C2006-900059-X

Cover design by Susan Thomas/Digital Zone
Cover photo: "Women Doing War in Marelco Factory (ca. 1940)." Reprinted by permission of the Archives of Ontario; "Dilapidated Wall" by Richard Mallison
Page design and layout: Brad Horning

06 07 08 09 10 5 4 3 2 1

Printed and bound in Canada by Marquis Book Printing Inc.

Canada

Table of Contents

PART II
THE INDUSTRIAL AGE (1890–1939)

PART III
WARTIME AND POST-WAR PROSPERITY (1939–74)

Copyright Acknowledgements

Chapter 1 by Rusty Bitterman, "Farm Households and Wage Labour in the Northeastern Maritimes in the Early Nineteenth Century," *Labour/Le Travail* 31 (Spring 1993): 13–45. Reprinted by permission of *Labour/Le Travail*.

Chapter 2 by Ruth Bleasdale, "Class Conflict on the Canals of Upper Canada in the 1840s," *Labour/Le Travail* 7 (Spring 1981): 9–39. Reprinted by permission of *Labour/Le Travail*.

Chapter 3 by Gregory S. Kealey, "'The Honest Workingman' and Workers' Control: The Experience of Toronto Skilled Workers, 1860–92" from *Labour/Le Travail* 1 (1976): 32–68. Reprinted by permission of *Labour/Le Travail*.

Chapter 4 by Lynne Marks, "The Knights of Labor and the Salvation Army: Religion and Working-Class Culture in Ontario, 1882–90," from *Labour/Le Travail* 28 (Fall 1991): 89–127. Reprinted by permission of *Labour/Le Travail*.

Chapter 5 by Peter DeLottinville, "Joe Beef of Montreal: Working-Class Culture and the Tavern, 1869–89," from *Labour/Le Travail* 8, 9 (Autumn/Spring 1981/82): 9–40. Reprinted by permission of *Labour/Le Travail*.

Chapter 6 by John Lutz, "After the Fur Trade: The Aboriginal Labouring Class of British Columbia, 1849–90," from *Journal of the Canadian Historical Association* 3 (1992). Reprinted by permission of the Canadian Historical Association.

Chapter 7 by Craig Heron and Steve Penfold, "The Craftsmen's Spectacle: Labour Day Parades in Canada, The Early Years," from *Histoire Sociale/Social History* 29 (1996): 357–89. Reprinted by permission of Les Publications Histoire Sociale — Social History, Inc.

Chapter 8 by Graham S. Lowe, "Class, Job, and Gender in the Canadian Office," from *Labour/Le Travail*leur 10 (Autumn 1982): 11–37. Reprinted by permission of *Labour/Le Travail*.

Chapter 9 by Gillian Creese, "Exclusion or Solidarity? Vancouver Workers Confront the 'Oriental Problem,'" from *BC Studies* 80 (1988): 24–51.Reprinted by permission of *BC Studies*, University of British Columbia.

Chapter 10 by Donald Avery, "The Radical Alien and the Winnipeg General Strike of 1919" from *The West and the Nation: Essays in Honour of W. L. Morton,* Carl Berger and Ramsay Cook, eds. (Toronto: McClelland and Stewart, 1976): 209–31. Reprinted by permission of McClelland & Stewart.

Chapter 11 by H.M. Grant, "Solving the Labour Problem at Imperial Oil: Welfare Capitalism in the Canadian Petroleum Industry, 1919–29," from *Labour/Le Travail* 41 (Spring 1998) 69–95. Reprinted by permission of *Labour/Le Travail*.

Chapter 12 by Bonita Bray, "Against All Odds: The Progressive Arts Club's Production of *Waiting for Lefty*" from *Journal of Canadian Studies* 25:3 (Fall 1990): 106–122. Reprinted by permission of *Journal of Canadian Studies*.

Chapter 13 by Laurel Sefton MacDowell, "The Formation of the Canadian Industrial Relations System during World War II" from *Labour/Le Travail* 3 (1978): 175–96. Reprinted by permission of *Labour/Le Travail*.

Chapter 14 by Ann Porter, "Women and Income Security in the Post-War Period: The Case of Unemployment Insurance, 1945–62" from *Labour/Le Travail* 31 (Spring 1993): 111–44. Reprinted by permission of *Labour/Le Travail*.

Chapter 15 by Mercedes Steedman, "The Red Petticoat Brigade: Mine Mill Women's Auxiliaries and the 'Threat from Within,' 1940s–1970s" from *Whose National Security?: Canadian State Surveillance and the Creation of Enemies,* Gary Kinsman, Deter K. Buse, and Mercedes Steedman, eds., (Toronto: Between the Lines, 2000): 55–71. Reprinted by permission of Between the Lines.

Chapter 16 by Ross Lambertson, "The Dresden Story: Racism, Human Rights, and the Jewish Labour Committee of Canada" from *Labour/Le Travail* 47 (2001): 43–82. Reprinted by permission of *Labour/Le Travail*.

Chapter 17 by Franca Iacovetta, "Defending Honour, Demanding Respect: Manly Discourse and Gendered Practice in Two Construction Strikes, Toronto, 1960–61" from *Gendered Pasts: Historical Essays in Femininity and Masculinity in Canada,* Kathryn McPherson, Cecilia Morgan, and Nancy M. Forestell, eds., (Toronto: Oxford University Press, 1999): 199–222. Reprinted by permission of Oxford University Press.

Chapter 18 by Ralph Peter Güntzel, "The Confédération des syndicats nationaux (CSN), the Idea of Independence, and the Sovereigntist Movement, 1960–80" from *Labour/Le Travail* 31 (Spring 1993): 145–72. Reprinted by permission of *Labour/Le Travail*.

Chapter 19 by Rebecca Priegert Coulter, "Alberta Nurses and the 'Illegal' Strike of 1988," from *Women Challenging Unions: Feminism, Democracy and Militancy*, Linda Briskin and Patricia McDermott, eds., (Toronto: University of Toronto Press, 1993): 44–61. Reprinted by permission of University of Toronto Press.

Chapter 20 by Laurel Sefton MacDowell, "Greening the Workplace: Unions and the Environment" from *Sustainability the Challenge: People, Power, and the Environment* (Montreal: Black Rose Books, 1998): 167–76. Reprinted by permission of Black Rose Books.

Chapter 21 by Ester Reiter, "Life in a Fast-Food Factory" from *On the Job: Confronting the Labour Process in Canada* (Kingston and Montreal: McGill-Queen's University Press, 1986): 309–26. Reprinted by permission of McGill-Queen's University Press.

Chapter 22 by Sam Gindon, "Globalization, Nationalism, and Internationalism" from *The CAW: Birth and Transformation of a Union* (Toronto: Lorimer, 1995): 199–227. Reprinted by permission of James Lorimer & Company, Ltd.

Tables and Figures

Table 4.1: "Sex of Salvation Army Converts in Selected Corps, 1887–1900" from Corps Records, Salvation Army Archives, Toronto. Reprinted by permission of the Salvation Army Archives, Canada and Bermuda Territory.

Table 4.2: "Occupations of Salvation Army Converts in Selected Corps, 1887–1900" from Corps Records, Salvation Army Archives, Toronto. Reprinted by permission of the Salvation Army Archives, Canada and Bermuda Territory.

Table 4.3: "Occupations of Ontario Salvation Army Officers Upon Becoming Officers, By Sex 1882–1890" from Corps Records, Salvation Army Archives, Toronto. Reprinted by permission of the Salvation Army Archives, Canada and Bermuda Territory.

Table 4.4: "Selected Occupations of Male Officers Who Had Been Skilled Workers/Artisans" from Corps Records, Salvation Army Archives, Toronto. Reprinted by permission of the Salvation Army Archives, Canada and Bermuda Territory.

Table 8.1: D.B.S. Census Branch; N.M. Meltz, "Growth of the Clerical Labour Force, Canada, 1891–1971" from *Occupational Trends in Canada, 1891–1931* (Ottawa 1939), Table 5; *Manpower in Canada, 1931-1961* (Ottawa 1969); and 1971 Census of Canada, vol. 3, part 2, table 2. Reprinted by permission of Statistics Canada.

Table 8.7: "Average Annual Salary Ranges for Various Head Office Clerical Jobs, Major Canadian and American Insurance Companies, 1930" from "Clerical Salaries in the Life Insurance Business," Proceedings of the 1932 Annual Conference of the Life Office Management Association, September 1932 (Fort Wayne, IN: LOMA, 1932), 276. Reprinted by permission of Life Office Management Association.

Table 8.8: "Annual Family Budget in 60 Canadian Cities, 1900–31," from *Canada Year Book, 1921* (Ottawa: Statistics Canada, 1922), 649; *Canada Year Book, 1932* (Ottawa: Statistics Canada, 1932), 692. Reprinted by permission of Statistics Canada.

Table 11.1: "Share of Market Supplied by Imperial Oil's Refineries, 1900–1929" from *The Petroleum Industry and Canadian Economic Development: An Economic History, 1900-1960*; Ph.D. Thesis, 1987. Reprinted by permission of University of Toronto.

Table 11.2: "Output per Worker, Canadian Petroleum Refineries, 1900–1929" from *The Petroleum Industry and Canadian Economic Development: An Economic History, 1900-1960*; Ph.D. Thesis, 1987. Reprinted by permission of University of Toronto.

Table 11.3: "Imperial Oil Company, Ltd. Estimated Cost of Safety and Benefits Plans, 1920–1929" from *Imperial Oil Review*, 14 (4). Reprinted by permission of Imperial Oil Company, Ltd.

Table 11.4: "Imperial Oil Company, Ltd. Manufacturing and Marketing Earnings, 1900–1939 ($1,000)" from *The History of the Imperial Oil Company*, Ltd., Ch. VIII, Sect. I, 73. Reprinted by permission of Imperial Oil Archives.

Ch. 16, Cartoon 1: "The Real Target." from *Canadian Labour Reports*. Reprinted by permission of Canadian Jewish Archives.

Ch. 16, Cartoon 2: "Discrimination Costs YOU Money" from *Canadian Labour Reports*. Reprinted by permission of National Archives (CLC Papers).

Ch. 16, Cartoon 3: "Labor...Intolerance" from *Canadian Labour Reports*. Reprinted by permission of Canadian Jewish Archives.

Ch. 16, Cartoon 4: "Don't Be a Pushover!" from *Canadian Labour Reports*. Reprinted by permission of Canadian Jewish Archives.

Preface to the Third Edition

In recent years, many students have displayed great interest in the history of Canada's working people in courses in Canadian labour history. Scholars have turned as never before to research and to probe the history of Canada's working class. Using a host of different approaches, historians, sociologists, and political scientists have studied workers on and off the job, in paid and unpaid work, in domestic and community life, in unions and in political movements. This collection provides a sample of the best in this recent scholarship.

The wide range of topics covered by the articles that follow indicates the impressive number of issues and developments currently capturing the attention of scholars. Specific unions or left political parties remain of central interest, as does the analysis of dramatic moments of labour strife. Articles in this collection discuss, for instance, the emergence of modern industrial unions, the Winnipeg General Strike, and aspects of legislation affecting workers. Some scholars have turned to other themes related to working life. The culture of the working-class tavern and agitprop theatre, and workers' attitude to religion in Canada are topics taken up by authors in our selection. State policies with regard to women workers are analyzed, and women's work is examined in various settings: on the farm, in factory and office, and within the union movement. Scholars are carefully reconstructing the experiences of particular ethnic and racial groups, as is evident here in the articles on Irish canal builders, Asian workers in Vancouver, and Italian immigrant and Aboriginal workers. In each case, the authors weave the factors of race, class, and gender into working-class history and explore their interconnections.

Not only are the topics diverse, but so too are the approaches and methods used by labour scholars active in Canada today. The authors represented in this collection draw on international intellectual currents and a range of political traditions which include liberal, social democratic, and Marxist. Some are committed to an "engaged scholarship" that seeks to radicalize; others follow a more detached, scholarly analytical style. The sources used include radical newspapers, oral interviews, diaries, and government documents. The form of presentation ranges from the analytical to the gripping narrative. All the authors, however, write effectively and make their arguments clearly and forcefully.

We hope that readers will find these studies interesting and intellectually challenging. They cover a long period of time—from the pre-industrial early nineteenth century to the 1990s—and diverse local, regional, and national developments. For students in courses, we have included in this edition a brief introduction to each section, which explains how the individual articles fit in with larger themes in each period, and a brief bibliography of recent studies. We are confident that students who read these articles will gain a better understanding of the history of Canada's working people in all its variations and complexities.

Laurel Sefton MacDowell
Ian Radforth

A Note from the Publisher

Thank you for selecting this third edition of *Canadian Working-Class History: Selected Readings* edited by Laurel Sefton MacDowell and Ian Radforth. The editors and publisher have devoted considerable time and careful development (including meticulous peer reviews) to this book. We appreciate your recognition of this effort and accomplishment.

Teaching Features Added to the Third Edition

This volume distinguishes itself on the market in many ways. One key feature is the book's well-written and comprehensive part openers, which make the readings more accessible to undergraduate students. These section openers provide both clear presentations of the themes of the collection, as well as cohesion to the different viewpoints.

The general editors have also added useful pedagogical material at the end of each section, including critical-thinking questions and annotated further readings.

PART I

The Pre-Industrial and Early Industrial Eras (1830–1890)

Immigrants from Europe began to arrive in Canada during the seventeenth and eighteenth centuries, when France and Britain colonized parts of North America; in the process these immigrants confronted and displaced many of the original inhabitants. The diverse native peoples had their own well-established ways of labouring to ensure survival, but, for many of them, economic life was fundamentally and permanently altered by the arrival of the Europeans. Settlers from France and Britain quickened the pace of change: they put new pressures on the environment by farming on a much wider scale than First Nations communities, and by intensifying the exploitation of natural resources and the trading opportunities of each region. The toil of working people—both indigenous inhabitants and newcomers, who included a few hundred African slaves—was crucial to the transformation of the land and its cultures.

By the beginning of the nineteenth century, agriculture lay at the heart of colonizing endeavours. In the white-settler colonies of Canada's Maritime region (Nova Scotia, New Brunswick, and Prince Edward Island), farming was essential to the survival of most of the inhabitants. In chapter 1, Rusty Bittermann examines the strategies of farming folk who lived in the Maritime colonies during the early nineteenth century. As in other agricultural districts throughout Canada at that time, the inhabitants turned to wage-earning opportunities in order to supplement their incomes, pay down debts, and bring the elusive dream of independence a little closer. This held true as much for free blacks as for whites. Settlers had to be flexible, taking paid jobs when available on nearby farms, seeking work further afield (including even outside the region), and tackling additional tasks at home when other family members were away. Occupational pluralism characterized the lives of many working people, who developed extensive information networks that led them to paid employment in many different settings.

In addition to working in the open air on farms, men had access to a range of outside occupations in early Canada. In Newfoundland and other coastal areas, fishing drew boys and men to the sea, while work opportunities for women in the fisheries were on shore, drying the cod. In the fur trade—which propelled the westward expansion of Canada—Native women and men trapped the animals, prepared the pelts, and traded them, while men of French-Canadian, British, and Métis background found employment in transporting the cargoes of furs and provisioning those who worked in the trade. In the timber industry, which thrived in New Brunswick and the Ottawa Valley especially, men worked for wages felling trees, preparing the wood for transport, and rafting it downstream to market and export centres. Construction work, too, provided men with outside jobs.

On the giant canal-building projects of the 1840s in central Canada, contractors hired thousands of strong-backed navvies. Many of these were Irish immigrants with experience in heavy construction gained from building canals in the United States. In chapter 2, Ruth Bleasdale describes the brutal conditions under which they worked, and the raw injustices that, under the right circumstances, sparked riots and strikes. She shows how Irish cultural traditions shaped the form of labour protest among the canal workers. Insofar as these workers organized, they made ephemeral alliances that never resulted in the formation of lasting labour organizations.

Enduring labour unions emerged in nineteenth-century Canada among an altogether different stratum of the working class: the highly skilled workmen who laboured for wages in workshops, on building sites, and in mining. When the Canadian economy began to industrialize in the second half of the nineteenth century, many craftsmen found that their skills were much in demand. In such circumstances, the craftsmen succeeded in gaining or retaining considerable control over their jobs and terms of employment. In Chapter 3, Gregory Kealey examines three groups of skilled male workers who struggled in different ways with the challenges that Toronto's industrial revolution posed for them. While certain groups of craftsmen succeeded much better than others in protecting themselves and advancing their interests, in each case that Kealey studies, the craftsmen used their trade unions to make a stand. From their struggles, skilled workers gained knowledge and forged links that laid the basis for the labour movement.

Nineteenth-century Canada was a patriarchal society in which women lacked access to most skilled jobs and thus to the higher pay, better security, and craft-union culture that were part and parcel of such jobs. Paid work for women was typically an activity confined to the life stage that preceded marriage. (Widowhood or spinsterhood often required women to break with the norm, however.) Most wage-earning women in nineteenth-century Canada worked as live-in domestic servants, cleaning and cooking for strangers at meagre rates of pay and in lonely, isolating situations. Young women also took jobs in the manufacturing sector of the economy, notably in the garment industry and in textile mills, where employers believed nimble fingers were an asset. After a day of drudgery, young women sought diversions from toil. In chapter 4, Lynne Marks analyzes two social institutions that attracted wage-earning women as well as men in late nineteenth-century Ontario: the Knights of Labor, a form of early labour unionism, and the Salvation Army, which at the time was a Christian revivalist movement. Marks explores the ways in which religious values and rhetoric, which were so central to Victorian Ontario's dominant culture, shaped how workers saw their own place in society and how they viewed and criticized the wider society.

In chapter 5, Peter Delottinville turns to another institution of importance to many working-class people in the late nineteenth century: the tavern. He presents a lively case study of one popular watering hole in Montreal, Canada's largest city at the time. Located on the waterfront, Joe Beef's Tavern provided alcohol along with a range of social services to its male clientele of sailors, casually employed dock workers, and petty thieves. The antics of its irrepressible owner, Charles McKiernan, captivated journalists, whose stories drew the moral indignation of respectable, middle-class Montrealers. DeLottinville demonstrates how Joe Beef's Tavern nevertheless defended and protected the working-class interests and values of its neighbourhood.

Canada expanded "from sea to sea" when British Columbia entered Confederation in 1871. As John Lutz shows in chapter 6, Aboriginal people, who made up the majority of B.C.'s population in the Confederation era, sought opportunities in the new, industrial-capitalist enterprises. As wage labourers, Aboriginal men and women contributed greatly to the development of the province's industries: agriculture, fishing, lumbering, mining, and trapping. Native people played a dynamic role in creating the capitalist economy of the region and, for a time, they succeeded in using the new economy for their own cultural purposes.

Chapter 1

Farm Households and Wage Labour in the Northeastern Maritimes in the Early Nineteenth Century

Rusty Bittermann

One of the most enduring mythologies of rural life in the temperate regions of North America has centred on the freedom resulting from easy access to land. In the New World, unlike the Old—the story goes—land was plentiful, free from the encumbrances of a feudal past; and common folk might gain unimpeded access to its abundance and carve an independent niche for themselves. In the eighteenth and nineteenth centuries, this mythology was fostered by the effusions of travel accounts and emigrant manuals as well as by the writings of immigrants themselves. Since then it has been broadly sustained in North American historiography.

In keeping with the larger trend, the myth of the independent yeoman has held a prominent place in Maritime literature. It can be found in the works of such Gaelic bards as Allan the Ridge of Mabou, himself one of the many immigrants who arrived in the region from Scotland early in the nineteenth century. In the New World, he lyricized, "free land" gave rise to "riches and herds of cattle" for common folk: "Now that you have come across the sea/to this fair land,/you will want for nothing the rest of your life;/everything prospers for us."[1] It figures in Joseph Howe's "Western Rambles." With "a wife and an axe," Howe maintained, an industrious man might carve out a handsome competence and become "truly rich and independent."[2] Thomas McCulloch's Mephibosheth Stepsure, too, sustains the contention that in the Nova Scotian countryside a natural abundance ensured that those with frugal and industrious habits would be rewarded with economic security and independence.[3] The theme of yeomanly independence emerges as well in the writings of these men's descendants: "Every man in Washabuckt," wrote Neil MacNeil recalling his experiences in a turn-of-the-century Cape Breton rural community, "was his own boss, for he got his livelihood from nature and did not have to work for any other man or thank any one but God for it."[4] And so it is still told to younger generations by older folk in Cape Breton: there was a time before the dependence of the contemporary era when those willing to work might combine their labour with an abundant land to derive a livelihood and secure independence for themselves. In contemporary regional historiography it re-emerges in the works of those who emphasize the insularity and self-sufficiency of rural households in the early nineteenth century. We also see it in the works of those who conceptualize the history of the countryside during subsequent decades in terms of the loss of an earlier independence rooted in the direct fulfilment of needs through access to the land.[5]

That the image of the independent yeoman was to a certain degree a reflection of a reality experienced by some rural residents in the Maritimes is indisputable. The opportunities for acquiring an independent rural livelihood were relatively greater in British North America than they were in the Old World. Many transformed these possibilities into reality, and achieved a "propertied independence."[6] Those who enjoyed such circumstances, however, were but in reality one component of a larger farming population. And many who came to enjoy a modicum of yeomanly independence only experienced this condition for a fraction of their lives. Like any powerful and pervasive mythology, the image of the independent yeoman is partly rooted in fact. Problems arise, though, when a fragment of the rural experience becomes a characterization of the whole. It is not my intention here to consider how this mythology developed, or to unravel the various strands of peasant dream, liberal ideology, and social critique that have sustained it. Rather, I want to examine what it has obscured, indeed, what it still tends to deny: the importance of wage labour to farmfolk in the northeastern Maritimes in the first half of the nineteenth century.[7] The survey which follows underlines the significance of wages to the farm population and highlights the profile of farm dwellers within the larger labour force.

Much of the rural population of the Maritimes began farm-making in the New World by spending part of their time as employees. In his study of rural life in Ontario, Robert Leslie Jones suggested a three-tier typology of new agricultural settlers: those with the capital (or credit) to hire others to speed construction and land clearing, those with the means to support themselves during the start-up period of farm-making, and, lastly, those who found it necessary to engage in off-farm work in order to sustain themselves while farm-making.[8] Given what we know of the economic circumstances of many of those who settled in the northeastern Maritimes in the late eighteenth and early nineteenth century, it is clear that thousands in Atlantic Canada fell in the latter category.[9] Rev. George Patterson's description of the adaptive strategies employed by the passengers who arrived on the *Hector* reflects the difficulties and possibilities available to other emigrants who came to the region under similar circumstances. Initially lacking the means to establish themselves on the land, Patterson noted, they spread out to places distant from Pictou where they could find work: "Not only men, but mothers of families, hired out, and their children, male and female, they bound out for service, till they should come of age."[10] As John Cambridge, a Prince Edward Island landlord, observed in the first years of the nineteenth century, those who arrived with little or no capital "generally work for others till they have acquired a little stock" and in the years that follow they "get assistance by working for the neighbouring farmers, till they have brought their own farms gradually forward."[11]

A good account of the settlement process in Pictou County in the early nineteenth century is provided by Lord Selkirk. Describing the farm-making labours of a household from Perthshire, he noted that the man of the house was "obliged to work for hire" to feed his family and sustain the credit necessary for purchasing the articles needed for capitalizing his farm. This particular household had the advantage of being settled on good land adjacent to West River and its occupants had the potential, one would imagine, of escaping from the necessity of wage dependence, but in the early years of establishment, Selkirk estimated that the Perthshire man spent "full half his time employed at wages off the farm."[12]

The ledger book of Cape Breton merchant Lawrence Kavanaugh provides insights into the process as well. In 1818, Kavanaugh recorded the influx of a number of settlers from Prince Edward Island who took up lands along the eastern shoreline of the Bras d'Or Lakes. Several opened accounts in St. Peters with Kavanaugh shortly after their arrival. James Corbit began his dealings with Kavanaugh by depositing £5 in cash and selling him a saddle for £2 1/2.[13] In return Kavanaugh provided Corbit with provisions and supplies—flour, meal, codfish, tea, vinegar, rum, tobacco, a pipe, salt, cod line, shoes, and calico—as well as the financing necessary to buy out a previous occupant of the lot he had occupied. Corbit's account with Kavanaugh was a relatively modest £33 (provisions plus interest) during the next six years, suggesting—particularly given the quantities of goods and the absence of building materials and tools on the account—that he was dealing with others as well to obtain his household supplies. To meet these particular debts, Corbit worked for Kavanaugh, 2 1/2 days in 1819, 33 days repairing and building a boat in 1821, 1 day sawing planks in 1822, 24 days sawing the following year, and half a day sawing in 1824. A credit to his account by a man named McAdam for 29 shillings in 1820 probably represents yet another 12 days' work performed in this case for McAdam. The survival strategies of many countryfolk, as the landlord John Hill noted in the case of Prince Edward Island, commonly included temporary work for anyone who might give them "an order on the shopkeepers for cloathing and tools."[14] As well, Corbit sold Kavanaugh a couple of chickens in 1820, an ox and a small amount of fresh mackerel and chickens in 1823, and 6 shillings' worth of butter in 1824, leaving him still in debt to the St. Peters merchant for £8 at the end of the year. Lacking knowledge of Corbit's dealings with others, it is impossible to gauge how much off-farm work in which he in fact engaged during these years, or to calculate his progress in farm-making (though the nature and scale of farm produce suggest a rudimentary, perhaps a single-cow, holding). However, the evidence from Corbit's account, as well as from the other new arrivals from Prince Edward Island who appear on Kavanaugh's books, reinforce the observations made by Cambridge, Selkirk, Hill, and Patterson in regard to the importance of wage work to new settlers in the early stages of farm-making.

How long might immigrants—such as those appearing in Kavanaugh's ledgers, or observed by Selkirk and Cambridge—engage in wage work before they could sustain themselves and their households with the returns of their farms? The answer would vary, of course, depending upon their circumstances at the time of arrival, the natural resources of their farm properties, the annual returns that could be made from wage work, and the level of their commitment to acquire a self-sustaining operation. Peter Russell's calculation of an average clearing rate in Upper Canada during the early nineteenth century of 1.5 acres per year per adult male probably is a reasonable estimate for the Maritimes as well.[15] At such a rate, a minimal 25 acres of fields would, when additional labour could not be hired, typically be realized only after a decade of work. Often, it would seem, this took longer. The itinerant shoemaker and missionary, Walter Johnstone, estimated that on average, the first generation of settlers on Prince Edward Island would, "not clear more than 20 or 30 acres all their life."[16] Another observer noted that there were "many who have been 20 years in the colony" and "have no more than 5 acres cleared."[17] To the cost of sustaining a household while preparing the land base necessary for household subsistence were added the costs of stocking and equipping such a farm. S.S. Hill, the son of John Hill, one of Prince Edward Island's largest landlords, advised would-be immigrants to expect costs of roughly £200 for the livestock, tools, and supplies necessary for establishing a farm of 30 cleared acres.[18] Though it was not in his interest to exaggerate the costs of farm-making on the Island, Hill's figure seems high.[19] What is beyond doubt is that with wages typically averaging around two and a half shillings per day, with work sporadic and seasonal, and with the needs of daily subsistence having first claim on income, raising the monies necessary to equip a farm was, typically, the product of years of labour.

The cost of land, of course, had to be factored into the farm-making process as well. On Prince Edward Island, there was little Crown land and most immigrants found it necessary to obtain land from landlords. In the 1820s and 1830s, an unimproved freehold would, typically, cost somewhere from 10 shillings to one pound per acre.[20] By leasing land, a new settler might defer these start-up costs, but in time would incur a rental cost of around £5 per year for 100 acres of land.[21] In Nova Scotia, the costs of acquiring "free" Crown land probably ran around £20 for a typical 200-acre lot.[22] With the termination of a "free" Crown land policy in the late 1820s, these costs increased as lands were sold at public auction with a base price established at 2/3 to 2/6 per acre.[23]

Given the costs of land, stock, and equipment, and the labour required for preparing fields, even when a household managed to acquire good lands—and many in the region did not—years and probably decades elapsed between beginning the tasks of clearing and planting, and arriving at a condition where, as Neil MacNeil phrased it, one did not have to "thank anyone but God" for one's living.[24] We can take as examples the experiences of Corbit and his fellow Prince Edward Islanders newly arrived in Cape Breton whose wage work appears in Kavanaugh's books, the Perthshireman whom Selkirk observed, or those who took passage aboard the *Hector* described by Rev. Patterson, and multiply these by the thousands of emigrants of modest means who took up farms in the northeastern Maritimes in the late eighteenth and early nineteenth century—people who of necessity had to follow similar work strategies for many years. The ongoing process of settlement and farm-making was intimately linked with the maintenance of a vast pool of farm-based labourers in pursuit of work opportunities.

Weather conditions and the presence or absence of crop and animal diseases played a substantial part in expediting the progress of household independence or, alternatively, in dashing hopes of agricultural security. A household which enjoyed a margin of independence in a favourable year could be plunged into debt and dependence in another. The extraordinary frosts of 1816 and the 1830s, and the repeated failure of the potato crops due to blight in the 1840s in particular, forced large numbers of farm households into an increased reliance on purchased foodstuffs. Particularly vulnerable were the newer and poorer farm households with limited inventories of livestock and reliant almost exclusively on the harvest of their potato and grain crops. Such natural disasters swelled the numbers in pursuit of work and expanded the commitments many households found necessary to make to off-farm labour. Employment was needed to pay for provisions and to meet the costs and debts incurred during years of crisis.[25]

For many, the quality of land resources available—particularly when coupled with a poverty that diverted labour and capital away from farm improvements and toward the needs of basic sustenance—precluded ever escaping the necessity of engaging in extensive wage work.[26] As the Crown surveyor in Baddeck, D.B. McNab, noted in 1857, there were "hundreds" of farms in this region of Cape Breton where 10, 20, or 30 years after initial settlement their occupants remained heavily reliant on off-farm employment in order to "eke out the means of a scanty subsistence."[27] In general, he contended, such settlers occupied the difficult hill lands, the backlands, of the Island and tended to be squatters rather than freeholders. The Land Commissioners taking evidence on Prince Edward Island in 1860 heard similar testimony concerning areas of Prince Edward Island, often predominantly occupied by squatters, where few settlers successfully managed to derive the bulk of their livelihood from the soil.[28]

While some households made ends meet by combining wage work with the sale of selected farm "surpluses," often enough exchanging costly foods like butter and meat for cheaper breadstuffs and fish, there were others which appear to have been exclusively, or almost exclusively, reliant on the sale of labour to meet the costs of household goods and food and to procure seed and animal provisions. The ledger books of the North Sydney trader, John Beamish Moore,[29] for instance, reveal a number of backland households whose occupants had nothing but labour to sell during the years of their dealings with him.[30] During the period 1853 to 1860, the members of Angus Link's household paid for their supplies of oatmeal, barley flour, and oats through a combination of Angus's own labour and that of his wife and daughter.[31] So, too, did the Angus McDonald household pay its debts through Angus's own labour and that of his sons and daughter.[32] The debts of the Murdoch Ferguson household as well were repaid entirely by Murdoch's labour and that of a female member of the household.[33] Moore's account book reveals something of the seasonality of the pressures on these backland households as well. Between 1853 and 1861, the accounts of those identified as backlanders in his books reveal recurrent debts for hay, barley flour, and oatmeal needed in April and May to replenish exhausted winter supplies, and seed grain (barley and oats) needed in May and June to permit planting another season's crop. Merchant ledgers reveal only a fragment of these patterns. Wealthier members of rural communities as well often took on the role, and assumed the benefits, of acting as provisioners and sources of credit to poorer households through the months of greatest scarcity. It appears to have been particularly common for those acting as road commissioners to sell provisions on credit during the winter and to retain the road-work returns due to these households the following summer.[34]

Backlanders such as these, though possessing or occupying considerable acreages, were yet compelled by necessity to participate extensively in labour markets near and far in order to make up for the great inadequacies of their farm returns. They were, as the Crown surveyor in Baddeck, D.B. McNab, noted, the New World equivalent of Great Britain's day labourers: they "represent[ed] this class."[35] Quantitative analysis of census data from Middle River in Cape Breton and from Hardwood Hill in Pictou County suggests that in the third quarter of the nineteenth century, somewhere between a quarter and a third of the households in these agricultural districts of northeastern Nova Scotia needed to earn $100 or more in off-farm income in order to secure a minimal livelihood.[36] At the common agricultural wage rate of roughly 80 cents per day, this would be the equivalent of 125 or more working days.[37] Put differently, given an average family food requirement of roughly $200, these farms at best probably derived only half their food needs from their own resources.[38] Data from Middle River confirms as well D.B. McNab's assertion that reliance on off-farm sources of income most often occurred among those who occupied rough hill lands: 84 percent of the households with negative net farm incomes estimated to be greater than $100 in 1860–61 were those of backlanders.[39] Physical constraints necessitated much of the pattern of adaptation that McNab and others described.

Besides new settlers requiring an income during their years of farm establishment and backlanders grappling with chronic resource problems, analysis of the Middle River census returns indicates yet another stream of rural peoples being propelled into participation in the work force in the mid-nineteenth century and beyond. Estimates of the relationship between farm resources and household needs reveal three basic household categories. At one end of the spectrum there were households, primarily those of backlanders, where farm returns were chronically and substantially short of household subsistence needs—households that of necessity had to look for income beyond the farm across the full course of the family life cycle. On the other extreme there was a significant minority of households, the commercial core of the valley's agricultural economy, where farm production was well in excess of household subsistence needs and the returns from farm product sales were sufficient to permit substantial reinvestments in agriculture and in other pursuits. Members of such households had the option of working for themselves with their own resources or working for others. Wedged between these two strata were families whose condition more closely approximated the image of household self-sufficiency permeating so much of the literature on the rural Maritimes—farms on which the value of production roughly matched current needs. Although they possessed sufficient resources to derive a livelihood from the land, it is clear, however, from the census and probate returns that the resources of many of these households were not expanding at a rate sufficient to permit all their offspring to begin life in similar circumstances. Demographic growth was forcing, and would force, many individuals from an emerging generation within these middle strata households into participation in the labour force.[40]

Throughout the early nineteenth century, then, substantial numbers of the members of farm households situated in the northeastern Maritimes—new settlers, backlanders (along with others whose farm resources were chronically insufficient for household needs), and some of the offspring of middle-strata households—necessarily had to maintain a significant and regular involvement in the labour force, despite the fact that they had access to extensive tracts of land. Added to the ranks of these workers of necessity were many who were drawn for one reason or another by the opportunities afforded by off-farm work, people who might move in and out of the workforce at will alternately deriving a living from farm resources or choosing to participate in the labour force.

Those seeking employment might work in many different niches of the regional economy. Some of the Prince Edward Islanders who settled along Cape Breton's Bras d'Or Lakes in the second decade of the nineteenth century found jobs with Lawrence Kavanaugh, the merchant from whom they obtained provisions. John Corbit made ends meet in part by sawing lumber and doing boat-carpentry work for Kavanaugh. During the period 1818 to 1824, others worked for this St. Peters merchant building fences, mowing hay, planting potatoes, looking after livestock, driving cattle that he had purchased, rafting timber, and working in his fishing operations. Daily wages ranged from 1 shilling 4d. to the more common 2 shillings 6d. Some jobs, such as mowing, were arranged by piece work, 5 shillings per acre, while yet other workers were hired on a monthly basis. Women appear sporadically in Kavanaugh's ledger, "knitting" twine at a fixed price per length and doing washing of some sort, again being paid by the piece.

The variety of tasks for which Kavanaugh hired labour, the different rates and means of payment, and the diverse composition of his work force—both in terms of age and gender—help suggest the complexity of the labour market in this period. The different areas of economic activity noted in his ledger—agriculture, the timber trade, vessel construction, the fishery, and general tasks associated with operating a mercantile establishment—capture much of the array of work available to the farm-based labourer of the northeastern Maritimes in the first quarter of the nineteenth century. Timber, ships, fishing, and trade—the listing of occupations recalls T.C. Haliburton's description of the typical Nova Scotian who could be "found superintending the cultivation of a farm and building a vessel at the same time," adding that this worker "is not only able to catch and cure a cargo of fish, but to find his way to the West Indies or the Mediterranean." But we must underline an important distinction between Haliburton's figure and those whose lives are under discussion here.[41] The occupational pluralist figuring in the *Old Judge* is an extension of the independent yeoman of other regional literature; his life is grounded in his control over a material abundance. The goods with which he loads his vessel are the "surplus" remaining from the produce of his farm, and though Haliburton does not address productive relationships, the thrust of this passage is that woods work and shipbuilding, too, are rooted in family labour which is being applied to resources over which this Nova Scotian exercises ownership or control. Certainly there were such people scattered about the Maritime countryside, although as I have argued elsewhere and will argue below, family labour alone did not typically sustain this sort of productivity.[42] I am focusing here, though, on the property-poor farm dweller whose labour sustained the entrepreneurial pluralism of others. The capital barriers which prevented acquiring an independence in agricultural production tended to be similarly limiting in other sectors of the economy. Whereas, for instance, the household with an agricultural abundance might be in a position to send their oxen to the woods and equip a cutting crew, ultimately selling the endproduct in the timber market, the participation of the capital-poor in this trade was more likely to be for the wages gained from handling an ax.[43]

Although other facets of the regional economy probably rivaled it in terms of the amount of wage employment offered, during the first half of the nineteenth century, agriculture may well have been the pre-eminent type of wage work when measured in terms of sheer numbers of participants, even if the extreme seasonality of demand meant that few worked as farm hands for extensive periods. The labour requirements of agriculture in the Maritimes in the era before the mechanization of harvesting and planting were such that not only big farms with scores of acres in hay and crops but even many relatively small operations found it necessary to hire seasonal help. Harvesting operations in particular required the assistance of many hands. A small operation might hire an extra worker or two for a few days or weeks to assist with getting in the crops, while a larger operation might add many daily labourers to its more permanent workforce. Timber operators also sometimes employed large crews to gather hay for their woods operations.[44]

Peter MacNutt, for instance, a merchant and farmer living near Princetown, Prince Edward Island, harvested his crops in summer and autumn 1837 with the aid of his "own men"—household members and long-term employees—augmented by the daily labour of 30 workers drawn from neighbouring farms. During that autumn, some worked for only a day, while others worked for MacNutt for 10 or 11 days, though never at a continuous stretch. The patterns point to the varied nature of MacNutt's labour needs even during the harvest. There were some tasks that required few or no additional hands and others for which he would hire nine additional workers on a daily basis to complement household members and servants. The composition of his crews varied in accordance with the farm calendar and the progress of harvesting operations. For certain tasks, such as raking hay, bundling grain, and digging potatoes, MacNutt employed the cheaper labour of women, girls, and boys. A few men, for instance, might start mowing at the beginning of the week and be joined by a growing and more heterogeneous workforce later in the week as the mowed hay began to dry and required raking, hauling, and stacking.[45]

The patterns of wage work recorded in MacNutt's diary also reflect, one can be sure, the needs of the rural folk recruited to work on his farm. Having to attend to crops of their own, they moved back and forth first between hay-making on their own farms and MacNutt's, and later between the harvesting of their own grain and root crops and those of MacNutt. Records from the 1830s concerning the nearby David Ross farm show Donald MacLean, a casual labourer on the farm, alternately working on his own holding and that of the Rosses, at times spending half a day harvesting MacLean crops and the other working with David Ross. On other occasions he would work at the Ross farm in the evenings, though in general he, like the workers on Peter MacNutt's farm, spent an entire day or a cluster of days working for wages, returning, one assumes then, to the demands of the home harvest.[46] The degree of flexibility workers might have in moving between their own farm operations and that of their employer(s) varied, of course, as a function of proximity. Donald MacLean lived close to the Ross farm and might, if he could negotiate it, work on his own *and* his neighbour's farm in the course of a day. Many of the labourers appearing on the payroll of those harvesting the hay on William MacKenzie's fields in Middle River later in the century, though, had traveled greater distances to the farm. Workers such as these found it necessary to take up residence at the work site for the duration of the harvest.[47]

In the era before the mechanization of harvest operations, the demand for agricultural labourers during the late summer and autumn was extensive. Analysis of the crop returns and household composition of farm households in Middle River between 1850 and 1875 suggests that roughly one-quarter of the farms there required some help from beyond the household in order to harvest their crops.[48]

The labour demands for harvesting the crops on Middle River's farms were typical of those found elsewhere in the agricultural districts of Nova Scotia and Prince Edward Island. There was, as a Nova Scotian report on labour conditions noted at midcentury, "always a great cry for field labour" at harvest time.[49] Certainly the employment of the wage labour in the agricultural sector was concentrated in these late summer and autumn months. The difficulty for the worker who was also a member of a farm household was that this too was the busiest period on the home farm. Such conflicts of interest could be solved, as Donald MacLean did, by moving back and forth between the work demands of the home farm and wage labour on the harvest of an adjacent holding or, as it would appear that some of those working for Peter MacNutt did, by dividing the total household workforce between the limited requirements of home-farm crops and the wage opportunities on more prosperous farms.

Although the bulk of wage labour was drawn into agriculture during the harvest season, some daily employment was available for men, women, and children throughout the year. The David Ross farm hired help for fencing, ploughing, harrowing, sowing, quarrying stones, cutting and sawing firewood, and slaughtering livestock as well as for harvest operations. The record books of Alex McLellan at Indian River, Prince Edward Island and Joseph Dingwell at Little River in the same colony show both purchasing labour not only for the harvest but for threshing in the winter, ploughing in the spring, and for fence work and building construction at other times of the year.[50] Labourers also were hired for land clearing.[51] As well, some farmers found it expedient to maintain year-round servants. As with much daily work, the wage rates associated with these long-term contracts varied depending on age and gender. John Lewellin noted in 1832 that while "farming men-servants" were retained at 30 to 40 shillings per month, girls received 12 to 15 shillings.[52]

The use of agricultural machinery that sharply reduced the critical demands for harvest labour was not widespread until well into the second half of the nineteenth century. Thus the demands for agricultural labour grew at roughly the same pace as the expansion of agricultural output in the first half of the nineteenth century. Mechanical threshers which permitted grain to be readied quickly for market began to be used in the 1830s, but these reduced a labour demand that could, if necessary, be spread across late fall and winter. The mowers, rakes, reapers, and binders that would, when in place, reduce the enormous demands for labour during harvest season by as much as 80 percent were not a significant presence in the region until the 1860s and afterward.[53]

For many of the Maritime-born, agricultural work probably was their first taste of wage employment. There was demand for the labour of both girls and boys in the harvest fields, and the scale and nature of the work, coupled with the manner in which it was organized, made it a relatively small step from working on the home farm. Those engaged in agricultural employment might work as a lone addition to another family's workforce, or they might be part of a crew of a dozen or more working the harvest fields. In either case, though, they were likely to be working for someone they already knew in a familiar setting among familiar faces, with a heterogeneous workforce—both in terms of age and gender—and to be performing tasks that were the common stuff of agricultural life. The work contract was likely to be informal, struck on a daily basis, and to demand a transportation commitment no more onerous than a walk.

Wage work in the timber trade and the shipbuilding industry—agriculture's great rivals for labour in the first half of the nineteenth century—was, in general, quite different from that in agriculture. This was male employment, and much of the work in these industries was concentrated at sites at some distance from the farms from which many came. Such employment was often for extended periods of time, for woods work was available from late fall until spring, and shipbuilding, when the market dictated, might be conducted on a year-round basis.[54] There were, of course, considerable variations in the nature of the work experience in woods work and shipbuilding. Some of the employment available within these industries was local and organized in small, perhaps primarily family-based, crews. Hired hands might be added to a cluster of brothers cutting logs for the winter or be employed casually in one of the many lesser shipyards turning out modest numbers of smaller vessels. Employment with small local operations where one might return home on a daily basis aided the integration of wage work with farm work. The Irish who settled on the backlands of Lot 29 in southwestern Queen's County, Prince Edward Island, for instance, and who worked in W.W. Lord's timber and shipbuilding operations, were said to have been able to clear their lands and hoe their crops "in spare time."[55] Looking back on his Cape Breton childhood, Aeneas McCharles recalled that his father combined working on his farm in the Baddeck Valley with carpentry work at the shipyards four miles away in the port of Baddeck.[56] Labour in these pursuits, however, was also being organized by capitalists operating on a much larger scale, who relied upon recruiting labourers from beyond the immediate locality of their operations. Entrepreneurs like the Archibalds in Cape Breton and the Popes, Macdonalds, and Cambridges on Prince Edward Island hired scores of men to work at their shipyards, sawmills, and woods operations. So too did their counterparts elsewhere in the region who, even before steam vessels and rail transportation eased the burdens of travel, were drawing labourers from the farms of northern Nova Scotia and Prince Edward Island to work in their operations. By the 1820s and 1830s, farmers in significant numbers were traveling back and forth between the timber camps and shipyards of the Miramichi and their homes in northern Nova Scotia and Prince Edward Island.[57]

Many of those working in these operations were likely to spend part of their lives as bunkhouse men, living at the worksite and labouring on a regular schedule for extended periods of time.[58] In both logging and boat-building, wages might be paid partly in kind—shipyards tended to be organized around a truck store—and differentially paid in accordance with a division of labour along skill lines.[59] Farmers and farmers' sons working in the large shipyards shared their workspace with greater numbers than did those in woods camps, and were engaged in work that required more complex forms of organization.[60] The experience of work in the shipbuilding yards that produced large vessels was, as Richard Rice has argued, that of a large, complexly orchestrated manufactory.

In 1824 it was estimated that perhaps 1,000 men, drawn from a total Island population of roughly 20,000, worked in Prince Edward Island's shipyards to produce some 10,000 tons of shipping.[61] This figure excludes those working in the woods to supply materials for the shipyards, and those working in the woods to produce timber for export. If a similar worker/tonnage ratio held in Nova Scotia, the numbers employed at shipbuilding there would be roughly double those of Prince Edward Island. In both cases, the expansion of shipbuilding during the pre-Confederation decades took place at roughly the same pace as the growth of population in these provinces.[62] As a consequence, the percentage of those engaged in shipbuilding to the larger population probably remained more or less the same on average across these decades, while varying sharply, of course, from year to year as the tonnage under construction responded to external demand.

Despite a number of efforts, a commercial fishery based in Prince Edward Island developed slowly. Prior to 1850, the fishery conducted by Island merchants provided few job opportunities.[63] In Cape Breton, on the other hand, fishing was an enterprise of greater significance. Of particular importance were the Channel Island firms that conducted an extensive industry from their bases in Arichat and Cheticamp. Although the scale of operations was large, and the work labour-intensive, it does not appear that these firms drew substantial amounts of wage labour from among the farm population of the interior. Stephen Hornsby suggests instead that their operations were conducted by combining the independent commodity production of fisherfolk clustered in coastal communities, linked to the firms by ties of credit, with the work of a seasonal wage-labour force drawn from the Channel Islands rather than Cape Breton.[64]

The opportunities available for wage work with the American fishing fleet as it worked in Maritime waters may well have been of greater significance. Vessels working out of New England ports came by the hundreds to the small harbours of the Atlantic coast and the Gulf of St. Lawrence, where they picked up supplies of food and water, profited by smuggling, and often engaged additional hands both for fishing in Maritime waters and for pursuing the fishery off Labrador and Newfoundland.[65] At mid-century, it was estimated that perhaps 4,000 Nova Scotians were working with the American fishing fleet, typically labouring aboard vessels crewed by a dozen or so fishermen. Although the majority would have been drawn from fishing communities about the coast, some of these hands traveled from interior regions to join the fleet as it moved through the Strait of Canso region. Others traveled south to the fishing ports of Maine and Massachusetts to sign on.[66] While the labour of women was a significant component of the family-based in-shore fishery, recruitment for the American fishing fleet, as for the timber industry and the shipyards, and unlike wage labour in agriculture, almost exclusively tapped the male members of farm households.[67] Workers were paid, it would appear, either on a monthly basis or by a share in the value of the catch and were signed on for periods ranging from weeks to months.[68] Islanders working on American vessels in the late 1830s reportedly were paid at a rate of £6 per month.[69]

Beyond the labour required for the tasks associated with the production of commodities from fields, forests, and fisheries, the merchants and others involved in these trades required workers for the multitude of tasks associated with assembling, transporting, and managing these goods. The ledgers of merchants like Lawrence Kavanaugh, John Munro, Joseph Dingwell, Peter MacNutt, Peter Smyth, Robert Elmsley, and John Beamish Moore show wages paid for delivering messages, rounding up and driving livestock, hauling hay, "looking after timber," sorting fish, stacking deal, loading vessels, tending stock, both onshore and on voyages to market, and a host of other irregularly necessary tasks generated by the uneven rhythms of mercantile activity. Work might also be obtained aboard the vessels moving these goods between ports.[70]

Grist mills, saw mills, and other processing industries scattered about the coast and waterways provided work opportunities for farm-based labourers too. While most of those employed were men, women and boys as well sometimes found work in these enterprises. In 1871 nearly 20 percent of those working in the carding and fulling mills of the seven northeastern counties of Nova Scotia were women.[71] Many enterprises, either because they were reliant upon seasonally fluctuating water supplies for their power or because demand was irregular, were part-time operations requiring labour for limited periods. The ledger books of John Munro of St. Ann's Cape Breton, for instance, indicate that the labour he obtained for his grist and carding mill in 1851 and 1852 was hired on a daily basis putting in from 25 to 58 days of work over the course of the year.[72] Some coming from a distance to work for Munro, such as Alex McKenzie of Big Harbour, surely must have stayed in St. Ann's during the period when the mill was running. A similar pattern of part-time employment was followed as well by those whom Lawrence Kavanaugh hired for his sawmill operations in St. Peters earlier in the century, and in Middle River too.[73] In 1870 one of the saw mills in the community worked for two months, the other for four. The three grist mills in Middle River operated for seven months of the year on average.[74]

In the first half of the nineteenth century, farm-based labourers found wages in building construction and work on roads, wharfs, canals, and the first of the region's railways. State expenditures on public buildings—such as the construction of Government House and county court houses and jails in Prince Edward Island during the 1830s—played a significant, though often short-lived, role in generating demand for construction workers. So too did projects like the Shubenacadie Canal and the Albion Mines Railway, portents of the demand for labour that bigger transportation projects would engender in the third quarter of the nineteenth century. On a more regular and local basis, annual state appropriations for road, bridge, and wharf improvements created a substantial amount of wage employment. Such state-generated work was, as Murray Beck has noted, central to the household economies of many of the rural poor, and its interruption could be the cause of considerable deprivation in the countryside.[75] Privately funded rural and urban construction work also provided employment for farm-based workers. Most of this work, like the construction work associated with transportation systems, tended to be seasonal employment for males.[76] When the work was close to home, the remuneration to be gained at road work or on construction jobs might, for those who possessed draft animals, be broadened by bringing horses or oxen to the job. Many, though, took their skills further afield. By the 1840s, if not sooner, labourers from the farms of the northeastern Maritimes were moving seasonally to construction sites in Boston and to other distant centres. Though an urban Cape Bretoner it would seem, George Musgrave's description of employment with a crew of nine in Roxbury, Massachusetts beginning work at dawn with breaks at six for breakfast, noon for dinner, and supper after dark at the end of the day probably captures the experience of many farm-based workers as well. Working and lodging with other single young men, he set the relatively high wages he was earning, and the expectation that he would soon accumulate enough to enable him to quit, against the discomforts of his long days.[77]

The coal mining industry as well provided work for farm-based labourers, even as it increasingly came to rely upon a skilled workforce for the actual mining. In the first decades of the nineteenth century, few of those working the coal seams of Cape Breton or Pictou were skilled colliers. Men more accustomed to finding their way about fish flakes or over cutover ground might yet find work in the pit signing on for a few months or a year. The experience of work in the Cape Breton coal fields in this period paralleled in some ways the work in the timber and shipbuilding industries: bunkhouse life, an entirely male workforce, and the truck store.[78] With the arrival of the General Mining Association in the 1820s and the massive injections of capital that came with it, coal mining became technologically more sophisticated and corporate policy favoured reliance upon a professional core of miners imported from the British coal fields. There remained, however, much demand for less-skilled casual workers in and about the mines. Of the 335 employees on the payroll at the Albion mines in the mid 1830s, only 66 were actually colliers. Scores of others were involved in construction and transportation tasks.[79] To meet this demand, the General Mining Association drew from the surrounding countryside about their mines and yet farther afield.[80] As Abraham Gesner noted, the labour force employed at the mines was divided. There was a well-housed and well-paid professional core and then there were the others, the "labouring farmers," who received less-generous treatment and were paid at roughly half the rate of the skilled miners.[81] Over time both the General Mining Association and subsequent operators in the Nova Scotian coal fields would increasingly turn again to the countryside for the recruitment of miners as well as general labourers.[82]

Around 1,500 men found employment in and about Nova Scotia's coal mines in the 1830s. Thousands more would be recruited in the coal boom of the third quarter of the nineteenth century.[83] Some of these workers were young men from the farm communities of the region who were in the process of severing their ties to the soil. Some ultimately would return to the countryside with their savings.[84] Yet others continued to farm even as they worked for mining companies. In the 1860s it was reported in Cape Breton that surface workers by the hundreds "leave their work, at certain seasons, to attend to their crops."[85]

A more heterogeneous workforce found wages in employment as domestic servants and in textile work and factory work. With increasing urbanization and the growth of middle-class demand for domestic servants, both within the region and in more distant centres, many young farm men and women were drawn out of the countryside and into domestic service for at least part of their working lives.[86] Wanted "an active LAD from 14 to 16 years of age to be indented as a house servant. One from the country would be preferred," ran an ad in the Charlottetown paper.[87] By 1851, roughly 20 percent of Saint John households employed a servant, or servants, and one out of seven Haligonian households employed at least one servant.[88] Other farmfolk found employment as domestic servants in wealthier rural homes. Though putting-out work does not appear to have been conducted on a large scale in the northeastern Maritimes, some men and women were hired by merchants to weave homespun by the yard. Women were hired as well to knit and perform other hand-work.[89] More significantly, by the 1840s women were being recruited from the southern Maritimes to work in the factories of New England. In July 1849, the *Saint John Courier* reported the departure aboard the *Fairy Queen* of "upwards of 100 young women who had been engaged to work in a factory at Salmon Falls near Portland."[90]

Clearly, as the nature of off-farm work varied, so too the ways in which it was integrated into the household economy differed. Daily work close at hand, such as on a neighbouring farm or for a local merchant, permitted, at least in theory, a good deal of flexibility. That farmers and merchants alike required casual labour and employed adults and children, both males and females, meant that various household members might move back and forth between work on the home farm and wage employment. John Beamish Moore's ledger from North Sydney in the 1850s, for instance, shows that the backlander Archy McDonald's household earned wages alternately from Archy's work, that of "his boys," and that of "the girl."[91] The accounts of other backlanders on Moore's ledger show a similar heterogeneity in the composition of household labour made available to the merchant for wages. The same pattern of varying daily movement of different members of the same household in and out of the local agricultural labour force is apparent in the MacNutt farm ledger as men and children, male and female, appear in varying numbers from day to day. One day a father and a couple of sons might be on the pay-roll, another day perhaps only the sons or only the daughters would be employed. There is no way to know whether the pattern was set by demand or by supply, or to discern how in fact those who momentarily disappear from the day book deployed their labour, but clearly local work afforded the possibility of a varied and shifting household response to the needs of the home farm. Local contract work and putting-out work offered similar flexibility. A man who had been hired to mow a field, dig a cellar, or clear land might, particularly if the work was close at hand, exercise some discretion in choosing his hours of employment and integrating such work into other tasks concerning his own resources. As well, he might flexibly use the labour of other members of his household to complete the task. Such would also be the case with the farmer/tailors contracted to sew trousers or for shirtmaking, or the farm women employed by the piece for spinning, weaving, or knitting.

Other employments permitted less flexibility. Some types of work—such as that in shipbuilding, the timber industry, employment with the American fishing fleet, or the construction trades—provided employment almost exclusively for adult males and often entailed working at a considerable distance from one's residence. In homes where the male head engaged in such work, women often were left to manage household and farm for extended periods. Seeking lodgings at a farm house on the Cape Breton-side of the Strait of Canso in the summer of 1831, David Stewart, a Prince Edward Island landlord, and his traveling companion Richard Smith of the

General Mining Association, discovered that the man of the farm "was gone to Miramichi to cut lumber."[92] Only Mrs. MacPherson and her two children were home. At midcentury, the Crown surveyor in Baddeck, D.B. McNab, reported that there were "hundreds" of farms located on poorer lands in his region of the Island where the men of the household traveled to "distant parts of the province or to the United States" each summer and left the maintenance of the farm to "their wives and children."[93] With the boom in railway construction and coal mining in the third quarter of the nineteenth century, a local observer noted that Cape Breton farmers and their sons "by hundreds, nay, thousands, [were] leaving their farms to the women, and seeking employment at the colleries and railways."[94] Some, such as a Highlander born on Lewis residing in Middle River who planted his crop of oats and potatoes and then traveled on foot to Halifax to work on the railway each year, appear to have regularized their patterns of distant wage work so that they synchronized with the seasonal rounds of farming. Come harvest time, the Lewis man would be back in Middle River.[95] In other households the distant wage work of males was made possible because females and children assumed a full array of farm tasks.[96]

The types of employment possibilities available to farm-based labourers varied across place—though the mobility of labour minimized the significance of some of this—and across time as the economies of timber, ships, fish, and agriculture waxed or waned and as decisions of the state and the private sector shaped the demand side of the labour market. The possibilities for the integration of wage employment into the economies of farm households varied, too, across the cyclical passages of family time. In some households a wage supplement was obtainable only if the male household-head worked off the farm on a daily or more extended basis. In others further along in the family life cycle, younger members of the household, male and female, might take on the role of subsidizing the farm with wage work. As the Prince Edward Island Land Commissioners learned when they inquired into the survival strategies of the rural poor there, household budgets were balanced because "the boys hire out," the family had put their "children out to service," and/or wages were sent home by family members who had moved away.[97] Such possibilities were available to households only at certain points in the family life cycle. The Strait of Canso household David Stewart and Richard Smith visited—finding a woman and two children at home and the husband in the Miramichi woods—probably was a young family with limited options, but a household with older children might be sustained, in part, by the remittance of money from the earnings of children working at distant locales.[98]

Earnings gained by a younger generation working away for prolonged periods might be sent to support a home farm but might as well be saved to finance a new household.[99] For many, prolonged, and often distant, wage work, was an early phase in lives that ultimately would be lived out on the land. Young men or women might work away for years to accumulate the cash necessary to permit them to acquire the things needed to establish a household of their own. "Tell Mary MacDonald," wrote Thomas Murchison from Boston to his cousin on Prince Edward Island, "not to engage with any in marriage until my return."[100] Cousin Malcolm was instructed to look after Thomas Murchison's Island property in his absence as well. Further afield, Walter McDonald wrote home to Pictou from Melbourne, Australia concerning his impending return and his traveling companion's interest in marrying sister Marion who had remained in Nova Scotia.[101] Such requests surely must have been repeated again and again as young rural Maritimers sought to combine distant earnings with local ambitions. For many others, of course, off-farm work was the first step in lives that would ultimately be lived out elsewhere.

Although remote work sites could be attractive because of the wages being offered (and perhaps the fact that in most cases they were being offered in cash), the ability to gain continuous work was a drawing card for many as well. "It would surprise you," wrote Thomas Murchison on his arrival in Boston in January 1846, "to see all the work there is going on here. As far as I travelled I could not see an idle man that wished to work." He was, he reported, "in very good employment and making money fast" and intended to be back by spring.[102] George Musgrave wrote in a similar vein from Roxbury in August of 1842. Work had been easy to obtain, and though the hours were long he was making five dollars a week plus board and would not be returning to Cape Breton until the fall.[103] Such returns compared favourably to the wages offered in Prince Edward Island and Cape Breton, and the ability to obtain steady employment at cash wages meant that the migrant worker might return with substantial savings. The unusual opportunities for big wages drew others able to afford the passage monies yet further afield. A Yarmouth man working in the California gold fields wrote home in July of 1849 that labourers were receiving from eight to sixteen dollars per day. Although the cost of board was extraordinarily high and life precarious and violent, he would not, he thought, start making his way homeward until autumn because the opportunities for amassing a vast savings were unrivalled.[104]

One of the most striking things revealed by a survey of the waged work of farm-based labourers during this era is its multiformity. Employment might be on a daily basis or for extended periods of time. It might entail working with a small family unit or with a large, complexly organized, stratified workforce composed exclusively of wage labourers. It might involve working with those of the same age, gender, and class background or with a more heterogeneous grouping. And it might be found in staples production, construction, manufacturing, transportation, or in aid of the "self-sufficient" activities of other farm households. Remuneration might be in cash, in kind, as a positive ledger entry, or in a mixture of these forms.

Insofar as the terms of contract between employer and employee were concerned, working circumstances varied across a broad spectrum of personal and impersonal relationships. Wage work might be found locally with a relative or neighbour or with a previously unknown employer in a distant locale. In the case of a local employer, who was a friend or relative, mutually advantageous terms may have been negotiable. Employee choices concerning the timing and terms of work—and employer—may have been more sharply constrained, though, in other localized working circumstances when the resident elite, particularly those possessing the power of a ledger or rent book, or perhaps holding a mortgage, sought extra hands. Did those working for merchants like Lawrence Kavanaugh, John Beamish Moore, and Peter Smyth—workers whose wages were set against ledger debts already incurred—come seeking employment, or were they summoned? And, if they lacked the cash or commodities to clear their debts, did they have the freedom to say "no"? The same question clearly applies to the many tenants on Prince Edward Island employed by land agents for road work, land clearing, construction, and shipbuilding whose wages were directly set against their arrears on rent rolls.[105]

Although in theory they were working for wages, in practice many of these tenants came to be under a labour obligation to their landlords. At the other extreme were the farm-based labourers earning wages from strangers in distant work sites. The Cape Bretoner George Musgrave was initially put off by the long hours he was expected to work in Roxbury and in consequence quit his job. But, he wrote home, "on consideration of my employer adding a dollar per week to my wages I returned to work again."[106] Clearly, a cash nexus was at the heart of this work relationship and many others like it.

These variations in the labouring experiences of farm-based workers raise questions about the extent to which paternal or "personal" relations can be said to be broadly characteristic of the working experiences of British North Americans in this period. No doubt paternalism informed the relationship between employers and employees in many instances, and quite possibly in most. This model, however, with its emphasis on local power structures and non-economic forms of labour recruitment and control, does not effectively capture the labouring experiences of temporary workers, often originating in the countryside, who moved in and out of the work force. As Clare Pentland admitted in his exploration of the concept, their circumstances do not fit the model.[107] The issue of numbers is, of course, important here. If workers such as these represent a relatively insignificant part of the total labouring population, perhaps there is some justification for viewing the nature of their circumstances as marginal to the broader picture. Existing research does not provide a clear answer to the numbers question. It is perhaps significant, though, that seasonal employees equaled or outnumbered permanent workers at the St. Maurice forges and at D.D. Calvin's lumber operations at Garden Island, supposedly classic examples of paternalistic labour practices in action. These enterprises in fact employed more workers who fell outside the model than within it.[108] The pattern was repeated in the Maritimes. The General Mining Association in Nova Scotia, too, had its well-paid and well-housed skilled workforce operating within locally sustained, paternalistic structures, and a numerous body of differently treated "labouring farmers" who moved in and out of the mining towns. Such, to varying degrees, appears to have been the case in other Maritime industries as well. Perhaps the circumstances of a skilled fraction of the workforce have assumed too great a profile in our conceptualization of labour relations, and worker consciousness, during the first half of the nineteenth century. Greater attention to the lives of farm-based workers may force some reassessment in our understanding of the contours of the experience of work during this period.[109]

The issue of numbers emerges again with the broader argument being presented here. While it is relatively easy to assemble data pointing to the involvement of farm-based workers in a wide variety of wage labour, establishing the breadth of this is another matter. One way to approach the issue is from the supply side, from the perspective of the household. Where data—such as census returns—permit, it is possible to estimate farm production and consumption and to calculate the numbers of farms requiring an income supplement. Applying this sort of analysis to the census returns from Middle River and Hardwood Hill suggested that roughly one-quarter to one-third of households fell into this category. Though the ratios would vary, similar analysis of data from farming communities elsewhere in the northeast Maritimes almost certainly would reveal roughly comparable patterns. Perusal of the census returns from the region indicate the recurring presence of farms with insufficient resources to maintain their occupants. It does not require the application of a complex algorithm to discern that, given the climate and soils of this region, a family of eight would not have been able to make ends meet with five cleared acres and a single cow. But since wage work was not the only strategy for augmenting deficiencies in farm income, it is not safe to equate all farm deficits with a comparable involvement in wage labour. Moreover, there were inducements to wage work other than that of immediate necessity. Wage labourers were drawn from across the spectrum of farm types, not just from operations with annual deficits. Likely these numbers more than compensate for those who may have successfully managed to supplement insufficiencies of farm income without recourse to wages, judging from a reading of a variety of sources. What needs to be emphasized is that the analysis of farm deficits ultimately rests on a series of assumptions concerning patterns of production and consumption. No matter how carefully done, the resulting figures are estimates. Shave down the calculations for household consumption levels or increase the coefficients for livestock productivity and we arrive at new estimates for the numbers of farm households requiring income supplements. To test the accuracy of such estimates, we need close analysis of the economic behaviour of specific households.

The problems of quantifying workforce participation do not get any easier when approached from the demand side. Existing evidence concerning employee numbers, length of work, and origins is fragmentary, although there are some sectors for which we have contemporary estimates of the numbers of workers. Shipbuilding, according to the editor of the *Prince Edward Island Register*, employed 1,000 Islanders in 1824. The Island was a relatively small place and the editor took a keen interest in developments in the shipbuilding industry. His figure is probably well grounded. Assuming that perhaps one-quarter of the total Island population of 20,000 comprised adult males, this would mean that one-fifth of them were working at the shipyards for some period of the year. In adjacent New Brunswick two decades later, it was estimated that roughly 20,000 were employed in the timber industry.[110] Figures such as these can be set against production tallies to provide a starting point for compiling estimates of the labour force in other years and other locales. So, too, fragmentary evidence concerning the numbers of labourers employed on specific farms and in particular enterprises can permit, by extrapolation, the creation of rough estimates of the labour demands of the industry as a whole. Unfortunately, little such work has been done. The fragments of evidence concerning employment, however, suggest that a composite picture would reveal substantial numbers of farm-dwellers participating in near and distant labour markets. It needs to be emphasized, though, that for many participation was brief. The percentage of farm-dwellers engaging in the wage economy is a very different figure from the percentage of the total productive time farm folk spent within the wage economy. Which is the more important figure depends, of course, on the questions we ask.

The problem of attempting to quantify the extent of farm-based wage labour in the first half of the nineteenth century is a difficult one. With more research into the behaviour of particular households and the circumstances of specific communities or industries for which there are good records, it will be possible to obtain a better sense of the scale of the phenomenon. At best, however, the figures will be very rough estimates, reasonable guesses based on limited evidence. But what is clear is that—even given the limits of the existing state of our understanding—wage work needs to be carefully factored into our understandings of rural life.[111] Though an oft-noted reality, it has not always assumed the profile that it should. Too often the appealing vision of rural autonomy and insularity has nudged it aside. Drawn in by the image of the independent yeoman, we seek to explain his decline. Influenced by the mythology of the autonomous household, or by its more recent derivative, the autonomous community in which households achieved independence by equitable sharing, we examine rural life in terms of narrowly defined geographical communities. None of this is entirely wrongheaded, but we need to recognize more explicitly that the presuppositions guiding these questions and approaches originate in a powerful mythology—a mythology that is only partly based on the reality of early nineteenth-century rural Maritime life.

I am reminded of the discrepancies in the assumptions which the scholar Bernard Pares brought to his study of the Russian countryside and the reality that he encountered when he actually moved among rural folk on the eve of the Revolution of 1905. Arriving at a peasant meeting in Tver, miles from the nearest train station, he expected to find rural folk with but a dim perception of the world that lay beyond their village. He discovered instead that more than 40 percent had worked in either Petersburg or Moscow.[112] The rural world that he found was not the insular one he had expected. Charles Farnham had a similar experience in Cape Breton in the 1880s. Traveling across the remote northernmost highlands, he encountered a young woman along the road and gave her a lift. When she asked to be put down at an intersecting cart trail, Farnham, who had come to Cape Breton to experience life in its primitive purity, inquired as to the direction she was taking. "Where does that road go to Maggie?" "It goes to the Strait of Canso, sir, and on to Montana...."[113] Twenty years earlier, perhaps the answer would have been Boston and half a century before, as David Stewart and Richard Smith discovered when they wandered the island, the trails led to Chatham and the Miramichi. The paths, roads, and waterways of the northeast Maritimes took countryfolk in many directions. And they brought many of them back again, weeks, months, and years later. Work in a neighbour's field or house or mill provided training for, and gave way to, work in more distant settings. With their movements, farm-based labourers continuously integrated a host of near and distant economies and experiences into the fabric of rural life. In Margaree, Marshy Hope, and Bear River, life was shaped not just by local crop returns and the relations between neighbours, but also by wages remitted from away and by the experiences and ideas of those who worked elsewhere.[114] Externalities visited on familiar feet.

From a rural perspective, from the hearths of these workers, there is a central commonality in many of these work experiences: their function, their integration into the economies of households that maintained a commitment to (or reliance upon) a soil-based livelihood.[115] Many worked so that they might farm. For the new settlers that Lord Selkirk and John Cambridge observed, wage work was undertaken as a temporary means by which sufficient capital might be acquired to permit an escape from the necessity of working for others. So too for the young men and women labouring to acquire a nest egg, wage work was a necessary phase in a life that, it was hoped, might be lived primarily outside of it. The contemporary language of praise underscores the importance of the objective. Describing the agricultural prosperity that a cousin had come to enjoy on Prince Edward Island, John McRa indicated the extent of his accomplishments by reporting that he had become "very independent."[116] Joseph Howe spoke to the same goal and perhaps beyond when he argued that the industrious Nova Scotian yeoman might with "a wife and an axe" become "truly rich and independent." The Rev. John MacLennan, on tour in the 1820s from his parish in Belfast, Prince Edward Island, lauded the condition of some of Middle River's farm households by noting that they were in "very independent circumstances."[117] Donald Campbell indicated the extent of the good fortune he had obtained in Cape Breton by saying that he was free from the impositions of factor and laird and "any toilsome work but what I do myself."[118]

These people had to some extent gained what many sought. The dream of achieving control over one's labour and its product and of acquiring "independence" was, of course, a widely shared aspiration of rural and urban dwellers alike. The language and arguments used to articulate these ideals in the Escheat struggle on Prince Edward Island in the 1830s are not dissimilar to those employed by many urban workers in this period.[119] The belief that such goals of autonomy and independence might best be achieved by securing a land-based livelihood was both widespread and persistent even among those deeply imbedded in the industrial labour force. The Ohio labour commissioners who assembled the state's first annual labour report in 1877 estimated that roughly one-half the mechanics and labourers in Ohio's urban centres were working to accumulate the savings necessary so that they might acquire a farm.[120] Similarly, as Ewa Morawska has argued, the majority of East Central European peasants who traveled to American industrial centres at the turn of the twentieth century engaged in wage labour thousands of miles from home so that they and their families might become more securely established on the soil; they did so with the intention of returning to their rural communities.[121] Such was the case as well, Theodore von Laue has argued, with much of the industrial work force in late-nineteenth and early-twentieth century Russia.[122] For centuries peasants in the Friuli and Saxony have "consciously" chosen, Douglas Holmes and Jean Quataert contend, to integrate wage work with agrarian pursuits on their rural holdings as a way of resisting a "propertyless working-class existence."[123]

Other farm-based workers in the northeast Maritimes, of course, may have resigned themselves to the necessity of perpetually maintaining the dual commitments of self-employment and working for others, or may indeed have embraced wage work never seeking to attain a degree of choice over their involvement in the labour market.[124] Given the sporadic and uneven nature of the demand for labour in the region in the early nineteenth century, life without the fall-back of an agricultural holding could be precarious.[125] Rather than working so that they might farm, some, no doubt, farmed so that they might live to work. For many, however, access to the soil held out the hope of achieving control over their time and their labour, and persistence in straddling two worlds constituted a way of resisting the imperatives and dependence of wage work.[126]

We need to look more closely at the transformation of these dreams, which had been closely associated with the myth of the independent yeoman, and at changes in the strategies adopted by working people. Few still maintain that true independence is to be gained by eschewing wage work for agricultural pursuits and by struggling to gain a toehold on the soil. The goal of a "propertied independence" that was embedded in the mythology and once held such an important position in the aspirations of working people of the North Atlantic world has long since lost its lustre. And though many rural residents in the region continue to engage in seasonal work at near and distant job sites, fewer and fewer rely on farming as a means to survive periods when they are not engaged in wage work.[127] Surely these will be key themes for those who would write the environmental history of the region. The decline of the belief that the labourer's salvation was to be found on the land and the decline of agriculture as a safety net have profoundly affected our perception of the significance of arable soil, and of land more generally. For increasing numbers, even of rural residents, it is no longer a matter of importance.

The author wishes to gratefully acknowledge the assistance received from the Social Sciences and Humanities Research Council of Canada, whose financial support aided this research. I am also grateful to Carmen Bickerton, Michael Cross, Margaret McCallum, Danny Samson, and the participants in the Atlantic Canada Workshop (Lunenburg, September, 1990) and the Rural Workers in Atlantic Canada Conference (Saint Mary's University, October 1990) for their comments on an earlier version of this paper. By "northeastern Maritimes" I mean Prince Edward Island, Cape Breton Island, and the northern-most section of peninsular Nova Scotia. I take some liberties with the time frame indicated, occasionally drawing evidence from the late eighteenth century and beyond 1850. Nonetheless this essay is primarily about farm-based wage work in the first half of the nineteenth century.

Endnotes

1. Margaret MacDonell, *The Emigrant Experience: Songs of Highland Emigrants in North America* (Toronto 1982), 90–2.
2. Joseph Howe, "Western Rambles," in *Travel Sketches of Nova Scotia*, M.G. Parks, ed. (Toronto 1973), 95–6.
3. Thomas McCulloch, *The Stepsure Letters* (Toronto 1960).
4. Neil MacNeil, *The Highland Heart in Nova Scotia* (Antigonish 1948, 1980).
5. Charles W. Dunn, *Highland Settler: A Portrait of the Scottish Gael in Nova Scotia* (Toronto 1953); D. Campbell and R.A. MacLean, *Beyond the Atlantic Roar: A Study of the Nova Scotia Scots* (Toronto 1974); John Warkentin, "The Atlantic Region," in R. Cole Harris and John Warkentin, eds., *Canada Before Confederation: A Study of Historical Geography* (Toronto 1977), 169–231; Peter Sinclair, "From Peasants to Corporations: The Development of Capitalist Agriculture in the Maritime

Provinces," in John A. Fry, ed., *Contradictions in Canadian Society: Readings in Introductory Sociology* (Toronto 1984), 276–93.

6. The phrase is drawn from Daniel Vickers' superb analysis of the ideal and some of its implications. Daniel Vickers, "Competency and Competition: Economic Culture in Early America," *William and Mary Quarterly*, 3rd Series, 47: 1 (1990), 3–29.
7. The mythology is often incongruously juxtaposed with another reality. Neil MacNeil, for instance, even as he extols the independence Washabuckers achieved on the land, tells of the regular flow of labour southward and of his grandfather's difficult experiences commuting on foot between Washabuckt and a job many miles north in industrial Cape Breton.
8. Robert Leslie Jones, *History of Agriculture in Ontario 1613–1880* (Toronto 1946), 60.
9. J.S. Martell, *Immigration to and Emigration From Nova Scotia, 1815–1838* (Halifax 1942); R.G. Flewwelling, "Immigration to and Emigration from Nova Scotia," *Nova Scotia Historical Society Collections*, 28 (1949), 75–105; D.C. Harvey, "Scottish Immigration to Cape Breton," *Dalhousie Review*, 21: 1 (April 1941), 313–24; Barbara Kincaid, "Scottish Immigration to Cape Breton, 1758–1838," M.A. thesis, Dalhousie University, 1964; D. Campbell and R.A. MacLean, *Beyond the Atlantic Roar*, 7–75; Helen I. Cowan, *British Emigration to British North America: The First Hundred Years* (Toronto 1961), 172–227.
10. Rev. George Patterson, *A History of the County of Pictou Nova Scotia* (Montreal 1877; rept. ed. Belleville, Ontario 1972), 86.
11. [John Cambridge], *A Description of Prince Edward Island in the Gulf of St. Lawrence, North America with a Map of the Island and a Few Cursory Observations Respecting the Climate, Natural Productions and Advantages of its Situation in Regard to Agriculture and Commerce; Together with Some Remarks, as Instructions to New Settlers* (London 1805), 8. See too John Lewellin, *Emigration. Prince Edward Island: A Brief But Faithful Account of this Fine Colony* (1832), reprinted in D.C. Harvey, ed., *Journeys to the Island of St. John* (Toronto 1955), 199. Captain Moorsom provides evidence on the process as well, though in this case viewed from the vantage point of the agricultural employer. Moorsom notes that in the Windsor region agricultural labourers were primarily recruited from among new settlers who had not become established and from the younger members of poorer farm households who worked away in the summer and returned in the winter. Captain W. Moorsom, *Letters from Nova Scotia; Comprising Sketches of a Young Country* (London 1830), 207–8.
12. *Lord Selkirk's Diary, 1803–1804: A Journal of his Travels in British North America and the Northeastern United States*, Patrick C. White, ed. (Toronto 1958), 51.
13. For Corbit's account see the Kavanaugh Account Book, 1818–1824, MG3, vol 301, 212, Public Archives of Nova Scotia (pans).
14. John Hill, Memo on Quit Rents, [1802], CO 226/18/230.
15. Peter A. Russell, "Forest into Farmland: Upper Canadian Clearing Rates, 1822-1839," *Agricultural History*, 57: 3 (July 1983), 326–39. A listing of squatters on Indian lands in Middle River indicating length of settlement and the extent of their fields gives some indication of the clearing rates of Highlanders in Cape Breton. For the eleven households for which there was adequate data, the average rate of clearing was just under 2 acres per year. On average these households had been located on their lands for 6 years and had just under eleven acres of land cleared. If anything these particular rates could be somewhat inflated as the cleared acreages may include lands that natives had cleared and/or those improved by other squatters who were driven off prior to the settlement of these individuals. Nova Scotia House of Assembly, *Journals*, 1862, App. 30, Report of Indian Committee, 7.
16. Walter Johnstone, *A Series of Letters, Descriptive of Prince Edward Island* (1822) reprinted in D.C. Harvey, ed., Journeys to the Island of St. John, 126.
17. Rusticus to the editor, *Prince Edward Island Register* (Charlottetown), 29 November 1825, 1.
18. [S. S. Hill], *A Short Account of Prince Edward Island Designed Chiefly for the Information of Agriculturalists and other Emigrants of Small Capital* (London 1839), 66.
19. Graeme Wynn's estimate of a minimal outlay of £30 to £40 is admittedly a very conservative estimate of simple start-up costs. Working farms of 100 acres with 20 acres cleared would, he notes, have

fetched from £100 to £300 in New Brunswick in the 1830s. Graeme Wynn, *Timber Colony: A Historical Geography of Early Nineteenth Century New Brunswick* (Toronto 1981), 80.

20. George Seymour to T. H. Haviland, 5 February 1837, 114 A/508/3, Warwick County Record Office (WCRO); Robert Stewart to John Pendergast, 23 April 1834, Robert Stewart Letterbooks, Ms. 2989/1, PAPEI (Public Archives of Prince Edward Island); State of Sales of Land by Sir James Montgomery, Baronet and Brothers, gd1/409/15/C14568, Scottish Record Office (SRO).
21. Selkirk Papers, mg 19/E1/73/19302-13, National Archives of Canada (NAC); Rental of the Property of Sir James Montgomery, Baronet and Brothers, GD1/409/16/C14568, SRO.
22. Donald Campbell to [a relative in Lewis], 7 October 1830, reprinted in the *Stornaway Gazette*, 30 September 1972, MG 100, vol. 115, #33, PANS.
23. S. J. Hornsby, "Scottish Emigration and Settlement in Early Nineteenth Century Cape Breton," in Kenneth Donovan, ed., *The Island: New Perspectives on Cape Breton History 1713–1975* (Sydney, Nova Scotia 1990), 58.
24. Graeme Wynn's commentary on J. E. Woolford's 1817 watercolour, *"View on the Road from Windsor to Horton by Avon Bridge at Gaspreaux River,"* that behind the security portrayed in this image of a farm household which had achieved a comfortable competency there lay a "half-century of unremitting work," is acute. Graeme Wynn, "On the Margins of Empire, 1760–1840," in Craig Brown, ed., *The Illustrated History of Canada* (Toronto 1987), 256.
25. On the frosts of 1816, a year that became known as "eighteen hundred and froze to death" see Rev. George Patterson, *A History of the County of Pictou Nova Scotia* (Montreal 1877; reprint ed. Belleville, Ontario 1972), 286; Howard Russell, *A Long Deep Furrow: Three Centuries of Farming in New England* (Hannover, New Hampshire 1976), 136, 147–8. For discussions of those of the 1830s and government initiatives to ban exports of foodstuffs and provide relief see the *Royal Gazette* (Charlottetown), 12 August 1834, 3; 9 December 1834, 3; 26 July 1836, 3; 13 September 1836, 3; 14 February 1837, 3; 28 February 1837, 3; 7 March 1837, 1–2; 11 April 1837, 3. The impact the potato blight of the 1840s had on Cape Breton is dealt with in Robert Morgan, "'Poverty, wretchedness, and misery': The Great Famine in Cape Breton, 1845–1851," *Nova Scotia Historical Review*, 6: 1 (1986), 88–104 and S. J. Hornsby, *Nineteenth Century Cape Breton: A Historical Geography* (Montreal 1992), 111–20. For discussion of the impact of the potato failures of the late 1840s on Prince Edward Island see the *Islander* (Charlottetown), 26 November 1847, 2; 24 December 1847, 3; 7 April 1848, 3; 14 April 1848, 3; 3 November 1848, 2; 12 January 1848, 3.
26. In his study of farm-making in Upper Canada in this period, Norman Ball notes the presence of immigrants trapped by similar cycles of poverty there. Norman Rodger Ball, "The Technology of Settlement and Land Clearing in Upper Canada Prior to 1840," Ph.D. thesis, University of Toronto, 1979, 30–2.
27. D.B. McNab to Uniacke, 3 January 1857, Nova Scotia House of Assembly, *Journals*, 1857, app. 71, 421.
28. Ian Ross Robertson, ed., *The Prince Edward Island Land Commission of 1860* (Fredericton, 1988), 136.
29. A number of John Moores lived in and about North Sydney in the mid-nineteenth century. Stephen Hornsby treats this account book as being that of John *Belcher* Moore. The Public Archives of Nova Scotia, though, stand by their description of it as being that of John *Beamish* Moore. Stephen J. Hornsby, *Nineteenth-Century Cape Breton: A Historical Geography*, 72, 138–9; private correspondence with J.B. Cahill, 26 October 1992.
30. These backlanders may have been selling farm products elsewhere, perhaps closer at hand, but the fact that they routinely purchased bulky items, such as 1/2 barrels of flour and bushels of grain from Moore without ever selling farm goods seems to suggest that they had little or nothing to sell.
31. John Beamish Moore Account Book, 1848–67, 14, Micro Biography, PANS.
32. Ibid., 22.
33. Ibid., 23.
34. *Spirit of the Times* (Sydney), 19 July 1842, 347; Captain W. Moorsom, *Letters from Nova Scotia*, 288.
35. Nova Scotia House of Assembly, *Journals*, 1857, Appendix No. 72, 421.

36. Rusty Bittermann, Robert H. MacKinnon, and Graeme Wynn, "Of Inequality and Interdependence in the Nova Scotian Countryside, 1850–1870," *Canadian Historical Review* (March 1993).
37. The estimate of an average agricultural wage for Nova Scotia is drawn from Julian Gwyn, "Golden Age or Bronze Moment? Wealth and Poverty in Nova Scotia: The 1850s and 1860s," *Canadian Papers in Rural History*, 8 (1992), 195–230.
38. Charles H. Farnham, "Cape Breton Folk," *Harpers New Monthly Magazine* (1886), reprinted in *Acadiensis*, 8: 2 (Spring 1979), 100. These estimates are considered in detail in Bittermann, MacKinnon, and Wynn, "Of Inequality and Interdependence in the Nova Scotian Countryside," and Rusty Bittermann, "Middle River: The Social Structure of Agriculture in a Nineteenth-Century Cape Breton Community," M.A. thesis, University of New Brunswick, 1987, app. IV.
39. Rusty Bittermann, "Economic Stratification and Agrarian Settlement: Middle River in the Early Nineteenth Century," in Kenneth Donovan, ed., *The Island: New Perspectives on Cape Breton History 1713–1975*, 86–7.
40. Ibid.; Rusty Bittermann, "Middle River: The Social Structure of Agriculture in a Nineteenth-Century Cape Breton Community," 157–9.
41. Thomas Chandler Haliburton, *The Old Judge; or, Life in a Colony, ed. with an introduction and notes by M.G. Parks* (Ottawa 1978), xxi.
42. Rusty Bittermann, "The Hierarchy of the Soil: Land and Labour in a Nineteenth-Century Cape Breton Community," *Acadiensis*, 18: 1 (Autumn 1988), 33–55.
43. There were, of course, other ways by which impecunious farmfolk might participate in these economies including share systems and the acquisition of outfits on credit. In some regions, though, even the more prosperous farm households increasingly found it difficult to maintain an independent foothold in the logging business in the Maritimes. See Béatrice Craig, "Agriculture and the Lumberman's Frontier in the Upper St. John Valley, 1800–70," *Journal of Forest History*, 32: 3 (July 1988), 125–37.
44. James Yeo, for example, appears to have recruited large hay harvesting crews drawing extensively from among the Acadian and Native populations of Prince Edward Island. See George Seymour, *Journal of Tour of Canada and the United States* (1840), entry for 7 September, CR 114A/1380, WCRO; Robert Stewart to John Lawson, 7 October 1835, Robert Stewart Letterbooks, Ms. 2989/2, PAPEI.
45. Diary of Honorable Peter MacNutt, Sr., Ms. 3552, 7 August 1837–4 November 1837, PAPEI.
46. David Ross Diary, 3–5, Prince Edward Island Collection, University of Prince Edward Island (UPEI).
47. William MacLean versus William MacKenzie, rg 39, "C," #645, PANS.
48. Rusty Bittermann, "Middle River," 63.
49. Nova Scotia House of Assembly, *Journals*, 1867, Immigration Report, App. 7. See too Captain W. Moorsom, *Letters from Nova Scotia*, 206–7; *Abstract of the Proceedings of the Land Commissioners' Court Held During the Summer of 1860 to Inquire into the Differences Relative to the Rights of Landowners and Tenants in Prince Edward Island* (Charlottetown: *The Protestant, 1862), 101*, 141.
50. Alex McLellan Account Book, Ms. 2802/1, PAPEI; Joseph Dingwell, Ledger, Ms. 3554/1, PAPEI.
51. *Royal Gazette*, 15 March 1836, 2.
52. John Lewellin, *Emigration. Prince Edward Island*, 196. In 1851 John Lawson reported wages of £24 to £30 per year for farm servants. John Lawson, *Letters on Prince Edward Island* (Charlottetown 1851), 20.
53. *Royal Gazette*, 18 April 1837, 3; James Robb, *Agricultural Progress: An Outline of the Course of Improvement in Agriculture Considered as a Business, an Art, and a Science with Special Reference to New Brunswick* (Fredericton 1856), 18; Rusty Bittermann, "Middle River: The Social Structure of Agriculture in a Nineteenth-Century Cape Breton Community," 150–2.
54. A. R. M. Lower, *The North American Assault on the Canadian Forest: A History of the Lumber Trade between Canada and the United States* (Toronto 1938), 32–3; Graeme Wynn, Timber Colony, 54; Richard Rice, "Shipbuilding in British America, 1787–1890: An Introductory Study," Ph.D. thesis, University of Liverpool, 1977, 178–81.
55. Mary Brehaut, ed., *Pioneers on the Island* (Charlottetown 1959), 58. On the local organization of farm-based labour for Prince Edward Island's shipyards see too Basil Greenhill and Ann Giffard,

Westcountrymen in Prince Edward's Isle (Toronto 1967), 56–76; Malcolm MacQueen, *Skye Pioneers and "The Island"* (Winnipeg 1929), 26.

56. Aeneas McCharles, *Bemocked of Destiny: The Actual Struggles and Experiences of a Canadian Pioneer and the Recollections of a Lifetime* (Toronto 1908), 10–1.
57. *Prince Edward Island Register*, 20 October 1825, 3; John MacGregor, *Historical and descriptive Sketches of the Maritime Colonies of British America* (London 1828), 168; David Stewart's Journal, 31, PAPEI, 3209/28; *Royal Gazette*, 30 May 1837, 3. See too the *Royal Gazette* 26 June 1838, 3, on the theft of £35—a season's wages—from a lumberman returning from the Miramichi woods to his residence in West River, Pictou County.
58. Abraham Gesner, *The Industrial Resources of Nova Scotia* (Halifax 1849), 215–7; Graeme Wynn, *The Timber Colony*, 62; Arthur R. M. Lower, *Great Britain's Woodyard: British America and the Timber Trade, 1763–1867* (Montreal 1973), 189–96. On shipyard/bunkhouse deaths due to drunkenness and violence see the *Prince Edward Island Register*, 25 September 1824, 3; *Prince Edward Island Register*, 27 February 1827, 3.
59. Richard Rice, "Shipbuilding in British America, 1787–1890: An Introductory Study," Ph.D. thesis, University of Liverpool, 1977, 171, 186–92. The labour contracts from the 1840s entered in Joseph Dingwell's ledger indicate that he paid most of his labourers half in cash and half in "trade." Joseph Dingwell Ledger, Ms. 3554/1, PAPEI. Capt Moorsom's account of labour relations on the waterfront in Liverpool in the summer of 1828, suggests the reasons for Dingwell's clear indications of the mode of payment in his contracts. There were, he noted, "two scales of value," the "cash price," and the "goods price," and "the various gradations thereof distinctly marked in all transactions between employers and labourers." Moorsom reported a rate of exchange in favor of cash at a ratio of 3 to 4. Captain W. Moorsom, *Letters From Nova Scotia; Comprising Sketches of a Young Country*, 292. For information on Joseph Pope's shipyard and truck store see John Mollison, "Prince County," in D.A. Mackinnon and A.B. Warburton, eds., *Past and Present of Prince Edward Island* (Charlottetown 1906), 86. Lemuel and Artemas Cambridge offered their ship carpenters the choice of employment by the month or payment "by the seam." *Prince Edward Island Register*, 23 May 1826, 3.
60. According to Dougald Henry (b. 1817) the modest shipbuilding operation run by the Bells of Stanley River Prince Edward Island employed 30 or more men in the yards. Working days, he relates, began at six with a break for breakfast at 8. For Dougald Henry's account of shipyard life as compiled by Dr. Hedley Ross, see Mary Brehaut, ed., *Pioneers on the Island*, 47.
61. *Prince Edward Island Register*, 27 March 1824, 3. Shipbuilding declined precipitously after the depression of the mid 1820s. It would be more than a decade before output on Prince Edward Island would surpass these figures. Evidence compiled by Richard Rice from 3 Quebec shipyards suggest reasonably similar man/ton labour force ratios there in the mid 1850s varying from 8.6 to 16.3 tons per man. Richard Rice, "Shipbuilding in British America," 179.
62. Ibid., 15–6; John Warkentin, "The Atlantic Region," 180.
63. John MacGregor, *Historical and Descriptive Sketches of the Maritime Colonies of British America*, 63; *Prince Edward Island Register*, 24 March 1829, 3.
64. Stephen J. Hornsby, "Staple Trades, Subsistence Agriculture, and Nineteenth-Century Cape Breton Island," *Annals of the Association of American Geographers*, 79: 3 (1989), 415. Rosemary Ommer too notes the significance of wage workers drawn from Jersey in the Gulf fishery. Rosemary Ommer, "'All the Fish of the Post': Property Resource Rights and Development in a Nineteenth-Century Inshore Fishery," *Acadiensis*, 10: 2 (Spring 1981), 113. Father Anselme Chiasson, though, notes the exploitation of Acadian wage workers in the early nineteenth century by the Robin Company in Chéticamp. Father Anselme Chiasson, *Chéticamp: History and Acadian Traditions*, trans. by Jean Doris LeBlanc (St. John's 1986), 66–7. Certainly too resident fish merchants like Laurence Kavanaugh made use of local wage labour.
65. John MacDougall, *History of Inverness County*, 17; Abraham Gesner, *The Industrial Resources of Nova Scotia*, 104–10; *Colonial Herald* (Charlottetown), 17 October 1838, 3; *Colonial Herald* (Charlottetown), 5 June 1839, 4.
66. For the general patterns of recruitment see Paul Crowell to James Uniacke, 10 February 1852, Nova Scotia House of Assembly, *Journals*, 1852, app. 25 and the statements of David Bears, Nova

Scotia House of Assembly, *Journals*, 1852, app. 13. On some of the folklore arising from the involvement of Cape Bretoners in these patterns of work see John P. Parker, *Cape Breton Ships and Men* (Toronto 1967), 130–1 and John MacDougall, History of Inverness County, 123–4.

67. Marilyn Porter, "'She was Skipper of the Shore Crew': Notes on the History of the Sexual Division of Labour in Newfoundland," *Labour/Le Travail*, 15 (Spring 1985), 105–24.
68. Harold Innis, *The Cod Fisheries: The History of an International Economy* (Washington, D.C., 1940; reprint ed. Toronto 1978), 325, 326–7, 333–4.
69. *Journals*, Prince Edward Island House of Assembly, 1837, 81-2.
70. Lawrence Kavanaugh Account Book, 1817–24, MG 3, vol. 301–2, PANS; John Munro Daybook, 1851–55, Micro Biography, PANS; Joseph Dingwell Ledger, Ms. 3554/l, PAPEI; Diary of Honorable Peter MacNutt, Sr., Ms. 3552, PAPEI; Peter Smyth Ledger, 1833–6, MG 3 vol. 284, PANS; Robert Elmsley Diary, 1855–89, PANS; John Beamish Moore Account Book, 1848–67, Micro Biography, PANS; Eric Sager, *Seafaring Labour: The Merchant Marine of Atlantic Canada, 1820–1914* (Kingston 1989), 136–63.
71. Census of Canada, l870–71, vol. 3 (Ottawa 1875), 316.
72. John Munro Daybook, 1851–55, Micro Biography, PANS.
73. Lawrence Kavanaugh Account Book, 1817–24, MG 3, vol. 301, PANS.
74. *Canada, Census*, 1870/71, Schedule 6.
75. Beck perceptively notes the differential impact of the blockage of appropriations in the revenue dispute of 1830: wealthier farmers suffered because of the deteriorating condition of the roads and bridges they used to move their goods; the rural poor suffered because of the loss of wages gained from working on the roads. J. Murray Beck, *Joseph Howe*, vol. 1, *Conservative Reformer*, 1804–1848 (Kingston 1982), 72.
76. Those working on road crews gained income both directly from the state through the disbursement of government monies in wages (albeit through the often-sticky hands of local road commissioners) and indirectly through the performance of statutory labour requirements for wealthier rural residents. For examples of the latter see the David Ross Diary, 2, Prince Edward Island Collection, UPEI, and Lawrence Kavanaugh Account Book, 1817–24, MG 3, vol. 302, 99.
77. George Musgrave to Ann, 7 August 1842, Micro Biography: Moore, no. 10, PANS.
78. Richard Brown, *The Coal Fields and Coal Trade of the Island of Cape Breton* (London 1871), 70–2; J.S. Martell, "Early Coal Mining in Nova Scotia," in Don Macgillivray and Brian Tennyson, eds., *Cape Breton Historical Essays* (Sydney 1980), 41–53.
79. James M. Cameron, *The Pictonian Colliers* (Halifax 1974), 27.
80. The Albion Mines ran ads for "seasonal" labourers in Prince Edward Island in the 1830s. See the *Colonial Herald*, 4 May 1839, 4. See too Joseph Howe, "Eastern Rambles," in *Travel Sketches of Nova Scotia*, 163; James M. Cameron, *The Pictonian Colliers*, 102.
81. Abraham Gesner, *The Industrial Resources of Nova Scotia*, 273.
82. Del Muise, "The Making of an Industrial Community: Cape Breton Coal Towns, 1867–1900," in *Cape Breton Historical Essays*, 80.
83. Ian McKay, "The Crisis of Dependent Development: Class Conflict in the Nova Scotia Coalfields, 1872–1876," in Gregory S. Kealey, ed., *Class, Gender, and Region: Essays in Canadian Historical Sociology* (St. John's 1988), 21, 30–4; Richard Brown, *The Coal Fields and Coal Trade of the Island of Cape Breton*, 98, 111–39.
84. There were obviously other variations here as well. Some floated back and forth for years at a time between wage work in the mines and life on the land.
85. Nova Scotia House of Assembly, *Journals* 1864, app. 4, 3. On the continuing linkages some mine workers maintained between country home and mine and the significance of these to social relations in the working class communities about the mines in the late nineteenth and early twentieth centuries, see David Frank, "The Industrial Folk Song in Cape Breton," *Canadian Folklore*, Canadien, 8: 1–2 (1986), 21–42; Danny Samson, "The Making of a Cape Breton Coal Town: Dependent Development in Inverness, Nova Scotia, 1899–1915," M.A. thesis, University of New Brunswick, 1988.
86. Faye E. Dudden, *Serving Women: Household Service in Nineteenth-Century America* (Middletown, Connecticut 1983). Claudette Lacelle's study of domestic servants in Montreal and Quebec City in the second decade of the nineteenth century and Toronto, Quebec City, and Halifax in the 1870s,

suggests a reasonably equal split between men and women domestics early in the century. Over the next half century, though, the numbers of women in domestic service grew and rural recruitment became increasingly important. Claudette Lacelle, *Urban Domestic Servants in nineteenth-Century Canada* (Ottawa 1987), 18–20, 78. John Lawson reported that women servants were receiving £9 to £12 per year in Prince Edward Island at mid-century. John Lawson, *Letters on Prince Edward Island*, 20. For an insightful early twentieth-century account of a country woman's experience as a domestic servant in Charlottetown see Bertha MacDonald, *Diary of a Housemaid* (n.p. 1986).

87. *Prince Edward Island Register*, 23 May 1826, 3. See too *Prince Edward Island Register*, 20 January 1825, 3; 21 August 1827, 3.
88. T. W. Acheson, *Saint John: The Making of a Colonial Urban Community* (Toronto 1985), 233–4; Claudette Lacelle, *Urban Domestic Servants in nineteenth-Century Canada*, 81.
89. For examples, see John Munro Daybook, 1851–55, Ann McLeod's account, 2 November 1852, Micro Biography, PANS; John Beamish Moore Account Book, 1848–67, 11, 13, 16, 23, and 30, Micro Biography, PANS; Lawrence Kavanaugh Account Book, 1818–24, 193, MG 3, vol. 302, PANS; Lawrence Kavanaugh Account Book, 1817–24, 228, MG 3, vol. 301, PANS.
90. *Courier* (Saint John), 21 July 1849, 2.
91. John Beamish Moore, Account Book, 1848-67, 22.
92. David Stewart's Journal, 31, PAPEI, 3209/28.
93. Nova Scotia House of Assembly, *Journals*, 1857, Appendix No. 72, 421.
94. *Journal of Agriculture for Nova Scotia*, July 1871, 652.
95. Francis MacGregor, "Days that I Remember," January 1962, Mg. 12, vol. 71, 31, Beaton Institute, Sydney, Nova Scotia.
96. These different patterns of domestic life in poorer households no doubt underwrote the perception that backland women were particularly able workers. Backland girls, notes Margaret MacPhail's character John Campbell, made the best marriage partners as "They can work outside and in and keeps a fellow warm in bed. What else would you want!" Margaret MacPhail, *Loch Bras d'Or* (Windsor, Nova Scotia 1970), 84, 65.
97. Ian Ross Robertson, ed., *The Prince Edward Island Land Commission of 1860* (Fredericton 1988), 116–9.
98. Alan Brookes, "The Exodus: Migration From the Maritime Provinces to Boston During the Second Half of the Nineteenth Century," Ph.D. thesis, University of New Brunswick, 1978, 88; Bettye Beattie, "Going Up to Lynn: Single Women from the Maritime Provinces Working in Lynn, Massachusetts, 1870–1930," paper presented to the Atlantic Canada Studies Conference, Orono, Maine, 18 May 1990. In her insightful evocation of life in mid-nineteenth century rural Cape Breton, Margaret MacPhail relates how the MacKiel's, a backland family, survived in part because an older daughter working as a domestic in Arichat sent money home as did a son working with the Grand Banks fishing fleet. Margaret MacPhail, *Loch Bras d'Or*, 7.
99. These were not, of course, mutually exclusive endeavours. Labouring to support the home farm could affect one's inheritance and thus ultimately contribute to the ability to become established on one's own at a later date.
100. Thomas Murchison to Malcolm Murchison, 15 January 1846, Ms. 3084/1, PAPEI.
101. Walter McDonald to Mother, 25 December 1862, MG 100/184/13, PANS.
102. Thomas Murchison to Malcolm Murchison, 15 January 1846, Ms. 3084/1, PAPEI.
103. George Musgrave to Ann, 7 August 1842, Micro Biography: Moore, no. 10, PANs.
104. *Nova Scotian* (Halifax), 30 July 1849, 243, col 1 & 2.
105. The practice was widespread. Lord Selkirk's agent William Douse, for instance, had at least 80 men working off their rents at a rate of 3/6 for a 6 am to 7 pm working day in the summer of 1838. Selkirk Papers, MG 19, E1, v. 73, 19207, PAC. See too Robert and David Stewart's notice to tenants in *Royal Gazette*, 30 September 1834, 1 and the Worrell rent books, RG. 15, PAPEI.
106. George Musgrave to Ann, 7 August 1842, Micro Biography: Moore, no. 10, PANS.
107. H. Clare Pentland, *Labour and Capital in Canada, 1650–1860* (Toronto 1981), 45–6.
108. The majority of the work force at the forges appear to have been temporary. The division between permanent and temporary workers at D.D. Calvin's operations was roughly equal. H. Clare Pentland, Labour and Capital in Canada, 1650–1860, 42–5; Bryan D. Palmer, *Working-Class Experience: The Rise and Reconstitution of Canadian Labour, 1800–1980* (Toronto 1983), 15.

109. For a consideration of this issue in a European context see Jean H. Quataert, "A New Look at Working-Class Formation: Reflections on the Historical Perspective," *International Labour and Working-Class History*, 27 (Spring 1985) 72–6.
110. Report from the New Brunswick *Royal Gazette* cited in the Islander, 20 November 1846, 2.
111. Certainly too, as Larry McCann has noted, these patterns have implications for urban development in the Maritimes as well. Larry McCann, "'Living a Double Life': Town and Country in the Industrialization of the Maritimes," in Douglas Day, ed., *Geographical Perspectives on the Maritime Provinces* (Halifax 1988), 93–113.
112. Bernard Pares, *A Wandering Student: The Story of a Purpose* (Syracuse 1948), 127.
113. Charles H. Farnham, "Cape Breton Folk," 97.
114. For a splendid example of how a focus on migratory labour can deepen our understanding of change in agrarian and urban and industrial society, see Bruno Ramirez, *On the Move: French-Canadian and Italian Migrants in the North Atlantic Economy, 1860–1914* (Toronto 1991).
115. For Russian peasants, the perceived importance of the functional commonality of all such off-farm work is reflected in its designation by a single word, promysly, meaning all those activities necessary to round out the insufficient returns gained from the soil. Theodor Shanin, *Russia as a Developing Society*, vol. 1, *The Roots of Otherness: Russia's Turn of Century* (New Haven 1985), 68.
116. John McRa to Archibald McRa, 1 January 1817, ms. 3363/2, PAPEI.
117. Letter of Rev. John MacLennan, 1827, Glasgow Colonial Society Correspondence, M-1352, 129, PAC.
118. Donald Campbell to [a relative in Lewis], 7 October 1830, reprinted in the *Stornaway Gazette*, 30 September 1972, MG 100, vol. 115, #33, PANS.
119. Rusty Bittermann, "Agrarian Alternatives: The Ideas of the Escheat Movement on Prince Edward Island, 1832–42," *Acadiensis*.
120. Cited in Peter H. Argersinger and Jo Ann Argersinger, "The Machine Breakers: Farmworkers and Social Change in the Rural Mid West of the 1870s," *Agricultural History*, 58 (July 1983), 401.
121. Ewa Morawska, "'For Bread with Butter': Life-Worlds of Peasant Immigrants from East Central Europe, 1880–1914," *Journal of Social History*, 17: 3 (Spring 1984), 392.
122. Theodore von Laue, "Russian Peasants in the Factory, 1892–1904," *Journal of Economic History*, 21 (1961), 80.
123. Douglas R. Holmes and Jean H. Quataert, "An Approach to Modern Labor: Worker Peasantries in Historic Saxony and the Friuli Region over Three Centuries," *Comparative Studies in Society and History*, 28: 2 (April 1986), 202.
124. Many emigrants had experience with similar work patterns before they migrated. See Barbara M. Kerr, "Irish Seasonal Migration to Great Britain, 1800–38," *Irish Historical Studies*, 3 (1942–3), 365–80; A.J. Youngson, *After the Forty-Five: The Economic Impact on the Scottish Highlands* (Edinburgh 1973), 182–4; T.M. Devine, "Temporary Migration and the Scottish Highlands in the Nineteenth Century," *Economic History Review*, 32 (1979), 344–59; William Howatson, "The Scottish Hairst and Seasonal Labour 1600–1870," *Scottish Studies*, 26 (1982), 13-36; E.J.T. Collins, "Migrant Labour in British Agriculture in the Nineteenth Century," *Economic History Review*, 29 (1976), 38–59. As Maritimers moved on, some carried these patterns of work to new locales. See Aeneas McCharles, *Bemocked of Destiny*, 28; Neil Robinson, *Lion of Scotland* (Auckland 1952, 1974), 28, 80, 99.
125. Judith Fingard, "A Winter's Tale: The Seasonal Contours of Pre-Industrial Poverty in British North America, 1815–1860," *Historical Papers* (1974), 65–94; D.B. MacNab to Uniacke, 3 January 1857, Nova Scotia House of Assembly, *Journals*, 1857, app. 71, 421.
126. On the significance of agrarian strategies to working-class struggles in Great Britain and the United States in this period see Malcolm Chase, *"The People's Farm": English Radical Agrarianism, 1775–1840* (Oxford 1988); Sean Wilentz, *Chants Democratic: New York City and the Rise of the American Working Class, 1788–1850* (New York 1984), 164–216, 335–43; Paul Conkin, *Prophets of Prosperity: America's First Political Economists* (Bloomington 1980), 222–58.
127. The terms of eligibility for unemployment benefits have played a role here in forcing some to choose between a state-based or land-based safety net and/or to define themselves as workers rather than farmers.

Chapter 2

Class Conflict on the Canals of Upper Canada in the 1840s

Ruth Bleasdale

Irish Labourers on the St. Lawrence canal system in the 1840s appeared to confirm the stereotype of the Irish Celt—irrational, emotionally unstable, and lacking in self-control. Clustered around construction sites in almost exclusively Irish communities, they engaged in violent confrontations with each other, local inhabitants, employers, and law enforcement agencies. Observers of these confrontations accepted as axiomatic the stereotype of violent Paddy, irreconcilable to Anglo-Saxon norms of rational behaviour, and government reports, private letters, and newspaper articles characterized the canallers as "persons predisposed to tumult even without cause."[1] As one of the contractors on the Lachine Canal put it: "they are a turbulent and discontented people that nothing can satisfy for any length of time, and who never will be kept to work peaceably unless overawed by some force for which they have respect."[2]

Yet men attempting to control the disturbances along the canals perceived an economic basis to these disturbances which directly challenged ethnocentric interpretations of the canallers' behaviour. In the letters and reports of government officials and law enforcement agents on the canal works in Upper Canada the violence of the labourers appears not as the excesses of an unruly nationality clinging to old behaviour patterns, but as a rational response to economic conditions in the new world. The Irish labourers' common ethno-culture did play a part in shaping their response to these conditions, defining acceptable standards of behaviour, and providing shared traditions and experiences which facilitated united protest. But the objective basis of the social disorder along the canals was, primarily, class conflict. With important exceptions, the canallers' collective action constituted a bitter resistance to the position which they were forced to assume in the society of British North America.

Southern Irish immigrants flooding into the Canadas during the 1840s became part of a developing capitalist labour market, a reserve pool of unskilled labourers who had little choice but to enter and remain in the labour force.[3] Most southern Irish arrived in the new world destitute. "Labouring paupers" was how the immigration agent at Quebec described them.[4] They had little hope of establishing themselves on the land. By the 1840s the land granting and settlement policies of government and private companies had combined to put land beyond the reach of such poor immigrants. Settlement even on free grants in the backwoods was "virtually impossible without capital."[5] The only option open to most southern Irish was to accept whatever wage labour they could find.

Many found work in the lumbering, shipping, and shipbuilding industries, and in the developing urban centres, where they clustered in casual and manual occupations. But the British North American economy could not absorb the massive immigration of unskilled Irish.[6] Although the cholera epidemics of 1832 and 1834 and the commercial crisis of 1837 had led to a decline in immigration and a shortage of labour by 1838, a labour surplus rapidly developed in the opening years of the 1840s, as southern Irish arrived in record numbers.[7] Added to this influx of labourers from across the Atlantic was a migration of Irish labourers north across the American border. During the 1830s the movement of labourers across the border had usually been in the opposite direction, a large proportion of Irish immigrants at Quebec proceeding to the United States in search of employment on public works projects. But the economic panic of 1837 had put a stop to "practically every form of public work" in that country, and further stoppages in 1842 sent thousands of Irish labourers into the Canadas looking for work. Some new immigrants at Quebec still travelled through to the United States despite the dismal prospects of employment in that country; Pentland concludes, however, that the net flow into Canada from the United States in the years 1842–43 was 2,500.[8] Large-scale migration of the unskilled south across the American border revived in the latter half of the decade, but the labour market continued to be over-supplied by destitute Irish immigrants fleeing famine in their homeland.[9]

The public works in progress along the Welland Canal and the St. Lawrence River attracted a large proportion of the unemployed Irish throughout the decade. The Emigration Committee for the Niagara District Council complained that construction sites along the Welland operated "as beacon lights to the whole redundant and transient population of not only British America, but of the United States."[10] From the St. Lawrence Canals came similar reports of great numbers of strange labourers constantly descending on the canals. Even with little work left in the early months of 1847, labourers were still pouring into the area around the Williamsburg Canals. Chief Engineer J.B. Mills asked the Board of Works what could be done with all the labourers.[11]

Many did secure work for a season or a few years. The massive canal construction programme undertaken by the government of the Canadas during the 1840s created a demand for as many as 10,000 unskilled labourers at one time in Upper Canada alone. The work was labour intensive, relying on the manpower of gangs of labourers. While mechanical inventions such as the steam-excavator in the Welland's Deep Cut played a small role in the construction process, unskilled labourers executed most aspects of the work, digging, puddling, hauling, and quarrying.[12] The Cornwall Canal needed 1,000 labourers during peak construction seasons in 1842 and 1843; the Williamsburg Canals required as many as 2,000 between 1844 and 1847; while the improvements to the Welland employed between 3,000 and 4,000 labourers from 1842 to 1845, their numbers tapering off in the latter half of the decade.[13]

Despite this heavy demand, there were never enough jobs for the numbers who flocked to canal construction sites. Winter brought unemployment of desperate proportions. While some work continued on the Cornwall and Williamsburg Canals and on the Welland to a greater extent, the number of labourers who could be employed profitably was severely limited. Of the 5,000 along the Welland in January 1844, over 3,000 could not find jobs, and those at work could put in but few days out of the month because of the weather.[14] Even during the spring and summer months, the number of unemployed in the area might exceed the number employed if work on one section came to an end or if work was suspended for the navigation season.[15]

Only a small number of those unable to get work on the canals appear to have found jobs on farms in the area. Despite the pressing demand for farm labourers and servants during the 1840s, the peasant background of the southern Irish had not equipped them to meet this demand, and many farmers in Upper

Canada consequently professed reluctance to employ Irish immigrants.[16] The Niagara District Council's 1843 enquiry into emigration and the labour needs of the district noted that farmers were not employing the labourers along the canal because they did not know "the improved system of British agriculture." Four years later the emigration committee for the same district gave a similar reason as to why farmers would not hire the immigrants squatting along the Welland Canal: "from the peculiar notions which they entertain, from the habits which they have formed, and from their ignorance of the manner in which the duties of farm labourers and servants are performed in this country, they are quite unprofitable in either capacity."[17] In the last half of the decade, fear that famine immigrants carried disease acted as a further barrier to employment of the Irish on farms.[18]

Despite their inability to find work, the unemployed congregated along the canal banks. As construction commenced on the Welland, canal Superintendant Samuel Power endeavoured to explain why the surplus labourers would not move on: "the majority are so destitute that they are unable to go. The remainder are unwilling as there is not elsewhere any hope of employment." Four years later the situation had not changed. The Niagara District Council concluded that even if there had been somewhere for the unemployed to go, they were too indigent to travel.[19] Instead they squatted along the public works, throwing together shanties from pilfered materials—the fence rails of farmers and boards from abandoned properties.[20]

These shanties of the unemployed became a part of all construction sites. Their occupants maintained themselves by stealing from local merchants, farmers, and townspeople. According to government and newspaper reports, pilfering became the order of the day along public works projects, the unemployed stealing any portable commodity—food, fence rails, firewood, money, and livestock.[21] While reports deplored this criminal activity, observers agreed that it was their extreme poverty which "impelled these poor, unfortunate beings to criminal acts."[22] The *St. Catharines Journal*, a newspaper generally unsympathetic to the canallers, described the condition of the unemployed in the winter of 1844:

> .... [T]he greatest distress imaginable has been, and still is, existing throughout the entire line of the Welland Canal, in consequence of the vast accumulation of unemployed labourers.... There are, at this moment, many hundreds of men, women, and children, apparently in the last stages of starvation; and instead ... of any relief for them ... in the spring, ... more than one half of those who are now employed must be discharged.... This is no exaggerated statement; it falls below the reality, and which requires to be seen, in all its appalling features to entitle any description of it to belief.[23]

Such descriptions appear frequently enough in the letters of government officials to indicate that the *Journal* was not indulging in sensational reporting. The actual numbers of those on the verge of starvation might fluctuate—two years earlier 4,000 unemployed labourers, not a few hundred, had been "reduced to a state of absolute starvation."[24] But the threat of starvation was an ever-present part of life in the canal zones.

Upper Canada lacked a system of public relief which might have mitigated the suffering of the unemployed and their families. Only gradually between 1792 and 1867 was there a "piecemeal assumption of public responsibility for those in need" and not until the mid 1840s did the province begin to operate on the principle of public support.[25] Even had the principle of public relief been operative, the Niagara, Johnston, and Eastern District lacked the resources to provide a relief programme such as that offered by Montreal to unemployed labourers on the Lachine Canal.[26] Nor was private charity a solution to the endemic poverty of the unemployed. When thousands of destitute immigrants first arrived in St. Catharines seeking employment on the Welland Canal in the spring of 1842, many citizens in the area came to their aid. But as the *St. Catharines*

Journal pointed out in similar circumstances two years later: "Those living in the vicinity of the Canal [had] not the means of supporting the famishing scores who [were] hourly thronging their dwellings, begging for a morsel to save the life of a starving child."[27]

The suffering of the unemployed shocked private individuals and government officials such as William Merritt who led a fund-raising campaign for the starving and charged the Board of Works that it was "bound to provide provisions, in some way."[28] The crime of the unemployed became an even greater concern as desperate men violated private property in their attempts to stay alive. But for the Board of Works and its contractors the surplus labourers around the canals provided a readily exploitable pool of unskilled labour. From this pool, contractors drew labourers as they needed them—for a few days, weeks, or a season—always confident that the supply would exceed the demand. The men they set to work were often far from the brawny navvies celebrated in the folklore of the day. Weakened by days and months without adequate food, at times on the verge of starvation, labourers were reported to stagger under the weight of their shovels when first set to work.[29]

Contractors offered temporary relief from the threat of starvation; but they offered little more. The typical contractor paid wages which were consistently higher than those of farm labourers in the area of construction sites. But for their back-breaking, dangerous labour and a summer workday of 14 hours, navvies received only the average or slightly above average daily wage for unskilled labour in the Canadas.[30] Since individual contractors set wage rates, wages varied from canal to canal and from section to section on the same canal; however, they usually hovered around the 2s.6d. which Pentland suggests was the average rate for unskilled labour during the decade. On the Cornwall and Williamsburg Canals wages fluctuated between 2s. and 3s., and if on the Welland Canal labourers in some seasons forced an increase to 4s., wages usually dropped back to 2s.6d. at the onset of winter, when contractors justified lower wages on the grounds that labourers worked fewer hours.[31]

These wage levels were barely adequate to sustain life, according to an 1842 government investigation into riots on the Beauharnois Canal. Many of those who testified at the hearings—foremen, engineers, magistrates, and clergymen maintained that along the St. Lawrence labourers could not live on 2s.6d. per day. A conservative estimate gave the cost of food alone for a single labourer for one day at ls.3d., suggesting that at the going rate a labourer could only feed himself and his wife, not to mention children, and then only on days when he was employed.[32] Under the best of circumstances, with work being pushed ahead during the summer months, this would only mean 20 days out of the month. In winter, if he was lucky enough to get work on the canals, he could not expect to put in more than 10 days in a good month.[33] Inadequate as his wages were, the labourer could not even be certain of receiving them. After a few months in a contractor's employ, labourers might discover that they had worked for nothing, the contractor running out of funds before he could pay his men. Other contractors, living under the threat of bankruptcy, forced labourers to wait months on end for their wages. These long intervals between paydays reduced labourers to desperate circumstances. Simply to stay alive, they entered into transactions with cutthroat speculators, running up long accounts at stores or "selling their time at a sacrifice," handing over the title to their wages in return for ready cash or credit. Such practices cost labourers as much as 13 percent interest, pushing them steadily downward in a spiral of debt and dependency.[34]

Labourers might become indebted to one of the "petty hucksters who swarmed around public works, charging whatever they could get," or to one of the country storekeepers who took advantage of an influx of labourers to extract exorbitant prices.[35] Or frequently the contractor who could not find the money to pay wages found the means to stock a company store and make a profit by extending credit for grossly overpriced provisions. Although contractors claimed they set up their stores as a convenience to the labourers, a government investigation concluded that in actual fact, stores were "known to be a source of great profit on which all the contractors calculated."[36] Many contractors ensured a profit from the sale of provisions by paying wages in credit tickets redeemable only at the company store. This system of truck payment was so widespread along the canals, and so open to abuse,[37] that the Board of Works introduced into the contracts a clause stipulating that wages must be paid in cash. The Board's real attitude toward truck, however, was more ambivalent than this clause suggests. Its 1843 "Report to the Legislature" argued that "truck payment" was in many cases "rather to be controlled than wholly put down."[38] It did not put a stop to store pay, and according to its officials on construction sites it did not control it very well either.[39] The result was that many canallers worked for nothing more than the provisions doled out by their employer. They did not see cash. Few could have left the public works with more than they had had when they arrived. Many were probably in debt to the company store when their term of work ended.

The combination of low wages, payment in truck, and long waits between paydays kept canallers in poverty and insecurity, barely able to secure necessities during seasons of steady employment, unable to fortify themselves against seasons of sporadic work and the inevitable long periods when there was no work at all. Government commissions and individual reports detailed the misery of the labourers' existence. Drummond, member of the Legislature for Quebec, had served on the Commission investigating conditions along the Beauharnois. During debate in the House, his anger at the "grinding oppression" which he had witnessed flared into a bitter denunciation of "sleek" contractors who had "risen into a state of great wealth by the labour, the sweat, the want and woe" of their labourers. He charged the government with having betrayed and abused the immigrant labourers:

> They were to have found continued employment, and been enabled to acquire means to purchase property of their own. They expected to meet with good treatment and what treatment had they met with?—With treatment worse than African slaves, with treatment against which no human being could bear up.[40]

Drummond was backed up by Montreal MP Doctor Neilson, whose experience as medical attendant to the Lachine labourers prompted a less passionate, but no less devastating appraisal:

> Their wants were of the direst kind. He [Dr. Neilson] had frequently to prescribe for them, not medicine, nor the ordinary nourishments recommended by the profession, but the commonest necessaries of life; he daily found them destitute of these necessaries, and he was, therefore, most strongly of opinion that the system under which they were employed, and which afforded them such a wretched existence ought to be fully enquired into.[41]

Conditions were equally bad on canals further up the St. Lawrence system. Work did not guarantee adequate food even on the Welland, which offered the highest wages.[42] David Thorburn, Magistrate for the Niagara District, wondered how the labourers could survive, as he watched them hit by a drop in wages and a simultaneous increase in food prices, struggling to feed their families, unable to provide "a sufficiency of food—even of potatoes."[43]

Work did not guarantee adequate housing either. A few contractors lived up to the commitment to provide reasonable and "suitable accommodation," constructing barrack-like shanties along the works for the labourers and their families.[44] But as Pentland has pointed out, the bunkhouse, "a sign of some responsibility of the employer for his men," was a development of the latter half of the nineteenth century.[45] The typical contractor of the 1840s left his employees to find whatever housing they could. Since only a very small percentage of canallers found room and board among the local inhabitants, most built their own temporary accommodation, borrowing and stealing materials in the neighbourhood to construct huts and shacks, similar to the shanties thrown up by the unemployed.[46] A canaller usually shared accommodation with other canallers either in the barrack-like structures provided by contractors or in the huts they erected themselves. Of the 163 shanties built by labourers at Broad Creek on the Welland, only 29 were single-family dwellings. The rest were occupied by one, two, or three families with their various numbers of boarders. These dwellings formed a congested shanty-town typical of the shanty-towns which sprang up along the canals, and reminiscent of squalid Corktown, home of labourers on the Rideau Canal in the 1820s and 1830s.[47]

For the brief period of their existence, these shanty-towns along the canals became close-knit, homogeneous working-class communities, in which the bonds of living together reinforced and overlapped with bonds formed in the workplace. Canallers shared day-to-day social interaction and leisure activities, drinking together at the "grog" shops which sprang up to service the labourers and lying out on the hillsides on summer nights.[48] And they shared the daily struggle to subsist, the material poverty and insecurity, the wretched conditions, and the threat of starvation.

Bound together by their experiences along the canals, the Irish labourers were also united by what they brought from Ireland—a common culture shaped by ethnicity. Canaller communities were not simply homogeneous working-class communities, but Irish working-class communities, ethnic enclaves, in which the values, norms, traditions, and practices of the southern Irish ethno-culture thrived. Central to this culture was a communal organization which emphasized mutuality and fraternity, primarily within family and kinship networks.[49] While the persistence of kinship relationships amongst the canallers cannot be measured, many labourers lived with women and children in family units. In the winter of 1844, 1,300 "diggers" brought 700 women and 1,200 children to live along the Welland between Dalhousie and Allanburgh; and at Broad Creek in the summer of 1842, the Board of Works enumerated 250 families amongst the 797 men and 561 women and children. Shanty-towns around the Cornwall and Williamsburg Canals also housed many women and children who had followed the labourers from Ireland or across the Canadian–American border, maintaining the strong family structure characteristic of southern Ireland.[50]

Given the Irish pattern of migrating and emigrating in extended families, kinship networks may also have been reproduced on the canals. The fact that both newly arrived immigrants and labourers from the United States were from the limited region of Munster and Connaught increases the probability that canallers were bound together by strong, persisting kinship ties. But whether or not the labourers were bound by blood they brought to the construction sites traditions of co-operation and mutual aid in the workplace. As peasants in Munster and Connaught, they had held land individually, but had worked it co-operatively. When forced into wage labour to supplement the yields from their tiny holdings, the pattern of work again had been co-operative, friends, relatives, and neighbours forming harvesting or construction gangs which travelled and worked together throughout the British Isles.[51]

The clearest evidence of cultural unity and continuity along the canals was the labourers' commitment to the Roman Catholic faith. In contrast with the Irish Catholic labourers in the Ottawa Valley lumbering industry whom Cross found to be irreligious, canal labourers took their religion seriously enough to build shanty chapels for worship along the canals and to contribute to the construction of a new cathedral in St. Catharines. A stone tablet on the St. Catharines cathedral commemorates "the Irish working on the Welland Canal [who] built this monument to faith and piety" but who, in their eagerness to be part of the opening services, crowded into the churchyard 2,000 strong, destroying graves and markers in the process.[52]

Canallers were prepared to defend their faith in active conflict with Orangemen. Each July 12th brought violent clashes between Orangemen commemorating the Battle of the Boyne, and Roman Catholic labourers infuriated at the celebration of an event which had produced the hated penal code. The entire canaller community rallied to participate in anti-Orange demonstrations. In 1844 all the canallers along the Welland, organized under leaders and joined by friends from public works projects in Buffalo, marched to confront Toronto Orangemen and their families on an excursion to Niagara Falls.[53] Similarly, all labourers on the Welland were encouraged to participate in an 1849 demonstration. A labourer with a large family who was reluctant to march on the Orangemen at Slabtown was ordered to join his fellows or leave the canal. He should have left the canal. Instead he went along to Slabtown and was shot in the head.[54]

The canallers also demonstrated a continued identification with the cause of Irish nationalism and the struggle for repeal of the legislative union of Britain and Ireland. They participated in the agitation for repeal which spread throughout the British Isles and North America in 1843.[55] Lachine Canal labourers joined Irishmen in Montreal to call for an end to Ireland's colonial status; and labourers on the Welland met at Thorold to offer "their sympathy and assistance to their brethren at home in their struggle for the attainment of their just rights."[56] On the Williamsburg Canals, labourers also met together in support of Irish nationalism and Daniel O'Connell, the "Liberator" of Ireland. A local tavern keeper who interrupted a pro-O'Connell celebration by asking the canallers to move their bonfire away from his tavern, lived in fear they would be back to burn the tavern down.[57]

Strong, persisting ethno-cultural bonds united the canallers, at times in active conflict with the dominant Protestant Anglo-Saxon culture. But their ethno-culture was also a source of bitter division. A long-standing feud between natives of Munster County and those from Connaught County divided the labourers into two hostile factions. The origin of the feud is obscure. It may have developed during confrontations in the eighteenth and nineteenth centuries between striking agricultural labourers of one county and black leg labourers transported across county lines. Or possibly it dated as far back as the rivalries of the old kingdoms of mediaeval Ireland.[58] Whatever its origin, the feud had become an integral part of the culture which southern Irish labourers carried to construction projects throughout Britain and North America.[59]

The feud did not simply flare up now and then over an insult or dispute between men who otherwise mingled freely. Feuding was part of the way in which canallers organized their lives, membership in a faction dictating both working and living arrangements. Men of one faction usually worked with members of the same faction. At times Cork and Connaught did work together under one contractor on the same section of the work, particularly during the first few seasons of construction on the Welland when contractors hired labourers regardless of faction. But contractors quickly learned to honour the workers' preference to work with members of their faction, if only for the peace of the work.[60] Members of the same faction usually lived together also, cut off from the other faction in their separate Cork or Connaught community. Members of these communities offered each other material assistance in weathering difficult times. During summer and fall 1842 when half the Connaughtmen along the Broad Creek were ill with malaria, those Connaughtmen who were able to work "shared their miserable pittance," and provided necessities and medicine for the sick labourers and their dependants.[61] During the same season, the Connaughtmen also pooled their resources to retain a lawyer to defend 17 faction members in prison awaiting trial.[62]

The other side of this communal help and support, however, was suspicion of outsiders and intense hostility towards members of the rival faction. Hostility frequently erupted into violent confrontations between the factions. These confrontations were not a ritualized reminder of past skirmishes, but battles in deadly earnest, involving severe beatings and loss of life. The brutality of the encounters between Cork and Connaught led the *St. Catharines Journal* to denounce the participants as "strange and mad belligerent factions—brothers and countrymen, thirsting like savages for each other's blood—horribly infatuated."[63] Most participants in these skirmishes were heavily armed with "guns, pistols, swords, pikes, or poles, pitch forks, scyths," many of which were procured from local inhabitants or the militia stores. In preparation for their revenge on the Corkmen, in one of their more spectacular thefts, Connaughtmen on the Welland actually took possession of blacksmith shops and materials to manufacture pikes and halberds.[64] Usually they simply accosted citizens in the streets or raided them at night.[65]

Armed conflict between the factions could reduce the canal areas to virtual war zones for weeks on end, "parties of armed men, 200 or 300 in number constantly assembling and parading," planning attack and counter-attack, at times fighting it out on the streets of St. Catharines and smaller centres around the Williamsburg Canals.[66] As Power explained to military authorities in the Niagara District: "one riot is the parent of many others, for after one of their factional fights the friends of the worsted party rally from all quarters to avenge the defeat."[67]

The fighting of two drunken men might precipitate a clash between the factions.[68] But men who reported to the Board of Works concerning factional fights were unanimous in concluding that the underlying cause of feuding was the massive and chronic unemployment in the canal areas. David Thorburn, magistrate for the Niagara District, explained: "The first moving cause that excites to the trouble is the want of work, if not employed they are devising schemes to procure it, such as driving away the party who are fewest in number who are not of their country...."[69] Another magistrate for the Niagara District agreed that "the want of employment to procure bread" was the "principal root" of all the troubles; and Captain Wetherall, appointed to investigate the unrest along the canals, reached the same conclusion: "Strife to obtain work takes place between the two great sectional parties of Cork and Connaught.... The sole object of these combinations is to obtain work for themselves, by driving off the other party."[70] These observers appreciated the fact that the feud was a deep-seated hostility rooted in the southern Irish culture. They also believed that the Irish were given to letting their hostilities erupt into open conflict. Nonetheless, they were convinced that the problems associated with the feud, the open conflict and disruption of the work, would disappear if the problem of unemployment were solved.

This was the argument put forward by the labourers themselves at a meeting called by James Buchanan, ex-consul at New York and a respected member of the Irish community in North America. Buchanan posted notices along the Welland asking the "Sons of Erin" to meet with him to "reconcile and heal the divisions of [his] countrymen in Canada."[71] Corkmen refused to attend since the Connaughtmen's priest was helping to organize the meeting. But the Connaughtmen sent delegates to meet privately with Buchanan and assembled for a public meeting at Thorold. After listening to patriotic speeches and admonitions to peace and order, the Connaughtmen laid down their terms for an end to factional fights: "give us work to earn a living, we cannot starve, the Corkmen have all the work, give us a share of it."[72]

Thus, along the canals the feud of Cork and Connaught became the vehicle through which an excess of labourers fought for a limited number of jobs. In this respect, the feud was similar to other conflicts between hostile subgroups of workers competing in an over-stocked labour market. In the unskilled labour market of the Canadas, competition was frequently between French Canadians and Irish labourers. Along the canals, in the dockyards, and particularly in the Ottawa Valley lumbering industry, the two ethnic groups engaged in a violent conflict for work, at times as intense and brutal as the conflict of Cork and Connaught.[73]

Similar ethnic clashes occurred between Anglo-Saxon and Irish Celtic labourers competing in the unskilled labour market in Britain. Long-standing animosities between these two groups have led historians to emphasize the xenophobic nature of such confrontations.[74] But in an analysis of navvies on the railways of northern England, J.B. Treble argues that these superficially ethnic clashes were actually rooted in economic conditions which fostered fears that one group was undercutting or taking the jobs of the other group. Treble concludes that however deep the racial or cultural animosities between groups of labourers, "the historian would ignore at his peril economic motivation, admittedly narrowly conceived in terms of personal advantage, but for that very reason immensely strong."[75] Like the conflict between Irish and French and Irish and Anglo-Saxon labourers, the factional fights became part of a general process of fragmentation and subgrouping which John Foster sees developing during the nineteenth century in response to industrialization. By bringing hostile groups into competition with each other, the process militated against united action and the growth of a broad working-class consciousness.[76] The feud was one variation in this broader pattern of division and conflict amongst workers.

Yet the feud and the bitter fight for work did not preclude united action in pursuit of common economic goals. In a few instances the factions joined together to demand the creation of jobs. During the first summer of construction on the Welland thousands of labourers and their families repeatedly paraded the streets of St. Catharines with placards demanding "Bread or Work," at one point breaking into stores, mills, and a schooner. In a petition to the people of Upper Canada, they warned that they would not "fall sacrifice to starvation": "we were encouraged by contractors to build cantees [sic] on said work; now can't even afford 1 meals victuals ... we all Irishmen; employment or devastation."[77] Setting aside their sectional differences and uniting as "Irish labourers," Cork and Connaught co-operated to ensure that no one took the few hundred jobs offered by the Board of Works. Posters along the canal threatened "death and vengeance to any who should dare to work until employment was given to the whole." Bands of labourers patrolled the works driving off any who tried to take a job.[78] By bringing all construction to a halt the labourers forced the Superintendent of the Welland to create more work. Going beyond the limits of his authority, Power immediately let the contract for locks three to six to George Barnett, and began pressuring contractors to increase their manpower.[79] But as construction expanded the canallers began a scramble for the available jobs until the struggle for work was no longer a conflict between labourers and the Board of Works, but a conflict between Cork and Connaught, each faction attempting to secure employment for its members.[80]

The following summer unemployed labourers on the Welland again united to demand the creation of jobs. This was a season of particularly high and prolonged unemployment. In addition to the usual numbers of unemployed flooding into the area, 3,000 labourers discharged from the feeder and the Broad Creek branches in the early spring had to wait over three months for work to commence on the section from Allanburgh to Port Colborne. Incensed by the Board of Works' apparent indifference to their plight, the unemployed pressured officials until in mid-July Power again acted independently of the Board, authorizing contractors to begin work immediately.[81] Anticipating the Board's censure, Power justified his actions as necessary to the protection of the work and the preservation of the peace: "However easy it may be for those who are at a distance to speculate on the propriety of delaying the work until precise instructions may arrive, it is very difficult for me, surrounded by men infuriated by hunger, to persist in a course which must drive them to despair."[82] The jobs opened up by Power could employ only half of those seeking work, but that was sufficient to crack the canallers' united front and revive the sectional conflict.[83] In general, Cork and Connaught appear to have united to demand jobs only during periods when there was virtually no work available, and consequently no advantage to competing amongst themselves.

It was in their attempts to secure adequate wages that the canallers most clearly demonstrated their ability to unite around economic issues. During frequent strikes along the canals the antagonistic relationship between the two factions was subordinated to the labourers' common hostility towards their employers, so that in relation to the contractors the canallers stood united. A Board of Works investigation into one of the larger strikes on the Welland Canal found Cork and Connaught peacefully united in a work stoppage. Concerning the strike of 1,000 labourers below Marshville, the Board's agent, Dr. Jarrow, reported that the labourers at the Junction had gone along the line and found both factions "generally ready and willing" to join in an attempt to get higher wages:

> No breach of the peace took place, nor can I find a tangible threat to have been issued.... Several men have been at work for the last two days on many of the jobs.... Those who have returned to work are not interfered with in the least degree. Contractors do not seem to apprehend the least breach of the peace.... The workmen seem well organized and determined not to render themselves liable to justice.... Both the Cork and Connaught men are at work on different jobs below Marshville, and they seem to have joined in the Strick [sic] and I have not been able to find that their party feelings have the least connection with it.[84]

This was not an isolated instance of unity between the factions. Many strikes were small, involving only the men under one contractor, who usually belonged to the same faction; however, on the Welland in particular, Cork and Connaught joined in large strikes. Unity may have been fragile, but the overriding pattern that emerges during strikes is one of co-operation between the factions.[85] Not only did the factions unite in large strikes, but during a small strike involving only members of one faction, the other faction usually did not act as strike-breakers, taking the jobs abandoned by the strikers. What little information there is on strike-breaking concerns striking labourers confronting members of their own faction who tried to continue work, suggesting that the decision to work during a strike was not based on factional loyalties or hostilities.[86] Thus, most strikes did not become extensions of the bitter conflict for work. Rather strikes brought labourers together to pursue common economic interests. The instances in which Cork and Connaught united provide dramatic evidence of the ability of these economic interests to overcome an antipathy deeply rooted in the canallers' culture.

Canallers frequently combined in work stoppages demanding the payment of overdue wages. More often their strikes centred on the issue of wage rates. In a report concerning labour unrest on the canals of Upper and Lower Canada, Captain Wetherall concluded: "the question of what constitutes a fair wage is the chief cause from which all the bitter fruit comes." The priest among labourers on the Williamsburg agreed with Wetherall, going so far as to suggest that if the rate of wages could be settled once and for all troops and police would not be required for the canal areas. Similarly, Thorburn ranked wage rates with unemployment as a major cause of labour disturbances on the Welland.[87]

Since officials often reported "many" or "a few" strikes without indicating how many, the level of strike activity can only be suggested. Contractors expected, and usually faced, strikes in the late fall when they tried to impose the seasonal reduction in wage rates.[88] Strikes demanding an increase in wages were harder to predict, but more frequent. Each spring and summer on the Cornwall, Welland, and Williamsburg Canals work stoppages disrupted construction. Even in winter those labourers fortunate enough to continue working attempted to push up wages through strikes.[89] The degree of success which canallers enjoyed in their strikes cannot be determined from the fragmentary and scattered references to work stoppages. It is clear, however, that they forced contractors to pay wages above the level for unskilled, manual labour in general, and above the 2s. or 2s.6d. which the Board of Works considered that most labourers on public works could expect.[90] On the Cornwall and Williamsburg Canals, strikes secured and maintained modest increases to as high as 3s. and 3s.6d.[91] Gains were much greater on the Welland. As early as winter 1843 labourers had driven wages to what Power claimed was the highest rate being offered on the continent.[92] While Power's statement cannot be accepted at face value, wages on the Welland may well have been the highest for manual labour in the Canadas, and in the northeastern United States where jobs were scarce and wages depressed. Strikes on the Welland forced wages even higher during 1843 and 1844, until the Board of Works calculated that labourers on the Welland were receiving at least 30 percent more than the men on all the other works under its superintendence.[93]

How did the canallers, a fluid labour force engaged in casual, seasonal labour, achieve the solidarity and commitment necessary to successful strike action during a period of massive unemployment? Work stoppages protesting non-payment of wages may have been simply spontaneous reactions to a highly visible injustice, requiring little formal organization, more in the nature of protests than organized strikes. But the strikes through which canallers aggressively forced up wages or prevented contractors from lowering wages, required a greater degree of organization and long-term commitment. Labourers might be on strike for weeks, during which time they would become desperate for food.

In a variety of ways, the canallers' shared ethno-culture contributed to their successful strike action. Strikers found unity in the fact that they were "all Irishmen," in the same way that the unemployed identified with each other as "Irishmen" in their united demands for work. In the only well-documented strike by canallers, the Lachine strike of 1843, the labourers themselves stated this clearly. Corkmen and Connaughtmen issued joint petitions warning employers and would-be strike-breakers that they were not simply all canallers, they were "all Irishmen" whose purpose and solidarity would not be subverted.[94] Membership in a common ethnic community provided concrete aid in organizing united action. At least in summer 1844 on the Welland, leadership in anti-Orange demonstrations overlapped with leadership in labour organization. During this season of frequent strikes, as many as 1,000 labourers assembled for mass meetings.[95] The authorities could not discover exactly what transpired at these meetings, since admittance was restricted to those who knew the password; a military officer, however, was able to observe one meeting at a distance. Ensign Gaele reported witnessing a collective decision-making process in which those present discussed, voted on, and passed resolutions. He drew particular attention to the participation of a man "who appeared to be their leader," a well-spoken individual of great influence, the same individual who had ridden at the head of the canallers on their march to intercept the Orangemen at Niagara Falls.[96] The situation on one canal during one season cannot support generalizations concerning organization on all canals throughout the 1840s. It does, however, suggest one way in which unity around ethno-cultural issues facilitated unity in economic struggles, by providing an established leadership.

Of more significance to the canallers' strike activity was the vehicle of organization provided by their ethno-culture. Like other groups of Irish labourers, most notably the Molly Maguires of the Pennsylvania coal fields, canallers found that the secret societies which flourished in nineteenth-century Ireland were well adapted to labour organization in the new world.[97] At a time when those most active in strikes were subject to prosecution and immediate dismissal, oath-bound societies offered protection from the law and the reprisals of employers. The government investigation into disturbances on the Beauharnois found sufficient evidence to conclude that secret societies were the means by which the canallers organized their strikes. But it was unable to break through the labourers' secrecy and uncover details concerning the actual operation of the societies.[98] Similarly, Rev. McDonagh, despite his intimate knowledge of the canallers' personal lives, could only offer the authorities the names of two societies operating along the Welland, the Shamrock and Hibernian Societies. He could provide no information as to how they functioned, whether there were a number of small societies or a few large ones, whether all labourers or only a segment of the canallers belonged to them. And he "couldn't break them."[99]

The oaths which swore labourers to secrecy also bound them to be faithful to each other, ensuring solidarity and commitment in united action, and enforcing sanctions against any who betrayed his fellows. In addition, societies operated through an efficient chain of communication and command which allowed for tactics to be carefully formulated and executed.[100] Navvies did not develop a formal trade union. Consequently, in comparison with the activities of workers in the few trade unions of the 1820s, 1830s, and 1840s in British North America, the direct action of the Irish labourers appears "ad hoc."[101] But the fact that the navvies' organization was impenetrable to authorities and remains invisible to historians should not lead to the error of an "ad hoc" categorization. Although clandestine, secret societies were noted for the efficiency, even sophistication, of their organization,[102] and although not institutionalized within the formal, structured labour movement, they were the means of organizing sustained resistance, not spontaneous outbreaks of protest. Organization within secret societies, rather than within a formal trade union also meant that canallers did not reach out to establish formal ties with other segments of the working class. As a result, they have left no concrete evidence of having identified the interests of their group with the interests of the larger working class, no clear demonstration that they perceived of themselves as participating in a broader working-class struggle. But while their method of organization ruled out formal linking and expression of solidarity with the protest of other groups of workers, secret societies testified to the Irish labourers' link with a long tradition of militant opposition to employers in the old world. The secret societies which flourished in Dublin throughout the first half of the nineteenth century were feared by moderates in the Irish nationalist movement, because of their aggressive pursuit of working-class interests. During the same period, the agrarian secret societies of the southern Irish countryside primarily organized agricultural labourers and cottiers around issues such as rising conacre rents and potato prices. Although the ruling class of Britain and Ireland insisted that agrarian societies were essentially sectarian, these societies were, in fact, the instruments of class action, class action which at times united Protestant and Catholic labourers in a common cause.[103]

This cultural legacy of united opposition was invaluable to the canal labourers in their attempts to achieve higher wages. During their years of conflict with landlords and employers, the peasant labourers of southern Ireland acquired a belief system and values necessary to effective united action in the workplace. Their belief system probably did not include a political critique of society which called for fundamental change in the relationship between capital and labour. Although Chartist and Irish nationalist leaders worked closely in the mid-nineteenth century, none of the varied radical strains of Chartism made significant advances in Ireland, which suggests that Irish labourers may not have seen themselves as members of a broader class whose interests were irreconcilable to the interests of capital.[104] But if theory had not given them a framework within which to understand the conflict of capital and labour, experience had created in them a deep-seated suspicion of employers and a sensitivity to exploitation. They brought to the new world the belief that their interests were in conflict with the employers' interest. Wetherall tried to explain their outlook to the Board of Works:

> They look on a Contractor as they view the "Middle Man" of their own Country, as a grasping money making person, who has made a good bargain with the Board of Works for labour to be performed; and they see, or imagine they see, an attempt to improve that bargain at their expense ... such is the feeling of the people, that they cannot divest themselves of the feeling that they are being imposed on if the contractor has an interest in the transaction.[105]

In the labourers' own words, posted along the works during the Lachine strike: "Are we to be tyrannized by Contractors ... surrender/To No Contractors who wants to live by the sweat of our Brow."[106]

Irish labourers also brought to the new world a willingness to defy the law and, if necessary, use force to achieve their ends. Years of repression and discrimination had fostered what Kenneth Duncan has characterized as "a tradition of violence and terrorism, outside the law and in defiance of all authority."[107] In Britain the Irish labourers' willingness to challenge the law and the authorities had earned them a reputation for militance in the union movements, at the same time that it had infused a revolutionary impulse into Chartism.[108] In the Canadas, this same willingness marked their strike activity.

Newspapers and government officials usually reported the strikes along the canals as "rioting" or "riotous conduct," the uncontrollable excesses of an ethnic group addicted to senseless violence.[109] Yet far from being excessive and indiscriminate, the canallers' use of violence was restrained and calculated. Force or the threat of force was a legitimate tactic to be used if necessary. Some strikes involved little, if any, violence. Although he claimed to have looked very hard, Dr. Jarrow could find no instances of "outrage" during the first week of the Marshville strike, a strike involving 1,500 labourers along the Welland. In another large strike on the Welland the following summer, the *St. Catharines Journal* reported that there were no riotous disturbances.[110] When strikers did use force it was calculated to achieve a specific end. Organized bands of strikers patrolling the canal with bludgeons were effective in keeping strike-breakers at home.[111] Similarly, when labourers turned their violence on contractors and foremen, the result was not only the winning of a strike but also a remarkable degree of job control.[112] After only one season on the Williamsburg Canals, labourers had thoroughly intimidated contractors. One did not dare go near his work. Another said that the labourers "set at defiance" and worked "as they pleased."[113] Canallers also attacked the canals, but these were not instances of senseless vandalism. Power viewed what he called "extraordinary accidents" as one way in which labourers pressured for redress of specific grievances.[114] On the Welland a related pressure tactic was interfering with the navigation. During the strike of approximately 1,500 labourers in summer 1844, captains of boats were afraid to pass through because they feared rude attacks on their passengers. Such fears appear to have been well-founded. The previous winter, 200 canallers had attacked an American schooner, broken open the hatches, and driven the crew from the vessel, seriously injuring the captain and a crew member. Soldiers were required to keep "at bay the blood-thirsty assailants" while the crew reboarded their vessel.[115]

The canallers' willingness to resort to violence and defy authority antagonized large segments of the population who lamented the transplanting to the new world of outrages "characteristic only of Tipperary."[116] But despite the protestations of newspapers and private individuals that the canallers' use of force was inappropriate to the new world, the Irish labourers' militant tradition was well suited to labour relations and power relations in the Canadas. The canallers' experience with the government and law enforcement agencies could only have reinforced what the past had taught—that the laws and the authorities did not operate in the interests of workers, particularly Irish Catholic workers. In their strikes, canallers confronted not just their employers, but the united opposition of the government, courts, and state law enforcement officers.

The government's opposition to strikes was based on the conviction that labourers should not attempt to influence wage rates. To government officials such as J.B. Mills of the Williamsburg Canal, the repeated strikes along the canals added up to a general "state of insubordination among the labourers," an "evil" which jeopardized the entire Public Works programme. Reports of the Board of Works condemned strikers for throwing construction schedules and cost estimates into chaos, and applauded contractors for their "indefatigable and praiseworthy exertions" in meeting turnouts and other difficulties with their labourers.[117] Leaving no doubt as to its attitude toward demands for higher wages, the Board worked closely with contractors in their attempts to prevent and break strikes. On their own initiative, contractors met together to determine joint strategies for handling turnouts and holding the line against wage increases.[118] The Board of Works went one step further, bringing contractors and law enforcement officers together to devise stratagems for labour control, and assuming the responsibility for co-ordinating and funding these stratagems.[119] Contractors and the Board joined forces in a comprehensive system of blacklisting which threatened participants in strikes. Operating on the assumption that the majority of the "well-disposed" were being provoked by a few rabble-rousers, contractors immediately dismissed ringleaders. Even during a peaceful strike such as the one at Marshville, in winter 1843, contractors discharged "those most active."[120] For its part the Board of Works collected and circulated along the canals descriptions of men like "Patrick Mitchell, a troublesome character" who "created insubordination amongst labourers" wherever he went.[121] Once blacklisted, men like Mitchell had little hope of employment on the public works in Canada.

Many labourers thus barred from public works projects also spent time in jail as part of the Board's attempt to suppress disturbances. Although British law gave workers the right to combine to withdraw their services in disputes over wages and hours, employers and the courts did not always honour this right. When the Board of Works' chief advisor on labour unrest argued that the Board should suppress the "illegal" combinations on the Welland and Williamsburg Canals, he was expressing an opinion widely held in British North America and an opinion shared by many officials involved in controlling labour unrest on the Public Works.[122] While opinion was divided over the rights of workers, there was general agreement that employers had the right to continue their operations during a strike, the course of action usually chosen by contractors, who seldom opted to negotiate with strikers. Workers who interfered with this right, by intimidating strike-breakers or contractors or generally obstructing the work, invited criminal charges. Since the charge of intimidation and obstruction was capable of broad interpretation, including anything from bludgeoning a contractor to talking to strike-breakers, this provision of the law gave contractors and the Board considerable scope for prosecuting strikers.[123]

To supplement existing labour laws, the Board of Works secured passage of the 1845 Act for the Preservation of the Peace near Public Works, the first in a long series of regulatory acts directed solely at controlling canal and railway labourers throughout the nineteenth century.[124] The Act provided for the registration of all firearms on branches of the Public Works specified by the Executive. The Board of Works had already failed in earlier attempts to disarm labourers on projects under its supervision. An 1843 plan to induce canallers on the Beauharnois to surrender their weapons was discarded "partly because there [was] no legal basis for keeping them." The following year a similar system on the Welland was also abandoned as illegal. Magistrates who had asked labourers to give up their weapons and to "swear on the Holy Evangelist that they had no gun, firearm, or offensive weapon" were indicted.[125] The 1845 Public Works Act put the force of the law and the power of the state behind gun control.

Most members of the Assembly accepted the registration of firearms along the canals as unavoidable under circumstances which "the existing law was not sufficient to meet."[126] A few members joined Aylwin of Quebec City in denouncing the measure as a dangerous over-reaction to a situation of the government's own making, "an Act of proscription, an Act which brought back the violent times of the word Annals of Ireland."[127] A more sizeable group shared Lafontaine's reservations that the bill might be used as a general disarming measure against any citizen residing near the canals. But the Attorney General's assurances that the disarming clause would apply "only to actual labourers on the public works" secured for the Bill an easy passage.[128] Even a member like Drummond, one of the few to defend canallers' interests in the House, ended up supporting the disarming clause on the grounds that it would contribute to the canallers' welfare by preventing them from committing the acts of violence to which contractors and hunger drove them. Drummond managed to convince himself that disarming the labourers would not infringe on their rights. He believed that all men had the right to keep arms for the protection of their property. But the canallers had no property to protect; they were too poor to acquire any. Therefore they had neither the need, nor the right to possess weapons.[129]

In addition to disarming the labourers, the Public Works Act empowered the Executive to station mounted police forces on the public works.[130] Under the Act, Captain Wetherall secured an armed constabulary of 22 officers to preserve order among the labourers on the Williamsburg Canals. The Board of Works had already established its own constabulary on the Welland, two years prior to the legislation of 1845. Throughout 1843 and 1844 the Welland force fluctuated between 10 and 20, diminishing after 1845 as the number of labourers on the canals decreased. At a time when even the larger communities in Upper Canada, along with most communities in North America, still relied on only a few constables working under the direction of a magistrate, the size of these police forces testifies to the Board's commitment to labour control.[131] While the forces fulfilled various functions, in the eyes of the Board of Works their primary purpose was to ensure completion of the works within the scheduled time. Even protection of contractors from higher wages was not in itself sufficient reason for increasing the size of one of the forces. When Power asked for accommodation for a Superintendent of Police at the Junction, the Board answered that the old entrance lock was the only place where a strong force was necessary, since no combination of labourers for wages on the other works could delay the opening of the navigation, "the paramount object in view." A later communication expressed more forcefully the Board's general approach to funding police forces, stating that the only circumstances under which the expense of keeping the peace could be justified were that if it were not kept up the canals would not be "available to the trade."[132]

Despite these apparently strict criteria for funding police, the Board usually intervened to protect strike-breakers, probably because any strike threatened to delay opening of the navigation in the long, if not the short, term. Indeed, in their 1843 Report to the legislature, the Commissioners argued that it was part of their responsibility to help contractors meet deadlines by providing adequate protection to those labourers willing to work during a strike.[133] In meeting this responsibility the Board at times hired as many as 16 extra men on a temporary basis. When it was a question of getting the canals open for navigation, the government appears to have been willing to go to almost any lengths to continue the work. In the winter of 1845, the Governor-General gave Power the authority to hire whatever number of constables it would take to ensure completion of construction by spring.[134] Canal police forces worked closely with existing law enforcement agencies, since the common law required the magistrates to give direction in matters "relating to the arrest of suspected or guilty persons," and generally to ensure that the police acted within the law.[135] But Wetherall's investigation into the conduct of the Welland Canal force revealed that magistrates did not always keep constables from abusing their powers: "The constables oft exceed their authority, cause irritation, and receive violent opposition, by their illegal and ill judged manner of attempting to make arrests." In one instance, the constables' behaviour had resulted in a member of the force being wounded. In another, an action had been commenced for false imprisonment. Wetherall also drew attention to complaints that the police force was composed of Orangemen, at least one of whom had acted improperly in "publicly abusing the Roman Catholic Religion—damning the Pope—etc., etc."[136]

The Williamsburg Canal force also came under attack for its provocative behaviour. Inhabitants of Williamsburg Township petitioned the Governor-General concerning the conduct of Captain James Macdonald and his men during a circus at Mariatown:

> The police attended on said day where in the course of the evening through the misconduct of the police on their duty two persons have been maltreated and abused cut with swords and stabbed, taken prisoners and escorted to the police office that all this abuse was committed having the constables in a state of intoxication on their duty when the Magistrate who commanded them was so drunk that he fell out of a cart. A pretty representative is Mr. MacDonald.[137]

The Roman Catholic priest on the Williamsburg Canals joined in denouncing the police force, warning the labourers: "They are like a parcel of wolves and roaring mad lions seeking the opportunity of shooting you like dogs and all they want is the chance in the name of God leave those public works."[138]

Of invaluable assistance to the constables and magistrates were the Roman Catholic priests, hired by the Board of Works as part of the police establishment, and stationed amongst canallers. Referred to as "moral" or "spiritual" agents, they were in reality police agents, paid out of the Board's police budget, and commissioned to preserve "peace and order" by employing the ultimate threat: hell.[139] They were of limited value in controlling Orange/Green confrontations. They were actually suspected of encouraging them.[140] Their effectiveness in stopping factional fights was also limited, at least on the Welland where the Reverend McDonagh was suspected of harbouring sectional sentiments.[141] Their most important function was to prevent or break strikes. Intimate involvement in the canallers' daily lives equipped them as informers concerning possible labour unrest.[142] When canallers struck, authorities could rely on priests to admonish labourers to give up their "illegal" combinations and return to work, to show "that the Gospel has a more salutory effect than bayonets."[143] Priests were not insensitive to the suffering of their charges, and to its immediate cause. McDonagh repeatedly argued the canallers' case with government officials, contractors, and civil and military authorities.[144] On the Williamsburg Canals, the Reverend Clarke's criticism of the treatment of labourers became such an embarrassment to the government that he was shipped back to Ireland, supposedly for health reasons.[145] But at the same time that priests were protesting conditions along the canals, they were devoting most of their energy to subverting the protest of their parishioners. McDonagh fulfilled this function so successfully that the Superintendent on the Welland Canal told the Board he knew of "no one whose services could have been so efficient."[146]

By supplementing existing laws and enforcement agencies, the government was able to bring an extraordinary degree of civil power against the canal labourers. Even an expanded civil power, however, was inadequate to control the canallers and the military became the real defenders of the peace in the canal areas. As early as the first summer of construction on the Welland, the Governor-General asked the Commander of the Forces to station the Royal Canadian Rifles in three locations along the Welland, 60 men at St. Catharines, 60 at Thorold, and 30 at Port Maitland. In addition, a detachment of the coloured Incorporated Militia attached to the Fifth Lincoln Militia was stationed at Port Robinson. Aid was also available from the Royal Canadian Rifles permanently stationed at Chippewa.[147] From these headquarters, troops marched to trouble spots for a few hours, days, or weeks. Longer postings necessitated temporary barracks such as those constructed at Broad Creek and Marshville in fall 1842.[148] No troops were posted on either the Cornwall or Williamsburg Canals, despite the requests of contractors and inhabitants. Detachments in the vicinity, however, were readily available for temporary postings.[149]

With a long tradition of military intervention in civil disturbances both in Great Britain and British North America, the use of troops was a natural response to the inadequacies of the civil powers.[150] Troops were important for quickly ending disturbances and stopping the escalation of dangerous situations such as an Orange/Green clash or a confrontation between labourers and contractors.[151] The use of troops carried the risk that men might be shot needlessly. As Aylwin told the Legislature:

> If the constable exceed his duty there is a certain remedy; he may perhaps throw a man in prison; but if that man be innocent he will afterwards be restored to his family; when however, the military are called out the soldier is obliged to do his duty, and men are shot down who perhaps ... are quite as unwilling to break the peace as any man in the world.

Such had been the case during a confrontation on the Beauharnois Canal. Troops were called in and "bloody murders were committed." Labourers were "shot, and cut down, and driven into the water and drowned."[152] On the canals of Upper Canada, however, the military does not appear to have charged or opened fire on canallers. No matter how great their numbers or how well they were armed, canallers usually disbanded with the arrival of troops and the reading of the Riot Act.

Detachments were even more valuable as a preventive force. Before special detachments were posted along the Welland, the Governor-General explicitly instructed magistrates to use the troops in a preventive capacity, calling them out if "there should be any reason to fear a breach of the Peace, with which the civil power would be inadequate to deal."[153] Magistrates gave the broadest possible interpretation to the phrase "any reason to fear" and repeatedly called in the military when there had been merely verbal threats of trouble. When a large number of unemployed labourers appeared "ripe for mischief," when strikers seemed likely to harass the strike-breakers, magistrates requisitioned troops.[154]

Magistrates used the troops to such an extent that they provoked the only real opposition to military intervention in civil affairs—opposition from the military itself. Both on-the-spot commanders and high-ranking military officials complained that troops were being "harassed" by the magistrates, that the requisitions for aid were "extremely irregular," and that the troops were marching about the frontier on the whim of alarmists.[155] The expense of keeping four or five detachments on the march does not appear to have been a factor in the dispute over the use of troops, since the civil authorities met the cost of deploying troops in civil disturbances. The British Treasury continued to pay for salaries, provisions, and stores, but the Board of Works accepted responsibility for constructing barracks and for providing transportation and temporary accommodation at trouble spots when necessary.[156] The only point at issue appears to have been the unorthodox and unnecessary use of detachments.

This dispute was the only disharmony in the co-operation between civil and military authorities and even it had little effect on the actual system of control. At the height of the dispute, commanding officers still answered virtually all requisitions, although in a few instances they withdrew their men immediately if they felt their services were not required.[157] After the Provincial Secretary ruled that commanders must respond to all requisitions, whatever the circumstances, even the grumbling stopped.[158] Particularly on the Welland, regular troops were kept constantly patrolling the canal areas in apprehension of disturbances, "looking for trouble," as Colonel Elliott put it.[159]

With special laws, special police forces, and a military willing—if not eager—to help, the government of the Canadas marshalled the coercive power of the state against labourers on the public works. Yet the government failed to suppress labour unrest and to prevent successful strike action. Many officials and contractors accepted this failure as proof of the Celt's ungovernable disposition. Invoking the Irish stereotype to explain the disorder along the canals, they ignored their own role in promoting unrest and obscured the class dimension of the canallers' behaviour. They also misinterpreted the nature of the relationship between the canallers' ethno-culture and their collective action. What the southern Irish brought to the new world was not a propensity for violence and rioting, but a culture shaped by class relations in the old world. Class tensions, inseparably interwoven with racial hatred and discrimination, had created in the southern Irish suspicion and hatred of employers, distrust of the laws and the authorities, and a willingness to violate the law to achieve their ends. This bitter cultural legacy shaped the Irish labourers' resistance to conditions in the Canadas and gave a distinctive form to class conflict on the canals.

Endnotes

1. Public Archives of Canada, Record Group 11, Department of Public Works: 5, Canals (hereafter cited RG11-5), Welland Canal Letterbook, Samuel Power to Thomas Begly. Chairman of Board of Works (hereafter cited WCLB), Power to Begly, 12 August 1842.
2. Public Archives of Canada, Record Group 8, British Military and Naval Records I, C Series, Vol. 60, Canals (hereafter cited C Series, Vol. 60), Bethune to MacDonald, 31 March 1843.
3. H.C. Pentland, "Development of a Capitalistic Labour Market in Canada," *Canadian Journal of Economics and Political Science* 25 (1959), 450–61.
4. A.C. Buchanan, Parliamentary Papers, 1842, No. 373, cited in W.F. Adams, *Ireland and the Irish Emigration to the New World* (Connecticut 1932).
5. Gary Teeple, "Land, Labour, and Capital in Pre-Confederation Canada," in Teeple, ed., *Capitalism and the National Question in Canada* (Toronto 1972); Leo A. Johnson, "Land Policy, Population Growth and Social Structure in the Home District, 1793–1851," *Ontario History* 63 (1971), 41 60. Both Teeple and Johnson attach particular significance to the ideas of Edward Gibbon Wakefield who advocated a prohibitive price on land to force immigrants into the labour force. V.C. Fowke, "The Myth of the Self Sufficient Canadian Pioneer," *Transactions of the Royal Society of Canada* 56 (1962).
6. R.T. Naylor "The Rise and Fall of the Third Commercial Empire of the St. Lawrence," in Gary Teeple, ed., *Capitalism and the National Question in Canada* (Toronto 1972), 1–13; Teeple, "Land, Labour, and Capital," 57–62.
7. H. C. Pentland, "Labour and the Development of Industrial Capitalism in Canada," Ph.D. thesis, University of Toronto, 1960, 239. In the fall of 1840, contractors in the Chambly Canal could not procure labourers even at what the government considered most extravagant rates. Canada, *Journals of the Legislative Assembly 1841*, Appendix D.; W.F. Adams, *Ireland and the Irish Emigration* and Helen I. Cowen, *British Emigration to British North America: The First Hundred Years* (Toronto 1961).
8. Pentland, "Labour and Industrial Capitalism," 273. See also: Frances Morehouse, "The Irish Migration of the 'Forties,'" *American Historical Review*, 33 (1927–28), 579–92.
9. The best treatment of famine immigrants in British North America is Kenneth Duncan, "Irish Famine Immigration and the Social Structure of Canada West," *Canadian Review of Sociology and Anthropology* (1965), 19–40.
10. Report of the Niagara District Council, *Niagara Chronicle*, 4 August 1847.

11. RG11-5, Vol. 390, file 93, Williamsburg Canals, Estimates and Returns, 1844–58, Public Notice of the Board of Works issued by Begly, 26 February 1844; RG11-5, Vol. 390, file 94, Police Protection and the Williamsburg Canals, Mills to Begly, 16 February 1847.
12. J.P. Merritt, *Biography of the Hon. W. H. Merritt* (St. Catharines 1875), 310. Concerning the construction industry in Britain, Gosta E. Sandstrom has argued that the very existence of an easily exploitable labour pool deferred mechanization, relieving state and private management "of the need for constructive thinking." Gosta E. Sandstrom, *The History of Tunnelling* (London 1963). For a discussion of the relationship between labour supply and the development of mechanization in the mid-nineteenth century see Raphael Samuel, "The Workshop of the World: Steam Power and Hand Technology in mid-Victorian Britain," *History Workshop*, 3 (1977), 6–72. Labourers on North American canals in the 1840s were still performing basically the same tasks their counterparts had performed half a century earlier during the canal age in Europe. For a description of these tasks see: Anthony Burton, *The Canal Builders* (London 1972). Alvin Harlow describes a variety of new inventions used on the Erie Canal, which might have made their way to the canals of the Canadas. These ranged from a sharp-edged shovel for cutting roots to a stump-puller operated by seven men and a team of horses or oxen. Alvin Harlow, *Old Towpaths: The Story of the American Canal Era* (New York 1964), 53.
13. John P. Heisler, *The Canals of Canada*, National Historic Sites Service, Manuscript Report Number 64, December 1971, 220-1, 224-5, 226-7.
14. RG11-5, Vol. 407, file 113, Thorburn to Daly, 10 January 1844.
15. Ibid., Thorburn to Murdock, 18 August 1842; RG11-5 WCLB, Samuel Power to A. Thomas Begly, Chairman of Board of Works, Power to Begly, 20 March 1843; Ibid., Power to Begly, 17 July 1843.
16. Duncan "Irish Famine Immigration," 25–6. For a discussion of the application of the improved system of British agriculture to Upper Canada see: Kenneth Kelly, "The Transfer of British Ideas on Improved Farming to Ontario During the First Half of the Nineteenth Century," *Ontario History*, 63 (1971), 103–11.
17. *St. Catharines Journal*, 31 August 1843; *Niagara Chronicle*, 4 August 1847.
18. Duncan, "Irish Famine Immigration," 26.
19. RG11-5, WCLB, Power to Begly, 8 April 1843; *Niagara Chronicle*, 4 August 1847.
20. RG11-5, Vol. 390, file 94, Hiel to Begly, 16 February 1847.
21. RGl1-5, Vol. 390, file 93, Public Notice of Board of Works, 26 February 1844; *Legislative Journals* 1844–45, Appendix Y, Report of Mills, 20 January 1845; Ibid., Mills to Begly, 21 January 1845; Ibid., Jarvis to Daly, 28 October 1845.
22. *Niagara Chronicle*, 4 August 1847.
23. *St. Catharines Journal*, 16 February 1844.
24. Petition of Constantine Lee and John William Baynes to Sir Charles Bagot, cited in Dean Harris, *The Catholic Church in the Niagara Peninsula* (Toronto 1895), 255. Lee was the Roman Catholic priest for St. Catharines, Baynes the community's Presbyterian minister. See also: RG11-5, Vol. 389, file 89, Correspondence of Samuel Keefer, 1843–51, Superintendent of Welland Canal, 1848–52, Keefer to Begly, 1 February 1843; RGl1-5, Vol. 407, file 114, McDonagh to Killaly, 2 May 1843; Vol. 407, file 113, Thorburn to Daly, 10 January 1844; RG11-5, Vol. 381, file 56, John Rigney, Superintendent Cornwall Canal, 1841-44, Godfrey to Begly, 22 April 1843; Ibid., Godfrey to Begly, 8 June 1843.
25. Richard Splane, *Social Welfare in Ontario 1791–1893* (Toronto 1965), 68–9, 74.
26. *St. Catharines Journal*, 26 January 1844.
27. *St. Catharines Journal*, 16 February 1844.
28. Harris, *The Catholic Church in the Niagara Peninsula*, 255; RG11-5, Vol. 388, file 87, Correspondence of General Killaly, 1841–55, Welland Canal, Merritt to Killaly, 12 August 1842.
29. RG11-5 Vol. 389, file 89, Keefer to Begly, 1 February 1843. Terry Coleman discusses the stereotype of the navvy on construction sites in the British Isles in his chapter, "King of Labourers," in Terry Coleman, ed., *The Railway Navvies: A History of the Men Who Made the Railways* (London 1965), ch. 12.

30. Farm labourers' wages appear in RG5-B21, Emigration Records, 1840–44, Information to Immigrants, April 1843, for Brockville, Chippewa, Cornwall, Fort Erie, Indiana, Niagara, Port Colborne, Prescott, Queenston, Smith's Falls; Ibid. For the Information of Emigrants of the Labouring Classes, December 1840, the Johnston District. Wages were not consistently higher in the area round any one of the canals. Newspapers also maintain references to wage levels for farm labourers. Only newspapers appear to have paid much attention to the serious accidents on construction sites. Navvies crushed by stones, kicked by horses, and drowned in the locks made good copy. Work on the canals under consideration did not involve tunnelling, by far the most hazardous aspect of the navvy's work. But the malaria-producing mosquito which thrived on many canal construction sites in North America made up for this. In October 1842 Dr. John Jarrow reported to the Board of Works that "scarcely an individual" from among the over 800 men who had been on the Broad Creek works would escape the "lake fever." Three-quarters of the labourers' wives and children were already sick. Very few of those under two would recover. RG11-5, Vol. 407, file 104, Welland Canal Protection 1842-50, Memorandum of Dr. John Jarrow to the Board of Works, 1 October 1842.
31. H.C. Pentland, "Labour and the Development of Industrial Capitalism in Canada," 232. Pentland underlines the difficulty in making valid generalizations because of "considerable variation from time to time and from place to place." All wages have been translated into Sterling, using the conversion rate of 22s. 2 3/4 d. Currency per £ Sterling, published in Canada RG5-B21, Quarterly Return of Prices in the Province of Canada in the Quarter Ending 31 October 1844. The variation in wages along the canals was determined through the frequent references to wage levels in the records of the Department of Public Works and newspaper articles. Wages fluctuated within the same range on the Lachine and Beauharnois Canals in Canada East. H.C. Pentland, "The Lachine Strike of 1843," *Canadian Historical Review*, 29 (1948), 255–77; Legislative Journals, 1843, Appendix T, Report of the Commissioners appointed to inquire into the Disturbances upon the line of the Beauharnois Canal, during the summer of 1843. *Legislative Journals*, 1843, Appendix Q; Ibid., 1845, Appendix AA.
32. Given that labourers at Beauharnois used company stores and received store pay as did many canallers in Upper Canada and considering the fairly constant price of foodstuffs along the St. Lawrence system, the findings of the Beauharnois Commission can be applied to labourers on the Cornwall, Welland, and Williamsburg Canals. *Legislative Journals*, 1843, Appendix T; RG5-B21, Information to Immigrants, April 1843; Ibid., For the Information of Emigrants of the Labouring Classes, December 1840, the Johnston District; Ibid., Quarterly Return of Prices for the City of Montreal in the Quarter ended 31st October 1844.
33. These figures represent averages of the estimated number of days worked during each month on the Cornwall, Welland, and Williamsburg Canals.
34. WCLB, Power to Begly, April 1842; Ibid., Power to Begly, 10 March 1843; Welland Canal Commission, folder 8 (hereafter cited WCC-8), Begly to Power, 24 January 1844; RGl1-5, Vol. 390, file 94, Killaly to Begly, 26 March 1846; Vol. 381, file 56, Godfrey to Begly, 8 June 1843; Vol. 389, file 89, Keefer to Begly, 2 May 1848, RG11-5, Vol. 388, file 88, Correspondence of Hamilton Killaly, Assistant Engineer on Welland Canal, 1842-57, Keefer to Begly, 14 March 1849. Frequently the government withheld money from contractors, making it impossible for them to pay their labourers. The government also took its time paying labourers employed directly by the Board of Works.
35. *Legislative Journals*, 1843, Appendix Q; WCLB, Power to Begly, 1 October 1842.
36. C Series, Vol. 60, Memorandum of Captain Wetherall, 3 April 1843.
37. *Legislative Journals*, 1843, Appendix Q. WCLB, Power to Begly, 1 February 1844. Power draws attention to the public outcry, but does not elaborate.
38. *Legislative Journals*, 1843, Appendix Q.
39. RG11-5, Vol. 388, file 87, Correspondence of Hamilton Killaly, 1841–55, McDonagh to Killaly, 25 January 1843; WCLB, Power to Sherwood and Company, 1 February 1844; Vol. 390, file 94, Wetherall to Killaly, 2 March 1844.
40. Elizabeth Nish, ed., *Debates of the Legislative Assembly of United Canada*, Vol. IV, 1844–45, Lewis Thomas Drummond, 1460.
41. Ibid., Wilfred Nelson, 1511.

42. The cost of living does not appear to have fluctuated significantly from canal to canal. See note 32.
43. RG11-5, Vol. 407, file 113, Thorburn to Daly, 19 January 1844.
44. RG11-5, Vol. 388, file 87, Articles of Agreement between the Board of Works and Lewis Schiclaw, 1 April 1845. See Ruth Bleasdale, "Irish Labourers on the Canals of Upper Canada in the 1840s," M.A. thesis University of Western Ontario, 1975, 34–7.
45. Pentland, "The Lachine Strike of 1843," 259.
46. Bleasdale, "Irish Labourers on the Canals," 3–7.
47. RGll-5, Vol. 407, file 104, Memorandum of Dr. Jarrow, 1 October 1842. A.H. Ross, *Ottawa, Past and Present* (Toronto 1927), 109.
48. WCLB, Power to Begly, 17 January 1845; RG11-5, Vol. 390, file 93, Mills to Begly, 26 June 1845; RG11-5, Vol. 389, file 90, Miscellaneous, 1842–51, Keefer to Robinson, 1 March 1842.
49. Conrad Arensberg, *The Irish Countryman* (New York 1950), 66–8.
50. *St. Catharines Journal*, 16 February 1844; RG11-5, Vol. 407, file 104, Memorandum of Dr. Jarrow, 1 October 1842.
51. T.C. Foster, *Letters on the Condition of the People of Ireland* (London 1847); J. G. Kohl, *Travels in Ireland* (London 1844); K. H. Connell, *The Population of Ireland, 1760–1845* (Oxford 1950).
52. Michael Cross, "The Dark Druidical Groves," Ph.D. thesis, University of Toronto, 1968, 470; Harris, *The Catholic Church in the Niagara Peninsula*, 262–4; *St. Catharines Journal*, 25 August 1843; Harris, *The Catholic Church in the Niagara Peninsula*.
53. C Series, Vol. 60, Merritt to Daly, 21 September 1844; C Series, Vol. 60, Elliott to Young, 23 July 1844.
54. C Series, Vol. 317, MacDonald to Daly, l4 July 1849.
55. Adams, *Ireland and Irish Emigration*, 89.
56. *St. Catharines Journal*, 24 August 1843.
57. *Legislative Journals* 1844–45, Appendix Y, Gibbs to Higginson, 6 January 1845.
58. T.D. Williams, *Secret Societies in Ireland* (Dublin 1973), 31.
59. E.P. Thompson, *The Making of the English Working Class* (Middlesex 1972).
60. By commencement of the second season of construction, employers followed William Hamilton Merritt's suggestion to employ only Corkmen on the upper section and only Connaughtmen on the lower section of the Welland Canal. On the Williamsburg Canals also the factions laboured on different sections of the work.
61. WCLB, Power to Begly, 25 August l843.
62. RG11-5, Vol. 407, file 104, Robinson to Begly, 19 October 1842.
63. *St. Catharines Journal*, 7 July 1842.
64. RG11-5, Vol. 407, file 113, Thorburn to Daly, 10 January l844; Vol. 407, file 104, Hobson to Daly, 20 January 1844; Vol. 407, file 113, Thorburn to Daly, 17 January 1844.
65. Ibid., Thorburn to Daly, 10 January 1844; *Legislative Journals*, 1844–45, Appendix Y, Jarvis to Daly, 28 October 1844.
66. Ibid., Appendix Y, Killaly to Daly, 5 November 1844; RG11-5, Vol. 389, file 89, Power to Begly, 17 January 1845; Vol. 407, file 113, Thorburn to Daly, 10 January 1814; *St. Catharines Journal*, 7 July 1843; *Brockville Recorder*, 8 August 1844.
67. WCLB, Power to Elliott, 28 December 1843.
68. RG11-5, Vol. 407, file 113, Thorburn to Daly, 10 January 1844.
69. Ibid.
70. RG11-5, Vol. 407, file 104, Hobson to Daly, 20 January 1844; Ibid., Wetherall to Killaly, 26 March 1844.
71. RGl1-5 Vol. 407, file 113, Public Notice to the Sons of Erin, Engaged on the Welland Canal, who are known as Corkmen and Connaughtmen, 12 January 1844.
72. WCC-6, Thorburn to Daly, 19 January 1844.
73. Pentland, "The Lachine Strike of 1843"; J. I. Cooper, "The Quebec Ship Labourers' Benevolent Society," *Canadian Historical Review*, 30 (1949), 338–43; Cross, "The Dark Druidicial Groves"; Michael Cross, "The Shiners' War: Social Violence in the Ottawa Valley in the 1830s," *Canadian Historical Review* 54 (1973), 1–26.

74. E.L. Tapin, *Liverpool Dockers and Seamen, 1870–1890* (Hull 1974).
75. J.H. Treble, "Irish Navvies in the North of England, 1830–50," *Transport History* 6 (1973), 227–47.
76. Foster's comparative study of class consciousness in three nineteenth-century towns rests on an analysis of varying degrees of fragmentation and sub-group identification. For an argument see: John Foster, "Nineteenth-Century Towns—A Class Dimension," in H. J. Dyos, ed., *The Study of Urban History* (London l968), 281–99. See also John Foster, *Class Struggle and the Industrial Revolution: Early Industrial Capitalism in Three English Towns* (London 1974), and Neville Kirk, "Class and Fragmentation: Some Aspects of Working-Class Life in South-East Lancashire and North-East Cheshire, 1850–1870," Ph.D. thesis, University of Pittsburgh, 1974. Kirk endeavours to explain the decline of class consciousness in mid-nineteenth century England in terms of the fragmentation of the working class into subgroups, emphasizing the widening gap between "respectable" and "non-respectable" workers, and the bitter conflict between Roman Catholic Irish and other segments of the workforce.
77. Petition of Lee and Baynes, cited in Harris, *The Catholic Church*, 255; RG11-5, Vol. 407, file 113, Thorburn to Murdock, 18 August 1842; *St. Catharines Journal*, 11 August 1812; Vol. 388, file 87, Petition presented to Reverend Lee, 1 August 1842.
78. *St. Catharines Journal*, 11 August 1842.
79. WCLB, Power to Begly, 12 August 1842.
80. *St. Catharines Journal*, 11 August 1842; WCLB, Power to Begly, 15 August 1842.
81. Welland Canal Commission, folder 6 (hereafter cited WCC-6), Power to Begly, 14 February 1843; WCLB Power to Begly, 20 March 1843; Ibid., Power to Begly, 17 July 1843.
82. Ibid., Power to Begly, 1 August 1843. The following winter, Thorburn praised Power for his attempts to ease unemployment by ensuring that contractors hired as many labourers as possible. RGl1-5, Vol. 407, file 113, Thorburn to Daly, 19 January 1844. Of course Power may have been motivated equally by a desire to push the work ahead.
83. WCLB, Power to Begly, 25 August 1843.
84. RG11-5, Vol. 407, file 104, Jarrow to Merritt, 6 January 1843.
85. Pentland describes the betrayal of one faction by the other in one of the large strikes on the Lachine. Pentland, "The Lachine Strike."
86. For example: RG11-5, Vol. 407, file 104, Cotton and Row to Wheeler, 26 August 1846.
87. C Series, Vol. 60, Memorandum of Wetherall to the Board of Works, 3 April 1843; Vol. 90, file 94, Clarke to Killaly, 6 March 1845; RG11-5, Vol. 407, file 113, Thorburn to Daly, 10 January 1844.
88. See for example: *Legislative Journals*, 1844-45, Appendix Y, Jarvis to Begly, RG11-5, Vol. 390, file 93, Mills to Killaly, November 1844; Ibid, Mills to Killaly, 29 November 1845.
89. *Legislative Journals*, 1843, Appendix Q, *Legislative Journals, 1844–45*, Appendix AA; RG11-5, Vol. 381, file 56, Godfrey to Begly, 26 March 1844; Vol. 390, file 94, Wetherall to Killaly, 2 March 1844; Vol. 389, file 89, Power to Begly, 4 March 1845.
90. *Legislative Journals, 1843*, Appendix Q; *Legislative Journals, 1844–45*, Appendix AA.
91. *St. Catharines Journal*, 7 June 1841; RG11-5, Vol. 381, file 56, Godfrey to Begly, 9 April 1844.
92. RG11-5, WCLB, Power to Begly, 10 March 1843.
93. WCLB, Power to Begly, 17 July 1843; *St. Catharines Journal*, 16 November 1843; WCC-7, Power to Begly, 7 December 1843; *Legislative Journals, 1844–45*, Appendix AA.
94. Montreal Transcript, 28 March 1843, cited in Pentland, "The Lachine Strike," 266.
95. According to the *St. Catharines Journal*, 20 September 1844, there were four major strikes between 1 April and 20 July.
96. C Series, Vol. 60, Gaele to Elliott, 23 July 1844; Ibid., Elliott to Young, 23 July 1844.
97. For an analysis of secret societies in Ireland see Williams, *Secret Societies in Ireland*. For a study of the Molly Maguires see Anthony Bimba, *The Molly Maguires* (New York 1932).
98. *Legislative Journals, 1843*, Appendix T.
99. RG11-5, Vol. 407, file 113, Thorburn to Daly, 10 January 1844.
100. Williams, *Secret Societies in Ireland*, 31.

101. Stephen Langdon, "The Emergence of the Canadian Working Class Movement, 1845–75," *Journal of Canadian Studies* 8 (1973), 3–4.
102. Williams, *Secret Societies in Ireland*, 31.
103. Ibid., 7, 25–7.
104. Rachel O'Higgins, "The Irish Influence in the Chartist Movement," *Past and Present* 20 (196l) 83-96.
105. C Series, Vol. 60, Wetherall to Board of Works, 3 April 1843.
106. Montreal Transcript, 28 March 1843.
107. Duncan, "Irish Famine Immigration."
108. O'Higgins, "Irish in Chartist Movement," 83–6.
109. *St. Catharines Journal*, 31 August 1843; *Niagara Chronicle*, 10 July 1844; for further examples of the sensational manner in which newspapers reported labour disturbances see: *St. Catharines Journal*, 16 November 1843, 14 December 1843, 21 December 1843, 17 May 1844, 2 August 1844, 16 August l844, 20 September 1844; *Niagara Chronicle*, 20 February 1845; *Brockville Recorder*, 7 September 1843, 21 December 1843, 21 March 1844, 8 August 1844; *Cornwall Observer*, 8 December 1842, 9 January 1845.
110. RG11-5, Vol. 407, file l04, Jarrow to Merritt, 6 January 1843; *St. Catharines Journal*, 28 June 1844.
111. RG11-5, Vol. 407, file 113, Thorburn to Daly, 10 January 1844; C Series, Vol. 60, testimony of James McCloud, sworn before Justices Kerr and Turney, 14 September 1844.
112. *Legislative Journals*, Jarvis to Daly, 28 October 1844; WCLB, Power to Begly, 3 January 1844.
113. *Legislative Journals*, Jarvis to Daly, 28 October 1844.
114. WCLB, Power to Begly, 14 February 1843.
115. RG11-5, Vol. 407, file 113, Thorburn to Begly, 1 July 1844; *Cornwall Observer*, 8 December 1842. See also: WCLB, Power to Begly, April 1842.
116. *Cornwall Observer*, 9 January 1845.
117. RG11-5, Vol. 390, file 93, Mills to Killaly, 29 November 1845; Ibid., Mills to Killaly, November 1844; *Legislative Journals, 1845*, Appendix AA
118. RG11-5, Vol. 407, file 113, Thorburn to Daly, 10 January 1844; Vol. 407, file 113, Thorburn to Daly, 17 January 1844.
119. RG11-5, Vol. 407, file 113, Thorburn to Daly, 10 January 1844.
120. RG11-5, Vol. 407, file 104, Jarrow to Merritt, 6 January 1843.
121. WCC-7, Power to Begly, 10 February 1843; Ibid., Begly to Power, 8 April 1843; WCC-8, Begly to Power, 3 September 1845.
122. A. W. R. Carrothers, *Collective Bargaining Law in Canada* (Toronto 1965), 13–15. C Series, Vol. 60, Wetherall to Board of Works, 3 April 1843; *Legislative Journals, 1843*, Appendix T. Also see Pentland, "The Lachine Strike," for a discussion of the conflicting opinions concerning combinations and strikes.
123. Carrothers, *Collective Bargaining Law*, 14; Henry Pelling, *A History of British Unions* (Middlesex 1973), 31–2.
124. Act for the better preservation of the Peace and the prevention of riots and violent outrages at and near public works while in progress of construction, 8 Vic.c.6.
125. Pentland "Labour and the Development of Industrial Capitalism," 413; RG11-5, Vol. 407, file 113, Thorburn to Daly, 17 January 1844; WCC-6, Thorburn to Daly, 19 January 1844; WCLB, Power to contractors, 16 January 1844, Vol. 407, file 104, Wetherall to Killaly, 26 March 1844.
126. *Legislative Debates, 1844–45*, Attorney General James Smith, 1443.
127. Ibid., Thomas Aylwin, 1459.
128. Ibid., Louis Hippolyte Lafontaine, 1505; Ibid., Attorney General James Smith, 1515–17.
129. Ibid., Lewis Thomas Drummond, 1516–17.
130. Ibid., Drummond, 1515.
131. WCLB, Bonnalie to Begly, 12 March 1844; RG11-5, Vol. 388, file 89, Power to Begly, 11 February 1846; Ibid., Power to Begly, 17 January 1847; RG-8, C Series, Vol. 60, Daly to Taylor, 17 May 1845; RG11-5, Vol. 390, file 94, Hill to Begly, 16 February 1817; Ibid., Hill to Begly, 21 June 1847. Both forces continued until the great bulk of the work on their respective canals was finished,

the Welland Canal constabulary until 31 December 1849, that on the Williamsburg Canals until 31 October 1847, the month that the last of the canals was opened.

132. WCC-8, Begly to Power, 2 December 1845; Ibid., Begly to Power, 27 December 1845.
133. *Legislative Journals, 1843*, Appendix Q.
134. WCLB, Power to Begly, 3 March 1845; Ibid., Power to Begly, 14 February 1845.
135. Leon Radzinowicz, *A History of the Criminal Law and Its Administration from 1750*, Vol. 111 (London 1948), 284.
136. RG11-5, Vol. 407, file 104, Wetherall to Killaly, 26 March 1844.
137. RG-5, C1, Provincial Secretary's Office, Canada West, Vol. 161, #11,362, Memorial of Inhabitants of Mariatown to Lord Metcalf Governor General.
138. Ibid., Vol. 164, #11,61l, MacDonald to Daly, 12 September 1845.
139. Report of a Committee of the Executive Council, 31 July 1844, cited in Pentland, "Labour and Industrial Capitalism," 432. The Board of Works also employed moral agents on the Beauharnois and Lachine Canals in Lower Canada. Pentland, "Labour and Industrial Capitalism," 414; Reverend McDonagh received £200 per annum for his services on the Welland Canal.
140. C Series, Vol. 317, MacDonald to Begly, 14 July 1849.
141. RG11-5, Vol. 407, file 104, Wetherall to Killaly, 26 March 1844.
142. Ibid., Vol. 279, #2,195, Extract from Report of the Committee of the Executive Council, 25 October 1849; Vol. 407, file 114, McDonagh to Killaly, 2 May 1843; Vol. 407, file 104, Hobson to Daly, 20 January 1844.
143. RG11-5, Vol. 407, file 114, McDonagh to Killaly, 2 May 1843; Vol. 90, file 94, Clarke to Killaly, 6 March 1845; Vol. 90, file 94, Wetherall to Killaly, 2 March 1844; Vol. 388, file 87, McDonagh to Killaly, 25 January 1843; Vol. 407, file 113, Thorburn to Daly, 10 January 1844; Vol. 407, file 104, Killaly to Begly, 10 October 1849.
144. Ibid., McDonagh to Killaly, 25 January 1843; Vol. 407, file 114, McDonagh to Killaly, 2 May 1843; Vol. 407, file 104, Wetherall to Killaly, 26 March 1844.
145. PSO CW, Vol. 164, #11,611, MacDonald to Daly, 12 September 1845.
146. RG11-5, Vol. 407, file 104, Killaly to Begly, 10 October 1849.
147. C Series, Vol. 60, Daly to Armstrong, 19 August 1842; Ibid., Morris to Taylor, 19 August 1842; WCLB, MacDonald to Begly, 18 April 1843; C Series, Vol. 60, requisition Fitzwilliam, 12 July 1844.
148. RG-11, Vol. 407, file 104, Robinson to Begly, 1 October 1842.
149. RG11-5, Vol. 379, file 44, Magistrates of the Eastern District to Begly, 31 August 1842; *Journals of the Legislative Assembly, 1844–45*, Appendix Y, 8 January 1845; Ibid., Petition of the Justices of the Peace and other Inhabitants of the County of Dundas; RG11-5, Vol. 407, file 113, Thorburn to Murdock, 18 August 1842.
150. Radzinowicz, *A History of the Criminal Law*, Vol. IV, 115–39.
151. See for example WCLB, Power to Begly, 3 January 1844; Vol. 407, file 104, Hobson to Daly, 20 January 1844.
152. *Legislative Debates, 1844–45*, Thomas Aylwin, 1456.
153. RG11-5, Vol. 407, file 113, Thorburn to Murdock, 18 August 1842.
154. WCLB, Power to Elliott, 3 January 1844; C Series, MacDonald to Col. Elliott, 2 April 1844; Ibid., Merritt to Daly, 21 September 1844; PSO CW, Vol. 100, #4956, Milne to Bagot, 21 December 1842.
155. C Series, Vol. 60, Armstrong to Browning, Military Secretary, 11 January 1844; Ibid., Temporary Commander of Canada West to Elliott, 16 July 1844.
156. Ibid., Wm Fielder to Taylor, 8 September 1843; Vol. 379, file 44, Harvey to Killaly, 30 August 1842.
157. RG11-5, Vol. 379, file 44, Tuscore to Killaly, 5 September 1842; WCLB, Power to Elliott, 3 January 1844; Ibid., Power to Elliott, 28 December 1843.
158. C Series, Vol. 60, Elliott to Cox and Gaele, 30 September 1844.
159. Ibid., Temporary Commander of Canada West to Elliott, 16 July 1844.

Chapter 3

"The Honest Workingman" and Workers' Control

The Experience of Toronto Skilled Workers, 1860–92

Gregory S. Kealey

> And now Canadian workingmen,
> Arise and do your duty;
> Behold these massive towers of stone,
> In all their wondrous beauty.
> Who builds those lovely marble towers,
> Who works and makes the plans?
> 'Tis he who sleepless thinks for hours—
> The honest workingman.
>
> From "The Toilers" written for *The Ontario Workman*, 17 July 1873.

Skilled workers in the nineteenth century exercised far more power than scholars had previously realized. Through their trade unions, craftsmen played important roles in community affairs, in the world of politics, and especially on the job well into the industrial period. In Toronto work-places, craftsmen employed their monopoly on skill and experience to dictate terms to their employers in a wide array of areas which, in modern parlance, provided late nineteenth-century craftsmen a high degree of workers' control of production. To illustrate the extent of this control, this chapter will describe the practice of three Toronto unions active between the 1860s and the early 1890s.

The three unions under discussion have been chosen to exemplify significant variants of trade union power in Toronto. They include the relatively little-known Coopers International Union, Ontario No. 3, which played an important role in the Nine Hour Movement and the establishment of the Toronto Trades Assembly; the extensively studied International Typographical Union No. 91; and the Iron Molders' International Union No. 28, employed in Toronto's heavily capitalized stove, machinery, and agricultural implements industry. This great diversity of experience demonstrates that the crafts discussed here—although distinct from each other—are nevertheless not atypical of other Toronto skilled unions of this period. Other crafts could have been chosen, and although the details would differ, the overall patterns would remain much the same.

To date most discussion of artisanal resistance to the arrival of industrial capitalism has focused on the maintenance of pre-industrial work habits, the tenacious hold of ethno-cultural ties, and on craft-workers' deep suspicion of "the new rules of the game" demanded by the advent of the market economy.[1] This analysis applies to workers undergoing the process of industrialization and will account for the Coopers' early Toronto experience; however, in considering the history of Toronto moulders and printers, we will need other explanations.

David Montgomery has suggested that we must look beyond pre-industrial cultural forms if we are to understand the behaviour of skilled workers in late nineteenth-century America. These workers often were "veterans of industrial life" who "had internalized the industrial sense of time, were highly disciplined in both individual and collective behaviour, and regarded both an extensive division of labour and machine production as their natural environment."[2] This was the world of Toronto moulders; Toronto printers, or rather Toronto compositors, occupied a position somewhere between the experience of the cooper and that of the moulder. The world of moulders and printers certainly drew on old craft traditions, but it also transcended them. Although drawing on "residual" cultural categories, there was much about their world that was "emergent," if we can borrow the important theoretical distinction drawn by Raymond Williams.[3] In the late nineteenth-century Toronto skilled workers came to terms with the new industrial society, but those terms involved constant resistance and struggle. The successes that they and other workers achieved forced management and government to devise entirely new strategies, commonly known as "scientific management" and "progressivism." Those innovations remain, however, subjects for other papers; here we will limit ourselves to an analysis of how the workers struggled, often successfully, for control of the work-place.[4]

I.

The experience of coopers in Toronto and throughout Ontario in the late 1860s and early 1870s provides a classic case of the artisan response to industrial capitalism. Elsewhere I have described the confrontation that occurred between Toronto shoe manufacturers and the Knights of St. Crispin.[5] Although less dramatic in their response than the Crispins' Luddism, the coopers shared with the shoemakers the unfortunate fate of watching the destruction of their craft through a combination of mechanization, the rise of factory production, the depression of the 1870s, and an all-out employer offensive.

Originally organized on a shop basis, coopers enjoyed all the prerogatives of the skilled artisan. One vivid description of the old-time cooper's lifestyle follows:

> Early on Saturday morning, the big brewery wagon would drive up to the shop. Several of the coopers would club together, each paying his proper share, and one of them would call out the window to the driver, "Bring me a goose egg," meaning a half-barrel of beer. Then others would buy "Goose Eggs" and there would be a merry time all around.... Saturday night was a big night for the old time cooper. It meant going out, strolling around town, meeting friends usually at a local saloon, and having a good time generally after a hard week's work. Usually the good time continued over Sunday, so that on the following day he usually was not in the best condition to settle down to the regular day's work. Many coopers used to spend this day sharpening up their tools, carrying in stock, discussing current events and in getting things in shape for the big day of work on the morrow. Thus Blue Monday was something of a tradition with the coopers, and the day was also more or less lost as far as production was concerned. "Can't do much today, but I'll give her hell tomorrow," seemed to be the Monday slogan. But bright and early Tuesday morning "Give her hell" they would, banging away lustily for the rest of the week until Saturday, which was pay day again, and new thoughts of the "Goose Eggs."[6]

However these older artisanal traditions were coming under attack at mid-century from trade unionists as well as efficiency-minded manufacturers. A St. Louis cooper's 1871 letter depicts both the tenacity of the old tradition and the new attitudes of skilled workers:

> The shops are paid off every two weeks, on which occasion one of these shops is sure to celebrate that time-honoured festival, Blue Monday. When Blue Monday falls it usually lasts for three days. And the man who succeeds in working during the continuance of this carnival is a man of strong nerve and indomitable will. Mr. Editor, did you ever hear of Black Monday? Perhaps not. But I tell you wherever Blue Monday is kept, there is also Black Monday. The only difference is, Blue Monday is celebrated at the shop, while Black Monday is observed at the cooper's home. The man celebrates Blue Monday, but the wife and family observe Black Monday.[7]

In 1870 craftsmen created the Coopers' International Union in order, as the *Chicago Workingman's Advocate* so aptly put it, to avoid the fate of the ship caulkers and ship carpenters, artisanal victims of the new age of iron and steam.[8] The new union with head-offices in Cleveland was "in many ways the model of a successful organization of skilled mid-nineteenth century American craftsmen."[9] Its leaders were deeply embedded in the labour reform tradition which found its organizational expression through the National Labor Union in the U.S. In Canada the Coopers' International Vice-President John Hewitt, played an active role in organizing the Toronto Trades Assembly and the Canadian Labour Union and was one of the major theorists of the Nine Hour Movement of 1872. The C.I.U. created a union structure which provided sick and death benefits, an international strike fund, and a card system for tramping members. Entering Canada in 1870, the union organized 24 branches in the first two years of its existence.[10] In early 1872 on a visit to Chicago John Hewitt announced that "the coopers in Canada were alive and active and increasing their organization rapidly."[11] Their decline was to be equally precipitous; but let us first examine the basis of their strength.

Coopers, like most skilled workers in the late nineteenth century, can best be described as "autonomous workmen." This term, usefully defined by Benson Soffer, describes workers who possess:

> Some significant degree of control over the quantity and quality of the product; the choice and maintenance of equipment; the methods of wage payment and the determination of individual wages and hours; the scheduling and assignment of work; recruitment, hiring, lay-off and transfer; training and promotion of personnel; and other related conditions of work.[12]

A reading of *The Coopers' Journal*, the excellent newspaper of the C.I.U., provides copious evidence that Canadian coopers enjoyed most of these prerogatives.

As was the case with most unions of skilled workers in the nineteenth century, wages were not the subject of collective bargaining. The union met together, arrived at the "price" of its labour, informed management of its decision, and either accepted the new rate with gratitude or struck if the boss refused. Local unions had no trouble dictating terms in prosperous times as can be seen in the report of the Brantford Local of August 1871, which simply notes that they had imposed a new price list and expected no trouble.[13] In January 1872 representatives from seven of the fifteen existing Ontario C.I.U. locals met in Toronto to arrive at a province-wide price list.[14] This document imposed not only prices but also called for a maximum 10-hour day province-wide. It dictated prices for 37 different categories of piece work and added a day rate of $1.75 for work not included on the list.

In addition to assuming control of hours and wages coopers also restricted production especially when work was short. In this way they could spread the work around and also prevent speed-ups or other infringements of their shop-floor control. In the Ontario reports stints are mentioned by locals in St. Catharines, Seaforth, Oshawa, and London.[15] This union-dictated restriction of output was of course the greatest evil in the eyes of the manufacturer.

Coopers also struggled to control the methods of production as in this Brantford case:

> H.W. Read, a boss cooper of this place, has shown his dirty mean spirit by discharging three flour bbl. [barrel] makers from his shop; they were making bbls. at nine cts. jointed staves and circled heading. The boss took the jointer boy away, so that the hands had to join their own staves, which they did until noon, when they refused to make anymore barrels, unless the staves were jointed for them or they were paid extra. For thus demanding their rights, Boss Read discharged them.... But we fear him not, for no respectable cooper will take a berth in his shop under the circumstances.[16]

The union also enforced personnel decisions in the shop. The monitor of each shop assured that new workers' union cards were clear if members and that "nons" would abide by the shop rules. "Nons" who refused often found themselves moving on to the next town sooner than anticipated. In Brantford in 1891 for example:

> A scab in one of our shops, by the name of David Clawson, made himself very obnoxious to our men by his persistent abuse of the Union. At our last meeting it was ordered that the shop should strike against him, which was accordingly done, the consequence of which was that the mean tool of a man trampled and our men were out but half a day.[17]

One year later in Seaforth:

> J. Carter (who was suspended in Jan. 1872) got a berth at Ament's shop.... The monitor of the shop immediately went to him and asked him to pay up his dues.... And also that if he did not pay up, either he or they should not work there. [After he refused] the monitor of the shop went to the boss and told him that he must either sack Carter or they would take their tools out of the shop.... [When he refused] they did instantly.[18]

Equally the coopers controlled admission to the craft and their ritual pledged them to "allow no one to teach a new hand" in order "to control the supply of help."[19] Use of helpers and apprenticeship rules were tightly supervised by the union.[20]

But perhaps more striking even than the presence of workers' control is the pervasiveness of appeals to manliness evidenced throughout the coopers' materials. David Montgomery has argued that this was a crucial component of "the craftsmen's ethical code."[21] Skilled workers carried themselves with pride and felt themselves to be the equal of their boss. C.I.U. President Martin Foran's novel, *The Other Side*, illustrates this theme well.[22] The hero is a proud and respectable workman surrounded by unscrupulous capitalists and unmanly workers who have given up their self-respect in order to carry out the evil tasks of the monopolistic bosses. Foran in discussing his didactic novel claimed that:

> The main incidents of the story are founded upon "notorious fact," so notorious that anyone wishing it can be furnished with irrefragable, incontestable proofs in support of all the charges made against the typical employer, Revalson; that working men have been—because being trade unionists—discharged, photographed on street corners, driven from their homes, hounded like convicted felons, prevented from obtaining work elsewhere, arrested at the beck of employers, thrown into loathesome prisons on ex parte evidence, or held to bail in sums beyond their reach by subsidized, prejudiced, bigoted dispensers of injustice, & in every mean dishonourable manner imaginable, inhumanly victimized and made to feel that public opinion, law & justice were Utopian "unreal mockeries" except to men of position and money....[23]

Canadian coopers saw "manliness" as the keystone of their struggle and for them honour and pride were sacrosanct. "Owls" or "nons" who broke pledges or violated oaths were less than men:

> At our last monthly meeting, the name of George Morrow was erased from our books, it having been proven beyond a shadow of a doubt that he had violated his obligations by making known the business of our meetings to his boss. This thing Morrow, for I cannot call him a man, has never been of any use to us, he has not only betrayed us, but degraded himself in the estimation of every good man in our community.[24]

The Hamilton corresponding secretary went on to describe Morrow as a "compromise between man and beast."[25]

The traditions of autonomous work and the culture which grew from it made the coopers men to be reckoned with. Yet if the rise of the C.I.U. was rapid its decline was even more precipitous.

By late 1873 only 17 locals remained and by 1875 this number had plummetted to approximately five.[26] The Canadian case was in no way unique and from a peak membership of over 8,000 in 1872 the union's total membership had declined to 1,500 by 1876. In that year *The Coopers' Journal* suspended publication.

This disastrous decline was related both to the depression of the mid-1870s and to a concerted employers' assault on the trade. The best account of the coopers' demise describes the displacement of the hand cooper by machines in the Standard Oil works in New York and Cleveland. These cities, which contained the largest concentrations of coopers in North America, saw an epic struggle as Standard Oil moved to crush the C.I.U., the one remaining obstacle in its path to modernization and total monopoly.[27]

A similar process took place in Ontario. Coopering began to break out of its artisanal mold in the late 1860s in Ontario when the need for well-made, tight oil barrels in Western Ontario led the London firm of R.W. and A. Burrows to introduce stave-making and stave-dressing machinery.[28] Until then the entire process had been performed by hand. This innovation was adopted by larger cooperages in the province such as those at distilleries in Windsor and Toronto. These three shops, Burrows, Walker's, and Gooderham's, also differed from the old-time cooper's shop due to their larger size; they resembled small manufactories far more than artisans' shops. Gooderham, for example, employed 40 coopers in Toronto while the next biggest Toronto shop in 1871 held only seven.[29]

Although creating some problems for the C.I.U. these early machines did not abolish the need for skilled workers. Skill and knowledge were still important components of barrel making. Thus as late as 1871, Martin Foran was taking consolation in the cooper's skill:

> Many of our members place far too much significance on machinery as a substitute for their labour. I have given the subject much thought and consideration, and am unable to see any serious cause for apprehension in barrel machinery.... Ours is a trade that cannot be reduced to the thumbrule of unfailing uniformity. To make a general marketable piece of work, of any kind peculiar to our trade, it requires tact, judgement and discrimination on the part of the maker ... when the friends of barrel machinery succeed in inventing a thinking machine they will succeed in making a success.[30]

Within two years of this statement Standard Oil's version of "a thinking machine" was a complete success.

The process was less revolutionary in Ontario but the effects of increased mechanization can be seen in the reports of the Toronto Local. Gooderham's defeated the union between 1870,[31] when hours and wages were dictated by the workers and C.I.U. President Martin Foran acclaimed "Gooderman's [sic] shop as without exception the finest cooper shop [he had] ever seen,"[32] and late 1872 when John Hewitt reported that the shop:

> contained the most inveterate set of owls to be found on this continent and the few good men we have there, not being able to control

> the shop, have concluded to sacrifice their principles and work on for whatever price the great Godderham [sic] chooses to pay.[33]

At its peak strength in March 1872 the Toronto Local had had complete control over the trade.[34] The ability of the coopers to dictate terms was seriously undermined elsewhere in Ontario by the advent of machinery. In 1874 the Seaforth Local noted that the installation of two barrel machines would throw a great number of coopers out of work.[35] Six months later they reported their failure to control the machines due to non-union coopers taking their jobs at low rates.[36] By the 1880s the struggle was over; the cooper's craft was dead. In 1887 a Windsor cooper argued before the Labour Commission that machinery had "killed the trade" and that there no longer was "a man in the world who would send his son to be a cooper."[37]

The power that coopers had possessed as artisans they tried to adapt to the industrial age. Old models of the trade practices of independent craftsmen were transformed into union rules and struggled over with new style bosses. However one base of their power was disappearing rapidly in the 1870s as technological innovation stripped them of "their monopoly of particular technical and managerial skills."[38]

Yet we should always be careful in positing technological change as the crucial factor; it is worth nothing that other workers, as we shall see here, were more successful than the coopers. A Seaforth cooper, P. Klinkhammer, recognized this only too clearly:

> The men here have much to say about the barrel machine. The machine is not to blame. If the union men had been supported by the nons last fall and the latter had not taken the berths vacated by the union men and worked at 4 cents the machine would not be making barrels now.[39]

Their one real hope was to ally with other workers as Klinkhammer suggested. Their important role in the U.S. National Labor Union and the Toronto Trades Assembly, the Canadian Labour Union, and the Nine Hour Movement were steps in the right direction, but craft particularism remained very strong in the 1870s. However unionism did not disappear totally from the barrel factory with the demise of the C.I.U. Like the shoemakers, the coopers learned from their experience. Toronto coopers retained an independent union after the demise of the C.I.U. and were successful in raising their rates in the spring of 1882.[40] The next year they participated in attempts to create a new International.[41] In 1886 the Toronto Local joined the Knights of Labor as "Energy Assembly," LA 5742.[42] This path was followed by many other coopers' Locals throughout Canada and the U.S.

II.

Workshop control traditions were extremely strong in foundry work. Late nineteenth-century moulders displayed all the characteristics that Soffer and Montgomery identify as typical of "autonomous workmen." Two things distinguish them from the coopers. First is their impressive success in tenaciously maintaining these traditions on into the twentieth century. Second was their presence from the start of this period at the centre of the industrial capitalist world. Moulders were not artisans working in small shops reminiscent of pre-industrial society. In Toronto, Hamilton, and elsewhere throughout Ontario, moulders worked in the important stove, machinery, and agricultural implements industries. These firms, among the largest in nineteenth-century Ontario, led Canadian industry in attempting to fix prices and later to create multi-plant firms. Not surprisingly, these companies were also continually in the forefront of managerial innovations regarding labour.

Moulders in Toronto were first organized into a local union in 1857.[43] This Local joined the Iron Molders' International Union, organized in 1859, some time in 1860.[44] The International made clear its position on questions of shop floor control from its inception. The original constitution claimed for the union the power "to determine the customs and usages in regard to all matters pertaining to the craft."[45] This gave the union control over the price of the moulders' labour. In stove shops, the union shop committee would meet and discuss the price to charge for moulding new patterns as the boss brought them in. The committee would meet with the boss or foreman and arrive at a mutually acceptable overall price for the whole stove but as there were always a number of pieces involved in the assembly of any stove the committee would then decide amongst itself how to split this price among its members working on the different castings. This "board price," once established, was considered to be almost non-negotiable and these prices very quickly became recognized as part of the established customs and usages that were the union's sole prerogative. This price was not the only source of the moulders' wages for there was a second element termed the "percentage," which was a supplement paid in addition to the piece rate. This percentage was negotiable and wage conflicts in the industry generally revolved around the "percentage"—for very few bosses made the mistake of trying to challenge the "board price."[46]

This was one considerable area of strength for the union but there were others. The shop committee also dictated the "set" or "set day's work" which was the number of pieces that a member was allowed to produce in one day. Thus production control was also taken out of the bosses' hands. It was of course in the union's self-interest to "set" a reasonable amount of work which an average craftsman could perform. Craft pride would dictate against "setting" too low, but equally craft strength could prevent any attempt at a speed-up.[47] Peterborough moulders enforced the "set" and brought charges against members who "rushed up work."[48] Generally part of each local's rules, the "set" was made a part of the International Constitution at the 1886 convention in London: "Resolved that all molders working at piece work be not allowed to make over $3.50 a day." In 1888 this was struck from the Constitution and was again left to the discretion of each local. Canadian locals continued to enforce this control over production. In Peterborough, in June 1891 "Brother Burns brought a charge against Brother Donavan for earning over $3 a day."[49]

An additional area in which the union dictated terms was hiring. Members who made the mistake of applying to the foreman instead of to the shop committee were often fined.[50] In one such case in Toronto, moulders directly recruited by stove manufacturer Edward Gurney found themselves casually turned away by the shop committee (to whom they had been directed by the workers after asking for the foreman).[51] The number of apprentices allowed in a shop was also set by the union. The Peterborough Local in 1889 refused to allow "Mr. Brooks to bring in any more apprentices," and in 1891 reasserted that the union would "allow no more than the regular number of apprentices, one for every shop and one to any eight moulders."[52] The union also controlled the use of "bucks" or "berkshires" (unskilled labourers). When used they were traditionally paid directly by the moulder out of his wages and thus were employed by the craftsman not the employer. Later when bosses tried to use "bucks" to perform some of the work customarily performed by moulders, the latter did all in their power to prevent it.[53] This was the greatest area of contention with Toronto employers. Finally the union struggled to impose a closed shop on its employers and refused to work with non-union moulders. Thus in the moulding industry large areas of control in the setting of price, productivity, and hiring resided with the union.

The extent of the control that the union established was neither won nor maintained without constant struggle. Manufacturers used every device in their power to break the moulders' shop floor control. In 1866 the newly founded employers' association in the industry passed a resolution to

> proceed at once to introduce into other shops all the apprentices or helpers we deem advisable and that we will not allow any union

> committees in our shops, and that we will in every way possible free our shops of all dictation or interference on the part of our employees.[54]

The "Great Lock-out of 1866" that followed the employer's posting of the above "obnoxious notice," which extended into Canada, culminated in a costly victory for the union. Canadian stove manufacturers also organized and were active in the 1870s in fixing prices, advocating increased protection, and most significantly in pressing a concerted effort to deal the union a smashing defeat.[55] In this they too failed.

In the Toronto moulding industry, the union's claim to control was the central issue. Strikes were fought at least 14 times in the years between the founding of Local No. 28 and 1895.[56] The moulders engaged in the major strikes to resist demands by the manufacturers that the customs and usages of the craft be sacrificed. Thus in 1867 McGee demanded that he be allowed to hire as many apprentices as he wished;[57] in 1870 Gurney tried to force his moulders to work with "bucks;"[58] in 1890 both Gurney and Massey offered their moulders a choice of either a substantive cut in the previously unchallenged board price or accept "bucks;"[59] in 1892 Gurney demanded that his moulders not only accept a reduction on the percentage rate but also commit themselves to this rate for a year, a new scheme to prevent their raising the "percentage" as soon as the economic climate changed.[60] The same battles were to be fought yet again in 1903–1904.[61]

These strikes were not minor struggles in the history of the Toronto working class. In the general employers' offensive of the late sixties and early seventies to counter the emergence of a strong and newly self-confident working class movement the boss moulders used various techniques in their attempt to defeat the union. In this period they resorted most often to coercion, falling back on outmoded statutes and the power of the law. The frequently cited case of George Brown and the Toronto printers of 1872 was preceded in Toronto by numerous uses of the courts by stove manufacturers. In 1867 McGee charged six Buffalo moulders with deserting his employment. Recruited by his foreman for a one-year term they quit work when they discovered that they were being used as scabs. The magistrate claimed he was being lenient due to the implicit deception used and fined them only $6.00 each.[62] Two apprentices who left McGee's before their terms were up because of the union blacklist of the shop were not so lucky. They received 15 days in jail for deserting his employment.[63] Three years later Gurney, a large Toronto and Hamilton stove manufacturer, made use of the courts to fight the union in a slightly different way. He had two union members charged with conspiracy and assault for trying to prevent scabs from filling his shop after he turned out the union men for refusing to work with "bucks" and a large number of apprentices. After the men were found guilty the Toronto Grand Jury commented that:

> It is with sincere regret that the Grand Jury have had before them ... two persons charged with assault and conspiracy acting under the regulations of an association known as the Molders Union and they feel it their duty to mark in the most emphatic terms their disapproval of such societies being introduced into our new country calculated as they are to interfere with capital and labour, cramp our infant manufactures and deprive the subject of his civil liberty....[64]

During another strike that same summer Beard charged 10 of his apprentices with "unlawfully confederating to desert his service with the intent to injure the firm in their business." Their real offense had been seeking a wage increase and then using the traditional moulders' weapon of restricting their output to enforce their demand. On their last day on the job they all did the same limited amount of work. They were found guilty.[65] Nevertheless the founders' tactics failed. The victory that the moulders won here was especially sweet given the force brought to bear against them. This victory was quite clearly contingent on their monopoly of skill and their ability to control the labour market. Thus it was reported that Gurney was forced to resort to employing moulders such as "John Cowie who quit one job to go scabbing in Gurney's shop where he had never worked in before, simply because he was of so little account they would never hire him—circumstances sometimes make strange companions."[66] The union "defied anyone to produce such a lot of molders as were in Gurney."[67] But if the victory over Gurney was pleasing, that over Beard was valued even more highly:

> It appears that for a year or two past, Beard and Co. of Toronto, have been running an independent scab shop refusing to be "dictated to by the Union as they felt competent to conduct their business in their own way." They found that reliable men were all union men, they found that the sober men were all union men, and what was of more importance, they found that all the good moulders were union men and they were obliged to take the off-scourings of creation, all the drunken scallawags and botch workmen, that found their way to Toronto.... Their scab foreman was not equal to the situation and they found that their trade was fast leaving them and to save themselves from utter ruin the nauseous dose had to be swallowed....[68]

The 1880s saw the maturing of the system of industrial relations that was only emerging in the 1860s and 1870s. The foundrymen mounted no challenges to the basic rights of the union in 1880s and only the percentage came under consideration. In 1880 moulders sought and gained a 10 percent increase but when the economy turned in late 1883 they were forced to accept a 20 percent reduction. In 1886 they won a 12.5 percent advance but in 1887 their request for a 10 percent increase was resisted by Gurney and after a nine-week strike a compromise 5 percent advance was accepted. In early 1887 the Ontario branches of the I.M.I.U. came together to form a District Union. The 13 Ontario locals with over 1,000 members were brought together to organize more efficiently and to run joint strikes more effectively.[69] In 1887 for example the Hamilton moulders' strike against Gurney spread to Toronto when Gurney locked out his moulders there. Later in 1890 moulders at the Massey Hamilton plant refused to mould while their Toronto brothers were locked out. But perhaps the major example of these cross-industry strikes was the Bridge and Beach Strike of 1887 in the U.S. In March of that year moulders struck the Bridge and Beach Manufacturing Co. in St. Louis with the sanction of the International. Immediately the new Stove Founders National Defense Association attempted to manufacture the required patterns for the Company. Their moulders in turn refused to work on the patterns from the struck foundry. This process spread until at its height almost 5,000 moulders were locked out in 15 centres. Finally in June, the Defense Association called the patterns in and supplied the St. Louis company with a force of non-union moulders and work resumed as before at the other shops. Both sides claimed victory but most important was that each side had demonstrated to the other its respective strength and staying power. Almost immediately after the end of this strike negotiations were commenced which were to lead to the establishment of national conciliation in the industry through conferences of the contending parties.[70]

The Canadian industry did not take part in these conferences nor did conciliation apply to the machinery moulding branches of the trade. Until these industry-wide agreements in stove foundries, the strength of the moulders depended entirely on their skill and control of the work process and their ability through their union to maintain this and to exercise some degree of control over the labour market. This labour market control was of great importance and has been admirably discussed before with reference to the moulders.[71] The importance of the union card to the moulder has been summarized: "... within the jurisdiction of his own Local a union card was a man's citizenship paper; in the jurisdiction of other locals it was his passport."[72]

The early 1890s saw a new employer offensive in Hamilton and Toronto as Gurney and Massey both attempted to smash the moulders' continuing power in their plants. The Gurney strike, which commenced in February 1890, lasted an amazing 16 months before Local 28 ended it. The Massey strike covered 10 months from October 1890 to July 1891.[73] In both cases the companies pursued a similar strategy. They shut down their moulding shops ostensibly for repairs and, after a considerable lapse of time, called in the shop committees and asked them to accept either a sizeable reduction or work with "bucks."[74] In both cases the moulders refused, for "union rules did not permit 'bucks' and the men thought they saw in it their eventual displacement by these labourers and a menace to their trade."[75] Both Gurney and Massey claimed that they could no longer afford union rates and compete successfully but the moulders suspected "a long conceived plan in the attempt at a reduction."[76] In each case management and labour settled down for a protracted struggle. David Black, the secretary of Local 28, wrote after five months on strike:

> Our fight with Gurney still continues and bids fair to last quite a while longer, we succeed very well in relieving him of his good men, but he has plenty of money and it will take hard fighting and time to beat him.[77]

The Toronto Local spared no expense or risk in this struggle and a number of their members were arrested and tried for intimidating scabs.[78] In September the Local issued an appeal "To the Canadian Public" which complained they had been locked out "because they refused to make their work cheaper than for any other employer in the same line in the city; and thus assist them to destroy their competitors and monopolize the Canadian market at our expense." The public was called on to buy only union-made goods since:

> By this means our victory over monopoly will be assured; our right to organize and obtain fair wages for our labour will be vindicated; while the superior quality of your purchase will amply repay your preference.[79]

The union lost both these struggles but the cost to capital was also high. Gurney, in early 1891, when his victory seemed sure, brayed triumphantly that "the only change resulting from the strike is that he now controlled his shop." However when he continued to claim that things were "excellent," the *Globe* reporter noted that, faced with the open incredulity of the union representatives present, Gurney modified his statement mentioning "that of course the whole year had not been as smooth." The key in these struggles in the early 1890s was control. As capital entered a new stage where it recognized the necessity of supervising more closely the process of production, it had to confront and defeat its "autonomous workmen." This gives Gurney's parting chortle added significance:

> The men must work for someone else until they come to one of my proposals. I do not think (with a smile) that there is any likelihood of my going to Local 28 and asking them to come and take control of my foundry.[80]

Gurney's last laugh was too precipitous, however, for the I.M.I.U. came back strong in Toronto in the late 1890s and a new wave of struggle broke over the foundry business in the years 1902–1904.[81] While it is beyond the scope of this chapter to detail that struggle, it is important to emphasize that the power of the moulders was not broken in the struggles of 1890–92. Gurney and Massey delivered only a partial defeat, and the moulders came back strong. J.H. Barnett, Toronto I.M.I.U. secretary, described one 1903 struggle:

> Just after adjourning the meeting this afternoon the foreman of the Inglis shop, R. Goods, came to the hall and informed us that he had discharged all the scabs in his shop and that he wanted the union men in on Monday, that the firm was tired of the scabs and was willing to give the nine hours....[82]

One year later in yet another struggle with Toronto foundrymen now supported by the National Foundry Association, Barnett wrote again of the continued monopoly on skill that the moulders enjoyed:

> They are having greater losses in the foundry now than when they first started. They have been trying to make a big condenser and can't make it. They have started the old St. Lawrence shop with some of the old country moulders who refused to work with Ersig, the NFA foreman up in the new shop. Jas Gillmore and Fred McGill is instruction [sic] them but ain't doing any better.[83]

Iron moulders then, unlike coopers, maintained a high degree of work-place control well into the twentieth century. This was primarily due to their strong organization but an additional factor was that their skills were relatively slowly replaced by technology. Experiments were carried out on machines for moulding in the mid-1880s but were an extremely expensive failure.[84] Massey imported its first machines in 1889.[85] Thus, unlike the coopers and shoemakers, the moulders had time to perfect their organization before their major contest with machinery.

Moulders also developed an early understanding of the need for solidarity with their unskilled co-workers. Thus, when the Knights of Labor struck the huge Massey works in Toronto in 1886, moulders left the job in their support. Peterborough I.M.I.U. Local no. 191 also co-operated with the Lindsay Knights of Labor.[86]

III.

The workers' control enjoyed by Toronto moulders, and their struggle to retain it, were more than equalled by the experiences of Toronto printers. The printers' control of the shop floor demonstrates extremely well early union power. In the 1890s the President of the Toronto Local of the I.T.U. insisted:

> The work of the composing room is our business. To no one else can we depute it. It is absolutely ours. The talk of running another man's business will not be hold. It is ours; we learned it and must control it.[87]

Unionism among the Toronto Printers owed much to the customs and traditions of the craft. Organized first in 1832, the Society lapsed in 1836, but was refounded in 1844 to resist a new Toronto employers' departure from the "settled usages of the trade."[88] In 1845, when forced again to fight the initiatives taken by George Brown, the printers issued a circular to the Toronto public demanding only "to maintain that which is considered by all the respectable proprietors as a fair and just reward, for our labour and toil—'the labourer is worthy of his hire.'"[89] Here the tenacity of pre-industrial notions of traditional wages can be seen. Customary usage dictated wages—not any abstract notion of what the market might bear. Employers as well as workers had to learn the new rules of a market economy and the disruptions caused by the Browns' arrival in the Toronto printing trades in the 1840s, suggest that until then wages had been "largely a customary and not a market calculation."[90]

The printers possessed a strong tradition of craft pride and identification. In their 1845 statement to the Toronto public they resolved "to maintain by all legitimate means in their power their just rights and privileges as one of the most important and useful groups in the industrious community."[91]

Members of the "art preservative," they saw themselves as the main carriers of rationalism and the enlightenment. No trade dinner or ball—and these were frequent—was complete without a set of toasts to the printers' patron, Benjamin Franklin, and to Gutenberg and other famous printers. Franklin replaced the older European craft tradition of saints and his rationalism fitted very well with the printers' disdain for other societies' usage of secret signs and fiery oaths. The printers prided themselves on the fact that:

> initiation ceremonies melo-dramatic oaths, passwords, signs, grips, etc., though advocated

> by many worthy representatives and repeatedly considered by the national union, never found a place in the national or subordinate constitutions.[92]

The printers saw their craft as crucial in maintaining all that was best in the western literary tradition. As one printer toasted in an 1849 Anniversary Dinner: "To the art of printing—under whose powerful influence the mind of fallen and degraded man is raised from nature up to nature's God."[93] Thus printer's shop committees were "chapels" and the shop steward was "the father of the chapel." This pride in craft was manifested time and time again throughout the nineteenth century.

In 1869 the executive recommended the initiation of a reading room and library:

> where the members of the craft can have access in leisure hours for the enjoyment of study and mental recreation and where may be ever within their reach increasing facilities for the acquisition of whatever in our art it may be of advantage to know.... It is a laudable endeavour to support one's calling which two centuries age was deemed the most honourable of all professions....[94]

The union seal depicted a printing press with light emanating from all around it.[95]

The Toronto printers had a strong sense of the history of their craft and their union. They were particularly proud of being the oldest Toronto union and parts of their frequent fetes were often spent on these themes. The 1888 picnic programme, for example, contained original histories of both the art of printing and of the Toronto Typographical Union.[96] All these traditions were put to use by the printers and they brought the craft lore together in stirring addresses involving custom in the struggle against oppression:

> Fellow-workingmen, knights of the stick and rule, preservers of "the art preservative,"—ye whose honourable calling is to make forever imperishable the noblest, truest and most sublime thoughts of the statesman, the philosopher, and the poet,—to you is committed the mightiest agent for good or ill which has yet been pressed into the service of humanity. The printing press, the power mightier than kings, more powerful than armies, armaments, or navies, which shall yet overthrow ignorance and oppression and emancipate labour, is your slave. Without your consent, without the untiring labour of your skillful fingers and busy brain, this mighty giant, with his million tongued voices speeding on wings of steam all over this broad earth of ours, would be dumb. Shorn of his strengths which your skill imparts, his throbbing sides and iron sinews might pant and strain in vain; no voice or cry of his or your oppressors could ever reach or be heard among men. Realizing this my friends it is easy to determine our proper station in the grand struggle that is now in progress all over the civilized world, the effort of the masses to throw off oppression's yoke.... We belong in the front rank, at the head of this column. Since the discovery of printing humanity has made great progress and already we see the dawn of the coming day when light and knowledge shall illuminate all lands and men shall no longer oppress his fellowman.[97]

Central to the power of the International Typographical Union was the extent to which each Local maintained its control over production. The composing room was the preserve of the printer. Management's only representative there, the foreman, was a union member and subject to the discipline of his brothers. This was true in Toronto from the inception of the T.T.U. and was very important because the union also demanded that all hiring be done through the foreman.[98] In 1858 the I.T.U. convention had ruled that:

> The foreman of an office is the proper person to whom application should be made for employment; and that it is enjoined upon subordinate unions that they disapprove of any other mode of application.[99]

The new I.T.U. constitution of 1867 fined members who applied for jobs to anyone other than the foreman. Four years later this control was reasserted but foremen were also warned:

> It is the opinion of your humble servant that the foreman of an office belongs to the union under which he works and the union does not belong to the foreman ... and that no foreman has the right to discharge a regular hand ... on any other ground than that of shortness of work or willful neglect of duty....[100]

In an extraordinary 1873 case the I.T.U. ruled that the Ottawa Local was correct to strike against J.C. Boyce, the proprietor of *The Citizen*, when he took over operation of his own composing room. Only if Boyce submitted a clear card from the London (Eng.) Trades Society would he "be allowed to work under the jurisdiction of the Ottawa Union."[101]

This effective union control of the hiring practice was augmented by the role the foreman played in enforcing the printer's right to divide work. In newspaper offices each regular employee had a "sit" and with this place came the right to choose a replacement any time the regular wanted time off. Although not technically employed by the regular printer that was actually what the practice amounted to. In Toronto the *Mail* paid the money to the regular who then paid the subs from his salary.[102] When bosses tried to regulate this custom by utilizing "sublists" which delineated the substitutes from whom regulars were forced to choose, the International roundly condemned the practice and refused to allow locals to co-operate with it.[103] The union claimed ever more interest in the hiring process. In 1888 a resolution was introduced at the I.T.U. convention "that would have placed the regulation of hiring and discharging of employees entirely in the hands of the Local unions."[104] In 1890 "the priority law" was passed by which the grounds upon which foremen could discharge were even more tightly circumscribed. Only incompetency, violation of rules, neglect of duty, or decrease of labour force were acceptable causes for firing; and on discharge a member was entitled to a written statement of cause. In addition, the final part of the law ruled that "subs" in an office had priority when positions became available.[105] The power of the union then, in controlling the selection of printers, was almost total.

The union also retained a strong position in bargaining. The union would first arrive at an approved scale of prices unilaterally and would then take it to the employers.[106] Some negotiation was possible but much of the scale was regarded as non-negotiable. For example, following the strike of 1872 for the nine-hour day, never again were hours subject to consideration; having been won once they were off limits for further discussion.[107] The scale was a complex document divided into three major sections: time work; piece work, news, and magazines; and piece work and books. Time work was not the traditional method of payment in the printing industry but throughout the late nineteenth century more and more job shops adopted it. However the time rate was closely tied to the piece rate. In Toronto where the piece rate was 33 1/3 cents per 1,000 ems, the time rate was 33 1/3 cents an hour the general assumption being that a hand compositor averaged 1,000 ems an hour. In newspaper offices the usual method of payment was by the piece, which in the compositor's case was measured by the area of type that he composed and expressed in "ems." Printers were thus paid per 1,000 ems of matter. There were a number of areas of conflict implicit in this type of payment. Rates were set for the newspaper as a whole but special rates were set for material classified as difficult, such as foreign languages or tables or even for illegible copy.[108] As the century progressed more and more newspaper work consisted of advertising which contained far more blank space than regular material. This copy became known as "fat" matter and was the most lucrative for the printer. The printers insisted that rates were set for the paper as a whole thus retaining the higher rate for fat matter as well. The traditional way of distributing the material was that all copy was hung on the "hook" as it arrived in the composing room and the compositors picked it up in order thus insuring an even distribution of the "fat." Bosses began to object to this and tried to create "departments" by which specific printers did the special composing. The union resisted this new approach strenuously, and forbade locals from accepting "departments." They offered, as a compromise, to allow members to bid for the "fat" matter. The successful bidder who gained the ads then paid back the union the amount of his bid, usually a percent of his earnings, which was then used to buy things in common for all the printers, to hire a person to clean everybody's type, or was distributed equally among the members.[109] The Toronto Local however resisted all employer incursions in this area. Toronto employers certainly tried. In 1882 the *Mail* offered its printers an advance but in return demanded the return of the ads. Instead the new scale of 1883 reiterated that "where weekly and piece hands are employed the piece hands shall have their proportionate share of 'fat' matter."[110] Seven years later another new scale still insisted that "compositors on newspapers were entitled to equal distribution of any 'phat.'"[111] The complexity of the Toronto printer's scale is suggested by the 39 sections of the 1883 and 35 sections of the 1890 contracts.[112] All this led one managerial strategist named DeVinne, who was later to play a major role in the United Typothetae, to moan that "It is the composition room that is the great sink-hole. It is in type and the wages of compositors that the profits of the house are lost."[113]

So far we have spoken entirely of only one branch of printing—the compositors. Until the middle of the century in the cities (and until much later in small shops), a printer ran the press as well as composing. With the rise of power presses, the pressman's role became more and more complex and increasingly, the old time printer who did both jobs disappeared and new specialists took over. By 1869 the Toronto Local had special piece rates for pressmen and the job definition of the compositor prevented him from performing press work. The pressmen's new consciousness led the I.T.U. to begin to charter Pressmen's locals separately in 1873 and 10 years later the Toronto Pressmen set up their own local. Disputes with Local 91 however led them to join the new International Printing Pressmen's Union in 1889. This splintering of the printing crafts caused many problems, but the pressmen as an equally skilled group carried with them the traditions of printers' unionism. Time was spent at meetings, for example, in designing outfits for the various marches and parades that were so much a part of working-class life in Toronto in the 1880s."[114]

Although the major focus of this paper is the skilled worker's power on the job, one cannot discuss the Toronto printers without at least a brief consideration of their political strength in the city, in provincial and even in national politics. They provided the Toronto working-class community and movement with important leadership. It was natural for these literate, working-class intellectuals to play key political roles; but the extent of their dominance is striking nevertheless. Although not the initiators of the Toronto Trades Assembly (this honour belongs to John Hewitt of the Coopers International Union) they did play an important part in this organization and in the Canadian Labour Union. In the 1880s they helped found the Toronto Trades and Labor Council after the meeting of the I.T.U. in Toronto in 1881, and later were quite active in the meetings of the Trades and Labour Congress. Moreover, of the six labour papers published in Toronto between 1872 and 1892, three of them were published and edited by printers—*The Ontario Workman* under J.S. Williams, J.C. MacMillan, and David Sleeth, all prominent members of Local 91; *The Trade Union Advocate/Wage Worker* of Eugene Donavon; and D.J. O'Donoghue's *Labour Record*. Other members of Local 91 also enjoyed prominent careers in labour reform—John Armstrong, a former International President of the I.T.U. (1878–89) was appointed to Macdonald's Royal Commission on the Relations of Labour and Capital in 1886; D.J. O'Donoghue, prominent as an MPP, leading Canadian Knight of Labor and later collector of labour statistics for the Ontario Bureau of Industries; E.F. Clarke, arrested in 1872 and later Mayor of Toronto, MPP and MP; and W.B. Prescott, International President of the I.T.U. from 1891–98. This was just one generation of Local 91's membership: the next was to include two mayors of Toronto and a senator.[115]

Local 91's political role stemmed from its union activities. Toronto printers, for example, had little use for George Brown's brand of Liberalism. As early as 1845 they had noted the irony implicit in his labour relations policies:

> A person from the neighbouring Republic commenced business here and has ever since been unremitting in his Liberal endeavour to reduce as low as possible that justly considered fair and equitable rate of remuneration due to the humble operatives.[116]

His "Liberal" endeavours were to lead him into conflict with the printers time and time again, culminating in the Printer's Strike for the nine-hour day in 1872.[117] Brown's use of antiquated British laws to arrest the leaders of the I.T.U. was turned against him by Macdonald's passage of the Trade Union Act. The Tories controlled Toronto working-class politics for a number of years following until D.J. O'Donoghue, the Knights of Labor, and the legislative responsiveness of the Mowat Ontario government started a swing towards the Liberals.

The political expertise of the printers had of course grown throughout their various struggles and the tactics perfected in 1872 were used again in the 1880s. Thus when John Ross Robertson's *Telegram* came under union attack in 1882 the union first turned to the boycott to bring pressure on the owner. They decided that in this way they could expose

> the treatment which union printers have received at the hands of JRR for many years past, and the manner in which that gentleman (?) invariably casts aspersions upon the union mechanics of this city generally through the columns of his vasculating [sic] paper.[118]

John Armstrong and D.J. O'Donoghue were appointed to visit the merchants who advertised in the *Telegram* and convince them to place their ads elsewhere. The next year when I.T.U. No. 91 passed a new scale of prices they struck the *Telegram* pulling most of the compositors out on strike. They then received the endorsement of the whole Toronto Trades and Labor Council for the boycott and late in March held a mass meeting at which speeches were delivered by most of the prominent Toronto labour leaders pledging support for Local 91.[119]

The strikes the following year against the *Mail* and the *Globe* were even more eventful and suggestive of the printers' political acumen. The papers united with other Toronto publishers and print shops to demand a 10 percent reduction in the printers' wages and gave only a week for consideration. The printers refused and struck. The union was successful in forcing job offices and smaller papers to withdraw the reduction but the *Globe* and the *Mail* held out. The *Globe* insisted that it had never become a union shop because "the boss needed absolute control in a newspaper office."[120] The morning papers after a hard fight won the reduction to 30 cents per 1,000 ems down from 33 1/3 cents but their victory was short-lived. In 1885 the *Globe* reversed its position of a year before and the political game of the 1870s by becoming a union shop for the first time. This left only the Tory *Mail* holding out against the typos. The *Mail* succumbed in February 1886 and became a union shop, withdrawing the iron-clad contract that it had adopted after the troubles in 1884.

What tactics had the I.T.U. used to win these long-range victories after their apparent defeat in 1884? The printers had employed their usual measures against the papers. They first withdrew all their members from the shops and when they failed to prevent the shops' filling up with the much despised "country-mice," non-union printers from small towns, they turned to the boycott and mass demonstrations of workingmen.[121] But this time they also requested all workingmen to boycott any candidates supported by the *Mail* in the municipal election campaigns of the winter of 1885/86.[122] Local 91 passed a resolution: "That this union will oppose to its utmost any candidate for municipal honours who may be supported by the *Mail* newspaper."[123] The following weeks saw union after union endorse the I.T.U. motion and also saw a number of Tory ward heelers running for cover and abandoning the *Mail*. The union issued a circular exposing its dealings with the *Mail* since 1872 and then placed advertisements in the Toronto papers in January of 1886 strongly attacking Manning, the *Mail*'s candidate for Mayor:

> Resolved that this union consider Mr. Manning a nominee of the *Mail*, he having advertised in that paper ... and having been editorially supported by it, particularly so on Saturday morning January 2; and therefore we call on all workingmen and those in sympathy with organized labour to VOTE AGAINST MANNING, THE NOMINEE OF THE *MAIL*.[124]

The same Local 91 meeting also decided to blacklist aldermanic candidates who had not broken with the *Mail* and decided to issue 10,000 circulars denouncing Manning and these candidates. After Howland's stunning election as mayor, widely regarded as a working class victory, the I.T.U. issued this statement:

> To the Trades and Labour organizations of Toronto—Fellow unionists: Toronto Typographical Union No. 91 takes this opportunity of thanking the labour organizations of this city and their friends who so nobly supported us at the polls in our effort to defeat the Mail. To the workingmen of Toronto who have had the honour and manhood to rise above party ties in the cause of the labour, the heartiest thanks of the 300 members of the TTU are due.... At a time when we needed your assistance you have shown that the mottoe of our union "United to support not combined to injure" is the guiding stone of the honest toiler everywhere.[125]

This electoral defeat led to the *Mail*'s total reversal in February 1886 when it surrendered to the Union. Local 91 had had to prove its strength at the polls, however, for as early as 1884 leading Tory printers had warned Macdonald of the possible repercussions of the *Mail*'s adventure. J. S. Williams had written in August, 1884:

> Not only will the matter complained of [*Mail* lock-out] alienate a very large proportion of the working men who have hitherto nobly supported the party, but it places a barrier in the way of any prominent or representative workingman actively working or speaking in the future.

Moreover he predicted that the *Mail*'s reactionary policies could cost the Tories two to three seats in Toronto and perhaps seats in other urban centres as well. E.F. Clarke, a prominent politician and member of Local 91, wrote to the same effect:

> A reduction of wages at a week's notice and a refusal of the Mail to leave the settlement of the question to arbitration will alienate the sympathies of a large number of workingmen who have hitherto supported the Conservative cause, and will weaken the influence of the journal with the masses....

A non-working class Tory politico wrote that the labour friends of the party were now in an impossible position since they "cannot support the party that treats them so shabbily" and expressed the fear that the loss of the whole Toronto Trades and Labor Council might result in electoral defeat in the City.[126] Nevertheless these warnings were ignored until the humiliating defeats of January 1886. Then the party rushed in to settle the matter once and for all. Harry Piper, a Tory ward heeler, wrote to Macdonald in February to inform him that the I.T.U.-*Mail* fight "had of late assumed a very serious aspect" since a number of old party workers had clearly transferred their allegiance in the election. As a result he arranged a meeting with John Armstrong, a Tory leader of Local 91 who had lost his own job at the *Mail* during the strike. Piper convinced Armstrong that "the Union was *killing our Party* and the Grits were reaping the benefit of the trouble and using our own friends." Armstrong promised to help if the iron-clad was removed. Piper then arranged with the manager and directors of the *Mail* that the document be ceremoniously burned before the printers and Armstrong agreed to have the union lift the boycott.[127] Thus the seeming defeat of the summer of 1884 had been translated by political means into a striking victory for Local 91. Neither the *Globe* nor the *Mail* were to cause the union difficulty again in the late nineteenth century.

Similar tactics were employed successfully against J.H. Maclean of the *World* in 1888 when he tried to defeat the union's control of "fat" matter. The struggle was precipitated by a fight over the price to be paid for an advertisement that was inserted twice. The union rule was that if the advertisement was run in an identical manner then the compositor was only paid once but that if any changes were made the compositor was paid again for the whole advertisement. The foreman supported the printers' case but the Maclean faction, after paying the money owed, locked out the union. The I.T.U. then reiterated its position on "fat" matter:

> Only by the getting of the advertisements and other "fat" matter are the men able to make anything like living wages, and this fact is recognized by all fair-minded employers as well as the men.[128]

In late July after filling his shop with "country-mice" Maclean sought an injunction against the I.T.U.'s boycott of the *World*. It was granted on an interim basis and then made permanent in mid-August.[129] The injunction did not solve Maclean's problems:

> The World is in sore straights as a result of the law compelling union men not to buy it or patronize merchants who advertise therein. Internal storms are of such common occurrence that a couple of weeks ago the vermin employed there went out on strike even but returned to the nest again.[130]

A few months later Maclean again sought to make his paper a union shop. Again the political dimensions of the settlement are clear. W.B. Prescott, the President of Local 91, wrote John A. Macdonald, seeking intervention with Maclean to ensure that the *World* came around. Prescott pointed out that "the cheap labour policies of the *World* antagonized organized labour."[131] Perhaps one reason that Maclean and the *World* felt the pressure was the Local had quickly found a way to circumvent the injunction by promoting union papers rather than naming those boycotted. They continued to use this technique especially in a political context. In the municipal campaigns of 1891–92, for example, they issued the following circular:

> Having been informed that you are seeking municipal honours, we desire to call your attention to the fact that there are a few printing and publishing houses in this city who do not employ union labour, and we, believing it would be to your advantage to patronize only those who do employ such, request you to place your patronage and advertising in union offices only, as we can assure you that from past experience, your chances of election are greater by so doing.[132]

The circular then listed the dailies that were union shops which by 1891 included all but the *Telegram*, which was shortly to enter the fold. In March, 1892 the T.T.U. also began the use of the union label.[133] Thus the power of the Toronto printers continued to grow throughout the late nineteenth century and a larger proportion of Toronto printers were unionised in the early 1890s than had been at any previous date.[134]

The initial encounter with mechanization served to strengthen their position. Until the invention of linotype and monotype machines in the late 1880s, typesetting had remained unchanged from the sixteenth century.[135] In Toronto the *News* introduced the Rogers typograph machine in 1892 and offered the printer operators 14 cents/1,000 ems. The I.T.U. had recommended in 1888 "that subordinate unions ... take speedy action looking to their [linotype machines] recognition and regulation, endeavouring everywhere to secure their operation by union men upon a scale of wages which shall secure compensation equal to that paid hand compositors."[136] This was amended in 1889[137] to demand that in all union offices only practical printers could run the machines and that the rates on the machines would be governed by the Local unions.[138] In Toronto the union's right to control the operation of the machine was not challenged initially and their *Typographical Journal* correspondent reported in March of 1892 "that so far we have not suffered from their use." However that summer the *News*, appealing to the craft custom of piece rates, refused to pay operators by the day. After a seven-week strike the union won its demand that the printers be paid by time. They were to receive $12.00 a week for six weeks while learning the machine operation and then $14.00 after they demonstrated their competency, which was set at 2,000 ems per hour or 100,000 ems per week. This settlement brought the union not only control of the machine and the wage style it sought, but also implicitly recognized the printers' right to limit production since the rate of competency set was far below the actual capabilities of the machine which were estimated to be anywhere from 3 to 8 times as fast as hand composition.[139] The International was also concerned to prevent any proliferation of speed-ups with the new machine and ruled that "no member shall be allowed to accept work ... where a task, stint, or deadline is imposed by the employer on operators of typesetting devices."[140] The union later successfully resisted any attempts by employers to speed up work totals. The victory over the *News* and the union's previous success with Robertson's *Telegraph* also brought Local 91 control of all Toronto newspapers for the first time in its history.[141] The printers had learned their lessons well. They left the century not only with their traditions intact but also with their power actually augmented. They had met the machine and triumphed.[142]

IV.

What ramifications did shop floor power have in terms of how workers thought about their society, how it was changing, and their own role in it? David Montgomery has argued that the major impact of this early workers' control was the skilled workers' growing awareness that the key institution for the transformation of society was the trade union.[143] From their understanding that through their unions they controlled production, it was a relatively easy step to the belief that all the capitalist brought to the process was capital. Thus an alternative source of capital would transform society, ending the inequities of capitalist production and creating the producer's society—a dream come true. This ideology looked to co-operation administered through the trade union as the major agent of change. All the unions we have discussed favoured co-operation.

John Monteith, President of Toronto I.M.I.U. Local 28, wrote *Fincher's Trades Review* in 1863 to describe the work of Canada West members in discussing and investigating co-operation. A union moulders' committee had contacted Rochdale and now recommended both producers' and consumers' co-ops to their Local unions. They sought co-operation because "our present organization does not accomplish what we want. That is to take us from under the hand of our employers and place us on an equal footing."[144] Co-operation of course would accomplish this very end. Five years later another Toronto moulder complained that "We are but little better off than our forefathers who were serfs to the feudal barons. We are serfs to the capitalists of the present day...." His solution:

> Let the next conviction create a co-op fund to be devoted entirely to co-operation.... We have

> been co-operating all our lives, but it has been to make someone else rich. We have been the busy bees in the hives while the drones have run away with the honey and left us to slave in the day of adversity.... Day after day the wealth of the land is concentrating in the hands of a few persons. The little streams of wealth created and put in motion by the hard hands of labour gravitate into one vast reservoir, out of which but a few individuals drink from golden cups; while labour, poor, degraded and despised labour, must live in unhealthy hovels and feed upon scanty, unhealthy food from rusty dishes....[145]

The I.M.I.U. founded as many as 20 co-operative foundries in the 1860s.[146]

Toronto printers started three co-operative newspapers. At the height of the nine hour struggle in 1872 *The Ontario Workman* was started as a co-operative venture as was D.J. O'Donoghue's *Labor Record* of 1886. In 1892 during the strike at the News a group of printers banded together and founded the *Star*.[147] The *Ontario World* operated as a co-op paper for only six months and the *Labor Record* and the *Star* each lasted about a year. Capital for the *Star* was raised from the T.T.U. and T.T.L.C. They initially used the presses of the *World* since W.F. Maclean offered them his facilities in return for 51 percent of the operation. This "Paper for the People" enjoyed quick success in winning the readership of the *News* which had from its inception in 1882 posed as the paper for Toronto workers.[148] Riordan, the owner of the *News* attempted to buy the operation and Maclean tried to merge it with the *World*; but the printers refused both offers and instead bought a press. However they failed to make a go of it and the paper suspended publication in June 1893. It was continued after its purchase as a pro-labour paper but control had passed out of the printers' hands.[149]

Machinists and blacksmiths in Toronto organized a co-operative foundry early in 1872 after losing a strike at the Soho works.[150] Six years later Toronto cigar makers established The Toronto Co-operative Cigar Manufactory Association. Here, as with the moulders in the 1860s, the push for co-operation came as a logical extension of their knowledge of the trade and their refusal to accept management's reduction of wages. Alf Jury, a Toronto tailor and labour reformer, denounced "the wage system as a modified form of slavery" and demonstrated that there could be "no fraternal feeling between capital and labour" at a cigar makers' strike meeting that year. Jury then cited production statistics to repudiate the employers' claims that the reduction was necessary. A number of bosses who had agreed to pay union rates supported this assertion. Jury's logical solution was the great aim of working class struggle: "to do away with the capitalists while using the capital ourselves"—the establishment of a co-operative factory.[151] An association was founded, shares were issued, a charter was obtained and the factory opened for business in March 1879. About a year later the Toronto Local of the C.M.I.U. reported that the co-operative was "progressing finely" and "doing a good trade."[152] Stratford cigar makers also founded a co-operative factory in 1886 which was owned by the Knights of Labor and run under C.M.I.U. rules. It employed between 20 and 30 men and produced a brand known as "The Little Knight."[153] Toronto Bakers Assembly LA 3499 also set up a co-operative bakery which lasted about two years in the mid-1880s.[154]

The successes or failures of these co-operative ventures are of less importance than the ideological assumptions on which they were based. With their origins often in crisis situations, they nevertheless flowed directly from the shop floor experience of skilled workers and the practices of their unions in struggling to control production. It was a relatively easy step from there to envisioning a system that was free of the boss (who did so very little). A Chatham moulder wrote in 1864:

> This then shows both classes in their just relations towards each other—the capitalist

and the mechanic; the one, the mechanic is the moving power—the capitalist bearing about the same relation to him that the cart does to the horse which draws it—differing in this respect, that the mechanic makes the capitalist and the horse does not make the cart; the capitalist without the mechanic being about as useful as the cart without the horse. The capitalist no doubt at times increases the sphere of usefulness of the mechanic; so does the cart that of the horse, and enables him to do more for his owner than otherwise he could do; but deprive him of it, and there is little that he can do with it that he could not accomplish without it. In short the workingman is the cause the capitalist the effect.[155]

The syntax may be confused but the moulder's meaning comes through clearly. In 1882 at the time of a Toronto carpenters' strike, during discussion of a co-operative planing mill, a reporter asked union leader Thomas Moor if the carpenters had the requisite skills. Moor's response was simple but profound: "If the men can manage a mill and make it a success for their employers, surely they can do the same thing for an institution in which they have an interest."[156]

Co-operation was one extension of workers' control; socialism was to be another.[157] Capital, however, also began to respond to the challenges raised by the growing tradition of workers' control. F.W. Taylor, capital's main workplace ideologue, understood very well the power of the "autonomous workman":

Now, in the best of the ordinary types of management, the managers recognize the fact that the 500 or 1,000 workmen, included in the 20 or 30 trades, who are under them, possess this mass of traditional knowledge, a large part of which is not in the possession of management.... The foremen and superintendents know, better than anyone else, that their own knowledge and personal skill falls far short of the combined knowledge and dexterity of all the workingmen under them.[158]

Taylor also reminisced at length about his first job experience in a machine shop of the Midvale Steel Company in the late 1870s:

As was usual then, and in fact as is still usual in most of the shops in this country [1912], the shop was really run by the workmen, and not by the bosses. The workmen together had carefully planned just how fast each job should be done, and they had set a pace for each machine throughout the shop, which was limited to about one third of a good day's work. Every new workman who came into the shop was told at once by the other men exactly how much of each kind of work he was to do, and unless he obeyed these instructions he was sure before long to be driven out of the place by the men.[159]

After his appointment as foreman, Taylor set out to increase production. He fired some of the men, lowered others' wages, hired "green" hands, lowered the piece rate—in general engaged in what he described as a "war." He attributed his limited success in this "bitter struggle" to not being of working-class origin. His middle-class status enabled him to convince management that worker sabotage, not the speed-up, was responsible for a sudden rash of machine breakdowns.[160]

The new popularity of Taylor and the other proponents of "scientific management" in the early twentieth century was indicative of capital's new attempt to rationalize production.[161] This, combined with the rise of the large corporation, the rapid growth of multi-plant firms, and the ever-increasing extension of labour-saving machinery, challenged directly not only workers' control traditions but also the very existence of the labour movement.

Toronto workers, who had struggled throughout the late nineteenth century for shop floor control, were about to face new, more virulent battles. The custom of workers' control, widely regarded as a right, had become deeply embedded in working-class culture. The fight—initially to maintain and later to extend—this control, became the major focus of class struggle in the opening decade of the twentieth century.

Thus even in the cases where craft unions abandoned the traditional practices of the "autonomous workman" in return for concessions (or out of weakness), the leadership could not always assure management that the membership would follow union dictates. As one investigator noted about the foundry business:

> The customs of the trade ... do not always vanish with the omission of any recognition of "the standard day's work" in wage agreements. Nor can it be expected that the entire membership of an organization will at once respond to the removal of limitations on output by a national convention of that organization. Trade customs, shop practices grow; they become as much a part of the man as his skill as a moulder....[162]

Written in 1904 these cautions were as true of other skilled workers as they were of moulders. Customs of control, established by struggle, would not vanish; they had to be vanquished by persistent management assault.

Endnotes

1. See Herbert Gutman, "Class, Status and the Gilded Age Radical: A Reconsideration" in Gutman and Kealey (eds.), *Many Pasts: Readings in American Social History*, Vol. 2 (Englewood Cliffs 1973), pp. 125–151 and his "Work, Culture, and Society in Industrializing America 1815–1919," *American Historical Review*, 78 (1973) pp. 531–588; see also E. J. Hobsbawm, "Custom, Wages and Workload," in *Labouring Men: Studies in the History of Labour* (London 1964), pp. 344–370.
2. David Montgomery, "Workers' Control of Machine Production in the Nineteenth Century," *Labor History*. 17 (1976) 485-509. See also by Montgomery, "Trade Union Practice and the Origins of Syndicalist Theory in the United States," unpublished paper; and "The 'New Unionism' and the Transformation of Workers' Consciousness in America, 1909–1922," *Journal of Social History*, 7 (1974), pp. 509–529. All these are part of Montgomery's ongoing study, tentatively titled *The Rise and Fall of the House of Labor, 1880–1920*.
3. Raymond Williams, "Base and Super-structure in Marxist Cultural Theory," *New Left Review*, 82 (Nov.–Dec. 1973), pp. 3–16. For an application of these categories to U.S. working-class history see Leon Fink, "Class Conflict and Class Consciousness in the Gilded Age: The Figure and the Phantom," *Radical History Review* (Winter 1975).
4. On scientific management in the U.S. see Milton Nadworny, *Scientific Management and the Unions* (Cambridge, M.A.1955); Katherine Stone "The Origin of Job Structures in the Steel Industry," *Radical America*, 7 (1973), pp. 19–66; and Bryan Palmer, "Class, Conception and Class Conflict: The Thrust for Efficiency Managerial Views of Labor and the Working Class Rebellion, 1903–1922," *The Review of Radical Political Economics*, 7 (1975), pp. 31–49. For Canada see Bradley Rubin "Mackenzie King and the Writing of Canada's (Anti) Labour Laws," *Canadian Dimension*, 8 (Jan. 1972); Michael Piva, "The Decline of the Trade Union Movement in Toronto, 1900–1915," unpubl. paper, CHA, 1975; and Craig Heron and Bryan Palmer, "Through the Prism of the Strike: Industrial Unrest in Southern Ontario, 1901–1914." *Canadian Historical Review* 58 (1977): 423-458.
5. Gregory S. Kealey "Artisans Respond to Industrialism: Shoemakers, Shoe Factories and the Knights of St. Crispin in Toronto," Canadian Historical Association, *Historical Papers* (1973), pp. 137–57.
6. Franklin E. Coyne, *The Development of the Cooperage Industry in the United States, 1620–1940* (Chicago 1940), p. 24.
7. *Coopers' Journal* [henceforth *CJ*] May 1871, pp. 210–211.
8. *Chicago Workingman's Advocate*, March 19, 1870.
9. H.G. Gutman, "The Labor Policies of the Large Corporation in the Gilded Age: the Case of the Standard Oil Company," unpublished paper, October 1966, p. 10.
10. Organizational data is drawn from *CJ*, 1870–1875; Coopers' International Union of North America, Proceedings, 1871 and 1873; and Coopers' International Union of North America, Executive

Department, *Names and Addresses of the Cor[responding] Secretaries of all the Unions* (Cleveland 1873).

11. *Workingman's Advocate*, Jan. 20, 1872.
12. Benson Soffer "A Theory of Trade Union Development: The Role of the Autonomous Workman," *Labor History*, I (1960), p. 141.
13. *CJ*, August 1871. p. 319.
14. Ibid., April 1872, p. 254 and Coopers' International Union of North America, Executive Board. Price List (Cleveland 1872), pp. 32–33.
15. *CJ*, October 1872, p. 633; March 1873, pp. 133–134; June 1873, p. 278.
16. Ibid., Sept. 1872, p. 566.
17. Ibid., June 1871, p. 248.
18. Ibid., June 1872, p. 373.
19. *Coopers' Ritual* (Cleveland 1870), pp. 8–9.
20. *CJ*, May 1871. p. 211.
21. Montgomery, "Workers' Control of Machine Production," pp. 7–9.
22. Martin Foran, *The Other Side: A Social Study Based on Fact* (Washington, 1886). The novel originally appeared in serial form in *CJ* commencing in December 1871 and was reprinted in the *Ontario Workman* in 1872.
23. *CJ*, July 1872, pp. 426–429.
24. Ibid., March 1871, p. 153.
25. Ibid.
26. Ibid., and *Proceedings*.
27. Gutman, "Standard Oil."
28. H.B. Small, *The Products and Manufactures of the New Dominion* (Ottawa 1868), pp. 139–141. For a good description of hand production see T.A. Meister, *The Apple Barrel Industry in Nova Scotia* (Nova Scotia Museum, Halifax n. d.).
29. For Gooderham's see *CJ*, Oct.–Nov. 1870, p. 25; July 1871, p. 268; April 1872, p. 235; August 1872, p. 500; September 1872, p. 566; December 1872, p. 741; March 1873, p. 133; Toronto *Mail*, April 23, 1872. For Walker's see *CJ*, January 1872, pp. 47–48. For other Toronto shops see Canada, Census 1871, Industrial Mss.
30. C.I.U., *Proceedings*, 1871.
31. CJ, Oct.–Nov. 1870, p. 25.
32. Ibid., July 1871, p. 268.
33. Ibid., December 1872, p. 741.
34. Ibid, March 1872, p. 182.
35. Ibid., December 1874.
36. Ibid., June 1875.
37. Greg Kealey (ed.), *Canada Investigates Industrialism* (Toronto 1973), pp. 113–116.
38. B. Soffer, "The Autonomous Workman," p. 148.
39. *CJ*, June 1875.
40. *Globe*, April 15, 24, 1882.
41. *Iron Molders' Journal*, August 1883.
42. G. S. Kealey, "The Knights of Labor in Toronto," unpublished paper, 1974.
43. Paul C. Appleton, "The Sunshine and the Shades: Labour Activism in Central Canada, 1850–1860," M.A. thesis, University of Calgary, 1974.
44. The best work on the Iron Molders International Union [henceforth I.M.I.U.] in Canada is C.B. Williams, "Canadian–American Trade Union Relations: A Study of the Development of Binational Unionism," Ph.D. thesis, Cornell, 1964, chs. 3–4. Although limited in scope the discussion of the Union is insightful.
45. I.M.I.U., *Constitution* 1859 as cited in Williams, "Canadian–American," p. 105.
46. The discussion of wages in the industry is drawn from John P. Frey and John R. Commons, "Conciliation in the Stove Industry," *Bulletin of the Bureau of Labor*, 62 (1906), pp. 124–196, especially pp. 125–130 and Frank T. Stockton, *The International Molders Union of North America* (Baltimore 1921).

47. Carroll D. Wright, "Regulation and Restriction of Output," *Eleventh Special Report of the Commissioner of Labor* (Washington 1904), pp. 149–185.
48. Peterborough Iron Moulders International Union, No. 191, *Minutes*, September 4, 1882, in Gainey Collection, Trent University Archives [henceforth Minutes, no. 191].
49. Ibid., June 19, 1891.
50. Jonathan Grossman, *William Sylvis, Pioneer of American Labor* (N.Y. 1945), p. 153.
51. *Globe*, January 21, 1871.
52. *Minutes* no. 191, February 8, 1889; May 15, 1891.
53. Frey and Commons, "Conciliation," pp. 126–127, 176; Stockton, *International Moulders Union*, pp. 170–185.
54. Williams, "Canadian–American," pp. 120.
55. *Iron Moulders Journal*, August–December 1874; February 1876; May 1876.
56. Strike date drawn from Toronto press, 1867–1892 and from *Iron Moulders' Journal*, 1864–1895 and I.M.I.U., *Proceedings*, 1864–1895.
57. *Globe*, March 22, April 3, 1867.
58. Ibid., December 21, 23, 27, 1870; January 20, 1871. I.M.I.U., *Proceedings*, 1872.
59. *Globe*, May 24, June 2, September 26, 1890; January 10, 1891; Massey Clipping Files, Vol. 1, 1886–1891, Massey Archives, Toronto. I.M.I.U., *Proceedings*, 1890.
60. I.M.I.U., *Proceedings*, 1895.
61. See especially J.H. Barnett to John Robertson, Toronto, August 20, 1903 and May 30, 1904 in I.M.I.U. no. 191, *Correspondence*, Gainey Collection [henceforth *Correspondence* no. 191].
62. *Globe*, March 22, 1867.
63. Ibid., April 3, 1867.
64. Ibid., January 20, 1871. See also December 21, 23, 27, 1870; April 21, 1871.
65. Ibid., July 15, 18. November 18, 1871; For the moulders' response to these legal initiatives see *Iron Molders Journal*, January 31, 1871.
66. Ibid., February 28, 1871. For other similar cases see IMJ, September 30, 1871; December 31, 1870.
67. Ibid., September 30, 1871.
68. Ibid., December 31, 1871.
69. *Globe*, January 8, 1887; January 6, 1888; *Canadian Labor Reformer*, January 8, 1887.
70. Frey and Commons, *Conciliation*, pp. 104–147.
71. Williams. "Canadian–American," passim.
72. Grossman, *Sylvis*, p. 110.
73. Ontario Bureau of Industry, *Annual Report*, 1892; I.M.I.U., *Proceedings, 1892–1895*.
74. *Globe*, February 27, 1890; August 22, 1890; September 26, 1890; October 3, 1890; January 10, 1891; News, August 25, 1890; *Monetary Times*, October 31, 1890.
75. *Globe*, January 10, 1891.
76. Ibid., August 22, 1890.
77. David Black to F. W. Parkes, Peterborough, June 29, 1890, *Correspondence*, no. 191.
78. *Globe*, May 24, June 2, 1890.
79. "To the Canadian Public," Toronto, September 1, 1890, *Correspondence*, no. 191.
80. *Globe*, January 10, 1891. Encouraged by his temporary victory in Toronto Gurney attacked his Hamilton moulders the next year. For this bitter struggle see I.M.I.U., *Proceedings, 1895*; Fred Walters to F.W. Parkes, Peterborough, March 20, 1892; Executive Board I.M.I.U., "Circular letter," March 3, 1892; Hamilton I.M.I.U. Local No. 26, "Labor Struggle Against Capital," March 28, 1892. The last three items are in Correspondence, no. 191.
81. For general material on the employee offensive see works cited in note 4, supra.
82. J.H. Barnett to John Robertson, Jr., Peterborough, August 20, 1903, *Correspondence*, no. 191.
83. Barnett to Robertson, May 30, 1904, Ibid.
84. Robert Ozanne, *A Century of Labour–Management Relations at McCormick and International Harvester* (Madison 1967), ch. I.
85. Massey Account Books, Massey Archives, Toronto. For the best discussion of technological innovation in the moulding industry see James Cooke Mills, *Searchlights on Some American Industries* (Chicago 1911), ch. 7.

86. For Massey Strike see Kealey, "Knights of Labor," pp. 23–27; for Peterborough-Lindsay connection see *Minutes* no. 191, 1886–1887. Ozanne, *A Century*, provides similar evidence of co-operation between Chicago moulders and the Knights.
87. From William Powell's address to the fifty-first annual convention of the I.T.U. Cited in Wayne Roberts, "The Last Artisans: Toronto Printers, 1896–1914," in Kealey and Warrian (eds.), *Essays in Working Class History* (Toronto 1976).
88. Toronto Typographical Union, *Minutes*, March 5, 1845 [henceforth T.T.U., *Minutes*].
89. Ibid., July 2, 1845.
90. Hobsbawm, "Custom Wages and Work-load," p. 347. See also Sally Zerker, "The Development of Collective Bargaining in the Toronto Printing Industry in the Nineteenth Century," *Industrial Relations*, 30 (1975), pp. 83–97.
91. T.T.U., *Minutes*, July 2, 1845.
92. George E. McNeill, *The Labor Movement* (Boston 1887), p. 185.
93. T.T.U., *Minutes*, March 7, 1849.
94. Ibid., January 1869.
95. Ibid., June 6, 1891.
96. *Globe*, July 27, 1888. The extensive historical interests of printers are also evidenced by two early official I.T.U. histories: John McVicar, *Origins and Progress of the Typographical Union, 1850–1891* (Lansing, Mich. 1891) and George A. Tracey, *History of the Typographical Union* (Indianapolis 1913).
97. International Typographical Union, [henceforth I.T.U.] *Proceedings*, 1881, p. 46.
98. Carroll Wright, "Restriction of Output," pp. 88–91.
99. National Typographical Union, *Proceedings, 1858*, pp. 45–46.
100. I.T.U., *Proceedings*, 1871, p. 47.
101. Ibid., 1873 and Elizabeth Baker, *Printers and Technology: A History of the Printing Pressmen and Assistants' Union* (New York 1957), p. 215.
102. *Globe*, July 21, 1884.
103. George A. Barnett, "The Printers: A Study in American Trade Unionism," *American Economic Association Quarterly*, 3rd series, X (1901), esp. pp. 218–221.
104. Ibid., p. 230.
105. Ibid., pp. 228–242 and *Typographical Journal*, July 15, 1890.
106. Zerker "Development of Collective Bargaining," pp. 84–88.
107. Sally Zerker, "George Brown and the Printers' Union," *Journal of Canadian Studies*, 10, I (1975) p. 47.
108. A humorous example of the last was the Vancouver "cap 'I' strike" of 1889. The printers struck the *World* for two days when management refused to pay for corrections in faulty copy. See George Bartly, *An Outline History of Typographical Union*, no. 226, Vancouver, B.C., 1887–1938 (Vancouver 1938), p. 8.
109. Barnett, "The Printer," pp. 108–142, and Sally Zerker, "A History of the Typographical Union," Ph.D. thesis, University of Toronto, 1972, pp. 1–14.
110. T.T.U., "Scale of Prices" in *Minutes*, March 17, 1883.
111. Ibid., December 20, 1890.
112. Ibid., March 17, 1883; December 6, 20, 1890; March 28, December 5, 1891.
113. Baker, *Printers and Technology*, p. 69. For a discussion of the historical roots of I.T.U. strength and for contemporary twentieth century examples see S.M. Lipset, M.A. Trow, J.S. Coleman, *Union Democracy: The Internal Politics of the I.T.U.* (Glencoe, IL 1956), ch. 2.
114. Toronto Printing Pressmen's Union, No. 10, [henceforth T.P.P.U.] *Minutes*, March 1883–December 1890, P.A.C. and Baker, *Printers and Technology, passim*.
115. Roberts, "Toronto Printers" and Ross Harkness, *J.E. Atkinson of the Star* (Toronto 1963), p. 28.
116. T.T.U., *Minutes*, July 2, 1845.
117. Zerker, "George Brown," *passim*, and for greater detail on T.T.U. struggles in the 1850's see Appleton, "The Sunshine and the Shade," pp. 103–116.
118. T.T.U., *Minutes*, June 3, 1882.

119. *Globe*, March 21, 23, 30, 1882.
120. Ibid., July 5, 1884.
121. Ibid., July 5, 6, 21, 22, 1884 and I.T.U., *Proceedings*, 1885, 1886.
122. T.P.U., *Minutes*, December 11, 1885.
123. *Globe*, December 8, 11, 15, 16, 19, 22, 1885.
124. Ibid., January 4, 1886. Emphasis in original.
125. Ibid., January 5, 1886.
126. J. S. Williams to John A. Macdonald, Toronto, August 5, 1884, pp. 196358–60; John Small to Macdonald, Toronto, August 5, 1884, pp. 196369–70. Macdonald Papers, P.A.C.
127. Harry Piper to Macdonald, February 2, February 3, 1886, pp. 205474-6, *Macdonald Papers*.
128. *Globe*, July 18, 1888.
129. Ibid., July 26, 27, August 8, 15, 1888.
130. *Typographical Journal*, September 15, 1889.
131. W. B. Prescott to Macdonald, Toronto, May 5, 1890, p. 241968, *Macdonald Papers*.
132. T.T.U., *Minutes*, December 5, 1891.
133. Ibid., March 5, 1892.
134. Zerker, "A History," ch. 3.
135. For the best discussion of the effects of mechanization on printers see George E. Barnett, "The introduction of the Linotype," *Yale Review* (Nov. 1904) 251–273. A good summary of all the literature on printers and mechanization is Harry Kalber and Carl Schlesinger, *Union Printers and Controlled Automation* (N.Y. 1967), especially ch. 1.
136. I.T.U., *Proceedings*, 1888 and Barnett, "The Printers," p. 197.
137. I.T.U., *Proceedings*, 1889. For the struggle in New York which set the continental pattern see Kalber and Schlesinger, Union Printers, ch. 1.
138. I.T.U., *Proceedings*, 1891.
139. For a similar success in Vancouver see Bartley, *Outline History*, p. 12.
140. I.T.U., *Proceedings*, 1893.
141. Zerker, "A History," pp. 160–165; 202–207; Harkness, *Atkinson*, pp. 25–26; Barnett, "The Printers," ch. 11, and Wright, "Restriction of Output," pp. 35–55.
142. For the English response to typesetting machines see Ellie Howe (ed.), *The London Compositor* (London 1947), ch. 19. For an excellent autobiographical account of an Edwardian British compositor which illustrates many of the themes discussed here see John Burnett (ed.), *The Annals of Labour: Autobiographies of British Working Class People, 1820–1920* (London 1974), pp. 330–340.
143. David Montgomery, "Trade Union Practice," pp. 16–25.
144. *Fincher's Trades Review*, August 15, 1863.
145. *Iron Moulders Journal*, February 1868.
146. James C. Sylvis, *The Life, Speeches, Labors and Essays of William H. Sylvis* (Philadelphia 1872), p. 390.
147. For similar events in Vancouver see Bartley, *Outline History*, p. 11. There, during a strike in 1892, the printers founded *The New World*.
148. Russel Hann, "Brainworkers and the Knights of Labor: E.E. Sheppard, Phillips Thompson and the Toronto *News*," in Kealey and Warrian (eds.), *Essays*.
149. Harkness, *Atkinson*, pp. 25–47.
150. *Machinists and Blacksmiths, Journal*, December 1871, p. 451; January 1872, p. 486.
151. *Globe*, October 30, November 5, 18, 27, December 14, 1885.
152. *Cigar Makers Journal*, March 1879; April 1880.
153. *Palladium of Labor*, May 29, July 3, 10, 1886.
154. *Globe*, January 30 31, February 5, 8, 22, 28, March 17, April 28, May 9, 15, 1884; see also *Journal of United Labor*, Oct. 25, 1885.
155. *Fincher's Trades Review*, April 23, 1864.
156. *Globe*, April 5, 1882.
157. David Frank, "Class Conflict in the Coal Industry: Cape Breton 1922," in Kealey and Warrian (eds.), *Essays*.

158. F.W. Taylor, *The Principles of Scientific Management* (New York 1967), p. 32. For a brilliant discussion of modern management strategies see Harry Braverman, *Labor and Monopoly Capital* (N.Y. 1974).
159. Taylor, *Principles*, p. 49.
160. Ibid., p. 53.
161. Palmer, "Class, Conception and Conflict," pp. 31–33.
162. Wright, "Restriction of Output," p. 174.

Chapter 4

The Knights of Labor and the Salvation Army

Religion and Working-Class Culture in Ontario, 1882–90

Lynne Marks

In 1883 the Salvation Army marched on Kingston. Intense excitement pervaded the town, with the Army hall packed night after night. As was the case in towns and cities across Ontario, most of the men and women who flocked to the Salvation Army's tumultuous all-night meetings and rowdy parades were working class. In Kingston, working-class involvement is seen most vividly in reports that in the town's major factories, "noon day prayer meetings amongst the working men are established ... and conducted by the men themselves."[1] By 1887 a very different working-class movement gripped the same workplaces. Workers at Kingston's Victoria Foundry, the Locomotive Works, and the cotton mill, who had organized Salvation Army prayer meetings four years earlier, now had joined the Knights of Labor (K of L). In May 1887, they were out on strike.[2]

Both the Knights of Labor, a major working-class organization, and the Salvation Army, which in this period was an exclusively revivalistic movement, drew mass support from Ontario's working class. It is no coincidence that both movements appeared in the 1880s, and saw their period of greatest strength in this decade. Industrialization first emerged in Ontario after mid-century, but was not well established until the 1870s and more particularly, the 1880s. In tiny villages and small towns across the province, as well as in larger centres, industrial wage work had become a way of life for many Ontarians.[3]

The existence of a class of people who sell their labour power to survive, a working class, does not necessarily mean that these people will identify themselves as a separate class. Historians have argued that when members of a class share distinct values, interests, and lifestyles—what some have termed a culture—they tend more readily to identify themselves with this class.[4] In *Dreaming of What Might Be*, the major study of the Knights of Labor in Ontario, authors Greg Kealey and Bryan Palmer have argued that the Knights, if only fleetingly, provided Ontario workers with a distinct "movement culture," which drew on working-class values and beliefs. One aspect of working-class belief that received minimal attention in their study was religion, which was central to the dominant culture of nineteenth century Ontario. While Kealey and Palmer acknowledged that religion was not irrelevant to the Knights, they downplayed its significance.[5] The mass popularity of the Salvation Army, which provided a distinct working-class religious alternative in the 1880s, strengthens arguments regarding the existence of working-class culture, but also forces us to recognize that religion was integral to the lives of many Ontario workers.

This paper examines the role of religion within the Knights of Labor and the Salvation

Army, assessing its relationship to working-class values, beliefs, and culture. Canadian historians' failure to examine religion within the Knights of Labor and their lack of interest in the Salvation Army may be linked to a broader reluctance among both religious historians and working-class historians to explore the subject of religion and the working class.[6] The majority of Canadian religious historians have focused on either institutional histories of the development of Canadian churches, or histories of religious ideas.[7] The relationship between religion and labour has been studied only in terms of the social gospel movement, with historians focusing on the attitudes of middle-class social gospellers towards the working class, rather than on the working class itself.[8] English Canadian labour historians have also neglected the religious dimensions of male and female workers' lives, choosing instead to study workplace experience and union activism.[9] Those few historians who have examined working-class participation in non-workplace activities have focused on leisure rather than religion.[10] The reluctance of religious historians to examine workers' religious experience can be traced to a lack of interest in class-based issues, while the explanation for labour historians' lack of interest may lie in their thoroughly secular outlook. Labour historians may also have avoided this topic from a sense that any working-class religious involvement was imposed on workers as part of a middle-class strategy of social control, and could only sully the purity of a distinct working-class culture and retard the development of class consciousness.

This paper will argue that religion was important to many Ontario workers, but that religious involvement among workers cannot in itself be viewed as evidence that workers completely accepted the dominant cultural system, in which Christian belief and practice played such a major role. Many of the same Christian beliefs professed by middle-class Canadians did appear to have been important to the workers who joined the Knights of Labor and the Salvation Army. However, as we will see through this study of religion within the two movements, these beliefs could be used by workers to help them stake out an independent respected place for themselves within an increasingly unequal society, and could also fuel a working-class critique of this society.

In examining the Knights and the Army at the local level, this study will focus particularly (but not exclusively) on small-town Ontario, since despite the significant level of industrialization in these centres, we know very little about working-class life here.[11] Historians and contemporaries alike have pointed to an apparent working-class shift away from the churches within the large cities. We have few insights, however, into the nature of religious life in smaller centres, beyond the monolithic image of dour and devout, small-town Protestant Ontario.

Origins and Membership

The Salvation Army began in London, England in 1878, but emerged from an earlier organization known as the Christian Mission, founded in 1865 by William Booth, a former Methodist preacher. The dominant principle in Booth's life was said to be the need to convert the poorest groups in society, who were generally untouched by the churches.[12] While Booth's earliest efforts were based in traditions of Methodist revivalism, his work soon became distinctive through his willingness to use a variety of unconventional methods to reach the poor. A key method was the adoption of military organization and military trappings. Army structure was firmly hierarchical, with all members being expected to obey the orders of superior officers. Supreme power was vested in Booth, who as General commanded an Army which by the 1880s had spread around the world. The Army's military trappings included brass bands and uniforms, as well as a distinctive vocabulary in which prayer services were called "knee drills" and saying "Amen" was known as "firing a volley." Those who joined the Salvation Army after conversion were known as "soldiers"; preachers were called "officers" and congregations were "corps." In the 1880s the English Salvation Army was already involved in the social rescue work for which the Booth's legions were to become famous. It must be emphasized, however, that in this decade the Canadian Salvation Army was very different from the present-day "Sally Ann" in that it remained almost exclusively a revivalistic movement, and focused on saving souls through preaching rather than through social service.[13]

The Knights of Labor's origins are better known. This organization, which combined struggles to improve workers' conditions at the local level with a broader critique of industrial capitalist society, was founded in 1869 in Philadelphia by Uriah S. Stephens. Within the Knights, workers were organized into Local Assemblies (LAs) either by trade or as mixed assemblies. LA meetings incorporated ritual similar to that of the numerous nineteenth century fraternal orders, while assemblies also provided various educational and social activities for their members. LAs were led by locally elected Master Workman, while the overall leader of the Order was the Grand Master Workman, based in the United States. In the 1880s, the annual General Assembly of the Order regularly re-elected Terence V. Powderly to this position.

While the Knights organized a secret assembly in Hamilton in 1875, both movements arrived publicly in Canada in 1882. In this year the Knights organized a number of local assemblies, including the Hamilton painters Alliance LA 1852, and mixed assemblies like St. Catharines Fidelity LA 2056 and Ingersoll's Pioneer Assembly 2416.[14] Kealey and Palmer suggest that links with the nearby United States, where the Knights already were fairly strong, help to explain the formation of the earliest Ontario LAs.[15]

A similar pattern emerges in the case of the Salvation Army. In 1882, Army services were begun in both London and Toronto by recent English immigrants, who had been converted in England. While these meetings were not officially sanctioned by Army Headquarters in England, General Booth soon sent American Army officers to Toronto to institute an official corps there and to commission those who had begun the meetings as full-time officers.[16]

It is difficult to compare the popular impact of the two movements, given their very different natures. Newspaper reports make it clear that when the Army first entered many Ontario towns, hundreds and sometimes thousands would rush to Army meetings.[17] Often the majority of the audience were curiosity seekers. But at least some of "those who came to scoff remained to pray," and the Army did make many converts. Some converts returned to the mainstream churches, but many became soldiers—the Army's equivalent of church members. The most conservative estimates of Salvation Army impact thus would be based on the number of Army soldiers. Measurement of Knights of Labor popularity have been based on membership tallies.

Membership in both organizations was extremely volatile. Although Salvation Army officers were instructed not to enroll converts as members until they were sure of the seriousness of an individual's conversion, the limited local evidence suggests that the majority of soldiers did not remain in the Army for more than three to four years, while many "backslid" much sooner, as was common in revival movements which focused on conversion.[18] K of L membership was at least as volatile, with many remaining in the Order only during the peak 1886–87 period. Kealey and Palmer argue that in Ontario "over the course of their history the Knights organized a minimum of 21,800 members."[19] An opponent of the Army recognized that at its height in 1885–86 the Army had enrolled 25,000 soldiers, mainly in Ontario, but by 1889, it was reduced to 9,000 soldiers across the country.[20] Certainly by the time of the 1891 census, just over 10,000 Ontarians are listed as Salvationists, and this, of course would include the children of adult soldiers.[21]

The basis for comparing the geographical strength of the Knights and the Army is again problematical. For an assembly of the Knights to exist in a particular centre, it required the active support of at least a core of members.

The Salvation Army could claim to have a corps in a particular town simply by sending two officers there. Nevertheless, there are ways of determining the relative strength of the Army in different centres. Despite the fact that the 1891 census was taken several years after the peak of Army popularity, an analysis of the proportion of Salvationists in local communities in 1891 can provide some insights, particularly when linked to other indices of Army support.[22] As in the case of the Knights, local newspapers occasionally provide evidence of the Army's numerical strength.[23] Since Army officers were recruited from among soldiers, analyzing the geographical origins of officers who joined up between 1882 and 1890 can provide further evidence of the relative enthusiasm the Army engendered in different locations.[24]

Both the Knights and the Army were successful in cities like Hamilton, Toronto, London, and Kingston. Although S.D. Clark, one of the few Canadian students of the Salvation Army, has characterized the movement primarily as a big-city phenomenon, the Army, like the K of L, was also successful in many smaller centres.[25] The Salvation Army had corps in most of the towns and villages where Knights assemblies existed (57 out of 74). The Army appears to have enjoyed considerable popularity within at least 36 of these communities.[26] The Army also established corps in many towns and villages where the Knights had no foothold. While the Army did not thrive in all of these communities, at least 32 show evidence of local support. The proportion of the population in the industrial workforce tended to be as great in these communities as it was in those that welcomed both the Knights and the Army. On average, however, industrial establishments were smaller in towns which only supported the Army, suggesting that these communities were not at the forefront of industrialization. Communities that welcomed the Army but not the Knights also tended to be less populous, with more than 40 percent having fewer than 1,500 inhabitants. Some small communities, like Bothwell and Dresden, reflect especially fervent support for the Salvation Army, with almost one percent of their populations becoming officers. Small communities which did not contain a significant number of Army supporters were not financially viable, and many of these corps were disbanded during the 1890s.[27]

In certain Knights of Labor strongholds, the Salvation Army appears to have had little success. This was the case in the Niagara area (outside of St. Catharines) and in the communities surrounding Ottawa.[28] In other areas, however, where the Knights of Labor attracted a large proportion of the town's workforce, the Salvation Army also did very well. This was particularly true in the region immediately east of Toronto and in Western Ontario. In the small town of Ingersoll, the Salvation Army claimed to have converted almost 700 people in 1883, while hundreds more had attended its parades and services.[29] The Knights of Labor, which arrived in town a year earlier, also developed a significant presence over the next few years, sponsoring balls and lectures, and organizing a mass celebration on Dominion Day 1887. In the oil-producing town of Petrolia crowds flocked to Salvation Army meetings in 1884; more than 200 became soldiers in the Army's first year, while only a year later 500 townspeople joined the local Knights of Labor assembly.[30] In other K of L towns—such as Woodstock, Seaforth, Chatham, Lindsay, and Belleville—the Army attracted large crowds, while in each town more than 20 soldiers were sufficiently committed to the Army to take up careers as full-time officers.[31] This compares quite favourably with the numbers of officers recruited in larger centres such as London (32), Hamilton (47), and Kingston (21).

At this point, the reader may wonder if there was any overlap between the K of L and Army memberships. This question is very difficult to answer directly, given the lack of local membership lists. Very few such lists exist for the Salvation Army, while none have been discovered for the Knights.[32] Yet less-direct evidence does suggest that the two movements' support-bases were not wholly distinct. Workers at Kingston's three largest factories became actively involved in both organizations, organizing Salvation Army prayer meetings and Knights of Labor strikes. There is also some evidence to suggest that ironworkers belonging to a Belleville local assembly attended Army meetings.[33] A closer look at the class-bases of these movements provides further clues about the probable extent of their overlap in membership.

Although some small merchants and employers joined the Knights of Labor, the Order was primarily a working-class organization. Skilled workers appear to have dominated the leadership of the movement even at the local level, and many LAs were organized on the basis of craft skills.[34] However, the K of L was the first major labour organization that attempted to organize all workers regardless of skill level, and there were many unskilled workers within various mixed assemblies. Unlike earlier trade unions, the K of L was also open to women, who organized both within mixed assemblies and in separate women's assemblies. Kealey and Palmer have estimated that women were involved in at least 10 percent of Ontario locals.[35]

The Salvation Army was also primarily a working-class movement. Newspaper reports such as that of the *Toronto Mail* reported that Salvation Army soldiers "are chiefly working people, who give what little leisure they have to helping the cause...."[36] An examination of three surviving converts' rolls for the 1887–1900 period further reinforces this evidence. In all three corps women made up slightly more than half of all converts, and over half of all women for whom an occupation was listed were servants. (See Tables 4.1 and 4.2.) In the small towns of Petrolia and Listowel, just over half of all male converts were labourers, while most of the rest worked in a variety of skilled or semi-skilled jobs.[37] Only in rural Feversham did the Army draw a significant number of farmer converts. (See Table 4.2.)

Information on the occupations of the 1,228 officers who entered the Army in Ontario during the period 1882–90 provides further evidence of the class background of Army members, since officers were recruited from the membership and in the early years of the movement there appear to have been few barriers to soldiers becoming officers. As was the case with converts, over half (55 percent) of all officers were female. These women, almost all of whom were single, were far more likely to be employed than the average single women.[38] Almost 40 percent had been domestic servants prior to entering the Army, while most of the rest were employed in traditionally feminine working-class jobs.[39] (See Table 4.3.) More than 40 percent of male officers had been skilled workers prior to entering the Army.

A wide range of skilled trades, traditional and more representative of the emerging industrial age, are found among male officers. (See Table 4.4.) Another one-quarter of male officers had been employed in other working-class occupations, while the remaining third were primarily farmers (at 23 percent) with a small number of businessmen and a more significant representation of clerks. (See Table 4.3.) The class background of officers demonstrates clearly that the Army did not simply attract working-class followers, but also had a predominantly working-class leadership.[40]

The occupational differences between converts and officers do suggest that officers may have come from a slightly higher strata within the working class than converts. Surviving converts' rolls, however, may not be representative of Army membership across Ontario. The information gleaned from the officers' roll suggests that in larger and more industrialized towns the Army attracted more skilled workers than it did in Petrolia, Listowel, or Feversham. It is also true however that the Army was popular in many smaller, less-industrialized communities. In such communities the Army would have attracted many nonindustrial workers such as servants, labourers, and farm labourers.

The Salvation Army appears to have drawn in more of the unskilled and of the nonindustrial workforce than did the Knights of Labor. The Army also attracted many more women. The different composition of Salvation Army support

Table 4.1 Sex of Salvation Army Converts in Selected Corps, 1887–1990*

Sex	Petrolia		Listowel		Feversham	
	#	%	#	%	#	%
Men	236	46	129	47	65	44
Women	274	54	144	53	84	56
Total	510	100	273	100	149	100

Source: Corps Records, Salvation Army Archives, Toronto.
Note: Petrolia and Listowel both had populations of under 5,000 in this period, while Feversham was a very small rural community.
* These are the only corps for which converts' rolls have survived for this period.

Table 4.2 Occupations of Salvation Army Converts in Selected Corps, 1887-1990*

Women						
Occupation	Petrolia		Listowel		Feversham	
	#	%	#	%	#	%
At Home	39	39	22	31	24	48
Dressmaker	4	4	1	1		
Servant	52	52	38	53	26	52
Other	5	5	11	15		
Total	100	100	72	100	50	100

Men						
Occupation	Petrolia		Listowel		Feversham	
	#	%	#	%	#	%
Clerk	3	2	1	1		
Skilled Worker	24	18	14	16	1	2
Semi-Skilled	12	9	1	1		
Labourer	83	60	51	59	23	41
Farmer**	9	7	16	12	31	55
Other	6	4	4	5	1	2
Total	137	100	87	100	56	100

Source: Corps Records, Salvation Army Archives, Toronto.
* These are the only corps for which converts' rolls appear to have survived for this period. This table does not include those converts for whom occupation was not reported.
** Including farm labourors (only in Feversham was this a significant group).
Note: Does not include those for whom no occupation is listed.

Table 4.3 Occupations of Ontario Salvation Army Officers upon Becoming Officers, By Sex 1882–1890*

Women	#	%	Men	#	%
At Home	137	28	At Home	2	-
Clerks	10	2	Businessmen/Professionals	14	4
Nurses	7	1	Clerks	31	8
Teachers	16	3	Teachers	4	1
Dressmakers/Tailoresses/Milliners**	98	20	Farmers	91	23
Factory Workers	37	8	Skilled Workers/Artisans***	164	41
Servants	186	38	Semi-Skilled Workers	22	6
Other	2	-	Factory Workers	30	7
			Labourers/Unskilled	39	10
			Servants	6	2
Total	493	100	Total	403	100

Source: Officers' Rolls, Salvation Army Archives, Toronto
* Includes only those officers who joined up in Ontario, not those transferred from England or from elsewhere in Canada
** Some of these women probably worked in factories, but this is impossible to determine.
*** Some of these men may have been self-employed, or even small masters, while many probably worked in factories. The poll only provided occupational titles.

Table 4.4 Selected Occupations of Male Officers Who Had Been Skilled Workers/Artisans*

Occupation	#	%	Occupation	#	%
Baker	9	6	Painter	12	7
Blacksmith	11	7	Printer	11	7
Butcher	6	4	Railwayworker**	9	6
Carpenter	16	10	Shoemaker	6	4
Harness maker	6	4	Tailor	8	5
Moulder	5	3	Tinsmith	7	4
Machinist	5	3	Total	164***	

Source: Officers' Rolls, Salvation Army Archives, Toronto
* Occupations listed are those held by five or more officers.
** Includes brakemen, engineers and not specified.
*** Includes all male skilled workers, not just those listed above.

meant that the Army was popular in many towns that remained untouched by the Knights. Even in towns that attracted both movements they would have drawn on somewhat different groups. For example, in many communities in which working-class husbands and fathers were active in the Knights, their wives and daughters may have found the Army more appealing.

While the Salvation Army and the Knights did attract somewhat different working-class populations, it is also true that both movements included skilled and unskilled workers, women and men. At the rank-and-file level, then, there may have been some overlap between the two movements. In the American context, Kenneth Fones-Wolf has noted that the strong Christian faith of the majority of American workers led many to see no contradiction between union membership, and even union activism, and involvement in fundamentalist Christianity.[41] It is reasonable to assume that this may also have been true in Canada.

The volatility of membership in the K of L and the Army means that even if few workers were simultaneously Knights and soldiers, many more may have been touched by both movements over the course of the 1880s. This is most likely truest in towns like Woodstock, Petrolia, and Gananoque, where the Army was strong and where Kealey and Palmer suggest that a large proportion of the workforce was involved in the Knights.[42] In these small communities, many Knights (or potential Knights) probably would have been attracted to the popular Salvation Army services. At such services some may have been converted, and made the decision to join the Army.

Christianity and the Knights

The extent to which Knights of Labor were involved in the Salvation Army is likely to remain a fascinating but largely unanswerable question. An assessment of the role played by Christianity within the Noble and Holy Order of the Knights of Labor, however, may make any possible overlap more explicable by demonstrating the importance of Christianity both to the Order, and to the workers who joined it. In *Dreaming of What Might Be*, Kealey and Palmer do note that religious zeal was part of the residual culture out of which the K of L fashioned their distinct "movement culture." However, this religious legacy merits very brief mention in their study of the Order. A closer look at this issue suggests that religion was more central both to the ideology of the Order and to the lives of individual Knights than historians have acknowledged.

Religious issues certainly were not absent from the K of L press. Newspapers were careful to avoid sectarian controversy, noting that such conflict only served to divide the working class.[43] However, the Hamilton-based *Palladium of Labor*, the Ontario K of L's principal newspaper, regularly contained reports of various sermons, both supportive of and opposed to the labour movement, with appropriate editorial commentary. The churches were not irrelevant here—their attacks were responded to while their support was applauded. The *Palladium*'s "Local News" department periodically reported on the social and religious activities of various Hamilton churches, most commonly featuring the working-class Primitive Methodist church and the Salvation Army.

In Canadian and American labour papers alike, journalists frequently expressed their hostility to the current economic system in terms of the Christian belief which they obviously assumed that their readers shared. The rhetoric identified here reinforces Herbert Gutman's argument in "Protestantism and the American Labor Movement" that while many Gilded Age labour leaders had little respect for the church, their profound belief in Christianity fueled their battles for social justice.[44] For example, a poem in the *Journal of United Labor* proclaimed: "We'll fight in this great holy war till we die/No longer in silence we'll whimper and sigh/No longer we'll cringe at the proud tyrant's nod/ But defy him, and fight 'neath the banner of God ... King Labor is ruler of earth of God's word...."[45] The *Palladium* is also full of the kind of religious rhetoric identified by Gutman. The editor was particularly fond of arguing that true Christianity was allied with the workers' cause. He frequently pointed out that "the doctrines of Jesus Christ, the carpenter—who would have been called a tramp and a Communist had he lived in these days—if applied to the present conditions would solve the question satisfactorily."[46] Christ was also described as "the greatest social reformer that ever lived. He had nothing but words of bitter Scorn and scathing indignation for the idle and luxurious classes who oppressed the poor...."[47]

In assessing similar rhetoric within the Canadian labourist tradition, Craig Heron concludes that "the crucial question remains whether working-class leaders got their politics from Christianity, or turned to a common cultural reservoir to express their politics."[48] This question could perhaps be put less starkly. The material deprivation which workers experienced and saw around them no doubt provided the primary basis for their opposition to the capitalist system. But, in the K of L's case at least, it seems that the religious imagery used did not merely reflect a routine acceptance of the dominant mode of discourse, but that it was based in fact, as Gutman suggests, on strongly held Christian beliefs. In the American context, Kenneth Fones-Wolf has argued that Christianity was at the core of the Knights' cultural system and that "... a deep religious inspiration and a commitment to Christian beliefs pervaded the Order's distinctly working-class program."[49] The Knights' Christian beliefs probably did not kindle their anger against the capitalist system, but the disparity between the Christian message and nineteenth-century capitalism would have fueled such anger.[50]

The significance of Christianity and of the churches to the Knights of Labor is also revealed through a brief look at K of L activities within certain small communities. Kealey and Palmer argue in their book that "there is evidence that in many communities the Knights of Labor usurped the traditional role of the church."[51] At the local level, no evidence has been found to substantiate the interpretation that the Knights, by acting as a kind of "secular church," came to replace the mainstream churches for small-town workers. The evidence cited by Kealey and Palmer points instead to the attendance of LA members at local ministers' special sermons on topics related to Christianity and the Knights of Labor.[52] The attendance by the Knights in a body at such sermons in towns like Ingersoll and Merritton parallels the annual attendance of fraternal orders like the Orangemen and the Oddfellows at their own special sermons.[53] On such occasions, the fraternal orders would march in a body to the church to hear a sermon that would interpret the activities of the particular order in Christian terms. This annual ritual of collective church attendance asserted these fraternal orders' position within the respectable culture of the town, which was most clearly symbolized by the institution of the church and the dominant ideology of Christianity.

The Knights' attendance at such sermons suggests that the Order was not usurping the role of the church in the local communities. The leaders of the Ingersoll Knights, who requested that the town's Presbyterian minister preach a sermon on a labour topic, probably saw that as with the fraternal associations, collective attendance at church would assert the Order's position within the respectable culture of the town.[54] Evidence for Ingersoll and Thorold (and from Kealey and Palmer's study) demonstrates that some K of L leaders also were officials in various fraternal associations, making the adoption of this ritual by the Order even more explicable. While there is still much more to learn about working-class church attendance, we do know that within some small towns, workers—particularly skilled workers—were often church members.[55] The forging of links with the churches thus may have also been viewed as a way of reassuring potential Knights that involvement with the Order would not conflict with their religious belief or involvement.

The Knights' march into the local church thus symbolizes their links to the dominant, respectable Christian culture. Like the Knights' dances, concerts, strawberry socials, and

Dominion Day celebrations, which in their external form are patterned on standard components of local respectable culture, it may also mean something more. The speeches delivered at these social activities may reflect the Knights' alternative vision; what they also demonstrate are workers organizing for themselves, and in their own interests, events which in the past had been dominated by the local middle class.

Workers who were church members worshipped within churches dominated by the local elite. When they were officials within local fraternal orders, they shared such positions with local merchants and professionals. However, when they marched into church as part of the Knights of Labor contingent they were not simply members of another fraternal order. They were part of an organization of working-class townspeople who were asserting their class identity and their equal place within the dominant respectable culture. They did not want to reject Christianity, but neither did they wish to remain any longer in the galleries of the local churches.

Leon Fink has argued that the Order did not oppose many aspects of the dominant culture of respectability, but instead sought to assert working people's place within this culture, in the face of declining working-class living standards and increasing middle-class pretensions.[56] What Fink and other historians have been less interested in exploring is the extent to which this assertion of respectable, "manly" equality and independence included the acceptance of an active role within the dominant religious institutions of the community.

In proclaiming themselves full and equal members of respectable Christian culture, the Knights could then go on to assert their rights on this culture's own terms, as they clearly did in the Ontario small towns of Petrolia and Thorold. In 1888 the federal government permitted the opening of the Welland Canal on Sundays for a few hours in the morning and the evening. Mountain Assembly No. 6798 of Thorold unanimously passed a resolution condemning this action, declaring "that such order will conflict with both the social and religious liberty of many of our members who are the servants of the government and as such will be compelled to perform duties which their consciences cannot approve of...."[57] In Petrolia, it apparently was common for certain companies to operate their oil wells on Sundays. Soon after the Knights of Labor arrived in town they sent a letter to all offending companies requesting that they cease this practice. The grounds on which they made this demand are worth quoting. "The laws of both God and man demand the due observance of the Lord's day, and the moral sentiment of the entire community.... It is believed that it is only necessary to appeal to the respect and reverence which, living as you do in an enlightened and Christian community, you must feel for God's law ... in order to secure your unhesitating consent to this reasonable request of your fellow citizens."[58] No mention was made of the men affected by this request. It was only the editorial in the *Petrolia Advertiser* (not a particularly pro-labour paper) which, in supporting the Knights' letter, pointed out that "[the] most powerful reason why this should be done is that a large number of men, greatly against their wishes, in violation of conscience and in opposition to their sense of moral right, are compelled either to violate the laws of both God and man and desecrate the Lord's day, or be discharged from their situation and thus deprived of the means of learning an honest livelihood."[59]

Why did the Knights press their demand against Sunday labour largely in religious terms? Was this simply a matter of tactics, a recognition that only an appeal to religious sentiment would be effective here? This would certainly be part of the answer. Phillips Thompson argued in the *Palladium* that "It is only that sacred character [of Sunday] which has secured to the working men the invaluable boon of a respite from toil in one day out of seven.... Only the religious sanction was powerful enough to interpose this barrier between the insensate greed of the money power and the rights of the toilers...."[60] While tactical concerns no doubt played a role here, it is also important to recognize that at the local level most Knights probably accepted the dominant Christian values. But, in affirming that everyone had a right to the religious liberty and day of rest ordained "by God's law," they were using such values to affirm the dignity and worth of all, within the context of communities characterized by hierarchy and inequality.[61]

While ministers allied themselves with the Knights in battles over Sabbath observance, several of the sermons preached to K of L audiences, or more generally on the topic of "Capital and Labour," reinforce the popular impression that the church was not sympathetic to Knights' efforts to combat inequality. While the "large number of knights" present at the Pine Street Methodist church in the industrial village of Merritton to hear a sermon by a Rev. Mr. Snider "seemed very much pleased with the discourse,"[62] their brother and sister Knights in neighboring Thorold had much less to be pleased about in the sermon by the Methodist minister Rev. Lanceley. Lanceley preached a strongly anti-labour sermon. "Let me warn you," he thundered, "against the cry of 'our rights'; it will spread like a fever.... It is an inflammation, a burning, that is set on fire of hell." He said that capital and labour should make common cause together and warned against discontent and covetousness, telling his listeners that "God will reward the meek and trusting spirit with its own reward."[63] Not all sermons were so extreme but few provided wholehearted support. Although the Rev. T. Atkinson of Ingersoll cautiously praised the aims of the K of L, he also talked of the interdependence of all classes, and the need for capitalists not to oppress labourers and for labourers to obey their masters.[64]

Local Knights who subscribed to the *Palladium* would have pointed out to their sisters and brothers after the service that the minister preached in this way because he was under the influence of the local elite who paid his salary. One frequently saw in the labour press variations on the argument that "the paid teachers of Christianity dare not quote the Biblical denunciations of land grabbers, usurers and oppressors of the poor, and apply them personally to wealthy supporters of the church. If they did they would soon preach themselves out of their pulpit."[65]

The message of such preachers may have led some labour activists to reject not simply the church, but Christianity itself. The *Palladium* argued that "There is no cause which has contributed in greater measure to the spread of rationalistic views and the indifference to popular religionism which paves the way for full blown Secularism, than the manner in which modern so-called Christianity has become identified with wealth, position and power."[66] There clearly were freethinkers within the Order. One of the arguments put forward by T.V. Powderly in asserting that Local Assemblies should not begin or end their meetings with prayer was that "we have members who believe that the dancing of a jig would be as appropriate as the use of prayer...."[67]

One must be careful, however, not to exaggerate the extent to which the Knights and labour reform generally were associated with secularism. In response to a letter asking Powderly to issue a circular stating that the word God in the Knights of Labor ritual [the Adelphon Kruptos] meant Good, Powderly responded that "the being whom God created with so little sense as to deny His existence is a fool. He may, if he chooses, have a spite against God for not furnishing him with a full stock of wit; but he should not ask others (who have) to take sides with him against their Maker."[68] Powderly may have been more conservative than many of his followers, but closer to home the *Palladium* also attacked freethought. When one member of the "Social Club" featured in the *Palladium* said that he was starting to move towards freethought, since freethinkers "are not always on the side of oppression and tyranny as religion is," Freeman, who spoke for the author, agreed that many modern ministers were self-serving hypocrites but argued that he was "confounding two different things. True religion is never on the side of tyranny."[69]

Labour activists also denied that freethought was particularly common among workers. In assessing the reasons why increasing numbers of working people were staying away from the churches, the *Palladium* recognized that "'infidelity' ... may have something to do with it," but argued it could be much more readily linked to the fact that "many of our places of worship have become simply Sunday Clubs or opera halls, intended to attract rich congregations, where the poor are neither invited nor welcomed...."[70] A letter to the *Palladium* similarly argued that workers were not becoming freethinkers and that "the muscle and sinew of Hamilton still pins its hope of emancipation to the doctrine preached from the cross," while pointing out that if workers no longer attended church it was because the church has allied itself with capital against labour, and that ministers who dared alienate their wealthy parishoners by preaching the Bible's true pro-labour message would bring workers back into the churches.[71]

A letter from "Well Wisher" states that he had once attended church regularly but "for want of that brotherly society and sympathy fell away" and found the "human love and desire to help my fellow man" which was missing from the churches through his involvement in the Knights of Labor. Kealey and Palmer use this letter to buttress their argument that for many workers the Knights displaced the church.[72] While this is a fascinating argument and probably was true for some workers, we must be careful here. Even "Well Wisher," who had found brotherly love in the Knights, still sought something more and "would fain cry out with thousands of my fellow workmen, O for a warm kindly Christ like church, a common plane where we could all meet on an equality and be brothers in Christ in this world, even as we hope to be in the next...."[73]

At the local level we have seen that the Knights did not appear to replace the churches, but used them to legitimate the Order's position within the local community. The *Palladium* also provides evidence that many Knights remained reluctant to abandon the churches. In response to a minister who preached against the labour movement that "this democratic spirit scoffs at religion," the *Palladium* responded that "this is merely an assertion without any argument whatever to bear it out. Our churches are as well attended—with perhaps one exception (the Centenary) as they were before we had any organization among our work people...."[74] In describing female Knights at the Dundas Cotton Mills, the reporter noted that these women "go to make up the well dressed congregation in some of the churches...."[75]

Assertions that the Knights did indeed go to church may have been intended partly to provide a respectable counter-image to the common portrayal of labour activists as Godless, bomb-throwing anarchists. However, such assertions also reflected a reality that labour historians have been reluctant to recognize. Workers were not isolated from the Christian-dominated world in which they lived. They sought an independent, respected place within it, and were as critical of churches where ministers preached the gospel of Mammon and relegated working people to the galleries as they were of the capitalist system which shaped such churches. This does not mean, however, that they abandoned Christianity, or the churches. On special occasions K of L assemblies marched in a body to local churches, asserting their equal participation within them, while many individual Knights appear to have attended church regularly. Many, and perhaps most of those who no longer attended church, still saw themselves as Christians. They shared with their middle-class contemporaries a belief in many basic Christian tenets, while also holding to distinct working-class values and beliefs, both religious and otherwise. In this context we have seen how Christian beliefs provided an important source, although certainly not the only source, of the Knights' challenge to the broader social and economic inequalities of Canadian society.

The Salvation Army and the Working Class

The Knights of Labor was not the only working-class movement of the 1880s that used Christianity in its critique of the inequalities of contemporary society. As Engels pointed out in 1882:

> ... the Salvation Army ... revives the propaganda of early Christianity, appeals to the poor as the elect, fights capitalism in a religious way, and thus fosters an element of early Christian class antagonism, which one day may become troublesome to the well-to-do people who now find the ready money for it.[76]

While Engels was describing the British Salvation Army, his insight is also relevant to the Salvation Army in Ontario, which in a variety of ways both promoted and fed into a certain form of class identity among Ontario Salvationists.

Like the Knights of Labor, the Salvation Army provided a very trenchant, class-based critique of the mainstream churches. The mere existence of the Salvation Army points to a belief that the churches had failed in their responsibility to minister to all classes. But many Salvationists and their supporters were much more explicit in opposing the churches. In the first few years after the Army's appearance in Ontario, local newspapers were filled with letters both attacking and defending the Army. The defense of the Army frequently included an attack on the churches as middle-class institutions which ignored Christ's true teachings. The letter from "Spectator" of Belleville is representative in this regard:

> ... Of all the denominations whose worship I have attended that which suffers least by comparison with the precepts and example of Christ is the Salvation Army.... As to the empty pews in the churches, they were so before the Army came to this city, and why? Because Sunday after Sunday they serve out the dry bones of sectarianism for the living truths of Christianity.... I see the haughty "Miss Shoddy" sweep up the aisle and recoil in poorly concealed discomfort lest her costly robes should touch the threadbare garments of some poor sinner who had the temerity to enter therein. I hear the doctrine of Dives preached in the name of Christ.... I see the Almighty blasphemed by the erection in His name of costly edifices, wherein are exclusive and costly people who worship in a costly style, while orphans cry for bread....[77]

"A Salvation Army Soldier" from Woodstock defended the Army that "reaches classes of people who have precious souls but whose burden of sin the clergy will not touch with even their little finger!," and attacked the "pew-renting and so-called respectable congregations of town and country, whose very respectability has crushed many a bruised reed...."[78] James Smith, a London Salvationist wrote of "the Salvation Army, who without money and without price are nobly bearing their crosses, fighting the Lord's battles; while the sluggish churches and overpaid ministry thereof have been asleep and drunken in their opulence."[79] Complaints from Ingersoll churchgoers make it clear that Captain Annie O'Leary preached a similar message, frequently attacking local ministers for being more interested in collecting their salaries than in saving the souls of the poor.[80]

The Salvation Army's class-based critique of the churches does echo in some ways that of the Knights, particularly in attacking the churches' emphasis on money and appearance to the exclusion of both the true word of God and the honest workingman. But, for the Salvation Army the true sin here lies in the churches' neglect of the souls of the poor, while for the Knights it lay in the churches' refusal to speak out for workers' social and economic interests. An article by Commissioner Railton in the Army's *War Cry* makes explicit this focus on spiritual rather than temporal concerns, while at the same time drawing certain parallels between the two. Railton argued that as society is moving away from accepting "the sight of poor creatures toiling from early morning till late at night ... for a few cents, neither will religious society ... tolerate the cold blooded existence of a Christian congregation, assembling twice or thrice a week for the worship of the Lord, and making no effort to make known His Salvation to thousands who are without it all around them."[81]

While the Ontario Salvation Army of the 1880s was largely unconcerned about the temporal welfare of the poor, its emphasis on spiritual equality and its willingness to appeal to the working class on their own ground attracted many Ontario workingmen and -women. The Army's evangelical emphasis on the salvation of souls, with its assumption of spiritual equality, may have tapped into or strengthened an emerging class consciousness. The Army explicitly discouraged involvement in political movements, since its followers were to focus on the state of their own souls and the salvation of others. But, as historians such as E.P. Thompson and Bernard Semmel have argued in the case of other highly evangelical religious movements, the Army's message of spiritual equality could perhaps have spilled over into the secular realm, fueling working-class anger at a society characterized by profound inequities.[82] At a minimum this message would have reinforced a sense of self-worth among the Army's working-class adherents, who were increasingly subordinated and devalued within the larger society.

In its focus on the equal value of all souls and in its acceptance of emotionally charged methods of bringing "the perishing" to salvation, the Army was very similar to earlier revival movements. By the 1880s, however, "emotionalism" had become anathema even among Ontario Methodists, who once had preached a "fire and brimstone" message across Upper Canada. By this period, middle-class Ontarians equated true religion with sedate church services, where they listened to rational learned sermons. Religion was respectable; indeed, was an integral element of respectability.[83] For this reason alone the intensely emotional appeal of Army services was interpreted as a class-based challenge to respectable middle-class churchgoing by middle class and working class alike.

While part of the Salvation Army's appeal to working-class people was its "blood and fire" revivalism, the Army's emotionalism was not all that distinguished it from respectable middle-class religion. Unlike earlier revivals, the Army drew explicitly on working-class popular culture as a means of attracting converts. The Army's methods included open-air meetings and parades, with colourful banners, the music of tambourines, triangles, and drums, the singing of hymns to the tunes of popular songs, and a variety of events, many of which were intended to provide a religious alternative to popular amusements, including Hallelujah Sprees, Popular Matinees, Hallelujah Picnics, Free and Easy Meetings, and Grand Tea Fights. A service in Kingston was advertised as "Superior to any show on earth" in an effort to compete with the visiting circus.[84] Some officers, like "Happy Bill" Cooper, who stood on his head and did cartwheels while preaching, clearly delivered on such advertising.

The Army's success attests to the efficacy of such methods. In pointing up the appeal of popular culture, it also suggests the distance of many Ontario workers from the more respectable culture to which the Knights' leadership sought to lay claim. In its own way, however, the Army's popularity does demonstrate a distinct class identity, a rejection of middle-class domination, and an assertion of working-class dignity and independence.

The periodic "Trades Meetings" in which all soldiers marched in their workday clothes, gives us a visual demonstration of the way in which the Salvation Army provided a space for workers to assert their distinct identity, as do the frequent advertisements that officers such as "Billy the Tinker," the "Happy Shoemaker," "Wright the Printer," and the "Hallelujah Blacksmith" would be featured at various Army events.[85] The Army's flouting of middle-class standards of respectability which marginalized the language of working-class Ontarians is seen in the comments of Captain Hall of London East:

> We are accused of being illiterate and not using the Queen's English properly. Who cares for grammar. The Devil has his grammar, so has the Salvation Army. We have just been singing that good old hymn "Better and Better Every Day" let us change it brothers and sisters, and sing "Gooder and Gooder every day" and it was sung....[86]

The equal value of workers' language in the sight of God was also asserted by "Hallelujah Jack" of Lindsay. "It is true I have not got the best of grammar, but I have got the love of God in my heart."[87] The primacy of salvation and the resultant irrelevance of mere earthly standards and social divisions was affirmed by "Shouting Annie" who proclaimed "there are no social distinctions in Heaven."[88]

The Salvation Army's appeal as a distinct working-class space is affirmed by the prevalence of domestic servants among its adherents, both as soldiers and as officers. Servants were among the lowest on the social hierarchy, and evidence suggests that they were among the least likely to be members of the mainstream churches.[89] Rather than sitting in church where she would be treated with disdain and watched closely by her mistress, the Salvation Army offered the domestic servant freedom from such control, and a space where she would not be looked down upon, but could proclaim her equality in the context of her own distinct culture and language. The Army also provided such women with a unique opportunity to play an active leadership role, strengthening their own sense of value and self-respect in a society which devalued them.[90] Such an opportunity clearly appealed to many other workers, both women and men, skilled and unskilled.

Victor Bailey, an historian of the British Salvation Army, has noted the primarily working-class nature of Army membership, and has argued that involvement in such a distinctively working-class organization reflects the emergence of class consciousness.[91] Roland Robertson, who has also studied the Army in the British context has suggested that for many working-class Salvationists "allegiance to the Salvation Army offered an opportunity of maintaining religiosity within the Protestant tradition but in opposition to the middle class identified denominations."[92] The evidence suggests that a similar dynamic existed within the Ontario Army. Army membership may not have implied an active opposition to the middle-class-dominated churches by all soldiers, but it would certainly reflect an alienation from class-based institutions in which workers were both subordinated and marginalized. The Salvation Army provided Ontario workers with a religious alternative which spoke to them in terms of their own cultural values, and provided a separate religious space in which they could feel comfortable and in control. The popularity of the Army points to the existence of some form of distinct culture and class identity among Ontario workers, while the Army's activities would themselves reinforce such consciousness.

It is important to remember that the Salvation Army's success points not only to working-class consciousness, but also to working-class religiosity. The Army's message was delivered in working-class cultural forms, but remained the message of evangelical Protestantism. This message was clearly a familiar one to those workers who were swept up in the Salvation Army. Some Salvation soldiers had formerly been church members, and had either drifted away from the churches or found the Army's "blood and fire" methods more appealing than sedate church services. Many other Army soldiers and officers never had been church members, but had had a Christian, very often a Methodist upbringing.[93] Even those who had never even attended Sunday School lived within a society in which Christianity (in particular Protestantism) was integral to the dominant culture. Anyone who had attended the public schools even briefly had been exposed to basic Christian teachings.[94] Like the workers identified by Gutman and the *Palladium*, many may have felt alienated from the churches while remaining committed to Christianity. The instant popularity of the Salvation Army certainly suggests that the basic message of evangelical Christianity was a familiar and welcome one to most workers, when presented within a culture and language with which they could identify.

The Army's message had a particular appeal to working-class women, as the gender distributions of converts and officers demonstrate. The relative over-represention of women within the Army is similar to that found within the mainstream denominations, suggesting at first glance a shared, cross-class feminine religiosity.[95] The behaviour expected of women in the Salvation Army was quite different, however, from the more passive, ladylike piety expected of women within the mainstream churches. Like male soldiers, female soldiers ("Hallelujah Lasses") were expected to stand up in crowded halls, testify to their faith in Jesus, and describe the sinfulness and misery of their past lives. They also marched through the streets, beating drums or tambourines to attract attention to the cause. The Army also provided many such women with the opportunity to defy more concrete, gender-based constraints. Many female soldiers challenged both the authority of husbands and fathers and their relegation to the narrow confines of the domestic sphere.[96] "Drum-Major Annie" of Petrolia proclaimed the importance of her efforts to save the souls even of unappreciative and undeserving men, defending such efforts as much more significant than "wash[ing] the crude oil out of the shirt of some dirty beast."[97]

Female soldiers who became officers posed an even greater challenge to dominant feminine roles by usurping the traditional male role of religious leader. Many such officers became Captains, and thus were in charge of local corps that could include up to several hundred soldiers and adherents. They were expected to follow the directives issued by Headquarters in Toronto, and were subject to transfer at any time. However, their work required considerable initiative and effort, not just in preaching to crowds every night of the week and three times on Sunday, but also in leading parades, visiting converts, managing the corps's finances, and planning innovative methods of drawing crowds.

As previously demonstrated, prior to becoming officers the majority of female Salvationists worked outside the home, labouring for long hours in factories, or as servants or seamstresses. Like the women who joined Knights of Labor assemblies during the same period, the image of the fragile, passive Victorian lady in the home thus may have had little relevance to the reality of female officers' lives, making them more willing to flout dominant gender roles.

Why did so many more women defy such roles through involvement in the Army than in the Knights? One reason is that while the Knights did welcome married women who worked in the home, their main female recruits were single wage earners. While this was also true of Salvation Army officers, a significant minority of female converts and soldiers appear to have been married.[98] As a result the Army had a larger pool of women to draw on.

However there is some evidence to suggest that the constraints of the dominant feminine ideology did prevent many women from joining the Knights. Certainly Leonora Barry, Organizer of Women's Work for the Knights, saw this as an issue and cited "natural pride, timidity and the restrictions of social custom" as a barrier to women's organization.[99] Some women who did join the Knights were able to overcome such concerns, like Katie McVicar, who organized the first woman's assembly in Canada. A female co-worker in denying working women's ability to organize suggests that McVicar may have been quite unusual. Her friend commented that

> Organization ... was all very well, but how were girls to accomplish it; were they to advertise mass meetings, mount platforms and make speeches? If so, the Canadian girls, at least, would never organize.[100]

The fact that upon McVicar's death, the assembly petitioned Powderly to appoint a man to chair their meetings reflects the truth of such sentiments.[101]

The Knights' own ambivalence about women's sphere may not have helped here. As Karen Dubinsky has demonstrated, while welcoming women and championing suffrage, equal pay, and temperance reform, the Order often called for the family wage, and argued that in an ideal world women would not work outside the home.[102] The Knights' assertions of manly respectability, which explain their commitment to reforms such as temperance also led them to buy into certain aspects of the dominant gender ideology. A Knights of Labor parade in St. Catharines, in which the "lady Knights" rode in carriages, while their brothers marched beside them, provides a visual reminder of such values.[103]

This image can be contrasted with Salvation Army parades, in which, as one observer commented: "there's a brave lot of lasses in the ranks, and they walk just as bravely as the men, and just take as big a step."[104] What is one to assume here? That middle-class conceptions of femininity were less relevant to the working-class women in the Salvation Army than to those in the Knights? There may be some truth to this argument, given the Army's greater willingness to reject the trappings of respectability. However, there is something else going on here. Unlike women in the Knights of Labor, Salvation Army women were not marching in parades and making speeches to improve their own lives and their own working conditions. As the Salvation Army paper, the *War Cry*, continually reminded them, by joining the Army they had abandoned all self-interest and dedicated their entire lives to Christ. For some women the public behaviour required of them may have been justified as part of a most appropriately feminine Christian submission to God's will.[105] However, the evident reluctance of female officers to enter social service work once it was introduced into the Canadian Army in the late 1880s shows that women preferred active public roles as preachers to more private, self-denying, and suitably feminine ones as "angels of mercy."[106] For many women, feminine self-denial provided more a justification than a motivation for their willingness to "mount platforms and make speeches."

Women's participation in the Army hints at the existence of a distinct working-class conception of femininity, which more readily acknowledged women's strength, assertiveness, and involvement in the public sphere. The willingness of many working-class women to become "Hallelujah Lasses," however, may also demonstrate the continued relevance of aspects of the dominant feminine ideal to at least some working-class women. The Army probably was more popular with working-class women than the Knights, since as a religious movement, it was a more familiar forum for feminine energies than was a trade-union movement. For some, too, it may have been considered a more suitable forum.

While some female Salvationists may have viewed their involvement in the Army as demonstrating appropriate feminine piety, many middle-class observers felt otherwise. For critics like Rev. A. Wilson of Kingston, "female preaching and fantastic dressing, the outrageous talk and singing of doggerel hymns" combined to render the Army completely unacceptable.[107] The Army's class-based critique of the churches was more than fully reciprocated by ministers and other middle-class observers across Ontario. These men clearly saw the respectable trappings of the mainstream churches as being integral to Christianity as they defined it. The Army was frequently accused of treating Christianity with vulgarity, levity, and frivolity, and Army activities were disparagingly compared to working-class entertainments.[108] A common, and telling comparison identified the Army as being worse than "a negro minstrel show."[109] The adoption of the cultural forms of the marginal and the devalued, whether by class or race, placed the Army beyond the pale of true Christianity, which in the dominant discourse of the period was inextricably linked with respectable middle-class culture.

Hostility to the Army was also fueled by fears of disorder and loss of middle-class control.[110] Common complaints about the Army included the lack of order at their meetings, and in particular their habit of marching through the streets with drums and tambourines. For example, in Ingersoll, a letter to the editor complained of the "infernal drum beating and parades" that forced "ladies" off the sidewalk into the gutter, while the *Newmarket Era* attacked the "abominable nuisance of singing and howling ... after orderly people have retired to rest" and the "drum and symball (sic) playing and singing, on the streets on Sunday."[111] Middle-class citizens frequently attempted to regain control over public space by petitioning town councils to pass by-laws prohibiting the Army from marching and beating their drums. In some cases Salvationists were arrested for refusing to comply with such laws.[112]

Outraged middle-class churchgoers and town councils were not the only Ontarians to oppose the Salvation Army. In most towns, the Army also faced considerable hostility from local young men, who appear to have been predominantly working class. This opposition took a variety of forms, from throwing rocks and rotten eggs, to putting cayenne pepper on a stove during Army meetings, to assaulting officers, to scoffing and heckling during meetings.[113] A major confrontation between the Army and these men occurred in Ingersoll in December 1883:

> During the parade of the Salvation Army on Monday evening an "indescribable" meeting took place between this and another body headed by a brass band composed of members of our town band and others. When the Salvationist started from the market square the other body, composed principally of working men to the number of several hundreds, also started from an opposite point, the band playing vigorously ... [when] opposite the Salvationists ... both bodies commenced to play with renewed vigour and to emit the most hideous yells.[114]

While some of this behaviour was probably just considered "all in good fun" by the perpetrators, some of the attacks do appear to reflect real hostility to the Army. Catholic hostility to the Army's active Protestant revivalism may have been behind these activities, as they certainly were in Quebec. There is no evidence of this, however, in Ontario. It is more likely that such attacks reflect a hostility toward the Army for its efforts to transform the lifestyle of working-class men.[115] Local young men may have been particularly hostile to Army claims that through conversion they were able to transform the most hardened drinker's life to one of piety and sobriety. In this regard it is interesting to note that the behaviour of local "roughs" towards the Army parallels in certain ways the near-riots that were touched off by efforts to enforce the Scott Act in the same period.[116] Opposition to the Army also may have been grounded in a popular anti-clericalism (and perhaps anti-religiosity) among certain young working-class men that did not differentiate the Salvation Army from the churches because of its working-class composition, but for this reason saw it as more vulnerable to attack.

While many local roughs remained hostile to the Army, others were at least temporarily converted at Army meetings. Such conversions gradually transformed middle-class attitudes toward the movement. The Salvation Army was increasingly praised for its ability to bring Christianity to those who would never enter the mainstream churches.[117] Middle-class observers were no doubt genuinely pleased by the Army's ability to save the souls of "the perishing masses." However, for these middle-class supporters, "getting religion" meant considerably more than accepting Jesus Christ. The Army was praised for reducing working-class drunkenness and crime, for increasing the industriousness of workingmen, and for providing an alternative to working-class movements that sought collective salvation on earth rather than individual salvation in heaven.[118] Such middle-class support was not misplaced. The Salvation Army did in many ways bring its followers more firmly within the dominant value system. Salvationists were expected to eschew drinking, smoking, dancing, and any interest in "worldly" issues. An organization which, while denying that it provided strikebreakers, went on to say "if [we have] anything to say in reference to the strike and the strikers it would be get converted, strike against sin, and use the cash as God directs you after you have earned it," would certainly appeal to middle-class Ontarians.[119] However, the Salvation Army cannot simply be dismissed as a manifestation of working-class false consciousness and middle-class social control. The Salvation Army was a working-class organization—while it did attract a minority of farmers and middle-class converts, the vast majority of both officers and soldiers were working-class. It spoke to workers in terms of their own language and culture, and asserted the equal value of their souls to those that were ministered to in costly middle-class churches. The Army tapped into and reinforced a sense among working-class Ontarians of their own value and dignity within a society characterized by increasing inequality. The Army also provided the kind of space sought by "Well Wisher" in the *Palladium of Labor* where "we could all meet on an equality and be brothers in Christ in this world, even as we hope to be in the next."

Conclusion

Neither the Knights nor the Army retained the promise of the 1880s. The Knights declined rapidly in the late 1880s as a result of poor economic conditions, external attack, and internal weakness. While the Salvation Army remains active today, it is a very different movement from the one described in these pages. By the early 1890s, the Ontario Salvation Army had been transformed into a primarily social rescue organization along the lines of the British Salvation Army. With this change, one finds growing class divisions within the Army itself, with increasingly respectable officers ministering to the "submerged tenth." The loss of evangelical zeal which accompanied the shift to rescue-work precipitated a major schism within the Army, led by Brigadier P.W. Philpott. Philpott opposed the Army's new emphasis on social work. Most tellingly, he also attacked the appearance of class divisions within the Army. He pointed to the inconsistency of the fact that senior officers travelled first-class while local field officers often lived on less than a dollar a week, although "we have always preached so much self-sacrifice and professed to the world to have all things in common."[120]

The transformation of the Army and the decline of the Knights does not negate, however, their importance to Ontario workers of the 1880s. Thousands of Ontario workers were influenced by these movements. While each movement did have greater appeal to different strata within the working class, the popularity of both the Knights and the Army demonstrate the importance of class identity and religious belief within the Ontario working class.

Skilled working men, who had bargaining power in the workplace and often a tradition of organized resistance, more commonly turned to the Knights. Here the Christian beliefs held by many workers were used to challenge the increasingly hierarchical social order they saw around them, both within the mainstream churches and in the larger social and economic sphere. The Knights demanded the consistent application of Christian values to all Ontarians, which, by their interpretation of Christianity, would lead towards the millennium on earth.

Ontario's more powerless unskilled workers, male and female, were more likely to be attracted to the individual heavenly salvation offered by the Salvation Army. The otherworldly emphasis of the Army negated the importance of a secular world where their lot was hard, their position lowly, and the prospects of material improvement slight. In flocking to the Army, workers demonstrated the importance of Christianity to their lives. At the same time, by turning to the Salvation Army, these workers were not demonstrating simply that religion was "the opium of the masses," and that piety undermined or precluded class consciousness. In joining the Army, Ontario workers were rejecting the hierarchical mainstream churches, choosing instead a religious movement which attacked respectable middle-class Christianity, and preached the equality of all souls. The popularity of the Salvation Army, a religious movement which provided workers with their own space and spoke to them in their own language, points to the existence of distinct working-class beliefs and cultural forms among the unskilled male and female workers who made up the bulk of Salvationists.

While different strata and genders within the Ontario working class tended to find that either the Knights or the Army meshed more readily with their own values and experiences, it is also true that many Ontario skilled workers became Salvationists, and that the Knights boasted a considerable following among the unskilled. During the 1880s, some of these people may have been drawn to both movements. In small towns across Ontario as the hope of collective salvation faded with the local defeat or dissolution of the Knights, some workers may have turned to the Salvation Army. More commonly, since the Salvation Army more often preceded the Knights within Ontario communities, the Army may have contributed to the development of a sense of class identity among local workers, and when the fires of revivalism died out, certain of these workers may have turned to the social Christianity of the Knights.

While we cannot know how many workers were touched by both movements, this examination of the Salvation Army and the Knights of Labor clearly demonstrates the importance of religion to working-class life in late nineteenth century Ontario. The religion of these workers was not totally distinct from that of their middle-class neighbours, of course, for workers did not live in a completely separate cultural world. At the same time, working-class piety did not guarantee shared values and class harmony. As Kenneth Fones-Wolf has argued, religion "was truly a contested terrain."[121] Certainly, in 1880s' Ontario, as in many other times and places, religion did not act simply to buttress the social order, but also to challenge it.

I would like to thank former Salvation Army archivist Johanne Pelletier for all her help. I would also like to thank John Blakely, Karen Dubinsky, Susan Houston, Greg Kealey, the members of the Labour Studies Group (Ruth Frager, Charlene Gannage, Craig Heron, Chris Huxley, Franca Iacovetta, Kathryn McPherson, Jim Naylor, Ian Radforth, Esther Reiter, Mark Rosenfeld, Bob Storey, and Eric Tucker) and the anonymous readers from *Labour/Le Travail* for their comments on earlier drafts of this paper. I am also grateful to the IODE for their financial support through a War Memorial Scholarship and to CRIAW for their assistance with research costs through the Marta Danylewycz Memorial Award.

Endnotes

1. *Thorold Post*, 23 March 1883 (letter from Kingston). Also see *The Daily British Whig* (Kingston) 12 March 1883.
2. Gregory S. Kealey and Bryan D. Palmer, *Dreaming of What Might Be: The Knights of Labor in Ontario, 1880–1900* (Toronto 1982), 347–8.
3. Despite the increasing prominence of Hamilton and Toronto manufacturing remained relatively decentralized in this period. See Kealey and Palmer, 27–56.
4. In some cases the existence of a distinct class culture can help lay the basis for an oppositional class consciousness, in which the members of a class see themselves as sharing common class interests opposed to those of other classes. For an exploration of working-class culture and consciousness see for example Richard Johnson, "Three Problematics: Elements of a Theory of Working-Class Culture," in John Clarke, et al., eds., *Working-Class Culture* (London 1979); E.P. Thompson, *The Making of the English Working Class* (New York 1963); and Bryan D. Palmer, *A Culture in Conflict: Skilled Workers and Industrial Capitalism in Hamilton, Ontario, 1860–1914* (Montreal 1979).
5. Kealey and Palmer recognize that religion was part of the residual culture out of which the Knights forged their "movement culture." They acknowledge that "religious motivation clearly served as a vital plank in the appeal of the Hamilton Knights" (145). Religion, however, receives only brief mention in their study.
6. S. D. Clark's *Church and Sect in Canada* (Toronto 1948) still provides the best scholarly discussion of the Canadian Salvation Army within a social history context, despite Clark's overly functionalist approach. Stephen M. Ashley's M.A. thesis, "The Salvation Army in Toronto, 1882–1896," (Guelph 1969) also contributes some valuable insights, while R.G. Moyles, a Salvationist, provides a useful and fairly balanced history of the *Army in The Blood and Fire in Canada: A History of the Salvation Army in the Dominion, 1882–1976* (Toronto 1977).

7. See for example John Webster Grant, *The Church in the Canadian Era* (Toronto 1972), John S. Moir, *Enduring Witness, A History of the Presbyterian Church in Canada* (Canada 1975), A. B. McKillop, *A Disciplined Intelligence: Critical Inquiry and Canadian Thought in the Victorian Era* (Montreal 1979), Ramsay Cook, *The Regenerators: Social Criticism in Late Victorian English Canada* (Toronto 1985). Two recent books which try to extend the bounds of these approaches are John Webster Grant, *A Profusion of Spires: Religion in Nineteenth Century Ontario* (Toronto 1988) and William Westfall, *Two Worlds: The Protestant Culture of Nineteenth Century Ontario* (Kingston and Montreal 1989).
8. See for example Richard Allen, *The Social Passion: Religion and Social Reform in Canada, 1914–1928* (Toronto 1973) and William H. Magney, "The Methodist Church and the National Gospel," *United Church Archives*, Bulletin, 20 (1968).
9. See for example Craig Heron and Robert Storey, eds., *On the Job: Confronting the Labour Process in Canada* (Kingston and Montreal 1986), Ian McKay, *The Craft Transformed: An Essay on the Carpenters of Halifax, 1885–1985* (Halifax 1985), Ian Radforth, *Bushworkers and Bosses: Logging in Northern Ontario, 1900–1980* (Toronto 1987), Craig Heron, *Working in Steel: The Early Years in Canada, 1883–1935* (Toronto 1988) and Ruth Frager, "No Proper Deal: Women Workers and the Canadian Labour Movement, 1870–1940," in Linda Briskin and Lynda Yanz, eds., *Union Sisters: Women in the Labour Movement* (Toronto 1983). Studies of the household economy, which focus on the household as women's primary workplace could be included here. See for example Bettina Bradbury, "Pigs, Cows and Boarders: Non-Wage Forms of Survival among Montreal Families, 1861–1891," *Labour/Le Travail*, 14 (1984), 9–46, and Bradbury, "The Family Economy and Work in an Industrializing City: Montreal in the 1870s," Canadian Historical Association, *Historical Papers* (1979).
10. See Bryan Palmer, *A Culture in Conflict: Skilled Workers and Industrial Capitalism in Hamilton, Ontario, 1860–1914* (Montreal 1979). Unlike Palmer, American historians who examine working-class leisure do not completely ignore religion. However, it generally merits only a brief discussion. See for example Roy Rosenzweig, *Eight Hours for What We Will: Workers and Leisure in an Industrial City, 1870–1920* (Cambridge 1983); Francis G. Couvares, *The Remaking of Pittsburgh: Class and Culture in an Industrializing City, 1877–1919* (Albany, NY 1984); and Steven J. Ross, *Workers on the Edge, Work, Leisure and Politics in Industrializing Cincinnati, 1788–1890* (New York 1985). Some very recent work both in Canada and the United States does examine religion as a significant element of working class life. See for example Mark Rosenfeld "'She was a hard life': Work, Family, Community and Politics in the Railway Ward of Barrie, Ontario, 1900–1960," Ph.D. thesis, York University, 1990; Doris Mary O'Dell, "The Class Character of Church Participation in Late Nineteenth-Century Belleville, Ontario," Ph.D. thesis, Queen's University, 1990; and Kenneth Fones-Wolf, *Trade Union Gospel: Christianity and Labor in Industrial Philadelphia, 1865–1915* (Philadelphia 1989).
11. In *Dreaming*, Kealey and Palmer provide the best available overview of working class activism in small town Ontario. This study will focus particularly closely on the towns of Ingersoll, Thorold, Petrolia, and Campbellford. (Ingersoll, Thorold, and Campbellford are the focus of my forthcoming Ph.D. thesis, "Gender and Class Dimensions of Religion and Leisure in Small Town Ontario, 1882–1896"). For the Salvation Army section of this paper information concerning other towns has also been drawn from selected Ontario newspapers. A Salvation Army officer has gone through over thirty Canadian newspapers for the first few years of the Army's presence in each town and has copied out all references to the Army in the local papers. This was the source used in references to the mainstream press, other than within the towns mentioned above.
12. Moyles, *Blood and Fire*, 5.
13. The Salvation Army founded a rescue home in Toronto in 1886, but such work did not begin in a major way in Canada until 1890.
14. Kealey and Palmer, *Dreaming*, 66–9.
15. Kealey and Palmer, *Dreaming*, 67.
16. Moyles, *Blood and Fire*, 6–9.
17. See *Daily British Whig* (Kingston), 26 March 1883; *London Advertiser*, 27 March 1883; *Newmarket Era*, 13 June 1884; *Northern Advance* (Barrie), 22 November 1883.

18. For a discussion of the short term nature of conversion within highly revivalistic religious movements see Westfall, *Two Worlds*, 50–81. For evidence of the short term nature of many Salvation Army conversions, see the converts' and soldiers' rolls for the towns of Listowel, Petrolia, and Chatham for the 1886–1900 period, Salvation Army Archives, Toronto.
19. Kealey and Palmer, *Dreaming*, 65.
20. A. Sumner, *The New Papacy: Behind the scenes in the Salvation Army by an ex-Staff Officer* (Toronto 1889), 7. Sumner, who denounced the Army in this pamphlet, would have insider knowledge of Army figures, as well as no reason to make the Army look good.
21. Canada, *Census of Canada 1891*. Volume 1, Table IV. The Army stated that in 1890 over 60,000 people, the majority being non-members, attended Salvation Army services across Canada each Sunday. This figure may well be inflated, however (Moyles, *Blood and Fire*, 11.)
22. The 10,320 Ontarians listed as Salvationists in 1891, reflects at most a fifth to a quarter of Salvationist support at its height in the mid 1880s, given the fact that the census figures includes the children of Salvationists, while there appear to have been at least 20,000 adult Salvationists in Ontario in the mid 1880s. (Sumner, *New Papacy*, 7.)
23. Army reports regarding the sales of the *War Cry*, the Army newspaper, sold in a particular location can provide further clues, but such evidence may suggest as much about the relative enthusiasm of the vendors as the buyers.
24. It must be recognized that if an officer was recruited from a particular town she or he may not have lived there, but may instead have lived in the surrounding countryside.
25. See Clark, *Church and Sect*, 420.
26. While there are some regional differences between K of L towns where the Army was also popular and those where it was not there do not appear to be other significant differences. In K of L towns there does not appear to be any correlation between the proportion of population involved in the industrial workforce, or the average size of industrial workplace and Army popularity.
27. See Moyles, 270–7.
28. In the Niagara area the Knights organized a number of small communities (Beamsville, Chippewa, International Bridge, and Queenston) which never had Army corps. Although the Army had some initial popularity in Thorold and Welland, it died out fairly rapidly in these communities. The unpopularity of the Army in the Ottawa region can be linked to the relatively large French Canadian Catholic population in the towns near the Quebec border, as well as to the fact that the Army did not establish corps in these communities until relatively late, by which point the novelty of the Army may have worn off for many.
29. *The Sentinel Review* (Woodstock), 15 February 1884.
30. *Petrolia Advertiser*, 28 June 1884 and Kealey and Palmer, 82.
31. See for example, *The Belleville Daily Intelligencer*, 26 November 1883; *The Sentinel Review* (Woodstock), 15 February 1884 and 4 July 1884; The Canadian Post (Lindsay), 26 October 1883; *The London Advertiser*, 8 January 1883. During 1882–90, 20 officers were recruited from the Belleville corps, 22 from Chatham, and 23 each from Lindsay, Seaforth, and Woodstock. (Source: "C" Roll, Salvation Army archives, Toronto.)
32. A very limited amount of data of this kind is available for the Western Ontario town of Petrolia, including lists of those who were Salvation Army soldiers in the late 1880s and the names of a small number of Knights of Labour leaders that were gleaned from the local newspaper. No overlap was discovered between these two lists. However, the K of L leadership appears to have been among the most skilled and well established workers within the Order. They may have been less likely to join the Army than the rank and file Knights.
33. *Belleville Intelligencer*, 15 October 1883.
34. Leon Fink, *Workingmen's Democracy: The Knights of Labor and American Politics* (Urbana 1983) argues that the Knights' leaders were primarily skilled workers (13).
35. Kealey and Palmer, *Dreaming*, 323.
36. *The Toronto Mail*, 17 July 1882. In a few towns both middle and working class people appear to have been attracted to the Army, see for example Kingston's *Daily British Whig*, 17 July 1883.
37. Many of the labourers in Petrolia probably worked in the dominant oil industry of the town, and an additional 6 percent of workers here are clearly identified with the industry as drillers or oil well workers.

38. In 1891 less than eleven percent of Canada's female population engaged in paid employment. Most of those who were employed were unmarried. However, although the 1891 census does not provide a breakdown of female employment by marital status we can be relatively certain that less than half of the unmarried female population was employed in this period, since in 1921, when over fifteen percent of the female population was gainfully employed, only forty-nine percent of unmarried women between the ages of fifteen and thirty-four were employed. Canada, Dominion Bureau of Statistics, Census of Canada, 1921. Canada, Dominion Bureau of Statistics, Occupational Trends in Canada, 1891–1931 (Ottawa 1939).
39. Many of the nurses or teachers who joined the Army may have come from working class backgrounds, although these jobs are generally considered middle class. Large numbers of women from working class backgrounds were becoming teachers in this period. See Marta Danylewycz and Alison Prentice, "Teachers, Gender and Bureaucratizing School Systems in Nineteenth Century Montreal and Toronto," *History of Education Quarterly*, Vol. 24, No. 1 (Spring 1984), 75–100. Nursing was only beginning to become a more professionalized middle class occupation in Canada in this period, and most nurses came from working class backgrounds. See Judi Coburn, "'I See and am Silent': A Short History of Nursing in Ontario," in *Women at Work, Ontario 1850–1930* (Toronto 1974), 127–64.
40. This was true in all Army ranks. While women seldom were found above the rank of Captain an examination of the twenty-four Ontario male officers who attained a rank higher than Captain shows that two thirds (66 percent) of these men were clearly working class, although predominantly skilled workers.
41. Fones-Wolf argues that this may have been true at least of many rank and file unionists even in cases when fundamentalist preachers preached actively anti-union messages. See Fones-Wolf, 192.
42. For a list of towns in which a high proportion of the workforce became involved in the Knights of Labor see Kealey and Palmer, *Dreaming*, 67.
43. See for example, *The Palladium of Labor*, 18 July 1885 and 4 December 1886.
44. Herbert Gutman, "Protestantism and the American Labor Movement: The Christian Spirit in the Gilded Age," in *Work, Culture and Society in Industrializing America* (New York 1966), 79–117.
45. *Journal of United Labor*, 25 May 1884.
46. *The Palladium* (Toronto), 13 February 1886.
47. *The Palladium* (Hamilton), 27 October 1883. See also 22 May 1886, 20 March 1886, 14 March 1885, 29 December 1883, 8 September 1883.
48. Craig Heron, "Labourism and the Canadian Working Class," *Labour/Le Travail*, 13 (Spring 1984), 65.
49. Fones-Wolf, *Trade Union Gospel*, 79 and 84.
50. The disparity between the Christian message and social inequality has certainly fueled oppositional consciousness in other contexts. See for example, E.P. Thompson, *The Making of the English Working Class* (New York 1963), 431, 438; and Thomas F. O'Dea and Janet O'Dea Aviad, *The Sociology of Religion* (New Jersey 1983), 15.
51. Kealey and Palmer, *Dreaming*, 311. In *Trade Union Gospel*, Fones-Wolf argues that the Knights took on the qualities of a millenarian sect. However, while he provides some fascinating arguments to buttress his assertion he makes no effort to prove that the Knights actually usurped the role of the church among workers, in that they left the churches for the Knights. They may however have provided a semi-religious parallel institution for many workers that did not necessarily lead them away from the churches.
52. See for example, *Ingersoll Chronicle*, 3 June 1886, 27 May 1886. *The Stratford Beacon*, 16 April 1886, also cited by Kealey and Palmer records a unanimous resolution of thanks by the local Knights of Labor Assembly to Rev. Gordon-Smith for his sermon on the topic of the Knights of Labor. He was thanked for "his earnest and eloquent defence of our rights, also for his effort to instruct us in our duty both to our employers and as citizens of the great commonwealth of Ontario."
53. See *Thorold Post*, 25 November 1887 regarding the Merritton Knights of Labor sermon. Also see *Ingersoll Chronicle*, 20 May 1886 regarding the Knights of Labor sermon there. Examples of fraternal orders' annual church sermon can be found in the *Ingersoll Chronicle*, 30 April 1885, 11 June 1885 and the *Thorold Post*, 14 December 1883.

54. *Ingersoll Chronicle*, 3 June 1886.
55. See O'Dell, "The Class Character of Church Participation," and Marks, "Gender and Class Dimensions of Religion and Leisure in Small Town Ontario, 1882–1896."
56. Fink, *Workingmen's Democracy*, 3–15.
57. *Thorold Post*, 13 July 1888.
58. *Petrolia Advertiser*, 24 September 1886.
59. *Petrolia Advertiser*, 24 September 1886.
60. *The Palladium*, 10 January 1885.
61. For a discussion of battles over Sunday streetcars in Toronto in the 1890s in which the labour movement at first opposed Sunday cars and later supported them see Christopher Armstrong and H.V. Nelles, *The Revenge of the Methodist Bicycle Company* (Toronto 1977). In *Trade Union Gospel*, Fones-Wolf demonstrates that Philadelphia workers sometimes used Sabbatarian arguments to protect workers from Sunday labour, but more often opposed Sabbatarianism as an interference in working class leisure.
62. *Thorold Post*, 21 October 1887.
63. *Thorold Post*, 21 October 1887, 28 October 1887.
64. *Ingersoll Chronicle*, 3 June 1886. The American churches may have been better than the Canadian ones in regard to their attitudes towards the Knights. Fones-Wolf suggests that in certain areas the churches appear to have supported the Knights. See Kenneth Fones-Wolf, "Religion and Trade Union Politics in the United States, 1880–1920," *International Labor and Working-Class History*, No. 34, Fall 1988, 43.
65. *The Palladium* (Toronto), 13 February 1886. Also see Palladium, 27 October 1883 and 8 September 1883.
66. *The Palladium*, 20 December 1884.
67. *Journal of United Labor*, June 1883.
68. *General Assembly of the Knights of Labor*, Proceedings, 1880.
69. *The Palladium*, 27 October 1883.
70. *The Palladium*, 8 September 1883.
71. *The Palladium*, 20 March 1886. In *Trade Union Gospel*, Fones-Wolf argues that workers remained committed to Christianity even if they did not attend church, and suggested that working class religion was characterized by "a lack of concern for such traditional gauges of religiosity as church attendance" and demonstrated "a greater reliance on direct Scriptural inspiration," xviii.
72. Kealey and Palmer, *Dreaming*, 311–2.
73. *The Palladium*, 28 November 1885.
74. *The Palladium*, 17 May 1884.
75. *The Palladium*, 15 May 1886.
76. F. Engels, *Socialism, Utopian and Scientific* (London 1892), xxxi, cited in Victor Bailey, "'In Darkest England and the Way Out': The Salvation Army, Social Reform and the Labour Movement, 1885–1910," in *International Review of Social History*, 29 (1984), Part 2, 133.
77. *Belleville Daily Intelligencer*, 5 December 1883.
78. *Woodstock Sentinel Review*, 6 June 1884.
79. *London Advertiser*, 14 July 1883.
80. *Ingersoll Chronicle*, 1 November 1883 and 10 January 1884.
81. *War Cry*, 27 August 1887.
82. Semmel and Thompson make this argument for early Methodism. Thompson, *The Making*, 399, and Bernard Semmel, *The Methodist Revolution* (New York 1973), 193.
83. See for example Neil Semple, "The Impact of Urbanization on the Methodist Church of Canada, 1854–1884," Papers, *Canadian Society of Church History*, 1976.
84. *Daily British Whig* (Kingston), 14 July 1883.
85. See for example *War Cry*, 25 June 1887, *Daily British Whig* (Kingston), 14 July 1883.
86. *The Dumfries Reformer* (Galt) 24 April 1884.
87. *Canadian Post* (Lindsay), 14 March 1884.
88. *The London* Advertiser, 16 November 1882.
89. Marks, "Class and Gender Dimensions of Religion and Leisure."

90. Thompson makes a similar argument regarding the role of Methodism in *The Making*, 44. Also see E.J. Hobsbawn, *Primitive Rebels* (London 1959), 132, and Robert Colls, "Primitive Methodists in the northern coalfields," in Jim Obelkevich, Lyndal Roper and Raphael Samuel, eds., *Disciplines of Faith: Studies in Religion, Politics and Patriarchy* (London 1987), 326.
91. Bailey, "In Darkest England."
92. Roland Robertson, "The Salvation Army: The Persistence of Sectarianism," in Bryan Wilson, ed., *Patterns of Sectarianism* (London 1967), 94.
93. For biographies of officers that give some sense of their religious background see for example *War Cry*, 4 December 1886, 19 February 1887, 19 March 1887, 18 June 1887.
94. Susan E. Houston and Alison Prentice, *Schooling and Scholars in Nineteenth Century Ontario* (Toronto 1988), 240, 248.
95. The percentage of women in mainstream English Canadian denominations was consistently above fifty percent, but differs in extent of female over-representation by denomination. See Marks, "Gender and Class Dimensions of Religion and Leisure" and Rosemary Gagan, Presentation to Gender and Religion Group, Toronto, March 1990.
96. See Lynne Marks, "Working Class Femininity and the Salvation Army: 'Hallelujah Lasses' in English Canada, 1882–1892," in Veronica Strong-Boag and Anita Clair Fellman, eds., *Rethinking Canada: The Promise of Women's History*, 2nd edition (Toronto 1991).
97. *Petrolia Advertiser*, 8 August 1884.
98. The proportion of married female converts varies from 56 percent of all female converts in Petrolia to 33 percent of female converts in Listowel.
99. Cited in Karen Dubinsky, "'The Modem Chivalry': Women and the Knights of Labor in Ontario, 1880–1891," M.A. thesis, Carleton University 1985, 141. Barry argues that the selfishness and injustice of men also played a major role in explaining the inequality of women in the workplace.
100. In a letter to *The Palladium of Labor*, Katie McVicar quotes a co-worker as making this comment. Quoted in Dubinsky, "'The Modern Chivalry,'" 32.
101. Kealey and Palmer, 144.
102. Dubinsky, "'Modern Chivalry.'"
103. *Thorold Post*, 19 August 1887.
104. *The London Advertiser*, 18 April 1884.
105. This was clearly the official Salvation Army position, as illustrated by a story in the War Cry of an officer's wife whose refusal to preach and testify publicly is presented as evidence of disobedience to God's will and a refusal to give herself completely to God. *War Cry*, 1 December 1888.
106. See Marks, "Hallelujah Lasses," 194.
107. *Daily British Whig* (Kingston), 31 August 1883.
108. Comments regarding the Army's levity and vulgarity can be seen for example in the *Daily British Whig* (Kingston) 30 April 1883; *London Advertiser*, 7 April 1884; *Sarnia Observer*, 16 May 1884.
109. *St. Thomas Times*, 17 August 1883; *Toronto World*, 5 September 1884.
110. For a discussion of middle class efforts to control working class behaviour in this period see for example Graeme Decarie, "Something Old, Something New ... Aspects of Prohibitionism in Ontario in the 1890s," in D. Swainson, ed., *Oliver Mowat's Ontario* (Toronto 1972), Christopher Armstrong and H.V. Nelles, *Revenge*, and Susan E. Houston, "The 'Waifs and Strays' of a Late Victorian City: Juvenile Delinquents in Toronto," in Joy Parr, ed., *Childhood and Family in Canadian History* (Toronto 1982).
111. *Ingersoll Chronicle*, 1 November 1883, *Newmarket Era*, 13 June 1884, also see *The London Advertiser*, 7 April 1884.
112. For a petition to pass such a by-law see *Ingersoll Chronicle*, 27 March 1884 and 10 April 1884, also see *The London Advertiser*, 19 and 20 June 1884.
113. See for example *British Whig* (Kingston), 31 January 1883 and 3 October 1883, *Barrie Northern Advance*, 30 August 1883, *Renfrew Mercury*, 15 April 1887, Woodstock *Sentinel Review*, 14 December 1883, *Huron Signal* (Goderich), 13 February 1885 and *Thorold Post*, 14 March 1884.
114. *Ingersoll Chronicle*, 13 December 1883.

115. Victor Bailey argues that this was the primary motivation for working class opposition to the Salvation Army in England. See Bailey, "Salvation Army Riots, the 'Skeleton Army' and Legal Authority in the Provincial Town," A. P. Donajgrodzki, *Social Control in Nineteenth Century Britain* (London 1977), 241.
116. For opposition to the Scott Act see *Ingersoll Chronicle*, 14 January 1886, 25 February 1886 and 10 March 1887. In the English context opposition to the Army was at least partially funded by tavern keepers, who perceived the Army as a threat to their business. See Bailey, "Salvation Army Riots," 239.
117. *Daily British Whig* (Kingston), 7 May 1883; *London Advertiser*, 3 March 1883; *Whitby Chronicle*, 4 April 1884.
118. For comments regarding the reduction in drunkenness see *London Advertiser*, 17 July 1883, *Belleville Daily Intelligencer*, 4 December 1883, *Hamilton Spectator*, 25 January 1884. For statistics pointing to a reduction in crime see *London Advertiser*, 30 November 1882, *Northern Advance* (Barrie), 25 October 1883, *Hamilton Spectator*, 5 May 1884. For the testimony of businessmen regarding increased industriousness see *London Advertiser*, 17 July 1883, *Petrolia Advertiser*, 28 June 1884, *Toronto World*, 17 December 1883. For a discussion of how the Army was preferable to revolutionary movement see *Toronto Week*, 10 January 1884.
119. *War Cry*, 4 July 1885.
120. P.W. Philpott and A.W. Roffe, New *Light, Containing A Full Account of the Recent Salvation Army Troubles in Canada* (Toronto 1892),17.
121. Fones-Wolf, *Trade Union Gospel*, xvii.

Chapter 5

Joe Beef of Montreal

Working-Class Culture and the Tavern, 1869–89

Peter DeLottinville

Montreal was a city of contrast. The casual tourist, following the advice of his *Strangers' Guide to Montreal*,[1] would spend days viewing florid Gothic and ornate Italian church architecture, the engineering marvel of Robert Stevenson's Victoria Bridge, and the various monuments to commercial power. This faithful *cicerone*, however, would not give the tourist the total picture of a nineteenth-century urban landscape. The official face of Canada's first city consisted of monuments to individual industry, public morality, and social harmony. Absent from the official guide were the inhabitants of the narrower streets—the factory workers, the frequenters of taverns, the waterfront street gangs, or the crowds of longshoremen outside the Allen Line office waiting for work. What the tourist needed to see was a monument to Montreal's working class. Had he accidentally wandered into Joe Beef's Canteen, the tourist might have found it, where the rules and procedures of official Montreal had little value.

During the late nineteenth century, Joe Beef's Canteen was a notorious part of that underworld which existed in the Victorian city.[2] Located in the centre of the waterfront district, the Canteen was the haunt of sailors and longshoremen, unemployed men and petty thieves. Middle-class Montreal saw this tavern as a moral hazard to all who entered and a threat to social peace. Yet if critics called the Canteen's owner, Charles McKiernan, the "wickedest man" of the city, working-class residents along the waterfront claimed McKiernan as their champion. His tavern was a popular drinking spot, but also a source of aid in times of unemployment, sickness, and hunger. For its patrons, Joe Beef's Canteen was a stronghold for working-class values and a culture which protected them from harsh economic times.

Primarily, this essay describes the working-class culture which grew around Joe Beef's Canteen and analyzes that culture in terms of the community which supported it. The efforts of middle-class organizations to improve the conditions of the waterfront labourers are examined in the light of this culture. Finally, by placing this culture within the major developments influencing Montreal during the 1880s, the decline of Joe Beef's Canteen can be understood. Through this process a clearer understanding of the relationship between cultural change and historic development can be reached.

As the recent lively debate bears witness,[3] the concept of working-class culture in historical analysis is both fruitful and problematic, and before entering into a detailed discussion of the working-class tavern, it is necessary to define this concept and establish the limitations of its application. Working-class culture covers a wide range of recreational, social, and job-related activities—from labour day parades and trade union picnics to charivaris and the secret ceremonies of the Knights of Labor. While each form of culture can only be understood within its specific time and place, there was a common thread which made particular cultures working-class cultures. As Raymond Williams has stated, working-class culture embodies "a basic collective idea and the institutions, manners, habits of thought and intentions which proceed from this."[4] By assuming an "active mutual responsibility"[5] between workingmen, working-class culture offered an alternative to the individualist, competitive philosophy of the nineteenth-century middle class. Nothing was as common as a tavern in nineteenth-century Montreal, and because of this, working-class taverns probably represented one of the most basic forums of public discussion. Drawing their customers from the neighbouring streets, such meeting places were the first to sense a change in mood, or experience the return of economic prosperity. Joe Beef's Canteen, while attracting a wider clientele than most taverns, was essentially the same type of focal point for the dockyard workers. The uncommon aspect of the Canteen was the remarkable ability of Charles McKiernan, the tavern's owner, to transform this rather commonplace forum into a dynamic force for the working class of Montreal.

The depression which accompanied the 1870s had a great impact on those who, like the patrons of Joe Beef's Canteen, were at the bottom end of the economic scale. Gareth Stedman Jones, in his study of casual labour and unemployment, *Outcast London*, demonstrated that middle-class London saw the casual labourers of East London as unregenerated workers who had yet to accept the industrious habits of their fellow workingmen of the factories.[6] These "dangerous classes," much like the patrons of the Canteen, were perceived as a threat to social order. While Montreal's waterfront could not compare to the horrors of East London, Montreal's middle classes were concerned about a "dangerous class" united by a forceful, if eccentric, spokesman who articulated labourers' frustrations and demands. Joe Beef would have been taken much less seriously had his success not coincided with the increasing number of factory workers, both skilled and unskilled, who appeared on the streets of Montreal. Municipal authorities, encouraged by middle-class reformers, paid more attention to questions of public order and morality in the face of such a mass of new residents. Drunkenness, blood sports, and street brawls associated with the waterfront taverns could not be permitted to flourish if all workers were to adopt the disciplined virtues of the new industrial society.

Charles McKiernan was born on 4 December 1835, into a Catholic family in Cavan County, Ireland. At a young age, he entered the British Army and, after training at the Woolwich gunnery school, was assigned to the 10th Brigade of the Royal Artillery. In the Crimean War, McKiernan's talent for providing food and shelter earned him the nickname of "Joe Beef," which would stay with him for the rest of his life. In 1864, McKiernan's Brigade was sent to Canada to reinforce the British forces at Quebec. By then a sergeant, McKiernan was put in charge of the military canteens at the Quebec barracks and later on St. Helen's Island. If army life had seemed an alternative to his Irish future, then McKiernan saw better opportunities in North America. In 1868, McKiernan bought his discharge from the Army and with his wife and children settled in Montreal, opening the Crown and Sceptre Tavern on St. Claude Street.[7]

By settling in Montreal, McKiernan joined an established Irish community which accounted for 20 percent of the total population. Centred in Griffintown, the largely working-class Irish had their own churches, national and charitable societies, political leaders, and businessmen.[8] And as a tavern owner, McKiernan entered a popular profession in a city with a liquor license for every 150 inhabitants.[9] The increasing number of taverns caused one temperance advocate to lament that if trends continued Montreal was destined to become "the most drunken city on the continent."[10] The Crown and Sceptre, commonly known as "Joe Beef's Canteen," had a central location with Griffintown and the Lachine Canal to the east and the extensive dockyards stretching out on either side. Business was good for Charles McKiernan.

In spite of the large numbers of taverns, Joe Beef's Canteen had an atmosphere, and a reputation, which was unique. Located in the waterfront warehouse district and at night identified only by a dim light outside the door, the Canteen housed a fantastic assortment of the exotic and the commonplace. One visitor described it as, "a museum, a saw mill and a gin mill jumbled together by an earthquake; all was in confusion."[11] The bar-room was crudely furnished with wooden tables and chairs, sawdust covering the floor to make cleaning easier. At one end of the bar, great piles of bread, cheese, and beef supplied the customers with a simple meal. Behind the bar a large mirror reflected a general assortment of bottles, cigar boxes, and curios. One bottle preserved for public display a bit of beef which lodged—fatally—in the windpipe of an unfortunate diner. The quick-witted McKiernan served his patrons with an easy manner. An imposing figure with a military bearing and fierce temper, the owner had few problems with rowdyism.[12]

Joe Beef's Canteen had a special type of patron, and McKiernan aptly referred to his establishment as the "Great House of Vulgar People." His clientele was mostly working class. Canal labourers, longshoremen, sailors, and ex-army men like McKiernan himself were the mainstays of the business. Along with these waterfront workers, Joe Beef's Canteen attracted the floating population along the Atlantic coast. W.H. Davies, in his *Autobiography of a Super Tramp*, remarked that "not a tramp throughout the length and breadth of the North American continent ... had not heard of [Joe Beef's Canteen] and a goodly number had at one time or another patronized his establishment."[13] McKiernan's tavern was also a well-known *rendezvous* for the "sun-fish" or "wharf-rats" of the harbour who lived a life of casual employment and poverty. Newspaper reporters often dropped into the tavern to check on petty criminals who mingled with the crowd. Unemployed labourers visited the Canteen in the early morning to look for a day's labour and often remained there throughout the day in the hope of something turning up. In all it was not a respectable crowd[14] and, no doubt, was shunned by the more self-respecting artisans of the neighbourhood.

For working-class Montreal, the tavern held attractions beyond the simple comforts of food and drink. With no public parks in the immediate area, and only occasional celebrations by national societies and church groups, their daily recreational activities were centred around places like Joe Beef's Canteen. McKiernan's tavern was exceptionally rich in popular recreations. A menagerie of monkeys, parrots, and wild cats of various kinds were from time to time exhibited in the Canteen, but it was McKiernan's bears which brought in the crowds. Joe Beef's first bear, named Jenny and billed as the "sole captive" of the "courageous" 1869 expedition to the North West, never retired sober during the last three years of her life. One of her cubs inherited the family weakness. Tom, who had a daily consumption of 20 pints of beer, was often as "drunk as a coal heaver" by closing. Indeed, Tom was one of the regulars, usually sitting on his hind quarters and taking his pint between his paws, downing it without spilling a drop. Local temperance men had always pointed out that drink turned men into animals, but in observing Tom's habits Joe Beef could point out this curious reversal of behaviour which the Canteen produced.[15] Other bears were kept in the tavern's cellar and viewed by customers through a trap door in the bar-room floor. Occasionally, McKiernan brought up the bears to fight with some of his dogs or play a game of billiards with the proprietor.

The tavern was not an ideal place for animals and one observer remarked on the mangy, dirty, and listless character of the bears.[16] Beatings were often used to rouse the animals into their "naturally" ferocious state. Sometimes McKiernan was mauled during these demonstrations and once a buffalo on exhibit sent him to hospital for a number of days.[17] A Deputy Clerk of the Peace, inspecting the tavern to renew its license, was bitten by one of Joe Beef's dogs.[18] There was little public outcry over these conditions. Montreal's Royal Society for the Prevention of Cruelty to Animals was still a fledgling organization in the 1870s which spent its time regulating butchers' practices and prosecuting carters for mistreatment of their horses. As long as they presented no public danger, McKiernan's menagerie was left undisturbed.

Although lacking formal education, Charles McKiernan considered himself a man of learning and regularly read the *New York Journal*, the *Irish American*, the *Irish World*, and local newspapers. He employed a musician (which was illegal under the terms of his license) to entertain his customers. Regular patrons played the piano in the tavern. McKiernan, however, led much of the entertainment. Drawing on personal experience and varied readings, McKiernan eagerly debated topics of the day, or amused patrons with humorous poems of his own composition. He had a remarkable ability to ramble on for hours in rhyming couplets. Sometimes to achieve this end, he distorted the accepted English pronunciation beyond recognition. This disgusted some middle-class visitors to the Canteen, but regular customers clearly enjoyed these feats of rhetoric.[19] Behind the bar, two skeletons were hung from the wall and served as props for McKiernan's tales. From time to time, the skeletons represented the mortal remains of McKiernan's first wife, his relatives in Ireland, or the last of an unfortunate temperance lecturer who mistakenly strayed into Joe Beef's Canteen one night.

From the occasional poetry which McKiernan printed in the newspapers, the style and subjects of these evenings can be seen. Concentrating on the figures of authority in the workingman's life, the employer, the Recorder, the landlord, or the local minister, McKiernan's humour allowed his patrons a temporary mastery over the forces which dominated their lives outside the Canteen doors. Inside the Canteen, the rights of the common man always triumphed. On local issues, McKiernan complained about the lack of municipal services for the waterfront community. He demanded,

> Fair play for Sammy, Johnny and Pat as well
> as the Beaver Hall Bogus Aristocrat![20]

Legal authority, most familiar to his patrons through the Recorder's Court, was also denounced, but feared. An engraving of the Recorder looked down on the patrons from above the bar, and wedged into the frame were a number of dollar bills and notes which served as a reserve fund. McKiernan used this fund to pay fines imposed upon his regular customers.[21] Since most depended upon day labour, even a short jail term could spell disaster for the labourers' families. Imprisonment in lieu of fines was a very contentious issue, as the vehemence of the following poem illustrates.

> They have taken me from my father,
> They have taken me from my mother,
> They have taken me from my sister,
> They have taken me from my brothers,
> In this wintry season of woe
> And for the sake of *one* paltry, lousy *Dollar*,
> Down to jail, for to die, like a Dog, amongst
> *Bugs* and *Vermin*,
> I had to go.
> I died amongst howling and laughter,
> I died howling for a drink of water.
> But you living *Tyrants*, and *Two Legged*
> *Monsters* take warning and remember that
> cold, cold Saturday Morning!!!
> For man's vengeance is swift, though God's
> vengeance is with some, rather slow.[22]

McKiernan himself was no stranger to the Recorder's Court. In July 1867, the tavern keeper faced charges from a disgruntled patron who had been roughly thrown into the street for rowdyism. On different occasions, McKiernan's musician and a former servant complained of beatings they had received for drunkenness on the job.[23] Along with the violations of his liquor licence, such incidents illustrated that Joe Beef's legal opinions were grounded in experience.

Another prominent subject in Joe Beef's Canteen was the economic depression which hovered over Montreal for much of the 1870s. As casual labourers, the Canteen's patrons were severely affected by commercial slumps. In "Joe Beef's Advice to Biddy, the Washerwoman," McKiernan wrote,

> I must tell you that Kingston is dead, Quebec is Dying and out of
> Montreal, Ottawa and Toronto hundreds are flying
> In the country parts unless you can
> Parlezvous, There is nothing for you to do
> And in John's office it is all the cry
> No Union printers for work need apply
> And if the landlord his rent you cannot
> Pay your sewing machine he will take
> Away. So in the fall God help the
> Poor of Montreal.[24]

The unwillingness of the private and public authorities to provide adequate relief systems also attracted Joe Beef's notice. In a parody of the economic histories of industrialists, McKiernan professed,

> Joe Beef of Montreal, the Son of the People,
> He cares not for the Pope, Priest, Parson or King
> William of the Boyne; all Joe wants is the Coin.
> He trusts in God in the summer time to keep him
> from all harm; when he sees the first frost and
> snow poor old Joe trusts to the Almighty Dollar
> and good maple wood to keep his belly warm....[25]

These were problems which his patrons had little difficulty in understanding.

Central to all of McKiernan's pronouncements was the belief that the common problems of casual labourers and the poor of Montreal should overcome the religious and national differences which separated them. Joe Beef did "not give a damn Whether he is an Indian a Nigger a Cripple a Billy or a Mich"[26] when attempting to help the unemployed. What the unemployed and casual labourer lacked, in McKiernan's opinion, was a common voice. Since no one else was likely to assume that role, Joe Beef became the self-appointed champion of the waterfront workers. His success was remarkable as he gained the confidence of his neighbours and attracted the attention of many residents who were unaware of the poor conditions on their doorstep. Making friends with both English and French journalists, Joe Beef's Canteen and the waterfront community appeared regularly in the press. While such publicity was good for the Canteen, few accused McKiernan of self-interest. "Joe Beef" became so well known that few knew precisely who Charles McKiernan was. And despite his Irish background, Joe Beef had considerable appeal to French Canadian workers as well, if one can judge popularity from the coverage Joe Beef received in the French language press.

The recreational aspects of Joe Beef's Canteen covered only a narrow spectrum of the interaction between the tavern owner and his patrons. As the focal point of social activities, Joe Beef's Canteen also provided the initiative for a number of social services which were a logical outgrowth of the close relationship between McKiernan and his neighbourhood. His role in alleviating problems of housing, job hunting, health care, and labour unrest indicated the possibility of a collective response to the common problems among casual labourers of Montreal's waterfront.

The most visible service which Joe Beef's Canteen offered was a cheap place to stay for transient and single workers. In the Crown and Sceptre, the bar-room was situated next to a dining room and sleeping quarters. The sleeping area contained about 40 wooden sofas which served as beds. At eleven o'clock, boarders deposited 10 cents at the bar and were handed a blanket. The men then spread a mattress over the wooden sofa, stripped off all their clothes and went to sleep. McKiernan insisted that all his boarders sleep naked as a matter of cleanliness. Those found dirty were ordered upstairs to use one of the wash tubs. Each boarder also had to have his hair cut short, and those failing to meet the standards were sent to Joe Beef's "inspector of health," or barber, to comply. No conversation was permitted after eleven o'clock and everyone was roused out of bed at seven sharp. These rules were enforced personally by McKiernan in his best British Army sergeant's manner. Three-quarters of the tavern's boarders were boys between the ages of 12 and 14 who earned their living selling newspapers. For 20 cents a day, they received their food and lodging and, although the conditions set down by Joe Beef might be draconian, they were clearly preferred to similar facilities offered by church organizations. Indeed, the Crown and Sceptre proved such a popular place that one of the prime reasons for moving to Common Street in 1876 was the lack of space. His waterfront location had room for 200 men.[27]

Fees for room and board were often waived for those without the means to pay such modest sums. McKiernan's tavern was also close to the sources of casual employment which was an important consideration when a day's work might depend on arriving early on the job site. McKiernan often loaned shovels to men engaged in snow shovelling and other jobs. And as the natural resting place for all types of labourers on the docks, Joe Beef's Canteen was an ideal location to learn who might be hiring in the future. In this way, the tavern allowed transient workers to familiarize themselves with the local labour market and to make a decision whether to stay in Montreal or move on.[28]

Other social services grew informally as local residents turned to McKiernan for assistance in times of trouble. When a Lachine canal labourer was injured during a blasting operation, fellow workers brought him to Joe Beef's to recuperate. After two men got into a drunken brawl and the loser was left stripped naked in the street, the crowd brought the man to Joe Beef's for care. A young immigrant who collapsed on the docks also ended up in the tavern for convalescence. While Joe Beef's served as a neighbourhood clinic, McKiernan's folk cures left much to be desired. The young immigrant was treated with a vinegar-soaked towel bound tightly around his head. McKiernan also professed faith in cayenne pepper and whiskey to cure cramps and Canadian cholera. All this in 20 minutes.[29] Still, many people in the nineteenth century attributed medicinal powers to alcohol, and McKiernan did state an intention to take courses at the Montreal General Hospital to improve his knowledge of basic medicine.

These experiences led the tavern owner to lobby established medical institutions to improve health care services for waterfront residents. In December 1879, he set up a collection box in his tavern for the Montreal General Hospital and invited his customers to contribute. Donating one-tenth of his receipts from all his dinners and a similar share of his boarding house income, McKiernan hoped to raise $500 a year. In the following years, McKiernan offered $100 to the Montreal General if they would provide a doctor to attend the poor in their homes. The hospital declined the offer. Unsuccessful in a more formal improvement of health care services, McKiernan continued to provide emergency relief. When the body of a suicide was buried in August 1883, the tavern keeper provided a tombstone.[30]

The question of class allegiance was most clearly defined by the incidents of labour unrest which periodically disrupted the city. In December 1877, over 1,000 labourers working on the enlargement of the Lachine abandoned their picks and shovels after a reduction in wages. The Irish and French workers paraded behind a tricolour flag along the canal banks and drove off those who refused to participate in the strike. Following a riot at the offices of canal contractor William Davis, during which the strike leader was shot, the Prince of Wales Rifles were called out to protect the canal and those workers who continued to work at reduced wages.[31] The strikers demanded a wage increase to a dollar a day, a nine-hour day, regular fortnightly payments, and an end to the "truck system" of payment.[32] Among the

Montreal citizens, there appeared to be some sympathy with the poor working conditions of the labourers, notably from the *Montreal Witness* and local MP Bernard Devlin,[33] but the militant behaviour of the strikers was generally condemned.

Strongest support for the strikers came from the waterfront community. Practical in all things, McKiernan realized that strikers, like the army, travel on their stomachs. On the morning of 20 December, he sent 300 loaves of bread, 36 gallons of tea, and a similar quantity of soup. These supplies required two wagons to be delivered. In addition to feeding the strikers, McKiernan took in as many as the Canteen could hold. One night 300 people found shelter under his roof. Throughout the strike McKiernan was observed, "carting loaves and making good, rich soup in mammoth boilers, as if he were a commissary-general with the resources of an army at his back."[34] No doubt his military training was put to the test in maintaining order in his kitchen. That background also made the tavern keeper aware of the awkward position of the Prince of Wales Rifles who had been hastily summoned to guard the canal. To ensure that the soldier ate as well as a striker, McKiernan dispatched a wagon of bread to the men on duty. The soldiers saw the humour in Joe Beef's assistance and gave most of the bread away to the crowd.[35] Some of the tension between striker and soldier was successfully released.

McKiernan, of course, was not popular with the canal contractors for his wholehearted support of the labourers. William Davis, pointing suspiciously to the 14 taverns in the immediate area, wrote that the strike was caused by outside troublemakers. Another contractor was more direct in his accusations. "All of the trouble which we have had on the canal this winter has been caused mostly by men that never worked a day on the canal and have been started in a low Brothel kept by one *Joe Beef* who seems to be at the head of it all."[36] Despite this claim, McKiernan had only a supporting role in the labourers' actions, but such comments indicated the success of McKiernan's efforts to aid the strike.

Besides using his Canteen to take care of the strikers' physical needs, McKiernan also used his skills as an orator to attract public attention to the strikers' demands. By 1877, Joe Beef was a figure of some notoriety in Montreal and the local press found that his exploits made good copy. His support of the strike was reported extensively in Montreal and even in one Ottawa newspaper. The strikers' first meeting took place outside Joe Beef's Canteen and the tavern owner was asked to say a few words. Those nightly discussions in the tavern had given McKiernan a remarkable ease with language, and his talent for speaking in rhyming couplets was not wasted. Most of his speech to the crowd was in rhyming form, which so impressed the *Montreal Witness* reporter that he apologized for only reporting the substance of the speech and not its form as well. McKiernan explained his actions in the following terms.

> I have been brought up among you as one of yourselves since I was a boy running about bare-footed. When I heard of the strike on the Lachine Canal, I thought I would try to help you, for I knew that men employed there had much to put up with. So I sent you bread to help you hold out. I could not send you whiskey, because you might get drunk, and commit yourselves. In this way you might have injured your cause, and perhaps made the volunteers fire on you. (Laughter).... The greatest philanthropists in the world are in Montreal, and the public here will sympathize with you. They will not see you tyrannized over. But if you are riotous, depend upon it, as sure as you are men before me, the law will take it in hand and crush you. I have nothing against the contractors and you will succeed by speaking rightly to them. You will get your $1 a day for nine hours, or perhaps for eight hours (cheers) or perhaps more (loud cheers). But keep orderly; mind your committee.[37]

The speech was received with "deafening" cheers.

These mass meetings organized by the strike committee were an important part of their efforts to secure better working conditions. Since the canal enlargement was a federal project, Alexander Mackenzie's government was anxious to have it completed before the next election. Failure to live up to this previous election promise would cost the Liberals votes in Montreal.[38] By rallying public support for their cause, the strikers hoped that Ottawa would intervene on their behalf and compel the contractors to make concessions. As the strike continued, the size of the mass meetings grew. In Chaboillez Square 2,000 people assembled to hear McKiernan and other speakers. Joe Beef lectured on the theme of the "Almighty Dollar."

> My friends, I have come here tonight to address you on "the Almighty Dollar." The very door bells of Montreal ring with the "Almighty Dollar." The woodenheaded bobbies nail you, and you have to sleep on the hard floor provided by the City Fathers, and the next morning the fat Recorder tells you: "Give me the 'Almighty Dollar,' or down you go for eight days." The big-bugs all have their eyes on the "Almighty Dollar," from the Bishop down, and if you die in the hospital, they want the almighty dollar to shave you and keep you from the students. No one can blame you for demanding the "Almighty Dollar" a day. The man who promises 90¢ a day and pays only 80¢ is no man at all. The labourer has his rights.[39]

Public support for the strikers did not alter the fact that the labourers were without income, and after eight days on strike, they returned to the canal at the old wages.[40]

The canal labourers, however, refused to admit defeat. In mid-January, a strike committee went to Ottawa with funds raised by McKiernan and others in order to plead their cause before Alexander Mackenzie. They reduced their demands to the single request that the contractors pay them every fortnight in cash.[41] Mackenzie was sympathetic but non-committal. When the committee returned to Montreal, the mass meetings became overtly political and the problems of the canal labourers were attributed to the inaction of the Liberal government.[42] Meanwhile, Mackenzie had ordered an investigation into the Lachine situation which revealed the widespread use of store payment which considerably reduced the real wages of the labourers. Sensing a political disaster in the making, the government ordered the contractors to end store payments.[43] All contractors complied immediately and the labourers won a modest victory. McKiernan's efforts, while not the only factor in this outcome, did help the strikers publicize their demands and eased their physical hardships. In doing so, he demonstrated the potential strength of a waterfront community united in a common cause.

The canal labourers' strike was McKiernan's most extensive effort in aiding strikers, but not his only involvement. During a strike against the Allen line, ship labourers used the Canteen as a rallying point and the flag they used in their parades came from the tavern. In April 1880, when the Hochelaga cotton mill workers struck, Joe Beef again assumed his role as people's commissary-general by supplying the strikers with bread.[44] Such incidents illustrated how the working-class culture which centred around the tavern could be mobilized to produce benefits for the Canteen's patrons. But in doing so, McKiernan also attracted the criticism of middle-class reformers who felt that such a culture encouraged workers in a dangerous behaviour which threatened the social stability of Montreal.

During the 1870s, middle-class reformers began to enter into the waterfront community to assist the workingman in overcoming his social and economic poverty. The YMCA, the Salvation Army, as well as local employers and clergy, all found themselves confronted by an existing culture and community services centred around Joe Beef's Canteen. Their response to McKiernan's activities illustrated the immense social differences between the middle and working class of Montreal. One visitor to the city described Joe Beef's Canteen as a "den of robbers and wild beasts" over which McKiernan presided, "serving his infernal majesty in loyal style." The patrons were "unkempt, unshaven, fierce-looking specimens of humanity," and "roughs of various appearances, ready apparently, either to fight, drink, or steal, if the opportunity offered." In conclusion, this visitor wrote, "As we came away from his canteen where we felt that dirt, bestiality, and devilment held high carnival, my friend said, 'I believe Joe is worse than his bears and lower down in the scale of being than his monkeys. No monkey could ever be Joe's ancestor, though he is the father of wild beasts that prey on society.'"[45] While Montreal's middle class did not engage in the "slumming parties" which were popular in London, portrait painter Robert Harris and his companion William Brymmer visited the Canteen to satisfy their curiosity.[46] The actions of middle-class men on the waterfront revealed a fundamental misunderstanding of the nature of the working-class behaviour which they observed.

The common middle-class picture of the waterfront community was one of drunkenness, immorality, and lawlessness. Waterfront taverns like the Canteen, or French Marie's, were described by the Montreal Police Chief as "hot beds of all that is vicious" whose patrons were "always on the look out for mischief, and whose chief and most relished pastime seems to consist in attacking the police, rescuing prisoners, and spreading terror."[47] Sub-Chief Lancy responded that the only reason why police did not close down Joe Beef's Canteen was that "it is better to have all these characters kept in one place so that they might be dropped upon by the detectives."[48] Indeed, there was much truth to police complaints about public order on the waterfront, but they were less than candid in public statements about the role which men like Charles McKiernan played in the maintenance of order. The Black Horse Gang, composed of working-class youths, roamed the waterfront for years, extorting drinking money from lone pedestrians and robbing drunken sailors. Implicated in at least one death, the Black Horse Gang rarely faced prosecution because their violent reputation intimidated many witnesses from pressing charges. And the Black Horse Gang did frequent Joe Beef's Canteen, or at least until October 1876, when McKiernan threw four of its members out into the street for rowdiness. Ironically, one of the gang members attempted to lay charges against the tavern owner for injuries resulting from the incident.[49] The waterfront also harboured "Joe Beef's Gang" which in November 1878 was involved in a market square battle with local butchers.[50]

Violations of public order, however, must be distinguished from acts of criminality. Indeed, McKiernan was known to assist the police in their efforts to capture criminals. Police arrested 10 men on charges of highway robbery in September 1880 following a tip from McKiernan. In minor cases, the tavern owner was called upon to give character references for waterfront residents. McKiernan's censure was enough to send a local street gang leader to two months' hard labour. When the prisoner tried to retaliate by charging Joe Beef's Canteen with violations of its liquor licence, the judge, grateful for the favour to the court, refused to admit the evidence.[51] McKiernan, like many working-class people, did not consider occasional drunkenness or acts of rowdyism sufficient cause to send men to jail, especially if imprisonment meant certain ruin for a laborer's family. The informal, if sometimes rough, justice which McKiernan enforced upon his patrons was obviously preferable to the legal penalties of the court. While not publicly admitting such an accommodation, the Montreal police found that such informal co-operation worked in their favour.

The difference between the middle-class attitude towards the police and that of the waterfront residents was illustrated by the experience of the YMCA's first venture into the area. As an alternative to the saloon, the YMCA established a reading room on Craig Street. In January 1877, eight men were arrested there for creating a disturbance, and the *Montreal Witness* accused McKiernan of offering a reward to the men who closed down the operation. The tavern owner refuted these charges by pointing out that the incident had occurred only because of the YMCA's mishandling of the situation. As McKiernan explained, "Joe Beef never called on one policeman to arrest any of those men who frequent his place. If those eight had only been sent to him he would have given them work and food and sent them back better behaved."[52] By using the police to settle their problems, the YMCA violated one of the unwritten rules of behaviour on the waterfront.

The influence of waterfront taverns upon sailors visiting Montreal was a constant concern amongst ship owners. Searches for deserting sailors often started with a visit to Joe Beef's Canteen and a quick check of its customers. As an alternative to the tavern, the Montreal Sailors Institute was established in 1869 "a stone's throw" from nine taverns. Open from May to November, the Institute had a reading room, writing desks, stationery, and sabbath services. Food, for a price, could be bought, but not alcohol. In 1879, the Institute sold 4,885 cups of coffee and confidently concluded that, "Every cup lessening much the demand for whiskey." Encouraging sailors to sign abstinence pledges, the Institute recognized that sober sailors were dependable sailors.[53] But like the YMCA, the Institute had little understanding or sympathy for the working-class culture of the neighbourhood. The Institute manager, Robert R. Bell, described tavern patrons as "the lowest and most depraved human beings."[54] Dock workers, in particular, he found "a class much given to alcoholic liquors."[55] Bell lamented the inability to enforce the Sunday liquor laws and suggested the local policemen were in league with the tavern keepers. In his attempts to save the waterfront workers from their own culture as well as from economic hardship, Bell was typical of the middle-class professionals who came into the area. With 60 percent of the Institute's budget earmarked for the salary of Bell and his two assistants, and liberal contributions from local ship owners,[56] the motives behind such projects were viewed suspiciously by the waterfront workers.

The most ardent attempts to reform the moral and social habits of the waterfront workers came from Montreal's clergy. The importance of the church in nineteenth-century social welfare services need not be recounted here,[57] but the resources of Montreal's various churches dwarfed anything which the waterfront community could organize on its own. McKiernan's public attitude towards all denominations of clergy was openly hostile. He wrote that "Churches, Chapels, Ranters, Preachers, Beechers and such stuff Montreal has already got enough."[58] The cartoon from *Le Canard* illustrated quite clearly that Joe Beef would look almost anywhere for salvation before turning to the church. Respectable Montreal was shocked in 1871 when McKiernan buried his first wife. On leaving the cemetery, he ordered the band to play the military tune, "The Girl I Left Behind Me." This so outraged the *Montreal Witness* that its editor only described the funeral as a "ludicrous circumstance" without going into details.[59] And, probably to his great delight, McKiernan actually convinced the census taker in 1881 that he was a practising *Baptist!*[60]

Clergy who ventured onto the waterfront, however, were sometimes pleasantly surprised at McKiernan's behaviour. John Currie, a Presbyterian minister, ventured into Joe Beef's Canteen to preach to its patrons as an "act of Faith." After some initial heckling from the tavern owner, Currie was allowed to finish his sermon. On its conclusion, McKiernan offered any man who went to Currie's services a dinner and night's lodging for free.[61] The YMCA and a "Hot Gospeller" at different times held religious services in the dining room attached to Joe Beef's Canteen. The apparent contradiction in McKiernan's public and private behaviour originated with his general distrust of a clergy which was essentially middle class. Once he viewed individual ministers at close range and found them willing to treat his patrons as their equals—at least before the eyes of God—then the tavern keeper had no objection to their work. As Joe Beef reported to the press,

> A preacher may make as many proselytes as he chooses in my canteen, at the rate of ten cents a head. That's my price ... for if I choose

> to give myself the trouble I could make them embrace any faith or none at all or become free thinkers.[62]

Not all preachers received a welcome into Joe Beef's Canteen. Mr. Hammond, a travelling revivalist whose views on tobacco and drink were at odds with McKiernan's, was invited to the Canteen for a debate. Before the evening was out, Mr. Hammond had been chased around the Canteen by a pack of Joe Beef's bears and dogs to the general amusement of the tavern's patrons.[63] When the Salvation Army first appeared in Montreal, McKiernan supported them. With their military bearing and brass-band approach to salvation, they were a natural to play outside the Canteen, and McKiernan paid them to do so. This harmonious relationship abruptly ended when an Army officer called the Canteen "a *notorious rendezvous* of the vicious and depraved."[64] Shortly afterwards the band was arrested for disturbing the peace and McKiernan was suspected of being behind the complaint.

These clashes between the local clergy, reform groups, the police, and Joe Beef were carefully chronicled by the editor of the *Montreal Witness*, John Dougall. Dougall founded the *Witness* to instruct the general public in the Christian way of life and frequently drew upon Joe Beef for examples of modern depravity. Dougall was not unsympathetic to the economic hardships of Montreal's working class. He gave extensive coverage to the 1877 canal labourers' strike and attacked industrialists for their lack of concern over the moral implications of modern industry upon employees. But Dougall was convinced that the working-class culture which centred around taverns was a dangerous influence for all workingmen. As one contemporary described Dougall, he was "a fighter in the cause of temperance, of political purity, of public morals, of municipal righteousness, of Free Trade and of aggressive Christianity."[65] The unyielding earnestness of Dougall's public statements made him a frequent target for Joe Beef's satires. A typical verse stated,

> Bitter beer I will always drink,
> and Bitter Beer I will always draw
> and for John and his song singing
> Ranters never care a straw.[66]

When the *Witness* dismissed six of its printers for belonging to the International Typographers Union, McKiernan naturally sided with the union's efforts to have the men reinstated.[67]

Dougall characterized Joe Beef as the "hunter for the souls of men"[68] and, instead of seeing the social services which surrounded the Canteen as a positive contribution to the community, believed that these were merely clever ways of entrapping unsuspecting workers into a world of drink and sin. The death of John Kerr in April 1879 confirmed Dougall's conviction. Kerr was a regular at the Canteen who made his living doing odd jobs around the docks. One day in April, Kerr did not go out to work and by nightfall had drunk himself to death. During the Coroner's inquest, McKiernan explained his policy of never calling in the police. When men got rowdy, he simply put them in a room under the bar to sleep it off. Customers, McKiernan went on, were never treated roughly and they were "all in good health. We never club them; you know you can squeeze a man to make him do what you want, without beating him."[69] Kerr, a well-behaved man and often sick, was never treated in this manner. Yet the existence of the "Black Hole" (as the jury foreman described it) caught Dougall's attention. In a scathing editorial, the *Witness* charged that McKiernan preyed on the unemployed in a merciless way:

> What an empire within an empire is this, where law is administered and Her Majesty's peace kept without expense to Her Majesty. How joyfully should Government renew the licence of this carer of the poor, who can squeeze a man even to the last cent he wants, even to go uncomplainingly to prison, or to working for him all day with the snow shovel he provides, and bringing home his earning daily and nightly to hand over the counter for the poison which is his real pay.[70]

Dougall demanded the Canteen's licence be revoked. The coroner's jury, however, did not see anything illegal in the unconventional practices of Joe Beef.

"Into Africa" was the phrase that one visitor to the waterfront used to describe his experience, and the social isolation of the middle and working classes of Montreal in the 1870s was quite remarkable. Yet these initial failures for the reformers did not stop their efforts, and throughout the coming decades they continued to establish links between the waterfront and the rest of the city. McKiernan, though suspicious, was not entirely hostile to these men addressing themselves to the obvious problems of the casual labourers. Their working-class culture was still strong enough to ensure that social assistance did not mean social control. Forces beyond the control of the waterfront community, however, were already weakening that culture.

The world of Joe Beef, which developed during the 1870s, continued to function throughout the 1880s, but its dynamic qualities appeared to be on the wane. Joe Beef's public profile certainly declined in the 1880s. The eventual disintegration of this culture cannot be attributed to any single factor either within the working-class community or from some of the larger developments of the decade. A combination of factors, including a decasualization of dockwork, the rise of the Knights of Labor, plus new attitudes towards leisure and urban conditions, made the survival of Joe Beef's Canteen beyond the death of its owner unlikely.

As a waterfront tavern, Joe Beef's Canteen depended upon the patronage of the longshoremen who unloaded and loaded the ships in the Montreal harbour. Longshoremen worked irregular hours, sometimes as long as 36 hours at a stretch. Crews were hired by stevedores who contracted with a ship's captain to unload the vessel for a fixed price and provided the necessary equipment. Longshoremen, therefore, spent long periods of time on the docks either working, or contacting stevedores about the prospects for employment. With between 1,700 and 2,500 men competing for work, individuals had to spend much of their time ensuring that they earned the average wage of $200 per season.[71] Given these job conditions, the attraction of a waterfront tavern where one could eat, sleep, drink, and scout around for employment can not be underestimated.

The nature of employment on the docks began to change in the mid-1880s. H.&A. Allen Company, one of the larger shipping firms in the port, introduced a system of contract labour. Over 100 longshoremen signed contracts directly with the shipping company which guaranteed steady employment for the season. The contract specified that each contract employee would have to pay one percent of his wages towards an accident insurance plan, as well as agree to have 10 percent of his total wages held back until the end of the season. Any man who left before the term of his contract forfeited claim to these wages. With a rate of 25 cents per hour, the pay of the Allen contract employees was slightly better than regular longshoremen, but these relinquished their traditional rights to refuse work which did not suit them.[72] Longshoremen testifying before the 1889 Royal Commission on the Relations of Capital and Labour were certainly critical of the contract system, which most felt gave the company a guaranteed labour supply without contributing greatly to the welfare of the longshoremen.[73] While the contract system accounted for only a fraction of the total labour force on the docks, the Allen Company's desire to "decasualize" their labour force was an indication of the future. Such a system made a convenient tavern unnecessary.

It was no coincidence that the Allen Company attempted to introduce the contract system among longshoremen at the same time that labour organizations appeared on the waterfront. Edmund Tart told the Royal Commission that he belonged to a "secret trades organization" which existed on the docks.[74] Possibly a local of the Knights of Labor, the union had its own benefit plan to offset the Allen Company insurance scheme. Patrick Dalton, a longshoreman for the Allen Company, testified against the contract system. Pointing to the organization of the Quebec City longshoremen, Dalton stressed that only the organization of all longshoremen could guarantee higher wages. Dalton concluded by saying "that labour unions were not fundamentally concerned with wages, but with bettering the condition of the men, socially and morally."[75]

The rise of the Knights of Labor in the mid-1880s produced profound changes in the dynamics of working-class development, and the culture surrounding Joe Beef's Canteen was shaken up by their emergence. Along with lawyers, bankers, and capitalists, the Knights of Labor banned tavern owners from their ranks. Testifying before the Royal Commission on the Liquor Traffic, Louis Z. Boudreau, president of the Montreal Trades and Labour Council, reflected this attitude towards drink when he stated that "people we meet in the Trades and Labor Council are not drinking men as a whole. They are a good class of men."[76] As skilled workers accepted the need for temperance, the unskilled waterfront labourers might also re-examine the benefits of tavern life. This did not signal an alliance between organized labour and the temperance advocates who attacked Joe Beef in the 1870s. Spokesmen for organized labour criticized most of these temperance workers for failing to realize that much of the drunkenness among workingmen resulted from economic hardship. Clearly, William Darlington, a prominent Montreal Knight of Labor, shared McKiernan's distrust of the clergy's attempt to reform the workingman. Darlington told the Liquor Commission that "the workingmen feel that the church is a religious institution without Christianity, and that the clergy is simply a profession, got up for the purpose of making money in some instances, and in other, for preaching in the interest of capital against labour.... They find out in reality that the Knights of Labor preach more Christianity than the churches."[77] Despite such similarities, there was no room for Joe Beef in the Knights of Labor.

Outside of the working-class neighbourhoods, other forces were emerging which shaped public attitudes towards Joe Beef's Canteen. Throughout the 1880s, Montreal's middle-class residents grew more critical of the police force's inability to enforce the liquor laws. This new mood was captured by the Law and Order League (also known as the Citizens League of Montreal) which was formed in 1886. The League's purpose was to pressure police to enforce the liquor and public morality laws by publicizing open violations. Operating in co-operation with the Royal Society for the Prevention of Cruelty to Animals, the League was able to effect a dramatic increase in the number of prosecutions against tavern owners.[78] Under such pressure, the police were less likely to work informally with Joe Beef on matters of public order.

New attitudes towards leisure activities were also coming to the fore during the 1880s. With the growth of the YMCA and the Amateur Athletic Associations, urban youths were encouraged to spend their time in organized sport and develop the socially useful traits of "teamwork, perseverance, honesty and discipline—true muscular Christianity."[79] As one YMCA lecturer told his audience, recreation had to "invigorate the mind and body, and have nothing to do with questionable company, being regulated by Christian standards."[80] While such campaigns were not designed to recruit former members of street gangs, but rather the middle-class youth and clerks from the new industrial factories, these new approaches to recreation did have an impact on general tolerance of the waterfront culture. Prize fighting, probably a favoured sport of Joe Beef's patrons, was publicly denounced as a barbaric and dangerous sport.[81] With the growing alliance between the RSPCA and the Law and Order League, the Canteen's menagerie could not have survived a public outcry. New recreational opportunities for working-class Montreal, such as the opening of Sohmer Park in the early 1890s,[82] indicated that the necessity to centre all recreational life around the tavern was diminishing.

There was also a perceptible shift in public attitudes towards poverty and the city slums.

With the reformers' concentration on the physical aspects of their city—clean water, paved streets, public parks, and adequate fire protection—urban slums were no longer seen only as places for poor people to live, but as potential threats to public health. Herbert Ames, a pioneer in efforts to clean up Montreal, stated that in matters of public health a simple rule existed—"the nearer people live to each other, the shorter they live."[83] Such programmes as the Fresh Air Fund, which sent mothers and children of the slums to a country retreat for temporary escape from the noise and smoke of the city, testified to the concern among middle-class reformers about the dangerous effects of an industrial city.[84] The *Montreal Star* carried a series of reports on the terrible living conditions in Montreal's slums.[85] In 1885 during a smallpox epidemic, riots broke out when health authorities tried to vaccinate working-class people against the disease.[86] The great physical dangers which the slums created for the city, let alone the social danger, forced local authorities to take a closer look at the waterfront neighbourhoods.

Many of these fears and developments seem to have been familiar to the reporter who visited the Canteen in 1887. While the bears received the familiar treatment, the reporter was quite disturbed at the new attitude among the patrons. He wrote, "Nothing is more striking than the demeanor of the poor folk who fill the room. No oaths are uttered, no coarse jests, no loud talking, and never a laugh is heard. A very quiet, not to say sombre, lot of men. One would like to see a little more animation and liveliness, to hear now and then a good hearty laugh."[87] Nor was this brooding silence unique to Joe Beef's Canteen, as the reporter found several other taverns similarly devoid of their regular good cheer. These dull vacant looks, the reporter went on, "are the kind of faces one meets in the east end of London and other similar districts; but we should hardly expect to find them here. They are here, though, you see."[88] The reporter's reference to East London was repeated a few years later by the author of *Montreal by Gaslight*, a muckraking study of the city's "underworld." For the local observer, the most frightening prospect for his city was to duplicate the urban miseries of the East End of London. In *Montreal by Gaslight*, the author warned against the social consequences of drink and crushing poverty. "Last and greatest of all, think you that the modern plague of London is not known to us? Are we not infected?"[89] Along the waterfront, the silence of the labourers was feared to be the incubation period of this great urban disease. Of its eventual outbreak, the author wrote, "It may be that some day labor will raise and demand that for which it now pleads. That demand will mean riot, strike, and even civil war."[90] *Montreal by Gaslight* was written as a warning that a solution must be found before it was too late. The general outcome of such fears was that middle-class Montreal began to pay more attention to its waterfront area just as the social and economic circumstances which gave rise to Joe Beef's Canteen were changing.

The rough life along the waterfront had its own hazards and on 15 January 1889 Charles McKiernan died of heart failure in his Canteen, only 54 years old. His death was received with great sadness in many quarters of the city and the funeral attracted large crowds. As the *Gazette* reporter commented, "Every grade in the social scale was represented in those assembled in front of the 'Canteen.' There were well known merchants, wide awake brokers, hard working mechanics and a big contingent of the genus bum, all jostling one another for a glimpse of the coffin containing what remained of one, whatever may have been his faults, who was always the poor man's friend."[91] After a short Anglican service, McKiernan's body was carried out of the tavern and the procession started for Mount Royal Cemetery. Among those in the procession were representatives from 50 labour societies who acknowledged for the last time Joe Beef's support of the trade union movement. The exception to this general sympathy was the *Montreal Witness* which published its own death notice.

> Joe Beef is dead. For twenty five years he has enjoyed in his own way the reputation of being for Montreal what was in former days known under the pet sobriquet of the wickedest man. His saloon, where men consorted with unclean beasts was probably the most disgustingly dirty in the country. It has been the bottom of the sink of which the Windsor bar and others like it are the receivers. The only step further was to be found murdered on the wharf or dragged out of the gutter or the river, as might happen. It was the resort of the most degraded of men. It was the bottom of the pit, a sort of *cul de sac*, in which thieves could be corralled. The police declared it valuable to them as a place where these latter could be run down. It has been actively at work over all that time for the brutalizing of youth—a work which was carried on with the utmost diligence by its, in that sense, talented proprietor.[92]

Perhaps more than any of Joe Beef's lampoons, this editorial showed the limits of the *Witness's* Christian charity.

With McKiernan's death, Joe Beef's Canteen declined. The transient customers were the first to suffer. Thomas Irwin, a "protégé" of the Canteen, was arrested a few days after McKiernan's death for stealing a piece of flannel. In explaining his crime, Irwin stated "There is no use for me trying to make my living now that poor old Joe is dead and gone. I must get a home somewhere in winter; won't you admit that? Well, I stole to get a lodging."[93] For the wharf-rats and sun-fish, Joe Beef's was closed. His bears met an ignoble end as well. In April police officers shot Joe Beef's bears on the request of McKiernan's widow. She planned to have them stuffed.[94] By 1893 the Canteen was gone. The Salvation Army bought the tavern and under the banner of "Joe Beef's Converted" continued many of the services to transient workers which McKiernan had pioneered. Masters at adapting popular culture to their religious beliefs, the Salvation Army transformed one of their most troublesome enemies into a prophet for bread and salvation.[95]

In assessing the significance of Charles McKiernan to the Montreal working class in the 1870s and 1880s, one must remember that when McKiernan arrived in 1868 he did not create the working-class culture associated with Joe Beef's Canteen. That culture, which had grown out of the daily routines of the casual labourers on the docks, already existed. What Joe Beef accomplished was to give that culture a public face and voice, a figure upon which the local press and reformers could focus. In doing so, Joe Beef saved that culture from the obscurity which generally surrounds work cultures. The material necessary for that culture was amply demonstrated by the numerous community services which grew up around the tavern. This waterfront culture possessed its assistance, hard work, good cheer, and a sense of manly dignity. The necessity to "act like men," which McKiernan urged upon striking canal labourers, was an important code of ethics which the tavern owner used as a measure of all things. Clergy who treated his patrons "as men" were allowed into the Canteen, but organizations which resorted to the police to settle problems deserved condemnation for such unmanly behaviour. Even McKiernan's denunciations of Montreal industrialists, the "Big Bugs," or John Dougall were denunciations of individuals and not social classes. Indeed, the tendency to personalize every problem facing the waterfront community pointed out the necessity for longshoremen to find some larger institutional framework through which they could preserve the values that their work culture generated. The Knights of Labor provided this opportunity, but the Knights built upon the traditional values preserved and strengthened by Joe Beef.

While Joe Beef's controversies with the middle-class reformers who entered into his neighbourhood were genuine, the lasting influence of such incidents appeared small. For all his bluster, Joe Beef was a limited threat to the social order of Montreal. As a spokesman for rough culture, Joe Beef satirized only the pretensions and hypocrisy which he saw in the smooth behaviour of middle-class men. He did not advocate class antagonism, but a fair deal. For a short time, Joe Beef's influence was able to reach a fair deal with municipal authorities. What frightened some observers was the possibility that the growing numbers of unskilled factory workers, that unknown quantity of industrial transformation, would adopt the working-class culture of Joe Beef, with its violence and disregard for legal and moral authority. No doubt these observers were pleased that the new factory hands followed the lead of respectable skilled workers within the Knights of Labor.

The culture represented by Joe Beef was certainly different than that of the skilled tradesmen of Montreal. Only with difficulty can one imagine an experienced typographer making regular trips to the Canteen to see the bears. Though rough and respectable cultures interacted, they were clearly separate.[96] The culture surrounding the casual labourers grew out of a physically demanding life of marginal economic benefit, obtained through the common exertion of labour. In these respects, Joe Beef's world was closer to the world of Peter Aylen and the Shiners of the Ottawa Valley than to the typographers in the offices of the *Montreal Witness*, or the cotton mill workers of Hochelaga.[97] The waterfront world had its own internal hierarchy as Joe Beef vigorously defended his patrons against middle-class charges of drunken violence, but then threw them into the street when they got rowdy. While McKiernan's background, as his Irish verses confirm,[98] was rural, he lived in an industrial city and had to contend with the economic and social restrictions which this implied. Realizing the growing power of the police and social reformers to define the limits of acceptable behaviour, Joe Beef attempted to convince these men of the validity of working-class culture. He was not very successful. To the very end, McKiernan was rooted in the culture of his tavern and neighbourhood. For him, the liquor business was not a means of upward mobility and the tavern owner's sons remained working class.

Joe Beef's Canteen illustrated the complex nature of working-class culture. In the narrow, traditional sense of culture as artistic creation, the satiric verses, engravings or cartoons by McKiernan and others about Joe Beef contributed in a minor way to the nineteenth-century radical literature in Canada. Local historians of Montreal were well aware of this tradition left behind by Joe Beef.[99] In the broader sense of culture as popular culture, the tavern life of bears, debates, and songs acknowledged a recreational culture created by the working class and not for them. The coming of rational recreation would weaken this tradition, but McKiernan's death had little long-term effect on this level. Finally, Joe Beef's Canteen represented a material culture of community services relating to the employment, housing, and health of the working-class neighbourhood. This culture was the most important manifestation of the Canteen in terms of class conflict.[100] All aspects of culture surrounding Joe Beef's Canteen demonstrated the integral nature of the life of the labouring men along the waterfront who would probably not have recognized distinctions between recreation and work, between a popular and material culture.

To label Joe Beef's Canteen a "pre-industrial" fragment in an industrial world obscures the fact that working-class culture was a fluid culture borrowing from its own past and from contemporary middle-class culture. Middle-class disgust at Joe Beef's antics largely grew out of his ability to parody their most pious thoughts. While Joe Beef rejected these new industrial virtues, this hardly distinguished him from thousands of other Montreal labourers and skilled workers. In many ways, the culture of Joe Beef had reached its own limits. Successful in bargaining social questions of public conduct and order, McKiernan played only a supporting role in the economic struggles in the factories and on the docks. The attempt to form new alliances between skilled and unskilled, men and women, tradesman with tradesman, would be made not by the Joe Beef's of the nineteenth century but by the Knights of Labor.

Endnotes

1. *Montreal Illustrated or The Strangers' Guide to Montreal* (Montreal 1875). For a more thematic guide to the city in the 1880s, see S. E. Dawson, *Hand-Book for the City of Montreal and its Environs* (Montreal 1883). *Lovell's Historic Report of the Census of Montreal* (Montreal 1891), is a good example of how the material progress of Montreal was equated with social and moral improvements. As Lovell stated "Peace, happiness and prosperity abound, and brotherly love forms a link that might be prized in any city. The policeman is seldom needed. Intemperance is becoming a thing of the past." (45) Lovell's private census should not be confused with the Dominion census conducted that same year. *The Montreal Star*, in its 16 September 1886 issue, carried special stories on the city's capitalists and their contribution to social development.
2. This underground Montreal is given a muckraker's treatment in *Montreal by Gaslight* (Montreal 1889), which contains a chapter on Joe Beef's Canteen. Charles McKiernan's landlord, F.X. Beaudry, was closely connected with the local prostitution trade, as his obituary (*Montreal Witness*, 25 March 1885) details. On gambling dens, see *Montreal Witness*, 14 September 1876, and the *Montreal Star*, 30 October 1889. The *Star*, 23 January 1872, carries an article on a local cockfight.
3. The most recent contributions to this debate are Kenneth McNaught, "E.P. Thompson vs. Harold Logan," *Canadian Historical Review*, 62 (1981), 141–68; Gregory S. Kealey's "Labour and Working-Class History in Canada: Prospects in the 1980s," and David J. Bercuson's, "Through the Looking Glass of Culture," both from *Labour/Le Travailleur*, 7 (1981), 67–94, 95–112. The history of Joe Beef hopefully shows some of the merits of a cultural approach to working-class history.
4. Raymond Williams, *Culture and Society* (London 1960), 327.
5. Ibid., 330.
6. Gareth Stedman Jones, *Outcast London* (Oxford 1971). Comparisons between Montreal and London, at least on general terms, are not as tenuous as might first appear. Contemporary observers of the waterfront often compared these slums to those of East London. Herbert Ames' attempt to introduce model housing for the workingman was modelled on the efforts of Octavia Hill's plan to help the London poor (*The City Below the Hill* [Toronto 1972], 114). McKiernan received his training at Woolwich, which William Booth studied before founding his Salvation Army. The Salvation Army was one of the more successful groups in the waterfront neighbourhood.
7. *Montreal Star*, l6 January 1889. See also Edgar A. Collard's *Montreal Yesterdays* (Toronto 1962) for a good general assessment of Charles McKiernan, and the Montreal City Archives clipping file-R. 3654. 2 "Rues, Commune, Rue de la," for general press coverage of McKiernan by Collard and other Montreal historians.
8. Dorothy Suzanne Cross, "The Irish in Montreal, 1867–1896," (M.A. thesis, McGill University, 1969) gives a general account of the Montreal Irish community. For contemporary descriptions, see John Francis Maguire's *The Irish in America* (Montreal 1868), and Nicholas Flood Davin, *The Irishman in Canada* (Toronto 1877).
9. *Montreal by Gaslight*, 10. Other well known taverns were Tommy Boyle's The Horseshoe, which catered to those who followed prize fighting, and the Suburban, which had a reputation for giving the poor man a helping hand. Ibid., 94–105.
10. *Montreal Star*, 14 February 1888. Liquor licenses, which included hotels, restaurants, saloons and groceries, increased from 723 in 1879 to 1,273 in 1887. Joe Beef's Canteen had a hotel licence.
11. *Montreal Witness*, 4 April 1881.
12. *Toronto Globe*, 14 April 1876; *Halifax Herald*, 28 June 1880; *Montreal Star*, 3 October 1887.
13. W. H. Davies, *The Autobiography of a Super-Tramp* (London 1964), 131, cited in Clayton Gray, *Le Vieux Montreal* (Montreal 1964), l6.
14. *Montreal Witness*, 4 April 1881. In an account of Joe Beef's encounter with the census taker, the problems of tracing the transient population were made clear. Of all the one-night guests which the Canteen provided for, only ten men were found by the census taker. Two of these, an Irish musician and a Spanish cook, were probably employees of the tavern. Also listed were an English coachmaker, an Irish blacksmith, an American barber, a Scottish commercial agent, an English (Quaker) leather merchant, an Irish accountant, an English labourer, and an Irish tanner. McKiernan's fifteen-year-

old son was listed as a rivet maker and was likely serving an apprenticeship. See Public Archives of Canada (hereafter PAC), RC 31, *Census of Canada, 1881*, Manuscript, Montreal, West Ward, Division 3, p. 1.

15. *Toronto Globe*, 14 April 1876.
16. *Montreal by Gaslight*, 115.
17. *Montreal Star*, 10 September 1883; 11 September 1883; 3 October 1883.
18. *Montreal Witness*, 17 March 1881; 22 March 1881.
19. *Montreal Herald*, 21 April 1880; *Montreal Witness*, 6 August 1875. Jon M. Kingsdale, "The Poor Man's Club: Social Functions of the Urban Working Class Saloon," *American Quarterly*, 25 (1973), 472–89, provides an excellent background to the discussion which follows and demonstrates that many of the Canteen's services were common to nineteenth-century taverns.
20. *La Minerve*, 2 August 1873.
21. *Toronto Globe*, 14 April 1876; *Halifax Herald*, 28 June 1880; *Montreal Star*, 3 October 1887.
22. *La Minerve*, 20 January 1874.
23. *Montreal Star*, 14 July 1876; *Montreal Witness*, 22 October 1873; 12 November 1877.
24. *La Minerve*, 7 November 1873. John was John Dougall of the *Montreal Witness* who had recently dismissed some union employees. Although the Canteen was a male bastion, McKiernan was not unaware of the growing number of women workers in the Montreal labour force. For the employment of women, see Dorothy Suzanne Cross, "The Neglected Majority: The Changing Role of Women in Nineteenth Century Montreal," *Social History*, 12 (1973), 202–3.
25. *Montreal Yesterdays*, 273–4.
26. *La Minerve*, 28 December 1878.
27. *Toronto Globe*, 14 April 1876.
28. The integration of transient labour into urban centres was very important and a failure to do so is described in Sydney L. Harring's "Class Conflict and the Suppression of Tramps in Buffalo, 1892–1894," *Law and Society Review*, 11 (1977). 873–911. See also James M. Pitsula's "The Treatment of Tramps in Late Nineteenth-Century Toronto," *Historical Papers* (1980), 116–32.
29. *Montreal Star*, 5 February 1877; *Witness*, 2 August 1876; *Star*, 3 October 1879.
30. *Star*, 15 January 1878; 29 December 1879; 27 February 1880; 25 March 1880; 1 April 1880. H.E. MacDermot in his History of the Montreal General Hospital (Montreal 1950) wrote that Joe Beef's Canteen was "a particularly staunch supporter, and entries of donations from 'Proceeds of iron box, bar-room, of Joe Beef's are frequent or from 'his own skating Rink,' as well as contributions for the care of special patients" (55). MacDermot's work was cited in Edgar Collard's "All Our Yesterdays," Montreal Gazette, 9 January 1960. William Fox Beakbane, who drowned in Allan's wharf on 29 July 1883, was buried in the McKiernan family plot in Mount Royal Cemetery (*Star*, 10 August 1883).
31. *Witness*, 17 December 1877; 19 December 1877. Strike leader Lucien Pacquette spent several days in hospital recovering from his wound. For contractor William Davis, this was not the first time his workers reacted violently to his labour practices. A year earlier someone tried to blow up the contractor's house and severely damaged the building (*Witness*, 20 December 1877).
32. *Witness*, 17 December 1877.
33. Ibid., 19 December 1877; 20 December 1877. Bernard Devlin (1824–80) came to Quebec in 1844 and published the *Freeman's Journal and Commercial Advertiser*. He ran unsuccessfully for the 1867 Parliament against Thomas D'Arcy McGee who accused Devlin of being secretly in support of the Fenians. Devlin served as a Liberal MP for Montreal West from 1875 to 1878 (DCB, X, 250).
34. *Star*, 20 December 1877, *Witness*, 24 December 1877.
35. *Star*, 19 December 1877.
36. PAC, Dept. of Public Works, RG11, B1(a). Vol. 474, p. 2534, Whitney & Daly to F. Braun, 22 January 1878.
37. *Witness*, 21 December 1877.
38. Ibid., 22 December 1877.
39. Ibid., 21 December 1877.
40. Ibid., 26 December 1877.
41. *Ottawa Citizen*, 18 January 1878. The *Citizen* carried a copy of a strikers' petition to Mackenzie which was signed by 122 people including McKiernan. Most of the signers were untraceable in

local business directories, but some local grocers and dry goods merchants did support the strikers' demands and this suggests some degree of neighbourhood support. Original petition in PAC, RG11, B1(a), Vol. 473, pp. 2514–20.

42. *Ottawa Citizen*, 24 January 1878. An admitted weakness of this study is the failure to document the political connections which McKiernan had with municipal politicians. Federally, McKiernan was a Conservative and this no doubt played some part in his attack on Mackenzie. During the 1872 election, McKiernan led a group of sailors into a Liberal polling station and began serenading them with a concertina. When surrounded by an angry crowd, McKiernan pulled out a pistol and fired into the air. In the tumult which followed McKiernan and his companions were beaten and had to be rescued by the police. *Montreal Witness*, 28 August 1872.
43. PAC, RG11, B1(a), Vol. 473, pp. 2514–69. Not all contractors paid their workers in truck, and those who did argued that the workers benefited from the arrangement. Davis argued that monthly pay periods increased productivity. "On Public Works as a Rule, a large number of men lose time after pay day, and, thereby disarrange and retard the progress of the Works." (Davis to Braun, 21 January 1878, p. 2532). John Dougall of the *Montreal Witness*, however, published an account of the supplies given to a labourer instead of cash. For $1.75 owing in wages the worker received whiskey, sugar, tobacco, cheese and bread valued at $1.05. The goods were on display throughout the strike at Joe Beef's Canteen (*Witness*, 22 January 1878).
44. *Star*, 17 April 1880; *Witness*, 21 April 1880.
45. *Halifax Herald*, 28 June 1880.
46. PAC, MG28, 1 126, Vol. 15, Royal Canadian Academy of Art scrapbook, *Montreal Gazette*, 7 February 1916, cited in *Montreal Yesterdays*, 271.
47. "Third Report of the Select Committee of the House of Commons respecting a Prohibitory Liquor Law," *House of Commons Journals*, 1874, Testimony of F. W. Penton, 9.
48. *Montreal Gazette*, 22 April 1880. The importance of battles between the police and working-class people is illustrated by Robert D. Storch in "The Policeman as Domestic Missionary: Urban Discipline and Popular Culture in Northern England," *Journal of Social History*, 9 (1976), 481–509.
49. *Star*, 30 October 1876. The Black Horse Gang's activities are reported in the *Witness*, 26 May 1875; 27 May 1875; *Star*, 1 February 1876; *Witness*, 24 July 1880; 10 May 1882. Street gangs in general are discussed in the *Witness*, 31 May 1875.
50. *Witness*, November 1878; 18 November 1878. The *Witness* story on the incident was protested by "Joe Beef's Gang" who turned up in the editor's office and claimed that they were "respectable mechanics and that the butchers are on the contrary not noted for their respectable behaviour."
51. *Witness*, 8 September 1880; 24 July 1879.
52. Ibid., 8 February 1877.
53. Annual Report of the Montreal Sailors Institute for the Year Ending January, 1870 (Montreal 1870), 5; *Annual Report of the Montreal Sailors Institute of 1870* (Montreal 1871), 8.
54. Royal Commission on the Liquor Traffic, House of Commons Sessional Paper, No. 4, 584.
55. Ibid., 589.
56. Ibid., 586.
57. The difference of religious sentiment was reflected in the organization of benevolent associations. Roman Catholic Montreal had its own hospitals and dispensaries, 13 benevolent institutions caring for the aged, orphaned, and widowed. Nine Catholic charitable societies also contributed to the welfare of the impoverished citizens. Protestant Montreal, besides having its hospitals, had 16 benevolent institutions for the same clientele as the Catholic institutions as well as homes for female immigrants and sick servant girls. Religious differences were further complicated by the national origins of Montreal residents. To aid fellow countrymen there were several national societies including the St. George, St. Andrew, St. Patrick, St. Jean Baptiste, Irish Protestant, Italian, Welsh, Scandinavian, and Swiss benevolent organizations. See Lovell's Historic Report of the Census of Montreal (Montreal 1891), 62–3, 72–3. See also Janice A. Harvey's "Upper Class Reaction to Poverty in Mid-Nineteenth Century Montreal: A Protestant Example," (M.A. thesis, McGill University, 1978) for descriptions of Protestant charities.
58. *Montreal Yesterdays*, 273–4.

59. *Montreal Star*, 29 September 1871: *Montreal Yesterdays*, 272–3. McKiernan's 25 year old wife Mary McRae and her baby died on 26 September 1871, and it is uncertain whether the contemporary accounts correctly interpreted McKiernan's actions. Interestingly enough, McKiernan's republican sentiments exhibited themselves on his wife's gravestone. Her inscription read in part,
    I leave a husband and four orphan babes
    To mouth their mother's loss
    Who will never return.
    But let that tree, which you see
    Be the tree of Liberty
    And in its stead never let the tree of [Bigotry]
    Be planted between them and me.
60. *Montreal Witness*, 4 April 1881; PAC, RG3l. Census of Canada, 1881 Manuscript, Montreal, West Ward, Division No. 3, p. 1.
61. *Montreal Yesterdays*, 279–80.
62. *Toronto Globe*, 14 April 1876; *Montreal Star*, 31 July 1876.
63. *Halifax Herald*, 28 June 1880. For Mr. Hammond's preaching style see *Montreal Star*, 18 March 1880.
64. Edgar Collard, "Of Many Things," *Montreal Gazette*, 28 February 1876. For the legal problems of the Salvation Army, see the *Montreal Star*, 19 August 1886; 3 September 1886; 14 September 1886.
65. *Montreal Star*, 9 January 1911. See J. I. Cooper's "The Early Editorial Policy of the *Montreal Witness*," *Canadian Historical Association Report* (1947), 53–62 and Dougall's obituary in the *Montreal Star*, 19 August 1886.
66. *La Minerve*, 13 March l873.
67. *Montreal Star*, 26 November 1872; 27 November 1872; 28 November 1872.
68. *Montreal Witness*, 8 February 1877.
69. Ibid., 4 April 1878.
70. Ibid., 5 April 1879.
71. Royal Commissions on the Relations of Capital and Labour, 1889, Quebec Evidence, Vol. 1, pp. 150–86.
72. Ibid., Testimony of R. A. Smith, 156–60; James Urquhart, 173–5.
73. Ibid., Testimony of Patrick Dalton, 183–5.
74. Ibid., Testimony of Edmund Tart, 175–81.
75. Ibid., Testimony of Patrick Dalton, 186.
76. Royal Comission on the Liquor Traffic, 512.
77. Ibid., 583.
78. *Montreal Star*, 28 January 1886. On the Law and Order League, see Star, 16 August 1887; 24 January 1889; 16 February 1889; 10 March 1887.
79. Alan Metcalfe, "The Evolution of Organized Physical Recreation in Montreal, 1810–1895," *Social History*, 21 (1978) 153. For the role of the YMCA in the new attitude towards leisure activities, see David Macleod, "A Live Vaccine: The YMCA and Male Adolescence in the United States and Canada, 1870–1920," *Social History*, 21 (1978) 5–25. An excellent study of recreation in England is Peter Bailey, *Leisure and Class in Victorian England* (Toronto 1978).
80. *Montreal Star*, 15 November 1873.
81. For denunciations of prize fighting see *Star*, 4 January 1887; 9 May 1887; 20 May 1887; 23 May 1887; 15 September 1887.
82. *Montreal Star*, 6 June 1893; 13 July 1893. Richard Bell of the Montreal Sailors Institute preferred that sailors drink at Sohmer Park rather than in the waterfront taverns. Royal Commission on the Liquor Traffic, 584–9.
83. Herbert B. Ames "Why We Should Study the Municipal System of Our City," *Abstract of a Course of Ten Lectures on Municipal Administration* (Montreal 1896).
84. *Montreal Star* contains several articles promoting the Fresh Air Fund, see 11 June 1887; 18 June 1887; 25 June 1887; 6 July 1887. On the Fresh Air Home, see *Star*, 23 June 1888.
85. Ibid., 24 December 1883; 29 December 1883.

86. Ibid., 29 September 1885.
87. Ibid., 3 October 1887.
88. Ibid.
89. *Montreal by Gaslight*, 10.
90. Ibid., 35.
91. *Montreal Gazette*, 19 January 1889.
92. *Montreal by Gaslight*, 119.
93. *Star*, 24 January 1889.
94. Ibid., 29 April 1889.
95. *Star*, 26 May 1893; 27 May 1893. R. G. Moyles, in *The Blood and Fire in Canada* (Toronto, 1877), remarked that this was a new venture for the Salvation Army. "Whereas other men's hostels had been designed as rescue centres for ex-prisoners and for total derelicts, Joe Beef's was a hostel for transients, providing a cheap bed for the unemployed man with little money and a cheap meal for the poor city labourer" (69).
96. Peter Bailey's "Will the Real Bill Banks Please Stand Up? Towards A Role Analysis of Mid-Victorian Working-Class Respectability," *Journal of Social History*, 12 (1979) offers some interesting insights into the differences between rough and respectable workingmen.
97. Michael S. Cross, "The Shiners War: Social Violence in the Ottawa Valley in the 1830's," *Canadian Historical Review*, 54 (1973), 1–26. For a description of an early Ottawa tavern, see W.P. Lett, "Corkstown," *Recollections of Old Bytown* (Ottawa 1979), 81–6.
98. See the attitudes reflected in "Spurn Not the Poor Man," *La Minerve*, 7 January 1874; "I am Long Past Wailing and Whining," *La Minerve*, 27 January 1874; and "The Big Beggarman," *La Minerve*, 13 January 1874. Poetic style makes it unlikely that these verses are from McKiernan's pen, but by printing them with his advertisements he demonstrated a sympathy with their author.
99. Frank W. Watt, "Radicalism in English Canadian Literature Since Confederation" (Ph.D. thesis, University of Toronto, 1957). Watt does not mention McKiernan but Watt's description of a literature disillusioned with nation building and inclined to associate patriotic feelings with the motives and methods of capitalist exploitation could accommodate much of McKiernan's verse.
100. Bryan D. Palmer's *A Culture in Conflict* (Montreal 1979), contains the fullest discussion of the importance of culture in Canadian class conflict. See also Gareth Stedman Jones, "Working-Class Culture and Working-Class Politics in London, 1870–1900," *Journal of Social History*, 7 (1974), 460–508.

Chapter 6

After the Fur Trade

The Aboriginal Labouring Class of British Columbia 1849–90

John Lutz

Aboriginal history is usually considered in isolation from mainstream Canadian history, as though it were about aboriginal people and nobody else. But the major issues of native studies—such as the appropriation of aboriginal land and resources, the denial of citizenship rights to a large segment of the Canadian population, the conditions under which aboriginal people would agree to trap, hunt or do wage-work for a capitalist economy—are major issues of national development and central to Canadian history.

This paper takes up questions about aboriginal wage labour and applies them to a 40-year period on the west coast of North America from the creation of the Colony of Vancouver Island in 1849, through the gold rushes, the founding of the giant export sawmills, Confederation, the development and spread of the salmon canning industry, to just past the completion of the Canadian Pacific Railway in 1885—an event which tied the province of British Columbia to the North American continental economy. Throughout this period, aboriginal people in British Columbia comprised the majority of the population. Despite introduced diseases (which reduced the aboriginal population by approximately two thirds), when British Columbia entered Confederation in 1871 it was in many important respects an "aboriginal province"—there were three times as many aboriginal people as all the non-aboriginals taken together.[1]

Although one might suppose historians would have turned their attention to the majority before examining minority groups, in British Columbia historiography the reverse has happened: only a few historians, notably Robin Fisher and Rolf Knight, have given their attention to the majority population in this era.[2] Most general accounts follow Fisher's pioneering work on aboriginal–non-aboriginal relations which argued that aboriginal peoples retained control of their lives during the fur trade, and had considerable influence over the trade itself. Fisher states that, with the gold-rush, the colonies which comprise modern British Columbia changed from "colonies of exploitation, which made use of indigenous manpower, to colonies of settlement, where the Indians became at best, irrelevant."[3] By contrast, this paper argues that aboriginal people were not made irrelevant by the coming of settlement. In fact, they were the main labour force of the early settlement era, essential to the capitalist development of British Columbia. With other recent scholarship, this paper takes a step towards rediscovering the largest component of British Columbia's early labouring class, and highlighting one element—paid work—of the lives of the majority aboriginal population.[4]

Even in the 1860s, opinion among white notables was divided about the usefulness and importance of aboriginal people to the British Columbia economy. While Charles Forbes' 1862 guide to Vancouver Island argued resolutely that "their labour cannot be depended on, and with one or two slight exceptions at present forms no point of consideration in the labour market," and A.A. Harvey described aboriginal people as "valueless in the labour market,"[5] in his 1871 report on British Columbia the federal minister of public works observed that "the Indians have been, and still are, and will long continue an important population for [British] Columbia, in the capacity of guides, porters and labourers."[6]

Who was right? Were aboriginal people "valueless in the labour market" or "an important population of ... labourers"? How important was their labour to British Columbia's nineteenth-century economy? How important was wage and contract labour to the aboriginal economy? What motivated aboriginal people to join the early paid labour force?[7] Who, and how many, were recruited? Based on a varied sample of aboriginal voices captured in biographies, ethnographies, and in letters to government and church officials, as well as the correspondence of colonial officials, fur traders, missionaries, and travelers, together with the records of the Department of Indian Affairs, this paper not only attempts to answer these questions, but in doing so provides a fresh perspective from which to view the early years of capitalist development in British Columbia.

Labourers of the Aboriginal Province

Of the 34,600 or so inhabitants of the Colony of Vancouver Island and its adjacent islands and shores in 1855, all but 774 were aboriginal. Outside the colony there were probably an additional 25,000 to 30,000 aboriginal people living in the remainder of what became British Columbia. This vast population was extremely heterogeneous, both culturally and historically. It was comprised of 10 distinct nations or ethnic groups, speaking 26 distinct—and for the most part mutually unintelligible—languages. Each nation had its own customary laws that defined property rights and social and gender relations, and by 1849 each village had its own history of relationships with non-aboriginal people or their trade goods.[8]

Victoria, the west-coast headquarters for the Hudson's Bay Company (HBC), became the capital when the colony was established in 1849. As the largest community of non-aboriginal people north of Oregon, it became "the great emporium" for aboriginal people from all over the Pacific Northwest, from Russian America (Alaska) down. The mass migrations to Victoria began in the summer of 1853, when Governor Douglas reported a gathering of 3,000 "Indians" at a potlatch hosted by the local Songhees people living across the harbour.[9] The next year aboriginal people from "all parts of the mainland coast south of Cape Spencer, in north latitude 59 degrees" dropped in on Victoria itself. Annually, from 1853 through the 1880s, 2,000 to 4,000 aboriginal people canoed their way to Victoria to trade or spend part of the year, travelling as much as 800 miles to do so.

Why did thousands of aboriginal people, between five and ten percent of the whole aboriginal population north of Puget Sound, paddle so far to visit a community that in 1855 numbered only 232?[10] Trading was undoubtedly a major attraction—the variety in Victoria was greater, alcohol was more easily available, and the prices of goods were perhaps better than at closer trading posts; and in the beginning at least curiosity to see this alien community was, no doubt, another factor.

There was nevertheless a third and key reason why aboriginal people returned year after year. As Governor Douglas explained in his dispatches to the Colonial Office, he was not unduly alarmed about being out-numbered ten-to-one during these seasonal visits by "ignorant and barbarous people.... For the object of the Indians in visiting this place is not to make War upon the White man, but to benefit by his presence, by selling their Furs and other commodities."[11]

One of the commodities aboriginal people sold was labour, a practice well established as early as 1853, when Douglas had reported that "a great part of the agricultural labour of the colony, is at present performed by means of the Natives, who though less skilled and industrious than the white men, work at a comparatively much cheaper rate, so that on the whole, they are exceedingly useful to the colonists."[12] Indeed, nearly all early accounts mention the hiring of aboriginal labour. The first *bona fide* colonist, W.C. Grant, hired aboriginal people on his farm and reported in 1853 that "with the proper superintendence [they] are capable of being made very useful. They all live by fishing but take kindly to any kind of rough agricultural employment, though their labour is not to be depended on for any continuous period." Similarly, colonist J.S. Helmcken used Indians "chiefly from the north" to clear land for his home, while the colony itself paid "scores of Indians" in HBC blankets to clear the land around the surveyors office and to build roads. The Puget Sound Agricultural Company also hired aboriginal labour on their farms, and by 1857 missionary William Duncan observed that around Victoria "most of the Farm Servants employed here ... are Chimsyan (Tsimshian) Indians—and they all give them a good character."[13]

The issue of wage labour was raised formally when, at the start of his 1856 seasonal visit, Douglas called the chiefs together and "spoke to them seriously on the subject of their relations with the whites, and their duties to the public, and after exacting a pledge for the good behaviour of their respective Tribes, *I gave them permission to hire themselves out as labourers to the white settlers, and for the public works in progress.*" He reported at the end of August that "the greater number of those people have lately departed *with their earnings* to their distant homes, and will not return to Vancouver's Island, before the spring of 1856; those who still remain about the settlements will spend the winter here...."[14]

Although the economies of the aboriginal peoples varied from the coast to the interior and even within these divisions, generally they were based on a seasonal migration cycle from permanent winter villages to harvesting sites for fishing in the fall, hunting and trapping in winter, and harvesting roots and berries in the summer. From 1853 onwards, however, a spring and summer visit to Victoria became a part of the seasonal cycle, and those who could not find work in Victoria often continued south into the American territory of Puget Sound. John Fornsby, a Coast Salish living in Puget Sound first saw these "Northern Indians" when 40 to 50 of them came to work at a Puget Sound sawmill around 1858, while James Swan wrote from Port Townsend that the Northern Indians "yearly come to Victoria and whenever they get a chance, come over here to work—the men at our mills or among the farmers, where they prove themselves faithful and efficient; and the women, by their cleanly habits, their bright dresses and hoop skirts ... winning the hearts or purses of the bachelors."[15] Others, who did not join the migration, found work closer to their own villages in the expanding activities of the Hudson's Bay Company posts, cutting shingles, spars, picking cranberries, harvesting ice, as well as gardening, fishing, preserving food, and doing general construction.[16]

While the summer migrants from the north worked on the farms and public works, some of the local Songhees people became established in year-round employment in the homes of the better-off colonists as servants and cooks. Reverend Staines wrote in 1852 that his Indian servant procured meat each day by trading with other Indians, and that he was teaching his Indian cook how to prepare beef, mutton, and venison. Other aboriginal people supplied venison, partridges, salmon, potatoes, and berries to the colonists, as well as shingles, lathes, mats, and baskets.[17]

With the 1858 gold rush and the consequent growth of Victoria came even more opportunities for work, and by 1860 whole villages might be deserted for the capital. Making for the Queen Charlotte islands in the *Alert*, James Cooper met the entire population of Masset heading for Victoria. At Skidegate, meanwhile, Chief "Estercana" asked the officials to "tell Mr. Douglas and the man-of-war to send my people home; I wanted to build a house this summer [but] nearly all my people are away at Victoria."[18] That summer, the governor reported over 4,000 visiting Indians at Victoria, double the number of non-aboriginal inhabitants in the town.[19] Despite the large gold-induced increase in the non-aboriginal population, Douglas was still not concerned about its relations with the majority. "When not under the influence of intoxication," he told the Colonial Office in 1860, "[the aboriginal people] are quiet and well conducted, make good servants and by them is executed a large proportion of the menial, agricultural, and shipping labour of the Colony. Besides their value as labourers they are of value commercially as consumers of food and clothing...."[20] He was not alone in his view. The *San Francisco Times*, for example, described the Indians around gold-rush Victoria as "industrious," which "alone establishes their superiority to the California aborigines."[21] Moreover, it was not just Victoria that felt their presence, as aboriginal people were also relocating seasonally, or even for several years, to the gold-mining communities of Fort Hope, Lytton, Yale, and New Westminster, the capital of the new colony of British Columbia.[22]

Despite claims by historians, aboriginal people were not made redundant by the influx of non-aboriginals to the gold fields, just less visible in the increasingly polyglot society of the colonies. Nor had they been bystanders as gold and coal became focal points of the economy of the Pacific Northwest between the 1840s and 1880s: in both cases, aboriginal people were the discoverers and the first miners, and they continued to work the mines throughout the century.

Coal was first discovered by aboriginal people on northern Vancouver Island. In 1846 the Royal Navy vessel *Cormorant* stopped there and "with the assistance of the Indians they collected about 60 tons."[23] The Kwakwaka'wakw (Kwakiutl) at this site told the HBC that "they would not permit us to work the coal as they were valuable to them, but that they would labor in the mines themselves and sell to us the produce of their exertions."[24] Between 1849, when the HBC established Fort Rupert at the coal mines, and 1851 when the seam was exhausted, the Kwakwaka'wakw people mined 3,650 tons of coal for which they were paid the handsome price of "one blanket 2 1/2 pt.s or equivalent in Grey Cotton for every two tons delivered at the Fort."[25]

Starting in 1852, the Fort Rupert experience was repeated in Nanaimo after trader Joe McKay, and then Governor Douglas, were led to various seams of coal by the local people. Douglas sent the HBC's *Cadboro* to the spot "and succeeded in procuring, with the assistance of Indians, about 50 tons of coal in one day." "The natives," he reported, "who are now indefatigable in their researches for Coal, lately discovered a magnificent seam over six feet in depth.... Such places are left entirely to the Indians, who work, with a surprising degree of industry, and dispose of the coal to the Agents of the Hudson's Bay Company for clothing and other articles of European manufacture."[26]

With the removal of the surface coal and the need to dig shafts and use pumps, the Hudson's Bay Company brought skilled miners from Great Britain. However, as Douglas noted in 1857, aboriginal people remained crucial to the underground operations:

> the want of Indian labor is certainly a great inconvenience for the miners but really they must learn to be independent of Indians for our work will otherwise be subject to continual stoppage.[27]

In the 1850s the coal mines regularly stopped production when the local people went to their seasonal fisheries, potlatched, or were attacked by illness. Although partly displaced by Chinese labour in the various coal mines that subsequently sunk shafts around Nanaimo, in 1877 it was noted that "the Nanaimo Indians ... have hitherto been chiefly employed about the coal mines as labourers." In 1882 the Indian Agent overseeing Nanaimo noted that the aboriginal people there "find constant employment at the coal mines and wharves," and in 1888 "many Indians are again working at the coal mines at Nanaimo, taking the place of the Chinese; the fear of accident by explosions deterred them for some time, but now the high wages paid has attracted them again to the mines."[28]

Gold, meanwhile, was first offered to the HBC in trade by the Haidas of the Queen Charlotte Islands in 1851, and in the mid-1850s by the Interior Salish of the Fraser and Thompson Valleys. In both cases white men were "obstructed by the natives in all their attempts to search for gold," and "when [the whites] did succeed in removing the surface and excavating to the depth of the auriferous stratum, they were quietly hustled and crowded by the natives who ... proceeded to reap the fruits of their labours."[29] In 1858, however, some 30,000 non-aboriginals surged into the Fraser Valley and up the Thompson, completely overwhelming the few thousand aboriginal inhabitants, who continued to work alongside them. In 1858 James Moore reported that the "whole tribe of Yale Indians moved down from Yale and camped on Hill's bar, about three hundred men, women and children, and they also commenced to wash for gold," and Governor Douglas reported that "it is impossible to get Indian labor at present, as they are all busy mining, and make between two and three dollars a day each man."[30]

Within the decade the gold rushes had passed and while most of the aliens had abandoned the diggings, aboriginal people continued to include gold mining as part of their modified seasonal cycle. In 1871 Alfred Selwyn of the Geological Survey of Canada remarked that "nearly all the Indians of the Fraser above Yale have now become gold washers. They return to the same spot on the river year after year, at the season of lowest water, to wash the sands, and, it is asserted, can almost always earn for a day's labour from one to two dollar's worth of gold." The next year the *Victoria Colonist* reported that "from $15,000–$20,000 is annually contributed to the wealth of the Province by mining on the Thompson and Fraser Rivers, which is carried on almost exclusively by the Natives at low water."[31] The Indian agents and the mining department regularly recorded the bands along the Fraser and Thompson panning gold into the twentieth century.[32] In addition to mining, many bands along the Fraser, Thompson and Nicola rivers took up packing supplies as a vocation. Chief Justice Begbie, who travelled this circuit, recalled that "no supplies were taken in [to the gold districts] except by Indians.... Without them ... the country could not have been entered or supplied in 1858–1860."[33]

Besides mining and packing, the aboriginal people of the southern Interior took up farming on their own behalf and worked as farm labour for others. In 1874 the Catholic missionary C.J. Grandidier wrote from Kamloops that "The Indians in this part of the country are now quite awake to the necessity of working, of following the examples of the whites, they look to the future and are afraid for their children's sake if they do not work." Acting on behalf of the people of the Fraser Valley Alexis, chief of Cheam, asked the Indian agent for advance warning if he visited "in order to unite our people who are now a little dispersed as they are working for the whites."[34] "Every Indian ... who could and would work—and they were numerous," the provincial attorney general recalled in 1875:

> was employed in almost every branch of industrial and domestic life, at wages which would appear excessively high in England or in Canada. From becoming labourers, some of the Natives ... engaged on their own account in stock breeding, in river boating, and in 'packing', as it is termed, as carriers of merchandise by land and water; while others followed fishing and hunting with more vigour than formerly to supply the wants of the incoming population. The Government frequently employed those living in the interior as police, labourers, servants, and as messengers entrusted with errands of importance.[35]

Did they also engage in more industrial pursuits? Martin Robin has argued that "it was not merely the shrinking numbers ... which accounted for the low participation of the Indians in the new industrial system. By inclination and habit, the Indian did not fit the industrial mould. His customary and casual and seasonal work schedule hardly prepared him for the discipline, pace and rhythm of industrial employment."[36] Yet, the evidence shows aboriginal people were among the region's first factory workers.

The "modern" factory arrived on Vancouver Island in 1861 when Captain Stamp commenced operation of the largest sawmill on the west coast of North America, a steam-powered facility that cost $120,000 to build, and was eventually capable of cutting 100,000 feet of lumber a day. For the Tseshaht people of the Albemi Inlet, where the mill was located, the industrial revolution arrived at the end of a cannon. When the white labourers arrived to set up the mill they chose the site where the local people were camped. The mill's operators were satisfied that they had "bought" the site from the local people for "Some 50 blankets, muskets, molasses and food, trinkets etc...."; but the Tseshaht clearly had a different view of the transaction than the mill owners—they refused to leave. They were introduced to capitalist property relations when the mill managers trained their cannons on them.[37] Ultimately they agreed to move, and when they returned to the mill site it was as workers. The mill manager subsequently recorded that when he "first employed Indians at Albemi, the price of their labour was two blankets and rations of bisquits and molasses for a month's work for each man, if he worked the whole time." One source reports that over its operation, the mill paid out close to $30,000 in wages, and a considerable portion of that was likely paid to the local Tseshaht people.[38]

Two more giant export sawmills were established on Burrard Inlet between 1863 and 1867. Both rivalled the Albemi mill in size, but unlike their predecessor, they continued to operate into the next century. Together, these mills were the largest industrial operations in the colonies, each employing between 75 and 100 mill hands, exclusive of loggers and longshoremen.[39] As with other settlements around the colonies, whole aboriginal communities relocated to the sawmills, and in Burrard Inlet, most of the workers inside and outside the factory were aboriginal.

"While Europeans or at least Whites fill the responsible posts," geologist George Dawson observed in 1875, "Indians [Squa'mich], Chinamen, Negroes & Mulattoes & Half breeds & Mongrels of every pedigree abound." That year George Walkem, Attorney General of British Columbia, wrote that "our lumber mills alone pay about 130 Indian employés over $40,000 annually. Each individual receives from $20 to $30 per month and board." Recalling this period R.H. Alexander wrote: "Our mill hands were largely composed of runaway sailors and Indians and I have known the mill to shut down for several days because all the hands were engaged in an interesting poker game." By 1877 the Indian commissioner for the province found it "difficult to imagine" what "indeed in any part of the Province ... the miner, the trader and the farmer, the manufacturer, the coast navigator, or almost any other vocation would do without the assistance of the Indian element."[40]

Inquiring into the income of the Musqueem band that worked in the Burrard Inlet the Indian Reserve Commission reported in 1877 that from the "saw mills and other concomitant interests ... a sum variously computed at from $80,000 to $ 100,000 finds its way annually into the hands of the natives. The mill owners, too, and the shipping frequenting the mills, are benefitting by a corresponding degree, by having a local source of labour constantly available." The Indian Commissioner remarked that in 1881 aboriginal sawmill workers were preferred to whites, and workers of both races earned up to $2.50 per day.[41] (For comparison of wage rates see appendix 6.2.)

At the same time sawmills in Puget Sound, Washington Territory, employed hundreds of British Columbia aboriginal people. William Pierce, a Tsimshian from Port Simpson, remarked that in the mid-1870s his co-workers in a Puget Sound sawmill included Haida from the Queen Charlottes, Tsimshian from the north coast, Nass, and Skeena Rivers, as well as Bella Bella, Bella Coola, Kitamaat, and Kwakwaka'wakw from the central coast and Tlingit from Alaska.[42] A decade later, one of these migrants, Charles Nowell, a 17-year-old Kwakwaka'wakw from Fort Rupert recalled arriving in Vancouver after returning empty-handed from seeking work in Washington State:

> ... I was dead broke, and went over to North Vancouver in a small canoe to the sawmill and asked the manager if he could give me a job. He told me I could be a fireman in the sawmill. I says, "I never did it before, but I will try and do my best." He says there is another Indian there who has been working there for two years and will tell me what to do.[43]

As Nowell's reference to "firemen" suggests, these mills were large factories operated by steam power. Morley Roberts worked alongside the crew of "Indians, half-breeds and Chinamen" at a New Westminster sawmill in the 1880s and his description leaves no doubt that sawmill work was among the most "industrial" in British Columbia.[44]

Some aboriginal people moved into skilled jobs but the majority of the aboriginal workers, like the non-aboriginals, were unskilled. Many aboriginal people, including the entire male population of the Sechelt band on the Sunshine Coast north of Burrard Inlet, cut wood for the mills. In addition to working for the big export mills, aboriginal people worked and ran several smaller sawmills that were scattered throughout the province, many of them first established by missionaries in order to encourage aboriginal people to adopt capitalist-Christian ethics. Not only was sawmill labour predominantly aboriginal but so were the longshoremen and women.[45]

While the sawmills of Burrard Inlet were getting into full swing, the second major factory-based industry—salmon-canning—was in its infancy. First attempted in 1867, it was not until 1870 that continuous production started. Within a decade, however, the canneries were large, modern factories employing hundreds of people and using steam boilers and retorts to heat and cook the salmon and to seal the cans.[46] The early canneries relied almost exclusively on aboriginal men to do the fishing and a workforce comprised of aboriginal women and Chinese men to do most of the canning. Like the big export sawmills, they were frequently located in coastal inlets, remote from white settlement but in, or close to, aboriginal communities. One estimate suggested that the 11 canneries operating on the Fraser River in 1883 employed 1,000 to 1,200 aboriginal fishermen plus hundreds of aboriginal women to process the fish.[47]

By 1885 a crude estimate based on the reports of the Indian Agents suggests that of the 28,000 aboriginal people in British Columbia in 1885, over 85 percent belonged to bands that earned substantial incomes through paid labour. The remaining 15 percent, although not wage labourers, participated to a lesser degree in the economy as fur traders.[48] More telling than the numbers are the accounts of whole villages being emptied by aboriginal people engaged in paid work. One surveyor reported, for example, that he did not know where to lay out a reserve because all the Haida were away at the canneries or the mills, while an ethnographer from the Berlin Museum was unable to trade artifacts in villages emptied by all who were mobile. One of the most interesting accounts is by Sayach'apis, a Nuu-cha-nulth, whose invitations to a potlatch in the mid 1880s were spurned by the Songhees, the Saanich, the Cowichan, and the Hikwihltaah: "You are too late," they told him; "we are going to the hop fields," to harvest the crop.[49]

Twenty-five years after the gold rush, aboriginal people had not been marginalized—rather they remained at the centre of the transformed, capitalist, economic activity. "Almost all the labour of the province is done by Indians and Chinese, the federal minister of justice reported in 1883."

> All the steamboats in which we travelled were manned by Indians—the Stevedores and

> longshoremen and the labourers you find about the streets are for the most part Indians. All the fishing for the canneries is done by them and in all these occupations they compare favourably with the labouring classes elsewhere ... they get good wages, frequently $2.00 a day and over....[50]

"The stranger coming for the first time to Victoria is startled by the great number of Indians living in this town," wrote ethnologist Franz Boas in 1886. "We meet them everywhere. They dress mostly in European fashion. The men are dock workers, craftsmen of fish vendors; the women are washerwomen or working women.... Certain Indian tribes have already become indispensable on the labour market and without them the province would suffer great economic damage."[51] Moreover, Chinook, the *lingua franca* of the fur trade (not English) was the language of the canneries, the docks, the sawmills, the hop-fields and many other sites where large amounts of labour were performed.[52] At no time since have aboriginal people been so central to the province-wide capitalist economy than in the early 1880s, though they continued to be vital to specific industries long after.

Recruitment and Composition of the Aboriginal Workforce

There is virtually no information on how aboriginal people were recruited into the pre-industrial labour force for agriculture and public works, or the manifold handicraft industries sponsored by the Hudson's Bay Company and others. It seems clear, however, that with aboriginal labour abundant in and around the settlements of British Columbia, recruitment was not difficult. Moreover, in addition to the nearby bands, often whole communities moved to white settlements, some seasonally and others permanently, to trade and work. The slim evidence available suggests that, in this period, chiefs acted as labour brokers for their local groups. As we have seen, Governor Douglas held chiefs responsible for the behaviour of those of their people who hired themselves out, and the Fort Rupert journals record that chiefs were paid at the same rate as labourers, to supervise. Similarly, sealing schooners would negotiate with chiefs to bring a whole crew from a single village.[53]

Recruitment became more of an issue with the advent of large sawmills and canneries—the factories—because they demanded an unfamiliar work discipline. For one thing, it was critically important to have a large, regular workforce gathered at a single site for extended, and in the case of the salmon canneries, very precise periods; for another, everyone had to start and end work at the same time. In retrospect, however, it should come as no surprise that aboriginal people were recruited and employed in these factories in large numbers. They dominated the population and either lived close to the new industrial sites (since the canneries, especially, located specifically to take advantage of aboriginal labour) or had their own means of transport to and from them. In addition, aboriginal people, under some circumstances, could be paid less than "White" labour.

Yet little is known about the different methods used to bring aboriginal people into the factories or how they made the transition to factory labour discipline. At the beginning of the industrial era, chiefs were still relied upon as labour agents. We know, for example, that white recruiters visited the Sliammon chiefs on the Sunshine Coast in 1882 and told them that their people would earn $3 a day at the Fraser River canneries.[54] Evidence from the early twentieth century shows that canneries employed "Indian bosses" who would be given cash advances for themselves and others, and who would be responsible for getting a specified number of fishermen and inside workers, particularly women, to come to individual canneries. Employers also used Indian Agents as informal recruiters, and large hop growers would send agents to visit bands and sign up workers in advance of the season.[55] However, it would seem from Charles Nowell's experience with the Burrard Inlet sawmill that as the number of industrial sites increased, local groups tended less to act as units; instead, individuals began to take control of their own labour and sell it independent of "Indian Bosses."[56] By the late 1880s, it was common for aboriginal women to be hired by Chinese labour contractors in the canneries on the Fraser and Skeena Rivers.[57] Whether as individuals or groups, Alfred Niblack noted in October 1886, aboriginal people were aggressive and creative about finding work:

> It was just at the end of the hop-picking season around Puget Sound, and hundreds of Indians were coming into Port Townsend en route to their villages to the north. A party of Young Haida stopped, and one of their number telegraphed over to Whidbey Island to offer the services of the party to a farmer to dig potatoes for him. In view of the glut in the labour market, due to the presence of so many idle Indians just then, this clever bit of enterprise ... secured them the job ahead of their rivals.[58]

The incorporation of aboriginal people into the capitalist labour force was a spatially discontinuous process that did not affect all aboriginal groups simultaneously or in the same way. Industry did not spread out gradually from the central settlements of Victoria, New Westminster, and Nanaimo; rather it arrived suddenly on inlets far removed from settlement. Moreover, many aboriginal groups opted to travel long distances to obtain employment while their neighbours did not. Those aboriginal groups that had previous exposure to working with or for non-aboriginal people were the first to take up the long migrations to find wage labour in the south.[59]

Participation also varied across generations and gender. Overall, the industrial workplace favoured younger people; agriculture, on the other hand, did not discriminate between young and old or between men and women.[60] The contrast was captured by William Lomas, the Cowichan Indian Agent: "All the younger men can find employment on farms or at the sawmills and canneries, and many families are about to leave for the hop fields of Washington Territory...." The elderly he saw were not faring so well:

> The very old people who formerly lived entirely on fish, berries and roots, suffer a great deal through the settling up of the country.... With the younger men, the loss of these kinds of foods is more than compensated by the good wages that they earn, which supplement what they produce on their allotments; but this mode of life does away with the their old customs of laying in a supply of dried meat, fish and berries for winter use, and thus the old people again suffer, for Indians are often generous with the food they have taken in the chase, but begrudge what they have paid money for.[61]

The British Columbia aboriginal societies had their own gender-based division of labour which were largely appropriated into the canneries.[62] Although, generally speaking, native men would fish and women would mend nets and work in the canneries, some women also fished with their husbands (the boats required a puller and a fisher)[63] and some, particularly older, men would mend nets and work inside. The infirm would look after the infants, while even young children had work in the canneries cleaning cans. In peak cannery periods, every possible person would be brought in to work and infants were placed in a corner where they could be watched.[64]

The traditional division of labour between male hunters and female processors of the catch was generally carried over into the capitalist economy of the sealing industry as well. When the local seals were hunted-out and schooners called at west coast villages to pick up crews, as many as 870 aboriginal people were hired, most of them men, although women were sometimes employed as boat-handlers. On the other hand, "the Indian women and children are always the most eager to go to the hop fields, where they always earn considerable sums of money, and, among these Indians, the wife's purse is generally entirely separate from the husband's."[65]

In some cases, however, aboriginal gender divisions of labour could not be grafted directly onto the capitalist economy. Were women or men better suited to work on steamships, in sawmills, or to sell food in the street markets? In the era 1849–90, both men and women worked at non-industrial occupations such as gold mining, farming, agricultural labour, rendering oil, and loading coal. With regard to the service trades, men are more often mentioned as cutting and selling firewood while women are commonly recorded as bringing fish and game to urban markets. In urban areas women did domestic work such as washing clothes, taking in ironing, and cleaning house,[66] and they were also employed to make fishnets.[67] Prostitution was an additional source of income for hundreds of aboriginal women from the late 1850s through the 1880s.[68] But in keeping with the gender divisions of labour prevalent in capitalist society, I have found no mention of aboriginal women being employed in the sawmills, coal mines, and on railroad crews.

The effect on aboriginal social and familial relationships of different participation rates by age and gender deserves more scholarly attention. The one study that has been done, of the Carrier people of the Chilcotin, where there was more demand for males in wage-occupations, shows that aboriginal women carried on and even enlarged their role as providers for households in the subsistence economy. Among the Carrier people, this had the effect of increasing the social status and power of women.[69] Among the coastal people women were gaining more prominence as "title holders" or "chiefs." Further research may reveal whether this was due to depopulation, their new incomes, their increased role as providers of subsistence, or other factors.

Why did Aboriginal People Work for Wages?

It is noteworthy in itself that aboriginal people in British Columbia chose, in large numbers, to work for pay. Indeed, in 1852, one of the HBC agents wondered if they could get the west coast people interested in any work besides fishing:

> ... when they can get all their wants and even a superfluity by a course congenial to them (fishing), it would be erroneous to suppose that they may be easily persuaded to follow an occupation they dislike and which is less remunerative, merely to gratify our will.[70]

Certainly in the 1840s and 1850s there was no pressure on the traditional resource base or subsistence economy which had sustained them for eons.[71] Even by the 1870s and the beginning of truly industrial labour, only a few of the aboriginal groups on southern Vancouver Island and in the Fraser and Thompson valleys were finding their traditional resource-base eroded to the point that they could not have reverted to a totally subsistence economy if such was their preference. Nor did evangelism have a significant impact until the 1860s and then only in a few locations, by which time church representatives were merely reinforcing an existing desire to participate in wage labour.

Prior to the wide-scale opportunities for wage labour most of the peoples of the west coast participated in the fur trade for reasons which, according to the "enrichment thesis," were broadly based in their own culture's traditions. Moreover, the new wealth generated by the fur trade, the relocation of bands to common sites around forts, population decimation from disease and firearms led to an enrichment of cultural activities, including, on the west coast, the potlatch.[72] "The arts and crafts, trade and technology, social and ceremonial life were all brought to new peaks of development. The climax of Indian culture was reached well after the arrival of the white man on the scene."[73]

Potlatch is a word in the Chinook jargon that refers to the different ceremonies among many nations of the Pacific Northwest that included feasting, dancing, and the giving of gifts to all in attendance. The potlatch was a central feature of the lives and economy of, especially, the coastal Indians. It was only through potlatches that one's hereditary status and rights to resources, property (including songs and dances), and names could be claimed and maintained. The more guests and the more gifts, the higher the relative status of the person giving the potlatch. High-status recipients of potlatch gifts were expected to reciprocate with potlatches in order to maintain their own relative position, and to protect their claims to traditional prerogatives.[74] All the evidence suggests that the fur trade intensified potlatching, and along with it the carving of totems and masks, the weaving of blankets, and all the other arts that were associated with the ceremony.[75]

Because of the cultural necessity to periodically distribute valuable gifts in a potlatch, the west coast people were a natural trading market. They had uses for property, possessions, and wealth which, while very different from those of the traders themselves, were nevertheless complementary. The traditional potlatch goods were valuable precisely because they were rare, or because they took much time and laborious effort to make. "On the other hand, the intrusive white civilization offered its goods for things that were relatively abundant": fur, fish, and unskilled labour.[76] Manufactured blankets and other mass-produced goods were substituted as potlatch goods for locally made, hand-produced items.

With some exceptions, aboriginal people welcomed the arrival of traders on boats and the establishment of trading posts in their territories. They were equally jealous of trading posts in their rivals' territories, or territories that they considered their hinterland.[77] Thus, in the 70 years prior to 1849, and since the first direct trading with Europeans, the society of the aboriginal people had changed so that trade with the foreigners had become an integral and largely welcome part of their culture.[78]

It appears that the same cultural forces that drew aboriginal people into the fur trade continued to operate and draw them into the wage and industrial labour force. Aboriginal people permitted, if not welcomed, initial non-aboriginal expansion into their territories to take advantage of the wealth-generating potential that the aliens offered. In 1843 the Songhees people helped the HBC build Fort Victoria.[79] In the 1850s the Haida and the Cowichan both appealed to Governor Douglas to establish a settlement among them that they might find work.[80] When he first visited them in 1881, although their village was still suffering from an unprovoked attack by the Royal Navy, the Kitamaats asked Indian Commissioner Powell if he would establish a sawmill in their community.[81] Even in the 1880s, when Port Simpson Tsimshian people refused to accept an Indian agent, refused to be administered under the Indian act, and prevented surveyors from assigning reserves, they permitted salmon canneries into their territory. Different bands of Kwakwaka'wakw refused to allow a priest into their village yet they too permitted the canneries, sawmills, and logging camps.

Aboriginal people apparently found that these new forms of work could be used like the fur trade, to enhance their position in their own society. In 1853, for example, using the wealth they had accumulated from working around Victoria, the Songhees people hosted a potlatch. Three thousand aboriginal people, perhaps a tenth of the population of the entire coastal area, attended this feast.[82] Having seen Victoria, the wealth of the Songhees, and the opportunities for work, the steady flow of thousands of coastal people to Victoria started the following season. Wage work became another adaptation of the seasonal subsistence round that had already been modified to include an extended trapping season, when furs were the easiest route to accumulation.

White employers, government officials, and missionaries noticed that aboriginal people worked to be able to potlatch. But the non-aboriginal immigrants could not reconcile their own work ethic with the motivations that led aboriginal people into the work force. The Indian Agent for Fraser Valley, James Lenihan, expressed his confusion this way:

> The Indians generally have views peculiar to the country as to the value of money. One band, numbering about fifteen families, applied to me in the spring for some agricultural implements and seeds. I questioned the Chief respecting a "potlatche" which he had held the previous winter, and ascertained that he

himself and two of his headmen had given away in presents to their friends, 134 sacks of flour, 140 pairs of blankets, together with a quantity of apples and provisions, amounting in value to about $700, for all of which they had paid in cash out of their earnings as labourers, fishermen and hunters.[83]

George Grant, who accompanied Sanford Fleming on his cross-country inspection of possible routes for the CPR, exhibited his puzzlement in describing the aboriginal work force at the Moodyville sawmill on Burrard Inlet in 1872:

> The aborigines work well till they save enough money to live on for some time, and then they go up to the boss and frankly say that they are lazy and do not want to work longer.... Another habit of the richer ones, which to the Anglo-saxon mind borders on insanity, is that of giving universal backshish or gifts to the whole tribe, without expecting any return save an increased popularity that may lead to their election as Tyhees or chiefs when vacancies occur.

Of particular interest was the story of "big George," who had

> ... worked industriously at the mill for years until he had saved $2,000. Instead of putting this in a Savings Bank, he had spent it all on stores for a grand "Potlatch".... Nearly a thousand assembled; the festivities lasted a week; and everyone got something, either a blanket, musket, bag of flour, box of apples, or tea and sugar. When the fun was over, "big George," now penniless, returned to the mill to carry slabs at $20 a month.

Similar comments can be found scattered throughout the accounts of missionaries, government agents and travellers.[84]

Aboriginal accounts confirm that income from wage work was used to enhance the prestige of the labourers. Charley Nowell recollected that between 1870 and 1876 his brother had regular employment as a cook: "That's why my brother was the richest of all the Indians at Fort Rupert. Every payday he used to be paid with trade—in blankets.... When the people of Fort Rupert know that my brother is paid, they come and borrow blankets from him.... My brother keeps on loaning until he has got enough (principal and interest) to collect and give a potlatch."[85]

In addition to accumulating wealth for potlatching, many aboriginal groups had other traditional uses for wealth. James Sewid, a Kwakwaka'wakw, told the story of his great-grandfather who trapped for several winters in order to hold a potlatch needed to recruit a war party to revenge his son's life. Northern men especially paid a substantial bride price to the families of their future wives. Shamans were paid to cure illness, and compensation was often demanded as restitution for intentional or unintentional killing or wounding of another.[86]

Helen Codere, who has made an intensive study of the Kwakwaka'wakw, has noted that while fur-trade wealth increased the frequency of potlatches, wage labour increased the number of guests and the wealth distributed to an even greater extent, and to her the years between 1849 and 1921 could justifiably be called "the potlatch period."[87] Her conclusions are borne out by Kwawkewlth (Kwakwaka'wakw) district Indian agent George Blenkinsop's 1881 observation that potlatches, "of late years, increased to a very great extent." He explained that among the Kwakwaka'wakw "the custom was formerly almost entirely confined to the recognized chiefs, but that of late years it has extended to the people generally, and become very much commoner than before.... [the Potlatch] has spread to all classes of the community and became the recognised mode of attaining social rank and respect."[88] Codere charted the increases in the number of blankets given at Kwakwaka'wakw potlatches going back over a century, numbers which were well remembered by her informants owing to the importance of establishing relative prestige levels. The number of blankets distributed at the greatest single potlatch in the following

20-year periods gives an indication of the striking increase in wealth available and distributed: 1829–48: 320 blankets; 1849–69: 9,000 blankets; 1870–89: 7,000 blankets; 1890–1909: 19,000 blankets; 1910–29: 14,000 blankets; 1930–49: 33,000 blankets. The first memories of Billy Assu, a Kwakwaka'wakw from Cape Mudge, were of his father's 1911 potlatch: "My father worked for the money to give that potlatch for many years. He gave away goods and money to the value of more than $10,000."[89]

The same phenomenon appeared to be drawing other aboriginal groups into the paid labour force. In 1881 Cowichan Indian agent Lomas predicted that a significant proportion of the $15,000 earned by the Cowichan people at the canneries that season would be given away at potlatches. Similarly, in 1884 a delegation of Nuu-chah-nulth chiefs explained that they worked for their money "and like to spend it as we please, in gathering our friends together; now whenever we travel we find friends; the 'potlatch' does that." Among the Haida the number of new totems being raised with the accompanying ceremonies reached its peak in the period 1860–76. Writing generally of this period missionary William Pierce, a converted Tsimshian wrote: "In these days, any man of a common order may give a potlatch if he is rich enough."[90] In short, it would appear that aboriginal people were not just servants of industry but also made industrialization serve their interests as well.[91]

However, the fact that aboriginal people had their own reasons for working for wages, and therefore chose when they would both enter and leave the labour force was a source of constant frustration to white employers. Indeed, the fact that aboriginal peoples had their own agendas probably accounts for the schizophrenic comments of white employers who spoke about them as "indispensable" while condemning their "unreliability" and "laziness."

Like most other groups outside the urban area, the Kwakwaka'wakw, for example, "continued to earn their own subsistence, which meant that earnings could go to the purchase of manufactured goods. Since they required only a limited amount of manufactured goods for consumption needs and since they did not hoard, any surplus could be and was used in potlatching."[92] Because of their subsistence cycle, winter was the main ceremonial season—and few aboriginal people were willing to work year-round and miss the winter festivities. In the beginning this was not a problem in labour-intensive activities like fishing, canning, harvesting, and logging, which were not conducted in the winter. Increasingly, however, the sawmills, the railways, the steamboats and other large employers were anxious to have a year-round and stable labour force so that seasonal labour, the choice of large numbers of aboriginal people, was becoming less compatible with the demands of capitalism.

It is no coincidence, then, that the federal government passed a law banning potlatch in 1884, just as aboriginal peoples reached their peak importance in the economy. Although the potlatch had drawn many aboriginal people into paid labour, by the mid 1880s it was inconsistent with the "stable" habits of industry that both missionaries and government agents saw as essential to the development of a Christian capitalist society. Seeing the potlatch as a bulwark which enabled the aboriginal people to resist acculturation since the seasonal cycle kept them mobile and away from schools and churches, missionaries and the Indian agents argued that it kept aboriginal people poor and mitigated against the accumulation of individual dwellings, land holdings, and private property.

Although the law proved ineffectual, and was not successfully enforced until 1908, it did provide government agents and missionaries with powerful suasion against potlatching.[93] Some of the bands responded to government pressure, others that had been christianized gave up the institution at the insistence of their ministers;[94] some bands in urban areas seemed to be slowly adopting the more individualistic and acquisitive ideals of the new majority. So, despite the ineffective laws, the 1880s were also the climax years of the potlatch along the coast generally.[95] Ironically, the very cultural imperative that had brought aboriginal people into the workforce was outlawed because, due to changing circumstances, it was no longer sufficiently compatible with the requirements of capitalism.

Conclusion

In the period 1849–90 the connections to the capitalist economy varied widely among the many nations and linguistic groups that comprised the aboriginal people of present day British Columbia. Depending on particular circumstances, integration into the paid labour force also had different effects on the social relations between men and women, youth and elderly, and nobles and commoners. Some patterns are nevertheless emerging as research in these areas moves ahead. West coast aboriginal people joined the international economy when Captain Cook first traded sea otter pelts with the natives of Yuquat (Nootka) in 1778, but their relationship to the economy changed dramatically in the mid-nineteenth century. Before the 1850s they were largely hunters, fishermen, trappers, and gatherers who exchanged the products of the land for products of the European market. By 1890, however, the industrial revolution having arrived on many of their inlets, bays, and rivers, most aboriginal people were trading their labour for wages.

Aboriginal people were central, not marginal, to the development of new industries and the spread of capitalism in the province-to-be. Coal would not have been mined in British Columbia in the 1840s and 50s, export sawmills would not have been able to function in the 1860s and 70s, canneries would not have had a fishing fleet, or the necessary processors in the 1870s and 80s, without the widespread participation of aboriginal people. The gold rush may have diverted the attention of historians, but it did not divert aboriginal people from the economy. It was the aboriginal workforce that allowed the creation of a capitalist regional economy based on fur trade, then coal mining, sawmilling, and salmon canning. This was the regional economy that kept the Hudson's Bay Company on the Pacific coast, persuaded Britain that the establishment of colonies could be profitable as well as strategic, and ultimately ensured that British Columbia would be *British* Columbia.

While the capitalist economy needed the vast pool of aboriginal labour, aboriginal people used the capitalist economy for their own cultural purposes. Wage labour was one juncture where the potlatch system and capitalism were curiously complementary. Aboriginal people fitted seasonal paid work into their own economic cycle and, in the era described, were able to maintain a level of control over their participation in both. However, the compatibility of capitalism and the aboriginal economy was breaking down by 1884, when the anti-potlatch laws were passed by the federal government: eager to participate in seasonal wage activities from spring to fall, aboriginal people were less interested in participating in the year-round employment that the economy was increasingly demanding.

By the taking of the census of 1891, British Columbia was no longer an "aboriginal province." Aboriginal populations had nearly reached their nadir and alternative pools of labour were becoming available. Since then, although aboriginal people have not comprised the majority of the labour force, they have been consistently important in key sectors, namely fishing, canning, and agricultural sectors. In this way, as well as others, the aboriginal and non-aboriginal histories of British Columbia are still inextricably linked.

Acknowledgements: James Hendrickson, Lorne Hammond and Peter Baskerville have all generously given me access to their unpublished research while Cheryl Coull, Cairn Crockford, Donald Davis and Richard Mackie have offered valuable suggestions. The research has been financially supported by the Social Sciences and Research Council of Canada and the Association of Canadian Universities for Northern Studies. My thanks to all.

Appendix 6.1

Aboriginal and Non-Aboriginal Population Estimates for British Columbia, 1835–1901[96]

Year	Aboriginal Population	Non-Aboriginal Population
1835	70,000	-
1851	65,000	-
1856	62,000	1,000
1861	60,000	13,624
1871	37,000	13,247
1881	29,000	23,798
1885	28,000	-
1891	26,000	72,173
1901	25,488	153,169

Appendix 6.2

Average Rates of Pay, Various Professions in British Columbia, 1864–90 (dollars per day unless specified)[97]

Occupation	1860	1864	1883	1890
Indian Agent			200/month	
Indian Dept. Constable			40/month	
General Labourers	2.50	3.00–4.00	1.75–2.00	1.25–2.50
Coal Miners			3.00–4.00	
Gold Miners				1.75–3.00
Colliery Labourers			2.50	
Skilled Tradesmen	5.00	?–4.85	3.40–4.00	4.00–6.00
Laundresses		2.10/doz. Shirts		10.00–18.00/mth
Longshoremen				50¢/hr.
Lumbermen		48.50/mth		1.50–2.25
Milkhands				2.50

Endnotes

1. A fuller discussion of population estimates is taken up in Appendix 6.1.
2. Robin Fisher, *Contact and Conflict: Indian European Relations in British Columbia, 1774–1890* (Vancouver, 1977); Rolf Knight, *Indians at Work: An Informal History of Native Indian Labour in British Columbia, 1858–1930* (Vancouver, 1978).
3. Fisher, *Contact and Conflict*, 96, 109, 111. For other statements along these lines see David McNally, "Political Economy Without a Working Class," *Labour/Le Travail* 25(Spring 1990): 220n;

Paul Phillips, "Confederation and the Economy of British Columbia," in W. George Shelton, ed., *British Columbia and Confederation* (Victoria, 1967), 59; Martin Robin, *The Rush for the Spoils: The Company Province 1871–1933* (Toronto, 1972), 30.

4. Alicja Muszynski, "Major Processors to 1940 and the Early Labour Force: Historical Notes," in Patricia Marchak et al, eds., *UnCommon Property: The Fishing and Fish Processing Industries in British Columbia* (Agincourt. Ont., 1987), 46–65; Richard Mackie, "Colonial Land, Indian Labour and Company Capital: The Economy of Vancouver Island, 1849–1858" (M.A.thesis, University of Victoria, 1985); James K. Burrows, "'A Much Needed Class of Labour': The Economy and Income of the Southern Interior Plateau Indians, 1897–1910," B.C. *Studies* 71 (1986): 27–46.
5. Charles Forbes, *Vancouver Island, its Resources and Capabilities as a Colony* (London, 1862), 25; A.A. Harvey, A Statistical Account of British Columbia (Ottawa. 1867), 9.
6. H.L. Langevin, *British Columbia: Report of the Hon. H. L. Langevin* (Ottawa, 1872), 28; A.C. Anderson, *Dominion on the West* (Victoria, 1872), 80.
7. For simplicity's sake, I have combined in the term "paid labour": wage work (whether paid in kind, scrip, or cash), piece work, and independent commodity production (hand logging for example), although each system produced its own set of social relations.
8. For an introduction see William C. Sturtuvant, *Handbook of North American Indians* (Washington, D.C.), vols. 4, 6, 7. For population estimates see Appendix I.
9. The Songhees, a band of the Coast Salish, were an amalgamation of several nearby villages that relocated to a site across the harbour from Fort Victoria after the latter was founded in 1843.
10. Great Britain, Colonial Office, Original Correspondence, Vancouver Island, 1846–l867 (CO) 305/6, 10048, Governor James Douglas to Russell, 21 August 1855. Colonial Office correspondence (with a CO number) cited here was made available to me by James Hendrickson from his unpublished manuscript "Vancouver Island: Colonial Correspondence Dispatches."
11. CO 305/14, 9267, Douglas to Colonial Office, 8 August 1860.
12. CO 305/4, 9499, Douglas to Newcastle, 28 July 1853.
13. The Tsimshian were from the Skeena River area around Fort Simpson; William Duncan, "Journal," 11 July 1857, cited in Jean Usher, *William Duncan of Metlakatla: A Victorian Missionary in British Columbia* (Ottawa, 1974), 40; W. C. Grant in William Grew Hazlitt, *British Columbia and Vancouver Island* (London, 1858), 179; Dorothy B. Smith, *The Reminiscences of Doctor John Sebastian Helmcken* (Vancouver, 1975), 134.
14. CO 305/6, 10048, Douglas to Lord Russell, 21 August 1855; CO 305/4, 12345, Douglas to Newcastle, 24 October 1853, emphasis mine.
15. June Collins, "John Fornsby: The Personal Document of A Coast Salish Indian," in Marian Smith, ed. *Indians in the Urban Northwest* (New York, 1949), 30l; "Northern Indians," *San Francisco Evening Bulletin* (October 4, 1860) reprinted in James Swan, *Almost Out of This World* (Tacoma, 1971), 99; CO 305/7, 3963, Douglas to Sir George Grey, 1 March 1856; and CO 305/7, 5814, 10 April 1856.
16. Mackie, "Colonial Land, Indian Labour."
17. CO 305/3, Rev. R. J. Staines to Thomas Boys, 6 July 1852; Smith, *Reminiscences*, 134; CO 305/3 Douglas to Earl Grey, 31 October 1851.
18. British Columbia Archives and Record Services (BCARS), Colonial Correspondence, F347/26a James Cooper, "Report by the Harbor Master at Esquimalt to the Acting Colonial Secretary"; Usher, *William Duncan of Metlakatla*, 58.
19. CO 305/14, 9267, Douglas to Colonial Office, 8 August 1860.
20. CO 305/14, 8319, Douglas to Colonial Office, 7 July 1860. One major change during the gold rush was that aboriginal labour was increasingly being paid in cash instead of goods. Previously the goods most sought after as pay were blankets, which were commonly used as "potlatch" gifts.
21. *San Francisco Times* (August 27, 1858) in Hazlitt, *British Columbia*, 208, 215. See also Robin Fisher, "Joseph Trutch and the Indian Land Policy," in W.P. Ward and R.A.J. McDonald, eds., *British Columbia: Historical Readings* (Vancouver, 1981), 155; Sophia Cracroft, *Lady Franklin Visits the Pacific Northwest: February to April 1861 and April to July 1870* (Victoria, 1974), 79.
22. Cracroft estimates 1,000 aboriginal people living at Yale in 1861 and mentions that some were engaged as servants. Lady Franklin, 53–3; at Lytton, the population of 250 was 80 percent aboriginal

and "the Indians [are] ... very industrious and peaceable. Their chief employment is gold mining and packing supplies to and from the interior with their own horses of which they have in great numbers," *Lovell's Gazetteer* 1870–3, 181: Fisher, *Contact and Conflict*, 111.

23. James Douglas to the Governor and Committee of the Hudson's Bay Company, 7 December 1846, in Hartwell Bowsfield, *Fort Victoria Letters 1846–1851* (Winnipeg, 1979), 4.
24. E. E. Rich, ed., *The Letters of John McLoughlin from Fort Vancouver ..., 1825–1838* (Winnipeg, 1941), 335.
25. The reference is to a blanket of 2 1/2 points specifying a particular quality of blanket. Douglas to the Governor and Committee, 3 September 1849, 3 April and 16 November 1850 in Bowsfield, *Fort Victoria Letters*, 46, 84, 132; William Burrill, "Class Conflict and Colonialism: The Coal Miners of Vancouver Island During the Hudson's Bay Company Era, 1848–1862" (M.A.thesis, University of Victoria, 1987), 54.
26. CO 305/3, 10199, Douglas to Pakington, 28 August 1852; also CO 305/3, 933, 11 November 1852.
27. Douglas to Stuart, 22 August 1857 in Burrill, "Class Conflict," 127.
28. Canada, Parliament, House of Commons, Sessional Papers (hereafter Canada, SP) 1878, 8, 1x; 1883, 54; 1889, 13, 100–102. The 1877 annual report of the B.C. Minister of Mines records 51 Indians working as coal-miners in the Nanaimo area plus an unrecorded number working as miner's helpers. These annual reports show some aboriginal people working in the coal mines into the twentieth century. British Columbia. Legislative Assembly, Sessional Papers (hereafter BC, SP) 1877, 617.
29. Quote from CO 305/3, 3742, Douglas to Earl Grey, 29 January 1852; CO 305/3, 9263, Staines to Boys, 6 July 1852; CO 305/3, Douglas to Earl Grey, 31 October 1851; CO 305/3, 8866, Captain A. L. Kuper to Admiralty, 20 July 1852; CO 305/9, 5180, Douglas to Labouchère, 6 April 1858.
30. James Douglas, in T. A. Rickard, "Indian Participation in the Gold Discoveries," *British Columbia Historical Quarterly* 2 (1938): 13; and *British Columbia Historical Quarterly* 3 (1938): 218. There are other estimates of between 200 and 500 aboriginal people mining at Hill's Bar compared to 50–60 white miners in Hazlitt, British Columbia and Vancouver Island, 137.
31. Alfred C. Selwyn, "Journal and Report of Preliminary Explorations in British Columbia," *Report of Progress for 1871–72* (Ottawa, 1872), 56; *Victoria Colonist* (26 November 1872).
32. Canada, SP 1886, 4, 87–92; BC, SP 1900, 724.
33. M. B. Begbie in Langevin, *British Columbia*, 27.
34. Canada, National Archives (NA), RG10, Department of Indian Affairs, Vol. 1001, items 82, 186, C. J. Grandidier to I. W. Powell, 2 July 1874 and Alexis to James Lenihan, 5 September 1875.
35. BC, SP 1875, George Walkem, "Report of the Government of British Columbia on the Subject of Indian Reserves," 3.
36. Robin, *The Rush for the Spoils*, 30.
37. BCARS, Colonial Correspondence, File 107/5, W. E. Banfield to the Colonial Secretary, 6 September 1860, from Lorne Hammond, unpublished manuscript on W.E. Banfield; James Morton, *The Enterprising Mr. Moody and the Bumptious Captain Stamp* (Vancouver, 1977), 22–3; H.C. Langely, *Pacific Coast Directory for 1867* (San Francisco, 1867), 158.
38. G.M. Sproat, *Scenes and Studies of Savage Life* (London, 1868, reprinted in Victoria, 1989), 40; G.W. Taylor, *Timber, History of the Forest Industry in B.C.* (Vancouver, 1975), 23.
39. Morton, *Enterprising Mr. Moody*, 33–7, 59; Taylor, *Timber*, 28.
40. Douglas Cole and Bradley Lockner, eds., *The Journals of George M. Dawson: British Columbia, 1875–78* (Vancouver, 1989), 115; R. H. Alexander, "Reminiscences of the Early Days of British Columbia, Address to the Canadian Club of Vancouver," *Proceedings of the Canadian Club of Vancouver 1906–1911* (Vancouver, 1911), 111; Walkem, "Report of the Government of British Columbia," 3; James Lenihan, *Canada*, SP 1876, 56; Powell, *Canada*, SP 1877, 33–4.
41. Canada, SP 1877, 8, "Report of the Indian Reserve Commissioners," lii; Powell in Canada, SP 1884, 107.
42. J.P. Hicks, ed., *From Potlatch to Pulpit: The Autobiography of W. H. Pierce* (Vancouver, 1933), 15. In 1876 "Hundreds and sometimes thousands of northern Indians congregate every spring" to trade

and work at Puget Sound mills, according to J.G. Swan, "The Haida Indians of Queen Charlotte's Islands, British Columbia," *Smithsonian Contributions to Knowledge* XXI (1876): 2, 8.

43. Nowell found working as a fireman too hot so he switched to loading lumber onto the ships, for $2 a day, then became a tally man for $7.50 per day. Clellan Ford, *Smoke from their Fires: The Life of a Kwakiutl Chief* (Hamdon, Conn., 1968), 134.
44. Morley Roberts, *The Western Avenues or Toil and Travel in Further North America* (London, 1887), 181–2.
45. In 1876 the 55 men of the Sechelt band cut 1,300,000 cubic feet of saw logs for the mills for which they received $3 per thousand, the same rate paid to white loggers; Canada, SP 1878, 8 "Report of the Indian Reserve Commissioners," lix: Knight, *Indians at Work*, 114, 123–4. Missionary William Duncan established a sawmill and a soap factory at Metlakatla by 1871. Other mission-mills followed at Alert Bay, Glen Vowell, Hartley Bay, and Kispiox. A description of the latter can be found in Hicks, *From Potlatch to Pulpit*, 69–70.
46. Duncan Stacey, *Sockeye & Tinplate: Technological Change in the Fraser Canning Industry, 1871–1912* (Victoria, 1982).
47. "Salmon Pack for 1883, Fraser River Canneries," *Resources of British Columbia* 1 (1883): 4; aboriginal cannery labour has been considered in some detail by Muszynski and Knight.
48. This estimate subtracts the population figures of the Indian Affairs census for the bands listed as living primarily or exclusively on trapping, hunting and fishing, from the total aboriginal population. The bands subtracted are: 239 people in Chilcotin, 600 on the coast, 300 of Kootenays and 2,000 for tribes not visited. See Wilson Duff, *The Indian History of British Columbia: The Impact of the White Man* (Victoria. 1965), 35–40 for estimates of tribes not visited.
49. J.A. Jacobsen, *Alaskan Voyage, 1881–83: An Expedition to the Northwest Coast of America, translated from the German text of Adrian Woldt by Erna Gunther* (Chicago, 1977), 13 and passim; Canada, SP 1888, 13, 109, 157–8; Edward Sapir, *Nootka Texts* (Philadelphia, 1939).
50. BCARS, A/E/Or3/C15. Alexander Campbell, "Report on the Indians of British Columbia to the Superintendent General of Indian Affairs," 19 October 1883.
51. R. P. Rohner, *The Ethnography of Franz Boas* (Chicago, 1969), 6, 9; Ernst von Hesse Wartegg, "A visit to the Anglo-Saxon antipodes (Chapter XVIII of Curiosa aus der Neuen Welt, 1893, translated by John Maass)," *B.C. Studies* 50 (1981): 38; Jacobsen, *Alaskan Voyage*, 5.
52. Chinook was made up of words from aboriginal languages, French and English. A provincial business directory for 1877/78 published a Chinook-English, English-Chinook dictionary for the benefit of its readers: see T. N. Hibben, *Guide to the Province of British Columbia for 1877–78* (Victoria, 1877) pp. 222–249. Franz Boas noted in 1889 that it was impossible for someone to get around British Columbia outside the major cities without knowledge of the language. See Rohner, *Ethnography*, 9 and BCARS, Add. Mss. 2305, Alfred Carmichael "Account of a season's work at a Salmon Cannery, Windsor Cannery, Aberdeen, Skeena," ca. 1885, which records the widespread use of Chinook in the Skeena canneries in the mid-1880s.
53. *Fort Rupert Post Journal*, 22 November 1849, in Burrill, "Class Conflict," 34; for the sealing Industry see C.E. Crockford, "Changing Economic Activities of the Nuu-chah-nulth of Vancouver Island, 1840–1920" (Hon. thesis, University of Victoria, 1991), 58.
54. Although they went, they did not like canning. The elders "did not like to expose their young men and women to the temptations of city life," thus few Sliammon people returned the next year, Canada, SP 1883, 61.
55. NA, RG10, Vol. 1349, items 85, 255, 290, 483, 501.
56. Clellan, *Smoke from their Fires*, 134.
57. Canner F.L. Lord told the B.C. Fishery Commission in 1892 that Chinese contractors hired the native women and "of course these Chinamen pay the klootchmen," in BC, SP 1893, 178: "When the fishing commences the boss chinaman hires Indians to clean the fish and their squaws to fill the cans," according to Carmichael, "Account of a Seasons Work."
58. A. P. Niblack, "The Coast Indians of Southern Alaska and Northern British Columbia," *U.S. National Museum Annual Report* (1888): 339.
59. The Tsimshian that lived around the HBC post at Fort Simpson went to Victoria before other Tsimshian groups not living at the fort. Similarly it was the Fort Rupert Kwakwaka'wakw, and the southern Haida around Skidegate (who had exposure to white miners and whalers in addition to itinerant sea-borne

fur-traders) that were the first of their respective "nations" to begin labour migration. For the Fort Rupert people see Philip Drucker and R. F. Heizer, *To Make My Name Good: A Re-examination of the Southern Kwakiutl Potlatch* (Berkeley, 1976), 215; For the Haida see J. H. Van Den Brink, *The Haida Indians: Cultural Change Mainly Between 1876–1970* (Leiden, 1974), 51.

60. Jacobsen, *Alaskan Voyage*, 13.
61. Lomas in Canada, SP 1888, 13, 105.
62. Jo-Anne Fiske, "Fishing is Women's Business: Changing Economic Roles of Carrier Women and Men," 186–197 and Lorraine Littlefield, "Women Traders in the Fur Trade," 173–183 both in Bruce Alden Cox, ed., *Native People, Native Lands: Canadian Indians, Inuit and Metis* (Ottawa, 1988); Marjorie Mitchell and Anna Franklin, "When You Don't Know the Language, Listen to the Silence: An Historical Overview of Native Women in B.C.," in P.E. Roy, ed., *A History of British Columbia: Selected Readings* (Toronto, 1989), 49–68.
63. Canada, SP 1883, 60 records an aboriginal husband and wife fishing team, the wife pulling the boat and the husband handling the net and making $240 in 14 days.
64. Carmichael, "Account of a Season's Work."
65. Canada, SP 1887, 5, 92; 1888, 13, 105. In 1913 Indian Agent Charles Cox reported that Nuu-chah-nulth men and women keep their incomes separate, in Royal Commission on Pelagic Sealing, Victoria, Indian Claims, December 1913, Vol. 8, 135, in Crockford, "Changing Economic Activities," 43. The Department of Fisheries Annual Reports in Canada, Sessional Papers, record the number of aboriginal people involved in pelagic sealing, 1882–1910.
66. Canada, SP, 1888, 13, 106; Cracroft, Lady Franklin, 79. W.F. Tolmie wrote in 1883 that the aboriginal women in Victoria worked "as washerwomen, seamstresses and laundresses, earn much and spend it all in the city." BCARS A/E/Or3/C15.
67. Canada, SP 1884, 106; Carmichael. "Account of a Seasons Work;" Indian women "knit" nets that "will average from 120–150 fathoms [long and 16 and a half feet deep], at the cost of one dollar per fathom," *Resources of British Columbia* 1 (December 1, 1883).
68. By 1865 the Victoria police were writing the Colonial Secretary that some 200 Indian prostitutes lived in "filthy shanties owned by Chinese and rented ... at four to five dollars a month," in Peter Baskerville, *Beyond the Island, An Illustrated History of Victoria* (Windsor, Ont., 1986), 39–44. For the 1880s see John A. Macdonald, Canada, SP 1885, lix. For an aboriginal account of prostitution, see Franz Boas, *Contributions to the Ethnography of the Kwakiutl* (New York, 1925), 93–4.
69. Fiske, "Fishing is Women's Business," 186–197.
70. J. M. Yale, 1852 in Mackie, "Colonial Land, Indian Labour," 89.
71. J. A. McDonald, "Images of the Nineteenth-Century Economy of the Tsimshian," in M. Seguin, ed., *The Tsimshian: Images of the Past: Views for the Present* (Vancouver, 1984), 49.
72. Philip Drucker, *Cultures of the North Pacific Coast* (New York, 1965), 129; Fisher, *Contact and Conflict*, 47–8.
73. Duff, *Indian History of B.C.*, 55.
74. There is an enormous ethnographic literature on the potlatch: a good bibliography can be found in D. Cole and I. Chaikin, *An Iron Hand upon the People* (Vancouver, 1990), 213–23.
75. Fisher, *Contact and Conflict; Duff, Indian History of B.C.*; Cole and Chaikin, *An Iron Hand*; Helen Codere, *Fighting With Property: A Study of Kwakiutl Potlatching and Warfare, 1792–1930* (Seattle, 1966).
76. Drucker and Heizer, *To Make My Name Good*, 15.
77. Fisher, *Contact and Conflict*, 27–49.
78. This is particularly true of the west coast people, and to a lesser extent, those of the interior.
79. Thomas Lowe, *Victoria Colonist* (29 October 1897); Paul Kane, *Wanderings of an Artist* (Edmonton, 1968), 145.
80. CO 305/4, 12345, Douglas to Colonial Secretary, 24 October 1853; Margaret Ormsby states that when the Haidas were unable to mine gold on the Queen Charlotte Islands for lack of tools they offered to sell their rights if the HBC would form an establishment. Bowsfield, *Fort Victoria Letters*, xci.
81. Canada, SP 1881, 5, 143. This was also the wish of the Kincolith people of the Nass River. NA, RG10, Vol. 11007, W. H. Collinson to the Reserve Commissioner, 10 October 1887.
82. CO 305/4, 12345, Douglas to Newcastle, 24 October 1853.

83. Lenihan says that on reasoning with the chief he agreed to discontinue the Potlatch and was given $80 in seeds. Canada, SP 1877, 38.
84. George M. Grant, *Ocean to Ocean: Sir Sanford Fleming's Expedition through Canada in 1872* (Toronto, 1873), 319–20; Knight has a similar story from a completely different source that seems to describe a response to Big George's Potlatch by a rival; *Indians at Work*, 114; Capt. C.E. Barrett-Lennard, *Travels in British Columbia with the Narrative of a Yacht Voyage Round Vancouver's Island* (London, 1862), 60.
85. Ford, *Smoke from Their Fires*, 54–5.
86. James Sewid, *Guests Never Leave Hungry: The Autobiography of a Kwakiutl Indian*, ed. James Spradley (Kingston, 1989), 27; Victoria Wyatt, "Alaskan Indian Wage Earners in the nineteenth Century," *Pacific Northwest Quarterly* 78 (1987): 43–49.
87. "The Kwakiutl had a potential demand for European goods in excess of any practical utility the goods might have possessed. This can be seen both as a stimulus to the Kwakiutl integration in their new economy and as a direct stimulus to the potlatch," Codere, *Fighting with Property*, 126.
88. George Blenkinsop, *Indian Agent* and Rev. A.J. Hall cited in G.M. Dawson, "Notes and Observations on the Kwakiool People of Vancouver Island and Adjacent Coasts made during the Summer of 1885," *Transactions of the Royal Society of Canada*, Section 2 (1887): 17.
89. Codere, *Fighting With Property*, 124; Harry Assu with Joy Inglis, *Assu of Cape Mudge: Recollections of a Coastal Indian Chief* (Vancouver, 1989), 39.
90. Canada, SP 1882, 160, 170; Canada, SP 1885, 3, 101; Brink, *The Haida Indians*, 42; Hinks, *From Potlatch to Pulpit*, 126.
91. Another indication of this is that traditional raiding of enemies was performed en route to and from their seasonal wage labour until the early 1860s; See for example CO 305/7, 9708, Douglas to Labouchere, 26 August 1856; CO 305/8, 7950, 13 June 1857; CO 305/10, 6949, 25 July 1859.
92. Codere, *Fighting with Property*, 126.
93. Cole and Chaikin, *An Iron Hand*, 19–20.
94. With the acceptance of Christianity "modified potlatching" continued in some places, but the new Christians also had new imperatives to work. New houses built with milled lumber, nails, and glass windows, as well as new standards for clothing, contributions to build a church or purchase musical instruments etc., all demanded cash incomes.
95. Although the Kwakwaka'wakw proved an exception in this regard.
96. Aboriginal population from Duff, *Indian History of British Columbia*, 39–35, and for 1901, from Canada Census. Non-aboriginal population is taken from Douglas's census of Vancouver Island in 1854 which gave 774 whites on Vancouver Island, plus an estimate for the mainland. The 1861 population estimate is from Phillips, "Confederation and the Economy of British Columbia," 59. Other estimates are from Canada Census for 1871, 1881, and 1891. Since racial information was not tabulated in 1891 the non-aboriginal population given here is the total population less Duff's estimate for the aboriginal population. See also CO 305/7, 11582, Douglas to Labouchere, 20 October 1856 and CO 305/6, 10048, Douglas to Russell, 21 August 1855.
97. 1860 wages from Bishop Hill to the Secretary, Society for the Propagation of the Gospel, 8 May 1860 in Bishop Hill Collection, Text 57, Box 3, File 3 Anglican Diocese of British Columbia, courtesy of Ira Chaikin; 1864 from Matthew McFie, *Vancouver Island and British Columbia* (London, 1865), 499–500; 1883 from Canada, Province of British Columbia, Information for Intending Settlers (Ottawa, 1883), 23; and for 1890 from Canada, SP 1891, "Immigration Agents' Reports," 95–7. Longshoreman rate from Biggar, *Canadian Handbook*, 20. The figures for 1860–64 are converted to dollars at the rate of one pound to $4.85. Indian agent's salary from Indian Affairs Annual Reports.

Critical-Thinking Questions

1. Did working for wages conflict with the agricultural settlers' goal of achieving a "propertied independence?"
2. Career advisors today urge people to update and broaden their skills and to be flexible in seeking work opportunities in the new "Information Economy." What evidence is presented in chapter 1 that demonstrates that early nineteenth-century farmers acted as if similar advice applied in their world?
3. Discuss how the Irish background of Canada's canal navvies affected their class behaviour on the construction projects of the 1840s.
4. Why was it that, in an era of "laissez-faire" and limited government, the state moved so forcefully to suppress the canal strikers?
5. Account for the different results in the three case studies of Toronto skilled workers' encounter with industrialization.
6. To what extent were the craft unions' goals and methods narrowly self-interested, and to what extent did they fundamentally challenge capital and lay the basis for the labour movement?
7. Compare and contrast the Knights of Labor with the Salvation Army in late-nineteenth-century Ontario, taking into account their goals, membership bases, methods of organizing, and rhetoric.
8. In taking up the language of Christianity used by the dominant, middle-class culture of late Victorian Ontario, were working people in the Knights of Labor and the Salvation Army showing that they shared the values of the wider society? Or did they use this language for different purposes? Discuss.
9. Why did journalists find Charles McKiernan and Joe Beef's Tavern so fascinating?
10. To what extent can we speak of a distinct working-class culture in Victorian Canada, when cultural expressions were as varied as those of Joe Beef's patrons and the members of the Salvation Army?
11. In seeking economic opportunities in the colonial economy of British Columbia, were Aboriginal people unintentionally undermining their own culture or demonstrating their adaptability by finding ways to preserve what they valued most?
12. Why do histories of Canada so frequently ignore the work of Aboriginal people "after the fur trade?"

Further Readings

Bradbury, Bettina. *Working Families: Age, Gender and Daily Survival in Industrializing Montreal* (Toronto: McClelland and Stewart, 1993). Drawing on both quantitative and qualitative sources, Bradbury shows how men, women, and children contributed to the survival of their families as Canada's largest city industrialized.

Burley, Edith. *Servants of the Honourable Company: Work, Discipline and Conflict in the Hudson's Bay Company* (Don Mills: Oxford, 1997). A study of work, authority, and labour relations in the fur trade. Burley relies on the extensive records of Canada's oldest company.

Burr, Christina. *Spreading the Light: Work and Labour Reform in Late Nineteenth-Century Toronto* (Toronto: University of Toronto Press, 1999). Burr investigates how class, gender, and race informed the politics of work and labour reform. Both the experiences of working men and women and the rhetoric of reformers are analyzed.

Cadigan, Sean T. *Hope and Deception in Conception Bay: Merchant-Settler Relations in Newfoundland, 1785–1855* (Toronto: University of Toronto Press, 1996). Cadigan examines the rise of the household fishery in a context where agricultural prospects remained poor. Family labour systems and relations with merchants and politicians are studied.

Cohen, Marjorie Griffin. *Women's Work, Markets, and Economic Development in Nineteenth-Century Ontario* (Toronto: University of Toronto Press, 1988). An economic history of Victorian Ontario that highlights the role of women. Agriculture is given special emphasis.

Craven, Paul. *Labouring Lives: Work and Workers in Nineteenth-Century Ontario* (Toronto: Ontario Historical Studies Series and the University of Toronto Press, 1995). A collection of essays on several occupational groups—workers in agriculture, lumbering, homes, factories, and on the railways. Included, too, are chapters on labour and the law, and on religion, leisure, and working-class identity.

Errington, Elizabeth Jane. *Wives and Mothers, Schoolmistresses and Scullery Maids: Working Women in Upper Canada, 1790–1840* (Montreal and Kingston: McGill-Queen's University Press, 1995). Errington studies work in the home done by housewives, daughters, and servants; she also studies wage-earning women in various jobs, including teaching, and women in small businesses. Issues relating to femininity and marriage are examined.

Judith Fingard. *Jack in Port: Sailortowns of Eastern Canada* (Toronto: University of Toronto Press, 1982). Case studies of sailors in the ports of Quebec, Saint John, and Halifax. The book highlights the sailor labour market, the law and the sailor, and attempts to reform sailors and their world.

Kealey, Gregory S. *Toronto Workers Respond to Industrial Capitalism, 1867–1892* (Toronto: University of Toronto Press, 1982). A local study of the emergence of industrial capitalism. Chapters analyze workers in particular trades, the role of Irish immigrants, the Knights of Labor, and workers in politics.

Kealey, Gregory S. and Bryan D. Palmer. *Dreaming of What Might Be: The Knights of Labor in Ontario, 1880–1900* (New York: Cambridge University Press, 1982). Kealey and Palmer study the Knights of Labor against the backdrop of the rise of industrial capitalism. Membership, ritual, reform, and corruption are examined.

Marks, Lynne. *Revivals and Roller Rinks: Religion, Leisure, and Identity in Late Nineteenth-Century Small-Town Ontario* (Toronto: University of Toronto Press, 1996). Marks explores the role of Christianity in working-class culture. Issues of gender and leisure are also analyzed.

Palmer, Bryan D. *A Culture in Conflict: Skilled Workers and Industrial Capitalism in Hamilton, Ontario, 1860–1914* (Montreal and Kingston: McGill-Queen's University Press, 1979). A community study of class formation in which skilled, male workers play the leading part. Palmer shows how workers developed a culture that buffered them from the upheavals of industrialization. Leisure activities, workplaces, union halls, and politics are examined.

Pentland, H. Clare. *Labour and Capital in Canada, 1650–1860* (Toronto: James Lorimer, 1981). An early (1961) overview of labour that includes chapters on slavery, paternalist labour relations of the pre-capitalist era, and the formation of an industrial proletariat. The role of Irish immigrants is highlighted.

Way, Peter. *Common Labour: Workers and the Digging of the North American Canals, 1780–1860* (Cambridge and New York: Cambridge University Press, 1993). The canal builders of Canada appear in a wider, North American context, where their vulnerability to exploitation and repression is emphasized.

Sager, Eric W. *Seafaring Labour: the Merchant Marine of Atlantic Canada, 1820–1914* (Kingston and Montreal: McGill-Queen's University Press, 1989). A study of industrialization aboard ship. Chapters cover the labour force, the organization of work, wages, community, and conflicts with authority.

Wynne, Graeme. *Timber Colony: A Historical Geography of Early Nineteenth-Century New Brunswick* (Toronto: University of Toronto Press, 1981). A study of changes in the landscape, economy, and society of New Brunswick brought about by forest exploitation. It examines transformations in logging and saw-milling techniques, the organization of the timber trade, and the lives of men who worked in the industry.

PART II

The Industrial Age (1890–1939)

CANADIANS RODE A ROLLER-COASTER ECONOMY DURING THE HALF CENTURY FOLLOWING 1890. LARGE PARTS of the country enjoyed unprecedented expansion at times: throughout the first dozen years of the twentieth century, during the latter part of the First World War (1914–18), and in the mid-to-late 1920s. At such times, immigration soared as people from Britain and continental Europe settled the Prairie West, carved out new resource frontiers in northern Quebec, Ontario, and British Columbia, and landed jobs in burgeoning cities such as Montreal, Toronto, Winnipeg, Calgary, and Vancouver. But there were bad times, too. Widespread unemployment sank hopes in the early 1890s, in 1913–15, in the early 1920s, and especially during the Great Depression of the 1930s. In some parts of the country—notably the Maritime provinces—hard times outnumbered the good. Working people everywhere bore the brunt of the sharp, painful fluctuations in the capitalist economy.

Craft unionism, which had its roots in earlier decades, expanded and consolidated in this period. Canada's skilled workingmen (and some working women) joined craft unions in particularly large numbers during times of industrial expansion, when their skills were most in demand. Overwhelmingly these unionists opted to belong to international unions with large union memberships and headquarters in the United States. The Canadian locals of international unions often had links to other craft unions in town through city labour centrals, to other unions in Canada through affiliation with the Ottawa-based Trades and Labour Congress of Canada, and to other international unions as affiliates of the Washington-based American Federation of Labor. Craft unionists were proud of their skills, which earned them good wages (ideally, a "family wage" that enabled a husband and father to provide for his wife and children), full citizenship rights, and social respectability. In Chapter 7, Craig Heron and Steve Penfold describe how craft unionists in the era before the First World War proudly displayed their manliness and important place in their communities during public celebrations, which they organized annually on Labour Day (a statutory holiday created by Parliament in 1894).

The great majority of wage earners in early twentieth-century Canada were excluded from membership in the craft union movement. The expansion of industrial Canada created countless jobs for unskilled male labourers, many of them foreign-speaking immigrants who did the grunt work in heavy construction, mining, lumbering, and railway building and track repair. In the eyes of most craftsmen, such workers lacked the skills, respectability, and "whiteness" commensurate with craft unionism. Trade unionists said the same about most semi-skilled machine tenders who were employed in increasing numbers by large corporations in the gigantic mills and factories of such industries as steel, automobile, and pulp and paper. Most women workers also fell outside the parameters of the craft union movement. The manly pride of craftsmen and the cigar-smoking atmosphere of union halls kept women out. Moreover, women workers toiled in workplaces that most craft unionists believed were unorganizable: private homes (the workplaces of domestics and needle-trades home-workers), sweatshops in the garment industry, department and other stores, and increasingly in offices. The early twentieth-century expansion of banks and insurance companies and of corporations with their need to track production and sales created many more opportunities for white-collar employment. White, Canadian-born, young women flocked to office work, not because it was especially well paid or interesting, but because it offered more social cachet than factory work; it also provided the opportunity to dress nicely as well as a great deal more sociability than domestic service. In Chapter 8, Graham Lowe traces both the rise of office employment in Canada in the early twentieth century and the feminization of clerical work.

Mass immigration in the years 1900–1913, and again in the 1920s, signalled both the attractiveness of Canada as a land of opportunity and the intensification of social tensions. Many working people living in Canada knew that to prosper, the country needed immigrants, and yet they worried that newcomers would flood labour markets, threatening hard-won wage-rates and working conditions. Echoing the ethnic prejudices and racism of Canadian society more widely, labour spokesmen in the late nineteenth and early twentieth centuries voiced particular objections to newcomers arriving from non-traditional sources of immigration: Asia, as well as central, eastern, and southern Europe.

Opportunities on Canada's Pacific coast drew male workers from China, Japan, and India to jobs in railway and other construction, mining, lumbering, and household service. In British Columbia white workers' organizations joined with groups of middle-class people in demanding that governments stop Asian immigration and bar Asians living in Canada from access to various jobs and citizenship rights. In chapter 9, Gillian Creese documents the anti-Asian activities of white labour organizations in Vancouver from the 1880s to the 1930s. White labour leaders justified these activities by claiming that Asian workers were unorganizable, and thus a persistent threat to organized workers—a fact belied by the actual record of Asian workers' militancy in Canada.

The arrival in turn-of-the-century Canada of immigrant workers from central, eastern, and southern Europe also posed challenges to the development of worker solidarity. Excluded from craft unions because of the work they did and also because of the ethnic and racial prejudices of craft unionists, many continental European immigrants gravitated to more radical labour organizations. Some Ukrainian, Finnish, and Jewish workers, for instance, brought left-wing ideas with them from Europe, and they struggled to build left political parties and militant industrial unions here in Canada. They worked to establish these unions both among their compatriots and more broadly within the Canadian working class as a whole. In the latter endeavour they worked alongside Canadian- and British-born radicals. Several left-wing organizations emerged on the scene, including ethnic-specific ones (such as the Ukrainian Labour-Farmers' Temple Association) and ones that brought people of various backgrounds together (such as the Industrial Workers of the World, the Social-Democratic Party, and the Communist Party of Canada). Not surprisingly, employers and other defenders of the propertied interest attacked the "Reds" as serious threats to the status quo, a position echoed by some Canadian-born workers and politically moderate labour leaders. As Donald Avery demonstrates in Chapter 10, tensions peaked in Winnipeg during the city's famous general strike of 1919. Middle-class opponents of the massive walkout sought to undermine support for it by depicting it as largely the work of dangerous foreigners bent on fomenting revolution. Their depiction helped to justify the state's fierce suppression of the strike.

The 1919 general strike in Winnipeg was labour's most exhilarating event during a short period of extraordinary labour unrest that began near the end of the First World War in 1918. Strikes erupted in hundreds of workplaces across the country as workers demanded wage increases to keep pace with inflation and union recognition (i.e. that employers bargain with the union representatives chosen by employees). Coming out of a war fought "for democracy," working Canadians demanded a voice in decisions affecting them on the job (or democracy in the workplace) and various enhancements to political democracy promised by reform-minded labour politicians. Before long, however, a sharp economic downturn that began in 1921 took the wind out of the militants' sails. Employers took advantage of the situation, firing "troublemakers," refusing to bargain with union representatives chosen by workers, rolling back wages, and devising clever new schemes for keeping their workplaces union-free even when business revived. In Chapter 11, H.M. Grant explains how executives at Imperial Oil sought to avoid union recognition in 1919 by introducing its "Industrial Representation Plan." The introduction of employee-representation plans, which were taken up by several large, corporate employers in the 1920s, relied on company-dominated unions to foster labour harmony through employer-initiated consultation with employees. Many of the plans also aimed to foster employee loyalty by offering accident, sickness, death, and pension benefits and assisting with the purchase of shares in the company. By these and similar means, some corporations succeeded in avoiding genuine collective bargaining for decades. Other companies, however, soon ended up contributing to employee disillusionment either by refusing to comply with the demands of employees after consulting with them or by discontinuing popular benefits when the Depression hit in the 1930s.

Canada was wracked by economic problems during the "Dirty Thirties": collapsed demand for vital exports such as wheat, lumber, and newsprint; natural disasters in vast agricultural districts on the Prairies; and unprecedented levels of unemployment. For countless working people, the hard times were disastrous both economically and personally. Especially hard hit were young men, who could find no work and for whom government relief meant sojourns in remote work camps run by the military.

When the layoffs began during the winter of 1929–30, labour militancy all but disappeared, but as unemployment ballooned in the next few years, some workers—particularly those on the political left—began to fight back. They reasoned that the Depression demonstrated the failure of capitalism and that sweeping economic and social changes were needed to bring about equality and social justice. Organizers mobilized the unemployed into a force for progressive change, most notably during the famous On-to-Ottawa Trek begun by striking relief-camp workers in 1935. Organizers on the left took charge of the restlessness among industrial workers, who were fed up with wage cuts and speed-ups on the job. New industrial unions—much more broadly based and socially conscious than the old craft unions—rallied first under the communist-led Workers' Unity League in the early part of the decade and then, later in the decade, under the successful American-based movement, the CIO. Innovations on the labour scene extended into the cultural sphere. In Chapter 12, Bonita Bray describes the success of *Waiting for Lefty*, a play that was part of a new movement in popular entertainment: agitprop theatre. Whereas Hollywood films of the 1930s encouraged moviegoers to escape the harsh realities of their lives, agitprop theatre compelled audiences to engage with the pressing social issues of the time. Even during the darkest decade for Canadian workers, a belief in the possibility of social justice glowed brightly.

Chapter 7

The Craftsmen's Spectacle

Labour Day Parades in Canada, The Early Years

Craig Heron and Steve Penfold

The marshals had their hands full pulling together the 3,000 wage-earners who converged on Market Square in London, Ontario, on 3 September 1894, the first nationally recognized Labour Day in Canada. In due course the first union contingents headed off down the city's main streets under the blazing noonday sun. The first was a group of 75 butchers on horseback, who set the tone of respectable craftsmanship with their crisply white shirts and hats and clean baskets on their arms. Several other groups presented themselves in identical outfits: the firemen from the railway car shops in their white shirts and black felt hats; the printers in their navy blue yachting caps (the apprentices wore brown); the barbers in their plug hats and white jackets. Each group of well-dressed unionists sported at least a distinctive badge. At intervals in the procession, floats depicted the craftsmen at work as they rolled along the streets. The plumbers showed men working around "a statue of Venus taking a shower bath in public." The Industrial Brotherhood injected a political message with a small but impressive float, which "conveyed a world of meaning," according to a local newspaper: under the banner "Strike Here," a large ballot was suspended over a ballot box with the words "Masses" and "Classes" and a large X beside the "Masses." Another display was described simply as "Coxey's Army on a wagon." The city firemen and their various fire-fighting equipment also caught plenty of attention. Spread throughout the parade were several marching bands and the decorated delivery wagons of three butchers, a brewery, three steam laundries, a fuel company, a newspaper, a roofing company, and two furniture companies, whose exhibits "gave the young people matrimonially inclined something to talk about in their evening rambles." The press reported that thousands had greeted the marchers along the route and followed them into Queen's Park, where, after brief words of welcome from the mayor and labour leader Joseph Marks, they cheered the victory of the Patrons of Industry tug-of-war team over the Grand Trunk railwaymen and watched Norval Wanless easily win the 100-yard race and Mrs. A. Lockwood triumph in the married ladies' race, along with numerous other amateur sporting events. The day concluded with a "burlesque entitled 'China vs. Japan,'" in which mock battles were waged by participants in oriental outfits.[1]

This was the public programme organized by workers, without any national co-ordination and with many minor local variations, in industrial towns and cities across the country to celebrate Canada's first national Labour Day.[2] It soon became the most widespread form of collective working-class cultural creation in the country. The essential shape of the festivities had emerged over the previous decade in unofficial or merely local events as part of the working-class upsurge often called the "Great Upheaval." From the beginning, however, the project of creating this workers' holiday was inherently ambivalent. Labour Day embodied two distinct demands—one for public recognition of organized labour and its important role in industrial-capitalist society, and the other for release from the pressures of work in capitalist industry and for expanded leisure time. Once Canadian labour leaders had won an official public holiday, it was up to unionists to shape the day's events to serve labour's needs. That task could often prove too much for local workers' movements with limited resources, whose confidence and morale could be sapped by unemployment, bitter strikes, hostile courts, and transient members. It could also be frustrated by the open-endedness of a public holiday that allowed wage-earners and their families to turn the time off the job to private pleasures, rather than cultural solidarity. The tension between celebration and leisure eventually undermined the grand ideals of the original proponents of Labour Day. In many parts of the country it died out completely as a workers' festival or limped on as a spiritless exercise in commercialized civic boosterism on a public holiday without focus or common purpose. Moreover, Marxist workers' movements would mount serious cultural alternatives, especially in western Canada, that drained away much of the festival's early vitality.

The Birth of a Workers' Festival

In June 1894 the Canadian House of Commons passed legislation making the first Monday in September a statutory holiday alongside only three other secular celebrations—New Year's Day, Victoria Day, and Dominion Day.[3] Labour Day thus became the only legal public holiday in Canada devoted to the interests of a specific class or group. Canadian labour leaders had been lobbying for this legislation since the mid-1880s and had won the support of both panels of the Royal Commission on the Relations of Labour and Capital in 1889.[4] Legalizing this labour festival was only to confirm what it had already become—an established event on the local holiday calendar in several cities and towns. It was first celebrated in Toronto in 1882, Hamilton and Oshawa in 1883, London and Montreal in 1886, St. Catharines in 1887, Halifax in 1888, and Ottawa and Vancouver in 1890. Typically it was either a self-declared day off work or a local civic holiday proclaimed by the mayor. In many smaller towns and cities, however, the local labour movements used the new legal recognition in 1894 to launch their first annual celebrations; others would not follow this example until the turn of the century.[5]

This kind of event must have been in widespread discussion within the North American labour movement, especially the Knights of Labor, in the early 1880s. The Central Labor Union of New York City is usually credited with declaring the first North American Labour Day and holding the first labour festival with a parade and picnic in September 1882, but the Toronto unions took to the streets several weeks before the New York "pioneers."[6] Local labour organizations evidently responded to this inspiration at their own pace, though there was a more centralized call in 1884 from the Federation of Organized Trades and Labor Unions of the United States and Canada (the predecessor to the American Federation of Labor), which urged its affiliates to organize their own Labour Days. In 1885 it was widely celebrated in the United States. City councils and, after 1887, state governments legalized the holiday. In 1894, in the same month that the Canadian Parliament took action, the American Congress declared Labor Day a national holiday in the District of Columbia and the territories.[7]

Labour Day emerged out of the more aggressive, class-conscious workers' movements of the 1880s. They were drawing together a broad range of workers into new craft unions, local assemblies of the Knights of Labor, trades and labour councils, the first independent labour political campaigns, and, beginning in 1886, the Trades and Labor Congress of Canada.[8] Like so much else in this "Great Upheaval," the new workers' festival marked a major shift in the consciousness of many wage-earners—a rejection of industrial paternalism and a recognition that they had separate interests in industrial capitalist society that had to be promoted and defended. The first unofficial Labour Days were often appropriately called "Labor Demonstrations"[9] and were intended to be a public show of strength, determination, and high moral tone. Organizers hoped these events would build stronger bonds among unionists, inspire the unorganized to join the movement, and impress the general public with the worthiness of their cause. "The demonstration is an object lesson to the public and to the participants is very valuable," a Halifax unionist explained in 1890. "The public see the power of unions and the workers themselves get a new idea of their importance in society."[10] In Toronto's first celebration, a labour leader went further: "Such a demonstration," he thought, "would teach their detractors that within the workshops there were men of sufficient executive ability to plan and carry out works of magnitude and importance," including filling public office. [11]

Labour Day was a bold act of public cultural creation. Neither the federal government nor civic leaders prescribed any official programme for the day. Any public events would have to be organized by the unions themselves. Labour leaders thus set out to invent a new labour festival built on well-established traditions of public celebration but designed to serve new needs. In this process they parallelled other social groups that in this late-nineteenth-century period also undertook to redesign annual public holidays for their own large purposes, notably Anglo-Canadian imperialists who transformed Victoria Day into Empire Day[12] and francophone Catholics who refashioned Saint-Jean-Baptiste Day.

The rationale for the timing of this labour festival is not immediately apparent. Unlike May Day, it does not correspond with any well-established pre-industrial celebration. Initially it was a mid-summer event. The Toronto workers kicked off the country's first "labor demonstration" in late July 1882, and most of the Labour Days of the 1880s were held in July or early August, sometimes piggy-backing onto regular half-holidays on Saturday or Wednesday or on municipal civic holidays.[13] Yet gradually the timing shifted to the end of the summer and was eventually fixed on the first Monday in September by Parliament, probably to correspond to the American holiday. This was a date chosen by labour leaders, not politicians, and it suggests a working-class interest in regularizing leisure time alongside capitalist worktime—like the parallel demand for the shorter work week with a Saturday half-holiday.[14] Labour Day fell at the end of what would normally be the effective change of seasons and rhythms of manual work in the communities where it first took hold. It was also a convenient time to fill a hole in a rationalized holiday calendar between Dominion Day and Thanksgiving that did not interfere with the many local civic holidays.

Agitating for this late-summer holiday set the Canadian and American labour movements apart from most of the rest of the industrialized world, where the workers' holiday most often became May Day. Eventually, as we will see, this difference would become overtly political, but in the late nineteenth century Canadian and American workers were not rejecting May Day in favour of Labour Day.[15] In fact, the first May Day was declared in 1886 in the United States in the same working-class upsurge that created the demand for a labour festival in the fall. The nascent American Federation of Labor declared a "day of revolt—not of rest" on 1 May 1886, to demand the eight-hour day for wage-earners, and continued to call for such annual spring protests until the turn of the century. Beginning in 1890, European socialists and anarchists emulated the American example and embraced May Day as an occasion to demonstrate for shorter hours and other political demands, only intermittently rolling recreational and folkloric dimensions into the event. (The initial 1889 resolution calling for the first European May Day made no mention of a festival, which was actively opposed ideologically by some elements.) May Day, then, was a day of protest, Labour Day one of celebration. In practice, the major difference was that May Day was a voluntary, one-day work stoppage often launched in defiance of government edict and employer wrath, not a state-sanctioned holiday—a distinction that would have considerable implications.[16]

The first Labour Day, organizers created a festival of several parts that borrowed from the standard set by other holidays and community events—a parade, speeches, spectator sports, concerts, dancing, and more.[17] Each reflected a social and political vision of a properly ordered world. As the holiday evolved into a full-fledged, legalized shutdown of all workplaces, however, the labour-sponsored events would face increasingly stiff competition: not from a manipulative bourgeoisie (who undertook to inject little of their own culture into this new workers' holiday), but from new political foes within the house of labour and from the merchants of working-class leisure.

The Craftsmen's Spectacle

The centrepiece of the first Labour Day celebrations in Canada was the parade. Here was the public face that organized workingmen wanted to present to their fellow citizens and that drew far more attention than any other part of the day's festivities. The labour leaders who put together these events were making use of a well-established, extremely popular form of public display in the streets of nineteenth-century Canadian towns and cities. Civic leaders and voluntary societies occasionally organized parades to celebrate both the Canadian and the imperial public holidays—Dominion Day and Victoria Day (often known as "Queen's Birthday" and later in some parts of the country as Empire Day), as well as municipal anniversaries. The Irish paraded on their respective religious holidays, St. Patrick's Day and the "Glorious Twelfth." The Catholic Church staged huge public processions, especially in Quebec, where religion and ethnicity were interwoven, particularly on Saint-Jean-Baptiste Day. Politicians and political parties mobilized their supporters into parades before and after elections. Some voluntary associations, from fire companies and fraternal orders to Sunday Schools and temperance groups, also developed their own parading traditions. Funerals produced parades of varying size depending on the social status of the deceased. In the first hint of commercialization of these events, circuses also heralded their arrival in town with exotic, colourful parades. There were also much more disorderly parades—burlesques of public events or rowdy protests, from charivaris to spontaneous marches of angry strikers. There were clearly many reasons for parading in urban streets and many different ways of doing so. In constructing their first parades in the 1870s, 1880s, and 1890s, Canadian labour leaders selected judiciously from among these many traditions and assembled their own unique version.[18]

Parades were an important form of communication in nineteenth-century North America. As public events that passed by the doorsteps of households, shops, and manufactories in compact nineteenth-century urban spaces, they were intended to convey powerful symbolic, largely non-literate messages about appropriate social and political values and acceptable social relationships. Parades, however, were a privileged mode of communication with urban populations, since not everyone could have this kind of access to the streets. They began as spectacles of pageantry designed by the dominant classes to legitimize their class rule. Some elements of subordinate classes could be incorporated into these ceremonies, but their only independent access to this kind of street theatre was either through outlandish, carnivalesque mockery (sometimes shading over into ritualized violence) or through emulation of the traditions of the powerful.[19]

In shaping a new tradition of parading, labour leaders, like parade-makers of ethnic and other voluntary organizations, took the second route.[20] They drew primarily on nearly half a century of British North American experience of "trades processions," a parading tradition stretching back through generations to the processions organized by craft guilds in early modern Europe. These European craft organizations had not reappeared in the New World to any significant extent, but organizations of artisans had emerged and reasserted what they understood to be the symbolic and ceremonial forms of the craft. Trades processions became familiar features of important public celebrations, in which master craftsmen and early industrialists led their journeymen and apprentices through the streets as part of civic events. As the crafts began to splinter along the rupture between capitalist employer and waged worker, the new unions adopted some of the "ancient" symbols of the craft. They, too, were often incorporated into such public ceremonies as welcoming a new governor general, opening a new railway, burying a prominent politician, or launching a new nation-state in 1867.[21] In the 1860s and 1870s craftsmen in Canada began to hold their own street processions as part of their first struggles for rights and recognition. In June 1867 a huge procession through the streets of Montreal organized by the *Union nationale* and the charismatic Médéric Lanctot was undoubtedly the first craftsmen's parade wrenched out of its previous place in the hierarchically structured civic and religious parades.[22] Similarly, five years later, the Nine-Hour Leagues in southern Ontario and Quebec sponsored public demonstrations in support of shorter hours. The most celebrated, held in Hamilton on 15 May 1872, was a strike parade that wound through the industrial district of the city with dramatic, colourful craft and industrial displays.[23] A decade later the practice was revived as the workers' movement in the larger cities again found its feet. Unions would often rejoin civic processions in the future,[24] but the custom of holding their own parades was soon firmly established. Indeed, strike parades remained a separate and recurring tradition throughout the twentieth century. By the turn of the century labour processions were a central feature of Labour Day events in industrial communities across the country.[25]

The late nineteenth-century Labour Day parade was the collective creation of many different groups within the scattered working-class communities, each with its own special flavour based on local industries and occupations, cultural mix, recent industrial relations, and resident artistic talent. Local Labour Day Committees co-ordinated the overall shape of the event and determined the order of the participants, perhaps giving the oldest union or a group of newly organized workers a place of prominence at the head of the parade. They would also attempt to stimulate creativity with prizes for the best displays. But individual unions and groups of company employees generally organized, designed, and most often built their own contributions (no doubt with some help from the women in their families). Collectively they shaped the ceremonial form for their new public celebration. They did so, however, within broader social constraints that defined public order and limited use of the streets. Municipal ordinances and professional policing had brought new definitions of acceptable collective behaviour in public.[26] Beyond getting parade permits, avoiding repression on the one hand and being recognized as respectable on the other meant conforming to well-established conventions about orderly processions.

The parade was designed to send a series of messages. Above all, it was meant to show the massed strength of the local labour movement, but it was also to convey the meaning of the movement to the wage-earners' families, neighbours, and fellow citizens. The first Labour Day organizers were centrally concerned with presenting the respectability of workingmen within a democratically constituted society of producers. They wanted to ensure that workers could lift their heads proudly and march through the main streets of the town or city as full citizens without scorn or condescension and with respect for their valuable contributions to the evolving urban society. In the process they also implied what in their eyes constituted the legitimate elements of this society. The most important step towards respectability came when workingmen shed grubby overalls and aprons and strode forth in their best shirts, ties, jackets, and hats. Although some wore special outfits to symbolize their particular trade, they never marched in their actual working clothes. Some even donned fancy-dress clothes with silk top hats.[27] They also insisted on full public acceptance by marching along the main public streets of the towns and cities, not merely in the working-class districts where they lived.

Respectability was inherent in the very structure of the Labour Day parades. Like so many other parade-makers in the period, labour leaders took military processions as a legitimizing model.[28] Each procession was headed by a marshal mounted on a horse, often followed by a contingent of mounted policemen or uniformed firemen. All participants marched in disciplined and orderly formation, kept in line by assistant marshals, "marking time with soldierly precision," according to one reporter.[29] The bands interspersed through the parade specialized in heavily syncopated marching music. The various kinds of uniforms on display had some military inspiration. The bands were invariably clad in quasi-military outfits, while specific unions often turned the work clothes of their trade into a stylized, though certainly non-military, uniform that all their members would wear. Little or nothing in the parades drew on the more disorderly customs of masking, mocking, and defaming that had flourished on urban streets throughout the nineteenth century.

Yet emulation of the powerful had its limits. Despite the debt to military conventions, the militia itself, with all its pomp, hierarchy, and weaponry, was never invited to participate (that is, until veterans joined the processions after World War I).[30] The lack of military content is a significant departure from the parading traditions of other public holidays, where the military might be the only institution sustaining a formal recognition of the holiday in the locality. The lack of military content also seems to be a departure even from the tradition of trades processions, which might occasionally contain the local regiment or military band.[31] Nor were the clergy invited to participate. Until the Catholic labour movement reached sufficient strength in the 1920s to hold separate mass processions, Labour Day parades were thoroughly secular and contained no religious imagery. Catholic bishops could bless the marchers beforehand, as they often did in Montreal,[32] and clergymen might grace Labour Day platforms later in the day. But churches and their various moral-reform offshoots were never invited to contribute floats or marching contingents to the parades.[33]

The parade-makers were quite prepared to highlight workers' identities as citizens in a democratic country. Generally the only non-unionists regularly included were the mayor and aldermen, who were invariably given places of prominence, generally in carriages near the head of the parade, as the popularly elected representatives of the people. The Union Jack appeared prominently at many points in every procession, though in many English-Canadian cities it was frequently paired, or "entwined," with the Stars and Stripes in an assertive declaration of international labour solidarity.[34] In Quebec parades the flag most often displayed was the French tricolour (which often flew in Ottawa parades as well).[35] At the turn of the century, working-class citizenship in Canada could have another international dimension—membership in the British Empire. Beginning with Queen Victoria's Diamond Jubilee and extending through the Boer War, some paraders introduced the imperial theme into their presentation. Union Jacks fluttered from many more floats, and portraits of the Queen and figures of Britannia looked down from a few floats. In 1902 a section of the Winnipeg parade was devoted to a presentation of the British Empire in which a float with Britannia enthroned was followed by several marchers costumed to represent the various ethnic groups within the Empire.[36] This whiff of jingoism was rare before the war, however. In fact, in the early years of Labour Day parading and from time to time thereafter, there could be hints that citizenship was a contested concept. The Saint John ship labourers carried a banner in 1883 with the inscription "We demand universal suffrage," and another in 1894 declaring, "The bone and sinew of this country must be recognized in its politics." The slogans in a Montreal procession included "We Want to Be Aldermen," "We Want Honest Government," and "Abolish Property Qualifications for Aldermen" (along with calls for free public education, playgrounds, and free libraries). As we have seen, some London workers used their float in 1894 to assert the rights of the "masses" over the "classes."[37] In London in the 1890s and in Toronto and Port Arthur just before the war, suffrage organizations joined the parades with their provocative slogan "Votes for Women," though these were rare moments in the long series of parades.[38] Overall the emphasis on democratic citizenship declined in the 1890s along with the Knights of Labor.

Craftsmen were more than citizens, however: they were producers. Their parade organizers aspired to artistic representation of the distinct and "ancient" traditions of specific trades and the values and practices they carried forward into the new industrial period. By the end of the nineteenth century there were still some visible forms of craft symbolism in the parades. King Crispin, for example, appeared in the first Labour Day procession in Toronto in 1882.[39] In a similar vein, butchers kept alive their tradition of participating in the parades on horseback and dressed in white.[40] Printers frequently brought along one or more boys dressed in red and adorned with horns and tail as "printer's devils."[41]

More commonly craft-workers unfurled beautiful silk banners with striking symbolic depictions of their craft and its central symbols, along with slogans declaring universal principles. Their themes and images had Christian and masonic inspiration, but increasingly reflected the new industrialism of the period. Typically local artists commissioned to produce the banners incorporated some combination of the tools and products of the trade. The Halifax shipwrights' and caulkers' banner, for example, bore a shield showing the tools of the two crafts and "a marine view having a schooner on the slip abreast of the lighthouses, shortening sail as she approaches the harbor." Some dealt more directly with immediate issues. The Halifax carpenters and joiners carried "a representation of two men working on an arch, and another about to put on his coat, at the same time pointing to a clock in the background and exclaiming: 'Nine hours constitutes a day's work.'" The labourers' new banner was more conciliatory, displaying two happy human figures representing labour and capital.[42]

The inscriptions beneath this imagery declared either universal principles—"Unity Founded on Equity is the Strongest Bond of Society," "By Diligence and Perseverance We Overcome All Things," "Labor Creates All Wealth," or the ubiquitous "Labor Conquers All"—or more specific claims of one craft group, such as the printers' claims to be "The art preservative of all arts." The banners floating over early Labour Day parades increasingly contained less allegory and more slogans and allusions to current concerns. They announced themes of craft brotherhood, the value of the manual producer and his toil, a commitment to shorter hours, and a determined but open-handed approach to employers.[43] By the turn of the century, more of these messages were appeals to consumers to buy goods marked with the union label or to support the early closing of retail shops.[44] The artistry and mythology were also fading by this point. They more often contained only the names and numbers of the union locals with a simple emblem of an international union.[45]

In most Labour Day parades, skilled workmen also carried on the tradition of putting their craftsmanship on display as a kind of street theatre, to the evident delight of spectators.[46] Some proudly carried the tools of their trades—the moulders' tampers or the boilermakers' hammers.[47] Others showed off the equipment they worked with—the longshoremen's huge model ships,[48] the firemen's glittering wagons and apparatus, and the electrical workers' blazing electrified floats,[49] among others.[50] Other groups showed off heaps of the products of their crafts.[51] Occasionally skilled men presented a symbolic creation constructed from the materials of their trade—such as the Toronto and Winnipeg carpenters' intricate banners of the 1890s made of different coloured wood shavings and the Ottawa tinsmiths' 1898 float constructed entirely of zinc in the patterns of fancy cornice work.[52]

Most fascinating for the crowds were the more animated floats that showed craftsmen at work—what late-nineteenth-century journalists liked to call "allegorical cars." Printers often manned a press from which a printed sheet was thrown to the crowds.[53] Cigarmakers and bakers tossed out samples of the goods they also made as they rolled through the streets.[54] Barbers could sometimes be seen shaving faces or cutting hair.[55] Almost everywhere, building tradesmen put on a good show: bricklayers put up walls, chimneys, or even small cottages; stonecutters shaped granite; lathers nailed up their wooden frames; plasterers fashioned fancy arches; painters slapped on paint or papered a room; and carpenters constructed small buildings, all while riding atop a wagon.[56] Blacksmiths, boilermakers, and moulders could put on dazzling displays of sound and light with their small furnaces and hot iron.[57] In Nanaimo coal miners presented a tableau of their work underground, "even to the miner with his fuse about to set off a blast, and an immense lump of coal," while fishers from the Fraser valley had two boats on their floats in the 1900 Vancouver parade "illustrating the catching of sockeye."[58] Even some new skills working with machinery in lumber mills or machine shops were on display.[59]

In the second half of the nineteenth century, this craft cultural tradition had taken a new turn as exhibitions of workmanship were often set up on floats bearing a company name, a visible symbol of the widespread industrial paternalism of the early industrial era in Canada. The working-class paraders thus simultaneously demonstrated their technical skills and advertised their employers' products. When wage-earners began to construct their own street spectacles, they incorporated both craft and commercial forms of display and even encouraged local firms to contribute decorated floats or carriages purely aimed at advertising their products.[60] Sometimes these businesses provided entertainment with employees working on the back of a float, occasionally offering free samples.[61] Again, however, the working-class parade-makers had recast the traditions. They rejected the older industrial paternalism and celebrated independently the high value of skilled manual labour to the specific firms for which they worked and to the well-being of their communities in general. As much as the practice of their craftsmanship might be tied to specific local firms, their employers were not invited to march with them.[62] This was a parade of wage-earners.

Not just any wage-earners, however: more specifically, it was a parade of wage-earning craftsmen who had organized themselves into unions. Above all else, Labour Day in its infancy was a celebration of craft unionism. It flourished only where craftsmen had reached sufficient numbers and shared a sufficient sense of injustice in their workplace to organize successful unions. It never appeared in company towns, and much less often in resource-based communities, such as mining towns.[63] The organizers were generally a committee of the local trades and labour council, and, aside from the commercial floats, participation in the procession was normally limited to unionists.[64] Prizes for the largest union turnout were part of the incentive to present a show of impressive strength, so that the entire community could be reminded of how big and powerful the local craft union movement was. It was not uncommon to read a journalist's report on popular amazement at the actual size of the local labour movement that marched through the streets.[65] Here, then, was a crucial ingredient in the working-class definition of respectability. These men were not just scrubbed, sober, and orderly; they were organized, determined, and proud of their collective independence of their employers' paternalistic, authoritarian control.

The exclusiveness of these organizations was clear to all those who watched them march by.

At a minimum, each contingent of paraders had special badges and sometimes colourful sashes. More striking were all the uniform-like costumes that individual unions wore and that set them apart as occupations. Boilermakers in "spotless overalls of blue," painters in "natty white uniforms," blacksmiths in "coarse brown aprons emblazoned with a horseshoe," and fur workers in "the regulation costume of white, not omitting caps and aprons" in the 1900 Toronto parade were typical. Alternatively a union might decide to deck out all its marching members in the same distinctive outfits. In the same Toronto procession, for example, the cigarmakers wore black alpaca coats and white trousers, the bread drivers straw hats and white coats, the machinists blue coats and matching caps, the moulders "neat dark suits," and the plumbers straw hats, dark suits, and matching ties.[66] This kind of costuming both accented the tight bonds among the group of marchers and set them apart from their audience. A Labour Day parade was not a participatory event; there were no calls for onlookers to join in—in contrast to the first European May Day marches. This was instead a spectacle to be watched and admired and to convey important lessons.

Most striking, perhaps, was what was missing from this presentation of "Labour."[67] Occasionally in the 1890s and at the end of World War I, farmers' organizations were invited to join as fellow "producers."[68] But, until at least the 1930s, the only white-collar workers who found a place in these spectacles were a few male retail clerks (most unionized clerical and quasi-professional workers, including teachers, kept their distance from the labour movement in any case). Rarely did less skilled wage-earners find their way into the parades before World War I. Typically those who did were specialized workers such as builders' labourers, whose close working relationship with the craftsmen in their industry gave them some leverage in organizing and bargaining, or particular groups of transportation workers such as longshoremen, trainmen, or street-railway conductors and motormen who struggled to adapt the craft union model to their needs.[69] Unlike the craftsmen, poorly paid seasonal workers might not even be able afford the time off for an unpaid holiday.[70]

By the early 1900s the absence of the less skilled meant that these were preponderantly parades of white anglophones and francophones, inaccessible to African and Native Canadians, and the newcomers from southern and eastern Europe and Asia who increasingly filled the jobs at the bottom of the occupational ladder and who were rarely unionized before World War I.[71] On the few occasions when people of colour appeared in these marches, they were presented as curiosities, not fellow workers. "It ... amused some spectators to see White's express led by a black man," a Saint John reporter noted in 1894. The "coloured gentlemen" who threw out plug tobacco at the end of Montreal's parade the same year were also an unsual sight and were, in fact, on board a company, not a union, float. Two "coloured men" marching with the Ottawa local of the builders' labourers in 1901 caught the eye of an obviously amazed reporter.[72] Plumbers' unions sometimes used black youngsters as comic accents to the gleaming white enamel fixtures on their floats. In one case in Toronto, the tableau was an older women trying to scrub the "dirt" off the black boy.[73] The few Native people who appeared were incorporated as exotic athletes and as circus clowns: the 1883 and 1884 parades in Hamilton integrated an "Indian Band of musicians and their dusky comrades in feathers and paint, who were to contribute to the afternoon's amusement, a game of lacrosse"; the *Spectator* reporter recorded their image as "quite ferocious and romantic and all that sort of thing." Several years later the Vancouver parade organizers awarded a prize for the "most comical Indian float," and the three Natives who appeared on a float of the Montreal Harbour Commission employees were reported to have "caused lots of amusement with their antics."[74] No Asian workers from British Columbia's fish-packing plants and sawmills ever got invitations to join the west-coast marchers. In fact, Victoria's tailors carried a banner in 1901 blaming the Chinese for their plight: "Only a few of us left; the rest driven out by Mongolian competition."[75]

Women were equally rare sights in the labour parades, though they were crucial participants in the cheering crowds. The few spaces they found in the processions epitomized the gender identities taking shape in working-class communities. No more than a handful of the thousands of "working girls" who were filling industrial jobs in Canada's First Industrial Revolution participated.[76] They entered the parades as wage-earners in two different ways depending on whether employers or unions had organized their participation. Long before the emergence of distinct Labour Day celebrations, some firms had incorporated women into the working tableaux on their company floats.[77] On the rare occasions when unions organized a contingent of female unionists (they seem never to have been allowed to organize themselves in these early parades), the women were almost never shown at work or in any version of their work-clothes.[78] Instead they were presented as respectable, well-dressed young ladies. In the first Labour Day march in Hamilton in 1883, the Knights of Labor gathered "a representative body of female operatives in the shoe and other factories of the city" and paraded them "with true gallantry" in union cabs. The next year, according to the local press, "whenever the ladies in the procession passed along they were greeted with loud cheers and continued applause" (they were led by the Knights' only prominent female activist in Canada, Katie McVicar). The featured speaker in the 1884 event, Henry George, also praised the female participants in the procession and quoted one local unionist: "The women are the best men we have." Yet, a decade later, a man in the Toronto parade also won applause for cross-dressing to clown as a woman on a bicycle, no doubt mocking the pretensions of the "New Woman" of the late nineteenth century.[79] In a more serious vein, the Winnipeg tailors arranged an unusually provocative melodrama on a moving wagon in 1898 to attack the sweating system, which highlighted the victimization of working women and, presumably, the degradation of the craft: "Several women, young and old, were busily plying their needles while over them stood the foreman whip in hand, ready to lay it across the shoulders of the first unfortunate wretch whom he should discover straightening her back for an instant."[80] Women were treated with similar patronizing ambivalence elsewhere in succeeding years.[81]

Generally, as paraders, they were constrained both by the masculine aura of military-style processions and by the nineteenth-century bourgeois standards of feminine respectability that frowned on women walking in the street.[82] Only two parades before World War I had women actually walking in the street. In Montreal in 1907 the garment workers included "a strong contingent of women, who all walked, and were ornamented with brilliant sashes, thrown over one's shoulder and knotted at the waist."[83] Six years later one female shoemaker created a sensation in London by marching with her fellow unionists and carrying "her share of the regalia." Despite the applause she received, her action was rare.[84] Well into the twentieth century, women in Labour Day parades would normally only be seen waving safely and primly from union carriages or automobiles.

In a few other instances, women appeared not as workers but as symbols of some higher principles—including nationalism or imperial sentiment. They would then play the role of a classically draped symbolic figure.[85] In 1872 the Hamilton sewing-machine manufacturer presented six women not only as seamstresses but also as clearly labelled symbols of the Canadian provinces. At the turn of the century the Winnipeg draymen's union put a woman at the centre of heaps of Manitoba grains to represent Canada, while the Ottawa painters' union sat a female statue of "Art" on its white and gold float, with "four little girls in white and wreathed in flowers." In Nanaimo a woman posed as the "Goddess of Commerce" and in Victoria as Queen Titania.[86] On a number of occasions, women on floats played the familiar role of Britannia.[87]

Aside from promotion of some products for domestic use such as sewing machines or furniture, no floats or carriages in these early Labour Day parades ever gave symbolic or ceremonial recognition to the domestic labour that working-class women were expected to perform for the collective survival of the working-class family. Nor did floats recognize or portray women's work in the home.[88] In a few places, they were honoured in the role designated for them by the male union leadership's role as supportive housewives, namely, as ladies' auxiliaries or as members of Union Label Committees. Again, they had to climb into the respectable patriarchal safety of carriages in order to participate.[89] Of course, behind the scenes, women often played a vital role in these labour festivals in preparing food for the spectators of the sporting events later in the day.[90]

Children were equally rare in the parades as clearly defined wage-earners. In some cases, apprentices might march behind the journeymen in their craft (actually, few crafts still had them), and in a few cities a contingent of newsboys might appear.[91] But the labouring children from large textile, tobacco, or lumber mills never marched with their fathers, brothers, and neighbours.[92] In early Montreal parades banners decried child labour, and in 1893 London cigarmakers carried a large imitation cigar bearing the motto, "No child labor."[93] Children typically found a role only as symbols or ornaments—the printer's devil, the driver of a tiny pony cart, or figures in a symbolic tableau or a display of products.[94]

It is clear, then, that these processions were affirmations of respectable white working-class "manhood"—from the pride in manual strength and craft skill, to the message that these men were the breadwinners of their families who did not need other family members in the paid labour force. In the words of an Ottawa labour columnist, Labour Day was the "practical recognition of brotherhood and fatherhood."[95] None of these features should be particularly surprising. Labour Day emerged out of the milieu of determined craft unionists and "Labour Reformers," who were appalled at the degradation of their workplace customs and routines brought about since mid-century by the first generations of industrial capitalists. They had strengthened their craft organizations (in some cases by joining hands with their American counterparts) and had established tighter procedures for controlling their craft practices. They had also built organizational links of solidarity across occupational boundaries. In Canada the "Great Upheaval," at the centre of which stood the Knights of Labor, was an expression of outrage at the accelerating pace of capitalist industrialization and the hollow promises of an earlier form of industrial paternalism. It was also a vigorous reassertion of the dignity of the respectable workingman, the wage-earning craftsman. Holding onto that respectability meant standing tall against the use of cheaper labour to degrade their crafts, including women and children.

Labour Day marchers nonetheless kept their demonstration polite. Parading through the streets on a labour holiday was intended as an implicitly political act aimed at publicizing the positive alternative to the apparent degradation of work in this new industrial order that this labour movement offered. Unlike the May Day demonstrations, in which the marchers carried a petition to state authorities, the Labour Day parade was not intended as an overt act of protest. In the words of the Toronto *Globe* in 1894: "With us Labor Day is less a demonstration of labor militant than of labor argumentative."[96] Initially, then, Labour Day was the symbolic representation of the working-class struggle for independence from paternalistic or repressive control and for recognition as a secure, respected place in a reformed industrial society. It carried the clear message that securing that status would require separate, collective organization and solidarity. Labour Day was thus the cultural expression of the sober determination and optimism that also built craft unions, independent newspapers, labour-controlled co-operative businesses, and the independent labour parties in the 1880s.[97]

Decline and Decay

Labour Day processions seem to have been quite popular with the broader public—indeed, local reports suggest they were among the most popular street events on the holiday calendar.[98] Well into the early 1900s, the parades and other official Labour Day activities were front-page news in local newspapers. Shopkeepers readily strung up coloured bunting along the parade route, and thousands of spectators packed the sidewalks each year to watch and often to applaud or cheer particular union contingents. Here in particular, local journalists noted, were the women and children of working-class families waving at their menfolk, demonstrating the bonds of community between paraders and their audience.[99] Certainly the parade-makers had public support for continuing their annual processions. At the turn of the century, in a new burst of economic activity and craft-union organizing, Labour Day parades were staged in far more industrial centres across the country, drew in many more workers, and blossomed into impressive street performances.

Yet the craftsmen's spectacle was in trouble in many communities in the decade before the war. Some unions began ignoring the call to participate, and those that did sometimes had to threaten fines for members who failed to appear for the march.[100] Journalists in many places also reported fewer floats and uniforms. The sparkle was disappearing from the spectacle. In this context, the surviving parades frequently took on a more commercial cast. Labour leaders came to see Labour Day programmes as a major source of funds for their other activities throughout the year and often grumbled about the poor returns for all the effort and expense involved in putting together these street spectacles.[101] In order to stimulate competition among the unions to create interesting displays, cash prizes had to be offered.[102] The money for prizes most often had to be raised from local merchants and businessmen, who had to be convinced that holding a parade would keep townsfolk in town and even draw in visitors to stimulate the local economy. This fundraising became time-consuming and often unrewarding work for the volunteers on the Labour Day Committees.[103] Many trades and labour councils eventually cancelled their processions to concentrate on sports and entertainment, or gave up holding any kind of "demonstration" at all. There was a small revival that paralleled the renewed militancy of the immediate prewar years, but, in most of western Canada in particular, Labour Day parades died out forever with World War I.[104] What had gone wrong?

Organizing parades with limited funds and volunteer labour had always taxed local unions. Few trades and labour councils could pull together a march every year before the turn of the century.[105] Often factors such as heavy rain, or commentary in the local press criticizing a parade for not measuring up to past performances, could be demoralizing.[106] In some smaller centres, instead of making their own parade each year, a large contingent of marchers might leave town to join a procession in a neighbouring town.[107] But there were deepening problems. The deterioration of the parading tradition often reflected what has been called the "crisis of the craftsman."[108] The first Labour Day parades had always drawn on the buoyancy and confidence of local craft unions, and it was the revival of these organizations across the country at the turn of the century that had temporarily reinvigorated the celebrations. After 1903, however, these unions were increasingly on the defensive in the face of employer hostility and state indifference. In fact, the foundations of craft unionism were under systematic attack. Many skilled men witnessed their role in industrial production destroyed or diminished in an emerging second industrial revolution. Across the evolving industrial landscape, fewer workers probably felt the craftsman's independent pride in their contribution to industry and may well have been more interested in escape than in celebration. In this context, craft unions could often ill afford the time and money to prepare for a parade that seemed to be doing little to strengthen their positions in the community.

Many Canadian unionists seemed to quietly abandon the expectations of the earnest Labour Day founders that public displays of pride and determination could make much difference to the ongoing battles for the well-being of workingmen.[109]

It is not entirely surprising, then, that the surviving union-sponsored parades often lost much of their original working-class vitality. With the emergence of more mass-production labour processes, it was increasingly more difficult to present small tableaux of workers practising their trade on the back of a wagon. Reporters across the country noted with regret the gradual disappearance of the "allegorical cars." There was a noticeable shift to emphasizing the product, rather than the process, of workers' labour and thus a higher identification with specific firms.[110] More and more, the parades relied for their colour and attractiveness on the company-sponsored floats, carriages, and cars that had always been woven through or tacked on to the end of the parade.[111] Ultimately, these commercialized parades became increasingly a form of civic boosterism. Municipal governments added their support with regular contributions of firefighting equipment and floats from various works departments.[112]

Increasingly, moreover, craft union leaders were not alone in defining the meaning of this holiday. Invariably local newspapers published editorials reflecting on workers and work, and some local clergymen preached "Labour Sermons" on the day before the festivities, often prompted by requests from local unions and, in many Protestant churches, eventually following guidelines distributed by the Social Service Council of Canada.[113] Politicians invited to address Labour Day crowds added their perspectives. These community commentators frequently hyperbolically proclaimed the great strides workers had made in overcoming oppression and exploitation, and commended the labour leadership for their accomplishments. Yet these were also regular occasions to interpret the polite respectability of the parades as evidence of the alleged "prosperity" of Canadian workers and, by extension, of the local economy.[114] Frequently, too, commentators contrasted the "contentment" of these respectable workingmen with the radicalism of Europe's May Day marchers.[115] They also seized the occasion to expand the definition of "Labour" to include more than unionized manual labour, since—as they argued—this was a holiday for the whole population, and lectured unions on the need for responsible, cautious behaviour in full co-operation with capital.[116] In fact, many newspapers liked to link the evident respectability of the event with class collaboration. In the words of a 1903 Toronto *Globe* editorial:

> Anything that serves to obliterate a feeling of inferiority and cultivate among workmen a pride in their work must ultimately tend to lessen the social cleavage and caste distinction that now lead to such class movements as the celebration of Labor Day.[117]

The public discourses on Labour Day thus quickly shifted beyond the confines intended by its founders.

Lots of workers had stopped listening anyway. The tension between a labour festival and a less structured public holiday increased after the turn of the century. Local labour leaders found themselves trying to hold workers' attention on the officially sponsored parades, amateur sporting events, concerts, and other activities, while other forms of holiday fun proliferated. Many other organizations started holding their own social and athletic events to draw crowds. Sports associations in particular took full advantage of this summertime holiday to stage competitions and meets, and in most major cities exhibitions ran during the week of Labour Day to drain away fun-seekers (the Canadian National Exhibition drew from towns across southern Ontario).[118] Taverns, pool-halls, vaudeville and movie theatres, amusement parks, and ice-cream parlours likewise opened their doors to eager holidaymakers. "Baseball, football, automobile racing, and hundreds of private picnics, ministered to the pleasure of the holiday makers," a Winnipeg reporter noted in 1905. "Performances were given afternoon and evening at the various theatres."[119] Many workers simply took to the streets to enjoy the holiday casually. In 1913 a *Globe* reporter found on Toronto's Yonge Street "one long incessant crowd wandering aimlessly for the most part, but apparently enjoying to the full this easy, innocent form of Labor Day recreation." He encountered congestion at the entrance to every restaurant and movie theatre, and was particularly struck by the steady streams of workingmen who "kept the doors in constant swing" outside bars.[120] Rather than spend the day in the town or city, more and more urban dwellers wanted to escape for the day. From the beginning, railroads and steamer companies arranged special Labour Day excursions to parks, beaches, or other points in the countryside.[121]

Labour Day thus lost its original focus. This was not the only public holiday drained of collective celebration. By the early years of the twentieth century, the main holidays on the Canadian calendar had similarly become occasions more for private pleasure than for public spectacle. Most years these holidays came and went with little or no attempt to use them for civic purposes.[122]

Some labour leaders had watched with amazement and disgust as workers drifted away from the forms of earnest, rational leisure envisioned by the founders of Labour Day toward more commercial and individualized pursuits. In 1903 the *Toronto Toiler* regretted that Labour Day had become "merely a day of meaningless parades and silly picnics.... The opportunity to set workingmen thinking when thus brought together is practically lost sight of."[123] One unnamed "prominent laborite" standing amid the bustle of activity outside a bar on Yonge Street in 1913 declared that "it was a shame the bars were allowed to keep open on Labor Day in view of the weakness of many who might better have been with their families spending the nickels on innocent and educative entertainment at the Exhibition."[124] Other more narrow-minded Labour Day organizers were simply frustrated at their inability to be better commercializers. All too often, their efforts to turn their programmes of sports and entertainment into successful fundraisers for local trades and labour council projects floundered in the face of competing activities. They added vaudeville shows, baby contests, and other commercial entertainment, with varying success.[125] Labour Day had become yet another terrain on which groups of workers split over an appropriate culture within industrial capitalist society, but it provided proof that after 1900, the moralists lost ground and the commercializers made rapid headway in providing leisure outlets.[126]

The most disgusted critics of the diluted, commercialized Labour Day programmes were Canada's early socialists. The editor of the *Western Clarion* referred to the holiday as "Slave Day" and to the parade as a "display of toadyism" and "a tawdry, vulgar display of commodities for sale, including the commodity labor-power."[127] Another thought Labour Day had become equivalent to "Dollar Day, Raisin Day, Mothers' Day and sundry other such days as Commercial Democracy bestows on us once in a while."[128] After 1906 socialists in some large cities began organizing alternative activities on May Day (usually bringing down the wrath of the local police forces). For the next half century there would be a tug of war between the right and the left in the workers' movement over which festival to honour, though May Day remained a more limited event until the 1920s and 1930s.[129]

Conclusion

Labour Day, then, began as the "invented tradition" of unionized craftsmen who created a popular festival of working-class pride, determination, and respectability and convinced the Canadian state to honour it. In its original design, parades were the most important public element in the day's planned activities. They became perhaps the richest collective art form that organized workers in Canada ever developed (though their dominant motif of orderly respectability certainly kept the fanciful and the fantastic under wraps). They were a dramatic public statement by organized craftworkers about themselves and their society. Within a decade after its official recognition by Canadian Parliament, however, Labour Day was losing much of its original earnest moral tone and symbolic impact. The public spectacles declined along with the craftsman and his vision. Soon after the turn of the century, craft unions found themselves driven from the heart of the new mass-production industries, and their ancient symbols meant less and less in the new industrial order that had so little respect for the "arts and mysteries" of craftsmanship. Their corporatist vision of co-operation and mutual tolerance with capital was shattered by aggressive industrialists and challenged by sceptical socialists, who organized an alternative festival. Ultimately, too, a workers' festival with its roots in the small-scale, community-based, public celebrations of the nineteenth century was swamped by the widening commodification of popular culture after the turn of the century. Many workers turned their backs on the earnest public moralism of the Labour Day pioneers and found more comfort in private pleasures and commercialized fun.

The original craftsmen's spectacle was thus moribund by World War I. Yet Canadian workers never allowed the idea of an annual workers' festival to die. A second phase in the history of Labour Day emerged after World War I, along with more militant and radical workers' movements. In several cities in central and eastern Canada, the September celebrations were revived or resuscitated and injected with a new note of protest alongside the merely colourful and festive. Throughout the twentieth century, the Labour Day parade was brought back as a theatre of protest in periods of intensifying industrial conflict. Thousands of working people in Canada apparently still believe that taking to the streets once a year will remind others that they are part of a movement united in pursuing common concerns and that they will not abandon hope of achieving them. In that sense, while their impact may be more limited, the spirit of the Labour Day pioneers is still alive and well.

Endnotes

1. *Advertiser* (London), September 4, 1894, p. 1.
2. Much of the following discussion is based on a review of annual reports on Labour Day events in local newspapers in major Canadian cities from Halifax to Vancouver. For the striking similarities in the celebrations in another part of the British Empire, see Bert Roth, "Labour Day in New Zealand," in John E. Martin and Kerry Taylor, eds. *Culture and the Labour Movement: Essays in New Zealand Labour History* (Palmerston North, New Zealand: Dunmore Press, 1991), pp. 304–314. Labour Day was even transported to colonial Africa by British and Australian miners as a festival of the white elite of the working class. Terence Ranger, "The Invention of Tradition in Colonial Africa," in Eric Hobsbawm and Terence Ranger, ads., *The Invention of Tradition* (Cambridge: Cambridge University Press, 1983), p. 213.
3. The first public holidays declared by Parliament in 1872 were Sundays, New Year's Day, Good Friday, Christmas Day, the birthday of the reigning sovereign, and an unspecified thanksgiving day. Dominion Day was added only in 1879. Quebec had several additional holidays—The Epiphany, All Saints' Day, The Ascension, Conception Day, The Annunciation, Corpus Christi, and St. Peter's and St. Paul's Day (the last three were removed from the list in 1890). Statutes of Canada, 1872, p. 33; 1879, p. 305; 1887, p. 4; 1893, p. 107.
4. Gregory S. Kealey, ed., *Canada Investigates Industrialism: The Royal Commission on the Relations of Labor and Capital, 1889* (abridged) (Toronto: University of Toronto Press, 1973), pp. 15, 36, 54. The only words exchanged in the House of Commons about the bill were a question about whether workingmen wanted the measure and Prime Minister Sir John Thompson's reply that there had been "hundreds of petitions presented to this House from all quarters." Canada, House of Commons Debates (Ottawa: Queen's Printer, 1894), vol. 1, p. 2410; vol. 2, p. 4594; Statutes of Canada, 1894, pp. 57–58. It is likely that the national executive of the Trades and Labor Congress ultimately pressed Thompson into recognizing the day as a public holiday, although it is not clear

that the TLC leaders felt it was a priority. Although the annual TLC convention passed resolutions calling for the executive to lobby for a Labour Day holiday on four occasions (1888, 1890, 1892, and 1893), the executive never reported doing so until 1894. See Public Archives of Canada, Trades and Labor Congress of Canada, Proceedings, 1886–1894.

5. *Globe* (Toronto), July 24, 1882, p. 6; August 4, 1883, p. 2; *Herald* (Halifax), August 3, 1888, p. 3; *Advertiser* (London), September 6, 1892, p. 5; *Spectator* (Hamilton), August 4, 1883, p. 1; *Palladium of Labor* (Hamilton), August 11, 1883, pp. 1, 6; August 18, 1883; *Journal* (Ottawa), August 30, 1890, p. 6; *Gazette* (Montreal), September 7, 1886, p. 3; September 3, 1889, p. 5; Bryan D. Palmer, *A Culture in Conflict: Skilled Workers and Industrial Capitalism, 1860–1914* (Montreal and Kingston: McGill-Queen's University Press, 1979), p. 57; Eugene Forsey, *Trade Unions in Canada, 1812–1902* (Toronto: University of Toronto Press, 1982), pp. 293–299, 302, 311–312, 315, 317–318, 320, 324–325, 330–331, 335, 339. Saint John also witnessed a labour demonstration in 1883, when a large trades procession was held in conjunction with the centennial of the United Empire Loyalists. This type of piggy-backing onto other events was not an uncommon form of "first" local Labour Day celebration. In Ottawa, for example, the first Labour Day was proclaimed by the city's mayor in 1890 to coincide with the national convention of the Trades and Labor Congress, which was held in the capital that year. The Saint John procession's connection to the Labour Day tradition seems tenuous, however, since no other Labour Day celebrations were apparently held there until the official declaration of the day in 1894. For details on the 1883 trades procession, see Bonnie Huskins, "Public Celebrations in Victorian Saint John and Halifax" (Ph.D. thesis, Dalhousie University, 1990).
6. Jonathan Grossman, "Who Is the Father of Labor Day?," *Labor History*, vol. 14, no. 4 (Fall 1973), pp. 612–623. Ironically, the supposed "father" of Labour Day in the United States, the New York carpenters' leader P.J. McGuire, was invited to speak at the 1882 Toronto "demonstration," but was unable to attend because of his wife's illness. *Globe* (Toronto), July 24, 1882, p. 6.
7. Michael Kazin and Steven J. Ross, "America's Labor Day: The Dilemma of a Workers' Celebration," *Journal of American History*, vol. 78, no. 4 (March 1992), pp. 1294–1323.
8. On Canadian workers' movements in the 1880s, see Forsey, *Trade Unions in Canada*; Gregory S. Kealey and Bryan D. Palmer, *Dreaming of What Might Be: The Knights of Labor in Ontario, 1880–1900* (New York: Cambridge University Press, 1982); Ian McKay, "'By Wisdom, Wile or War': The Provincial Workmen's Association and the Struggle for Working-Class Independence in Nova Scotia, 1879–97," *Labour/Le Travail*, vol. 18 (Fall 1986), pp. 13–62; Paul Phillips, *No Power Greater: A Century of Labour in British Columbia* (Vancouver: B.C. Federation of Labour, 1967), pp. 11–26; Bryan D. Palmer, *Working-Class Experience: Rethinking the History of Canadian Labour, 1800–1901* (Toronto: McCleiland & Stewart, 1992), pp. 117–154.
9. In the nineteenth century, the word "'demonstration' had not taken on its late-twentieth-century connotation of protest. Many other groups such as fraternal societies and the YMCA had "demonstrations."
10. *Herald* (Halifax), July 24, 1890. p. 3.
11. *Globe* (Toronto), July 24, 1892, p. 6.
12. Robert M. Stamp, '"Empire Day in the Schools of Ontario: The Training of Young Imperialists," *Journal of Canadian Studies*, vol. 8, no. 3 (August 1973), pp. 32–42.
13. See, for example, *Free Press* (London), July 10, 1886. p. 3.
14. Gary Cross, *A Quest for Time: The Reduction of Work in Britain and France, 1840–1940* (Berkeley: University of California Press, 1989), pp. 9–12.
15. It has too often been assumed that there was a right-left split from the beginning of May Day and Labour Day; see, for example, Claude Larivière, *Le 1er mai: fête internationale des travailleurs* (Montreal: Editions cooperatives Albert St-Martin, 1975), for a labelling of the first Labour Day as "une diversion des boss" (p. 24).
16. Philip S. Foner, *May Day: A Short History of the International Workers' Holiday, 1886–1986* (New York: International Publishers, 1986); Maurice Dommanget, *Histoire du premier mai* (Paris: Editions de la Tête de Feuilles, 1972); George Seguy, *Premier mai: les 100 printemps* (Paris: Messidor/Editions sociales, 1989); Michelle Perrot, "The First of May 1890 in France: The Birth of a Working-Class Ritual," in Pat Thane, Geoffrey Crossick, and Roderick Floud, eds., *The Power of*

the Past: Essays for Eric Hobsbawm (Cambridge: Cambridge University Press, 1984), pp. 143–171; Andrea Panaccione, ed.. *May Day Celebration* (Venice: Marsilio Editori, 1988); Eric Hobsbawm, "Mass Producing Traditions: Europe, 1870–1914," in Hobsbawm and Ranger, eds., *The Invention of Tradition*, pp. 283–291. Some Canadian workers at least tried to distance themselves from European socialist traditions in these parades: in Montreal in 1892, in the only known incident in which a union contingent showed up with a red flag, the parade's marshals swooped in and had it removed. *Gazette* (Montreal), September 6, JS92, p. 3.

17. A morning parade followed by afternoon leisure events (usually sports or a picnic) with a dance or concert in the evening was an extremely common way to commemorate significant days.
18. Peter G. Goheen, "Symbols in the Streets: Parades in Victorian Urban Canada," *Urban History Review*, vol. 18, no. 3 (February 1990), pp. 237–243, "Parading: A Lively Tradition in Early Victorian Toronto," in Alan Baker and Gideon Biger, eds., *Ideology and Landscape in Historical Perspective* (New York: Cambridge University Press, 1992), pp. 330–351, "The Ritual of the Streets in Mid-Nineteenth-Century Toronto," *Environment and Planning D: Society and Space*, vol. 11 (1993), pp. 127–145, and "Negotiating Access to Public Space in Mid-Nineteenth Century Toronto," *Journal of Historical Geography*, vol. 20, no. 4 (1994), pp. 430–449; Susan G. Davis, *Parades and Power: Street Theatre in Nineteenth-Century Philadelphia* (Berkeley: University of California Press, 1986); Mary Ryan, "The American Parade: Representations of the Nineteenth-Century Social Order," in Lynn Hunt, ed., *The New Cultural History* (Berkeley: University of California Press, 1989), pp. 131–153; Huskins, "Public Celebrations"; J. M. S. Careless, "The First Hurrah: Toronto's Semicentennial of 1884," in Victor L. Russell, ed., *Forging a Consensus: Historical Essays on Toronto* (Toronto: University of Toronto Press, 1984), pp. 141–154; Michael Cottrell, "St. Patrick's Day Parades in Nineteenth-Century Toronto: A Study in Immigrant Adjustment and Elite Control," *Histoire sociale/Social History*, vol. 25, no. 49 (May 1992), pp. 57–73; Cecil J. Houston and William J. Smyth, *The Sash Canada Wore: A Historical Geography of the Orange Order in Canada* (Toronto: University of Toronto Press, 1980), pp. 122–124; Gregory S. Kealey, *Toronto Workers Respond to Industrial Capitalism: 1867–1892* (Toronto: University of Toronto Press, 1980), pp. 115–123; Rémi Tourangeau, *Fêtes et spectacles du Québec: région du Saguenay-Lac-Saint-Jean* (Québec: Nuit Blanche Editeur, 1993); Bryan D. Palmer, *A Culture in Conflict: Skilled Workers and Industrial Capitalism, 1860–1914* (Montreal and Kingston: McGill-Queen's University Press, 1979), following p. 152; Earl Chapin May, *The Circus From Rome to Ringling* (New York: Dover Publications, 1963); Doug A. Mishler, "'It Was Everything Else We Knew Wasn't': The Circus and American Culture," in Ray B. Browne and Michael T. Marsden, eds., *The Cultures of Celebrations* (Bowling Green: Bowling Green State University Popular Press, 1994), pp. 127–144.
19. Davis, *Parades and Power*; Bryan D. Palmer, "Discordant Music: Charivaris and Whitecapping in Nineteenth-Century North America," *Labour/Le Travailleur*, vol. 3 (1978), pp. 5–62. These sorts of rougher traditions of street theatre should not necessarily be confused with social commentary. By the 1880s carnivalesque parading, stripped of its political bite, could fit comfortably into quite respectable public events, even those organized or sanctioned by prominent citizens and civic leaders. In Ottawa, for example, the Confederation parade of 1886 included prominent citizens in the grotesque garb of the "Terribles" marching alongside military bands and voluntary societies. The year before, the Terribles had a separate, night-time march with the mayor and several aldermen in grotesque garb alongside butchers on horseback and a shoemaking display including machines and workmen from Alderman W. E. Brown's factory. *Citizen* (Ottawa), July 2, 1886, and July 2, 1885. This combination of respectable marchers and "rougher" style (though not substance) in the same parade was not uncommon in this period. See, for example, *Globe* (Toronto), May 25, 1878 (report on Hamilton St. George's Society Victoria Day march with Calithumpians); May 25, 1875 and 1876 (reports on Chatham Victoria Day processions with Calithumpians alongside veterans and civic leaders).
20. On Labour Day, the "rougher" traditions of parading surfaced only in a few settings, usually small towns. At the turn of the century, in 1901 and in 1903, for example, press reports in Sydney, Port Colborne, Stratford, Victoria, and, oddly enough, Toronto mentioned "calythumpian" or "polymorphian" contingents, meaning some costumed paraders who engaged in mocking street theatre. *Herald* (Halifax), September 3. 1901, p. 1; *Globe* (Toronto), September 3. 1901. p, 12; September

6, 1904, p. 11; *Colonist* (Victoria), September 4, 1901. p. 5; Davis, *Parades and Power*, pp. 113–154. As noted above (note 19). Calythumpians occasionally appeared in the parades marking other holidays and anniversaries.

21. Huskins, "Public Celebrations," pp. 176–217; Forsey, *Trade Unions in Canada*, pp. 10–13, 311; Palmer, *A Culture in Conflict*, pp. 56–57.
22. Jacques Rouillard, *Histoire du syndicalisme québecois: des origines a nos jours* (Montreal: Boreal, 1989), pp. 25–26.
23. *Globe*, April 16, 1872; *Mail*, April 16, 1872; Palmer, *A Culture in Conflict*, pp. 141–142; John Battye, "The Nine-Hour Pioneers: The Genesis of the Canadian Labour Movement," *Labour/Le Travailleur*, vol. 4 (1979), pp. 25–56.
24. See, for example, Careless, "The First Hurrah," p. 150; Huskins, "Public Celebrations," pp. 205–206. The term "trades procession" seems to have been a relatively flexible one. On one hand, it could be applied to parades that combined manufacturing products, labour process, and union messages. On the other, the term was applied to parades that seemed to be simply rolling advertisements or display cases for manufacturers' products, with less emphasis on labour process and virtually no union content. See *Galt Reporter*, May 29, 1885, and July 5, 1889; *Globe* (Saint John), October 2, 1883; *Mercury and Advertiser* (Guelph), July 2, 1891. A *Globe* (Toronto) report on a Dominion Day trades procession in Norwich described it as having the "character of an industrial exhibition" (July 2, 1881). In Guelph, the *Mercury and Advertiser* used the phrase "Gypsy march and trades procession" to refer to a Salvation Army march where converts simply walked in the procession carrying their tools (May 25, 1887).
25. At various points before World War I, there were parades in at least 42 centres, namely St. John's, Sydney, Glace Bay, Halifax, Westville, Moncton, Saint John, Charlottetown, Quebec City, Sherbrooke, Montreal, Ottawa, Carleton Place, Brockville, Kingston, Peterborough, Toronto, Hamilton, St. Catharines, London, Brantford, Berlin, Guelph, Galt, Stratford, St. Thomas, Windsor, Samia, Fort William, Port Arthur, Winnipeg, Rat Portage, Saskatoon, Regina, Moose Jaw, Calgary, Edmonton, Lethbridge, Fernie, Vancouver, Nanaimo, and Victoria.
26. John Weaver, "Crime, Public Order, and Repression: The Gore District in Upheaval, 1832–1851," *Ontario History*, vol. 78, no. 3 (September 1986), pp. 175–207; Nicholas Rogers, "Serving Toronto the Good: The Development of the City Police Force, 1834–84" in Russell, ed., *Forging a Consensus*, pp. 116–140; Patricia E. Roy, "The Preservation of the Peace in Vancouver: The Aftermath of the Anti-Chinese Riot of 1887," B.C. *Studies*, vol. 31 (Autumn 1976), pp. 44–59.
27. For example, *Globe* (Saint John), September 3, 1894; September 2, 1895; September 1, 1902, p. 1; September 7, 1903, p. 1; *Herald* (Halifax), September 5, 1899, p. 1; September 3, 1901, p. 7; *Gazette* (Montreal), September 4, 1894, p. 5 (16 years later the same paper regretted that "the traditional silk hat only shone out occasionally in faded splendor," September 6, 1910, p. 6); *Advertiser* (London), September 4, 1894, p. 1.
28. Davis, *Parades and Power*, pp. 49–72. Mary Ryan has suggested that "This particular type of celebratory performance seems to have been an American invention." See Ryan, "The American Parade," p. 132.
29. *Manitoba Free Press* (Winnipeg), September 2, 1913, p. 1.
30. Hamilton workers provided an exception in 1895 when they integrated army and navy veterans into their Labour Day parade. *Spectator* (Hamilton), September 3, 1895, p. 5.
31. For military content in trades processions, see *Mercury and Advertiser* (Guelph), July 2, 1891; *Galt Reporter*, May 29, 1885, and July 5, 1889.
32. *Gazette* (Montreal), September 5, 1893, p. 5, and September 4, 1894, p. 5.
33. In Calgary local clergymen were invited to ride as guests in a carriage. *Herald* (Calgary), September 3, 1907, p. 1, and September 8, 1908, p. 1.
34. *Spectator* (Hamilton), August 4, 1883, p. 1.
35. *Gazette* (Montreal), September 4, 1888, p. 3; *Journal* (Ottawa), September 2, 1890, p. 1; September 7, 1891, p. 1; September 6, 1892, p. 1.
36. *Globe* (Toronto), September 7, 1897, p. 2; September 5, 1899, p. 7; September 4, 1900; *Journal* (Ottawa), September 6, 1898, p. 5; *Manitoba Free Press* (Winnipeg), September 6, 1898, p. 5; *Province* (Vancouver), September 7, 1898; September 5, 1899, p. 2.

37. *Globe* (Saint John), October 2, 1883, p. 1; September 3, 1894; *Gazette* (Montreal), September 8, 1891, p. 2.
38. *Manitoba Free Press* (Winnipeg), September 3, 1895, p. 1; *Globe* (Toronto), September 2, 1913, p. 9.
39. *Globe* (Toronto), July 24, 1882, p. 6. King Crispin (along with Queen Crispiana) reappeared, probably for the last time in a Canadian parade, in the Saint John trades procession in 1883. *Globe* (Saint John), October 2, 1883, p. 1.
40. *Spectator* (Hamilton), September 3, 1895. p. 5; September 2, 1902, p. 5; *Globe* (Toronto), September 4, 1894, p. 3; September 6. 1898. p. 2; September 6, 1904, p. 11. It is not clear why butchers paraded on horseback, but obviously this was their standard practice. For examples of butchers on horseback in other parades, see *Globe* (Toronto), July 2, 1889 and 1890 (Dominion Day); *Mercury and Advertiser* (Guelph), July 2, 1891 (Dominion Day); Leo Johnson, *History of Guelph 1827–1927* (Guelph: Guelph Historical Society, 1977), p. 261 (account of the celebration of attaining city status, 1879).
41. *Globe* (Saint John), October 2, 1883, p. 1; September 3, 1894; September 2, 1895; *Manitoba Free Press* (Winnipeg), September 3, 1895, p. 1; *Gazette* (Montreal), September 3, 1901, p. 7; *Spectator* (Hamilton), September 7, 1897, p. 7; September 2, 1902, p. 5; September 6, 1904, p. 9; September 5, 1905, p. 5; *Globe* (Toronto), September 4, 1900, p. 7; September 8, 1903, p. 16; September 5, 1911, p. 7; September 3, 1912, p. 8; *Herald* (Calgary), September 8, 1908, p. 1; September 6, 1910, p. 1; *Herald* (Halifax), September 7, 1909, p. 1.
42. The Saint John and Halifax press provided the fullest descriptions of the banners carried in labour parades there in the 1880s and 1890s; see *Globe* (Saint John), October 2, 1883, p. 1; September 3, 1894; September 2, 1895; *Herald* (Halifax), August 3, 1888, p. 3; July 24, 1890, p. 3. Virtually all these early banners have disappeared, but the one known to exist in Saint John and scattered references in nineteenth-century newspapers suggest that the first probably came from British banner-makers. Rosemary Donegan, "The Iconography of Labour: An Overview of Canadian Materials," *Archivaria*, vol. 27 (Winter 1988–89), pp. 36–45; R. A. Leeson, *United We Stand: An Illustrated Account of Trade Union Emblems* (Bath: Adams and Dart, 1971); John Gorman, *Banner Bright: An Illustrated History of the Banners of the British Trade Union Movement* (London: Allen Lane, 1973) and *Images of Labour* (London: Scorpion Publishing, 1985); Forsey, *Trade Unions in Canada*, pp. 10–13.
43. For examples, see *Globe* (Toronto), August 16, 1887, p. 3; September 3, 1896, p. 1; September 2, 1902, p. 12; *Gazette* (Montreal), September 3, 1889, p. 5; September 8, 1891, p. 2; September 5, 1893, p. 1; September 3, 1895, p. 6; *Globe* (Saint John), September 3, 1894; *Journal* (Ottawa), September 7, 1897, p. 6; September 5, 1899, p. 5.
44. *Herald* (Calgary), September 3, 1907, p. 1; *Herald* (Halifax), September 7, 1909, p. 1; *Globe* (Toronto), September 3, 1912, p. 8.
45. The shift away from the rich allegorical images of the nineteenth century is plainest in the Saint John parades; see *Globe* (Saint John), October 2, 1883, p. 1; September 3, 1894; September 2, 1895; September 1, 1902, p. 1; September 7,1903, p. 1. See also the description of the banners in the 1908 Calgary parade in the *Herald* (Calgary), September 8, 1908, p. 1; also Donegan, "The Iconography of Labour," pp. 45–48.
46. For early examples of these craft performances in Saint John and Halifax, see Huskins, "Public Celebrations," pp. 199–203.
47. *Herald* (Halifax), September 3, 1901, p. 7; *Colonist* (Victoria), September 4, 1912, p. 8; also the electrical workers' giant wrench and hammer, *Herald* (Halifax), September 7, 1909, p. 1.
48. *Spectator* (Hamilton), August 4,1883, p. 1; September 3, 1895, p. 5; September 2, 1902, p. 5; *Globe* (Toronto), July 24, 1882, p. 6; September 12, 1892, p. 6; September 7, 1897, p. 9; September 6, 1898, p. 2; September 5, 1899, p. 7; *Globe* (Saint John), September 3, 1894; September 2, 1895; September 1, 1902, p. 1; September 7, 1903, p. 1; *Province* (Vancouver), September 7, 1898; *Colonist* (Victoria), September 4, 1912, p. 8.
49. *Herald* (Calgary), September 5, 1911, p. 8; *Manitoba Free Press* (Winnipeg), September 5, 1911, p. 20; *Colonist* (Victoria), September 4, 1912, p. 8; *Leader* (Regina), September 3, 1913, p. 8; *Globe*, September 4, 1906, p. 14; September 5, 1911, p. 7; September 2, 1913, p. 9.

50. In 1910 Fort William's grain trimmers operated on their float "a miniature elevator from which grain was poured into a small counterpart of the steamer Ames." *Times Journal* (Fort William), September 6, 1910, p. 1. Even the less skilled could put their equipment on display, as the civic workers did in Winnipeg in 1899 with remarkable floats showing road building and laying of waterworks and as the maintenance-of-way men demonstrated with a hand car and signals several years later. *Manitoba Free Press* (Winnipeg), September 5, 1899, p. 1; September 5, 1911, p. 1; September 8, 1914, p. 14. See also *Province* (Vancouver), September 7. 1898; *Herald* (Calgary), September 6, 1910, p. 1.
51. See, for example, *Globe* (Toronto), September 4, 1900, p. 7; *Herald* (Halifax), September 8, 1903, p. 1; *Times Journal* (Fort William), September 8, 1903, p. 1.
52. *Manitoba Free Press* (Winnipeg), September 3, 1895, p. 1; *Globe* (Toronto), September 8, 1896, p. 1; September 7, 1897, p. 9; *Journal* (Ottawa), September 6, 1898, p. 5.
53. In London's 1892 parade, it was a special poem entitled "The Song of the Printer" and in Vancouver the same year a one-sheet newspaper called the *Vancouver Typographer*, Globe (Toronto), July 24, 1882, p. 8; *Palladium of Labor* (Hamilton), August 18, 1884, p. 7; *Free Press* (London), July 10, 1886, p. 3; *Journal* (Ottawa), September 7, 1891, p. 1; September 6, 1898, p. 5; September 7, 1909, p. 3; *Advertiser* (London), September 6, 1892, p. 5; September 3, 1893, p. 3; *Manitoba Free Press* (Winnipeg), September 6, 1898, p. 5; *Globe* (Saint John), September 3, 1894; *Province* (Vancouver), September 5, 1899, p. 2; Vancouver City Archives, copy of Vancouver Typographer, August 11, 1892.
54. For cigarmakers: *Journal* (Ottawa), September 6, 1892, p. 1; September 6, 1910, p. 3; *Globe* (Toronto), July 24, 1882, p. 6; July 23, 1883, p. 6; September 3, 1895, p. 6; September 4, 1900, p. 7; *Gazette* (Montreal), September 2, 1890, p. 5; *Globe* (Saint John), September 1, 1902, p. 1; *Manitoba Free Press* (Winnipeg), September 2, 1920, p. 7. For bakers: *Journal* (Ottawa), September 8, 1903, p. 6; *Globe* (Toronto), September 7, 1897, p. 9; *Manitoba Free Press* (Winnipeg), September 2, 1902, p. 7.
55. *Free Press* (London), July 10, 1886, p. 5; *Journal* (Ottawa), September 3, 1895, p. 5; September 2, 1902, p. 6; *Province* (Vancouver), September 4, 1900, p. 8; *Spectator* (Hamilton), September 5,1905, p. 5; *Colonist* (Victoria), September 4, 1912, p. 8; Whig *Standard* (Kingston), September 3, 1918, p. 3.
56. *Journal* (Ottawa), September 7, 1891, p. 1; September 5, 1899, p. 5; September 3, 1901, p. 6; September 7, 1909, p. 3; *Globe*, July 24, 1882, p. 6; September 3, 1895, p. 6; September 3, 1896, p. 1; September 7, 1897, p. 9; September 5, 1899, p. 4; September 3, 1912, p. 8; September 2, 1913, p. 9; *Gazette* (Montreal), September 2, 1890, p. 5; September 8, 1908, p. 7; September 2, 1913, p. 12; *Province* (Vancouver), September 7, 1898, p. 2; September 5, 1899, p. 2; *Manitoba Free Press* (Winnipeg), September 8, 1903, p. 8; September 5, 1905, p. 1; *Times Journal* (Fort William), September 8, 1903, p. 1; *Daily Examiner* (Peterborough), September 8, 1903, p. 5; *Herald* (Calgary), September 2, 1902, p. 4; September 3, 1907, p. 1; September 8, 1908, p. 1; *Leader* (Regina), September 2, 1907, p. 3; September 7, 1909, p. 9; September 3, 1913, p. 8; *Citizen* (Ottawa), September 3. 1912, p. 2; *Colonist* (Victoria), September 4, 1901, p. 5; September 4, 1912, p. 8; Working Lives Collective, *Working Lives: Vancouver, 1886–1986* (Vancouver: New Star Press, 1985), p. 140; Doug Smith, *Let Us Rise: An Illustrated History of the Manitoba Labour Movement* (Vancouver: New Star Press, 1985), p. 22.
57. For blacksmiths: *Globe* (Toronto), July 24, 1882, p. 6; September 12, 1892, p. 6; September 3, 1896, p. 1; September 7, 1897, p. 9; September 5, 1899, p. 7; September 3, 1901. p. 12; September 2, 1902, p. 12; *Journal* (Ottawa), September 3. 1895, p. 5; *Gazette* (Montreal), September 8, 1896, p. 6; September 2, 1902, p. 5; *Manitoba Free Press* (Winnipeg), September 6, 1898, p. 5; *Colonist* (Victoria), September 6, 1899, p. 8; September 4, 1912, p. 8; *Spectator* (Hamilton), September 5, 1905, p. 5; *Citizen* (Ottawa), September 3, 1912, p. 2. For boilermakers: *Province* (Vancouver), September 5, 1896; *Manitoba Free Press* (Winnipeg), September 7, 1897, p. 1; September 2, 1902, p. 7; September 5, 1905, p. 1; *Globe* (Toronto), September 5, 1899, p. 7; September 3, 1901, p. 12; *Gazette* (Montreal), September 3, 1901, p. 7; September 2, 1902, p. 5; *Colonist* (Victoria), September 4, 1901, p. 5; *Herald* (Halifax), September 6, 1904, p. 1; September 5, 1905, p. 1; *Journal* (Ottawa), September 3,1907, p. 10; *Herald* (Calgary), September 3, 1907,

p. 1. For moulders: *Globe* (Toronto), September 3, 1895, p. 6; *Daily Examiner* (Peterborough), September 3, 1903, p. 1; see also *Palladium of Labor* (Hamilton), August 18, 1883, p. 7; *Globe* (Toronto), September 3, 1896, p. 1; September 7, 1897, p. 9.

58. *Colonist* (Victoria), September 6, 1898, p. 6; September 6, 1899, p. 8; *Province* (Vancouver), September 4, 1900, p. 8. From time to time, there were tableaux of other old crafts rolling through the streets: carriage workers (*Globe* [Saint John], September 3,1894); coopers (*Advertiser* [London], September 6, 1892, p. 5); tanners (*Advertiser* [London], September 3, 1893, p. 3; *Globe* [Toronto], September 5, 1899, p. 4); tinsmiths (*Journal* [Ottawa], September 5, 1893, p. 5, and September 8, 1903, p. 6); butchers (*Colonist* [Victoria], September 3, 1902, p. 8); machine woodworkers (*Journal* [Ottawa], September 5, 1893, p. 5, and September 8, 1896, p. 1); tailors (*Globe* [Toronto], September 5, 1899, p. 7; *Journal* [Ottawa], September 8, 1903, p. 6; *Manitoba Free Press* [Winnipeg], September 5, 1911, p. 1).

59. Saint John millmen contributed a float in 1894 that showed all the stages of production of wood products from chopping a tree to sawing lumber on a small sawmill. *Globe* (Saint John), September 3, 1894; see also *Journal* (Ottawa), September 6, 1892, p. 2. Spectators could also sometimes see machinists handlings variety of lathes. *Globe* (Toronto), September 7,1897, p. 9; September 6, 1898, p. 2; September 5, 1899, p. 7; *Manitoba Free Press* (Winnipeg), September 7, 1909, p. 1; September 5, 1911, p. 1.

60. *Palladium of Labor* (Hamilton), August 11, 1883; *Globe* (Saint John), September 2, 1895.

61. In Winnipeg in 1895, for example, spectators got glimpses of workers making soda water, binding books, baking buns, shaving faces, making tents, and milling lumber—all on wagons sponsored by companies, not unions. Three years later, one of that city's brewers had quite a crowd following his wagon. *Manitoba Free Press* (Winnipeg), September 9, 1895, p. 1; September 6, 1898, p. 5. For years Winnipeg had the most elaborate company floats. See also *Journal* (Ottawa), September 5, 1893, p. 5; *Province* (Vancouver), September 5, 1896; September 7, 1898.

62. The only exception to this generalization that has been uncovered was in the first few Halifax parades starting in 1888. Here employers were often invited as "guests," who rode in carriages or led their own (apparently non-unionized) employees in the march. Working-class solidarity and industrial paternalism mingled comfortably here in the absence of any serious industrial conflict in several industries and in a context of fluid lines between journeymen and small-scale owners. The hated Moirs bakery and confectionery firm, the model of the new industrial capitalist workplace, did not appear, however. *Herald* (Halifax), August 3, 1888, p. 3; July 24, 1889, p. 1; July 24, 1890, p. 3; July 23, 1891, p. 3; July 21, 1892, p. 6; July 20, 1893, p. 6; Ian McKay, *The Craft Transformed: An Essay on the Carpenters of Halifax. 1885–1985* (Halifax: Holdfast Press 1985), pp. 1–26, and "Capital and Labour in the Halifax Baking and Confectionery Industry During the Last Half of the Nineteenth Century," *Labour/Le Travailleur*, vol. 3 (1978), pp. 63–108. In most cities, employers clearly co-operated in the production of the craftsmen's street theatre, allowing the men to use valuable machinery and raw materials and often company vehicles.

63. There were occasional Labour Day celebrations in coal-mining towns in Nova Scotia and British Columbia, but this labour festival never seems to have taken hold with the regularity of the celebrations in the metropolitan and larger manufacturing centres. Sydney, Nova Scotia, had a sporadic parading tradition, but this was mainly tied to the local Trades and Labour Council.

64. One of the earliest parades in the 1880s that emerged out of the more expansive spirit of the Knights of Labor made some space for a contingent of "'Unorganized Labour,'" but, with the consolidation of a more exclusivist craft unionism by the end of the decade, this opportunity never again opened up. *Spectator* (Hamilton), August 4, 1884, p. 4; *Palladium of Labor* (Hamilton), August 9, 1884, p. 7.

65. One in London wrote in 1886: "the proportions attained by the grand parade of yesterday must have proved extremely surprising to many" (*Free Press*, July 10, 1886, p. 3). "The capitalist, if he was looking on, as no doubt he was, got a very good idea of the strength of the united labor organizations of the city," the Montreal *Gazette* reported on September 4, 1894 (p. 5). The Ottawa *Journal* also saw "indications in the demonstrations in the large cities that the vitality of the labor organizations is steadily increasing" (September 4, 1894, p. 4). See also *Manitoba Free Press* (Winnipeg), September 3, 1901, p. 3.

66. In several cities, the tinsmiths used their skills to make some combination of identical hats, ties, cuffs, and canes out of tin. *Journal* (Ottawa), September 5, 1893, p. 5; September 4, 1894, pp. 3, 5; September 3, 1895, p. 5; September 5. 1899, p. 5; September 4, 1900, p. 3; September 3, 1901, p. 6; *Globe* (Saint John), September 2, 1895; *Spectator* (Hamilton), September 2, 1902, p. 5; *Herald* (Calgary), September 8, 1908, p. I; September 6, 1910, p. 1; *Globe* (Toronto), September 5, 1911, p. 7; *Citizen* (Ottawa), September 5, 1917, p. 3. Tailors in Ottawa and Toronto wore frock coats and silk hats to highlight their occupation. *Globe* (Toronto), September 12, 1892, p. 6; September 3, 1895, p. 6; *Journal* (Ottawa), September 8, 1903, p. 6.
67. Two studies of nineteenth-century parades, to our minds, exaggerate their participatory quality. See Ryan, "The American Parade," p. 137; Goheen, "Symbols in the Streets," p. 240.
68. *Globe*, September 2, 1919, p. 3.
69. In Saint John in 1902 and 1903, for example, freight handlers' and hod carriers' unions contributed major floats showing their work on trains and building sites respectively. *Globe* (Saint John), September 1, 1902, p. 1, and September 7, 1903, p. 1.
70. In 1900 the Montreal *Gazette* noted that waterfront workers were not even able to get off work, "the stevedores claiming that the season is too short for sentiment," according to a reporter. "If a man wants to get off there are others to take his place said a foreman yesterday, the absentee being simply checked for lost time." *Gazette* (Montreal), September 4, 1900, p. 8.
71. The only exceptions that have surfaced are in Montreal, where an "Italian Brotherhood," decked out in Italian army uniforms, marched in the 1901 and 1902 parades and where separate groups of English, French, and Jewish carpenters participated in the 1906 event. *Gazette* (Montreal), September 3, 1901, p. 7, and September 4, 1906, p. 5.
72. *Globe* (Saint John), September 3, 1894; *Journal* (Ottawa), September 3, 1901, p. 6.
73. *Globe* (Toronto), September 5, 1899, p. 7; September 3, 1901, p. 12; September 2, 1902, p. 12; *Spectator* (Hamilton), September 2, 1902, p. 5. In a similar vein, a float in the 1911 Calgary parade depicted what the newsman called "a big black nigger wench" trying to do her laundry amid domestic turmoil, in contrast to the electrical appliances on display at the other end of the float. *Herald* (Calgary), September 5, 1911, p. 8.
74. *Gazette* (Montreal), September 4, 1894, p. 5: September 8, 1903, p. 6; *Palladium of Labor* (Hamilton), August 11, 1883; *Spectator* (Hamilton), August 4, 1883, p. 1; August 4, 1884, p. 4; *Province* (Vancouver), September 5, 1899: see also *Evening Record* (Windsor), August 30, 1913, p. 1.
75. *Colonist* (Victoria), September 4, 1901, p. 5.
76. Susan Mann Trofimenkoff, "One Hundred and Two Muffled Voices: Canada's Industrial Women in the 1880s" in Michael S. Cross and Gregory S. Kealey, eds., *Readings in Canadian Social History, Volume 3: Canada's Age of Industry, 1849–1896* (Toronto: McClelland & Stewart, 1982), pp. 212–229; Bettina Bradbury, "Women and Wage Labour in a Period of Transition: Montreal, 1861–1881," *Histoire sociale/Social History*, vol. 17, no. 33 (May 1984), pp. 115–131: Sharon Myers, "'Not to Be Ranked as Women': Female Industrial Workers in Turn-of-the-Century Halifax" in Janet Guildford and Suzanne Morton, eds., *Separate Spheres: Women's Worlds in the 19th-century Maritimes* (Fredericton: Acadiensis Press. 1994), pp. 161–184.
77. In Halifax's first Dominion Day festivities, the Virginia Tobacco Company had women making tobacco and cigars, and in the Hamilton Nine-Hours march in 1872 the Wilson and Lockman float had six young women running the sewing machines that the firm manufactured. Several years later a Brantford rag merchant had six girls sorting rags on the back of a wagon, a Winnipeg bottler had women packing pickles, and Halifax's Moir's had six girls wearing sailor suits throwing candy kisses to spectators. Bonnie Huskins. "The Ceremonial Space of Women: Public Processions in Victorian Saint John and Halifax," in Guildford and Morton, eds., *Separate Spheres*, p. 154; Palmer, *A Culture in Conflict*, p. U2: *Globe* (Toronto), September 4, 1894, p. 3; *Manitoba Free Press* (Winnipeg), September 6, 1895, p. 5; *Herald* (Halifax), September 2, 1919, p. 1.
78. The inevitable exceptions were a Toronto bookbinder's float showing "a ruling machine which was being operated by a girl with flaxen ringlets" and a Winnipeg tailor's float showing men and women at work. *Globe* (Toronto), September 12, 1892, p. 6; *Manitoba Free Press* (Winnipeg), September 7, 1897, p. 1.

79. *Globe* (Toronto), September 3, 1895, p. 6.
80. *Manitoba Free Press* (Winnipeg), September 6, 1898, p. 5.
81. *Palladium of Labor* (Hamilton), August 11, 1883; August 9, 1884, p. 1; *Spectator* (Hamilton), August 4, 1883, p. 1; August 4, 1884, p. 4; *Globe* (Toronto), August 5, 1884, p. 5; September 2, 1902, pp. 4, 12; *Free Press* (London), July 10, 1886, p. 3; *Advertiser* (London), September 6, 1892, p. 5; September 3, 1900, p. 8; September 8, 1903, p. 3; *Manitoba Free Press* (Winnipeg), September 7, 1897, p. 1; September 5, 1899, p. 1; September 4, 1906, p. 1; September 7, 1909, p. 1; *Gazette* (Montreal), September 5, 1903, p. 7; September 8, 1908, p. 7; September 2, 1913, p. 12; *Leader* (Regina), September 3, 1913, p. 8; *Evening Record* (Windsor), August 30, 1913, p. 1. In 1899 the Ottawa labour leaders solicited an article for their Labour Day Souvenir from Lady Aberdeen, feminist wife of the governor general, rather than from a local working woman. *Journal* (Ottawa), September 2, 1899, p. 9.
82. Mary P. Ryan, *Women in Public: Between Banners and Ballots, 1825–1880* (Baltimore: Johns Hopkins University Press, 1990); Huskins, "The Ceremonial Space of Women."
83. *Gazette* (Montreal), September 3, 1907, p. 7.
84. *Advertiser* (London), September 2, 1913, p. 9.
85. *Advertiser* (London), September 6, 1892, p. 5; September 1, 1900, p. 8; September 8, 1903, p. 3; *Gazette* (Montreal), September 5, 1903. p. 7; September 2, 1913, p. 12; September 2, 1919, p. 5: *Herald* (Halifax), September 2, 1919, p. 1; *Manitoba Free Press* (Winnipeg), September 4, 1903, p. 2; September 2, 1919, p. 10; Ryan, "The American Parade," pp. 148–151.
86. *Colonist* (Victoria), September 5, 1900. p. 6; September 4, 1901, p. 5.
87. Huskins, "The Ceremonial Space of Women," p. 154; Palmer, *A Culture in Conflict*, p. 142; *Journal* (Ottawa), September 4, 1900, p. 3; *Globe* (Toronto), September 4, 1900, p. 7; *Manitoba Free Press* (Winnipeg), September 2, 1902, p. 7; *Herald* (Calgary), September 8, 1908, p. 1.
88. In a partial departure from this pattern, an Ottawa float in 1900 organized by the Ottawa Co-operative Store—essentially a commercial element in the parade—had "a dozen children ... being supplied with a substantial meal." *Journal* (Ottawa), September 4, 1900, p. 3.
89. *Herald* (Halifax), September 6, 1909, p. 3; September 7, 1909, p. 2.
90. *Manitoba Free Press* (Winnipeg), September 6. 1904, p. 7; September 6, 1910, p. 9; Daily Times *Journal* (Fort William), September 2, 1913, p. 1; *Examiner* (Peterborough), August 30, 1919, p. 1. Sometimes, too, they sold tags for labour causes. *Herald* (Halifax), September 3, 1920, p. 16.
91. *Spectator* (Hamilton), September 3, 1895. p. 5; September 7. 1897. p. 7; *Gazette* (Montreal), September 6. 1904, p. 5; September 5. 1905. p. 7: September 4, 1906, p. 5; September 3, 1907, p. 7; September 8, 1908, p. 7; *Journal* (Ottawa), September 6, 1910. p. 3; *Manitoba Free Press* (Winnipeg), September 9, 1914, p. 14. In Montreal newsgirls regularly joined the boys, but rode in carriages like the other female paraders.
92. The only exceptions we uncovered were the 200 boys from Tuckett's tobacco factory in the Hamilton parade in 1895 and a number from the local lumber mills in Ottawa the same year. *Spectator* (Hamilton), September 3, 1895, p. 5. Child labour in this period is discussed in Bettina Bradbury, *Working Families: Age. Gender, and Daily Survival in Industrializing Montreal* (Toronto: McClelland & Stewart, 1993), pp. 118–151; Loma F. Hurl, "Overcoming the Inevitable: Restricting Child Factory Labour in Late Nineteenth Century Ontario," *Labour/Le Travail*, vol. 21 (Spring 1988), pp. 87–121; Craig Heron, "Factory Workers" in Paul Craven, ed., *Labouring Lives: Work and Workers in Nineteenth Century Ontario* (Toronto: University of Toronto Press, 1995), pp. 479–590.
93. *Gazette* (Montreal), September 2, 1890, p. 5; September 2, 1902, p. 5; *Advertiser* (London), September 3, 1893, p. 3.
94. *Free Press* (London), July 10, 1886, p. 3; *Globe* (Toronto), September 4, 1894, p. 3; *Free Press* (Winnipeg), September 4, 1900, p. 2; *Spectator* (Hamilton), September 5, 1905, p. 5; *Herald* (Calgary), September 5. 1905, p. 1; Times *Journal* (Fort William), September 6, 1910, p. 1; *Citizen* (Ottawa), September 5, 1917, p. 3; *Whig Standard* (Kingston), September 3, 1918, p. 3; *Journal* (Ottawa), September 5, 1899, p. 5; September 6, 1904, p. 3. In 1910 the J.R. Booth company had five little girls sitting on its float, "wearing capes and hats made of light paper of variegated colors." *Journal* (Ottawa), September 6, 1910, p. 3. In the early 1900s Calgary's parade organizers introduced contingents of marching school children. *Herald* (Calgary), September 6, 1904, p. 1;

September 5, 1905, p. 1. Of course, gangs of boys might effectively join the parades by tagging along to beg for handouts from the merchants' floats. *Free Press* (Winnipeg), September 8, 1903, p. 8.

95. *Journal* (Ottawa), September 2, 1899, p. 2. On working-class masculinity in this period, see Christina Burr, "'That Coming Curse—The Incompetent Compositress': Class and Gender Relations in the Toronto Typographical Union during the Late Nineteenth Century," *Canadian Historical Review*, vol. 74, no. 3 (September 1993), pp. 344–366; Keith McClelland, "Masculinity and the 'Representative Artisan' in Britain, 1850–80" in Michael Roper and John Tosh, eds., *Manful Assertions: Masculinities in Britain since 1800* (London: Routledge. 1991), pp. 74–91; John Tosh, "What Should Historians Do with Masculinity? Reflections on Nineteenth-Century Britain," History *Workshop*, vol. 38 (Autumn 1994), pp. 179–202.
96. *Globe* (Toronto), September 4, 1894, p. 7.
97. The ideological similarities with the working-class liberalism that has come to be known as Labourism is striking. See Craig Heron, "Labourism and the Canadian Working Class," *Labour/Le Travail*, vol. 13 (Spring 1984), pp. 45–75.
98. The *Ottawa Journal* claimed that on the first Labour Day in 1890 the "procession was the finest ever seen in Ottawa" (September 2, 1890. p. I).
99. See, for example, *Herald* (Halifax), September 2, 1919, p. 1.
100. *Globe* (Toronto), September 7, 1920, p. 6; September 3, 1929, p. 16.
101. Sam Landers, "Labor Day and Its Origins: Why a Day is Observed," *Citizen* (Ottawa), September 2, 1911; *Herald* (Halifax), September 1, 1913, p, 4; September 6, 1937, p. 11.
102. When they were cancelled in Montreal in 1908 "to cease offering further encouragement to the circus parade features of the procession," the *Montreal Gazette* noticed a decline in quality: "there was practically no attempt at decorative effects; even the traditional silk hat only shone out occasionally in faded splendor" (September 6, 1910, p. 6). As floats began to dwindle in the Fort William and Port Arthur parade in 1913, the judges also concluded that larger prizes were needed "to encourage more decoration" (Times *Journal*, September 2, 1913, p. 1).
103. In Kingston the labour movement allowed the local Humane Society to organize the street spectacle in 1913 with a "Work Horse Parade." Immediately after World War I, the Labour Day parading tradition in several smaller communities passed briefly to veterans' organizations, which broadened the range of participants to include merchants, manufacturers, school children, and other community organizations, but few unions. Thereafter most small-town Labour Day parades, such as the perennial event in Bridgetown, N.S., had a variety of sponsors and a broad social mix of participants (that is, unless some serious labour struggle disrupted the community). *Standard* (St. Catharines), September 3, 1918, p. 3; September 2, 1919, pp. 1, 3–5; and September 4, 1920, p. 9; *Tribune* (Welland), August 28, 1919, p. U; *Herald* (Halifax), September 8, 1925, p. 2; September 4, 1929, p. 2; September 5, 1933, pp. 3, 14; September 4, 1937, p. 3; September 6, 1937, p. 11; August 31, 1944, p. 9; and September 3, 1946, p. 9; *Manitoba Free Press* (Winnipeg), September 1, 1919, p. 7.
104. Toronto and Calgary had no march in 1909, Halifax had only three between 1906 and 1913, Winnipeg had none in 1908 and none at all after 1919, Hamilton's 1906 march was the last for 40 years, and Vancouver had no parade after 1913. *Herald* (Halifax), September 1, 1913, p. 4; *Free Press* (Winnipeg), August 29, 1946, p. 3; *Gazette* (Montreal), September 3, 1956, p. 7; Working Lives Collective, *Working Lives*, p. 141.
105. Despite their well-established parading traditions, for example, Halifax, Hamilton, and Toronto workers had no procession for the first national Labour Day in 1894.
106. In 1895 the Halifax *Herald* published a blunt critique of that year's "demonstration," and no festivities were organized again until 1899. *Herald* (Halifax), September 4, 1985, p. 6; September 8, 1896; September 7, 1897, p. 8; September 6, 1898, p. 8; September 5, 1899, p. 1. For other mildly critical comments see *Herald* (Calgary), September 4, 1906, p. 1; September 8, 1908, p. 1.
107. *Globe* (Toronto), September 8, 1896, p. 9; September 7, 1897, p. 2; September 5, 1899, p. 4; *Spectator* (Hamilton), September 8, 1903, p. 1; September 6, 1904, p. 9.
108. Craig Heron, "The Crisis of the Craftsman: Hamilton Metalworkers in the Early Twentieth Century," *Labour/Le Travail*, vol. 6 (Autumn 1980), pp. 7–48.

109. These trends are discussed in Robert H. Babcock, *Gompers in Canada: A Study of American Continentalism Before the First World War* (Toronto: University of Toronto Press, 1974); Mark Leier, *Red Flags and Red Tape: The Making of a Labour Bureaucracy* (Toronto: University of Toronto Press, 1995); Ian McKay, "Strikes in the Maritimes, 1901–1914" in P.A. Buckner and David Frank, eds., *The Acadiensis Reader: Volume Two, Atlantic Canada After Confederation* (Fredericton: Acadiensis Press, 1985), pp. 216–259; Heron, "The Crisis of the Craftsman"; Craig Heron "The Second Industrial Revolution in Canada, 1890–1930," in Deian R. Hopkin and Gregory S. Kealey, eds.. *Class, Community and the Labour Movement: Wales and Canada, 1850–1930* (Aberystwyth: Llafur/Canadian Committee on Labour History, 1989), pp. 48–66, and *Working in Steel: The Early Years in Canada, 1883–1935* (Toronto: McClelland & Stewart, 1988); Craig Heron and Bryan D. Palmer, "Through the Prism of the Strike: Industrial Conflict in Southern Ontario, 1901–14," *Canadian Historical Review*, vol. 58, no. 4 (December 1977), pp. 423–458.
110. Rather than showing their actual work process, for example, Ottawa papermakers used the paper mass-produced in local mills to construct a colourful float with flowing streamers and a large paper canoe with two little girls seated in it. *Citizen* (Ottawa), September 3, 1912, p. 2.
111. By 1901, for example, the Toronto parade included 26 bakery wagons, 73 dairy wagons, 28 delivery vans from the Simpson's department store, and dozens more. *Globe* (Toronto), September 3, 1901, p. 12. "There were in the procession some features which were not, strictly speaking, illustrative of Labor," a Hamilton newspaper commented in 1902, "but as they helped to make up the show, their presence may be excused." *Spectator* (Hamilton), September 2, 1902, p. 4. As an Ottawa paper noted the next year: "This is usually done for advertising purposes and while it detracts somewhat from the real labor aspect of the demonstration it always lends bulk." *Journal* (Ottawa), September 8, 1903, p. 6. In 1903 the *Welland Telegraph*'s report on the floats in the "best trades procession ever seen in Port Colbome" said that "the business men are to be congratulated on the earnest manner with which they took hold of the affair" (September 10, 1903, p. 6). In 1918 the industrialists and merchants of Hull provided virtually the entire procession. *Journal* (Ottawa), September 3, 1918, p. 8. See also *Journal* (Ottawa), Septembers, 1892, p. 1; *Advertiser* (London), September 3, 1893, p. 3; September 2, 1913, p. 9; Free Press (Winnipeg), September 4, 1894, pp. 1–2; *Evening Record* (Windsor), September 8, 1903, p. 1; *Herald* (Halifax), September 2, 1919, p. 1; September 7, 1920, p. 10; *Manitoba Free Press* (Winnipeg), September 2, 1913, p. 3; *Cornwall Standard*, September 10, 1925, p. 2. In the early 1900s specific prizes were often awarded for merchant and industrial floats, decorated cars, and other specialized entries.
112. *Gazette* (Montreal), September 8, 1921, p. 5. The perennial Toronto march into the Canadian National Exhibition grounds and the tame speeches later delivered at the CNE directors' lunch were probably the clearest example of this trend. Vancouver's Labour Day parade was similarly shaped to promote the Pacific National Exhibition in 1913. *Sun* (Vancouver), September 2, 1913, p. 1.
113. *Gazette* (Montreal), September 2, 1895, p. 2; September 5, 1904, p. 5; September 4, 1905, p. 8; September 3, 1906, p. 4; *Globe* (Toronto), September 8, 1896, p. 9; *Manitoba Free Press* (Winnipeg), September 6, 1897, p. 1; *Colonist* (Victoria), September 3, 1900, p. 2; *Spectator* (Hamilton), September 2, 1901, p. 5; September 7, 1903, p. 8; *Leader* (Regina), September 1, 1913, p. 5; *Sun* (Vancouver), September 2. 1933. p. 8.
114. In a typical burst of boosterism, the *Globe*'s reporter scanned the assembled masses at the 1883 Toronto parade and concluded that "the crowds of well-dressed, intelligent men, attended by wives, sisters and sweethearts equally well dressed and as intelligent, show that elevating tendencies have been at work." Several years later, the same paper claimed to sense among the spectators a "thrill of pride in a city which can turn out such a large number of robust, intelligent, contented and well-dressed mechanics and workmen.... The Labor Day parade is a good barometrical index of the industrial progress of Toronto." *Globe* (Toronto), July 23, 1883, p. 6, and September 5, 1897, p. 7. See also *Manitoba Free Press* (Winnipeg), September 3, 1895, p. 1.
115. *Gazette* (Montreal), September 2, 1890, p. 4; *Journal* (Ottawa), September 7, 1897, p. 6; *Globe* (Toronto), September 7, 1897, p. 9: *Leader* (Regina), September 3, 1907, p. 4.
116. *Herald* (Halifax), September 5, 1921, p. 6; September 4, 1922, p. 4; *Colonist* (Victoria), September 4. 1899, p. 4.
117. *Globe* (Toronto), September 8. 1903.

118. John Withrow, ed., *Once Upon a Century: 100 Year History of the "Ex"* (Toronto: J.H. Robinson Publishing, 1978); David Breen and Kenneth Coates, *Vancouver's Fair: An Administrative and Political History of the Pacific National Exhibition* (Vancouver: University of British Columbia Press, 1982); *Herald* (Calgary), September 2, 1902, p. 4. The Calgary Stampede that started in 1912 had a similar drawing power.
119. *Manitoba Free Press* (Winnipeg), September 5, 1905, p. 1; see also September 3, 1907, p. 1.
120. *Globe* (Toronto), September 2, 1913, p. 8. Other retail outlets were closed on Labour Day, but, in keeping with the efforts of more and more retail trades to turn public events and celebrations such as Christmas, Valentine's Day, Mother's Day, and birthdays into occasions for special purchases, local merchants and major department stores urged shoppers to prepare for the holiday with a new tie or Kodak camera. Times *Journal* (Fort William), September 8, 1903, p. 1; *Gazette* (Montreal), September 4, 1920, p. 7; September 1, 1933, p. 5. (There is no record of any effort to market Labour Day greeting cards.)
121. *Journal* (Ottawa), September 2, 1919, p. 3. "Main Street presented a very quiet appearance except for an occasional pedestrian hurrying to catch the bus," the *Welland Telegraph* reported on September 6, 1910 (p. 2). "The entire population scattered through the waterways and trails of the neighbouring coast," the *Vancouver Sun* noted on September 4, 1918 (p. 9): "Every outdoor resort, every seaside and riverside picnic ground was utilized to the full extent. A great crowd went to Seattle, to Nanaimo, Victoria, and up the Chilliwack valley. The city beaches were black with pleasure-seekers, and the recreation grounds were jammed."
122. "Of late there has been some complaint of the paucity of local attractions on holidays," the Hamilton *Spectator* noted on September 3, 1895 (p. 5). "Of the many holidays during the summer Labor Day is one of the few where there is something going on here to keep citizens at home," it lamented a decade later (September 5, 1905, p. 5). A Peterborough editorialist also complained on September 8, 1925, in the *Examiner* that Victoria Day, Dominion Day, Civic Holiday, and Labour Day had "been allowed to become just holidays, that's all—meaning nothing save that the stores are closed, and the factory whistles cease to blow" (p. 4). See also *Spectator* (Hamilton), September 6, 1904, p. 9.
123. *Toiler* (Toronto), September 18, 1902, p. 2.
124. *Globe* (Toronto), September 2, 1913, p. 8. A few years earlier the Winnipeg Labour Day organizers had announced that only "hot tea and hot water" would be available on their picnic grounds. *Free Press* (Winnipeg), September 3, 1900, p. 6.
125. *Province* (Vancouver), September 7, 1898, p. 2; *Manitoba Free Press* (Winnipeg), September 3, 1900, p. 6; September 2, 1902, p. 7; *Advertiser* (London), September 4, 1900, p. 8; September 6, 1910, pp. 8, 10; *Telegraph* (Berlin), September 4, 1900, p. I; *Globe* (Toronto), September 8, 1903, p. 16; *Spectator* (Hamilton), September 5, 1911, p. 7; *Evening Record* (Windsor), September 2, 1913, p. 1; *Examiner* (Peterborough), August 30, 1919, p. 1; September 4, 1920, p. 11; *Free Press* (London), September 3, 1946, p. 24.
126. On this trend, see Roy Rosenzweig, *Eight Hours for What We Will: Workers and Leisure in an industrial City, 1870–1920* (New York: Cambridge University Press, 1983); Kathy Peiss, *Cheap Amusements: Working Women and Leisure in Turn-of-the-Century New York* (Philadelphia: Temple University Press, 1986); Lizabeth Cohen, *Making a New Deal: Industrial Workers in Chicago, 1919–1939* (New York: Cambridge University Press, 1990).
127. *Western Clarion*, September 10, 1904, p. 1; September 9, 1905, p. 1; September 10, 1906, p. 1; Semember 10, 1910. p. 1.
128. Quoted in Working Lives Collective. *Working Lives*, p. 141.
129. *Worker* (Toronto), May 15, 1922, pp. 1, 4; May 16, 1923, pp. 1, 4; May 17, 1924, pp. 1, 4; May 16, 1925, p. 1; May 15, 1926, pp. 1, 2; May 14, 1927, pp. 1, 2; May 19. 1928, pp. 1, 2; May 18, 1929, pp. I, 2; May 3, 1930, pp. 1, 2. 4; *Globe* (Toronto), September 7, 1920, p. 6: *Tribune* (Winnipeg), May 2, 1924, p. 8: *Sun* (Vancouver), May 2, 1920, p. 5; May 1, 1924, p. 2; May 2, 1927, p. 4; May 2, 1929, p. 7: Larivière, *Le 1er mai*; Rouillard, *Histoire du syndicalisme québécois*, p. 109; Smith, *Let Us Rise*, pp. 21, 79, 84; Working Lives Collective, *Working Lives*, pp. 178–179.

Chapter 8

Class, Job, and Gender in the Canadian Office

Graham S. Lowe

One of the most perplexing issues facing students of capitalist development is the impact of economic change on the class structure of a society. Since the late nineteenth century, the advancing capitalist division of labour has created new occupations as quickly as it has discarded old ones. This rise and decline of occupational groups has, in turn, recharted the map of class configurations and cleavages with, of course, major political implications. Marx's vision of a dichotomous class system composed of workers and capitalists has thus not been borne out. What has especially confounded Marx's predictions in this regard is the growth of a huge white-collar labour force occupying a middle terrain between the two principal classes. Where to locate the white-collar masses in the class structure has been a persistent source of debate in twentieth-century political and social theory.[1] The focal point of the debate is clerical employees, whose particularly ambiguous socio-economic status would appear to give them a foot in both working and middle classes. The erosion of the clerks' relative wage position, their growing unionization, and the factory-like conditions in many offices may be taken as proof of their descent into the working class. But at the same time, one can point to the clerks' greater mobility prospects, lifestyle differences, and generally more favourable working environment than blue-collar workers as indicative of middle classness. In short, the question of whether clerks are the new proletarians or members of a white-collar middle class is far from resolved.

The proletarianization thesis represents the most concerted attempt to account for the class position of the clerk. Neo-marxists use the concept of proletarianization to describe the deteriorization of white-collar working conditions and relative pay advantages over manual workers.[2] The proletarianization thesis derives its empirical support from historical wage trends and changes in the labour process. Advocates of the thesis posit a direct relationship between the development of rationalized office bureaucracies, a deterioration of clerical wages and working conditions, and the movement of clerical workers as a group into the working class. Income is the most widely used measure of the declining class position of the clerk. The general convergence of clerical and manual earnings since the turn of the century in western capitalist societies is adduced as solid evidence of the destruction of the clerks' once superior socio-economic position.[3] This is usually augmented by a description of the progressive rationalization of administration, such as Braverman's well-known account of the degradation of clerical work.[4] According to Braverman, as traditional managerial functions became part of the administrative labour process, they were delegated to a growing army of routine clerks and subjected to increasing rationalization, largely through mechanization and scientific management. The deskilling and regimentation of clerical tasks eliminated previous distinctions between mental and manual work. This loss of the job autonomy and skill typical of the nineteenth-century bookkeeper thus constitutes the major criterion for classifying clerks as proletarians.[5]

Essentially the proletarianization thesis infers class location of an occupational group from its changing market and work situations. It is precisely because of this assumed organic link between workers' class location on one land, and job and labour market conditions on the other that the thesis has been criticized.[6] One must thus bear in mind that "fluctuations in the market and work conditions of particular groups of workers are, of course a far more common recurrence than any 'radical' shifts in their class situation...."[7] An equally fundamental problem with the proletarianization thesis, yet to be explored, is the tendency to overlook how the changing labour market and job characteristics of clerical employees are directly tied to the dramatic shift in the sex composition of the office workforce during the early twentieth century. It is difficult to interpret the broader impact of the administrative revolution which transformed clerical work without carefully analyzing the process of feminization. This lacuna in the proletarianization debate largely reflects the dominant assumption in all forms of stratification theory that the economic and social experiences of males define the class structure.[8] It is thus taken for granted that females, the great majority of whom are married, depend directly on their husbands for their class position. These comments are particularly germane in the case of clerical workers; McNally, for example, observes that because of the male bias in sociological studies of work the female clerk remains something of a mystery.[9]

This blind-spot concerning the centrality of gender in the development of modern office work has led to three serious flaws in the clerical proletarianization thesis. In the first place, the tendency to examine wages for all workers in an occupation, rather than disaggregating data by sex, masks how the rapid influx of cheap female labour into the office depressed average salaries.[10] A second flaw stems from not explicitly examining the way in which office expansion and reorganization brought about a shift from a male to a female labour supply. Consequently, a defining feature of the administrative revolution is ignored: that the jobs into which women were increasingly being recruited could not be proletarianized to any great extent because most were mechanized, routinized, and generally unrewarding almost from their inception. Both oversights are evident in Braverman's analysis.[11] While acknowledging that declining wages and the entry of women into the office define the new clerical sector of twentieth-century monopoly capitalism, Braverman failed to explore how these two trends are interconnected. Instead, he treated clerks as an undifferentiated group and presented salary data for males and females combined to document the groups' descent into the working class. The third flaw, also found in Braverman, results from viewing clerks as a homogeneous group subjected to the all-encompassing onslaught of work rationalization. Certainly the administrative revolution wrought fundamental, enduring changes in the labour process, but the trend towards more fragmented, standardized, and regulated tasks occurred unevenly. Even within the female clerical sector there can be found pronounced differences in wages and working conditions across industries, within and among firms, and among occupational subgroups. The proletarianization thesis, in short, does not recognize the importance of gender as a major source of change and variation within the twentieth-century office.

In light of these weaknesses, the purpose of this paper is to advance the proletarianization debate by examining the transformation of the clerical labour market and office working conditions from the perspective of the feminization process. Focusing primarily on the administrative revolution in Canadian offices—roughly between the years 1900 and 1930—we will document how the segmentation of the office workforce along gender lines explains many of the characteristics which the proletarianization thesis erroneously interprets as signs of the clerks' declining class position. The discussion begins with an overview of the growth and rationalization of the office during the administrative revolution. We then examine comparative wage trends for the 1901 to 1971 period, highlighting the relative positions of male and female clerks. Next, inter-firm clerical salary differences are documented through a comparison of a bank and an insurance company. Following this, evidence of variations within the office hierarchies of specific organizations is examined. A final section of the paper places wage trends within a broader socio-economic context through an analysis of cost of living data for the first three decades of the century. Concluding comments underline the necessity of incorporating gender into future studies of the class position of clerical employees.

I. The Growth and Rationalization of the Office

The ascendancy of corporate capitalism in Canada precipitated a revolution in the means of administration.[12] Buoyed by the wheat boom on the western frontier, a growing population, and expanding markets, industrialization accelerated after 1900. By the end of World War I, Canada's modern industrial structure was largely in place. In both manufacturing and services the predominant form of organization became the modern corporation, a vast bureaucratic structure which separated ownership and control, delegating operating authority to specialized managers. Large administrative staffs were hired to handle the mounting flow of paperwork. This expansion of the office can be traced to the growing scale and complexity of economic activity, as well as to the extension of managerial control and co-ordination functions. The office became the managerial nerve centre through which voluminous information vital for controlling all aspects of business was compiled, processed, and stored. Adam Smith's self-regulating market place had been eclipsed; the twentieth-century office emerged as "the 'Unseen Hand' become visible as a row of clerks and a set of IBM equipment...."[13]

Turning to Table 8.1 we note that the most immediate impact of the administrative revolution was to expand significantly clerical employment.[14] Clerks now constitute the largest occupational group in the Canadian labour force, having increased their share of total employment from 2 percent in 1891 to 15.2 percent in 1971. Perhaps even more important, the data highlight the fact that most of this clerical growth can be accounted for by the rapid influx of women into the office. In 1891 there were 4,710 female clerks holding 14.3 percent of all clerical positions; by 1971 over 900,000 women filled close to 70 percent of available jobs. The feminization of the office was well underway by 1931, when 45.1 percent of all clerks were women. The two decades between 1910 and 1930 marked a period of transition from the old office to the new. As clerical jobs acquired a "female" label they replaced domestic work as the major female job ghetto. This can be seen from the jump in the proportion of employed women in clerical occupations, from 2.3 percent in 1891 to 17.7 percent in 1931.

Women did not simply replace men in existing clerical jobs. Rather, they were recruited into the new bottom layer of routine jobs produced by the administrative revolution. The typical nineteenth-century clerk was a male bookkeeper. A generalist, he practised a craft acquired through long apprenticeship and often became indispensable to the firm's owner, thereby increasing his chances of some day being made a partner. In stark contrast, the modern clerk is likely to be a young woman operating an office machine, monotonously processing a steady stream of words or figures which hold little meaning for her. The expansion of public education and the proliferation of private business colleges after the turn of the

Table 8.1 Growth of the Clerical Labour Force, Canada, 1891–1971*

	Clerical workers as a percentage of total labour force	Females as a percentage of clerical workers	Female clerks as a percentage of total female labour force
1891	2.0	14.3	2.3
1901	3.2	22.1	5.3
1911	3.8	32.6	9.1
1921	6.8	41.8	18.5
1931	6.7	45.1	17.7
1941	7.2	50.1	18.3
1951	10.8	56.7	27.4
1961	12.9	61.5	28.6
1971	15.2	68.9	30.5

* Data adjusted to 1951 Census occupation classification.

Source: D.B.S. Census Branch, *Occupational Trends in Canada, 1891–1931* (Ottawa 1939), Table 5. N.M. Meltz, *Manpower in Canada, 1931–1961* (Ottawa 1969), Section 1, Tables A-1, A-2 and A-3. 1971 Census of Canada, Volume 3, Part 2, Table 2.

century provided a ready pool of cheap, but reliable, female labour for the burgeoning office bureaucracies.[15] Males would not tolerate the poor conditions and lack of opportunity these subordinate tasks entailed and, furthermore, they were needed to fill the expanding upper clerical and supervisory ranks. Employers therefore began increasingly to recruit women for routine administrative jobs. Reinforcing this shift in labour supply was simple economics; the fact that the vast majority of women in the early twentieth century saw their jobs as "merely a fill-in before marriage" had the effect of suppressing wages through constant turnover.[16]

A major force in the creation of routine clerical tasks was the rationalization of the administrative labour process which accompanied the rapid expansion of the office. The cutting edge of this rationalization was what Bryan Palmer calls the "thrust for efficiency," a diverse collection of managerial assaults on the design, organization, and execution of work with the goal of increased productivity and lower costs.[17] The popularity which F.W. Taylor's doctrine of scientific management achieved immediately before World War I heralded an "efficiency craze" which became an ideological underpinning of the American progressive era.[18] These ideas spilled into Canada, transmitted by Canadian business publications and aided by the management practices of United States-owned branch plants. *Industrial Canada*, the foremost business journal of the day, published a series of articles by Taylor himself in 1913.[19] The managerial reforms initially devised for the factory were gradually introduced into the office. W.H. Leffingwell, a leading proponent of scientific office management, observed in 1917 that "many businessmen, after analyzing the remarkable results secured by applying Frederick W. Taylor's system of scientific management in factories, have asked whether or not similar betterments could be obtained in offices with the system. Their questions can now be answered, for the main principles of the Taylor system have actually been adapted and applied in office work."[20] While Leffingwell was referring to the United States and, moreover, overstated the diffusion of the Taylor system, there can be little doubt that work rationalization methods were being applied in major Canadian offices by the 1920s.

Office working conditions were dramatically altered as tasks were standardized, machines were introduced, the division of labour grew more specialized, and a rigid chain of command emerged. This combination of changes added a stratum to the bottom of the administrative hierarchy into which women were hired. The spread of office mechanization provides clear evidence of this. Machine-related job titles, such as stenographer and office appliance operator, first appeared in the census in 1921. By this time such jobs had a "female only" label firmly affixed to them. For example, Sun Life Insurance Company of Montreal hired its first female clerk in 1894; by 1914 many departments had "an army of typewriters," and there was a central typing pool with dictating machines—all operated by women.[21] According to the same report, many of the machines in the actuarial department seemed "capable of thinking," indicating the supplanting of mental by manual labour. Generally, the feminization of machine-related clerical jobs was completed by the end of the 1920s. The 1931 census shows, for instance, that women comprised 95 percent of all stenographers and typists and 86.3 percent of all office machine operators.[22]

One of the standard ways managers achieved greater overall efficiency was by carefully controlling cost through cost accounting systems. Perusing the pages of Industrial Canada after 1900, one is impressed by the growing number of articles describing various cost accounting procedures and proclaiming their advantages.[23] Often these schemes entailed an intensification of clerical operations, demanding that a greater volume of data be processed with increased speed and accuracy. This in turn accelerated the introduction of machines and encouraged the creation of separate accounting departments. When the Bell Telephone Company of Montreal set up a central accounting department in the early 1920s, key punch equipment was continually operated to record all expenses.[24] While the typewriter launched the first wave of office mechanization, the proliferation of menial accounting tasks precipitated a second wave in the form of Hollerith punch card equipment. Data pertaining to production costs, customer accounts, expenses, and so on, were punched onto an 80-column card and then processed in a variety of ways by ancillary machines. The women operating the Hollerith equipment fitted Marx's notion of the machine-minder. It is significant to note that this primitive computer technology was fairly widespread in Canada, with at least 105 major offices having adopted it by the early 1930s.[25]

Insurance is the prototype of a white-collar service industry. A successful insurance company resembles a finely tuned clerical machine, given the heavy reliance on efficient paper processing. Not surprisingly, insurance managers were at the forefront of office reform. Major Canadian and American life insurance companies organized the Life Office Management Association (LOMA) in 1924 with the explicit goal of solving the problem of "correct organization and administration of ... clerical activities."[26] Discussions of office organization and clerical methods were infused with the ideology of scientific management, and efficiency experts such as W.H. Leffingwell regularly addressed annual conferences. A clear outline of the central trends in insurance office management was presented by a London Life official (London, Ontario) in his 1927 presidential address to LOMA: 1) scientific training, selection, placement, and promotion; 2) a scientific basis for remuneration; 3) caring for the physical and social welfare of workers; 4) supplying adequate supervision over workers; 5) motivating workers; 6) mechanizing work and humanizing work relations; and 7) improving the calibre of management.[27] Some of these aims are seemingly contradictory, mixing elements of scientific management with the human-relations emphasis of the early personnel movement. But taken together, these policies constituted the broad "thrust for efficiency" in the office which underlay the administrative revolution.

We have sketched the growth and rationalization of the early-twentieth-century office in rather general terms. The new routine clerical jobs created by the development of the administrative apparatus of corporate capitalism constituted an expanding area of women's work. That these jobs were regimented, often mechanized, fragmented, low paying, and dead-end suggests the spread of factory-like working conditions. But to conclude further that the incumbents of such jobs were proletarianized in the process is erroneous. In fact, the shift in the sex composition of office staffs would indicate that neither males nor females were proletarianized in the neo-marxian sense of descending into the working class. On one hand, male clerks occupied the better clerical positions and some experienced upward mobility as the ranks of management expanded. On the other hand, very few women actually experienced the proletarianization of office working conditions simply because their recruitment was directly linked to the proliferation of these menial administrative tasks which, as we have seen, became labelled as "women's work." Admittedly the onslaught of managerial work rationalization strategies did introduce factory-like conditions into some areas of the office. But evidence presented below shows that the feminization of the office did not entail the creation of a homogeneous mass of unskilled, low-wage tasks. Granted that the basic structure of inequality in the modern office, revolving around the male manager-female clerk dichotomy, was forged during the administrative revolution. The experience of women clerks, however, was far from uniform—considering that the pay and working conditions for some female clerks was substantially better than for others.

In sum, the process of work degradation within the office proceeded unevenly across firms and industries, as well as within the clerical occupational structure itself. Braverman's model of the modern office—a paper-processing factory staffed by a uniform administrative underclass—does not bear up under careful empirical investigation. Pronounced inter-industry differences and salary variations within the offices of large organizations reveal stratification within the clerical labour market beyond the basic male–female division.

II. Clerical Earning Patterns, 1901–71

The administrative revolution, by creating a more complex office hierarchy with a greater proportion of simplified tasks, precipitated a decline in clerical earnings. But to what extent did this represent a marked departure from the relative labour market position of the nineteenth-century clerk? Unfortunately, the lack of reliable data makes it difficult to estimate any consistent white-collar wage trends for late-nineteenth century Canada. Available evidence portrays the clerks of this period as a small group of males who came from middle class backgrounds, possessed considerable skills, and had good advancement opportunities. A junior clerk hired by Consumers' Gas Company in Toronto started at $300 annually in 1855, rising to $600 after four years; chief clerks earned over $1,000. In contrast, the company paid the stokers in its gas works $364 and lamplighters received $260 annually.[28] It is difficult, however, to generalize on the basis of a single firm, considering that Lockwood's research reveals significant salary variations among British clerks in the latter half of the nineteenth-century.[29] He identifies essentially two groups of clerks, both better paid than artisans. Only the select group of financial, civil service, and mercantile clerks could support a middle-class lifestyle, the majority suffering a "respectable poverty."[30] Lockwood raises an important point (to which we will return in a later section of the paper) regarding the connection between salary and lifestyle. Comparing the earnings of various groups of employees ascertains their economic positions relative to each other, but says little about the actual standard of living, and therefore lifestyle differences, provided by these earnings.

Beginning with the census of 1901 we can trace wage patterns in Canada with reasonable accuracy. According to Table 8.2, the typical

Table 8.2 Average Annual Earnings for Labour Force and Clerical Workers, by Sex, and Production Workers in Manufacturing, Canada, 1901–71*

	Labour Force			Clerical Workers			
	1	2	3	4	5	6	7
	Total	Male	Female	Total	Male	Female	Production Workers in Manufacturing
1901	$384.53	$387.16	$181.98	$446.72	$496.49	$264.37	$375.00<2>
1911	542.17	593.31	305.71	611.91	757.02	449.50	417.00
1921	844.26	1,056.92	572.82	1,056.20	1,248.77	785.10	999.00
1931	847.00	925.00	559.00	1,007.00	1,153.00	830.00	950.00
1941	867.00	993.00	490.00	922.00	1,113.00	731.00	1,220.00
1951<1>	1,860.00	2,131.00	1,220.00	1,771.00	2,166.00	1,546.00	2,434.00
1961	3,170.00	3,660.00	1,993.00	2,743.00	3,381.00	2,339.00	3,762.00
1971	5,391.00	6,574.00	3,199.00	4,139.15	5,868.70	3,402.60	6,695.00

* Data for clerical occupations adjusted to the 1951 Census occupation classification.
<1> Median income, columns 1 through 6.
<2> For the year 1905.

Source: Columns 1 through 6 computed from the following:
1901 Census of Canada, Census and Statistics, Bulletin 1, *Wage Earners by Occupation*, Table II.
1911 Census of Canada, Unpublished working tables for wage earners, Statistics Canada microfilm roll #11001.
1931 Census of Canada, Volume 5, Table 33.
Meltz, *Manpower in Canada*, Section V, Table A-1.
1971 Census of Canada, Volume III, Part 6 (Bulletin 3.67), Table 14.

Column 7 compiled from the following:
M.C. Urquhart and K.A.H. Buckley (eds.), *Historical Statistics of Canada* (Toronto 1965), 99 [to 1951].
D.B.S., *Manufacturing Industries of Canada*, Section A, Summary for Canada (1961), 16 [for 1961].
Statistica Canada, *1971 Annual Census of Manufacturers*, Summary Statistics, Preliminary (July 1973), 3 [for 1971].

clerical employee earned more than the labour force average until 1941, and more than the average production wage until 1931. Through the depression and World War II, however, these clerical wage advantages disappeared. In 1941 clerks had an average salary of $922, considerably less than the $1,220 earned by production workers. And in 1951 clerks earned only $1,771, compared to the labour force average of $1,860. Over the following two decades clerks continued to lose economic ground, especially relative to production workers. Table 8.3 furnishes a concise summary: clerical earnings ranged from 13 to 29 percent above the labour force average from 1901 to 1921, then steadily declined to only 74 percent of the average wage in 1971.[31]

This precipitous drop in clerical earnings may be attributed to a number of factors. The expansion of public education enlarged the supply of suitably trained workers for office jobs. Equally decisive was the reduction of skill and educational requirements with the proliferation of routinized and mechanized clerical tasks. Gains in blue-collar wages, because of the mounting strength of unions and a dwindling

Table 8.3 Average Clerical Earnings Expressed as a Percentage of Average Labour Force Earnings, by Sex, Canada, 1901–71*

	1901	1911	1921	1931	1941	1951	1961	1971
Total	117	113	127	129	107	95	85	74
Male	116	129	119	126	107	102	92	89
Female	149	154	150	166	168	141	126	109

* Average labour force earnings exclude clerical earnings
Source: Computed from Table 8.2.

supply of cheap rural labour with the slowing of immigration after 1914, helped to narrow the wage gap with white-collar employees. But the central reason for the decline in clerical earnings was the recruitment of females into the lower ranks of administrative bureaucracies.

Two distinct labour markets emerged: one for males in more skilled and highly rewarding jobs, another for women in low-paying routine jobs. Discriminatory hiring and promotion practices became institutionalized as the economic advantages of hiring female clerks eroded the traditional social sanctions against employing women in business. In order to assess fully the impact of feminization on clerical wage trends we must separately examine male and female earnings.

There can be little doubt that a distinct labour market for female clerical employees has existed since the turn of the century. This is evident from comparing the male and female clerical earnings presented in Table 8.2. Female clerks earned 53 percent of the average male clerical salary, inching up to 58 percent by 1971. This persistently lower female wage accounts for the overall decline in clerical earnings, as women comprised a steadily growing proportion of the office workforce. Given that women are balkanized into subordinate sectors of the labour market, competing amongst themselves for jobs and not with men, it is noteworthy that during the first four decades of this century female clerks earned 49 to 68 percent more than the average female worker (Table 8.3). But this wage superiority diminished after 1941 as thousands of young women who previously would have remained at home acquired sufficient education to meet the minimal requirements for the booming white-collar sector.[32] The growing abundance of qualified female labour interacted with a reduction of skill requirements in many office jobs to depress clerical salaries to within nine percent of the female labour force average by 1971. Nonetheless, other than the female professionals, clerical work has been one of the most attractive areas of employment—at least from the point of view of wages and working conditions—for women in this century.

Looking now at male clerks, we note a sharp decline in earnings relative to both production workers and the labour force average. Table 8.3 documents that male clerks began to lose economic ground after 1911, regaining slightly in 1931, then sliding below the labour force average by 1961. When compared with production workers, in Table 8.4, male clerks could claim to be economically better off only up to the 1930s, after which time the situation was reversed. In the prosperity at the end of the wheat boom the scarcity of clerical labour was registered in relatively high wages for both males and females. But a steady decline then set in, and from 1941 to 1971 the average male clerk earned around 10 percent less than his blue-collar counterpart. This alone is insufficient grounds for concluding that a levelling of class differences had occurred. To be sure, a good number of individuals recorded as clerks in the censuses were embarking on careers that would elevate them into management. This

Table 8.4 Average Clerical Earnings, by Sex, Expressed as a Percentage of Average Earnings of Production Workers in Manufacturing, Canada, 1901–71

	1901	1911	1921	1931	1941	1951	1961	1971
Male	1.32	1.82	1.25	1.21	.91	.89	.90	.88
Female	.70	1.08	.79	.87	.59	.64	.62	.51

Source: Compiled from Table 8.2.

issue requires further attention, for as we noted above, little is known about the historical mobility patterns of male clerks in Canada. Scattered evidence raises the possibility that in some early-twentieth-century organizations avenues of clerical promotion were fairly restrictive.

For example, the British-style job hierarchy introduced into the federal civil service in 1882 inhibited promotion opportunities from the lower ranks.[33] In addition to facing low starting salaries and meagre annual increments, junior clerks had little hope of ascending through the ranks. The basic departmental organization was built around one chief clerk, two first-class clerks, four in the second class, and eight or more in the third and lowest class. The result, according to one observer, was that "nothing short of the chief clerks being stricken by paralysis every three or four years could create any hope for the scores who are submerged in the lower classes."[34] Even with regular promotions it would have taken 20 years of steady progress for a male clerk to reach the maximum salary of $1,400.[35] The junior positions became less attractive for aspiring young men, in part resulting in a shift toward a female labour supply. It is difficult to say how widespread this bureaucratic problem was, although we should hasten to add that rapid business expansion after 1900 provided mobility opportunities by creating new positions. For example, after examining census data pertaining to the Toronto banking industry in 1911 and 1921, Coombs estimates that the creation of new management positions during the decade could have provided upward mobility for over one quarter of the 1911 pool of Toronto-based bank clerks.[36] Whether this reflects conditions in a particular industry or the general economic climate of the war remains an open research question.

Our overview of clerical wage trends between 1901 and 1971 provides the foundation for an understanding of major transformations in the clerical labour market precipitated by the administrative revolution. The most dramatic change was the creation of non-competing and unequal male and female labour market segments. Females formed an expanding pool of cheap labour for routine office jobs, thereby depressing average clerical earnings. But when each segment is examined separately, a somewhat more complex picture emerges. Male clerks experienced an erosion of their relative wage position after 1911, at the same time as mobility prospects were improving. While female clerks lost some economic ground over the seven decades, most office jobs open to women offered above-average wages and working conditions. In short, the clerical labour market cannot be viewed as a homogeneous entity. The next two sections of the paper will advance this gender-based analysis, examining even finer variations in working conditions within specific organizations.

III. A Comparison of Earnings in a Bank and an Insurance Company

The clerical labour market is far from homogeneous, even within the major male and female segments. As with most occupational groups, clerical salaries vary regionally, by firm and

Table 8.5 Average Annual Earnings[1] of Male and Female Employees, Selected Occupations, Bank of Nova Scotia (Ontario) and Manufacturers Life Insurance Company (Toronto Head Office), 1911–13

	1911		1916		1921		1926		1931	
	BNS	MLI	BNS	MLI	BNS	MLI	BNS	MLI	BNS	MLI
Males										
Clerks[2]	$529.69	$630.62	$556.36	$985.95	$918.29	$1,063.23	$907.41	$1,128.10	$1,085.60	$1,328.66
Junior Clerks[3]	336.54	369.87	348.11	462.00	507.58	890.37	478.23	757.24	657.14	1,033.53
Stenographers, Typists	-	540.00[5]	1,000.00[5]	-	950.00[5]	-	-	1,293.33	-	1,550.00[5]
Jr. Stenographers, typists[3]	-	540.00[5]	-	-	-	-	-	-	-	-
Managers, Professionals[4]	2,601.25	3,850.00	2,211.50	3.687.50	3,008.37	5,056.43	3,153.79	5,537.50	3,458.27	6,431.94
Females										
Clerks	$603.50	$530.63	$456.27	$587.35	$865.43	$840.62	$917.54	$871.81	$993.83	$923.82
Junior Clerks[3]	598.00	412.52	419.70	457.78	900.00[5]	742.73	563.89	729.00	646.00	793.50
Stenographers, typists	610.00	562.36	615.29	660.56	1,001.79	998.53	950.27	915.00	1,023.49	1,403.33
Jr. Stenographers, typists[3]	560.00	486.00	489.25	520.00	908.57	-	672.77	797.14	730.00	-
Managers, Professionals[4]	-	-	1,400.00[5]	865.00[5]	-	-	-	1,300.00[5]	-	1,550.00[5]

[1] Includes average annual salaries, plus bonuses and living allowances, as of 31 December of each year. Earnings of temporary or part-time employees excluded.

[2] Includes all non-supervisory clerical employees (below the rank of assistant manager in the bank; below the rank of department head in the insurance company) excluding stenographers and typists. The 1951 Census definition of clerk was used as a guide for classification.

[3] The term "junior" simply denotes those employees with less than one year of service. It provides an approximation of starting salaries, although raises granted to some employees at the end of their probationary period are included.

[4] For the bank this includes branch managers, assistant managers, accountants, inspectors, and general office executives. For the insurance company this includes executives, department head, cashiers, actuaries, accountants, translators, medical doctors, and registered nurses.

[5] One employee only.

Source: Branch Staff Lists for 1911–31. Bank of Nova Scotia Archives, Toronto. *Head Office Salary Books for 1911-1931*. Manufacturers Life Company Archives, Toronto.

industry, and by the specific task performed. Regional differences, reflecting the specific interplay of supply-and-demand forces in local labour markets, will not concern us here.[37] Our primary interest is in salaries paid within individual firms and for specific tasks. This level of analysis, absent in most discussions of clerical proletarianization, is essential for determining how changes in office working conditions affected the clerical labour market.

There have been few attempts to establish earning patterns for individual firms, mainly because these types of historical data are often unobtainable. We are fortunate that two major employers of clerical workers, the Bank of Nova Scotia and Manufacturers Life Insurance Company, have maintained salary records from around the turn of the century.[38] Some of these data are presented in Table 8.5 for the 1911 to 1931 period when both organizations initiated major changes in the clerical labour process. Salary data for the bank include Toronto head office and branches throughout Ontario. In 1911 this encompassed a workforce of 151, of which 38 were in head office; by 1931 this had swelled to 1,102 employees with 219 in head office. The share of clerical positions held by women increased from 8.6 percent to 30.4 percent over this period, the majority being concentrated in head office. The Manufacturers Life salary data pertain to Toronto head office, which grew from a staff of 93 in 1911 to 445 by 1931. The proportion of all clerical jobs held by women was high in comparison to the bank, standing at 41.8 percent and 55.2 percent in 1911 and 1931 respectively. This alone attests to the uneven impact of the feminization process across firms.

Male clerical earnings in each firm roughly follow the male labour force trend (Table 8.2), except for insurance clerks in 1931. The earnings of these particular bank and insurance clerks were not significantly better than the wages received by production workers in manufacturing during the 1911 to 1931 period. Canadian bank and insurance clerks hardly constituted an "aristocracy of clerkdom," the term Lockwood applies to similar employees in Britain.[39]

A number of salient observations emerge from a comparison of male salaries in the bank and the insurance company. First, clerks and juniors in insurance appear to have been better off than their counterparts in banking throughout the period. This inter-firm wage spread is even greater in the managerial and professional category. Second, fluctuations in salaries follow a different pattern in each organization, suggesting that they may have been drawing upon different pools of labour. Canadian banks used apprenticeship systems which required young recruits to toil at subsistence wages for several years in order to prove themselves worthy of a banking career. Because low starting salaries failed to attract sufficient numbers of Canadian men with the type of solid middle-class background desired, banks were forced to recruit in England and Scotland before eventually turning towards women as a source of labour. Life insurance, by contrast, placed greater emphasis on formal education and consequently paid higher salaries. University commerce or mathematics graduates were considered ideal recruits because of the actuarial expertise required in many of the higher positions. Third, part of the salary differential may reflect the fact that the bank's salary data included many branches in small towns and rural areas where wage levels were lower than in Toronto.

The two firms were much closer together on female salaries in all clerical categories. Female employees in both organizations, except for new recruits, earned notably more than the average female clerk throughout the period (see Table 8.2). In fact, starting salaries in both institutions were close to the average clerical salary for the whole labour force. We should also mention that the gap between male and female clerical salaries was greater in insurance, mainly because of the higher male salaries paid by Manufacturers Life.

The difference between salaries for general clerks and stenographer-typists buttresses the argument that the female clerical labour market is internally stratified. Of all the office jobs available to women, stenography held out the greatest rewards. The special skills and greater responsibilities of stenographers placed them in a distinct labour pool. Stenographers tended to be more career-minded, having greater seniority than other female clerks in both firms. Indeed, the early-twentieth-century stenographer was the craft-worker of the office.[40] This accounts for the rather anomalous situation in the Bank of Nova Scotia where stenographers were the highest paid clerks of either sex throughout the 1911 to 1926 period. The accelerating drive for greater office efficiency, however, did fragment and de-skill the stenographer's work. Specialized jobs such as clerk typist, dictaphone typist, receptionist, and file clerk were carved out of the stenographer's general domain. Thus while the stenographer remained the administrative accoutrement of the manager in smaller branches, the banks had installed typing pools in their larger urban branches and head offices by the late 1920s. Until the 1920s, the Bank of Nova Scotia hired only stenographers, replacing them with the lower-grade clerk typist as the work became increasingly sub-divided and routine. The stenographer, although losing ground by 1930, was clearly at the top of the female office hierarchy. This position marked the limit of female advancement within the office given that women were virtually excluded from managerial and professional jobs.[41]

Our case studies of two major clerical employers underline the importance of shifting the focus of analysis away from the entire clerical labour force toward the division of labour within specific firms. Our research must be supplemented with case studies of other firms located in different industrial sectors before generalizations about the relationship between work and market conditions can be offered with any certainty. Nonetheless, it is possible to draw from our case studies some tentative conclusions about the general employment patterns of stenographers. From its origins in the late nineteenth century, stenography was labelled as "women's work," attracting young women with the lure of relatively high salaries and the prestige of an office job. But the explosion of paperwork increased repetitive typing tasks, thereby spawning the position of clerk typist. So widespread was the use of the typewriter that in 1912 the federal civil service began to hire only women with typing skills.[42] The market for stenographers became flooded by World War I with graduates from commercial courses in high schools and private business colleges.[43] Yet the potential for high salaries remained good for competent and experienced workers. For example, during the war the "exceptional stenographer" with "managing abilities" could command a salary in the $1,500 to $2,000 range annually.[44] This group must have appeared financially privileged in the eyes of women employees in other occupations. Just before World War I the earnings of female retail clerks fell considerably below those of office workers.[45] Moreover, nurses and teachers commanded salaries roughly on a par with those of female stenographers and bookkeepers. Even in 1921 the female office clerk earned more than 22 other female occupations. Only telegraph operators in Montreal and tailoresses, teachers, as well as telegraph operators in Toronto earned more.[46]

IV. Internal Job Hierarchies

Modern corporations and governments are bureaucratic organizations based on a hierarchical arrangement of specialized tasks. We have documented the existence of distinct groups of clerical workers in banking and insurance, defined by different functions and remuneration level. The gradual erosion of employee control over the execution of work, which paralleled office rationalization, no doubt exacerbated these trends. The administrative revolution degraded some tasks, but the fact that not all jobs were directly affected contributed to the development of elaborate clerical hierarchies within organizations. In addition, the bureaucratization of corporations employing both white- and blue-collar workers tended to accentuate the differences between these groups.

We have shown (Table 8.4) that the typical male clerk was economically better off than production workers until 1941. This broad trend, however, does not accurately reflect the experience of many clerks employed in large corporations. Table 8.6 clearly documents that the early-twentieth-century male clerk's salary lagged behind other major wage earning groups in the Canadian Pacific Railway. Of six major occupational groups in the railway, general office clerks (mainly males) received the lowest daily wage. And it is unlikely that the clerk's slightly better employment security would significantly alter this disparity on an annual basis. In 1911 clerks earned $2.17 daily compared with $4.40 for engineers and $3.76 for machinists. While these data only cover the 1909 to 1916 period, there is little indication that the situation changed appreciably in later years considering the general trends for clerical and manual earnings outlined above. It was not that the CPR unduly exploited its clerical employees; the railway clerks' 1911 salary was only slightly below the clerical labour force average. More plausible is that the powerful running trades and craft unions greatly increased the bargaining power of the blue-collar employees. It thus seems that in the CPR—one of the nation's largest employers at the time—it was the colour of the clerk's collar and not their economic status which separated them from manual workers. This underlines the general point that within-industry market conditions are a more fruitful level of analysis than aggregate labour force trends, especially considering that employees would tend to assess their economic standing relative to other groups within their immediate firm or industry.

The second example comes from the insurance industry, where we will examine the typical hierarchy of head offices in Canada and the United States. The white-collar job structure presented in Table 8.7 reflects the division of labour after extensive rationalization of the office. The Table is largely self-explanatory, but we should emphasize that the majority of the jobs up to the position of stenographer were performed almost exclusively by women. Interestingly, 10 of the 12 are machine-related. Even so, there is a salary range of $900 to $1,200 annually, well above the average female clerical salary of $830 in 1931 (Table 8.2). The jump in the salary scale between stenographer and lab technician, and again between clerk on special actuarial computations and legally trained clerk, demarcate three job clusters: routine female jobs, intermediate level jobs performed by either sex but usually by males, and exclusively male jobs at the top level. The income disparity between the first and third groups is great, as exemplified by comparing the salaries of any of the machine operators with that of the security analyst.

Table 8.6 Daily Earnings of Selected Occupations, Canadian Pacific Railway Company, 1907, 1911, and 1916

	1907	1911	1916
General Office clerks	$1.83	$2.17	$2.19<1>
Station agents	2.23	2.91	3.32
Telegraph operators and dispatchers	1.84	2.28	N/A
Locomotive Engineers	4.03	4.40	4.37<2>
Machinists	2.94	3.76	4.54
Carpenters	2.24	2.76	3.12

<1> Chief clerks earned $4.81 and stenographers and typists earned $2.10.
<2> Includes motormen.
Source: *Annual Report of the Canadian Pacific Railway Company to the Minister of Railways and Canals of Canada*, for the years 1907, 1911, and 1916.

Table 8.7 Average Annual Salary Ranges for Various Head Office Clerical Jobs, Major Canadian and American Insurance Companies, 1930

Keypunch operator	$900–$1,100
M.I.B. file clerk	900–1,200
Addressograph operator	900–1,200
Typist	900–1,200
Calculating machine operator – routine	1,000–1,300
Policy writer	1,000–1,400
Photostat operator	1,040–1,600
Premium posting clerk	1,040–1,600
Dictaphone operator	1,100–1,500
Telephone operator	1,100–1,600
Hollerith machine operator	1,200–1,500
Stenographer	1,200–1,600
Laboratory technician	1,750–2,500
Secretary to office	1,750–2,500
Clerk on special actuarial computations	1,800–2,600
Legally trained clerk	2,400–3,200
Travelling auditor	2,400–3,600
Lay underwriter – major responsibilities	2,500–4,500
Security analyst	3,000–4,750

Source: Life Office Management Association, *Proceedings* (1932), 276.

A third and final example extends the above analysis a step further, examining the job classification system for female employees introduced in 1929 in the head office of the Sun Life Insurance Company. With a Montreal head office staff of over 2,800, the company's personnel experts were constantly striving to streamline clerical operations through the introduction of "scientific methods for the selection of the staff and to promote the competence of its members."[47] The more immediate effect, however, was to specialize and standardize clerical tasks further.

Briefly, the plan classified clerks into five grades of permanent staff and a probationary grade.[48] The starting salary of $600 (rising to $720 after six months of good performance) was below the amount paid to juniors in the bank and insurance company examined above (Table 8.5). Senior grade clerks earned a maximum of $1,500 and those in a special grade could earn even more. Salaries were tied to the skill and responsibility requirements of the jobs, as well as to experience. Junior grade clerks performed "simple mechanical or clerical work requiring little previous training or experience," including routine typing. The middle level of the hierarchy consisted of clerks with "considerable experience operating bookkeeping machines; who are competent to perform more advanced stenographic work; or who can supervise more difficult office routines." And the special grade was composed of "experienced clerks who can perform secretarial work requiring the exercise of independent judgement and a complete knowledge of office procedures;

or who by reason of special training can supervise or undertake very advanced work." The numbers of staff thinned out as one proceeded up the hierarchy, and the top two grades covered supervisory duties that, if performed by males, would bring a higher rank and salary. Nonetheless, it is clear that not all office jobs involving women were routinized and de-skilled. A significant minority still demanded considerable expertise and judgment and therefore can in no way be considered proletarianized.

V. Living Conditions of the Canadian Clerk

Much of our discussion has focused on comparisons between various groups of clerks, or between clerks and blue-collar workers. But this type of wage trend analysis remains somewhat abstract unless placed within the broader context of the minimum standard of living deemed acceptable in a society. It is one thing to trace the historical relationship between manual and clerical earnings, but quite another matter to determine whether the salaries of either group were capable of maintaining a family above the poverty line. The debate on clerical proletarianization has thus far lacked this crucial dimension. We will now attempt to examine this issue by providing cost-of-living data against which earnings of various groups of workers can be measured. This approach is admittedly static insofar as changes in the living standards of individuals during their working lives are not measured. It augments the proletarianization debate, however, by documenting how specific jobs limited the ability of their occupants to achieve anything resembling a middle-class lifestyle. In brief, it is a major step towards evaluating the social significance and individual consequences of earning a particular income.

Table 8.8 presents the federal Department of Labour's annual budget for a "workingman's family of five," a fairly accurate estimate of a basic level of subsistence. Included were the average cost in 60 Canadian cities of 29 basic food items, laundry starch, coal, coal oil, wood, and rent. The cost of clothing, medical care, transportation, and other necessities was not included. Nor were provisions made for alcohol, tobacco, entertainment, and other "luxury" items. The budget would provide a basic working-class lifestyle, perhaps marginally better if the family was smaller. But a middle-class lifestyle, especially for a family, was simply out of reach on the budget allotted.

The stark economic reality facing the average male worker, according to Figure 8.1, was a chronic struggle to support a family at an acceptable subsistance level between 1900 and 1931. Production workers in manufacturing—the industrial proletariat—were even more disadvantaged during all but the end of the period. Only male clerks earned sufficient incomes to boost them above this official poverty line. Some groups of clerks, such as those in insurance, likely could afford the comfort and status of a middle-class lifestyle. Yet for the majority this probably remained an elusive ideal.

Table 8.8 Annual Family Budget in 60 Canadian Cities, 1900–31[1]

1900	1910	1916	1921	1926	1931
$487.24	$640.64	$849.16	$1,117.48	$1,116.44	$970.32

[1] Based on weekly costs of 29 food items, laundry starch, coal, wood, coal oil, and rent for the month of December 1900, 1910, and 1921. Data for 1921, 1926, and 1931 cover the entire year. The budget was compiled by the federal Department of Labour and was regularly published in the *Labour Gazette*. It was based on estimates of the weekly consumption of a "workingman's family of five." Rental costs were for "a representative workingman's dwelling of the better class" with "sanitary conveniences."

Sources: *Canada Year Book, 1921* (Ottawa 1922), 649. *Canada Year Book*, 1932 (Ottawa 1932), 691.

This conclusion is confirmed by contemporary reports of actual living conditions. J.P. Buschlen, a bank clerk turned novelist, gave the following account of the Canadian white-collar workers' lifestyle at the start of World War I: "Conditions in the modern business world continue to make it more and more difficult for the 'man without means' to live. He may exist—earn enough to pay for clothes, food and other bare necessities of life—but he cannot invest in a home, marry, and build for the future."[49] Buschlen's reference to marriage was a barb aimed directly at the banks' rule in force until the late 1940s, forbidding employees earning below a specified salary from marrying. The salary requirement was set at $1,000 in 1911, or about 32 percent higher than the average male clerk's salary and almost double that earned by the typical male Bank of Nova Scotia clerk. This notorious edict, enforced by threat of dismissal, ostensibly guarded against embezzlement, but it indirectly justified low salaries. Even the staid *Monetary Times* found Draconian overtones in the marriage regulation, proclaiming that it "smacks of the dark ages" and urging the banks to "raise clerical salaries in order to stem the growing employee dissatisfaction."[50]

Clerks employed in other industries also encountered economic hardships. When the Civil Service Association petitioned the federal government for higher salaries in 1907, it presented personal expense statements showing individual clerks facing deficits ranging from $9.42 to $31 monthly.[51] The association argued that a male clerk could support himself and his family only "by the exercise of prudence and, sometimes, rigid self-denial. Under existing conditions, having regard to the continuous increase in the cost of living, he finds the struggle growing harder and harder."[52] This situation apparently did not improve over the next few decades.[53]

As for female clerks, one might discount the fact that their earnings fell well below the subsistence level by arguing that the vast majority were young, single women gaining worldly experience before retreating into domesticity after marriage. Figure 8.1 suggests, however, that unless such employees boarded at home they would have faced

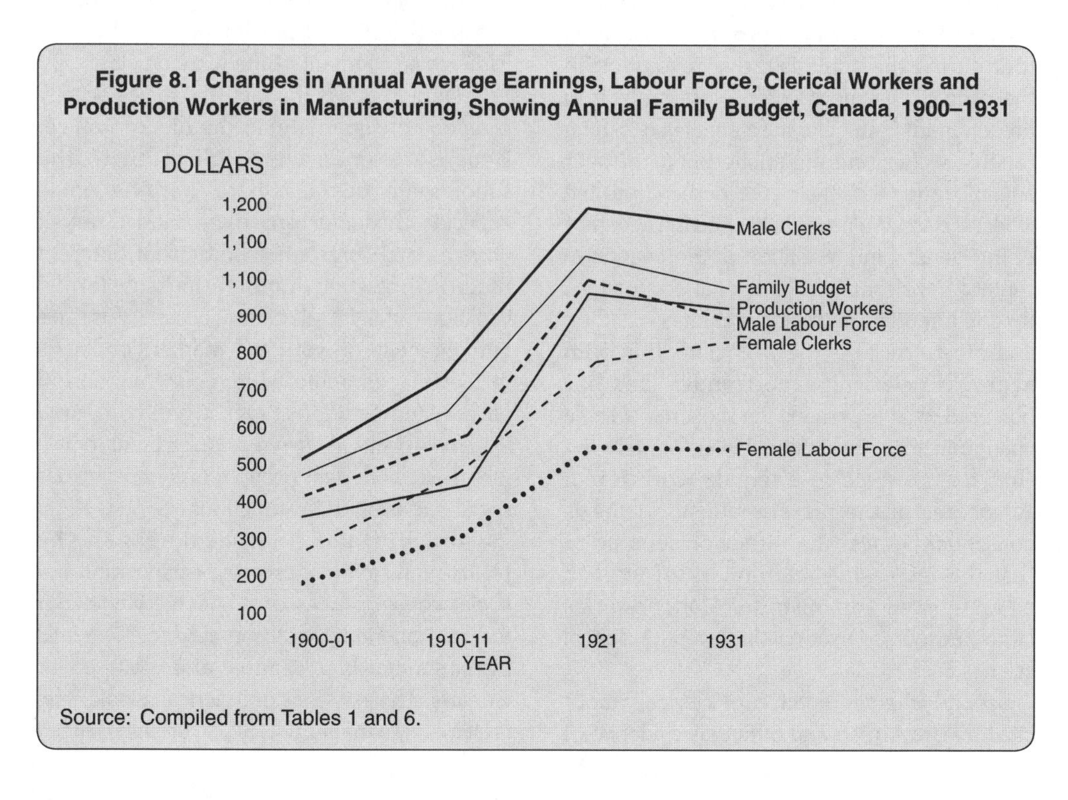

Figure 8.1 Changes in Annual Average Earnings, Labour Force, Clerical Workers and Production Workers in Manufacturing, Showing Annual Family Budget, Canada, 1900–1931

Source: Compiled from Tables 1 and 6.

economic difficulties. Indeed, the circumstances of widows, women with dependants, and others who were self-supporting were nothing short of tragic.[54] The Ontario Civil Service Association documented that female clerks were just as severely affected as men by the pincer-like squeeze of post-World War I inflation and lagging salaries.[55] The association lobbied the government at the end of World War I for a minimum annual salary of $1,000 for female civil servants. Budgets prepared by single, self-supporting women showed that even this substantial increase—about 25 percent more than the 1921 female clerical average—would leave "very little for saving" after necessary expenses had been met.[56] The popular notion at the time of the office girl who worked merely for "pin money" thus served as an ideological screen which masked the economic hardships endured by many office women.

VI. Conclusion

To summarize our discussion, this paper has presented a re-examination of the clerical proletarianization debate from the vantage point of the feminization process which took root during the administrative revolution in the office. The model of proletarianization predominant in the literature equates declining relative wages and diminished control over administration with the clerks' descent into the working class. We have challenged the accuracy of this general interpretation of the twentieth-century transformation of clerical occupations by documenting its major weaknesses. First and most crucial is the preoccupation with aggregate clerical wage trends. This has obscured what is perhaps the most remarkable change in the office since 1900, namely the shift from a male to a female work force. Advocates of the proletarianization thesis consequently miss the rather obvious point that the increasing recruitment of women as low-priced administrative functionaries largely accounted for declining average clerical salaries.

Second, the degradation of clerical labour cited by Braverman and others as evidence of the spread of factory-like conditions requires careful qualification. Admittedly some office jobs became part of a paper processing assembly-line, their incumbents experiencing the labour process as would any factory operative. Central typing pools and Hollerith machine rooms quickly come to mind here. Our evidence shows, however, that concerns with this mental–manual division tends not to be extended to the male–female cleavage within the office resulting from labour market segmentation. Yet even for male clerks, economic distance from the upper ranks of manual workers was never great during the early twentieth century. The extent and nature of their middle classness thus remains at issue. The growing importance of management functions within modern bureaucracies certainly offered a sizeable minority of aspiring clerks opportunities to improve their socio-economic status. While our evidence is tentative with respect to the lifestyle and mobility experiences of the male clerk, it does provide a fruitful working hypothesis for future research: that despite clerks' declining market position relative to manual workers, their better work environment, job security, and greater mobility prospects inhibited the formation of a new white-collar segment of the working class.

Related to this is the fact that males occupy positions of superiority in the modern office. Because women were relegated to the subordinate jobs, it is here that one would expect to encounter signs of proletarianization. Our research presents a somewhat different picture, however, highlighting substantial variation within female clerical occupations. This heterogeneity of work and market conditions in fact placed some white-collar women in advantaged positions, even when compared with male clerks. And in relation to other female job ghettos, clerical occupations had obvious social and economic attractions.

The third and final weakness in the proletarianization thesis revolves around the social consequences of a specific wage. Far too little attention has been paid to the actual living standards of manual and white-collar workers. The existence of a clerical middle class is ultimately a matter of lifestyle, broadly defined to include social relations, politics, and culture. But as our cost of living analysis revealed, the male clerk would have encountered difficulty supporting himself and a family at a living standard discernably better than the upper reaches of the working class. Whether this economic reality was mirrored in residential and consumption patterns or political attitudes and behaviour can only be determined through further investigation.

The above discussion underlines the need to rethink our approach to studying the relationship between changing working conditions and class structuration. The sex segregation of the office workforce demands that the experiences of male and female workers be examined separately but within a single theoretical framework focusing on structural factors in the work place.[57] For example, the superior positions male clerks have occupied in the clerical hierarchy bears directly on their future career prospects. A recent British study suggests that male clerks have diverse origins and destinations, rendering meaningless any blanket class label.[58] Stratification arrangements, the researchers conclude, are more fluid than static. Consequently, one must analyze career paths rather than inferring class position from the job an individual holds at one time. In other words, if an individual's career involves changes in lifestyle, social relationships, and other social experiences, then movement in the class structure may be taking place.

These arguments are much less applicable to the female clerk, largely because opportunities seldom exist for them. How, then, might we determine the class position of women in clerical jobs? A first step would be to highlight the connections between the sex structure of work arrangements, the family system and the subordinate position of women within it, and the persistence of class-based inequalities in the larger society. Heeding the caveat against "equating people with jobs," we must distinguish between changes in clerical jobs and the social position of those women who, at a given time, happen to be employed as clerks.[59] According to Braverman the most common occupational combination in the working-class family is a manual operative husband whose wife works as a clerk.[60] The presence of working-class women in the office may constitute the only real form of proletarianization. The fact that the majority of working wives typically have middle-class backgrounds lends a certain implausibility to the claim that when performing routine clerical work such women are transformed into proletarians. In short, the crux of the issue is how researchers can most accurately identify the class position of women. There are three basic approaches: focus solely on women and their work; use the family as the unit of analysis examining the economic activities of both spouses; or define women's class location in terms of their fathers or husbands. The extent to which each of these approaches reflects the realities of gender-based inequality is a contentious issue in class theory.[61] Any major advances in our understanding of the class-gender relationship require a creative interplay between theory and data. In this respect the office provides an ideal research laboratory.

Endnotes

1. For overviews of the pertinent literature, see Adam Przeworski, "Proletariat into A Class: The Process of Class Transformation from Karl Kautsky's *The Class Struggle* to Recent Controversies," *Politics and Society* 7(1977) 343–401; M.P. Kelly, *White-Collar Proletariat: The Industrial Behaviour of British Civil Servants* (London 1980) 6–24; A. Stewart, K. Prandy, and R.M. Blackburn, *Social Stratification and Occupations* (London 1980), 91–113.
2. Marx originally used the concept of proletarianization to explain the incorporation of the independent petit bourgeoisie into the expanding capitalist wage labour market. But because this process has now largely run its course, given that the vast majority of individuals are now propertyless employees, it is the neo-marxist version of the concept which predominates. Concise definitions of the term "proletarianization" are found in Przeworski "Proletariat into A Class," 353–67; and Giorgio Gagliani "How Many Working Classes?" *American Journal of Sociology*, 87(1981), 261.

3. This reflects the general reduction of the income gap between white-collar and blue collar workers in capitalist societies as documented by Colin Clark, *The Conditions of Economic Progress* (London 1940). For more detailed data pertaining to Britain and the United States see respectively David Lockwood, *The Blackcoated Worker* (London 1966) and R.K. Burns "The Comparative Economic Position of Manual and White collar Employees," *Journal of Business*, 27(1954), 257–67.
4. Harry Braverman, *Labour and Monopoly Capital* (New York 1974), 293–358.
5. This line of argument is found in recent contributions to neo-marxist class theory. See especially E.O. Wright "Class Boundaries in Advanced Capitalist Societies," *New Left Review*, 98 (1976), 3–41; and G. Carchedi, *On the Economic Identification of Social Classes* (London 1977). A similar but theoretically less rigorous argument is contained in Glenn and Feldberg's definition of clerical proletarianization as resulting from "changes in the organization of work designed to increase managers' control of the work process" (62). See Evelyn Nakano Glenn and Roslyn L. Feldberg, "Degraded and Deskilled: The Proletarianization of Clerical Work," *Social Problems*, 25(1977), 52–64.
6. There are some knotty theoretical problems, falling beyond the scope of this paper, involved in determining an individual's class position on the basis of present market situation and job characteristics. As David Lockwood reminds us in *The Blackcoated Worker*, despite the economic decline of once high-status British insurance clerks their jobs continued to offer better security, promotion opportunities, work environment, and benefits thereby socially differentiating them from manual workers. The argument that movement across class boundaries involves considerably more than changing income was first articulated in the British affluent worker studies. See John H. Goldthorpe and David Lockwood, "Affluence and the British Class Structure," *Sociological Review*, 11(1963) 133–63. A forceful elaboration of the basic point is presented by Stewart, Prandy, and Blackburn, *Social Stratification and Occupations*, 91–113 as the foundation of their critique of the clerical proletarianization thesis.
7. John H. Goldthorpe. "Class Mobility in Modern Britain: A Reply to Crompton," *Sociology* 14 (1980),122.
8. For a critical discussion of the effects of this male bias see Joan Acker. "Women and Social Stratification: A Case of Intellectual Sexism," *American Journal of Sociology*, 78(1973), 932–45; and Elizabeth Garnsey, "Women's Work and Theories of Class Stratification," *Sociology*, 12(1978), 223–43.
9. Fiona McNally, *Women for Hire: A Study of the Female Office Worker* (London 1979), 39.
10. This point is not a new one—although it seems to have been lost sight of in the proletarianization debate—having first been enunciated by Richard Hamilton in "The Income Differences between Skilled and White-Collar Workers," *British Journal of Sociology* 14 (1963), 363–73.
11. Braverman, *Labour and Monopoly Capital*, 296–8.
12. See Graham S. Lowe "The Administrative Revolution in the Canadian Office: An Overview," in Katherine L.P. Lundy and Barbara D. Warme (eds.), *Work in the Canadian Context: Continuity Despite Change* (Toronto 1981), 153–73.
13. C. Wright Mills, *White Collar: The American Middle Classes* (New York 1956), 189.
14. All census data pertaining to clerical employment presented in the paper have been standardized to conform with the 1951 census definition of clerk, thereby facilitating accurate intercensus comparisons.
15. For details of the development of commercial education in Canada see Graham S. Lowe, "The Administrative Revolution: The Growth of Clerical Occupations and the Development of the Modern Office in Canada, 1911 to 1931," unpublished doctoral thesis, University of Toronto, 1979, 145–9. Prior to 1900 vocational training for office workers was mostly limited to private business schools. The first public vocational school in the country opened in Toronto in 1901. Ontario quickly became the leader in the field; by 1917 all but two urban areas with populations over 8,000 had set up vocational schools. In 1910 the federal government appointed a Royal Commission on Industrial Training and Technical Education eventually leading, in 1919, to the Technical Education Act which gave nation-wide impetus for vocational education.
16. *Blue Bell* [Bell Telephone Company employee magazine] (August 1930), 8. According to Mary Vipond, "The Images of Women in Mass Circulation Magazines in the 1920s," in S.M. Trofimenkoff

and A. Prentice (eds.), *The Neglected Majority* (Toronto 1977), 117, approximately 90 percent of working women were single during this period. Reinforcing dominant sex role norms were the formal barriers erected by many employers, including the federal civil service and the Ontario school system, against employment of married women.

17. Bryan Palmer "Class, Conception and Conflict: The Thrust for Efficiency, Managerial Views of Labour and the Working Class Rebellion, 1903–22," *Radical Review of Political Economy*, 7 (1975), 31– 49.
18. See Samuel Haber, *Efficiency and Uplift: Scientific Management in the Progressive Era 1890–1920* (Chicago 1964).
19. "Principles of Scientific Management," (March 1913), 1105–6; "What is Scientific Management," (April 1913), 1224–5; "How Scientific Management Works" (May 1913), 1349–50. For details of the applications of American managerial innovations by Canadian businessmen see Paul Craven. *"An Impartial Umpire": Industrial Relations and the Canadian State* (Toronto 1980), 90–110; Craig Heron and Bryan Palmer, "Through the Prism of the Strike: Industrial Conflict in Southern Ontario, 1901–14," *Canadian Historical Review*, 58 (1977) 431–4; Graham S. Lowe, "The Rise of Modern Management in Canada," *Canadian Dimension*, 14, 3(1979), 32–8.
20. William H. Leffingwell, *Scientific Office Management* (Chicago 1917), 5.
21. *Sunshine* [Sun Life Insurance Company employee magazine] (November 1911), 142.
22. Lowe, "The Administrative Revolution," 280.
23. See, for example, Kenneth Falconer "Practical Value of Cost Accounting" (August 1903), 26; E.J. Hathaway, "Ascertaining the Cost of Production" (February 1905), 432–3; H.L.C. Hall, "Economy in Manufacturing" (February 1906), 430–1; L.E. Bowerman, "What a Cost System Will Accomplish" (May 1908), 774–5; C.S. Walters, "The Practical Cost System—Its Relation to the Office" (March 1909), 666–8; John C. Kirkwood's three-part series "A Standard Cost System for Manufacturers" (September 1918), 83–7; "Outlines of a Standard Cost System" (December 1918), 83–9; "A Cost System of Universal Application" (January 1919), 221–3, 226; G.M. Pelton, "Organization of An Efficient Cost System" (June 1924), 85–7, and (July 1924) 189–91.
24. *Blue Bell* (March 1923), 8–9.
25. For a full listing of these organizations see Lowe, "The Administrative Revolution," 379–81.
26. LOMA *Proceedings* (1924), 8.
27. LOMA *Proceedings* (1927), 6.
28. David Coombs, "The Emergence of a White-Collar Work Force in Toronto, 1895–1911," Ph.D thesis, York University (1978), 114.
29. Lockwood, *Blackcoated Worker*, 22.
30. Ibid., 24.
31. It should be noted that in computing Table 8.3 clerical earnings were excluded from the labour force totals to ensure that average labour force trends are not confounded by changes occurring in clerical occupations.
32. N.M. Meltz, *Changes in the Occupational Composition of the Canadian Labour Force, 1931–1961* (Ottawa 1965), 66.
33. R.M. Dawson, *The Civil Service of Canada* (London 1929); J.L. Payne, "The Civil Servant," *University Magazine*, 6(1907), 507–13.
34. Payne, "The Civil Servant," 508–9.
35. Ibid., 508.
36. Coombs, "Emergence of a White-Collar Work Force," 166.
37. In 1921 for example, weekly wages of male clerks in Canada's seven largest cities varied from $22.98 in Quebec to $28.23 in Vancouver; and for female clerks from $12.60 in Quebec to $19.02 in Winnipeg. See *Canada Year Book* (Ottawa 1928), 778–9.
38. The co-operation of the officials of both these companies in making the salary records available is greatly appreciated.
39. Lockwood, *Blackcoated Worker*, 67.
40. See Graham S. Lowe, "Women, Work and the Office: The Feminization of Clerical Occupations in Canada, 1901–1931," *Canadian Journal of Sociology*, 5(1980), 376–8.
41. The exceptions included a woman manager in the Bank of Nova Scotia stationery department, a non-banking service unit, and a nurse and a translator in Manufacturers Life (see Table 5).

42. Civil Service Commission of Canada, *Fourth Annual Report, House of Commons Sessional Papers, No. 31* (1913), xi. Also see *Report of the Ontario Commission on Unemployment* (Toronto 1916), 181–4.
43. By 1915 Toronto had 28 schools and business colleges turning out an estimated 2,000 stenographers annually, many of whom were poorly trained. This over-supply situation undoubtedly contributed to the 25 percent unemployment rate among female stenographers in Toronto at this time reported in the *Labour Gazette* (February 1915), 924.
44. *Report of the Ontario Commission on Unemployment*, 184.
45. *Labour Gazette* (April 1913), 1078–9.
46. *Canada Year Book* (Ottawa 1928), 799.
47. G.H. Harris, *The President's Book: The Story of the Sun Life Assurance Company of Canada* (Montreal 1928), 252.
48. The following details of the salary plan are found in two documents at the Sun Life Archives, Montreal: "Announcement to Women Employees Regarding Salary Grading," from E.E. Duckworth, 1 July 1929 "Renumeration (sic) of Female Employees," Head Office Circular from T.B. MacCauley, President and Managing-Director, 1 July 1929.
49. J.P. Buschlen, *Behind the Wicket* (Toronto 1914), 256.
50. *Monetary Times* (20 May 1911), 2021.
51. *Report of the Royal Commission on the Civil Service, House of Commons Sessional Papers*, No. 29A (1907–1908), 805.
52. Ibid., 1339.
53. Dawson, *Civil Service of Canada*, 189.
54. In June 1931 there were 256 married women employed in eleven major departments of the over 10,000-strong Ontario Public Service, of whom 1 was divorced, 46 were separated, and others were undoubtedly supporting disabled husbands or children. See Ontario Provincial Archives, RG25, Administrative Service Branch, Statistical Files, 1919–1968, "Report on Married Women in the Public Service as of June 1931."
55. Ontario Provincial Archives, Ontario Civil Service Association, "Statement Presented to the Government of Ontario" (Toronto 1919), 8. In 1918 the Ontario government established a Civil Service Commission in a move to rationalize the expanding bureaucracy in the interests of efficiency. J.M. McCutcheon, the first Commissioner, pressed for a standardized job classification system based on merit, recognizing that low salaries undermine morale and efficiency. His second annual report documented the problem facing most white-collar workers as a result of the War: "As a general rule, the compensation of salaried workers responds tardily to changing conditions in the cost of living, a fact which makes such employees in a peculiar measure the victims of the present rule of high prices. This is true of employees in the Public Service whose salaries have not kept pace with the high cost of living." See *Second Annual Report Civil Service Commissioner for Ontario* (Toronto 1920), 10. Arguing in his next report that the state should be a model employer, McCutcheon asserts the principle that salaries should be "adequate, fair, and equitable at least sufficient to enable the employee to maintain a proper standard of living." See *Third Annual Report Civil Service Commissioner for Ontario* (Toronto 1921), 10.
56. Ontario Civil Service Association, "Statement," 8.
57. See Rosabeth Moss Kanter, *Men and Women of the Corporation* (New York 1977) for an excellent analysis of how gender differences in occupational experiences and behaviour are linked to position in the organization.
58. Stewart Prandy and Blackburn, *Social Stratification and Occupations*.
59. Ibid., 112.
60. Braverman, *Labour and Monopoly Capital*, 354.
61. See for example Acker, "Women and Social Stratification"; Garnsey, "Women's Work and Theories of Class Stratification"; and Max Haller, "Marriage, Women and Social Stratification: A Theoretical Critique," *American Journal of Sociology* 86 (1981), 766–95; Heidi Hartmann, "The Family as the Locus of Gender, Class and Political Struggle: The Example of Housework," *Signs*, 6 (1981), 366–94; Nancy Halstrom, "Women's Work, The Family and Capitalism," *Science and Society*, 45 (1981), 186–211.

Chapter 9

Exclusion or Solidarity? Vancouver Workers Confront the "Oriental Problem"

Gillian Creese

> Vancouver, from its very beginning it may be stated, has always been thoroughly anti-Chinese in its sentiments.[1]

> The Chinese question was then constantly before the [Vancouver Trades and Labour] Council and many motions were made on the various phases of the question.[2]

The history of labour politics in early twentieth-century British Columbia was marked by periods of intense anti-Asian agitation.[3] Although the labour movement is commonly seen as an indication of developing working-class consciousness, white workers' consciousness of a common working-class interest in British Columbia did not extend to Asian workers.[4] This leads us to question why the white labour movement followed a strategy of excluding rather than including Asian workers in attempts to collectively improve their lives in British Columbia.

Those who have attempted to answer this question have focused on two different factors: social psychology and economic competition. W. Peter Ward is the strongest proponent of the psychological approach, suggesting that the "Oriental problem" was fundamentally a product of "the social psychology of race relations."[5] "At the bottom of west coast radicalism lay the frustrated vision of a 'white' British Columbia."[6] Ward sees ideas as historically free-floating and therefore sufficient explanation for social action. This argument is premised on the sociologically untenable assumption that social structures are primarily the outcome of the conscious creation of the human mind. The relationship between human agency, social structures, and ideas is a reflexive social process in which people are both the products and the producers of their social environment.[7] Ideological factors are important for understanding racism, but it is necessary to consider the social context in which ideas have efficacy in specific historical times and places.

The more common explanations for racial exclusion by white workers focus on economic factors, either alone or in combination with psychological or cultural differences. For Paul Phillips, Thomas Loosmore, Ross McCormack, Rennie Warburton, and Robert Wynne, economic competition between high-wage white workers and low-wage Asian workers explains racial exclusion by white workers.[8]

These authors agree that labour competition was the central feature of ethnic divisions in the working class, and that exclusion was the only viable strategy under those circumstances. Exclusion was the only viable strategy because Asians were, they suggest, unorganizable. As McCormack argues, Asians were "unassimilated and, therefore, impossible to organize."[9] Two factors make this explanation weak: white workers did not try to organize Asians and then exclude the latter when organization failed; and Asian workers showed greater involvement in labour militancy than conventional wisdom allows, suggesting that solidarity with Asians was a possible alternative to exclusionary practices. The exclusion of Asian workers was not, then, the automatic outcome of competition in the labour market; other factors, such as the denial of political rights to Asians and their status as permanent "foreigners," were important considerations that shaped the practices of white workers.

Other authors have attempted to combine economic and ideological explanations. Patricia Roy and Carlos Schwantes both argue that racism had two distinct loci: economic competition and the ideology of racism, or, in Roy's words, fear for the future of a "white" British Columbia.[10] Neither considers the relationship between economic and ideological factors, however, so an integrated analysis is undeveloped. David Bercuson and H. Clare Pentland consider cultural differences as emigrants from different ethnic origins compete with one another. Pentland argues that large numbers of low-status immigrants led to lack of solidarity, while few low-status immigrants facilitated labour radicalism.[11] British Columbia is placed in the latter category, ignoring the coexistence of radicalism and anti-Asian exclusion. Bercuson suggests that the key to intra-working-class conflict was immigrants' different expectations before arriving in Canada. Asians were cheap and docile because they faced worse conditions in their countries of origin and expected nothing better than they found in Canada; while European, especially British, immigrants expected better conditions and were radicalized.[12] Bercuson does not explain why radicalized white workers excluded rather than included Asians as a solution to cheap labour competition. He also seems to assume that Asian docility gave white workers no choice but exclusion.

What follows is a case study of patterns of racial exclusion and solidarity among one group of workers in an attempt to analyze the circumstances that shaped such actions. Practices of Asian exclusion and inclusion within the Vancouver labour movement are explored in the period prior to the Second World War. Racial divisions within the working class reflected the importance of race in defining workers' lives, not only in the workplace, but also in the political sphere, in civil society, and in prevailing ideologies through which people understood their lives. Race appeared more or less salient in workers' understanding of their lives and problems under different circumstances. As the following analysis will attempt to show, white workers' treatment of Asian workers varied with economic conditions, adherence to radical political ideologies, and the participation of Asian workers in labour conflicts. The white labour movement often pursued anti-Asian activities in the period before World War II. Yet racial solidarity grew during periods of heightened labour radicalism and Asian labour militancy, especially during the Great Depression, even though competition for jobs was at its most intense. At such times white workers no longer distinguished Asians as "foreigners" whose exclusion would advance the situation of "real" (white) workers; they were seen as members of the Vancouver working class with interests similar to other workers.

Cheap Labour/Foreign Workers

Patricia Roy, W. Peter Ward, Edgar Wickberg, Tien-Fang Cheng, Peter Li, Ken Adachi, and others have documented the pervasiveness of racism against Asians during the early twentieth century.[13] Racism was expressed both through dominant ideologies about the inferiority of non-Europeans and through discriminatory practices in the labour market, in the political system, and in most areas of daily life. Asians were not equal to whites in the province during the first half of this century, either in popular consciousness or in the social institutions of the society.

Racial inequality was firmly linked to (and much acrimony rested upon) the role of Asians as cheap wage labourers in the economy. The push and pull of Asian immigration was tied to their status as wage labourers. The first large-scale migration of Chinese recruited by the Canadian Pacific Railway was precipitated by the demand for cheap labour, and Chinese, Japanese, and East Indian migrants actively sought entry into Canada in pursuit of wage-labour opportunities. With a small indigenous population, immigration filled economic development needs, and the motivations for emigration were little different for European or Asian immigrants.[14] Immigrants of all lands sought better economic opportunities, and the vast majority would find those opportunities labouring for someone else. Capitalism was, and remains, a central organizing feature of Canadian society, and immigration patterns were, and are, closely linked to the demands of capitalist economic development.

What differentiated Asian migrants from Europeans was not only the precise role that the former played in the labour market, as an under-class of cheap labourers, but also their being denied political rights by the Canadian state. The mostly male Asian workers were largely confined to the least desirable unskilled labour and concentrated in the primary and service sectors of the economy; earned from one-half to three-quarters of the wages of unskilled white men in the same industries; and were typically hired under labour contractors rather than as individuals, a system that added to their lower standard of living and segregration from the white labour force.[15] Low wages and restricted employment opportunities were directly related to the second-class political status accorded Asians in Canada. Unlike other immigrants, Asians were denied the rights of political citizenship, restricted in areas of employment, regulated, taxed, and even prohibited from immigration to Canada.[16] In its policies the Canadian government clearly distinguished between desirable white settlers and Asian migrants who would be encouraged to work but not to settle in Canada.[17] Asians were considered unassimilable permanent "foreigners," irrespective of naturalization or place of birth.

The different treatment Asian and European immigrants received from employers and the Canadian state created a racially stratified society.[18] Asian subordination was an integral part of social relations in British Columbia. As a result, class relations were shaped by practices of white domination and Asian subordination.

Class relations of power and domination derived from the rights of private property and the pursuit of profit central to a capitalist economy, and were a part of the daily life (if not always daily consciousness) of all who laboured in the province.[19] Although class inequality was common to all wage labourers, however, practices attributed to the race and the gender of the worker shaped the nature of the subordination. To a considerable extent racial and gender characteristics defined the type of work available, the wages received for work, the ability to acquire various kinds of skills, and even conditions in the workplace.[20] White men monopolized the skilled trades, and received higher wages than other workers in unskilled labour. Some work was clearly classified as "women's work" and other work as "coolie labour," sometimes with overlapping boundaries.[21] Workers in British Columbia were not, then, neutral units of labour power: they were hired as "white" or "Asian" workers, male or female workers, and were treated differently by employers. In a society where racial and gender characteristics defined the nature of citizenship and political rights, women and Asian workers were socially defined as more exploitable than white male workers.[22] It should not be surprising, then, that both race and gender affected the development of labour movement in British Columbia, a movement dominated by white men, the strongest segment of the working class.

The Politics of Exclusion in the Vancouver Labour Movement

The Vancouver Trades and Labour Council (VTLC), founded in November of 1889, was the centre of the Vancouver labour movement and the centre of working-class anti-Asian activity. The "Oriental problem" was constantly before the council during its early years, as a review of its first year of operation shows. In February the VTLC supported an agreement between the City of Vancouver and Rogers Sugar Refinery granting the latter tax concessions in exchange for an all-white hiring policy.[23] In September 1890 the VTLC pursued a boycott of Chinese laundries and enforcement of Sunday closing bylaws against Chinese businesses.[24] In October VTLC delegates attended the Trades and Labour Congress convention in Ottawa to express their views on the dangers of Chinese immigration, and met with Prime Minister John A. Macdonald to demand an increase in the Chinese head tax from $50 to $500.[25] In November the VTLC formed a committee to investigate and compile statistics on Chinese labour to be used in its agitation for stricter immigration laws.[26] And in April of the following year the VTLC adopted a resolution calling for the total prohibition of Chinese immigration to Canada.[27]

Individual unions within the Labour Council regularly complained of cheap Chinese, and later Japanese and East Indian, competition undermining union workers. In a single council meeting on 4 June 1908, for example, three different unions identified Asian competition as the cause of poor labour conditions for the union concerned.[28] The Tailors' Union reported:

> Trade dull; Chinese competition displacing membership. Delegates urged the demand for their label, the only guarantee that their clothes were made outside Asiatic sweat-shops and non-union premises.

The Cooks and Waiters' Union reported:

> Asiatic competition was a continual menace to their organization. Complaint that white cooks could not be secured was due to higher wages demanded.... Many members out of employment; trade very dull.

The Typographical Union reported on the existence of Chinese and Japanese print shops "doing work for 'patriotic' local businessmen" that were putting union members out of work. Two motions were passed at the meeting concerning Asian competition. One motion was directed to the provincial Attorney-General to find out:

> why the Asiatic population is not compelled to comply with the civic Health by-laws the same as others ... [and] urged that prompt measures be taken to see that the Chinese disease-breeding sweatshops be at least cleaned up and made to comply with the law.

And the VTLC executive was directed to inquire why Japanese establishments were granted liquor licences. Although all VTLC meetings were not as preoccupied with the "Oriental problem" as this meeting in June 1908, Asian competition was a recurring concern for the Council.

The VTLC and its union affiliates engaged in numerous forms of anti-Asian activities. Exclusionary labour practices included boycotts against Asian businesses, campaigns to replace Asian labour with white labour, to disallow the employment of white women alongside Asian men, to restrict areas of Asian employment, areas of Asian residence and the hours that Asians could work, to prohibit further Asian immigration, and to prohibit Asian membership in trade unions. The labour movement tended to equate non-union labour with Asian labour, even though only a minority of white workers were unionized.[29] And while cheaper Asian labour was criticized for undermining union workers, Asian workers were explicitly excluded from membership in trade unions.

Concern with cheap Asian labour competition was pressed most strongly by unions faced with direct Asian competition, especially tailors, garment workers, laundry workers, and restaurant workers. The skilled craft unions, which made up the bulk of VTLC membership, were not often in direct competition with Asian workers, although skilled unions perceived potential Asian competition in their industries as a threat. For the unskilled unions, Asian labour competition was often a preoccupation, especially during periods of high unemployment. The minutes of the Hotel and Restaurant Employees' Union, for example, record persistent denunciations of union men patronizing "unfair" restaurants, referring to restaurants and hotels employing Chinese cooks, waiters, or bus boys rather than non-union establishments employing whites. Chinese waiters and cooks were identified as the major impediment to more successful union organizing in the culinary industry. The Hotel and Restaurant Employees' Union actively supported the Asiatic Exclusion League and tried repeatedly to persuade City Hall to tie licences to white-only hiring clauses and to disallow the employment of white women in Chinese restaurants. The union also directly lobbied hotels and restaurants to replace Chinese employees with whites in return for union patronage of their establishments. The Hotel and Restaurant Employees' Union did not try to include Chinese restaurant workers as a solution to cheap labour competition until 1938, when a Chinese union organizer was hired.[30]

The labour movement's rationale for excluding Asians was based not only on cheap labour competition but also included explicitly racist ideas. Asians were considered inferior social beings: "Japs," "Chinks," "Coolies," "Hindoos," "insidious Orientals." Just as the Canadian state distinguished between Asian immigrants without political rights and whites who would become "real" Canadians with political rights, so too did the labour movement define Asian workers as "foreigners" and whites as the "real" working class in Canada. Critiques of the oppression of workers were often linked to demands to hire "citizens" of one's own "race." In 1907 a petition was circulated among upper class women to repeal the $500 Chinese head tax because it contributed to a scarcity of servants in the city. In the VTLC's response to this petition, the importance of race is central to the definition of the working class:

> Thus we urge the present Government to disregard the petition of those ladies of British Columbia, who want Chinese servants. The women of the working class do their own work and when they need help, they employ their own race. Let these ladies who now waste their time ... [in] useless functions emulate the example of their poorer sisters and do a little of their own domestic work. If, however, they claim immunity from work, let them pay the price, or modify the conditions of service in such a manner as will secure for them girls of their own race. It is, we think, absurd that the working class of Canada should run the risk of having its standard of living degraded to the level of a Chinese coolie merely to gratify the whim of an aristocratic lady for a Chinese servant.[31]

For the labour movement, the essential factor defining membership in the Vancouver working class was not, apparently, union membership, length of residence, or Canadian versus foreign birth; it was race. Asians were considered nonassimilable "foreigners" who were undermining the living standards of real (white) workers in British Columbia. The problem was not immigration per se, but the type of immigration into British Columbia:

> The demand for Asiatic Exclusion can not be answered by a counter-demand for the exclusion of all immigration, upon the ground of equal treatment to the peoples of all nations. Admitting that European immigration, as it has recently developed, constitutes a problem demanding immediate attention, it is after all a problem of quantity, whereas Asiatic immigration is distinctly a problem of quality.[32]

The prevalance of racist attitudes about the inferiority of Asian workers in British Columbia was grounded in the social organization of Asians as cheap wage labourers at the bottom of the class structure, and the state's denial of citizenship rights. Racism was part of the dominant ideology of the period, a legacy of British colonialism, which found salience in the conditions of workers' lives since employment practices were explicitly race-conscious. White workers' experiences included witnessing the expansion of cheaper Asian labour in the primary and service sectors of the economy as employers sought to drive down the price of labour and undermine union organization. As an article in *The British Columbia Federationist* suggested, white workers feared that the long-term effect of this competition threatened to undermine their already inadequate living standards:

> It has been proved, time and time again, that when the Oriental once gets a foothold in a certain line, the standard of wage in that field at once drops because of his basing his wage demands according to his standard of living. It is not a case of possibly raising the Oriental to the white standard, it is a case of the certain lowering of the standard of the whites.[33]

In the context of a racially segregated labour market the strongest segment of the working class, white (male) workers, organized to exclude, rather than include, cheaper and politically weaker workers who were already defined as "foreigners" within Canadian civil society. In order to overcome racial exclusion, white workers had to begin to define Asian workers as part of the working class rather than as "foreigners" who were the cause of the former's insecurity.

During two brief periods between the First and Second World Wars, when many organized white workers pursued greater solidaristic practices with Asian workers, the labour movement did begin to redefine Asians as part of the Vancouver working class. At the end of World War I (1917–21) and during the Great Depression, the two most militant periods of Vancouver labour history, some white labour organizations actively set out to organize with Asians rather than against them. It was also during these periods that Asian workers were most actively involved in labour militancy.

Asian workers were always in a weaker position than white workers in Vancouver. They were less likely to engage in labour militancy and more vulnerable when they did so. This is not surprising. Asian workers lacked political and citizenship rights, possessed fewer economic resources than white workers, lacked well-developed trade union and socialist traditions, faced the resistance of the ethnic community elites (dominated by Asian employers), and were the object of exclusionary practices by white trade unions. Nevertheless, the image of Asians as strikebreakers but never labour activists during the early years of the labour movement is exaggerated. Although much less active in labour conflicts than white workers, there was a thread of Asian labour activism in Vancouver throughout the early twentieth century.[34]

In the Greater Vancouver area Chinese, Japanese, and East Indian workers took part in no fewer than 50 separate strikes between 1900 and 1939.[35] Seventy percent of these strikes involved the joint action of Asian and white workers, mostly in the lumber industry and the fisheries. Two-thirds of the strikes involving Asians were concentrated in two periods: Asian workers struck 12 times at the end of World War I (1917–21) and 20 times during the Great Depression (1921–37). In contrast, Asians engaged in only 13 strikes during the first 16 years of this century and in only six strikes between 1922 and 1930.

It is not coincidental that higher levels of Asian labour militancy occurred simultaneously with greater solidaristic practices by white workers. The position of Asian workers was strengthened considerably by common action with white workers, thereby encouraging Asian labour militancy. And the more militant Asians were in the workplace, the more likely that white workers would recognize their common interests and attempt to unite with Asian co-workers. For all workers, the state of the economy shaped labour activism: the labour shortage at the end of World War I strengthened the position of all workers, while the depth of the economic crisis during the 1930s had a general radicalizing effect. These three interrelated factors—economic conditions, the growth of radical labour politics, and increased Asian militancy—resulted in greater racial solidarity at the end of World War I and during the Great Depression.

There were, of course, instances of Asian-white co-operation during strikes in the period prior to World War I, especially, but not exclusively, in the salmon fishery.[36] Whatever co-operation occurred, however, was short-lived, lasting only during a particular labour conflict, and never involved organizational inclusion. Lack of organizational unity weakened joint strike activity, and employers often found it possible to break strikes by forcing weaker Asians back to work. White workers gave little consideration to the weaker economic and political position of Asian workers, and simply branded the latter as strikebreakers. In the fisheries, for example, the areas where Japanese fishermen could fish were restricted, while white and Native fishermen could fish throughout the coast. This had a profound effect on labour conflicts in that industry. As one Japanese fisherman remembered, Japanese fishermen could not strike for long because if they lost the season in their area they could not go elsewhere to recoup as could other fishermen. This made Japanese fishermen "the weak link in the chain" in spite of their commitment to improving fish prices and frequent involvement in fisheries strikes. When economic necessity forced the Japanese back to work, white and Native fishermen simply branded the Japanese as strikebreakers, even though the whites and Natives were instrumental in enforcing restrictive regulations against Japanese fishermen in the first place.[37]

On rare occasions some white labour organizations advocated organizing Asian workers as a solution to cheap labour competition. In 1903 The Western Federation of Miners suggested organizing Chinese coal miners to forestall strikebreaking during the Canadian Pacific Railway strike, but nothing came of it.[38] The WFM's successor, the International Workers of the World, also, on occasion, suggested organizing Chinese workers, but apparently never acted on the idea.[39] Apart from these two industrial unions, no other unions even considered Asian organization a possibility.

Exclusionary politics were much less prevalent in the more radical industrial unions and in the socialist political parties in the province than in the mainstream labour movement, even before World War I. The dominant socialist organization in British Columbia during the first two decades of this century was the Socialist Party of Canada (SPC). Like other labour representatives, SPC members of the Legislative Assembly supported legislation discriminating against Asians in the workplace and restricting further Asian immigration.[40] But while endorsing the labour movement's call for the abolition of Asian immigration, socialists also cautioned that this would not solve the labour problem; only the abolition of capitalism would accomplish that end. As the *Western Clarion* suggested:

> Organized workers are even now making loud complaints against what they term the "Sikh invasion." They are calling upon the powers that be to put a stop to it. They overlook the fact that the powers to whom they appeal, and the property interests which profit by the influx of this cheap and docile labor are identical. Their appeal thus of necessity must fall upon deaf ears. If the workers of this or any other country desire the exclusion of people from other lands they must first take possession of the reins of government in order to effect their purpose and enforce their will.[41]
>
> This race question is being agitated by the master class in order to delude the workers into participating in a trade war for their masters' benefit.... The longer that the hope of betterment by emigration is before the workers, the longer they will be in discovering that their one common hope of betterment lies in the overthrow of the wage system.[42]

By the beginning of World War I the Socialist Party's position on Asian workers had become clearly defined in the context of the international solidarity of all workers, and the politics of exclusion was rejected:

> What does it greatly matter who our masters import or exclude? We are slaves here. We are slaves in China or Japan; so our condition can be changed but slightly while the capitalist system lasts. We are not of any nationality; we are not white or black; but one thing suffices to make us all common; we are forced to sell labour power to another class in order to live.[43]

For those who embraced radical socialism there could be little rationalization for excluding some workers, whether socially defined as foreigners or not, from the collective working class when the abolition of the exploitation of all workers was the goal. Socialists more clearly defined the "enemy" as capitalist employers, not other workers.[44] But as Robert McDonald has recently pointed out, the labour movement in Vancouver was not dominated by socialists—it was dominated by "moderate labourism."[45] For the most part, Vancouver workers sought reform, not the abolition of capitalism; and one area where reform was pursued was the exclusion of "foreign" Asian workers from immigration to Canada and from more desirable jobs in the economy.

While the *Western Clarion* was calling on workers to recognize that all workers were the victims of capitalism, the VTLC continued to pass motions seeking the "abolition of Oriental labour in mines, lumbering, fishing and railways"; to legislate "white labour clauses" on public works projects and for the renewal of hotel and restaurant licences; and even to enforce "segregated areas" for Asian residence in Vancouver.[46] However, the shortage of labour and high rates of inflation created by World War I fostered labour militancy, among Asian as well as white workers, and when combined with the growth of radical socialism after the war, produced increased solidaristic practices within the Vancouver labour movement for a brief period of time.[47]

World War I marked a watershed in white–Asian solidarity. The post-war period was marked by general strikes in Vancouver in 1918 and 1919, the rapid growth of support for the One Big Union (OBU), massive organization in the largely unorganized lumber industry, and labour confrontations throughout the province. Asian workers participated in militant labour conflicts, including the 1919 general strike; played dominant roles in some strikes, particularly in the lumber industry; and, for the first time, were admitted into some white labour unions. Chinese and Japanese workers also organized their own trade unions within the lumber industry.[48]

The first confrontation in which Asian workers played a dominant role during the war was the shingle weavers' strike in the summer of 1917. Approximately 800 men, three-quarters of whom were Chinese, struck in dozens of shingle mills in the lower mainland for an eight-hour day with 10 hours' pay.[49] White workers were organized, separately, under the Shingle Weavers' Union, and Chinese workers were organized under the Chinese Canadian Labour Union, formed the previous year. According to *The Chinese Times*, the white union distributed leaflets in Chinese urging the Chinese to organize for shorter hours.[50] Once the strike began, however, Chinese workers were the main motivating force. As the *British Columbia Federationist* commented:

> Officials of the Shingle Weavers' Union assert that if they were as sure of some of the married white workers as they are of the Chinese, there would be no difficulty in enforcing union conditions throughout the jurisdiction.... Chinese employees are asking for two cents more per thousand than the whites. However, it is possible that the whites may be able to get the Chinese to come to a more "reasonable" frame of mind. But at that, it's a sight for the gods.[51]

The strike was not successful, but it marked the beginning of large-scale organization among

Asian workers in the lumber industry, and greater co-operation with whites.

In March 1919 Asian shingle weavers again launched a major strike in the industry. Approximately 1,200 Asian workers, mostly Chinese, struck up to 50 shingle mills in the lower mainland and on the coast to resist a 10 percent wage reduction. The strike lasted one month, with the old wage scale restored in April. In May, the Chinese Shingle Workers' Union, formed during the strike, demanded and won a further wage increase.[52] Incidents of this kind of Asian labour militancy led to calls for white workers to unite with Asians to improve the situation of all workers.

By 1919 *The British Columbia Federationist*, formerly affiliated with the VTLC, had adopted an explicitly socialist politics and would encourage the growth of the One Big Union. The paper both reflected and further encouraged greater Asian–white solidarity:

> Yes fellow workers, Asiatic workers should be encouraged as joining [sic] white unions for it is a class problem, and not a race problem that confronts the white mill-worker of B.C.[53]
>
> It is time that all workers in Canada realised that the "Chink" is as much a part of this country as the Scotchman [sic]; that the "Bohunk" is as necessary as the Englishman; that all of us are exploited by a master-class who cares not what nationality we are so long as we remain willing slaves.[54]

Asian workers, especially those in the shingle and saw mills, took an active part in the 1919 general strikes in Vancouver and New Westminster.[55] According to *The Chinese Times*, the VTLC "promised to treat the Chinese workers well after the strike was over ... [and] help the Chinese to fight against discriminatory laws."[56] Asian workers also played an active role in many OBU-organized strikes for the eight-hour day in the lumber industry during 1919 and 1920. In some instances Asian workers were members of the Lumber Workers Industrial Union (OBU), although more commonly joint labour agitation occurred with Asians organized separately in the Chinese Shingle Workers' Union and the Japanese Workers' Union.[57]

There were many instances of solidarity unparalleled in the past. In April 1920, for example, Chinese workers, at least some of whom were members of the OBU, struck Fraser Mills in Maillardville when a wage increase was refused. White workers quit work in solidarity with the Chinese, and a joint committee was formed that successfully negotiated a wage increase. *The British Columbia Federationist* commented that such incidents should help to educate white mill workers who mistakenly believed that "the reason they are so poorly paid is because they have to compete with Oriental labour." In this and other cases, the "splendid solidarity evidenced in the way in which the white workers, Japs and Chinese stood together" was recognized as an important factor in the gains being made in the lumber industry.[58]

Labour gains did not last long. By 1921 the post-war recession was producing an onslaught of wage reductions and the One Big Union, and radical socialist politics, dwindled almost as quickly as it had grown. The "moderate labourism" of the VTLC dominated Vancouver labour politics again and, with unemployment high and circumstances no longer advantageous for labour miltiancy among Asians or whites, Asian exclusion became a central focus of organized labour once again.[59] In May 1921 the VTLC launched a "Made in B.C. by citizens of Canada" campaign, suggesting that:

> the time has arrived when the citizens must draw the line more closely between our own nationals, and the aliens from other countries and particularly those from Asiatic countries with a lower standard of living, by replacing these men [with] returned men and citizens generally, with special regard for those who are suffering from handicaps incurred in the war.[60]

Two weeks later the Council struck an "Asiatic Committee" to gather data on Asian employment. In July the committee reported that Asian immigration "constitutes the most serious social menace facing the citizens of B.C." and demanded that Asian immigration be prohibited.[61] In August the VTLC, seven trade unions, five veterans' associations, and the Retail Merchants' Association formed the Asiatic Exclusion League at a meeting at the Labour Hall. The mandate of the Asiatic Exclusion League was threefold:

1. To educate the white population to the terrible menace of the Oriental immigration.
2. To pledge every candidate who is running for Dominion offices at the next election to give a stated policy for the exclusion of Orientals.
3. To press for immediate registration of all Orientals in British Columbia under the auspices of the government.[62]

Once the exclusion movement had succeeded with the passage of the Chinese Immigration Act in 1923 and the reduction of Japanese labourers to 150 per year, the Council concentrated on replacing Asian workers with whites and boycotting Asian businesses.[63]

In 1921 the Japanese Workers' Union applied for affiliation with the VTLC but was turned down. Six years later (now the Japanese Camp and Mill Workers' Union), the first Asian union became a member of the Vancouver Trades and Labour Council. This time only five of the 25 unions that voted in the referendum on Japanese union affiliation objected to the latter's inclusion.[64] Japanese affiliation indicated a greater degree of racial tolerance within the VTLC, but it did not end exclusionary practices. The Hotel and Restaurant Employees' Union, the Bakers' Union, the Domestic Workers' Union, and the Shingle Weavers' Union all undertook campaigns, endorsed by the VTLC, to replace Asian labour with white labour.[65] And when the Canadian Labor Party endorsed the enfranchisement of Asians in the spring of 1928, the VTLC withdrew its affiliation after 32 of 36 unions voted against the motion in a referendum.[66]

Class conflict within the Japanese community was the main outcome of Japanese union affiliation with the VTLC. The Japanese Merchants' Association condemned Japanese involvement in the trade union movement and mounted a campaign to weaken the Japanese Camp and Mill Workers' Union. Japanese employers fired members belonging to the union. Merchants withdrew all advertising from the union's newspaper, *The Daily People*, objecting to the paper's message that Japanese workers should unite against their employers. In response, the Japanese Camp and Mill Workers' Union organized a boycott of Japanese businesses and a food co-operative to supply their members' needs.[67] Anti-union resistance by Asian employers, who were powerful members of the Asian communities, probably mitigated greater Asian labour organization. In any event, Asian workers were involved in few strikes during the rest of the 1920s and still faced considerable anti-Asian activity among white workers. Although the Camp and Mill Workers' Union was a member of the VTLC, Asians were still not welcome in the white unions. As one Japanese labour activist commented, "without the cooperation of the white unions we could achieve nothing."[68]

As the economic crisis deepened and unemployment escalated during the early 1930s, labour militancy among whites and Asians, and radical socialist politics increased. The social dislocation was so severe during the 1930s that for many workers capitalism was clearly identified as the "enemy," and solidarity between white and Asian workers was actively pursued. By the end of 1930 there were more unemployed in Vancouver than there were union members.[69] The depth of unemployment generated two different forums for labour activism, the organization of the unemployed and its increasing demands for state action; and the organization of the unorganized, especially in the lumber industry again, under the Workers' Unity League (WUL). Both the organization of the unemployed and the WUL occurred under the auspices of the Communist Party of Canada.

The VTLC became increasingly irrelevant to labour activism during the depression. Maintaining its stance of "moderate labourism," the VTLC continued to pursue strategies to increase the security and standard of living of its employed members and remained separate from the unemployed organizations and from the "dual unions" that it condemned.[70] The issue of unemployment did dominate Council concerns, but until the late 1930s one of its major solutions was to demand the exclusion of Asian workers in preference for the employment of whites. As the VTLC's newspaper *The Labor Statesman* often proclaimed, Asians should not be employed when thousands of "Canadian boys" were out of work.[71] Moreover, it was up to the government to ensure the preferential hiring of whites:

> ... the Provincial Government should also require that goods or materials needed for public works should not be purchased from firms employing Oriental labor.[72]

In spite of the persistence of the view in the mainstream labour movement that Asians were "foreigners" and not "real" Canadian workers (so the lives of the latter could be improved if the former were eliminated), the 1930s witnessed the breakdown of racial divisions in a more profound way than the brief post-war radicalism had. In the unions of the Workers' Unity League and in the National Unemployed Workers' Association—the umbrella organization for various unemployed groups—Asians were not only accepted as members, they were actively recruited as equals, and issues specific to Asian workers were placed on the labour agenda during conflicts.

The National Unemployed Workers' Association called for the solidarity of all unemployed workers:

> The unemployed do not recognize any difference of race or color ... among the many thousands of unemployed workers organized in the NUWA there are many Oriental workers who are among the most highly respected in the organization.[73]

The situation faced by unemployed workers varied by marital status, race, and sex. Chinese workers, for example, were ineligible for city relief because almost all were single men (unlike the Japanese) and only married men qualified for city relief in the early years of the depression. Unemployed Chinese workers were also ineligible for the Relief Camps for single men because these only accepted white men. Thus Chinese workers found unemployment particularly difficult and, as the resources within the Chinese community were stretched beyond their limits, formed the Chinese Unemployed Workers' Protective Association (CUWPA). CUWPA fought for relief for the unemployed along with the Single Unemployed Protective Association, which organized single white men in Vancouver, and the neighbourhood Councils and Block Committees of the National Unemployed Workers' Association, which organized married families (including Asian, mostly Japanese, families). These organizations successfully pressed for city relief for destitute Japanese (and in at least one instance Chinese) families. They fought for equal relief rates for Asian and white families after the City of Vancouver deemed the former to require 20 percent less than the latter to live. They also lobbied for relief for single Chinese men and demanded (albeit unsuccessfully) improved conditions in a mission soup kitchen that was contracted to feed unemployed Chinese in 1933 but was so inadequate that over 100 Chinese men died of starvation by 1935. These organizations also demonstrated from time to time to reinstate Chinese men who were cut off from further assistance.[74]

Solidaristic practices were not confined to issues of unemployment. Between 1931 and 1939 Asian workers were involved in at least 20 strikes in the lower mainland area, three-quarters of which were in saw mills and shingle mills. Nearly half of these strikes took place in a single year, 1932, when Asian workers took part in eight strikes in local lumber mills. Most of these strikes were co-ordinated by the Lumber Workers' Industrial Union, affiliated with the Workers' Unity League. During some of these labour conflicts new demands for racial equality emerged.

In September 1931, 600 white, Chinese, Japanese, and East Indian workers struck Fraser Mills in Maillardville over a reduction in wages. Organized under the WUL, the strikers demanded a 10 percent wage increase, "equal pay for equal work," union recognition, the "abolition of the contract labor system for Oriental workers," and the immediate dismissal of the Japanese labour contractor.[75] The demands in this strike illustrate the extent to which Asian workers were integrated as fuller members of the union and strike committee, especially the demands for equal pay and the abolition of the contract labour system.[76] In August 1932 50 white and Japanese workers struck at Sterling Shingle Mills in Vancouver for a 10 percent wage increase and the reinstatement of workers discharged for union organization, most of whom were Japanese. According to *The Lumber Worker* (a WUL newspaper), this was the first strike where white workers went out in order to protect the jobs of Asian workers.[77] In September 1933, 1,000 white and Japanese men and women, organized under the WUL, struck a Fraser Valley hop farm demanding a wage increase and better living conditions, especially improvements in the Japanese living quarters. The strike committee included Japanese and white representatives, with the Japanese initially demanding higher wages than the white strikers.[78] Asian representation on WUL strike committees was common; in fact, it was an intentional strategy of the union and often resulted in placing demands specific to Asian workers on the strike agenda.

The most notable feature of Asian labour militancy during the 1930s was the degree to which Asians were included as equal members of (at least part of) the labour movement in comparison to previous periods.[79] At the end of the 1930s, after the WUL unions had merged into the international labour movement, even some of the most vocal anti-Asian unions in Vancouver began to include Asian workers within their ranks. The Hotel and Restaurant Employees' Union, for example, hired a Chinese labour organizer to help unionize Chinese cooks in 1938.[80] Asian workers were by no means fully integrated into the Vancouver labour movement during the 1930s, but the shift toward the acceptance of Asians as equal workers and citizens (rather than as "foreigners") was well underway within sections of the organized working class during the depression. The events of World War II demonstrate that racial equality had not yet been accomplished. As the depression ended with World War II, Japanese Canadians were again defined as the "foreign" enemy, not only by the Canadian state but also by the white labour movement in British Columbia.[81]

Conclusions

The politics of the Vancouver working class reflect the heterogeneity of the conditions experienced by workers. The labour movement in Vancouver, as in all capitalist societies, emerged out of the struggle over control in the workplace and the political sphere; but employment practices were neither colour-blind nor sex-blind. Male, female, white, and Asian workers did not receive equal treatment in the labour market, by the state, or in civil society. The material realities of working-class life included relations of white domination and Asian subordination (and male domination and female subordination) that, to a large extent, defined conditions of work and wages, and the nature of citizenship rights within civil society. It is little wonder, then, that working-class politics were structured by ethnic (and gender) relations of inequality.

Labour competition was indeed central to racial divisions within the Vancouver working class, but labour competition is not sufficient to explain these divisions. Common assumptions that Asian exclusion was the only possible outcome of labour competition while labour solidarity was impossible are challenged by the foregoing analysis. The extent of Asian labour militancy before World War II shows that assumptions about docile and "unorganizable" Asians are, at the very least, exaggerated.

Moreover, it should be recognized that the actions of white workers thwarted greater Asian labour organization in the first place. It is reasonable to assume that Asians would have been even more active in labour struggles if white workers had been more open to co-operation with Asians. Furthermore, if labour competition was a sufficient explanation for exclusionary practices we would expect such practices to be heightened during the depression of the 1930s, when labour competition was most intense. Instead, racial solidarity was strongest during this period. A fuller explanation for racial divisions, and the process of overcoming these cleavages, must include attention to the subordinate status of Asians within civil society, patterns of Asian labour militancy, and changes in the political/ideological orientation of white workers, since socialists and labour reformists pursued different strategies toward Asian workers.

Asian workers formed a pool of cheap labour whose social status within civil society, established through state immigration policies and the denial of political rights, was as permanent "foreigners." For white workers, whose own precarious existence was further threatened by cheaper Asian labour, the "foreigner" status of Asians led, at least for the majority who embraced labour reformism, to strategies of exclusion; as "foreign" workers, Asians were not considered part of the "real" (white) working class whose common interests organized labour sought to represent. A pattern of ethnic divisions developed in Vancouver whereby economically and politically stronger white workers sought to improve their lives by excluding Asian workers from better jobs and, preferably, from the country. Racist labour practices in turn reinforced the subordination of Asian workers in the labour market and in civil society, and ensured their persistence as cheap labour.

Asian labour militancy was hampered by lack of economic and political resources, the racist practices of organized white workers, and class conflict within the ethnic communities. Yet contrary to much of the literature on British Columbia labour history, there was a thread of Asian labour militancy throughout this century. At the end of World War I, increased Asian labour activism was facilitated by the war-induced labour shortage and inflation, greater militancy among white workers, and the strengthening of socialist politics advocating solidarity with Asians. The severity of the depression of the 1930s fostered even greater Asian labour activism, much of it organized by the Communist-led Workers Unity League and the organizations of the unemployed. During the 1930s, Asian workers began to place their own issues on the political agenda, an indication of their inclusion as more equal members of the labour movement compared to earlier periods of co-operation.

A necessary condition for bridging ethnic divisions among Vancouver workers was the redefinition of Asians as workers, like others in Canada, rather than as "foreigners." The adoption of socialist politics, with its sharper focus on class divisions and solidarity among all workers, and evidence of common class interests shown through Asian labour activism, helped to break down ethnic divisions within working-class politics even though differential racist treatment by employers and the Canadian state, and labour competition between white and Asian men, persisted.

Endnotes

1. *The British Columbia Federationist*, 18 November 1911, 4.
2. *The B.C. Trades Unionist and Union Label Bulletin*, September 1908, 1.
3. See Thomas Loosmore, "The British Columbia Labour Movement and Political Action," 1879–1906 (unpublished M.A. thesis, University of British Columbia, 1954); A. Ross McCormack, *Reformers, Rebels and Revolutionaries: The Western Canadian Radical Movement, 1899–1919* (Toronto: University of Toronto Press, 1977); Paul Phillips, *No Power Greater: A Century of Labour in British Columbia* (Vancouver: B.C. Federation of Labour Boag Foundation, 1967); Carlos Schwantes,

Radical Heritage: Labor, Socialism, and Reform in Washington and British Columbia, 1885–1917 (Seattle: University of Washington Press 1979); Robert Wynne, *Reactions to the Chinese in the Pacific Northwest and British Columbia* (New York: Arno Press, 1978).

4. There is a rich body of literature in Marxian theory on the relationship between class structures and class consciousness as well as a plethora of historical studies of working-class conflict in industrial-capitalist societies. Collective action dedicated to advancing the interests of workers in opposition to employers is commonly seen as an indication of some degree of consciousness of class divisions, although there is much disagreement about the "degree" of consciousness and its links to revolutionary social movements. See, for example, Adam Przeworski, "Proletariat into a class: the process of class formation from Karl Kautsky's The Class Struggle to recent controversies," *Politics and Society* 7 (1977): 343–401; and Nicolas Abercrombie and John Urry, *Capital, Labour and the Middle Class* (London: George Allen & Unwin, 1983).
5. W. Peter Ward, *White Canada Forever: Popular Attitudes and Public Policy toward Orientals in British Columbia* (Montreal: McGill-Queen's Press, 1978), ix.
6. Ibid., 22 and W. Peter Ward, "Class and Race in the Social Structure of British Columbia, 1870–1939," *B.C. Studies* 45 (Spring 1980): 17–36.
7. Anthony Giddens refers to this process as "structuration." People are the (material and ideological) products of the social structures into which they are born and live, but the structures only exist as the outcome of human actions. So we are, at the same time, structured by pre-existing social arrangements, and reproduce and change those social structures and cultural and ideological forms through human agency (Giddens, *Central Problems in Social Theory* [Berkeley: University of California Press, 1979]). Similarly, Marx observed that "men make their own history, but they do not make it just as they please; they do not make it under circumstances chosen by themselves, but under circumstances directly encountered, given and transmitted from the past" (Karl Marx, *The 18th Brumaire of Louis Bonaparte* [New York: International Publishers, 1963], 15). "New" social history, in an attempt to pursue Marx's historical method, is in essence the study of the structuration of classes, the interplay between the social relations that produce the working class and the social relations that the workers produce and reproduce through their actions. This seems a particularly fruitful approach to the study of ethnic divisions within the British Columbia working class.
8. Phillips, *No Power Greater*; Loosmore, "The British Columbia Labour Movement"; McCormack, Reformers Rebels and Revolutionaries; Wynne, *Reactions to the Chinese*; Rennie Warburton, "Race and Class in British Columbia:A Comment," *B.C. Studies* 49 (Spring 1981): 79–85.
9. McCormack, *Reformers, Rebels and Revolutionaries*, 10.
10. Schwantes, *Radical Heritage*; Patricia Roy, "The Oriental 'Menace' in British Columbia," in J. Friesen and H.K. Ralston (eds.), *Historical Essays on British Columbia* (Toronto: McClelland and Stewart, 1976), 243–55; and "British Columbia's Fear of Asians, 1900–1950," *Histoire sociale/social History* 13(25) (1980): 161–72.
11. H. Clare Pentland, "The Western Canadian Labour Movement, 1897–1919," *Canadian Journal of Political and Social Theory* 3(2) (1979): 53–78.
12. David Bercuson, "Labour Radicalism and the Western Industrial Frontier: 1897–1919," *Canadian Historical Review* 58(2) (1977): 154–75.
13. Roy, "The Oriental 'Menace'"; "British Columbia's Fear of Asians"; "The Illusion of Tolerance: White Opinion of Asians in British Columbia, 1929–37," in K. Victor Ujimoto and Gordon Hirabayashi (eds.), *Visible Minorities and Multiculturalism: Asians in Canada* (Toronto: Butterworths, 1980) 81–91; and "Citizens Without Votes: East Asians in British Columbia," in Jorgen Dahlie and Tissa Fernando (eds.), *Ethnicity, Power and Politics* (Toronto: Methuen, 1981) 151–71; Ward, *White Canada Forever*; Edgar Wickberg (ed.), *From China to Canada: A History of Chinese Communities in Canada* (Toronto: McClelland and Stewart, 1982); Tien-Fang Cheng, *Oriental Immigration in Canada* (Shanghai: The Commercial Press, 1931); Peter Li, *The Chinese in Canada* (Toronto: Oxford University Press, 1988); Ken Adachi, *The Enemy That Never Was: A History of the Japanese Canadians* (Toronto: McClelland and Stewart, 1976).
14. The context of emigration was not identical for all Europeans or all Asians: conditions inducing emigration from the home country varied enormously, some had stronger ties and obligations to kin left behind; no doubt some were "sojourners" without intentions of settling permanently in British Columbia; some had skills that were in demand while others did not. Yet the common thread inducing

emigration was the desire to improve one's life's chances. For a discussion of the concept of the sojourner in Chinese Canadian history, and questions about its efficacy, see Anthony Chan, "The Myth of the Chinese Sojourner in Canada," in *Visible Minorities and Multiculturalism*; and Jin Tan, "Chinese Labour and the Reconstituted Social Order of British Columbia," *Canadian Ethnic Studies* 19(3) (1987): 68–88.

15. Cheng, *Oriental Immigration*, 163–97; Ward, *White Canada Forever*, 17; Gillian Creese, "Working Class Politics, Racism and Sexism: The Making of a Politically Divided Working Class in Vancouver, 1900–1939" (unpublished Ph.D. thesis, Carleton University, 1986), 72–81; Li, *The Chinese in Canada*, 43–55; Canada, Report of the Royal Commission on Chinese Immigration (Sessional Papers, no. 54a, 1885); Canada, Report of the Royal Commission on Chinese and Japanese Immigration (Sessional Papers, no. 54, 1902).
16. Cheng, *Oriental Immigration*, 163–97; Roy, "Citizens Without Votes," 151–71, "The Oriental 'Menace,'" 243–44, and "British Columbia's Fear of Asians," 168–69; Ward, *White Canada Forever*, 33– 38; Peter Li, "A Historical Approach to Ethnic Stratification: The Case of the Chinese in Canada," *Canadian Review of Sociology and Anthropology* 16(3) (1979): 320–32, and *The Chinese in Canada*, 27–33.
17. See, for example, the conclusions in the 1902 Royal Commission on Chinese and Japanese Immigration, 272–79 and 397.
18. An explanation for the origins of this differential treatment must begin with the history of uneven capitalist development and colonialism conquest. Racial theories about the inferiority of non-Europeans emerged out of colonial conquest, a product of unequal power relations, European ethnocentrism, and justification for colonial domination. With the colonial settlement of Canada, British racial ideologies formed an integral part of civil society and structured immigration policies, thus shaping the treatment that immigrants from different origins experienced in Canada.
19. There is no direct relationship between objective class structures and subjective class consciousness. Przeworski has pointed out that classes are not simply derived from their objective position in the economy; classes, as social actors, are "the effects of struggles" structured by economic, political, and ideological relations. Rather than a unilinear progression of class consciousness, "classes are continually organized, disorganized, and reorganized." This suggests that economistic notions of the unilinear progression of working-class consciousness are too simplistic. See Przeworski, "Proletariat into a Class," 367–72.
20. For discussions of women's paid labour in early twentieth-century British Columbia and the differential treatment that men and women received in the labour market, see Josie Bannerman, Kathy Chopik, and Ann Zurbrigg, "Cheap at Half the Price: The History of the Fight for Equal Pay in B.C.," in Barbara Latham and Roberta Pazdro (eds.), *Not Just Pin Money: Selected Essays on the History of Women's Work in British Columbia* (Victoria: Camosun College, 1984), 297–313; Marie Campbell, "Sexism in British Columbia Trade Unions, 1900–1920," in Barbara Latham and Cathy Kerr (eds.), *In Her Own Right: Selected Essays on Women's History in B.C.* (Victoria: Camosun College, 1980), 167–86; Gillian Creese, "The Politics of Dependence: Women, Work, and Unemployment in the Vancouver Labour Movement Before World War II," *Canadian Journal of Sociology* 13 (1–2) (1988): 121–42; Star Rosenthal, "Union Maids: Organized Women Workers in Vancouver, 1900–1915," *B.C. Studies* 41 (Spring 1979): 36–55.
21. Muszynski has pointed out that during the late nineteenth century, Chinese male labour was in demand, not only to fill the "rough" unskilled male jobs in resource extraction and railway construction, but also to fill typically women's jobs in service occupations due to a shortage of women in the province. See Alicja Muszynski, "The Creation and Organization of Cheap Wage Labour in the British Columbia Fishing Industry" (Ph.D. thesis, University of British Columbia, 1986), 161–74.
22. Lacking the same political and civil rights as white men, both Asian men and all women were in a weaker bargaining position in any attempts to attain better wages in the labour market. The second-class citizenship status of women and Asians was also reflected in justifications for why white male labour was worth more than Asian (male) labour (because the latter had an innately lower standard of living) or (white) female labour (because women were dependants of male fathers/husbands). Thus women and Asian workers were cheap labour by definition. See Creese, *Working Class Politics*, 277–82.

23. Vancouver Trades and Labour Council Minutes, 14 February 1890.
24. Ibid., 30 September 1890.
25. Ibid., 30 October 1890.
26. Ibid., 14 November 1890.
27. Ibid., 24 April 1891.
28. Ibid., 4 June 1908.
29. In 1916 only 6.3 percent of the non-agricultural labour force in British Columbia was unionized, rising to 31.8 percent in 1919, dropping to 9.1 percent in 1921, 9.2 percent in 1931, and rising to 12.7 percent by 1939 (Paul Phillips, "The British Columbia Labour Movement in the Inter-War Period: A Study of its Social and Political Aspects" [Ph.D. thesis, University of London, 1967], 388). In Vancouver, union membership reached its pre-war peak with 15 percent in 1912 (Robert A.J. McDonald, "Working Class Vancouver, 1886–1914: Urbanism and Class in British Columbia," *B.C. Studies* 69–70 [Spring/Summer 1986]: 45). In 1931, 7.2 percent of the Vancouver labour force was unionized (calculated from the number of unionized workers as a percentage of the total Vancouver labour force in 1931). See Phillips, *The British Columbia Labour Movement*, 389; and *Census of Canada*, 1931, vol. 3, 756–63.
30. Hotel, Restaurant and Culinary Employees' Union, Local 20 Minute Books; 1910–1939.
31. VTLC Minutes, 21 March 1907.
32. *B.C. Trades Unionist*, April 1908, 6.
33. *British Columbia Federationist*, 24 March 1916, I.
34. In his recent study of the New Westminster labour movement, Allen Seager also points out that Asian workers were much more involved in labour conflicts than is generally supposed. See "Workers, Class and Industrial Conflict in New Westminster, 1900–1930," in Rennie Warburton and David Coburn (eds.), *Workers, Capital and the State in British Columbia* (Vancouver: University of British Columbia Press, 1938), 117–40.
35. The fifty-one strikes are labour conflicts where the involvement of Asian workers could be documented, and probably under-represents Asian labour activism. For a more detailed discussion of Asian labour activism in Vancouver prior to World War II see Creese, *Working Class Politics*, 93–172, and "Organizing Against Racism in the Workplace: Chinese Workers in Vancouver Before the Second World War," *Canadian Ethnic Studies* 19(3) (1987): 35–46.
36. Percy Gladstone and Stuart Jamieson, "Unionism in the Fishing Industry of British Columbia" in *Canadian Journal of Economics and Political Science* 16 (1950): James Conley, "Relations of Production and Collective Action in the Salmon Fishery 1900–1925," in *Workers, Capital, and the State*, 86–116.
37. Public Archives of British Columbia, Reynoldson Research Project, Oral History Tape 1462.
38. William Bennett, *Builders of British Columbia* (Vancouver: Broadway Printers, 1937), 115–20; Phillips, *No Power Greater*, 37–41.
39. Bennett, *Builders of British Columbia*, 40–42.
40. *The Western Clarion*, 1903–1914; Phillips, *The British Columbia Labour Movement*, 129–31.
41. *Western Clarion*, 1 September 1906, I.
42. Ibid., 12 September 1908, 2.
43. Ibid., 24 May 1913, 4.
44. Paul Phillips has suggested that the weakness of the labour movement is often a result of the failure to correctly "identify the enemy," leading to internal divisiveness. (See "Identifying the Enemy: Racism, Regionalism and Segmentation in the B.C. Labour Movement," unpublished paper, 1981).
45. McDonald, "Working Class Vancouver," 33–69. Seager argues that the New Westminster Trades and Labour Council was also dominated by moderates. See "Workers, Class, and Industrial Conflict," 125.
46. VTLC Minutes, 21 April 1910, 20 April 1911, 15 April 1915, and 18 June 1914.
47. The growth of radical socialism occurred throughout much of the western world at the end of World War I, as the common problem of economic and social dislocation was widespread. Compared to countries like Italy, Germany, and Hungary, the growth of radical socialism in Canada was weak. See, for example, Charles Bertrand, *Revolutionary Situations in Europe 1917–1922: Germany, Italy, Austria-Hungary* (Montreal: Inter-university Centre for European Studies, 1976).

48. In 1916 the Chinese Canadian Labour Union, later called the Chinese Workers' Union was formed. In 1919 the Chinese Shingle Workers' Union was formed. In 1920 the Japanese Labour Union, later called the Japanese Camp and Mill Workers' Union, was founded. All three unions were involved in strikes in the lumber industry during the post-war period.
49. PAC, Department of Labour, RG 27, Strikes and Lockouts File, Vol. 306, Strike 43; British Columbia Federationist, 27 July 1917, I; *The Chinese Times* (translations in UBCSC), 18 July 1917, and 24 July 1917.
50. *The Chinese Times*, 18 July 1917, and 24 July 1917.
51. *British Columbia Federationist*, 27 July 1917, I.
52. PAC, Department of Labour, RG 27, Strikes and Lockouts File, Vol. 310, Strike 27; *Chinese Times*, 7 March 1919, 9 April 1919, and 27 May 1919.
53. *British Columbia Federationist*, 17 September 1920, 7.
54. Ibid., 10 September 1920, 4.
55. PAC, Department of Labour, RG 27, Strikes and Lockouts File, Vol. 314, Strike 190; Vol. 315, Strike 221.
56. *The Chinese Times*, 10 June 1919.
57. Accepting Asian members into OBU unions reflected a greater degree of racial solidarity than limited joint action during a labour conflict. It is probably unlikely, however, that large numbers of Asian workers actually joined OBU affiliates, especially since Chinese and Japanese workers organized their own unions in the lumber industry during this period.
58. *British Columbia Federationist*, 16 April 1920, 1, 8; 21 May 1920, I.
59. The One Big Union movement had split the labour movement in Vancouver. The craft unions withdrew from the VTLC, controlled by the OBU, in August 1919 and established the VTLC (International). As the OBU rapidly declined after 1920, the international unions again dominated the Vancouver labour movement and a single VTLC reigned by the mid-1920s. All references to the VTLC in the early 1920s refer to the International Council. See VTLC Minutes, 7 August 1919–4 September 1919. Phillips, *The British Columbia Labour Movement*, 196, 389; David Bercuson, *Fools and Wise Men: The Rise and Fall of the One Big Union* (Toronto: McGraw-Hill, 1978), 155–70.
60. VTLC Minutes, 5 May 1921.
61. Ibid., 19 May 1921, and 21 July 1921.
62. *The British Columbia Labor News*, 19 August 1921.
63. Restrictions against Chinese immigration had been in effect since 1885, when a $50 head tax was imposed. The tax was raised to $100 in 1902, to $500 in 1904, and in 1923 the Chinese Immigration Act was passed prohibiting the further immigration of all Chinese to Canada, excepting students, diplomats, and some merchants. The number of Japanese labourers eligible to immigrate to Canada each year was set, by agreement between the Canadian and Japanese government, at 400 in 1908, and reduced to 150 in 1923; in 1928 "picture brides" were prohibited, ending further female Japanese immigration. East Indian immigration was halted by "continuous journey" legislation in 1908, which stipulated that immigrants must arrive in Canada by continuous journey from their country of origin. There were no direct shipping routes between Canada and India. By 1923, therefore, Asian immigration to Canada had all but ceased. See Adachi, *The Enemy That Never Was*, 81–92; Cheng, *Oriental Immigration*, 60, 66, 71, 92, 126, 136, and 145.
64. VTLC Minutes, 4 August 1921, 19 July 1927, and 2 August 1927.
65. Ibid., 1927–1939; *The Labor Statesman*, 1927–1934.
66. *Labor Statesman*, 6 April 1928, l, 4; 4 May 1928, l, 2; and 8 June 1928, I.
67. VTLC Minutes, February 1929–April 1929; Rolf Knight and Maya Koizumi, *A Man of Our Times: The Life History of a Japanese-Canadian Fisherman* (Vancouver: New Star Books, 1976) 38–57.
68. Ryuichi Yoshida, quoted in Knight and Koizumi, *A Man of Our Times*, 54.
69. Phillips, *The British Columbia Labour Movement*, 271–74.
70. Since the split with the OBU, the VTLC railed against the problem of "dual unions." During the early 1930s the Workers' Unity League and unemployed organizations (especially the National Unemployed Workers' Association) affiliated with the Communist Party repeatedly applied to speak at VTLC meetings and undertake joint actions, but were always turned down (VTLC Minutes, 1930–1936).

Not until the WUL was disbanded to merge into the international unions in 1936 did closer relations between moderates and socialists in Vancouver became possible.

71. *Labor Statesman*, 1 May 1931, 4; and 1930–1934.
72. Ibid., June 1932, I.
73. *The Unemployed Worker*, 26 September 1931, 5.
74. Ibid., 1931–1934; *The B.C. Workers' News*, 1935–1937; *The People's Advocate*, 1937–1939; Creese, *Working Class Politics*, 146–51, and "Organizing Against Racism," 43–44; Wickberg, *From China to Canada*, 181–85.
75. *Unemployed Worker*, 19 September 1931, l, 2, and 4; 26 September 1931, 4; and 3 October 1931, 2; *The Labour Gazette*, October 1931, 1071–72; and December 1931, 1302–03. For a detailed analysis of the Fraser Mills strike, see Jeanne Myers, "Class and Community in the Fraser Mills Strike, 1931," in *Workers, Capital, and the State*, 141–60.
76. The union strategy of equal pay was a response to differential wages based on marital status and race. The average hourly wage was 31 cents for married (white) men, 27 cents for single (white) men, and 20 cents for Asian men (Myers, "Class and Community," 146). Strategies of equal pay ran counter to continuing traditions of differential pay for whites and Asians, even when performing the same work. In mainstream trade unions these differentials were included within union agreements in the late 1930s, after the WUL unions had merged into the international unions and Asians were eligible for membership in the latter. For example, in a contract with the International Brotherhood of Papermakers in 1933 "the basic rate for Occidental workers was 51 cents per hour and for Oriental workers 41 cents per hour; from January 1, 1938 these basic rates were raised to 54 and 44 cents per hour respectively" (*Labour Gazette*, December 1933, 1405). Some union contracts even distinguished racial wage scales for each job classification, as a contract in Ocean Falls shows:

    ...logging (summer)-boommen 68 cents; sawmill-boommen (Oriental) 53 cents, pickers (Oriental) 44 cents, millwrights 68 and 82 cents, bargemen (Oriental) 44 and 58 cents .... (*Labour Gazette*, December 1933, 1406).

77. *Lumber Worker*, September 1933, 10; PAC, Department of Labour, RG 27, Strikes and Lockouts File, Vol. 353, Strike 140.
78. *Unemployed Worker*, September 1933, 7; VTLC Minutes, 19 September 1933; PAC, Department of Labour, RG 27, Strikes and Lockouts File, Vol. 356, Strike 102.
79. From the perspective of Asian workers, the solidaristic practices of working-class organizations espousing radical socialist views was double-edged. According to some Japanese workers, the socialist orientation of these groups probably deterred many Asians from more active participation in labour struggles. As one Japanese worker remembered, this was because Japanese workers recognized that the socialist movement was deemed illegitimate in the dominant society, and was even less acceptable to leaders of the ethnic community than the mainstream labour movement. This suggests that Asian labour militancy might have been enhanced considerably had the mainstream labour movement, rather than only its socialist wing, adopted solidaristic labour practices. See Public Archives of British Columbia, Reynoldson Research Project, Oral History Tapes 1462 and 1465.
80. Hotel, Restaurant, and Culinary Employees' Union, Local 28, Minute Books, 23 March 1938 to 17 July 1938.
81. As Werner Cohn has shown, even the CCF and the Communist Party in British Columbia supported the internment of Japanese-Canadians during World War II. See "The Persecution of Japanese Canadians and the Political Left in British Columbia, December 1941 to March 1942," *B.C. Studies* 68 (Winter 1985): 3–22.

Chapter 10

The Radical Alien and the Winnipeg General Strike of 1919

Donald Avery

The Winnipeg General Strike of 1919 has been one of the most intensively studied episodes in Canadian history.[1] Yet, it seems that the many analyses of this major confrontation between capital and labour have left a number of important questions unanswered. Why, for example, was there such a tragic breakdown in communication between the two major protagonists—the Central Strike Committee and the Citizens' Committee of One Thousand? And why were Dominion officials prepared to accept the allegation that the Strike was a prelude to revolution in Canada, when there was ample evidence that it was a legitimate industrial conflict? One factor that might help to answer these questions has hitherto received only superficial treatment from historians: the role of "radical" immigrant workers in the strike. Thus, despite the numerous charges emanating from the Citizens' Committee in regard to the subversive influence of these workers, very little is known about their role in the life of Winnipeg. In large measure, linguistic difficulties have been responsible for this neglect; not surprisingly, historians who are themselves English-speaking have concentrated on the role of the predominantly Anglo-Saxon leadership of the Central Strike Committee. Moreover, the crucial evidence about the role of the radical aliens which has been locked away in the confidential files of the Royal Canadian Mounted Police and military intelligence has only recently been made available to scholars. It is from the vantage point of this new evidence that the Winnipeg General Strike will be revisited.

I.

On the eve of the Great War Winnipeg had become a city of many solitudes; within its boundaries rich and poor, Anglo-Saxon and "foreigner" lived in isolation. More perhaps than any other city in Canada, Winnipeg had been permanently altered by the surge of immigration after 1896. In 1901 there had been approximately 3,000 Central Europeans in the city; by 1911 the number had grown to 22,296. This represented an increase of from 9 percent to 15 percent of the population. Class and ethnic segregation was very apparent; the vast majority of the white-collar Anglo-Saxon population was to be found in the South and West Ends; the continental European immigrants were "hived" in an ethnic ghetto known as the North End.[2]

Life for most of these immigrants was harsh and uncertain. The unskilled immigrant male was faced with the prospect of irregular employment. In part, this was because his labour was in demand in seasonal economic activities like railway construction, coal mining, lumbering, and wheat farming. Canada was indeed "an eight months' country."[3] The labour situation facing the immigrant worker was aggravated by the activities of private employment agencies operating in Winnipeg and other major distribution centres. It was to the advantage of these fee-charging agencies to maintain a constant flow of immigrant labour between their offices and the various construction camps scattered about the country. For thousands of immigrant workers, the North End of Winnipeg was an occupational and social base from which they ventured forth as the exigencies of the labour market demanded. Each spring these men set out from the North End in search of work in the coal mines and rail camps of western Canada and northwestern Ontario.[4] With the advent of winter they returned to their particular ethnic enclave. Some came home to wives and families; others to boarding houses in which the elements of kinship and ethnicity were very apparent.[5]

The adaptation of Ukrainian workers to the Canadian environment was also facilitated by the transfer of cultural institutions from the Old World. One of the most important of these was the Ruthenian Greek Catholic Church. In 1912 Bishop Nykyta Budka had arrived from Galicia to assume the leadership of the church in Canada. From his Winnipeg residence, working through the *Canadian Ruthenian*, Budka had attempted to foster a strong sense of religious nationalism among Ukrainian immigrants.[6] Of special concern to him was the preservation of Ukrainian bilingual schools in the three prairie provinces.[7] Another institution around which Slavs could unite was the Ukrainian Social Democratic Party. The appeal of this organization was both ideological and social. Within the party, workers were constantly reminded of their Ukrainian heritage and given promises of a Marxist Utopia. The socialist hall also provided them with an opportunity to talk to their fellow Ukrainian workers, to hear news from Galicia or Bukovinia, to stage plays and concerts, to hear lectures and to read socialist works in the Ukrainian language. Moreover, the socialist clubs offered the possibility of collective security; if a worker agreed to join the organization, he was assured of a 20 dollar benefit in the event of sickness or unemployment.[8]

In their recruitment campaign the Ukrainian Social Democrats were fortunate in having in their ranks many experienced socialists. Among these were Matthew Popovich and Hoyorg Tkachuk, both of whom had organized peasants and workers in Galicia before arriving in Winnipeg in 1912.[9] Many of these Ukrainian socialists quickly became involved with the *Robochny Narod* ("Working People"), the Winnipeg-based organ of the Canadian Social Democratic Party. This newspaper was highly ideological, although written in simple and colourful language. Frequent reference was made in it to the depravity of Canadian politicians, Ukrainian priests and Ukrainian national democrats. Ukrainian voters were constantly reminded by *Robochny Narod* that social justice could only be achieved through Marxian means: "The Capitalists do not know how to give, only to take," it argued. "Under the Conservative and Liberal Parliaments thousands of workers have perished in various mines and factories. Thousands live without arms and legs."[10] More specifically, the newspaper called upon Ukrainian voters to support Social Democratic candidates at election time, regardless of nationality. This class solidarity was clearly evident during the 1914 Manitoba provincial election when Ukrainian, Jewish, and Anglo-Canadian Social Democrats succeed in electing R.A. Rigg in the North End; ironically, his major opponent was Taras Ferley, a prominent Ukrainian intellectual, who was a candidate for the Liberal party.[11]

The attitudes of the more affluent members of Winnipeg's Anglo-Canadian community towards political and social ferment of the North End fluctuated between indifference and suspicion. J.S. Woodsworth and a few like-minded spirits aside, Anglo-Canadians in the city had shown little concern over appalling living conditions of the immigrants. There was, however, a general feeling in the local Anglo-Canadian population that the "foreigners" were highly susceptible to criminal behaviour.[12] To the English-speaking elite of Winnipeg the barbarism of the North End was shocking in itself; the thought that it might spill over into the rest of the city and lead to a general attack on property produced an even deeper and more profound anxiety. This sentiment was clearly evident in 1908 when strenuous efforts were made by civic officials to prevent the famous anarchist, Emma Goldman, from visiting the city. In April 1908, Mayor J.H. Ashdown, a wealthy Winnipeg merchant, protested this proposed visit in a strongly worded letter to the Minister of the Interior. Ashdown's claim was that Emma Goldman was coming to Winnipeg "to create trouble ... among the foreigners in our midst."[13] It would be dangerous enough to allow her to address an Anglo-Saxon audience, but for her to appear before a foreign group was to invite disaster:

> ... we have a very large foreign population in this City, it consists approximately of 15,000 Galicians, 11,000 Germans, 10,000 Jews, 2,000 Hungarians and 5,000 Russians and other Slavs and Bohemians. Many of these people have had trouble in their own country with their Governments and come to the new land to get away from it but have all the undesirable elements in their character that created the trouble for them before. They are just the right crowd for Emma Goldman or persons of her character to sow seeds which are bound to cause most undesirable growths in the future....[14]

Ashdown's protest was echoed by many Anglo-Canadian organizations in the city, including the local branch of the Women's Christian Temperance Union who denounced the presence of "a foreigner of such character and reputation," the more so since her appeal would be directed to people who had not been Canadianized.[15] In the event, Emma Goldman was able to enter the country since the Immigration Act made no provision for the exclusion of anarchists. Nevertheless, her visit proved abortive; she was harassed by the local police and had to cancel her lecture series. Moreover, in 1910 the Immigration Act was amended to provide for the exclusion and deportation of those professing anarchist views.[16] This amendment was a portent of what was to follow in 1919.

II

The coming of war in 1914 magnified many of the problems facing immigrants in Canada. The immediate effect of the conflict was the dismissal of large numbers of aliens from their jobs for "patriotic reasons"; these dismissals swelled the ranks of the thousands of aliens already unemployed because of the economic depression of 1913–14.[17] At the start of the war there was also agitation from prominent businessmen and local government officials for the mass internment of these "idle" and impoverished aliens, both for humanitarian and security reasons. The Dominion government, however, was not prepared to implement a mass internment policy, primarily because of the prohibitive cost of operating internment camps. On the other hand, Dominion security officials did maintain a close watch on potentially dangerous ethnic leaders such as ecclesiastics and newspaper editors. In each major urban centre in the country Special Registrars of Enemy Aliens were appointed; all who fell into the "undesirable" category were required to maintain close contact with these Officers.[18] Of special importance was the creation of a Press Censorship Branch in June 1915, under the auspices of the Secretary of State.[19]

In Winnipeg Anglo-Canadian concern over the potential disloyalty of the immigrant population, especially that part of it which came from the German and Austro-Hungarian Empires, had been evident even prior to the declaration of war. In July 1914, while the world waited for the Austrian reaction to the assassination of the Archduke Ferdinand, Bishop Nykyta Budka had issued a pastoral letter calling upon his Ukrainian parishioners to remember their duty to the Austro-Hungarian Empire if war should occur.[20] Budka's letter was angrily denounced by the Anglo-Canadian press with the *Manitoba Free Press* leading the attack. The *Free Press* predicted that other incidents would occur unless the Slavic immigrants were forcibly and quickly Canadianized.[21] Its prediction proved correct; as the demands of war grew during 1915 and 1916, the view that ethnic and cultural diversity was impeding the national war effort gained more and more ground among Anglo-Canadians. In Manitoba, this feeling was focused on a public school system which permitted instruction not only in English and French but in a host of other languages, including those spoken by the enemies of the British Empire. In this context it was easy to equate the creation of an English unilingual school system with the strengthening of national unity. In January 1916, the Minister of Education, in the newly elected Liberal government of Manitoba, announced that he intended to create a unilingual school system in the province, because "among so many different nationalities there is an absolute need of a common medium of communication."[22] Many ethnic leaders in Manitoba did not accept such reasoning. Bishop Budka, for example, asserted that bilingualism was "the right of Canadian Ukrainians."[23] Other ethnic spokesmen claimed that the abolition of bilingual schools was a diabolical plot on the part of "English jingoes and Orangemen ... who desire to deprive the Ukrainian youth from having an opportunity to enter any position above digging sewers and cutting lumber."[24] The response of Manitoba's Anglo-Canadian politicians and press to the protests coming from the ethnic community was unyielding. In March 1916, during the debate over the schools question, a Liberal member of the Legislature, D.A. Ross (Springfield) went so far as to charge not only that Bishop Budka was an Austrian spy, but that he was an officer of the Austrian Army, and not a Bishop at all.[25] Virulent remarks of this kind were accompanied by demands for the internment both of the Bishop and other outspoken members of the Ukrainian intelligensia. Although nothing was done about this, the Dominion press censorship authorities did inform several editors of the non-English-language newspapers that continued agitation over the abolition of bilingual schools would endanger national security and would lead to the suppression of their papers.[26]

Throughout 1917 and 1918 anti-alien sentiment continued to mount. The Conscription Crisis, the Wartime Elections Act, and the Dominion Election of 1917 significantly polarized the Anglo-Canadian and "foreign" elements in Canadian society. In Winnipeg both the *Telegram* and *Free Press* supported the disfranchisement of enemy alien voters to ensure that the forces of "justice and democracy" would emerge triumphant from the Dominion election.[27] Indeed, the vitriolic assault by these newspapers on the enemy alien community prompted even the moderate *Canadian Ruthenian* to protest strenuously about rampaging "Canadian Chauvinism."[28] Growing industrial unrest throughout the country—particularly in western Canada—provided an additional reason for Anglo-Canadians to demand greater control of the enemy alien community. Businessmen in labour-intensive industries charged that agents of the Industrial Workers of the World and socialist organizations were undermining the war economy. With the Bolshevik triumph in Russia these complaints became more shrill. Dominion security officials were also concerned about the possibility of industrial unrest and civil disorder in communities with large foreign-born populations: high on the list of such communities was the city of Winnipeg.[29]

During 1917 the growing militancy both of Slavic workers and the *Robochny Narod* had become a matter of grave concern for the Winnipeg business elite. These feelings had been dramatically brought to the surface by a construction workers' strike in July. In this instance the *Robochny Narod* had been a major force behind the attempt on the part of Slavic unskilled workers to secure better working conditions through collective bargaining.[30] The paper had also denounced the strikebreaking tactics of the Manitoba Builders' Exchange, and the appeal of the Exchange to Anglo-Canadian nativism:

> In the last few days there have appeared in the Anglo press public declarations of the ... Builders' Exchange. This gang of exploiters explains its reasons for refusing to carry out negotiations with the union ... because it is composed almost totally of Austrians and Germans, *who are calling for higher wages for the purpose of saving more money to send to the old country to help in the struggle of our land....* On the basis of this niggarly conceived lie, the contractors have gone to the government for aid. The strength of organizational unity of the construction workers causes them (the contractors) to lose their equilibrium and grab at extreme measures.[31]

In July 1917, violence had erupted between the strikers and the local police with the result that some 23 foreign strikers were arrested. Those immigrant workers from enemy countries were sent immediately to an internment camp at Cochrane, Ontario; the rest were charged in the Winnipeg courts. But despite these repressive measures and attempts by the Builders' Exchange to recruit strikebreakers, the workers had won a limited victory. The construction workers' union was eventually recognized, and working conditions in the industry gradually improved. Significantly, at a meeting of the jubilant strikers, a motion had been passed thanking the editor of *Robochny Narod*, Matthew Popovich, "for his help in the organization of the union, for his participation in many meetings during the Strike, and for his help" in aiding the families of the arrested strikers."[32]

By the fall of 1918 the industrial situation in Winnipeg had deteriorated further; indeed, there had been a brief General Strike during the month of May. Not surprisingly, enemy aliens were once again singled out by spokesmen of the business community as the instigators of the continuing unrest. A representative of the Manitoba Gypsum Company, one of the firms affected by the strikes, charged that "all of the men who have gone out are of alien nationality, many of them not naturalized."[33] Local military officials supported this view. Thus the Registrar of Enemy Aliens informed Colonel Sherwood, the Commissioner of the Dominion Police, that many prominent Anglo-Canadians were becoming impatient over the "lenience with which these Alien Enemies are treated." The Registrar recommended stronger measures, including the internment of enemy alien strike leaders. This, he argued, "would have a very beneficial effect upon the labour situation."[34]

In point of fact, the Dominion government, alarmed by reports about the activities of the Industrial Workers of the World and "Bolsheviks" among the foreign-born workers, was prepared to act.[35] In September 1918 a series of coercive measures were implemented: by two Orders-in-Council (P.C. 2381 and P.C. 2384) the foreign language press was suppressed, and a number of socialist and anarchist organizations were outlawed. Most of these organizations were composed of immigrants; the most prominent were the Ukrainian Social Democratic Party, the Russian Social Democratic Party, and the Finnish Social Democratic Party. Penalties for possession of prohibited literature, or continued membership in any of these outlawed organizations, were extremely severe: fines of up to $5,000 or a maximum prison term of five years could be imposed.[36]

Nor did this concern over a possible Bolshevik conspiracy subside after the Armistice. In December 1918, Prime Minister Borden, while attending the Paris Peace Conference, was informed by British intelligence officials "that the Bolshevik government of Russia is making a very active and to some extent a successful propaganda [effort].... Very large credits are placed in the hands of their agents. There is reason to believe that the same efforts will be extended to Canada and the United States soon."[37] It was generally agreed that New York City was to be the focal point of Bolshevik activity in North America. Winnipeg, because of its large Slavic and Jewish population, was generally regarded as the most likely "Bolshevik" base in Canada. This image of the city was strengthened by the activities of Ukrainian socialists like Michael Charitinoff, former editor of the *Robochny Narod*, who was described by Dominion Censorship authorities as "the ambassador of the Bolshevik government in Western Canada."[38] Another report suggested not only that Charitinoff had received instructions, but also financial aid from Bolsheviks in the United States:

> I learn from two sources that the sum of $7,000 has been, transmitted from the Bolshevist organization in the United States headed by L.A.C.K. Martens to Winnipeg to enable one Charitonoff [sic] 567 Selkirk Avenue, Winnipeg, to establish a revolutionary journal named "Novy Vek," I shall be grateful, for any information which you can give me regarding this matter, or regarding Charitonoff [sic]. I believe he was editor of "Robotchny Narod" [sic].[39]

The growing fear of Bolshevism produced further demands both from Dominion security officials and members of Winnipeg's Anglo-Canadian community for the strict enforcement of the orders-in-council of September 1918.[40] This trend was clearly revealed when Michael Charitinoff was arrested for possession of illegal literature. Judge Hugh John Macdonald, a prominent member of Winnipeg's Anglo-Canadian community, sentenced the young Ukrainian socialist to three years' imprisonment and a fine of $1,000.[41] Significantly, there was an immediate outcry from Anglo-Canadian trade unionists in the city against the severity of this sentence. The *Western Labor News*, the organ of the Winnipeg Trades and Labor Council, charged that "the only possible explanation for such a draconian sentence is that the magistrate who pronounced the sentence was obsessed with the mania of the war and for the moment had forgotten to be judicious."[42] This particular response on the part of the Anglo-Canadian socialists in Winnipeg suggests that class consciousness was becoming a stronger force in the city than ethnicity. Indeed, during a mass protest rally of the Socialist Party of Canada in the Walker Theatre on 22 December 1918, Charitinoff was very much the focus of attention.[43]

Members of the Winnipeg Trades Council also started a Defence Fund for Charitinoff. R.B. Russell, the Secretary of the Council's Press Committee and one of the leading Anglo-Canadian socialists in the city, assumed the responsibility of this fund. In January 1919, Russell sought assistance from other Western Canadian Socialists such as Joseph Knight, a radical Edmonton labour leader. In a letter to Knight, Russell emphasized the need for class solidarity, stresssing that immigrant workers would be a vital force in the building of a Socialist Canada.[44] Russell's idea found organizational expression in Calgary in March 1919, when the Western Labor Conference gave birth to the syndicalist *One Big Union*. A resolution was passed at this convention which declared that "the interests of all members of the working class were identical and that there was no alien but the capitalist."[45] This declaration ran counter to the nativism which was in full flood in some Anglo-Canadian areas of Winnipeg and which was having such an unsettling effect on Dominion policy.

In the early months of 1919, the Borden government was importuned again and again to deport enemy and radical aliens *en masse*. Various veterans' organizations now took the lead in advocating this policy.[46] While their objectives coincided with those of other nativist elements, the reason behind this position was very different. Indeed, the problem of fitting the returned soldier into Canadian society was producing almost as much anxiety among the economic elite of the country as were the controversies surrounding enemy aliens and radical unionists. The contrast between the savagery of the trench warfare which they had known in France and the affluence which the wartime boom had brought to many Canadian businessmen produced in the returned soldiers a deep sense of alienation. This manifested itself in a resentment against wealthy financiers and manufacturers, and made the veterans receptive to socialist allegations of a capitalist conspiracy.[47] There were, however, several factors preventing the large scale mobilization of veterans against the capitalist system. In the first place, both business organizations and pro-business newspapers urged employers to dismiss foreign workers and to replace them with returned soldiers. The anonymity of the "ruling class" was also a factor in the situation. It was one thing to denounce the rich and powerful, but they remained remote from the daily experience of the veteran. Not so the immigrant worker who seemed everywhere "babbling" in his foreign dialect and "peddling" his foreign papers. It was quite apparent to many veterans that the aliens had prospered during the war. The once-despised neighborhood "bohunk," who had been the object of disdain before 1914, now seemed prosperous, and what was even more important, had a job. Yet another factor influencing the political stance of the veterans in the post-war period was the hostility of the executive of the Great War Veterans Association (GWVA) towards radical labour organizations. The sharp distinction between officers and men, which characterized the Canadian Armed Forces had been carried over into the GWVA.[48] Moreover, many of the officers who stood at the head of this organization had close ties with business interests. This was especially true in Winnipeg, where J.O. Newton, the President of the local chapter of the GWVA, actively promoted anti-alien sentiment in order to divide the working class.[49] In this endeavour he had the strong support of the Winnipeg dailies, particularly the *Telegram*. The violent confrontation between veterans and foreigners which occurred in the city in January 1919 was indicative of the success of this campaign.

On 28 January 1919, an angry mob gathered at the Swift Company meat packing plant to protest against the company's retention of alien workers. According to one eye witness "they might have demolished the whole building ... had not the civic and military officials intervened."[50] Mayor Gray addressed the mob, urging them to respect private property, but supporting their anti-alien campaign: "We want to get the aliens out and I am with you in that, but let us do it constitutionally. Go back to the city and show them you will give them a chance to get rid of the aliens and if they don't do it, then is the time for reckoning."[51] Later the same day the German Club and the Socialist Party of Canada offices were wrecked; then the mob swept along Main Street "beating up foreigners, or apparent foreigners." An attack on the business establishment of Samuel Blumenberg, a prominent Jewish socialist, followed. Unable to find Blumenberg, the mob "seized the woman [Mrs. Blumenberg] and forced her to kiss the Union Jack." Finally the mob vented their wrath on the premises: "Everything possible to smash was smashed up...."[52] Newspapers such as the *Telegram* made no apologies for the violence directed against the alien. In reporting the riot, the newspaper contrasted the manly traits of the Anglo-Saxon veterans with the cowardly and furtive behaviour of the aliens: "It was typical of all who were assaulted, that they hit out for home or the nearest hiding place after the battle...."[53]

Clearly, many Anglo-Canadians in the city were prepared to accept mob justice. R.B. Russell reported that the rioting veterans had committed their worst excesses when "smartly dressed officers ... [and] prominent members of the Board of Trade" had urged them on.[54] Nor had the local police or military security officials made any attempt to protect the foreigners from the mob.[55] At the provincial level Premier Norris's response to the violence was not to punish the rioters, but to establish an Alien Investigation Board. This Board was instructed to issue registration cards only to those enemy aliens who were considered "loyal" Canadians. With these cards the "loyal" aliens would be able to secure employment, and would, ostensibly, be protected from physical intimidation. In practice, however, the hearings of the Board often degenerated into virtual "kangeroo" courts, with illiterate aliens being harassed both by members of the Board and crowds of hostile veterans who gathered daily at the Registration Hall. Many of the aliens deemed disloyal were subsequently scheduled for deportation along with interned enemy aliens.[56]

The extent of hysteria and misunderstanding about the immigrant community was intensified during the spring of 1919. Thus, despite clear evidence to the contrary, Anglo-Canadian demagogues such as D.A. Ross claimed that the entire Ukrainian community in Manitoba was dominated by Bishop Budka, and that this sinister prelate was deeply involved in a Bolshevik conspiracy. In particular, Ross indicated that he had irrefutable evidence that Ukrainians throughout the province "had machine guns, rifles and ammunition to start a revolution in May" and that they intended "to divide up property equally among everybody."[57] The stage was now set for the "Red Scare" of 1919.

III.

The Winnipeg General Strike of 15 May to 28 June 1919 brought the elements of class and ethnic conflict together in a massive confrontation. The growing hysteria in the city brought with it renewed anti-alien propaganda, a close co-operation between security forces and the local political and economic elite, and finally, attempts to use the Immigration machinery to deport not only alien agitators but also British-born radicals. The sequence of events associated with the Winnipeg Strike has been well documented: the breakdown of negotiations between management and labour in the building and the metal trades was followed by the decision of the Winnipeg Trade and Labor Council to call a general strike for 15 May. The response was dramatic: between 25,000 and 30,000 workers left their jobs. Overnight the city was divided into two camps.[58]

On one side stood the Citizen's Committee of One Thousand, a group of Anglo-Canadian businessmen and professionals who viewed themselves as the defenders of the Canadian way of life on the prairies. Their purpose was clear: to crush the radical labour movement in Winnipeg. In their pursuit of this goal, the Citizen's Committee demanded that all three levels of government act decisively against the strikers, in particular against those public employees who had gone out in sympathy with the metal and building trade workers. The first priority of the Citizen's Committee was the replacement of those members of the Winnipeg police force who were refusing to pledge themselves not to strike. When the majority of the city's 200 police were dismissed on 9 June, the Committee financed the enlistment of 1,800 special constables. Most of these men were drawn from the Anglo-Saxon middle-class regions of the city.[59] In the meantime, Major-General Ketchen, the Officer in Command of the Manitoba Military District, had brought local militia units up to full strength by requesting "all loyal citizens, through the Citizen's Committee, to offer their services."[60] The Citizen's Committee also engaged in a ferocious propaganda campaign against the opposing Central Strike Committee. This was conducted both through its own newspaper *The Citizen*, and through the enthusiastic support it received from the *Telegram* and the *Manitoba Free Press*. The Committee's propaganda was aimed specifically at veterans, and the strike was portrayed as the work of enemy aliens and a few irresponsible Anglo-Saxon agitators.[61] John Dafoe, the influential editor of the *Free Press*, informed his readers that "the five members of the Central Strike Committee—Russell, Ivens, Veitch, Robinson, and Winning—had been rejected by the intelligent and skilled Anglo-Saxon workers, and had gained power only through "the fanatical allegiance of the Germans, Austrians, Huns and Russians...." Dafoe advised that the best way of undermining the movement was "to clean the aliens out of this community and ship them back to their happy homes in Europe which vomited them forth a decade ago."[62]

But there was now evidence that the anti-socialist and anti-alien attitudes so assiduously being cultivated among the veterans by the Winnipeg dailies had begun to subside. This trend can be attributed, in part, to the active educational campaign launched by local socialists such as R.B. Russell, and, in part, to the growing resentment of the returned soldiers about the failure both of government authorities and business leaders to resolve their social and economic problems.[63] On the opening day of the General Strike, the major veterans' organizations in the city had endorsed the demands of the strikers; they had also accepted the pledge of the Central Strike Committee that law and order would be maintained.[64] Moreover, the *Western Labor News*, the official publication of the Winnipeg Trades Council, continually reminded the returned soldiers that the enemy aliens had been brought to the Dominion "by the men who are now prominent in the 1,000 Committees across Canada." The paper also charged that the current anti-alien campaign was directed against all workers: "so long as they were ... abject slaves, they were desirables; now that they have become a little better off and a little better informed they are aliens."[65] By early June security officials and members of the Citizen's Committee were alarmed by the success which strike leaders such as R.E. Bray and aliens such as Oscar Schoppelrie were having in establishing links between the strikers, ethnic organizations and the veterans. On 14 June, a secret agent of the RNWMP informed the Superintendent of the Winnipeg District that Bray was "at the present time the most dangerous person in the City, in view of the fact that he is a Returned Soldier and is using this to influence other Returned men."[66] The agent also alleged that Bray had organized alien "shock" troops, which would be used when the Bolsheviks seized full control of Winnipeg:

> In ... my conversation with Bray he stated that this affair was going to end in a fight and when I lamented the fact that we had no guns Bray said "Don't worry about guns, we'll have them. We have got between three and four, thousand men, ready and instructed to be in certain places when the 'Alarm' is sounded and they will get into the citizens cars which are to carry the militia to Minto Barracks, pass themselves off as Militiamen until they get inside the Barracks; get possession of the rifles, turn them on the real soldiers and seize the Barracks."[67]

The violent confrontation between the special police and the strikers that had occurred on 10 June provided additional evidence of impending anarchy. Not surprisingly, the *Telegram* placed the blame for the violence entirely on the foreign-born strikers, and angrily denounced any returned soldier "who supports these cowardly brutes."[68] But it was now apparent to the enemies of the strikers that the existing conflict could not be ended by playing the veterans off against the foreign workers and their Anglo-Canadian allies. There now seemed no alternative to direct intervention by the Dominion government. Significantly, the form of intervention which was favoured was the use of the Immigration Act to deport strike leaders.[69]

In point of fact, the Dominion government had already begun the deportation of enemy and radical aliens from the various internment camps which had been established during the war.[70] Moreover, in April 1919, a bill had been introduced into the House of Commons amending Section 41 of the Immigration Act. This amendment provided not only for the exclusion of self-proclaimed anarchists, but of "any person other than a Canadian citizen" who advocated revolution or who belonged to "any organization entertaining or teaching disbelief in or opposition to organized government."[71] Quite clearly at this stage the deportation policy was aimed at the radical alien, for in June 1919, the Naturalization Act was amended so that Bolshevik aliens could be denaturalized and then deported under Section 41.[72] These changes did not, however, satisfy either the Citizen's Committee or security authorities in Winnipeg, who argued vigorously that British-born radicals should also be liable for deportation.[73] Accordingly, Section 41 was amended a second time in a bill which was rushed through the Houses of Parliament in less than an hour. Under the terms of this legislation British-born radicals could expect the same fate as their foreign-born comrades.[74]

In the meantime, plans had been laid for the removal of the Winnipeg strike leaders whose influence seemed to be growing daily. Sympathetic strikes had been launched in other cities, and there was a distinct possibility of a nation-wide railway strike.[75] According to Gideon Robertson, the Dominion Minister of Labour, the only solution to the crisis was to arrest and deport the radical agitators in Winnipeg and to carry out similar actions across the country: "our plan will probably be to remove a considerable number directly to a train destined [to] Internment Camp Kapuskasing ... it being thought very desirable that they should be removed promptly from here [Winnipeg]."[76] On 16 June, RNWMP Commanding Officers across the country were provided with special authority to effect the necessary deportations. In the early hours of the next morning the officers of the force descended on the residences of 10 Winnipeg men: six Anglo-Saxon labour leaders and four "foreigners."[77] The Anglo-Saxons arrested were R.B. Russell, William Ivens, R.E. Bray, A.A. Heaps, John Queen, and George Armstrong. The four "foreigners" seized were Michael Charitinoff, Samuel Blumenberg, Moses Almazoff, and Oscar Schoppelrie, all of whom had been considered dangerous and had been placed under police surveillance weeks before the strike.[78]

But none of these men were summarily deported. In the case of the Anglo-Saxon strike leaders an immediate protest was registered by numerous labour organizations across the country, including the conservative Executive of the Trades and Labor Congress.[79] In Winnipeg itself even John W. Dafoe deplored the government's action arguing that the arrest of the strike leaders would "enable them to pose as martyrs in the cause of the working-men."[80] Alarmed by this uproar, the Borden government announced that it did not intend to employ Section 41 against the British-born agitators either in Winnipeg or any other centre. Of equal significance was the decision on 21 June to release on bail the Anglo-Saxon Winnipeg strike leaders, a gesture which was not extended to the four "foreign" radicals who remained lodged in the Stoney Mountain penitentiary.[81] The same day there was a violent confrontation between the strikers and the RNWMP. In the melee scores were injured on both sides and two "foreigners" were killed by gunfire. During this clash members of the special police and the RNWMP arrested some 31 "foreign rioters." Other police action soon followed. On 1 July, a series of raids were carried out across the country on the homes of known agitators and the offices of radical organizations.[82] These RNWMP forays resulted in the seizure of a great mass of "incriminating" material. In Winnipeg, the Ukrainian Labor Temple and the homes of 30 socialists were ramsacked.[83]

The stage was now set for the Dominion government to initiate legal action against those accused of radical activity. At this point, the Dominion authorities appear to have decided on two separate courses of action in dealing with the detained radicals: Anglo-Saxons would be given jury trials; aliens would be subject to deportation hearings before a Board of Inquiry. Samuel Blumenberg, Michael Charitinoff, Solomon Almazoff, and Oscar Schoppelrie appeared before an Immigration Board of Inquiry presided over by Judge R.M. Noble.[84] Crown council was A.J. Andrews, one of the leading members of the Citizen's Committee of One Thousand, and a confidant of Arthur Meighen, now acting Minister of Justice.[85] The defence was conducted by three lawyers, T.J. Murray, Marcus Hyman, and E.J. McMurray—appointed by the Winnipeg Trades and Labor Council. More than the fate of the accused was at stake at these hearings. If Section 41 could be made to stand up to the requirements of this situation, the way would be cleared for the deportation of hundreds of other immigrant agitators across the country. Moreover, the fate of the foreign strike leaders would obviously influence the outcome of the trial of their Anglo-Saxon counterparts which was to follow.[86] Section 41 was tested and found wanting. Initially, Almazoff was acquitted, and the other three ordered deported. Both Charitinoff and Blumenberg had their verdicts reversed on appeal. Of the four only Schoppelrie was deported, and he was sent out of the country not for having violated Section 41, but for having crossed the border illegally three years before.[87]

The aliens arrested in Winnipeg on 21 June were not as fortunate. Most of these men were denied the formal deportation proceedings specified under Section 41. Instead, they appeared before Winnipeg Magistrate Hugh John Macdonald who ordered them sent to the internment camp at Kapuskasing for "safe-keeping." Despite the angry protests of the defense council appointed by the Winnipeg Trades and Labour Council, these men were subsequently deported in secrecy.[88] This high-handed action by the Dominion authorities accorded well with the attitudes of the Citizen's Committee of One Thousand and public officials like Hugh John Macdonald, who presided over many of the alien trials in Winnipeg. In a letter to Arthur Meighen, dated 3 July 1919, Macdonald emphasized that only an uncompromising attitude towards the radical alien would end the current industrial disorder:

> ... as Police Magistrate I have seen to what a large extent Bolsheviki ideas are held by the Ruthenian, Russian and Polish people, whom we have in our midst ... it is absolutely-necessary that an example should be made ... they do not understand generous treatment and consider it is only extended to them because the Government is afraid of them: indeed, fear is the only agency that can be successfully employed.... If the Government persists in the course that it is now adopting the foreign element here will soon be as gentle and easily controlled as a lot of sheep.[89]

IV.

The historical evidence now available indicates that neither Anglo-Saxon nor foreign workers regarded the Winnipeg General Strike as the first stage in a national revolution. For most of Winnipeg's workers the General Strike was an attempt to improve local social and economic conditions through collective bargaining and nothing more. Why, then, did the Citizen's Committee of One Thousand and the Dominion Security officials maintain that Winnipeg was facing an incipient revolution with the radical foreigners in the vanguard? And why was "anti-foreign" sentiment so much more pronounced in Winnipeg than in any of the other Canadian cities that experienced industrial disorder during 1919? Part of the answer to these questions undoubtedly lies in the intensification of nativism in Winnipeg during the war. The bilingual school controversy, the tension created in Winnipeg over the Wartime Elections Act, and the "race riots" of January 1919, had all illustrated Anglo-Canadian hostility towards the "foreigner." Another factor which must be taken into account is the extent to which Anglo-Canadian businessmen had become concerned in the post-war period about the growing co-operation between English-speaking and "foreign" socialists. The impact of this co-operation was revealed during the General Strike. Thus, Ukrainian and other Slavic workers faithfully followed the guidelines of the Central Strike Committee even though the membership of this Committee was exclusively Anglo-Saxon. Moreover, the strong sense of community among Ukrainian workers helped to transform the strike into something more than a mere economic conflict; it became a life-and-death struggle in which any deviance from the ethnic norm was branded as traitorous. Organizations such as the Ukrainian Labour Temple Association maintained the *esprit de corps* of the Slavic community and seemingly provided a most effective link with the Central Strike Committee.[90]

Dominion security officials were also greatly alarmed over the activities of radical aliens both before and during the strike; this was clearly shown in the arrests of Charitinoff, Blumenberg, Almazoff, and Schoppelrie. These men were not arrested merely because they were "unfortunate in having non-Anglo-Saxon names," but because they were regarded as dangerous revolutionaries. On the other hand, there is little reliable evidence to support the view of the Dominion police and military intelligence officials that the alien leaders were subversives. Rather, the arrests were usually made on the basis of rumour and circumstantial evidence; this was clearly revealed during the July 1919 deportation hearings. Like their Anglo-Canadian counterparts, the "foreign" strike leaders, despite their radical rhetoric, were concerned with local issues, not general revolution.[91]

Yet if Dominion security officials misjudged the alien menace, the Citizen's Committee of One Thousand exploited it. The Committee's intent was clearly to tarnish the image of the Central Strike Committee in the eyes of the city's Anglo-Canadian population in general and with the veterans in particular. Not surprisingly, this appeal to ethnic and cultural bigotry left deep scars on Winnipeg society. Indeed, in many ways the Strike widened the gulf between the Anglo-Saxon South End and the immigrant North End of the city. Throughout the 1920s many middle-class Anglo-Canadians continued to regard the people of the North End as semi-barbarians whose rightful place was on the bottom rung of the social ladder.[92] The words of Sandor Hunyadi, the fictional character created by John Marlyn in his book *Under the Ribs of Death*, vividly describes what Winnipeg and the larger world looked like from the North End:

> "The English," he whispered. "Pa, the only people who count are the English. Their fathers got all the best jobs. They're the only ones nobody ever calls foreigners. Nobody ever makes fun of their names or calls them 'bologny-eaters,' or laughs at the way they dress or talk. Nobody," he concluded bitterly, "'cause when you're English it's the same as bein' Canadian."[93]

Endnotes

1. D.C. Masters, *The Winnipeg General Strike* (Toronto, 1950). W.L. Morton, *Manitoba: A History* (Toronto, 1957), pp. 356–379. Kenneth McNaught, *A Prophet in Politics* (Toronto, 1959), pp. 99–154. David Bercuson, "Labour in Winnipeg: The Great War and the General Strike," Ph.D. thesis, University of Toronto, 1971; Norman Penner (ed.)., *Winnipeg 1919: The Strikers' Own History of the Winnipeg General Strike* (Toronto, 1973); A.R. McCormack, "The Origins and Extent of Western Canadian Labour Radicalism: 1896–1919," Ph.D. thesis, University of Western Ontario, 1973, pp. 230–86, 401–498; David Bercuson and Kenneth McNaught, *The Winnipeg Strike: 1919* (Toronto, 1974).
2. Alan Artibise, "An Urban Environment: The Process of Growth in Winnipeg," Canadian Historical Association, *Historical Papers* (1972), Ottawa, 1974, pp. 119–124.
3. *The Christian Guardian*, July 16, 1913, pp. 9–10; Leonard Marsh, "The Problem of Seasonal Employment" (unpublished typescript), Research project No. 22, McGill Social Research Series, 1933, p. 100.
4. Donald Avery, "Dominion Control Over the Recruitment and Placement of Immigrant Industrial Workers in Canada, 1890–1918," Paper Presented at the Conference on Canadian Society in the Late Nineteenth Century, McGill University, January 18, 1975.
5. *Robochny Narod* ("Working People"), Winnipeg, Oct.; ibid., Dec. 14, 1916.
6. Paul Yuzyk, *The Ukrainians in Manitoba* (Toronto, 1953), pp. 74, 197.
7. J. Skwarok, *Ukrainian Settlers in Canada and Their Schools* (Toronto, 1959), pp. 60–67.
8. Marunchak, *Ukrainian Canadians*, pp. 265–67; A.R, McCormack, "Western Canadian Labour Radicalism," pp. 187–192.
9. *Robochny Narod* ("Working People"), June 9, 1915; ibid., Dec. 14, 1916.
10. Ibid., Dec. 17, 1913; Ibid., July 8, 1914.
11. Ibid., May 20, 1914.
12. Artibise, "An Urban Environment," p. 119–124, J.S. Woodsworth, *My Neighbour* (Toronto, 1972), pp. 60–78, 86–95, Ralph Connor, *The Foreigner* (Toronto, 1909), p. 326.
13. Immigration Branch Papers (hereafter IB), PAC, File 800111, J.H. Ashdown to Frank Oliver, April 9, 1908.
14. Ibid.
15. Winnipeg District Minute Book, Women's Christian Temperance Union, April 8, 1908, Public Archives of Manitoba.
16. IB, file 800111, W.D. Scott, Supt. of Immigration to Frank Oliver, Minister of the Interior, Dec. 15, 1908; *Statutes of Canada*, 9–10 Edward VII, Ch. 27, p. 14.

17. The 1911 Census shows that there were 393,320 residents of the country of German origin; 129,103 had come from the Austro-Hungarian Empire; 3,880 had come from the Turkish Empire; and several thousand from Bulgaria. *Census of 1911*, Vol. II, p. 367.
18. Major-General W.D. Otter, *Internment Operations, 1914–20* (Ottawa, Sept. 30, 1920), pp. 3, 6; *Canadian Annual Review*, 1914, pp. 277–281.
19. Secretary of State Papers, Chief Press Censor Branch (hereafter CPC), Public Archives of Canada, vol. 157, Colonel Chambers to J.W. Dafoe, Sept. 13, 1915.
20. *Canadian Ruthenian*, Aug. 1, 1914, translated and cited in Yuzyk, *Ukrainians in Manitoba*, p. 187.
21. *Manitoba Free Press*, Aug; 5, 1914.
22. Ramsay Cook, *The Politics of John W. Dafoe and the Free Press* (Toronto, 1963), pp. 8–101; *Manitoba Free Press*, Feb. 29, 1916.
23. *Northwest Review* (Winnipeg), Feb. 26, 1916.
24. *Manitoba Free Press*, Jan. 31, 1916. 25. Ibid., March 1, 1916.
26. CPC, 144-A-l, vol. 27, Colonel Chambers to Orest Zareboko, editor of the *Ukrainian Voice*, July 8, 1916.
27. *Manitoba Free Press*, Dec. 21, 1917; *Winnipeg Telegram*, Dec. 21, 1917.
28. *Canadian Ruthenian*, Dec. 10, 1917.
29. A.R. McCormack, "Western Canadian Labour Radicalism," pp. 401–468.
30. *Robochny Narod*, Jan. 15, 1917; ibid., July 18, 1917.
31. Ibid., July 25, 1917.
32. Ibid., Aug. 1, 1917.
33. David Bercuson, and Kenneth McNaught, *The Winnipeg Strike*, pp. 15–21., *Building Bulletin*, Aug. 15, 1918.
34. Department of Justice Papers, PAC, file 2059, for the year 1918, Registrar of Alien Enemies, Winnipeg, to Colonel Sherwood, Aug. 17, 1918.
35. Robert Borden Papers (hereafter Borden Papers), PAC, 56668, C.H. Cahan to Borden, Sept. 14, 1918.
36. Statutes of Canada (1919) 9–10 Geo. V. pp. lxxi–lxxiii, lxxvii–lxxx. *Robochny Narod* was one of the newspapers which was suppressed.
37. Borden Papers, 60920, Prime Minister Borden to Council, Dec. 2, 1918.
38. CPC, file 144-A-l, vol. 27 Fred Livesay, Western Press Censor to Colonel Chambers, April 24, 1918.
39. Ibid., A.A. McLean, Comptroller of the Royal North West Mounted Police to Colonel Chambers, June 9, 1919.
40. Department of Militia and Defence Headquarters Records (hereafter DNB), Public Archives of Canada, C-2665, Secret Agent #47, to Supt. Starnes, RNWMP, March 24, 1919.
41. CPC, file 144-A-2, vol. 28, Colonel Chambers to General Ketchen, Officer Commanding Military District # 10, Oct. 3, 1918.
42. *Western Labour News*, Oct. 5, .1918.
43. Ibid., Dec. 28, 1918.
44. Royal Canadian Mounted Police Records (hereafter RCMP), RCMP Headquarters, Ottawa, Files Re: Winnipeg Strike, vol. 7, R.B. Russell to Joseph Knight, Dec. 7, 1918.
45. CPC, file 279-12, col. 125. Excerpt memorandum prepared for Colonel Chambers, April 22, 1919. *Ukrainian Labour News* (Winnipeg), May 10, 1919 supported the One Big Union, and urged Ukrainian workers to join this labour organization.
46. Borden Papers, Series OCA, file 252, in passim.
47. *Canadian Annual Review*, 1919, pp. 46–49. Throughout 1919 there were reports of socialists activities among veterans organizations, DND, C-2817 (2) Comptroller RNWMP to Lt. Colonel Davis, Assistant Director of Military Intelligence, April 7, 1919.
48. D.H. Avery, "Canadian Immigration Policy and the Alien Question, 1896–1919: The Anglo-Canadian Perspective," Ph.D. thesis, University of Western Ontario, 1973, pp. 505–41.
49. OBU Collection, Public Archives of Manitoba, R.B. Russell to Victor Midgley, Jan. 30, 1919; *Western Labour News*, Feb. 14, 1919

50. RCMP, Records, Deportation Board of Enquiry, The Sam Blumenberg Enquiry, Aug. 1, 1919, Testimony of G. Batsford.
51. *Vancouver Sun*, Jan. 27, 1919.
55. Ibid., Russell to C. Stephenson, Jan. 30, 1919; *Western Labour News*, Jan. 31, 1919.
56. *Manitoba Free Press*, Feb. 4, 1919. In the first three months of the Board's existence approximately 3,000 cases were processed; of these 500 were denied certificates, ibid., May 7, 1919.
57. Arthur Meighen Papers (PAC), 000279, D.A. Ross to Arthur Meighen, April 16, 1919., ibid., Ross to Meighan, April 8, 1919. Ironically, Dominion security officials had regarded Bishop Budka as a firm ally against the Bolshevik element in the Manitoba Ukrainian community since the fall of 1918. CPC, file 144-A-2, Colonel Chambers to the Secretary of State, Sept. 29, 1918.
58. D.C. Masters, *The Winnipeg General Strike*, pp. 40, 44.
59. Murray Donnelly, *Dafoe of the Free Press* (Toronto 1968), p, 105; (OUPA) Bercuson and McNaught, *Winnipeg Strike*, pp. 68–76.
60. RCMP Records, 1919, vol. 1, Major General Ketchen to Secretary of the Militia Council, May 21, 1919.
61. McNaught, *Prophet in Politics*, pp. 107–112; *The Citizen*, June 5–20, 1919.
62. *Manitoba Free Press*, May 22, 1919.
63. OBU Collection, R.B. Russell to Victor Midgley, May 19, 1919.
64. Bercuson and McNaught, *Winnipeg Strike*, pp. 68–71.
65. *Western Labour News*, Special Strike Edition, #19, June7, 1919.
66. RCMP Collection, 1919, vol. 2, Special Agent W.H. McLaughlin, to Supt. Cortland Starnes, Manitoba Division, June 14, 1919.
67. Ibid.
68. *Winnipeg Telegram*, June 11, 1919. *The Free Press* account was equally vitriolic.
69. The use of the deportation weapon had been suggested by various security authorities during the early Spring of 1919. DND, 2817 (2), Major A.E. Jukes, D.I.O., to Major General Leckie, D.O.C., B.C., May 5, 1919.
70. Secretary of State Records, Public Archives of Canada, Internment Operations Files, F. 6 #6712, Lt. Colonel W. E. Date, Commandant, Kapuskasing Camp to Major-General Otter, May 12, 1919. 71. "An Act to amend the Immigration Act," *Statutes of Canada*, 9–10, Geo. v Chap. 38, s. 41.
72. "An Act to amend and consolidate the Acts relating to British Nationality, Naturalization and Aliens, 1919," Statutes of Canada, 9–10 Geo. v, Chap. 38, s. 2, s. 8.
73. Borden Papers, 61838, A.J. Andrews to Arthur Meighen, telegram, June 6, 1919.
74. "An Act to amend an Act of the present session entitled An Act to amend The Immigration Act, 1919," *Statutes of Canada*, 1919, 9–10 Geo. v, Chap. 26, s.41.
75. Borden Papers, 61913, Gideon Robertson to Prime Minister Borden, June 13, 1919.
76. Ibid.
77. RCMP Records, Criminal Investigation Branch, Public Archives of Canada (hereafter RCMP Records) 22/4, Vol. 70, 70, telegram, J.A. Calder, Minister of Immigration and Colonization to Commissioner Perry, RNWMP, June 16, 1919.
78. Police informer Harry Daskalud submitted several reports that Almazoff had given seditious speeches at the meetings of the Young Jewish Socialist Party. RCMP Records, Almazoff Enquiry.
79. Extract, letter Tom Moore, President of the T.L.C. to E. Robinson, Secretary, Winnipeg Trades and Labour Council, June 24, 1919, cited *Manitoba Free Press*, November 21, 1919, p. 11. The British Labour Party at its 1919 Convention actually passed a resolution calling upon the British Government to attempt to dissuade the Canadian authorities from carrying out the deportations. *Vancouver Province*, June 26, 1919.
80. *Manitoba Free Press*, June 18, 1919. A.J. Andrews admitted to Arthur Meighen that the opposition of the *Manitoba Free Press* to the use of Section 41 was a serious blow. Borden Papers, 62012, Andrews to Meighen, June 18, 1919.
81. Penner, *Winnipeg 1919*, pp. 175–181. A fifth radical alien arrested was listed in the *Western Labour News* as M. Berenczat, a returned soldier, ibid., p. 80. In other sources the fifth man was referred to as Mike Verenchuk. *Ukrainian Labour News*, July 16, 1919. However, only Blumberg, Almazoff, Charitinoff, and Schoppelrie were given formal deportation hearings under Section 41. Moreover,

Charitinoff was also spelled "Charitonoff," and Schoppelrie was referred to both as "Schiapparell" and "Choppelrie."

82. Bercuson & McNaught, *Winnipeg Strike*, pp. 86–97, RCMP Collection, vol. 2, Commissioner Perry to Comptroller McLean, July 6, 1919.
83. *Manitoba Free Press*, July 2, 1919, *Ukrainian Labour News*, July 14, 1919.
84. The preliminary trials for the eight Anglo-Saxon strike-leaders were held before Magistrate Noble during the latter part of July and August, overlapping with the deportation hearings. D.C. Masters, *The Winnipeg General Strike*, p. 115.
85. On May 26, 1919, Andrews had been appointed by Arthur Meighen, the Acting Minister of Justice, "To represent the Department in Winnipeg." RCMP Collection, Supt. Starnes to Commissioner Perry, May 27, 1919.
86. RCMP Records, C.I.B., 22/22 vol. 70, Commissioner Perry to Supt. Lethbridge District, July 5, 1919, ibid.. Vol. 4, Supt. Starnes to Commissioner Perry, July 24, 1919.
87. Almazoff Hearing, August 16; Blumenberg Hearing, August 15, Charitinoff Hearing, August 15; Schoppelrie Hearing, July 18, *Manitoba Free Press*, September 21, 1919.
88. I.B. 912971, #3, T.J. Murray, telegram, J.A. Calder, Minister of Immigration & Colonization, October 30, 1919. Department of Justice Files, 1919, file 1960, Deputy Minister Justice to Murray and Noble, November 5, 1919; ibid., Deputy Minister Justice, to Major General Otter, November 11, 1919.
89. Meighen Papers, 002537, Hugh John MacDonald to Arthur Meighen, July 3, 1919.
90. Bercuson & McNaught, *Winnipeg Strike*, pp. 52; *Ukrainian Labour News*, Aug. 20, 1919. *The Canadian Ruthenian*, organ of Bishop Budka, maintained a position of neutrality during the strike, a sharp contrast from its previous anti-socialist stance.
91. *Ukrainian Labor News*, July 16, 1919; Almazoff Hearings, July 16, Aug. 15; Charitinoff Hearings, July 16, July 17.
92. Vera Lysenko, *Yellow Boots* (New York, 1954), pp. 211–42; T. Peterson, "Ethnic and Class Politics in Manitoba," in Martin Robin (ed.), *Canadian Provincial Politics* (Scarborough, 1972), pp. 81–86.
93. John Marlyn, *Under the Ribs of Death* (Toronto, 1964), p. 24.

Chapter 11

Solving the Labour Problem at Imperial Oil

Welfare Capitalism in the Canadian Petroleum Industry, 1919–29

H.M. Grant

On the tenth anniversary of its "Industrial Representation Plan," the Imperial Oil Company's *Review* explained that: "The Plan was simply an expression of appreciation on the part of the Directors in connection with the length of service and the loyalty of their employees." It emphasized that its experiment with corporate welfarism "was not the outcome or the result [of] strikes or dissension in any way; fortunately, the Company had never experienced any difficulty in regard to labour."[1] In a similar vein, Reverend Dr. Daniel Strachan, the Presbyterian minister hired as "Assistant to the President on Industrial Relations," protested at the National Industrial Conference of 1919 that the Plan was not designed to usurp unionization: "I am not spending my time, as a serious man, to defeat any organization; I am not putting my life and my service into this work of industrial relations for the purpose of upsetting any plan of any organization. It would be foolish to do that."[2]

These public pronouncements stand in sharp contrast to the private concern expressed by executives of Imperial Oil over growing labour unrest in all of its refineries as World War I drew to a close. When informed of union activity on the west coast, Company President C.O. Stillman wrote to Strachan that:

> Our friends [at Standard] should understand that we are constantly struggling against the same problem [of labour unrest] ... it extends from the Ioco Refinery in British Columbia through to Regina, Sarnia and (from information we recently obtained that the labour organizations were organizing our men in Montreal), to the Montreal refinery, and, naturally, it will only be a short time when Halifax is in the same position.[3]

Strachan's response stressed the urgent need for action:

> I too learned ... that the unions were very active and I felt no time was to be lost in getting those plants organized on a non-union basis.... If we can get in before the unions have the balance of power we can organize on our own lines and they can simply whistle but if we wait too long, the labour end will have us by the throat.[4]

In 1919, therefore, Imperial Oil joined the ranks of the "progressive minority" of Canadian firms which embraced a "new industrial philosophy." Predicated upon the benevolent treatment of workers as an act of "enlightened self-interest," the logic was consistent: joint labour–management councils would replace industrial conflict with workplace harmony; accident, sickness, death, and pension benefits would reduce absenteeism and turnover; and a share-purchase plan would foster company loyalty and undermine class consciousness. In short, labour's co-operation could be purchased and trade unionism made redundant.

Welfare capitalism is portrayed as an aberration in the history of North American industrial relations. In the United States, it was seized upon in the wake of labour unrest during World War I, but largely repudiated by both managers and workers during the 1920s. According to Brandes, workers never "genuinely embraced" the paternalism of their employers; Montgomery concurs that workers were "not greatly impressed"; and Bernstein contends that welfarism failed because it never addressed shop-floor concerns.[5] Many employers were equally unconvinced. Proponents of scientific management labelled welfare experiments a "sociological joke," and once the pressure of tight labour markets abated, firms abandoned paternalist approaches in favour of traditional methods of close supervision, the drive system, and wage incentives to control worker effort.[6] Despite Brody's argument to the contrary, few company programs survived intact into the 1930s; and the myth of labour as "equal partners" was shattered as firms retrenched in the face of declining profits during the Great Depression.[7] If any semblance of life still remained, the death knell was sounded by Section 8a of the Wagner Act (1935), which defined employer support for a company union as an unfair labour practice.

Evidence for Canada is both more fragmentary and more ambiguous. In the aftermath of World War I, Canadian workers were poised to assert greater control over their economic and political lives. Naylor describes the "labour revolt" in Ontario, and Kealey documents how the rank-and-file across the country "defiantly challenged" the Royal Commission on Industrial Relations, and articulated coherent alternatives to industrial capitalism.[8] Corporate welfarism is one of several factors contributing to the decline of unionization in the 1920s and the failure to establish a "new democracy."[9] In simple quantitative terms, company unions were more prevalent in Canada than the United States, covering up to half as many workers as unions did in 1920. This is probably due to the predominance in manufacturing industries of subsidiaries of American corporations—International Harvester, General Motors, General Electric, U.S. Rubber, and Imperial Oil—that parroted the industrial relations initiatives of their parent companies.[10] But large Canadian-owned firms also adopted employee-representation plans and comprehensive welfare programs, albeit with mixed results. The industrial council at Massey-Harris, for instance, had little influence over wages and employment during buoyant economic times; completely broke down when production declined; and otherwise "limped along" until the plant was unionized in 1943.[11] In the steel industry, Heron notes that company unions and welfare schemes failed to address the shop-floor experience of workers and thus made few inroads in the face of demands for union recognition. Even the heralded employee-representation plan and profit-sharing scheme at Dofasco fits uncomfortably into the general pattern in that it was not introduced until 1936.[12]

This mixed evidence raises the question of why some firms adopted a paternalist approach to securing labour's co-operation at a time when others relied upon greater coercion; and why some workers apparently deferred to paternalist treatment when others rejected it. Zahavi argues that historians have drawn a false dichotomy—between acceptance and repudiation—in workers' response to corporate welfarism. His emphasis on "negotiated loyalty" underscores that the paternalism that provided ideological reinforcement for corporate welfarism was restricted in scope.[13] Managers and workers recognized their respective rights and obligations, but exercised them within strict limits defined by the unequal nature of the capital–labour relationship. Managers never hid their objectives of control over the labour process and worker subordination, and the threat of dismissal remained paramount; and workers remained cognizant of their economic power to disrupt production either through work stoppages or more informal resistance. The manager–worker relationship, therefore, was the subject of continual negotiation, with workers exerting their power to extract wage concessions and improvements in working conditions as the price of their loyalty. Welfare capitalism thus assumed a "bifurcated identity": firms with the "wherewithal to pay" espoused an image of employer benevolence and workplace harmony, while workers transformed the rhetoric of corporate welfarism to serve their own ends.[14]

This paper examines the interaction between managers and workers with the introduction of corporate welfarism at the Imperial Oil Company, Limited, between 1919 and 1929. More specifically, it focuses on how the Company articulated its industrial relations policy for public consumption and examines more limited evidence on workers' response. Despite this limitation, Imperial Oil's strategy represents an interesting case study for two reasons. Foremost is that it was a distinct success. In 1930, the Company boasted that: "We have never had a lockout, never had a strike."[15] Unionization was forestalled until 1946, and the non-union status of the majority of its refineries today is, in part, a testament to its ability to usurp legitimate worker organizations. Second, patterned after the renowned "Rockefeller Plan" or "Colorado Plan"—designed by Mackenzie King for his benefactor in the aftermath of the Ludlow Massacre of 1914—it permits an examination of the application of King's approach to industrial relations. Imperial Oil thus provides fertile ground for examining the conditions that permitted King's brand of corporate welfarism to flourish.

Imperial Oil and Petroleum Refining in Canada, 1898–1929

At the outset of the twentieth century, the petroleum refining industry in Canada was a textbook example of perfect monopoly. J.D. Rockefeller Sr.'s Standard Oil Trust purchased controlling interest in the Canadian-owned Imperial Oil Company, Ltd., in 1898 and centralized production at Sarnia, Ontario. Imperial Oil was the sole refiner of petroleum products in the country and, combined with imports from its American affiliates, supplied virtually the entire Canadian market. Sales approximated $2 million, with illuminating oil, for use in kerosene lamps, accounting for roughly two-thirds of the total.

Rapid growth in demand presented Imperial Oil with an opportunity to extend its market power. Between 1909 and 1920, the consumption of petroleum products grew dramatically—from $5 to over $83 million—or a remarkable rate of growth exceeding 25 percent per annum. The popularity of the automobile pushed gasoline sales to over one-half of total sales, while the increasing use of fuel oil in transportation and industry provided an outlet for heavier by-products of distillation.[16] Imperial Oil, however, was slow to respond to these opportunities. Despite predatory actions to restrict competition, a "competitive fringe" of domestic refiners emerged, including the Canadian Oil company (Petrolia, 1901) and British American Oil Company (Toronto, 1908).[17] But of greater concern to Imperial Oil was the rise in imports to claim 70 percent of the domestic market as international firms—Shell Oil and Union Oil—extended marketing operations into Canada.[18] Accordingly, the share of the market supplied by Imperial Oil's refinery fell sharply: on the eve of World War I, it accounted for only 20 percent of domestic consumption (see Table 11.1).

It was not until World War I that the Company undertook a substantial expansion program. When the U.S. Supreme Court forced the dissolution of the Standard Oil Trust in 1911, control over Imperial Oil passed to the Standard Oil Company (New Jersey) and expansion followed.[19] Sarnia's capacity was augmented in 1914, and new refineries were built at "Ioco," adjacent to Barnaby, British Columbia (1915), Regina (1916), Montreal (1917), and "Imperoyal" on the Dartmouth/Halifax harbour (1918). This expansion was fostered by the unique relationship the Company enjoyed with the Canadian and American governments during

Table 11.1 Share of Market Supplied by Imperial Oil's Refineries, 1900–29

Year	Other Domestic<1> Refineries	Imports<2>	Imperial Oil's Refinery Share
1900	0	34	66
1905	10	34	54
1910	10	56	34
1915	12	40	48
1920	6	32	62
1925	7	28	65
1929	10	23	67

<1> Percentage of market supplied by domestic refineries not controlled by Imperial Oil.
<2> Value of imported petroleum products as a percentage of total Canadian consumption. This includes imports by Imperial Oil and its American affiliates.
Source: H. Grant, "Petroleum Industry," ch. 3.

wartime mobilization. The U.S. Petroleum Advisory Committee, created as a private sector advisory board, was given a "free hand" in the organization and allocation of production and distribution among competing firms. Headed by A.C. Bedford, President of Jersey Standard, it operated out of Jersey Standard's New York office. Control extended to Canada where, with the assistance of Imperial Oil's President, W.C. Teagle, efforts were undertaken to meet the needs of allied shipping for fuel oil. Imperial sought to exploit this special arrangement, for as Teagle wrote to Bedford: "We want to be patriotic, but, at the same time, is it not misguided patriotism to overlook extremely sound business practice?"[20]

Imperial Oil also enjoyed access to cheaper crude oil, including exclusive ownership of concessions in Peru, Mexico, and Colombia. Its Peruvian properties were held by the International Petroleum Company (IPC), organized as a majority-owned affiliate of Imperial Oil to avoid potential anti-trust legislation in the United States. Low wages and unitized production made oil from Mexico and Peru less expensive relative to Texas, and less costly to refine than heavy California crudes. Jersey Standard's desire to find an outlet for its Latin American and mid-Continent crude oil output favoured Imperial Oil's refinery expansion. Ioco was supplied from Peru; Montreal and Halifax operated on Mexican crude from Jersey Standard's producing affiliate until IPC purchased monopoly concessions in Colombia in 1920; Sarnia was supplied by mid-Continent producing affiliates; and discovery of crude oil in Wyoming, where Jersey Standard's Carter Oil Company controlled the majority of the field's output, encouraged the construction of refining capacity in the prairies.[21]

Imperial Oil's growth, however, rested primarily upon its hegemony over new refining technology in Canada. Prior to World War I, petroleum refining remained essentially a "batch" operation: crude oil was pumped from underground storage tanks into one of a battery of stills mounted upon a brick "setting" and "fired" from tubular boilers. The crude still, a steel cylinder roughly 14 by 40 feet, had a domed top with a vapour pipe attached to condenser coils leading to a condenser box. Temperature was gradually increased until the various fractions of the crude oil were distilled and condensed, and sent to the appropriate finishing still for further treatment. The lightest fractions—naphtha, kerosene or "refined oil" and "engine distillate"—were drawn off first, followed by lubricating oils and paraffine waxes, gas oil, and fuel oil (or the liquid residuals), leaving a coke-like residue on the still bottom. After "charging" the main still with crude oil and distilling the various fractions of petroleum, the still was cooled, cleaned and the entire process repeated. The typical refinery had numerous finishing stills, agitators and storage tanks for the various grades of refined oil. Other facilities included a barrel-filling house, "canning and casing" and "mixing and compound" departments, warehousing and railway loading docks.[22]

Growing gasoline demand focused research upon increasing the yield of lighter fractions of crude oil in the distillation process. The first significant innovation was Indiana Standard's Burton-Humphrey process for "cracking" heavier hydrocarbons—particular "gas oils"—under high pressure and high temperature in order to increase the output of gasoline per barrel of crude. Licensing rights were restricted to former members of the Standard Trust, and Imperial Oil obtained a license in 1914. Thermal cracking units were eventually installed in all of its refineries and, estimated to reduce the cost of producing gasoline by 38 percent, ceded Imperial a substantial advantage over existing and potential competitors in Canada.[23] More dramatic changes were on the horizon. Continuous processing evolved to overcome higher fuel costs, down time and the strain on equipment from constantly cooling, cleaning and recharging batch-type equipment. Crude or gas oil charging stock was pumped through cracking "coils" in order to raise it to the appropriate pressure and temperature before being discharged into the main still for cracking, and then to secondary distillation units.[24] Standard's "Tube and Tank" method, developed in 1923, was immediately leased to Imperial Oil and the first continuous cracking units in Canada were installed at its new Calgary refinery in 1924, and cracking capacity units was introduced in all of its other refineries by 1927. Development of continuous-cracking technology by competing American refiners led to conflicting patent claims and the subsequent formation of the "Patent Club" that restricted the diffusion of this technology to smaller firms until the "Dubbs" process became widely available in the 1930s.[25] Imperial Oil's approach to research and development changed accordingly. Rising compression ratios in automobile engines required gasoline with a higher octane rating, and altered the character of the "Test House" in Imperial Oil's refineries. From routine adaptation of existing procedures, its first full-time research chemist was hired in 1924 and a research department was established at Sarnia in 1928. According to Purdy, "the 1920s and early 1930s were the golden years of petroleum engineering because almost every process could be improved by the application of engineering principle."[26]

Imperial Oil thus enjoyed both a quantitative and qualitative superiority in the Canadian petroleum refining industry. From a one-plant operation with a capacity of 4,000 barrels per day (bd) in 1911, it grew to become a nationwide company with five refineries boasting a total capacity in excess of 30,000 bd by 1920. Its share of domestic refining capacity rose to over 90 percent and imports dropped to less than one-fourth of total Canadian sales, such that the Company's refineries were supplying over two-thirds of the Canadian market. During the 1920s, Imperial Oil again doubled its refinery capacity and, despite the entry of a handful of Canadian competitors, continued to supply over two-thirds of the Canadian market.[27] Nor did this expansion go unrewarded: between 1914 and 1920 it amassed $52 million in earnings (contributing over 10 percent of Jersey Standard's global refining and marketing earnings), and during the 1920s its net income rose to over $120 million.[28]

Worker Militancy and the Production Process

Having restored its dominance over the Canadian petroleum market during World War I, another challenge remained to Imperial Oil's monopoly position: labour unrest. In the parlance of economists, petroleum refining underwent both "capital widening" and "capital deepening," or a more extensive and intensive use of capital. The net value of Imperial Oil's capital stock engaged in refining and marketing rose from $2.9 million (1911) to $44.8 million (1920), and to $74.4 million by 1929. A more intensive use of capital can be inferred from a steady increase in output per worker. Between 1900 and 1920, the workforce in refineries increased ten-fold, the volume of crude "run" per worker remained fairly constant, but output per worker rose from $5,500 to $14,500. During the 1920s, crude output per worker more than doubled, and the value of annual output per worker rose to $22,300 (see Table 11.2). Technological change in refining thus had a potentially contradictory effect upon Imperial Oil: intensification of work promised greater profits, but also left it more vulnerable to work stoppages. With more capital stock engaged at every stage of a vertically integrated operation, a strike threatened to shut down the Company's entire operations and leave expensive machinery and equipment lying idle. The major threat to Imperial Oil's profitability, then, was not competition from other capitalists, but from labour.

Little is written about the labour process in early North American petroleum refineries,[29] but much can be inferred from the nature of the technology used. Chandler observes that firms processing liquids were the first to achieve high rates of output due to the relative ease in organizing a steady flow of raw materials into finished products. In the petroleum industry, this was accomplished through a more intensive use of heat: new stills with seamless wrought-iron and steel bottoms permitted the application of higher temperatures in order to obtain a larger fraction of refined products by "cracking" residual oils. Plant designs better synchronized the movement of materials within the refinery, as the use of steam pumps provided more effective co-ordination of activities.[30] "Economies of speed" were critical to a successful operation and were reflected in the organization of the workforce. Men were employed in a variety of occupations: "stillmen" oversaw the distillation process; pipefitters and machinists maintained and repaired equipment; "pumpers" attended to the operation of engines: "firemen" fed the boilers; "gaugers" measured the flow of oil into various stills and storage tanks; "still cleaners" removed the coke residue on still bottoms; and labourers were employed in a number of capacities, including the packaging and shipping of end products.[31] Employment of women was restricted to clerical positions, to the "delicate art of packing candles" in the paraffin works, and in the chemical testing laboratories, where "it has been found that girls possess the qualities [required by the work] even in a greater degree than the men."[32]

Table 11.2 Output per Worker, Canadian Petroleum Refineries, 1900–29

Year	Wage Earner	Crude Run (m. gal.)	Output ($m)	Crude/Worker (1,000 gal.)	Output/Worker ($1000)
1900	345	23.4	1.9	67.8	5.5
1905	469	35.8	2.2	76.3	4.7
1910	457	40.3	2.8	88.1	6.1
1915	1,050	111.0	8.9	105.7	8.5
1920	3,889	902.4	57.3	77.8	14.7
1925	3,230	445.1	49.8	137.8	15.4
1929	4,420	1,072.8	98.4	242.7	22.3

Source: H. Grant, "Petroleum Industry," ch. 5.

The trend towards a "homogenization" of labour in factory production and continuous processes relied upon the "technical control" of semi-skilled workers. The "drive system," where the pace of work was regulated by machinery, placed greater pressure on foremen to maintain the intensity of work effort.[33] The harsh nature of working conditions was most apparent in the treatment of still-cleaners, required to enter the still through a man-hole in the end or top, and shovel out the coke-like residue. Economies of speed and fuel, and the cost of repeatedly cooling, cleaning, and reheating the still, dictated that workers were sent into the still at temperatures between 135ºF and 200ºF and, not surprisingly, were frequently overcome by the heat and gases.[34] Working conditions of this nature were responsible for the bloody strike in 1915 at Jersey Standard's refinery in Bayonne, New Jersey, where five strikers were killed. The Bayonne strike underscored the hazards of leaving employment, transfer discipline, and discharge decisions to shop-floor managers. As the strikers complained: "We request humane treatment at the hands of the foremen and supervisors in place of the brutal kicking and punching we now receive without provocation."[35] As the scale of operations increased, management complained of the loss of the "human touch" and the need to overcome growing worker animosity.

Sensitive to the criticisms of the U.S. Commission on Industrial Relations, Jersey Standard instituted a reduction in the work week and a wage increase. Imperial Oil, however, sought to resist the adoption of an eight-hour day—despite the fact that British American had done so in its Toronto refinery in 1913—arguing that it would be too disruptive for the entire Sarnia labour force. Nor were wages to be increased. Following the Bayonne strike, Teagle, now President of Jersey Standard, wrote to C.O. Stillman, Imperial Oil's new President: "I think in view of the number of idle men in Canada, there is no necessity of any increase in wages, that a man who had a steady employment was fortunate." He based this conclusion partly upon casual observation:

> When we were in Vancouver in April last there was a bread-line of considerable length. Under these circumstances, it would seem to me that there is no necessity of making any changes whatsoever in the scale of wages at Ioco.[36]

Thus for "process" workers, who constituted roughly one-half of Imperial Oil's workforce, an 84-hour work week—composed of six 12-hour days and a 24-hour Sunday shift every other week—remained the norm.[37]

This intransigence left Imperial Oil vulnerable to a growing threat of unionization as the labour market tightened during World War I. In December 1915, boilermakers at its Montreal refinery walked out during its construction, forcing the Company to institute a pay increase.[38] Evidence presented at the Royal Commission on Industrial Relations (Mathers Commission) confirmed the trend towards unionization. Imperial Oil's pipefitters, machinists, boilermakers, and masons at Sarnia belonged to their respective craft unions, and in January 1919 the Sarnia trades federation undertook a unionization drive in the refinery. Of the 1,600-member workforce, estimates of union membership ranged from 50 to 75 percent.[39] Four months later, workers at the Regina refinery formed the short-lived Local 62 of the Oil Workers International Union.[40] But Imperial Oil faced its greatest challenge at Ioco. On 15 February 1918, workers in the barrelling, casing, and shipping departments went on strike in support of wage demands. They were soon followed by "process" workers—boilermakers, stillmen, and pumpers—seeking a reduction in their 84-hour work week. After a 12-day work stoppage by the 170-member labour force, workers gained a 14 percent wage increase for labourers and prevailing union rates in Vancouver for skilled workers. Process workers secured the modest concession of 24 hours off every 7, instead of 13, days. The strike's success encouraged Ioco's workers to form the short-lived Oil Refinery Workers Union, subsequently chartered as Local 4 of the AFL's newly-formed International Association of Oil Field, Gas Well and Refinery Workers of

America.[41] But none of these union locals was recognized by the Company.

A capital-intensive form of production based upon continuous processing, coupled with growing discontent among its workers, equalled a potential threat to Imperial Oil's highly-profitable operations. As World War I drew to a close, the Company recognized that "there must be freedom from interruption of operations."[42]

Corporate Welfarism: The Company Way

Jersey Standard was prominent among American companies in the adoption of a more systematic approach to industrial relations during World War I and Imperial Oil, its majority-owned affiliate, played a similar role in Canada. In January 1919, Imperial Oil embarked on a wide-ranging "Industrial Relations Plan" to win the loyalty of workers. Its approach was threefold: a) the establishment of employee-manager "joint councils" to give workers an outlet to voice shop-floor discontent; b) an array of welfare programs to increase the Company's influence over workers' lives both inside and outside of the workplace; and c) a share-purchase plan to vest workers with a sense of ownership in the Company. Equally important was the Imperial Oil Review, which maintained an unrelenting propaganda assault on its employee-readers. Its rhetoric combined an explicit recognition of existing class antagonisms with the declaration that capital and labour must work together to replace the "old spirit of suspicion and bitterness in Industry." The basis for co-operation was explained in the following terms:

> [The worker] has the right to ask for a square deal, a little time to rest, a little time to work, a little time to meet the obligations of citizenship. But on the other hand, it will not do to look upon capital as only greedy, and corporations as supremely soulless.[43]

The centrepiece of Imperial Oil's approach was the joint council, introduced at the Sarnia refinery in January 1919, in Halifax two months later, and eventually throughout all of its refinery and larger marketing departments. With an equal number of employee-elected and management-appointed delegates, and chaired by the refinery supervisor, industrial councils met monthly to offer suggestions to senior management on wages, hours of work, housing, and working conditions. This satisfied the Company's definition of collective bargaining: a forum for settling inevitable problems that arise in the day-to-day operation of a large, complex industrial enterprise. Placing senior management in direct contact with workers would allow the Company to regain the "human touch."[44]

This was complemented by the formation of Employment Departments in each major branch of operation to systematize hiring and firing, oversee all personnel affairs, and offer "friendly counsel in personal matters."[45] Jacoby points out that personnel departments of this nature were couched in the ethos of "professional neutrality": they were to function as both union and management in giving an impartial hearing over shop-floor disputes.[46] This included a non-discrimination clause in hiring on the basis of union membership, expected to win employee confidence without interfering with the maintenance of an open shop.[47] Defining clear and consistent work rules was intended to counter the arbitrary authority exercised by foremen and supervisors; for instance, in the Sarnia refinery 75 different pay rates existed among the 175 boilermakers.[48] The effort to mediate the worker–foreman relationship and provide a sense of "fairness" was reinforced by having Strachan oversee industrial relations matters and report directly to the President.

Hastily instituted to counter union activities in the plant, however, the employee-representation plan got off to a rocky start in Sarnia. Workers complained that they were "ignorant" about the joint council, with elections "sprung kind of sudden."[49] The Employees Federation—a coalition of trade unions active in the plant—seized the opportunity to elect an active union member to the joint council, who promptly placed the union's salary demands on the table for discussion at the first meeting. He was subsequently dismissed and only reinstated following the threat of a walkout.[50] In contrast to the laudatory testimonials published in the *Review*, evidence given at the Mathers Commission revealed its ambivalent reception by workers at Sarnia. Harry Steel, President of the local Trades Council, stated that "the other side of the table does all the talking" and that 300 men had joined unions since the Plan's introduction. At a meeting convened by the Employees Federation, the 400 to 500 employees of the Sarnia refinery voted to press their wage demands through the union rather than the industrial council.[51] According to Bert Bazeley, Air-Brakeman, men had little faith in the welfare committee and preferred unionization: "They seem to think it is [a] scheme to break unions."[52]

In order to buy goodwill, therefore, Imperial Oil instituted an eight-hour day, six-day work week and a pay increase across the country. Stillman conceded that "I believe, as we all agree, that the best way to handle the present disturbed labour position is to anticipate a raise to our employees before a flat demand is made on us."[53] And while workers in Sarnia interpreted the raise as an attempt to pre-empt union demands,[54] it initiated the pattern of high wages that saw workers in petroleum refineries earning over 40 percent more than the average manufacturing wage.[55]

Imperial Oil's preoccupation with maintaining an open shop heightened with the Winnipeg General Strike. Stillman sought to reassure readers of the *New York Sun* that the cause of the strike was limited to "a handful of extremists, largely of foreign birth" seeking to establish a "new despotism."[56] The Company drew solace when Imperial's Vancouver marketing division "weathered the strike storm" of sympathy walkouts. Its unionized employees—including teamsters, chauffeurs, and tank-car drivers—had, "with one exception," refused to join the walkout, "standing staunch in defense of a company that has treated them as fellow-men and partaken a personal interest in their welfare." The *Review* mentioned in parenthesis that Company vehicles were given police escorts, its bulk plant was accorded police protection and "at the same time the volunteers, which we had to fill in vacancies that might take place on account of the union men leaving, were far more than there was any possibility of our requiring."[57] Nonetheless, the Company declared that its reputation as "one large happy family" remained intact and attributed this to its employee-representation plan.

The authority of industrial councils, however, was strictly confined by the terms of the accompanying "Joint Agreement" (issued by the Company and "approved" by joint councils) that detailed management's rights.[58] The offenses leading to immediate dismissal or suspension—including violation of safety laws, insubordination, profanity, absenteeism, sleeping on duty, possession of liquor, or habitual use of drugs—were enumerated and, more significantly, wages were decided unilaterally by the Toronto head office. Joint councils' role was restricted to ensuring that foreman interpreted Company norms and rules in a fair and consistent manner. But even in this respect, here were obvious shortcomings. While workers were given the power to grieve disciplinary action meted out by foremen and line supervisors, they were obliged to first take up their complaint with the foreman before carrying it to the joint council. And no company was likely to consistently overturn a line manager's decision at the risk of ceding too much shop-floor authority.

As Imperial Oil's approach evolved, the relationship between paternalism and profit became more clearly articulated. Early expressions of welfare capitalism, according to Brody, "lacked any functional relationship to industrial operations";[59] instead, they were embraced by firms with a rather vague sense of the relationship between employer benevolence and industrial efficiency. Imperial Oil acknowledged that in inaugurating its Industrial Representation Plan it was "just feeling its way" in the attempt to "create a community of interest and feeling between labour and capital" and that it offered no "panacea for industrial ills."[60] Such a program was unlikely to be successful, either from the point of view of the employer or employee, without more tangible benefits: it needed to address the real concerns of workers to win their support, as well as yield greater productivity to justify the cost for the employer. As Strachan emphasized: "it is not philanthropy and it is not benevolence: it is a cold-blooded business proposition."[61]

To this end, the employee-representation plan was accompanied by a package of welfare benefits. Life insurance was purchased for all employees with more than 12 months of continuous service, to a maximum of $2,000.[62] Sickness/disability benefits were established equal to one-half of an employee's pay for a period ranging from 6 to 52 weeks, depending upon years of service. And retirement benefits were paid in the form of an annuity equal to two percent of the employee's average annual earnings during the last 10 years of service, multiplied by the years of service. The paternalist nature of these concessions is evident in the fact that they were non-contributory and compulsory for all employees, while the payment of benefits remained at the discretion of the Company.[63] In each case, however, the rhetoric of Company largesse was accompanied by two "riders": the firm's demand for reciprocity, and the continual reminder that non-compliance could be remedied through dismissal.

In return for providing accident, sickness, and life insurance benefits, management expected greater productivity through lower absenteeism's "contraction in the cost of replacement," and reduced time lost due to accidents. According to Strachan, "We expect through this insurance and through sickness benefits, etc., that we are profited by it at the end of the year."[64] Imperial Oil acknowledged that industrial accidents were "a production problem due to the development and speeding up of industry and transportation and rules, like the manufacturing processes, become more complicated"; nonetheless, workers were chastised for failing to act "sensibly" and costing the Company "large losses in time and money."[65] The *Review* regularly published a "meat chart" displaying the distribution of injuries by body parts: eye injuries were blamed on workers not wearing their goggles; and hand, foot, and leg injuries to a lack of employee "foresight." Claiming that 75 to 90 percent of industrial accidents were due to worker carelessness, "it is surely not too much to ask that all employees ... insure that our casualty records are considerably reduced." This was reinforced with the reminder that "a pay envelope is much fatter than a compensating check" and the threat that "a careless man and his job are soon parted."[66] To remove any ambiguity, it was reiterated that: "For the protection of the safe workers and good name of the plant, the troublemaker should be requested to call at the paymaster's office on the way out and reminded that the plant gate is a one-way thoroughfare for him."[67]

The same dynamic between employer benevolence, reciprocal rights and obligations, and the threat of dismissal pervaded the pension plan. The Company reported that the plan recognized that "some enduring obligation exists to the employee who has given long and faithful service to the Company."[68] But it also served two other objectives for the firm. The retirement plan compelled workers to retire at the age of 65, and thus addressed the problem of terminating older workers in a manner that did not undermine worker morale. More significantly, pension benefits were a form of deferred wages with eligibility based upon 20 years or more of "continuous active service," free of layoff, discharge, or suspension. As a prize for loyalty, reductions in the rate of labour turnover were anticipated. "There is no room in our organization for weaklings and failures," declared the *Review*, and in excess of 10 percent of Imperial's permanent workforce experienced "termination" each year.[69] Placing the efficiency loss at $100,000 to $500,000 per year, it hoped that more rigorous screening of potential employees, coupled with long-term incentives, would result in greater workforce stability. And when the number of terminations declined in 1919, it was interpreted as "a testimonial to our Annuities and Benefits Plan and to the Industrial Representation Plan."[70]

Enhanced benefits were also initially greeted by workers with skepticism. Thomas Noble, an elected delegate to the Sarnia industrial council, acknowledged that "it is a good scheme in the right direction," but preferred unionization. "The majority of men," he stated, "seem to appreciate it for the simple reason that if they are sick they get benefits."[71] Similarly, Fred Stuchberry, also an employee delegate on Sarnia's industrial council, complained that he "only gets abuse for his efforts" from fellow workers: "the majority say they have to die before they get anything." Nor did they defer to the Company's paternalism: "They could carry their own insurance if they got the money, and their own sick benefits, too, if they wanted to."[72] But there was no ignoring the tangible benefit to workers. Over half of those who died in the Company's employment held no other life insurance, and the pension annuities were not "scanty" as Brandes suggests was the general case.[73]

Welfare initiatives also extended beyond the plant. Imperial Oil introduced the ubiquitous company picnic, and bolstered its support of social clubs and sports teams to encourage the "esprit-de-corps, the co-operation, the team-work reflected in a baseball team or a social organization."[74] (The crowning achievement occurred when the Sarnia Imperials football team captured the Grey Cup in 1934.) The most concerted efforts came with the construction of townsites at Imperoyal and Ioco replete with playgrounds, bowling greens, and tennis courts. The long-neglected camps surrounding the Imperoyal refinery—created to house temporary workers during construction in 1917—were abolished in 1921 and replaced with nearby cottages.[75] But the Company's claim over the daily life of workers reached its zenith at Ioco. In 1919, the shantytown of cabins, shacks, and "chicken houses" adjacent to the refinery was converted into the "jewel of Vancouver's suburbs." Imperial Oil purchased land on the hillside overlooking the refinery and provided financial assistance to employees who wished to construct a house. A community centre and government-built school followed. With limited road connections to Vancouver, almost every aspect of workers' social life—dances, sports, and more casual socializing—occurred within the Company's purview. Members of the Ioco Tennis Club competed for the "Stillman Cup"; Company-sponsored teams competed in local baseball, curling, soccer, and hockey leagues; and when the land occupied by the baseball diamond was required for plant expansion, the solution was to build a new diamond within the plant, with the outfield walls surrounded by oil storage tanks.

Amidst the barrage of initiatives directed at male production workers, surprisingly scant attention was directed specifically towards women employees. The exception was a special "Woman's Number" of the *Review*, issued in January 1925, with a portrait of "The Wise Virgin" adorning the cover. This rather meagre "gift of appreciation for endeavours in the past" reflected management's view that women had a "brief and uncertain stay in the business world." It reported that all of the female office staff were "engaged ... Of course, to Imperial Oil." Left to wonder why they were unmarried, the *Review* concluded that: "The only explanation is that they like their work and the Company so well, that it would be a very exceptional kind of man that would induce them to leave." But resigned to the high turnover of female office staff, the Company only hoped that not too many left at one time.[76]

The third aspect of Imperial Oil's industrial relations program was the "Co-operative Investment Trust," a share-purchase plan. Beginning in 1920, workers with more than 12-months of service could deposit up to 25 percent of their wages into the Trust and the Company contributed 50 cents for every one dollar of employee contribution. Imperial Oil stock was then acquired and held in trust, along with accumulated dividends, for a period of five years after which shares were issued to individuals. The plan was explicitly structured to further foster labour stability: "Those who have studied the Plan have probably not failed to note that its principal benefits are reserved for those who remain in the service of the Company for five years."[77] Depositors leaving before two years received their money back plus six percent interest; those dropping out after two years received stock of a value equal to his/her deposits plus six percent interest; and only by remaining with the Company for the duration of the Plan did an employee receive the employer's contribution. Workers were counselled to "be careful to establish what they can afford" if they were to be successful investors: "It was solemnly averred [by outside critics] that a capitalist was born and not made and that any attempt to make small capitalists out of wage earners who might have no real inclination or talent for saving was doomed to failure."[78] Making capital and labour "comrades" in enterprise was expected to have both immediate and long-term benefits:

> For the Company—that is, all of us—it will mean a more united effort as the result of the added common incentive to economical and efficient operation ...; it will make, we hope, for greater continuity of employment, with a minimum change in the personnel of the "Imperial" family, and will deepen the sense of partnership which has ever been the basis of the relations between us.[79]

Unlike the employee-representation plan and the welfare initiative, the Trust was an unambiguous success from the outset. It enjoyed a high rate of participation: in 1920, of 3,570 eligible employees (with more than one year of service), over 2,500 subscribed to the program. Subsequent share-purchase plans yielded even higher participation rates, with the number of depositors rising to 3,219 by 1925.[80]

As labour market pressures eased and union activity abated, Imperial Oil maintained its commitment to welfare programs. Joint councils proved to be effective as a vehicle for communicating Company policy from the top down, and for obtaining approval for unilateral decisions. As McCallum argues, industrial councils did little more than "cloak" management decisions in a rhetoric of employer-employee co-operation.[81] The refinery superintendent at Halifax offered a cogent example:

> From the beginning of our Plant in 1917 ... the cost of living advanced rapidly and to keep the wages in line it was agreed by our Company to add Bonuses to meet the increased cost of living. Therefore, in January, 1922, to bring the schedule of wages in line I held a meeting of the Industrial Welfare Council and explained to them the object of the meeting. I placed before the Council the figures issued from Ottawa, which showed the decrease in the cost of living since 1920 when our last 10% Bonus increase in wages was given. I asked them if they were willing to play the game fair with the Company by passing a Resolution asking the Company to withdraw the 10% Bonus and I am glad to state that the Council after discussing the proposition rose to the occasion and unanimously passed a Resolution to withdraw the 10% Bonus. This showed the Spirit of Brotherhood existing between the Company and its employees.[82]

Workers did achieve a reorganization of working hours at Ioco in 1925, and a rent reduction in Imperoyal in 1926; in general, however, joint councils lapsed into discussions of more routine matters concerning housing, sanitation, safety, and the industrial representation plan itself. During the first five years of operations, over 1,000 issues were addressed, but only 11 percent concerned wages, 3 percent dealt with promotions, suspensions, and dismissals; by 1930, of the 205 issues on the agenda, only five concerned wages, and four dealt with promotions and dismissals. Marketing divisions frequently had "nothing to report" and often found no reason to convene meetings.

While other firms were shedding the financial burden of welfare and share-purchase plans, Imperial Oil was relatively insulated from the stock market crash and the collapse of demand in the 1930s. Workers and managers adhered to the implicit contract struck in the 1920s: workers gained economic security and the

Company found its reward in the "intangible" returns. In 1930, it concluded that:

> While it is difficult even now to measure the results, as they are more or less intangible, the sober conclusion is that it has not only stood the acid test during a very critical period in the world's history, but in addition has created and maintained a finer sense of comradeship, and the Company has enjoyed a greater measure of loyalty, efficiency and continuity of service, in this attempt to recover the necessary "personal touch."[83]

Confident that the labour problem had been solved, the Company's emphasis upon narrowly defined industrial relations issues subsided. The *Review* increasingly targeted a more general readership, as did its distribution. In 1934, it ceased publishing statistics on its benefits and industrial representation plans, and reports on company picnics gave way to coverage of broader public relations initiatives, such as the Sunday night radio broadcasts of "The Imperial Oil Hour of Fine Music" and editorials on gasoline prices and provincial taxes.[84] Industrial relations became just one, albeit important, aspect of a larger publicity campaign to convince the Canadian public and governments of Imperial Oil's social responsibility.

The Dialectic of Deference

The welfare strategies pursued by other Canadian companies in the 1920s and 1930s highlight the distinct paths to soliciting worker loyalty. Sangster persuasively argues that the allegiance of the predominantly female work force at Westclox in Peterborough was sustained by a "powerful ideological hegemony." While the material rewards were significant—wages exceeded community standards and workers obtained paid vacations, group insurance, and sick leave—they were integrated within a nineteenth-century style and "patrician sense of patriarchy." Importing prevailing community norms of gender and hierarchy into the workplace "ultimately supported women's secondary status as daughters in the Westclox family."[85] Penmans Limited adopted a similar, though less successful, application of paternalism in an effort to recruit women for its Paris textile mills. It built the Young Women's Christian Association and directed its activities in order to provide suitable accommodation and recreational programs to ensure young women of the respectability of urban factory life. Penmans also introduced a non-contributory pension plan, but its focus was at the community level where it sought to create a "public countenance of helpfulness and concern."[86] Dofasco's capacity to "manufacture consent" also relied on ideological reinforcement, in this instance by identifying loyalty to the Company with loyalty to the war effort. According to Storey, however, it was the appeal to economic security through a profit-sharing fund—coupled with a "consistent and often ruthless policy of dismissing and intimidating those attempting to organize their fellow employees"—that offered the most powerful inducement.[87]

There was nothing qualitatively different in Imperial Oil's variant of corporate welfarism *per se* that accounts for its success. Other firms instituted similar welfare benefits, and profit-sharing or share-purchase plans; and the employee-representation plan at the Colorado Fuel & Iron Company upon which it was based suffered through four strikes during 12 years before lapsing into "innocuous desuetude."[88] What was distinctive was the high price that Imperial Oil was able and willing to pay—and that its workers had the capacity to extract—in order to maintain a loyal, union-free labour force.

In 1930, the Company calculated the total costs of its welfare initiatives—some required by legislation—at $2.6 million (Table 11.3). The first Co-operative Investment Trust (1920–25) was of greater monetary significance. Workers paid in a total of $4.4 million and the Company's dollar contribution was $2.2 million. The actual cost to Imperial Oil and the benefits to its employees, however, were much greater. When the First Investment Trust began, the nominal share value was far below its actual value ($25 as compared to $125), and Imperial permitted shares to appreciate to their market value over the five-year period. At the end of the five-year period, 347,000 shares were purchased at a total value of between $11 and $12 million, yielding a net return to its employees in the order of $7 million.[89] The returns on the Second Investment Trust (1925–28) were less generous, but still substantial.

These dollar figures can be placed in perspective by comparing them to Imperial Oil's reported profit. Between 1921 and 1929, its manufacturing and refinery earnings varied significantly, but averaged roughly $8 million per annum (Table 11.4), and the annual cost of its welfare and share-purchase programs exceeded $1.5 million. If the latter is seen as a deduction from the Company's profits it hardly threatened to drive it into bankruptcy; nonetheless, it constituted a sizable claim by labour to a share of profits. Alternatively, one can consider the benefits to the average wage paid to a refinery worker of $1,200 in 1920. The benefits package, valued at $66 per employee per annum, represented a modest 5.5 percent increase in in-kind remuneration. But those participating in the Trust received an average annual return of roughly $400, or a 33 percent bonus on top of their wage. When added to wage rates well above local and national standards, it is clear that labour harmony had its price, and Imperial Oil had both the capacity and resolve to pay.

Table 11.3 Imperial Oil Company Ltd. Estimated Cost of Safety and Benefits Plans, 1920–29

Program	Expenditure
Annuities Plan	$732,507.15
Death Benefits	363,600.85
Sickness Benefits	568,391.47
Accident Benefits	185,661.78
WCB Assessments	582,036.20
Medical Expenses	133,554.28
Total	$2,565,751.73

Source: *Imperial Oil Review*, 14(4) (Aug./Sept. 1930) 17.

Table 11.4 Imperial Oil Company Ltd. Manufacturing and Marketing Earnings, 1900–39 ($1,000)

Year	Earnings	Year	Earnings
1921	1,349	1930	7,215
1922	7,710	1931	8,915
1923	2,528	1932	4,331
1924	7,927	1933	3,927
1925	7,972	1934	3,023
1926	14,102	1935	2,900
1927	5,648	1936	3,082
1928	16,775	1937	3,527
1929	15,703	1938	3,473
		1939	5,368

Source: Ewing, *History*, Ch. VII, Appendix; Ch. XV, Sec. C, Tables 1 and 2.

But this does not imply a passive acceptance of the Company's paternalist rhetoric. In 1920, the Sarnia council responded to the 10 percent wage increase by expressing "their complete confidence that the Directors of the company are now, and will continue to give these matters the attention they deserve."[90] Nor could the Company be completely assuaged by the views of one Halifax worker who described the employee-representation plan as "perfectly satisfactory ... and capable of great development"; for he added, perhaps naively, that it was "the nucleus of something that can be broadened out into a democratic control of the Company by the men themselves."[91]

After 1919, Imperial Oil's workers rarely, if ever, stepped outside of the "dialectic of deference"—to borrow Parr's term.[92] Workers, however, remained cognizant of their power to resist through informal ways, and Imperial Oil eventually expressed disappointment at the failure of positive work incentives to reduce the rate of turnover, absenteeism, and lost time due to accidents. The annual number of "terminations" from permanent job positions remained relatively high and there was no obvious downward trend on accident rates.[93] The *Review* complained of the erosion of the work ethic by attendance at sporting events and movies, and by the "English weekend." Rising unemployment had partially remedied the problem; however, "in many cases three employees are doing indifferently well what two did before the saxophone displaced the dinner horn." The "menace of success" was that it fostered complacency.[94] In turn, the Company was never remiss in warning that punitive measures were ever present: "The morale of an organization must be kept up, and if the rank and file determine to be fair to the company employing them, the few exceptions can be taken care of through discharges without making it necessary to impose burdensome regulations upon the entire force."[95]

Imperial Oil's workers may be susceptible to the charge that they were "co-opted" or "sold out" by accepting the material rewards at the expense of industrial democracy. But this indictment, if it has validity, is appropriate to a later period. In the economic climate of the 1920s, described as "unpropitious" for labour gains, Imperial Oil's workers attained major concessions in wages, hours of work, benefits, and a lucrative savings plan.

The Legacy of Mackenzie King

In a rather roundabout way—from Ludlow, Colorado via Bayonne, New Jersey to Sarnia, Ontario—one aspect of Mackenzie King's influence upon Canadian industrial relations can be concretely observed. The "Colorado Plan" was adopted at several of Rockefeller's companies, including Jersey Standard's refineries following the notorious strike at Bayonne, and subsequently extended to its Canadian subsidiary. Executives at Imperial Oil were reluctant to compare their industrial relations program to that at Jersey Standard, adamantly declaring that "it is not the Rockefeller plan." King, however, claimed at least a share of authorship: "I have seen [Imperial Oil's] plan, and it seems to me in some particulars to be very much a copy of the [Colorado] plan."[96] And he was not wrong, for in his capacity as an industrial relations "consultant" King played a prominent role in the diffusion of corporate welfarism, and company unionism in particular, to several American firms, including International Harvester, Bethlehem Steel, Standard Oil of Indiana, and General Electric.[97]

In many respects, King reflects the "Janus face" of corporate welfarism—with its paternalistic benevolence on the one side and deception on the other. King is credited with creating the "velvet glove over the bloody iron fist" used to pacify workers in the wake of the Ludlow massacre: for Ferns and Ostry, he was the creator of "fake organizations" for "sapping the spirit of independent labour"; according to Craven, King's advocacy of employee-representation plans reflected his distrust of labour organizations; similarly, Gitelman notes that King tolerated the use of industrial spies in Colorado while the company union was in place; and Scheinberg, in a peculiar interpretation of Gramsci, excuses King for merely playing out his role as a ruling-class intellectual, to rationalize the use of force and to ensure consent and acceptance of the existing order.[98] Others interpret his actions as consonant with his vision of "capitalism with a human face" and his evolutionary model of industrial relations. Industrial conflict resulted from misinformation and misunderstanding that concealed the common interests of the two parties. Employee-representation plans were thus one stage in "metamorphosis" of the employer-employee relationship: if employers initiated co-operation, workers would reciprocate and "legitimate" unions would evolve into agencies for co-operation.[99] And there is support for the view that, although ultimately unsuccessful, welfare experiments in the 1920s and 1930s were important in paving the way for the post-World War II capital-labour accord. Edwards argues that employee-representation plans demonstrated to firms the value of a grievance process and welfare schemes served to confirm the value of positive work incentives; Brandes describes corporate welfarism as a "necessary step" in the road towards a bureaucratic solution to industrialism; King could champion the "corporatist" strategy described by McInnis in the formation of the wartime Labour–Management Production Committees; and Whitaker concedes the "astonishing prophetic quality" of King's vision reflected in the "corporatist" strategies of the 1970s.[100]

The experience in the Canadian petroleum industry, and Imperial Oil in particular, emphasizes the former face of welfare capitalism. From the National Industrial Conference in 1919, to the hearings of the National War Labour Board in 1943, Imperial Oil championed its industrial councils as an alternative to trade unions for all industries to imitate. When passage of the Wagner Act recognized workers' demands for the right to association and signalled the end of company-organized worker organizations in the United States, the Company successfully lobbied against the exclusion of company unions in comparable Canadian legislation.[101] Bernstein observes for the United States that "no [manufacturing] industry presented such massive roadblocks to unionization as petroleum,"[102] and the same can be argued for Canada. The first union contract in a Canadian refinery came in 1942, when the Saskatchewan Consumers' Co-operative Federation voluntary recognized the CCL-chartered union. Other small refineries in the prairies followed, but the persistence of company unions among the major refiners is blamed for the Oil Workers International Union "miss[ing] out on the mass organizing drives of the 1940s."[103]

It was not until 1946, at Ioco—ironically where the Company's paternalism had been the most pervasive—that Imperial Oil was forced to recognize unionization among refinery workers. And in 1951 and 1953, when workers at the Shell refinery in British Columbia went on strike in support of demands for a 28 percent and 5 1/2 percent wage increase, Imperial Oil's management finally ceded unilateral control over wage setting in the industry.[104] But the non-union status of the majority of Imperial Oil's refineries today is a testament to the Company's opposition to industrial democracy.[105]

A formal approach towards managing capital–labour conflict marked one aspect of the emergence of monopoly capitalism in Canada. As the scale of production increased, continuous processing evolved, and the "drive" system intensified work, the conditions for industrial unionism were created. By 1920, welfare capitalism—structured upon higher wages, a paternalistic benefits plan, profit sharing, and a limited worker voice over shop-floor concerns—emerged as the solution to forestall unionization and ameliorate industrial conflict in several firms. But welfare capitalism did not offer a general solution to the "labour problem" in Canada. Its application was largely restricted to firms operating in newer mass-production and monopolistic industries where the need and capacity to purchase labour harmony was predominant. The persistence of company unionism at Imperial Oil reflects the Company's resolve to maintain a union-free status, and the capacity of workers to extract a high price for their loyalty.

The author thanks Reg Basken, James Naylor, and the referees of *Labour/Le Travail* for their helpful comments.

Endnotes

1. *Imperial Oil Review*, 14, 4 (August-September 1930), 16.
2. Canada, Department of Labour, National Industrial Conference: Official Report of Proceedings and Discussion (Ottawa 1919), 163.
3. J.S. Ewing, *The History of the Imperial Oil Company, Limited* (Boston 1951; unpublished manuscript held in the Imperial Oil Archives), ch. VIII, sect. I, 73.
4. Cited in Ewing, *History*, 76.
5. S. Brandes, *American Welfare Capitalism, 1880–1940* (Chicago 1970), 6; D. Montgomery, *The Fall of the House of Labor: The Workplace, the State, and American Labor Activism, 1865–1925* (Cambridge, MA 1987); I. Bernstein, *The Turbulent Years: History of the American Worker, 1933–1941* (Boston 1970).
6. S. Jacoby, *Employing Bureaucracy: Managers, Union, and the Transformation of Work in American Industry, 1900–1945* (New York 1985), 205. Both Frederick Taylor and Robert Valentine viewed welfarism as a joke (Brandes, *American*, 36; H.M. Gitelman, *Legacy of the Ludlow Massacre: A Chapter in American Industrial Relations* [Philadelphia 1988], 200).
7. Brody cautions that: "In failure, welfare capitalism has been too casually dismissed" since, on the eve of the Great Depression, "the essential vitality of welfare capitalism seemed wholly undiminished." D. Brody, "The Rise and Decline of Welfare Capitalism" (1964), reprinted in *Workers in Industrial America: Essays on the Twentieth-Century Struggles* (New York 1980). But his peculiar counterfactual—if the Great Depression had not intervened, would welfare capitalism have persisted into the post-World War II period—is hardly germane. Business cycles are endemic to capitalism, and when the inevitable downturn occurred, the inherent contradictions in paternalistic corporate welfarism were laid bare. There was a brief revival in employer support of company unionism under the auspices of the National Industrial Recovery Act (1933), but these "cynical" initiatives were short lived. Daniel Nelson, "The Company Union Movement, 1900–1937: A Re-examination," *Business History Review*, 56 (1982), 335–57; Jacoby, *Employing Bureaucracy*, 226–7.
8. J. Naylor, *The New Democracy: Challenging the Social Order in Industrial Ontario, 1914–1925* (Toronto 1991); G.S. Kealey, "1919: Canada's Labour Revolt," *Labour/Le Travail*, 13 (1984), 11–44.
9. Repressive state measures in the wake of the Winnipeg General Strike, including the application of sedition laws and recourse to the militia, are discussed by D. McGillvrary, "Military Aid to Civilian Power: The Cape Breton Experience in the 1920s," *Acadiensis*, 3 (1974), 45–64; the rise of mass culture undermining the unity of working class experience is emphasized by B. Palmer, *Working-Class Experience: The Rise and Reconstitution of Canadian Labour, 1880–1980* (Toronto 1983), ch. 5; resistance of traditional craft unions to organize the unskilled, and a variety of demographic, industrial and economic circumstances are identified. S.M. Jamieson, *Times of Trouble: Labour Unrest and Industrial Conflict in Canada, 1900–1966* (Ottawa 1976).
10. M.E. McCallum, "Corporate Welfarism in Canada, 1919–39," *Canadian Historical Review*, 71 (1990), 46–79; B. Scott, "A Place in the Sun: The Industrial Council at Massey-Harris, 1919–1929," *Labour/Le Travailleur*, 1 (1976), 158–92.
11. Scott, "A Place in the Sun," 160.
11. C. Heron, *Working in Steel: The Early Years in Canada, 1883–1935* (Toronto 1988), 99–107; R. Storey, "Unionization versus Corporate Welfare: The Dofasco Way," *Labour/Le Travailleur*, 12 (1983), 7–42. The introduction of company unionism at Dofasco in 1936 is attributed to cyclical upturn in the industry and the unionizing drive of the Steel Workers Organizing Committee.
13. G. Zahavi, *Workers, Managers and Welfare Capitalism: The Shoeworkers and Tanners of Endicott Johnson, 1890–1950* (Urbana, IL 1988).
14. Zahavi, *Workers*, 54.
15. Canada, House of Commons Standing Committee on Banking and Commerce, *Minutes of Proceedings and Evidence: The Price of Gasoline* (Ottawa 1932), testimony of Victor Ross, 9.

16. H. Grant "The Petroleum Industry and Canadian Economic Development: An Economic History, 1900–1960," Ph.D. thesis, University of Toronto, 1987, ch. 4.
17. Canadian Oil Companies Limited, "Black Gold Victory: The Story of Canadian Oil Companies, Limited, 1908–1958," *Canadian Oil News* 19, 4 (1958); J.T. Saywell, "The Early History of Canadian Oil Companies: A Chapter in Canadian Business History," *Ontario History* 53 (1961), 67–72. The Standard Trust sought to restrict sales to independent jobbers in Canada and to secure discriminatory freight rates secured on railway shipments from Pennsylvania and Ohio to Canada, and from Sarnia to Montreal; National Archives of Canada (hereafter NAC), Canadian Transport Commission, RG 46, Series B.I.l, *Minutes and Proceedings of the Railway Committee of Privy Council*, vols. 718, 719, 781; United States Industrial Commission, Hearings, Standard Oil Combinations (Washington 1899), 378: United States Commissioner of Corporations, Transportation of Petroleum (Washington 1906), 129.
18. Shell Oil of Canada, incorporated in 1911, constructed an ocean terminal in Montreal to dispose of excess bunker fuel of its Indian Oil affiliate; and its American affiliate was selling gasoline supplied by its Asiatic Petroleum affiliate on Canada's west coast by 1912. K. Beaten, *Enterprise in Oil: A History of Shell in the United States* (New York 1957), ch. 2. Union Oil Company of California began marketing fuel oil in British Columbia in 1904, and secured the large CPR contract. Ewing, *History*, ch. IX, sect. C.
19. This followed an extensive reorganization of Imperial Oil that shifted a greater degree of control from New York to Toronto. See G.D. Taylor, "From Branch Operation to Integrated Subsidiary: The Reorganization of Imperial Oil under Walter Teagle, 1911–1917," *Business History*, 34 (1992), 49–68.
20. Ewing, *History*, ch. XVII. 3; H.F. Williamson, et al., *The American Petroleum Industry: The Age of Energy, 1899–1959* (Evanston, IL 1963), 269–72.
21. On IPC's activities in Latin America, see G.S. Gibb and E.H. Knowlton, *History of the Standard Oil Company* (New Jersey), *Volume 2: The Resurgent Years 1911–1927* (New York 1956), chs. 4, 13; and H. O'Connor, *World Oil in Crisis* (London 1962), chs. 9, 17, 18. Development of Colombia's oil resources is discussed by J.F. Rippy, *The Capitalists and Colombia* (New York 1931), ch. 7.
22. A detailed description of Imperial Oil's Ioco refinery and the distillation process is provided in the *Imperial Oil Review*, 3, 5 (May 1919), 7–8; 3, 8 (August 1919), 3–5; 4, 10 (November 1920), 7.
23. G.A. Purdy, *Petroleum: Prehistoric to Petrochemical* (Toronto 1958), 153–5; Williamson, *American Petroleum Industry*, 147, 269–72; Gibb and Knowlton, *History*, 118. Imperial Oil paid $15,000 for the first 50,000 barrels/year of crude refined and 30 cents for each subsequent barrel of crude.
24. Purdy, *Petroleum*, 43–5, 157–60.
25. Williamson, *American Petroleum Industry*, 375–95.
26. Purdy, *Petroleum*, 44; J.L. Hoggett, "The Transformation of the Test House," *Imperial Oil Review*, 15, 3 (December 1931), 5–8 and 15, 4 (January/February 1932), 13–5. Incidental to the evolution of cracking technology was the discovery that "cracked" gasoline had superior anti-knocking properties. From 1926 to 1929, Imperial had a semi-exclusive right to the use of tetraethyl lead in Canada as an additive to increase the octane rating of straight-run gasoline. Concerns over health and safety and the high cost of tetraethyl lead. however, contributed to a rather slow rate of adoption of leaded gasoline in Canada. Ewing, *History*, ch. IX, sect. B. Health concerns over the use of tetraethyl lead stemmed from the death from lead poisoning of several employees at Standard Oil's plant in Elizabeth, New Jersey. M. Ross. "The Standard Oil's Death Factory," in R. Engel, ed., *America's Energy: Reports from The Nation on 100 Years of Struggles for the Democratic Control of Our Resources* (New York 1980), 167–70.
27. A handful of competitors built refineries in the 192Os. McColl Brothers (a long-time Toronto marketer) erected a refinery in 1926. and then amalgamated with Frontenac Oil Company (the successor to National Oil Refineries, Ltd. of Montreal) in 1929; Union Oil operated a small topping plant at Port Moody, British Columbia between 1921 and 1926, until a production agreement with Imperial Oil was reached; North Star Oil and Refining Company constructed a tiny topping plant in Winnipeg in 1921 (Imperial Oil acquired a majority interest in North Star and concealed its ownership); and a number of small "scrubbing plants" in the Turner Valley gas field separated the sulphur from the crude naphtha at the well head prior to selling the highly-volatile output to local farmers. Grant, "Petroleum Industry," ch. 5.

28. Gibb and Knowlton, *History*, Tables 10, 17, 20, and 21.
29. The exception is H.G. Gutman, "The Labor Policies of the Large Corporation in the Gilded Age: The Case of the Standard Oil Company," in *Power and Culture* (New York 1987). He examines the erosion of the economic position of skilled coopers in the barreling departments of refineries, and how Standard Oil crushed the coopers' union in the 1870s.
30. A.D. Chandler, *The Visible Hand: The Managerial Revolution in American Business* (Cambridge, MA 1977), 240, 241, 255–56.
31. D. Horowitz, *Labor Relations in the Petroleum Industry* (New York 1957), ch. 1.
32. *Imperial Oil Review*, 2, 2 (February 1918); 7, 5 (June 1923), 21–2.
33. D. Gordon, R. Edwards, and M.R. Reich, *Segmented Work, Divided Workers: The Historical Transformation of Labor in theUnited States* (Cambridge MA 1982), 100; R. Edwards, Con*tested Terrain: The Transformation of the Workplace in the Twentieth Century* (New York 1979).
34. Gibb and Knowlton, *History*, 137–42.
35. Cited in S. Chase, *A Generation of Industrial Peace* (New York 1946).
36. Ewing, *History*, ch. VIII, sect. I, 69.
37. U.S., Department of Labor, Bureau of Labor Statistics, *Wages and Hours of Labor in the Petroleum Industry, 1920* (Washington 1922).
38. Ewing, *History*, ch. VIII, sect. I, 72.
39. Canada, Royal Commission on Industrial Relations (hereafter RCIR), *Evidence*, testimony of William Campbell, boilermaker (19 May 1919), 2022. Imperial Oil refused to recognize the union federation, allegedly firing one union member who was only rehired on threat of a refinery-wide strike.
40. H. O'Connor, *History of the Oil Worker's International Union-CIO* (Denver 1950).
41. NAC, Department of Labour, RG 27, v. 308, strike 97.
42. NAC, Tariff Board, RG 79, vol. 169, file 84, pt. 7, testimony of H.C.F. Mockridge, 1778.
43. *Imperial Oil Review*, 8, 2 (February 1924), 5. Early issues were replete with pithy slogans such as: "The man who habitually complains much will always find much to complain about."
44. Testimony of D. Strachan, National Industrial Conference, 150–2.
45. Imperial Oil's employment practices were far from enlightened. When Teagle recruited chemists from Cornell's graduating class in 1916, he specified that no applications from "Hebrews" would be entertained. Ewing, *History*, ch. VIII, Appendix 1, 86n. And as late as 1950, African-Canadians were only employed as uniformed porters at the head office building. Ewing, *History*, ch. XIX, sect. B, 20n. In 1936, L.C. McCloskey, Vice-President, described his pride in Imperial Oil's policy of paying high wages in Latin America, in the following terms: "I do not want to be like the cartoon I saw a short time ago of a nigger that went to a nigger church and his eyes were popping out and the preacher said to him 'Brother, you are not confessing, you are bragging.'" NAC, Tariff Board, RG 79, volume 69, file 84, pt.7, Ottawa hearings, 2305.
46. Jacoby, *Employing Bureaucracy*, 159.
47. Mackenzie King had insisted upon the inclusion of such a clause in the "Colorado Plan" and was adamant that it would not encourage unionization. Gitelman, *Legacy*, 246.
48. RCIR, *Evidence*, 2036.
49. RCIR, *Evidence*, 2089.
50. RCIR, *Evidence*, 2000, 2002, 2099.
51. RCIR, *Evidence*, 1997, 1999.
52. RCIR, *Evidence*, c 2072.
53. Stillman, cited in Ewing, *History*, ch. VIII. Sect. I. 73.
54. RCIR, Evidence, testimony of William Campbell. 2020.
55. In 1939, the average weekly wage of workers in the Petroleum and Coal Products industry was $35.31, compared to $22.79 in all manufacturing industries. F.H. Leary, ed., *Historical Statistics of Canada* (Ottawa 1983), E90, E110.
56. Reprinted in the *Imperial Oil Review*, 3, 7 (July 1919), 7–8.
57. *Imperial Oil Review*, 3, 8 (August 1919), 14.
58. "The Joint Agreement," *Imperial Oil Review*, 14, 4 (August–September 1930), 66.
59. Brody, "Rise and Decline," 52.
60. *Imperial Oil Review*, 14, 4 (August–September 1930). 62.

61. RCIR, *Evidence*, 2794.
62. This was augmented in 1930 with a Group Insurance plan, and additional benefits could be purchased by employees at a low cost. *Imperial Oil Review*, 14, 4 (August–September 1930), 62–6. McCallum in "Corporate Welfarism," 50, notes that company-sponsored insurance plans were encouraged by their treatment as a business expense. And by the push of the insurance industry for new markets.
63. Ewing, *History*, ch. XI. Sect. C.
64. RCIR, *Evidence*, 2777, 2794.
65. *Imperial Oil Review*, 2, 11 (April 1927), 11.
66. *Imperial Oil Review*, 7, 6 (July 1923), 14.
67. *Imperial Oil Review*, 9, 7 (July 1925), 7.
68. *Imperial Oil Review*, 14, 4 (August–September 1930), 17.
69. *Imperial Oil Review*, 5, 8 (August 1921), 14.
70. *Imperial Oil Review*, 4, 1 (January 1920), 4.
71. RCIR, *Evidence*, 2043, 2046.
72. RCIR, *Evidence*, 2068, 2064.
73. "Annual Benefits and Annuities Statistics," *Imperial Oil Review*, 1920–32, passim; Brandes, *American Welfare Capitalism*, ch. 11. The average annuity in 1927, for instance, was $875, roughly 60 percent of the average annual wage. What was surprising was the small number of annual retirees: between 1919 and 1927, the number ranked from 13 to 17, roughly half the number of men that died while in the Company's service.
74. *Imperial Oil Review*, 5, 5 (May 1921), 10.
75. Company housing was also maintained at the East Montreal refinery, primarily for its English-speaking management.
76. *Imperial Oil Review*, 3, 10 (October 1919), 6. Reports of the women's baseball team in Saskatoon were equally patronizing, inviting readers to look closely at the team photo and notice all the "curves" on the field.
77. *Imperial Oil Review*, 4, 2 (March 1920), 3.
78. *Imperial Oil Review*, 5, 5 (May 1921).
79. *Imperial Oil Review*, 4, 2 (March 1920), 4.
80. In 1921, Imperial Oil employed over 7,000 people, roughly half of which worked in its five refineries (Ioco, 325; Regina, 275; Sarnia, 1,400; Montréal, 450; Halifax, 1,000), *Imperial Oil Review*, 5, 7 (July 1921), 3.
81. Ewing, *History*, ch. XIX, sect. C; McCallum, "Corporate Welfarism," 61.
82. *Imperial Oil Review*, 9, 5 (May 1925), 7.
83. *Imperial Oil Review*, 14, 4 (August–September 1930), 16.
84. Pictures of the members of joint councils appeared for the last time in 1947, presumably to avoid explaining why there was no photograph for the newly unionized Ioco refinery.
85. J. Sangster, "The Softball Solution: Female Workers, Male Managers and the Operation of Paternalism at Westclox, 1923–1960," *Labour/Le Travail*, 32 (1993), 167–99. For an elaboration, see her *Earning Respect: The Lives of Working Women in Small-Town Ontario, 1920–1960* (Toronto 1995).
86. J. Parr, *The Gender of Breadwinners: Women, Men, and Change in Two Industrial Towns, 1880–1950* (Toronto 1990), 45–50.
87. Storey, "The Dofasco Way," 9.
88. Cited in Gitelman, *Legacy*, 338.
89. *Imperial Oil Review*, 9, 4 (April 1925), 1.
90. *Imperial Oil Review*, 4, 1 (January 1920), 9.
91. RCIR, *Evidence*, 4279.
92. Parr, *Gender of Breadwinners*, 50.
93. Annual terminations varied between 328 and 675 over the decade, equal to roughly ten percent of insured employees; this compares unfavourably to turnover rates in the American petroleum industry which ranged between four and five percent. There is no obvious trend in the time lost due to accidents ("Annual benefits and Annuities Statistics," *Imperial Oil Review*, 1920–32, passim).
94. *Imperial Oil Review*, 9, 10 (December 1925), 14.

95. *Imperial Oil Review*, 9, 10 (November 1925), 15.
96. See the comments of Strachan and King, National Industrial Conference, 160.
97. Gitelman, *Legacy*, 252–3.
98. H.S. Ferns and B. Ostry, *Age of Mackenzie King: The Rise of a Leader* (Toronto 1955), 216, 208; P. Craven, "King and Context: A Reply to Whitaker," *Labour/Le Travailleur*, 4 (1979), 182, and "An Impartial Umpire": *Industrial Relations and the Canadian State, 1900–1911* (Toronto 1980); Gitelman, *Legacy*, 191; S.J. Scheinberg, "Rockefeller and King: the Capitalist and the Reformer," in J. English and J.O. Stubbs, eds., *Mackenzie King: Widening The Debate* (Toronto 1978).
99. Gitelman, *Legacy*, 247, 257–8, 261.
100. Edwards, *Contested Terrain*, 108; Brandes, *American Welfare Capitalism*, 146; P.S. McInnis, "Teamwork for Harmony: Labour–Management Production Committees and the Postwar Settlement," *Canadian Historical Review*, 77 (1996), 317–52; R. Whitaker, "The Liberal Corporatist Ideas of Mackenzie King," *Labour/Le Travailleur*, 2 (1977), 137–69.
101. Section 8 of the Wagner Act deemed company unions to be an "unfair labor practice." Brandes, *American Welfare Capitalism*, 108.
102. Bernstein, *The Lean Years*, 110.
103. W. Roberts, *Cracking the Canadian Formula: The Making of the Energy and Chemical Workers Union* (Toronto 1990); O'Connor, *Oil Workers*, 57. On the Difficulties of unionizing in the face of company unions, see Warren Caragata, *Alberta Labour: A Heritage Untold* (Toronto 1979), 132–6.
104. NAC, RG 27, v. 486, strike 152; v. 504, strike 165.
105. Daphne Gottlieb Tara, "Managerial Intentions and Wage Determination in the Canadian Petroleum Industry, *Industrial Relations*, 36 (1997), 178–205.

Chapter 12

Against All Odds

The Progressive Arts Club's Production of *Waiting for Lefty*

Bonita Bray

When the Progressive Arts Club produced Clifford Odets's *Waiting for Lefty* in Vancouver at the height of the waterfront strike in October 1935, the play was an unlikely contender for success. All elements of the performance were problematic: the play itself, the players, and the reaction of the audience. *Waiting for Lefty* was the antithesis of the escapist fare to which Vancouverites were accustomed, for it was a militant, pro-union play which explored the capitalist system from the viewpoint of working people, and exposed its exploitive nature. The play examined the hardships that forced workers to take a stand, and ended with an uncompromising call to strike. The players were equally inauspicious: a group of young workers, many of foreign descent, unemployed, inexperienced on the stage, and drawn together as much by their political commitment as their love for the theatre. Audience support was also doubtful. The citizens of Vancouver, after six years of protests, demonstrations, and strikes that had polarized public opinion, were witnessing a violent waterfront strike which pitted the longshoremen against the powerful Shipping Federation and its allies. *Lefty* offered theatre-goers no diversion or respite from the struggle. Instead, its searing indictment of the capitalist system raised the issues of inequality and social justice in concrete, emotional terms that demanded political action. The play's radical subject matter, the players' inexperience, and the polarized political climate in Vancouver all mitigated against success. Yet the Progressive Arts Club succeeded in overcoming these obstacles to produce the hit of the 1935–36 theatre season.

An examination of how *Lefty*, despite numerous impediments, achieved a large measure of acclaim and popularity leads inevitably to an investigation of the changing nature of working-class protest and the impact of drama as a tool to educate, motivate, and organize. It also poses a number of intriguing questions regarding the resiliency and adaptability of working-class culture and its relationship to the dominant culture—questions which are beyond the scope of this paper.

To understand why *Lefty* succeeded, it is necessary to analyze the volatile social context in which the play was presented. In 1935, after six years of conflict between masses of unemployed and the authorities which frequently broke out into violent confrontation in the streets, Vancouver simmered with discontent and dissatisfaction. The general public, increasingly pushed to take sides in the debate, was frustrated by the intransigence and inaction of all levels of government despite an unemployment rate that hovered around 30 percent. Repeated investigations of the city's relief department and scandals within the police force further undercut the legitimacy of the status quo.[1] When 1,500 relief camp workers struck their isolated bush camps in April, and longshoremen attempted to win control of the dispatching hall by threatening to shut down the port, civic and business leaders made dire predictions of an impending general strike.

Polarization of public opinion was intensified in mid-May by the appearance of the Citizens' League, a vigilante-style group made up of the former chief of police, civic leaders, and members of the Shipping Federation. While ostensibly formed to "finance an intensive campaign to educate and inform citizens of the ... danger of radical control of labour unions,"[2] the League's main purpose was to enlist popular support for its strident "law and order" campaign which equated labour unions with communism. When the relief camp workers took their struggle On-To-Ottawa in early June, the Shipping Federation, supported by civic authorities, increased its red-baiting crusade and moved to crush the waterfront workers. Federation spokesmen informed the men that their contract was no longer in force, evicted the union from its offices in the Shipping Federation Hall, and, in conjunction with the Citizens' League, began advertising for special constables to "protect private property on the waterfront."[3] The position of civic authorities was clear since Mayor Gerry McGeer had already pledged that he would "mobilize 10,000 men to keep the port open and rid this city of the red menace." The union immediately sought to neutralize these imprecations and situate the dispute in a working-class framework, pointing out to the public that "our fight is with our employers" and warning that "it will be up to them to say whether there will be any violence."[4] But their appeal was to prove futile.

Despite the massive police presence on the waterfront, which discouraged effective picketing, protected strike-breakers, and "encouraged" the normal flow of traffic to and from the docks,[5] the strike held firm. But the authorities were not content with this show of strength. Barely two weeks into the strike, a massed force of city, provincial, and federal police with tear gas and batons attacked the strikers who were demonstrating on Ballantyne Pier. The city was polarized as never before. For some citizens, the sight of galloping horsemen pursuing unarmed strikers, seen either in person or through the horrifying picture on the front page of the *Sun* the next day, exemplified all that was wrong with the system, and they became even more convinced of the need for radical change.[6] Others called for action to repress the "red menace." The struggle continued for the hearts and minds of the citizens of Vancouver.[7]

The Progressive Arts Club's production of *Waiting for Lefty* was set against this backdrop of class conflict and was intended to add fuel to the fire. The primary force behind the club's formation was Garfield King, a progressive lawyer who was deeply committed to protecting the civil rights of left-wing protestors. As a past-chairman of the play selection committee for the Vancouver Little Theatre Association and producer of at least three of its plays, King was concerned that theatre in Vancouver was ignoring the realities people faced in the depression, and becoming increasingly conventional, comfortable, and irrelevant. He was determined to reverse that trend and to introduce Vancouver audiences to the vital, involved theatre which was making its debut in the United States.[8] In July 1935, armed with the text of *Lefty* published in the February 1935 issue of New Theatre, he discussed the project with Guy Glover, another progressive member of the Vancouver Little Theatre Association, and together they set about to form the Vancouver chapter of the Progressive Arts Club—a loosely linked organization that had established groups in Toronto, Montreal, and Winnipeg, dedicated to organizing a workers' theatre to produce plays "which tend to the achievement of social justice."[9]

For artistic and political reasons, both King and Glover were committed to using working people in the cast of *Lefty*. Since the very nature of the play demanded political commitment, they attempted to recruit people whose desire to be on the stage was matched by their commitment to the principles of social equity. To this end they advertised auditions in both the left-wing papers—*The Commonwealth*, published by the CCF, and *The B.C. Workers' News*, the official organ of the Communist Party—posted notices throughout the downtown area, and contacted the Ukrainian Labour Farmers' Temple Association, a left-wing, working-class organization supportive of progressive causes. The ULFTA was a natural source for recruiting the cast since its extensive theatre, music, and dance programmes attracted large numbers of young people, and its central downtown location acted as a focal point for much of the city's left-wing activity. The contact proved most fortunate since the ULFTA provided both free rehearsal space, which was most welcome given Lefty's limited prospects for commercial success, and volunteer actors from its Youth Section.[10]

Harry Hoshowsky and Mike Kunka were typical of those who volunteered. They were young—only 15 years old—and had little direct theatrical experience. But they had grown up singing, dancing, and playing music for audiences in the association's hall, and understood the dynamics between spectator and performer.[11] Others, like Sophie Rankin, had no experience on the stage, but auditioned for *Lefty* because they wanted to "do something positive to change the terrible situation we were all in."[12] Although two or three of the older actors were experienced, for the most part members of the cast, like the play they intended to produce, were unorthodox: they were young, working-class, unemployed, and inexperienced.

When the cast assembled for the first rehearsal at the beginning of August, the enormity of their task became apparent. Most of the prospective thespians had no idea of how to act on stage, learn their lines, or project their voices. Ironically, their youth, inexperience, and unstructured time turned out to be beneficial: they took direction willingly, and worked hard. According to Guy Glover: "There were no problems about turning out for rehearsals. We could really give the actors hell and they would take it. We had total discipline.... The cast was dedicated and we were ruthless in the way we worked."[13] And so the work progressed, with the actors rehearsing four nights a week and sometimes full days during the weekend. At the same time they also worked on a companion piece, *The Bear* by Anton Chekhov, which was chosen to "show the contrast both in subject matter and technique as compared with *Lefty*."[14] These two presentations, together with musical numbers by the Ukrainian members of the cast, provided a full evening's program.

By the end of September the productions were ready for the public, and the group scheduled its debut for October 13 and 14 at the Ukrainian Labour Temple—the same week the longshoremen voted to reject the Shipping Federation's latest offer. The cast was not surprised by the standing-room only crowd: they had anticipated a large, working-class audience, partly because they believed that the Left would support their venture, and partly because Garfield King's comments about the "Little Theatre's namby-pamby plays and the need for theatre with a little blood to it" had generated a great deal of controversy.[15]

The enthusiastic reaction they received, however, was beyond their wildest dreams. Even before the final lines of the play, the audience, composed mainly of progressives and friends of the Labour Temple, rose *en masse* and cheered. This was exactly the response that *Lefty* had been generating in the United States since its first performance in New York nine months earlier. *Lefty* represented the "new theatre"—in essence, a renaissance of involved and critical drama—that brought the protests of the day to the stage, criticizing the inequalities of the capitalist system, depicting the day-to-day problems of working people, and calling for corrective action. *Lefty* employed a strong story line, vernacular diction, and innovative staging to put across its uncompromising political message. Unlike so many of its predecessors in the contemporary social theatre mileau, *Lefty* was dramatically successful, marrying social concerns with gripping theatre to create a working-class blockbuster.

Lefty's plot is intense and melodramatic. Set in a taxi-drivers' union hall, the play opens with the strike committee debating a strike call. As they wait for *Lefty*, the leader of the pro-strike contingent, members of the committee relate, through a series of knife-edged blackout scenes, the crucial events that forced them to opt for strike action. Throughout these scenes the corrupt union boss, Mr. Fatt, and his gunman sidekick are a constant malevolent presence—an "ugly menace which hangs over the lives of all the people who act out their own dramas."[16] Fatt tries desperately to undercut the growing support for the strike by threatening and redbaiting. When these methods fail, he calls upon a union member, in reality an actor seated inconspicuously in the audience, to describe the devastating losses suffered in a similar strike the preceding year. This litany of failure and betrayal is interrupted by another union member, also seated in the audience, who angrily intervenes in mid-speech and unmasks the witness as a company spy, sent to dissuade the men from striking. Still, Lefty does not appear. Finally, Agate Keller, the elder statesman of the committee, takes control and calls for a vote. As he attempts to speak he is grabbed by Fatt and his henchman, but he breaks away and triumphant, his torn shirt the proud symbol of struggle, he addresses his fellow union members—the audience—drawing together their mutual experiences:

> These slick slobs stand here telling us about bogeymen. That's a new one for the kids—the reds is the bogeymen! But the man who got me food in 1932, he called me Comrade! The one who picked me up where I bled—he called me Comrade too! What are we waiting for.... Don't wait for Lefty! He might never come. Every minute—[17]

With these words still hanging in the air like a prophecy, Keller's appeal is interrupted by a driver who crashes through the back door of the hall and runs onto the stage, yelling, "Boys, they've just found Lefty!... Behind the car barns with a bullet in his head!" After a moment's shocked silence, Keller calls to the audience, "Well, what's the answer?" A split-second later the actors and some members of the audience raise their voices in a ringing "Strike! Strike! Strike!"[18]

The reason for the play's force lay in both its spirited plot and its innovative staging techniques, which broke down the curtain between actors and audience and encouraged everyone to be an active participant in the unfolding drama. During the production the entire theatre was transformed into a union hall, with dramatic action whirling from the stage to the body of the theatre and back again. As incognito actors, strategically placed throughout the crowd, shouted encouragement and derision at those on stage, and on occasion emerged from the audience to take their place on stage, people watching the play were slowly drawn from spectator to participant, creating a powerful emotional fusion between the author, actors, and audience. Guy Glover commented that "with that play, as distinct from other plays I did, you knew you were getting some kind of involvement from the audience that was unusual."[19] So intense was this involvement that patrons regularly stayed behind after performances to discuss both the play and its political implications with the actors.[20]

The colourful, vernacular language used in the play also increased the audience's involvement. The words of the young couple who, after a three-year engagement, finally realized that their dreams of marriage and a family were doomed by their miserable wages could have been spoken by any of the young adults in the theatre: "I'm so tired of being a dog, Baby, I could choke.... You and me—we never even had a room to sit in somewhere.... We got the blues, Babe—the 1935 blues."[21] All these elements—the powerful plot, the original staging, and the graphic language—made both *Lefty* and its message more potent.

Although *Lefty* attracted audiences with its passion and intensity, equally important for the play's popularity with working people was its realistic portrayal of their lives. The play focused on ordinary people, depicting their problems in a sympathetic manner and reflecting the tragic realities they faced every day. As Harold Griffin, the secretary of the Club, recalled: "The actors were living out a fiction on the stage which corresponded to their experience in real life, and the audience was witnessing a fiction on the stage which was almost a mirror of what they personally had lived through."[22] In 1935 working people readily identified with the father who, despite his 12 to 14 hour workday, could not provide enough food for his family or shoes for his children, and the desperate young actor, about to become a father, who was unable to find work in a system dominated by greed and an old-boy network. But *Lefty* offered more than poignant scenes. It revealed the causes of the hardships it chronicled and articulated a solution—collective action and worker solidarity. It also pointed to the tactics which would be used to impede such a resolution. These, too, were an everyday reality for working people in Vancouver who regularly heard about the deportations of "troublemakers," saw the police club demonstrators in the streets, and watched as the leaders of any movement that tried to improve their situation were labeled "reds." In essence, *Lefty* strengthened the working class by legitimizing their lives. It was, reported one woman who saw the play, "as if your own life was being played out on the stage ... it made your own problems seem more significant and understandable." By focusing on the real predicament of working people, the play "articulated those emotions which the injustices of the present day had laid in every heart."[23]

Although the play opened to packed houses, only the left-wing press noticed. Reviewers for those publications immediately hailed the production as a triumph. In the *Commonwealth*, A.M. Stephen noted that "The Progressive Arts Club made history and established a new standard in dramatic art" with *Lefty*. He described how the audience was "thrilled by the strength and emotional force with which the performers presented the smashing indictments of our present inhuman social order." In the same issue, A. Buckley reported that the 2,000 people who saw *Lefty* were "talking about it with sparkling eyes."[24] The reviewer for the B.C. *Workers' News* echoed Stephen's accolades, noting that "this proletarian play ... dwarfs all bourgeois plays ... making them seem flat and puerile in comparison." He foretold that, "In *Waiting for Lefty*, the *bourgeoisie* see how workers live, talk, act and learn what their hopes and purposes are."[25]

Not all reaction to the Club's performances was positive. The *Citizens' League*, in particular, was incensed that authorities allowed such a play to be produced in the city, and they were exceptionally vocal about their disapproval. In his weekly broadcast for the *Citizens' League*, Tom McInnis, a sometime poet and journalist, roundly condemned the play, labelling it the "red beast of Moscow."[26]

Controversy stirred such an interest in *Lefty* that the Club scheduled two more performances for 9 and 11 November.[27] Again, *Lefty*'s intensity provoked a heated response. As Harry Hoshowsky remembered:

> There was almost a riot during the spy episode, when I was making statements to the executive on stage and Mike Kunka was going to contradict them. He was already making preposterous asides to the audience. The people were almost sure they were at a meeting. They tried to contain him ... people moved right out of their seats and bodily tried to contain him ... he was a little afraid that he wasn't going to get up on the stage. We had others spotted around at later performances to ensure that he could get away.[28]

Additional dates were quickly booked in New Westminster for 22 and 23 November, to accommodate those who had been turned away at the door of earlier performances, and King and Glover set about to find accommodation for an extended run.

City authorities had other ideas. Fearing that the play's unequivocal message would lead to greater solidarity in support of the waterfront workers, they shut the play down and threatened to cancel the licence for the hall if the play were produced there again. While the police maintained that this action was motivated by "disgust for the violent expressions" used in the play,[29] the progressive press denounced the closure as fascist. They correctly concluded that the censorship of *Lefty* was prompted not by concern for the language but by complaints from the *Citizen's League* and the *Shipping Federation* regarding the play's militant thrust—particularly in light of the current waterfront strike. The mainline press concurred with this assessment. In his column on 22 November, James Butterfield of the *Vancouver Province* complained that "there were far more stout and ribald words in Shakespeare than there are in *Lefty*" and summed up the situation succinctly: "the whole trouble with this play and the touchy authorities is that it has a labor angle."[30]

As producer of the play, King was not easily silenced. The next day he met for two and a half hours with Inspector Darling, an RCMP officer who had recently been seconded to the Vancouver City Police to reorganize the Criminal Investigation Division.[31] The outcome was that two objectionable phrases—"God damn it" and "an ancient expression used commonly to cast aspersion upon the authenticity of parentage"—would be removed and the play would be allowed to proceed. But Darling still professed uneasiness and, without being very specific, felt that "considering existing local, social and labour circumstances, the expressions used might inflame emotions of *Lefty* patrons and lead to something not in the best interest of law and order."[32]

The Club quickly capitalized on the public interest generated by the attempted censorship. They began performing almost immediately, playing at the Victoria Road Hall on 29 November, in New Westminster three days later, and at Kitsilano High School on 8, 9, 11, 13, and 14 December—all to capacity crowds. Even their advertising took advantage of the closure—it featured three burly, scowling policemen wielding hefty batons lurking around an exit labelled "Stage Door."[33] The Club, anxious to undercut any future attempts at censorship and determined to reach larger audiences, applied to compete in the regional eliminations for the fledgling Dominion Drama Festival which were scheduled to take place at the end of January. Somewhat to their surprise, they were accepted, and their position was further strengthened when the official acceptance latter stated "Of course, we have absolutely no objection to the theme of the play."[34]

For members of the cast, January was filled with performances and rehearsals. They tightened up the play, cut two of the least successful scenes in order to comply with the time constraints of the competition, and ended up with an even more powerful production. To gain more experience, popularize the play, and "show what workers can accomplish," they toured extensively throughout the Lower Mainland, and even produced two acts of *Lefty* on radio station CJOR the night before the competition.[35] But not everyone was supportive: the week before the competition, an anonymous reviewer in *The Review*, a North Shore weekly, branded *Lefty* as "foreign," crude," "vulgar," "indecent," and "offensive" and asserted that the production "didn't have a chance in the regional contest."[36]

On the first night of the competition *Lefty* won praise from both the audience, which broke with tradition to applaud the production, and the adjudicator who, although personally eschewing "propoganda plays," described *Lefty* as a "magnificent work, acted in a manner which absolutely compelled my admiration." Although newspaper accounts made pointed references to the "large number of our Ukranian friends"[37] in the audience, most of those attending were "supporters of the theatre in evening gowns and dinner jackets." Yet even this audience was not immune to *Lefty*'s power. Fifty years later, a member of the crowd remembered *Lefty* as one of the best performances he experienced during a lifetime of theatregoing, ranking "Othello with Paul Robeson as a close second."[38]

At the time, however, most assumed that the really serious competition was scheduled for the second night, when the Vancouver Little Theatre Association's elaborate and artistic production of Eugene O'Neill's *Lazarus*

Laughed would battle the Strolling Players' *The Valiant* for first place and the right to represent British Columbia at the finals of the Dominion Drama Festival in Ottawa. To everyone's surprise, the adjudicator, British producer Allan Wade, awarded first place to *Lefty* and hailed it as "the nearest approach to professional standard I have ever witnessed by a group of amateurs." Wade noted that the work itself "was one of several plays written that will help make the theatre what in its great day it always was—a forum, a communal institution and instrument in the hands of the people for fashioning a sound society."[39]

With these remarks, Wade focused the debate on the real competition in the festival that year—the contending ideas about the *raison d'être* of theatre. Was it a tool for social progress, a way of exploring the injustices and exploitation of the system, and an inspiration for the creation of a better society? Or was it a diversion from the harsh realities of life, a celebration of truth and beauty in the abstract, a source of potential individual enlightenment? This debate between socially relevant, politically engaged theatre and a disengaged, pure art, which came to be characterized in Vancouver as propaganda versus art and beauty, was intensified by Butterfield's public criticism of Wade's decision. While Butterfield had been supportive during the censorship incident, he was incensed that *Lefty* had been chosen over "more artistic" presentations. In his column the day after *Lefty*'s victory, he stated that "there is a duty in the arts towards propaganding beauty and truth ... there is truth in *Lefty* but no beauty." His position was that "everyone knows that taxi drivers have a tough time of it, and the matter ends there."[40] This debate over the role of the theatre cut through the community during the coming months as the Progressive Arts Club prepared for the Ottawa competition.

For the Left, the success of *Lefty* signalled a victory for the social theatre's gritty realism and searing critique of the capitalist system, and an acknowledgement of the potential of working people. For members of the Vancouver Little Theatre Association, on the other hand, *Lefty*'s win elicited anger and resentment, since they felt that both the play and players had been inferior to their entry. The VLTA, which had traditionally played an important role in the theatrical life of the city, prided itself on its innovative productions and its large percentage of English-speaking members.[41] Yet its subtle, artistic production had been passed over in favour of "a cheap piece of stark realism"[42] that had "no demand in it for any great dramatic skill nor ... a demand for the exercise of any of the other arts of the theatre" and its acknowledged leadership had been supplanted by a neophyte group of largely ethnic actors. Although the VLTA was forced to accept its defeat gracefully in public, "behind the scenes a lot of muttering went on" and the cast of *Lefty* was pointedly excluded from a post-festival party organized by the President of the VLTA, Brigadier General Victor Odlum, where "the various groups of contesting players had an opportunity to discuss informally their entries of Friday and Saturday."[43]

For the Club, *Lefty*'s victory in the regional competition was only the opening shot. Now its battle to compete in Ottawa began on another front, since the Club had no money to take the play east. Because the majority of the cast were unemployed and some were even on relief, they had no resources to finance the trip, and the allowance offered by the Dominion Drama Festival was grossly inadequate to transport a cast of 15 from British Columbia to Ottawa. To raise money the cast went on tour, taking *Lefty*'s socialist point of view to numerous working-class audiences in community and labour halls throughout the Lower Mainland and Southern Vancouver Island. They even presented the play for prisoners at the Oakalla Prison Farm, where "the *revolutionary* song, the "Rebel Girl," was sung."[44] Reaction to the play was almost always enthusiastic: "ordinary people in the audience were delighted to see their own lives and problems on the stage,"[45] and the audience frequently became so involved that they intervened in the action of the play, shouting encouragement and disapproval to the actors on the stage.

While the cast gained experience and support for their trip east, the controversy surrounding their win, and the news that the University of British Columbia had prohibited a student production of *Lefty*, prompted requests for additional performances.[46] The Club responded by scheduling a combined performance and symposium to discuss the issue of propaganda in art on 11 March at the Empress, one of the city's largest theatres. By this time *Lefty* was something of a *cause célèbre* and the performance packed the 1,200 seat theatre.[47] As at the regional eliminations for the Dominion Drama Festival, the audience was largely middle and upper-class—a radical departure from the working-class, left-wing group the play usually attracted. The growing debate over the production generated intense public interest and, as a consequence, *Lefty* drew more and more people to the theatre. But this popularity was a double-edged sword. While those attending were still emotionally moved by *Lefty*, their reactions to the play had shifted to safer ground. Rather than confronting the play's criticism of the system—its contention that injustice and exploitation were inherent in the capitalist system, and that salvation for the workers lay in class struggle—their comments after the performance tended to emphasize the dramatic elements of the play itself and the propaganda-versus-art debate.

The symposium after the performance encouraged this stance. Entitled "Art and Propaganda in the Drama," it advertised three prominent speakers—Drs. G.G. Sedgewick and A.F.B. Clark, professors of literature at the University of British Columbia, along with James Butterfield, whose comments had prompted the public debate. Brigadier General Victor Odlum of the VLTA was to chair the discussion. On the program, quotations from reviews of *Lefty* illustrated the contending positions and set the stage for the debate. But the symposium fell flat. At the last minute, Butterfield withdrew without giving any reason. With the main protagonist absent, the thrust of the discussion shifted from criticism to praise, although Dr. Clark noted that, as effective as *Lefty* was, the play "would not stand the test of time." The tenor of the discussion was best summed up by Dr. Sedgewick's assertion that "If there is any group at Ottawa that can beat *Waiting for Lefty*, they will, in the idiom of the play itself, have to do damn well."[48]

As increasing numbers of Vancouverites came to accept this assessment of *Lefty*, rapprochement between the Club and the VLTA seemed necessary, and a joint performance of *Lefty* and Vancouver Little Theatre Association's *Pierrot the Prodigal* was scheduled for April 7 at the Empress Theatre. This presentation before a full house helped heal the rift between the two groups, and allowed the little theatre group to honour its promise to assist the Club with fundraising. The Club's farewell performance in Vancouver—a midnight show at the Orpheum—was so popular that B.C. Electric Railway scheduled special street cars to help people get home after the show.

Despite all this activity, the Club still had insufficient funds for the trip to Ottawa and asked the city for permission to hold a tag day. Its request was initially denied, but public pressure forced Mayor McGeer to relent. On 28 March, hundreds of taggers with banners across their chests blaring "Waiting for Lefty," many of them recruited by the left-wing press, flooded the streets calling "Send *Lefty* To Ottawa!" They collected over $600. While most people supported the cause, one tagger reported that some fellows he approached for donations wanted to know why *Lefty* couldn't ride the rods like everyone else![49] The revenue from the tag day pushed the Club close to its target, and King and Glover decided that the shortfall could be made up by performing at various cities along the route to Ottawa. Individual cast members hurriedly made arrangements for the trip[50] while King booked passage for everyone in the CPR colonist car that the cast would call home for the next two weeks.

In mid-April, approximately 10 months after the relief camp workers set out on their On-to-Ottawa Trek, the cast of *Lefty* began their journey—with much the same political message and aspirations. This time, however, the group travelled inside the train. Like the trekkers before them, the actors quickly realized that their cross-country excursion presented a tailor-made opportunity to publicize their cause. Relying primarily on local theatrical or political contacts to make arrangements, the cast performed in Kamloops, Calgary, Regina, and Winnipeg on the way to Ottawa, and, on the return trip, in Sudbury, Winnipeg and Calgary again, Edmonton, Penticton, and Abbotsford. No longer relegated to union and community halls, *Lefty*'s growing popularity often justified booking the town's largest theatre. Although a number of these performances were political events, for working-class audiences at community, ethnic, and union halls, the majority were played in mainline theatres to largely middle-class audiences who were attracted by the theatrical rather than the political element. In Winnipeg, for example, the play was presented twice: once, under the auspices of the Winnipeg Progressive Arts Club, at the Jewish Workers' Cultural Centre; the other, organized largely by the Manitoba Little Theatre Association, at the Walker Theatre, where the mayor welcomed the audience, and notables such as Lady Tupper, who was very active in the Manitoba Little Theatre Association, came backstage to congratulate King and the cast. Regardless of the venue, however, performances of *Lefty* continued to generate enthusiasm, excitement, and controversy. Over 50 years later Sophie Rankin recalled, "Everyone was always extremely excited to see the play—they had heard so much about it before we arrived, and they wanted to make up their own minds. There was also an element of working-class pride—they were proud that working people could do such a good job."[51]

Before the curtain rose on a performance, Garfield King or one of the actors commented on the controversy that *Lefty* had generated, tracing the recent revival of realistic theatre with its focus on "the social struggles of our present day" and contrasting it with more conventional drama that dealt with purely personal relationships. In addition, this introduction also outlined the dynamics of the propaganda-versus-art debate that had occurred in Vancouver, decrying the reaction of "'Ivorytower' dramatists who drew up their skirts in horror at the thought that their romantic absurdities might be replaced with realism which they characterized as propaganda ... unmindful of the fact that all great art was definitely propaganda in that it was objective, teaching a truth, propounding a cause, or furthering an ideal." The question of language was also addressed with the comment that "whilst the language may seem unusual to some ... [it] is the language of real life."[52]

In Ottawa the cast faced their final hurdle—the national competitions. Although the tours had given the production polish and the actors some measure of confidence, the Ottawa experience drew attention to their deficiencies and increased their apprehensions. Regardless of the successes with *Lefty*, they were neophytes and outsiders in the world of the theatre. Their experience was limited, their knowledge minimal, and their working-class background created a virtually unbridgeable social abyss that separated them from their fellow competitors. In addition, the group was painfully aware that, in the finals, *Lefty* would face not only the stiff competition and rigorous criticism inherent in competition at this level, but also an audience composed largely of prominent diplomats, politicians, and bureaucrats. Although they had received assurances that the festival committee "had no objections to the subject matter," they were unsure how *Lefty*'s message would be received by such an illustrious audience. Yet the cast believed passionately in what the play stood for and "were determined to go out and do a bang-up job."[53]

Despite their anxiety, when the Club performed in the Little Theatre on 22 April the audience, including Governor-General Lord Tweedsmuir, Lady Tweedsmuir, Prime Minister Mackenzie King, Opposition Leader R.B. Bennett, former Prime Minister Sir Robert Borden, and Lady Tupper, "really warmed to it quite well."[54] At the close of the performance, this "eminent and distinguished crowd," moved no doubt by the power of the drama rather than the content, rewarded the production with such prolonged applause that the cast was called back to the stage from the dressing rooms. Meanwhile, Lady Tupper, who was directing the Manitoba Little Theatre Association entry, paced back and forth at the front of the theatre muttering, "the God-damned hypocrites, the God-damned hypocrites." After the applause subsided, the adjudicator, Harry Granville-Barker, remarked that while *Lefty* was a "play of bitter irony," "the most ironical thing of all was the frantic applause of this comfortable audience."[55]

In fact, the reaction of the audience varied from grudging admiration to wild acclaim. Newspaper accounts noted darkly that "certain eminent personages commented highly on the performance though not agreeing altogether with its theme," and Mackenzie King noted unctuously in his diary that, although he found the language deplorable, the play "was a true picture of the hard life which men are encountering today, and the kind of thing which is bred therefrom."[56] The best summation came from Andrew Allan, a drama critic who would later become the head of the CBC's drama programming, who noted "when *Lefty* had come and gone there were as many shades of opinion as there were people in the house."[57]

In his adjudication the night of the performance, Granville-Barker commended the acting of the group and "unhesitatingly named *Lefty* the most interesting title of the evening." However, he noted that it was "a frank appeal to the emotions and the conscience"—an appeal that would "fall to the ground if it were in the slightest degree biased."[58] For Granville-Barker, the scene where a young doctor lost his position because of anti-semitism and political patronage was an unfair attack, a criticism on which the press was quick to capitatize. Two nights later, when Granville-Barker ranked the performances at the end of the festival, the cast learned of their success. Competing against the best amateur theatre groups in Canada, the Progressive Arts Club's presentation of *Waiting for Lefty* had won first prize for the best play in English, excluding the Bessborough trophy for the best play overall.

Although *Lefty*'s theme caused consternation among many connected with both the theatre and government, it was not the only play to portray the harsh realities of the Depression. The coveted Bessborough trophy went to Eric Harris's *Twenty-Five Cents*, a contemporary drama that illuminated the grinding poverty and smashed hopes that squandered the lives of ordinary working people during the Depression. At the closing ceremony Mackenzie King acknowledged this new element in theatre, noting that "the numerous presentations dealing with social problems were indications of how the minds of people were seeking solutions to these problems."[59] Unlike *Lefty*, however, *Twenty-Five Cents* took a subdued, individualist approach—it did not suggest any solutions or advocate militant action. Comparisons between the two productions were inevitable and, in an editorial, the *Ottawa Journal* praised both productions for shunning the trivial and portraying what were stark realities of the day for thousands. However, in a somewhat transparent attempt to minimize both *Lefty*'s success and the impact of its message, the writer quickly opted for the "restrained quality" of *Twenty-Five Cents* versus the "violence of protest" in *Lefty*.[60]

This ungenerous attitude toward *Lefty* was even more pronounced in the Vancouver press. Public interest in *Lefty*'s progress ran high, in part because of the production's controversial history, and in part because the play represented British Columbia in the festival. Civic pride dictated that *Lefty*'s win was front page news in both *The Sun* and *The Province*. However, the stories, editorials, and columns about *Lefty* in both papers were fraught with ambivalence: they revealed pride in the production's triumph and admiration for the cast's spirit and hard work in the face of seemingly insurmountable odds, but they tended to gloss over *Lefty*'s achievement and, after paying obligatory respects, quickly lapsed into praise for the previous successes of the Vancouver Little Theatre Association at the festival, pointing out that "in every one of the festivals ... a cast or an individual from Vancouver has been in the honours."[61]

While others pondered the implications of the play, the cast of *Lefty* was caught up in the whirlwind of social events that surrounded the Festival—teas, luncheons, and receptions. Although members of the group were scrupulously included in all formal activities, their presence tended to emphasize the class differences that separated them from other participants. They were invited to a luncheon at the Chateau Laurier with Opposition Leader R.B. Bennett, lunch in the parliamentary dining room with J.S. Woodsworth, and tea with the Governor General, but the luxurious surroundings were almost beyond their comprehension. As Harry Hoshowsky recalled, "we were poor, and the life that we saw there made us totally confused. Here we were, two kids who a couple of weeks earlier had been eating oranges in the vestibule of the train, sitting at the Chateau Laurier with seemingly endless amounts of wine and food, gleaming cutlery, shining crystal—and a code of behaviour that we didn't understand at all." The unreality of their situation was summed up by Denny Kristiansen who recalled, "here I was, twice to tea at Government House, and still on relief."[62]

When the Progressive Arts Club returned to Vancouver in mid-May, they immediately began planning their next production. Although Garfield King and Guy Glover left the group to continue their theatrical commitments elsewhere, and others left to find jobs outside the Vancouver area, new members came forward. The Club produced 11 more socially relevant plays, but the circumstances surrounding the production of *Lefty* had combined to make it their most successful venture, and they were never able to duplicate their achievement.

The Progressive Arts Club's production of *Waiting for Lefty* reveals much about the adaptability and resiliency of working-class protest. By 1935, the limitations of massed demonstrations, street parades, and strikes in the face of government intransigence and repression were painfully obvious. Yet, instead of quiescence, the spirit of protest remained strong. In its search for an alternate method of agitation, one segment of the working class turned to drama as a vehicle for protest. Enlisting drama in their struggle for a more equitable society, these workers began, in effect, to politicize culture. In opposition to the dominant culture's emphasis on material accumulation, personal fulfillment, and an imagined classless society, the cast of *Lefty* articulated an alternate vision of society: a vision that took into account the class nature of society and the everyday experience of working people. In *Lefty* and the other social dramas which followed it, the Club transcended the impersonal rhetoric of political meetings. Instead, the actors adapted a form of bourgeois culture to their own purpose, using the theatre's ability to communicate at an immediate, emotional level to create a culture of resistance that empowered working people, legitimized their aspirations, justified organization, and nourished class solidarity. The enthusiastic responses of *Lefty*'s audiences showed how welcome this counter-culture was.

While *Lefty*'s success attests to the potential of drama to educate and motivate, the varying responses the play evoked show the limitations of the cultural milieu. Once *Lefty* entered the cultural arena as a play and cultural artifact, it invited judgment of both its artistic and theatrical merits, and its content. In addition, it encouraged the audience to separate or disengage the message of the play—its content—from its dramatic presentation. The success of *Lefty* in the festival and the ironic reaction of the distinguished and comfortable audience noted by Granville Barker seem to suggest that this was, indeed, what was happening. While the cast saw the play's message as the reason behind the performance, its significance could be diminished in the eyes of festival audiences and judges because part of their judgment was the comparison of plays. This was also the case with the controversy surrounding the "art versus propaganda" debate. Attracted by the debate itself, more people attended the performances, but their comments were largely confined to the parameters of the debate that had drawn them to the theatre. Paradoxically, then, the two avenues the Club pursued to bring *Lefty*'s message to a broad spectrum of people in fact obscured the play's central tenet.

How then did *Lefty*, despite seemingly insurmountable obstacles, achieve such a large measure of success, not only with working-class audiences, but also with members of the middle-class and the bourgeoisie? The answer lies, in part, within the play itself: its subject matter, timeliness, authenticity, compelling plot, and dramatic power. *Lefty* dealt with issues that were of concern to everyone, regardless of their social position and political beliefs. And it did so in a compelling, dramatic fashion. Another element of *Lefty*'s success was the theatrical encounter—the unique emotional and social experience that occurred as spectators were drawn into the performance itself.

Yet *Lefty* had an impact that went beyond its individual successes. The saga of *Lefty*'s victory against all odds acted as a catalyst, stimulating the growth of progressive theatre. Similar drama clubs sprang up in Calgary, Edmonton, Victoria, Nanaimo, and Salmon Arm. In Vancouver, social theatre burgeoned after *Lefty*. During 1936, CCF and ethnic drama groups, in co-operation with the Club, organized individual productions, competitions, and festivals of progressive theatre. But the play had wider ramifications than the cultural scene—it also made an impact at the political level. In support of the Health Insurance Bill that he was introducing to the British Columbia Legislative Assembly, the Honourable Dr. George Weir noted that changing social needs had altered people's perceptions of what was acceptable. *Waiting for Lefty*, he stated, provided a forceful illustration that "life was pulsating with social and economic changes."[63]

Endnotes

1. John Belshaw "The Administration of Relief to the Unemployed in Vancouver During the Great Depression," M.A. thesis, Simon Fraser University, 1982, p. 129; *Vancouver Sun*, June 5,1935; and *B.C. Workers' News*, February 15, 1935.
2. Lorne A. Brown, "The Bennett Government, Political Stability and the Politics of Unemployment Relief Camps, 1930–1935," Ph.D. thesis, Queen's University, 1979, p. 62.
3. *Vancouver Sun*, June 5, 1935; John Stanton, *Never Say Die!: The Life and Times of John Stanton, A Pioneer Labour Lawyer* (Ottawa: Steel Rail Publishing, 1987), p. 8.
4. *Vancouver Sun*, May 27, June 5, 1935.
5. The provincial government provided at least 200 provincial police, the *Citizens' League*, 160 special constables while the city's additional costs for policing the waterfront during the period were estimated at $70,000. Directorate of History, Department of National Defence, 322.009, D(804), Report from Chief Constable Foster to Mayor McGeer, undated.

   A report to Mayor McGeer from the Vancouver City Police Department, Communist Activities Branch, dated July 24, 1935, reveals the intimidating nature of the police presence and the kind of personal information they were amassing. In addition, a letter from Chief Constable Foster to the Vancouver Harbour Commission, dated June l5, 1935, reveals that police were taking an active part in breaking up picket lines, encouraging people and vehicles to cross the line, and recording the license numbers of vehicles that turned around and left the dock after talking with pickets. This information was reported to employers. Directorate of History, Department of National Defence, 322.009, D(804) Aid to the Civil Power, MDll, August 3l, 1936.
6. Stanton, *Never Say Die!*, p. 6. Also, author's interview with Sophie Rankin, July 29, 1989.
7. Although the strike continued after the attack on Ballantyne Pier, it was seriously undermined by the arrest of all the union leaders after the incident. Deprived of their leaders, and facing an overpowering police presence, the intransigence of the Shipping Federation, and the co-operation of the city relief department which granted relief only to strikers who had been approved by the Shipping Federation, workers slowly drifted back to work, and port activity returned to normal. By December, at least 450 original employees had still not been rehired, For a full account of the strike, see R.C. McCandless, "Vancouver's Red Menace of 1935: the Waterfront Situation," *B.C. Studies* 22 (Summer 1976), pp. 56–71.

8. Interview with Sophie Rankin.
9. University of Guelph Library, Archival Collection, Toby Gordon Ryan Collection, "Constitution of the Progressive Arts Club," p. 2.
10. Nine of the fourteen actors were recruited through the ULFTA according to programmes of the early performances in the City Archives of Vancouver.
11. Interview with Harry Hoshowsky, February 22, 1989.
12. Interview with Sophie Rankin.
13. Toby Gordon Ryan, *Stage Left: Canadian Workers Theatre 1929–1940* (Toronto: Simon & Pierre, 1985), p. 65.
14. "Notes of Introduction," typescript from collection of Hilda Kristiansen, p. 1.
15. Interview with Sophie Rankin.
16. "Notes for Production" for "Waiting for Lefty," in Clifford Odets, *Three Plays* (New York: Random House, 1935), p. 53.
17. Clifford Odets, *Waiting for Lefty* (New York: Random House, 1935), p. 51.
18. Ibid., p. 52.
19. Ryan, *Stage Left*, p. 64.
21. Interview with Harry Hoshowsky.
21. Odets, *Waiting for Lefty*, pp. 27–29.
22. Interview with Harold Griffin, January 23, 1989.
23. Interview with Hilda Kristiansen, February 27, 1989; *Calgary Herald*, May 7, 1936.
24. "Music and Drama," *The Commonwealth*, Nov. 1, 1935; "Ironies," *The Commonwealth*, Nov, 1, 1935.
25. *B.C. Workers' News*, Nov. 1, 1935.
26. "Ironies," *The Commonwealth*, Nov. 22, 1935.
27. *The Commonwealth*, Nov. 1, 1935.
28. Interview with Harry Hoshowsky.
29. *The Commonwealth*, Nov. 22, 1935.
30. "Common Round," *Vancouver Province*, Nov. 22, 1935.
31. *Vancouver Sun*, May 5, 1935.
32. *The Commonwealth*, Nov. 22, 1935.
33. University of Guelph Library, Archival Collection, Toby Gordon Ryan Collection, File 3.1.
34. Letter from Osborne to King, quoted in "Ironies," *The Commonwealth*, Jan. 24, 1936.
35. Interview with Sophie Rankin; *B.C. Workers' News*, Jan. 31,1936.
36. "Proletarian Playwright and Renegade Reviewer," *B.C. Workers' News*, Feb. 15, 1936.
37. *Vancouver Province*, Feb. 1 and 2, 1936.
38. Letter to author from John S, Hall, Jan. 28, 1989.
39. *Vancouver Sun*, Feb. 3, 1936.
40. *Vancouver Province*, Feb. 3, 1936.
41. Vancouver City Archives, Vancouver Little Theatre Association, Add. Ms. 41,4, File 1.
42. Quote from Butterfield in "Ol' Bill," *B.C. Workers' News*, Feb. 23, 1936.
43. Interview with Hal Griffin; *Vancouver Sun*, Feb. 4, 1936.
44. Directorate of History, Department of National Defence, "Aid to the Civil Power—Report for Month Ending January 1936," p. 1.
45. *The Commonwealth*, Feb. 22, 1936, p. 4.
46. *B.C. Workers' News*, Feb. 7, 1936.
47. *The Commonwealth*, March 15, 1936.
48. *The Commonwealth*, March 15, 1936.
49. Ryan, *Stage Left*, p. 53; "Hammer Blows," *Sun*, March 13, 1973.
50. Some of the younger members of the cast were advanced money to buy appropriate clothes for the trip, while others who were on relief and married made arrangements for their relief payments to continue for their families while they were away. See Ryan, *Stage Left*, p. 59. Also interview with Harry Hoshowsky.
51. Interview with Sophie Rankin.
52. Notes of Introduction from Hilda Kristiansen, p. 2.

53. Interview with Harry Hoshowsky.
54. Ryan, *Stage Left*, p. 64.
55. *Vancouver Sun*, April 22, 1936; *Vancouver Province*, April 23, 1936.
56. W.L. Mackenzie King, *Diary*, Wednesday, April 22, 1936.
57. Untitled article by Andrew Allan in Anglin Scrapbook, Vol. 42, Dominion Drama Festival Papers, NAC.
58. *Vancouver Province*, April 25, 1936.
59. *Vancouver Province*, April 27, 1936.
60. *Ottawa Journal*, April 28, 1936.
61. *Vancouver Province*, April 29, 1936.
62. Interview with Harry Hoshowsky; "Hammer Blows," *Vancouver Province*, March 5, 1973.
63. *The Commonwealth*, March 27, 1936.

Critical-Thinking Questions

1. Discuss the ways in which Labour Day parades of the 1890s and 1900s reflected the values of craftsmen.
2. Account for both the vitality of Labour Day parades in the early years and their decline by the beginning of World War I.
3. What was the "administrative revolution?"
4. How does an awareness of gender difference enhance our understanding of the administrative revolution's impact on the work experiences of clerical employees?
5. What explains the prevalence of "anti-Orientalism" in early twentieth-century Vancouver?
6. Is there compelling evidence that labour solidarity was a genuine alternative to racial exclusion, given the racial politics of Vancouver in the early twentieth century?
7. Compare Anglo Canadians' views and treatment of Asian workers in early twentieth-century Vancouver with their representation of and behaviour towards "the foreigners" of Winnipeg's North End. Can you account for any differences?
8. What role did ethnic prejudice play in the Winnipeg general strike of 1919?
9. Assess the attractions and dangers of the Industrial Representation Plan for Imperial Oil's employees and for the company.
10. What might human resources managers today learn from studying the history of company unionism and corporate welfarism?
11. Why did audiences respond so favourably to *Waiting for Lefty*?
12. Discuss the differences between theatre with a social conscience and theatre as propaganda.

Further Readings

Donald Avery. *"Dangerous Foreigners": European Immigrant Workers and Labour Radicalism in Canada, 1896–1932* (Toronto: McClelland and Stewart, 1979). A study of the important role played by European immigrant workers during a period of economic expansion. Avery examines the backgrounds, migration, work experiences, and politics of the men, as well as the hostility they faced from the host society.

Baskerville, Peter and Eric W. Sager. *Unwilling Idlers: The Urban Unemployed and Their Families in Late Victorian Canada* (Toronto: University of Toronto Press, 1988). An analysis of who the unemployed were and how they survived their ordeal during the time of the "discovery of unemployment" in Canada.

Bercuson, David. *Confrontation at Winnipeg: Labour, Industrial Relations, and the General Strike*. Rev. ed. (Montreal and Kingston: McGill-Queen's University Press, 1990). A close examination of the origins, events, and impact of the Winnipeg General Strike.

Dumas, Evelyn. *The Bitter Thirties in Quebec* (Montreal: Black Rose, 1975). Brief accounts of strikes in Quebec during a period when labour militancy was fiercely repressed.

Endicott, Stephen. *Bienfait: The Saskatchewan Miners' Struggle of '31* (Toronto: University of Toronto Press, 2002). Coal miners in Saskatchewan struck in 1931 during a period of worsening poverty. Endicott explains the origins and events of the bitter strike, including the prominent part played by Communists.

Frager, Ruth. *Sweatshop Strife: Class, Ethnicity, and Gender in the Jewish Labour Movement of Toronto, 1900–1939* (Toronto: University of Toronto Press, 1992). An examination of Jewish labour activism in Toronto's garment industry, where many employers were also Jewish. Class, ethnic, and gender identities are explored against the backdrop of changing material conditions.

Heron, Craig, ed. *The Workers' Revolt in Canada, 1917–1925* (Toronto: University of Toronto Press, 1998). A collection of local and regional case studies of a period of unusual labour militancy and radicalism across Canada. Overviews of the Canadian scene and the impact of World War I and the "red scare" on workers are also included.

Heron, Craig and Steve Penfold. *The Worker's Festival: A History of Labour Day in Canada* (Toronto: University of Toronto Press, 2005). The festivities are vividly documented in this lavishly illustrated book. The authors analyze changes in working-class culture over a long sweep of time by focusing on Labour Day.

Kealey, Linda. *Enlisting Women for the Cause: Women, Labour, and the Left in Canada, 1890-1920* (Toronto: University of Toronto Press, 1998). Kealey examines the work of women and their contribution to labour organizations and left parties during an era of sweeping change. The back-room work of women in politics is noted, alongside the leadership roles of exceptional working-class women.

Naylor, James. *The New Democracy: Challenging the Social Order in Industrial Ontario, 1914–1925* (Toronto: University of Toronto Press, 1991). A regional case study of a period of intense labour militancy and growing radicalism. Politics, women, and corporate strategies are highlighted.

Parr, Joy. *The Gender of Breadwinners: Women, Men, and Change in Two Industrial Towns, 1880–1950* (Toronto: University of Toronto Press, 1990). A study of wage-earning and gender identities in two contrasting towns: a "women's town," where a knitting mill provided most jobs, and a "men's town," where furniture-making prevailed.

Roy, Patricia. *A White Man's Province: British Columbia Politicians and Chinese and Japanese Immigrants, 1858–1914* (Vancouver: University of British Columbia Press, 1989). Explores the economic and political circumstances behind anti-Asianism in British Columbia. The role of workers and labour activists in public campaigns is given close attention.

Ward, Peter. *White Canada Forever: Popular Attitudes and Public Policy Toward Orientals in British Columbia*. 3rd ed. (Montreal and Kingston: McGill-Queen's University Press, 2002). A study of racism among whites in British Columbia. Attitudes, popular movements, and public policies are explored.

PART III

Wartime and Post-War Prosperity (1939–74)

World War II ended the Great Depression by putting people back to work, either in the armed forces or in the massive industrial war production effort. The war was a crisis of a different nature, bringing anxiety about the military campaigns and the future, separations in families, and long working hours, often in dangerous jobs in munitions plants.

Women's work patterns changed when a serious labour shortage resulted after 1941. Many women, including married women with children, worked in jobs that traditionally were held by men. They were trained in new skills, their children went into the daycare centres provided, their wages increased despite the existing wage-control policy, and along with thousands of others they joined a union in this period of astounding union growth, especially in the industrial sector. Laurel Sefton MacDowell's chapter outlines the issues for workers in the wartime economy, the intense conflict between the labour movement and the Canadian government over the issues of collective bargaining legislation and wage controls, and the eventual resolution of these conflicts with the establishment of a legal framework for the conduct of industrial relations in the modern era.

At the end of the war, instead of the feared post-war recession many expected, the Canadian economy experienced phenomenal growth. After a brief disruption in employment in 1945, as the economy converted from wartime to peacetime production, conditions began to change. The needs of Europe, the pent-up consumer demand at home, the beginning of the Cold War in which Canadian companies filled some American military supply needs—all these factors contributed to an extraordinary prosperity (labelled in retrospect "the golden years" by historians), which lasted to 1973. Women were "bumped" from industrial jobs to make way for veterans and returned to lesser-paid traditional "pink ghetto" jobs. As Ann Porter's chapter indicates, older attitudes concerning gender—for example, that women were "secondary earners," working for "pin money," who did not need to work if they had husbands—reasserted themselves and were reflected in federal policy implementing and administering the Unemployment Insurance Act, 1940.

The Cold War between the United States and the Soviet Union and their respective allies intensified anti-Communism in the West. Though Canadian views were less extreme than American, nevertheless the RCMP resumed and increased its surveillance of "reds," which led them to investigate unlikely groups. Mercedes Steedman's chapter, which bridges the wartime and post-war periods, conveys the importance of ladies' auxiliaries in many unions, before most married women worked very much in the labour force themselves, particularly in resource-based communities. In northern mining towns, where available jobs were mostly for men, their wives' work in the auxiliaries was important in supporting the union, in running strikes, in educating wives about the labour movement's purpose, and in some cases in politicizing auxiliary members. During the Cold War, the RCMP considered the auxiliaries worth placing under surveillance, particularly those auxiliaries associated with unions such as Mine Mill, whose leaders were Communists.

At the end of World War II, citizens around the world were shocked by two events: the dropping of two atom bombs on Japan, and the revelation of the Holocaust—the Nazi death camps in which millions of Jews and other peoples were murdered. After the war, various forces in Canada became committed to creating a tolerant society as Canada became a more diverse community. They worked to bolster civil liberties and civil rights, and to push for human-rights legislation, much of which was passed in federal and provincial jurisdictions from the 1960s. The labour movement in the past had usually opposed immigration. Its concern to protect the labour standards of Canadian workers sometimes also reflected racism and distaste for immigrant minorities working in Canada. This complex attitude ranged from nativism against Asians in British Columbia to antipathy towards European immigrants. In the post-war period, organized labour substantially changed its position on immigration. It favoured positive treatment of new immigrants, wanted to unionize them, and actively supported human-rights legislation and protection of civil liberties in daily life. Ross Lambertson discusses a small part of this process in analyzing the work of the Jewish Labour Committee, whose commitment to human rights also related directly to the aftermath of the Holocaust. The labour movement's embrace of the human rights issue also was tied to its participation in the international labour movement (particularly the ICFTU) and to the adherence of many Canadian labour leaders to the social democratic CCF/NDP, which had been both international and progressive in its outlook in the area of human rights.

Immigrant workers arrived in Canada in droves as "DPs" ("displaced persons"), refugees, and as persons seeking jobs—of which there were plenty in post-war Canada. In this large immigration wave, many Italians came to Canada and settled in Toronto. Often the men worked in the booming construction industry, but as Franca Iacovetta indicates, in very poorly paid, dangerous jobs. Her article describes these workers' situations in cultural and social terms, and discusses a turning point resulting from the Hogg's Hollow Disaster. Thereafter working conditions began to improve as many Italians organized themselves into unions and connected with the larger labour movement in the city; in doing so, she argues, they asserted a new notion of masculinity.

Chapter 13

The Formation of the Canadian Industrial Relations System during World War II

Laurel Sefton MacDowell

I.

The war years were a period of antagonistic labour–government relations and serious industrial unrest, which the labour movement attributed to wage controls, the failure of the government to consult on policies that directly affected employees, and the inadequacy of the existing collective bargaining legislation. As a result, trade unions organized aggressively in the new war industries, struck with increasing frequency, and eventually became involved in direct political activity. At the centre of this conflict was the demand for collective bargaining. Collective bargaining was not just a means of raising wages and improving working conditions. It was a demand by organized workers for a new status, and the right to participate in decision-making both in industry and government. Thus, it became an issue not only on the shop floor where employers and unions met directly, but also in the political arena.[1] Eventually this demand for a new status in society was met by the introduction of a new legislative framework for collective bargaining, which has been modified only slightly since that time. Yet in order to appreciate the evolution of this policy, it is insufficient to consider simply the political debate or the crises which precipitated the change. Even the important strikes—those which crystallized labour's discontent and prompted specific concessions—took place within the special context of the war economy and a general realignment of industrial and political forces. Over a period of years, the economic tensions associated with the war generated pressures for reform, could not be contained.

The most dramatic change in these years was the growth of the labour movement itself. At the outbreak of the war, there were only 359,000 organized workers. During the war, union membership more than doubled, so that by 1946 there were 832,000 organized employees engaged in collective bargaining.[2] In 1939 there were still 900,000 registered unemployed in a workforce of approximately 3.9 million, but this labour surplus was quickly absorbed, and soon there was a labour shortage.[3] These conditions were very favourable for trade-union organizing.

The new industrial unions expanded with the industries from which they drew their support. The labour market conditions also produced higher wages, rising expectations and demands for better working conditions. Wartime wages were high by Depression standards, although in 1941 most industrial workers were still not earning an adequate wage, as defined by welfare agencies of the day.[4] Paradoxically, those industries with the highest and most rapidly increasing wage rates were also the industries being unionized most quickly. Wages were rising but apparently not as quickly as the expectations of workers, who were reacting to the tight labour market, the rising cost of living, and their experiences during the Depression. They were determined not to return to their situation in the 1930s. Some of the older workers remembered the extent to which real wages were undermined during World War I.[5] These insecurities prompted workers to join unions, even at a time when wages were strictly controlled, so that there was no guarantee of any immediate economic benefit. After the proclamation of the wage control policy in 1940, most wartime wage increases were not increases in the basic wage rates but in cost-of-living bonuses. Workers feared that even these wage gains would be rescinded at the end of the war.

This increased organizational activity met with considerable employer resistance and resulted in unprecedented levels of industrial conflict. Until the government passed legislation supporting collective bargaining in 1944, there was a continuous increase in the number of strikes, workers involved, and man-days lost. The peak of industrial unrest was reached in 1943. In 1943 one out of every three trade union members was involved in strike activity, a level of membership involvement exceeded only in 1919 (and then only by a small margin). Indeed, to the extent that membership involvement in industrial conflict is a measure of employee disaffection, 1919 is the only year with which 1943 can be compared.[6]

The growth of trade unionism during the war involved structural changes in the movement itself which had both organizational and political ramifications. Traditionally, the most effective unions had been organized on a craft basis. These craft skills could not be easily acquired so that by controlling the supply of labour and eliminating competition between tradesmen, the trade union could enhance its bargaining power and guarantee both employer recognition and collective bargaining. Its effectiveness depended upon its ability to define and protect their "job territory" against the encroachments of other craftsmen, mechanical innovations, or less skilled employees who were hired in order to reduce labour costs (and who subsequently provided the organization base for the industrial unions). The principles of craft exclusivity within carefully defined work justifications had been the basis for the successful early organization and expansion of trade unionism, and had ensured the survival of craft unions when broader-based industrial organizations had failed.[7] Moreover, the jurisdiction of each union defined by the trade unions themselves and jurisdictional disputes were resolved by their central organization, the AFL-TLC.

In contrast, the industrial unions proposed organization on an industry-wide basis, without regard to an employee's specific skills. Bargaining power was based on numbers, not on a monopoly of available skills. This fundamental difference in outlook made inter-union rivalry inevitable, and made the craft unions cautious about the legislative changes which the new unions proposed. Legislation such as the American "Wagner Act," which gave a government agency the authority to define the jurisdiction in which unions could organize, was as great a challenge as industrial unionism itself. It implied that an unskilled majority might "swamp" the less numerous craft employees. This conflict ultimately resulted in the expulsion from the TLC of the industrial unions affiliated to the American CIO,[8] but it was also evident in the legislative program of the TLC in the years immediately prior to the war.

By 1939 there were 22,000 members in the TLC who belonged to the CIO international industrial unions.[9] The industrial unions pressured the Congress to support legislation patterned after the American Wagner Act. The Congress responded by drafting a "model bill" in 1937 and presenting it to provincial governments. This bill was sharply criticized at two successive Congress conventions[10] for the following reasons: it did not compel employers to bargain with unions with majority support; it did not prohibit "company unions"; and it did not include machinery to determine the exclusive bargaining agent when jurisdictional disputes arose between unions. The new unions, which lacked the economic strength to establish collective bargaining relationships, required government intervention to protect their organizations. The craft unions, which were strong and entrenched, did not need government intervention to gain recognition from employers, and were wary of the increased role of government implicit in the "Wagner" principles. Later in the war, craft unions would unite with industrial unions in support of this legislative demand, but not until the craft unions had embarked on a more dynamic organizing policy and had begun to broaden their own organizational base.[11]

The conversion of the economy to a war footing required unprecedented government intervention and regulation of economic life. New policies administered through the National Selective Service (NSS) restricted workers' freedom in the labour market, since a worker could be frozen in his job, transferred, or placed in a military training plan.[12] This system was intended to distribute manpower more efficiently and increase production, but the essence of all these policies was to regard labour as a factor in production which could be regulated by legislative and administrative fiat.[13]

The regulation of wages and working conditions by the political authority inevitably brought trade unions into politics, and increased labour's criticism of the lack of labour representation on government policy-making bodies. Labour resented the anti-labour attitudes of many of the "new men" drawn from business into C.D. Howe's Department of Munitions and Supply. Labour developed a deep distrust of the personnel entrusted with administering government policy, since unionists remained outside the formal power structure. Business influence in the government and society was much greater, and that influence was reflected in the government's wartime labour policy.

The common effort industrial workers were making to wage war, their common insecurity with regard to wages and the status of their unions, their common resentment about their lack of influence on the government, and the inequities of the wage control policy led to union organization, industrial unrest, and ultimately political opposition. Labour's increasing resentment of the government's wage and collective bargaining policies caused the "labour problem" to escalate during 1941 and 1942, and to reach explosive proportions by 1943. In Canada, all were being asked to make a contribution and sacrifice as equals in a war effort for democracy, but this only heightened the dissatisfaction with "industrial autocracy." As "equal" participants in the war effort, industrial workers wanted equal rights on the job, in the economy, and in the councils of the nation. Strong unions were their vehicle to acquire those rights.

II.

In 1939, when the War Measures Act made the federal government pre-eminent in labour matters, the government had no positive collective bargaining policy. At a time when thousands of employees were joining unions, there was no legislative support for their endeavour, nor protection should their employer take reprisals. Section 502A of the Criminal Code made it an indictable offence for an employer to refuse to employ, dismiss, or intimidate any person for the "sole reason" that he was a member of a union; however, the wording of the section and the burden of proof made it virtually impossible to secure a conviction. Even if an employer were found guilty, he could be penalized; but there was no remedy (such as reinstatement) for the employee.

The Industrial Disputes Investigation Act (IDI Act) was extended by a 1939 order-in-council to cover 85 percent of all industrial activity; but it did not contain any provisions for union recognition, and was primarily concerned with avoiding strikes through the process of compulsory conciliation which was a necessary precondition for a lawful strike. Conciliation implied a built-in compulsory delay that was particularly troublesome in recognition disputes where the time factor was crucial. Timing of strike activity was of central importance and delay could interrupt the union's organizational momentum, as well as give the employer the opportunity to relocate production, recruit strikebreakers, and promote management-controlled "employees' committees" to compete for the loyalty of the workforce and to hinder the development of independent unions. The application of the IDI Act therefore handicapped trade union organization. Moreover the IDI Act took no account of the different types of industrial dispute. Disputes concerning union recognition and collective bargaining required different treatment from those primarily about wages and working conditions. The act proved "unsuited to deal with disputes arising out of the refusal of the employer to recognize and deal with trade unions."[14] Such disputes increased throughout the war but because they involved the very existence of the union and the legitimacy of its activities, they were not amenable to mediation and compromise. The very existence of one of the parties was not an issue for which there was a "middle ground." The result was that the IDI Act merely contributed to delay, and this inevitably benefited management, and undermined trade union activity.[15]

Despite its expressed concern about delay, the government created two further mechanisms which exacerbated the problem: the Industrial Disputes Inquiry Commission and compulsory strike votes. The former was supposed to provide a speedy pre-conciliation fact-finding procedure, while the latter was apparently based on the belief that the union leadership was fomenting discontent, and that if the rank and file were permitted to express their views they would exercise restraint.[16] In fact, neither mechanism was successful and such restrictions merely contributed to labour discontent.

In order to deal directly with the increasing number of disputes in which employers refused to bargain collectively, the government could have enacted legislation similar to that which was in force in the United States. Between 1937 and 1939, the provinces had enacted legislation providing for some recognition for trade unions and collective bargaining; but such laws were unenforced and therefore ineffective.[17] At the beginning of the war, however, the federal government had no intention of enacting a Canadian "Wagner Act." Instead, in June 1940, the government was persuaded to proclaim order-in-council P.C. 2685: a declaration of principles which the government hoped labour and management would adopt. The government wanted to prevent industrial unrest, which might prejudice the war effort. The order was an effort to furnish a voluntary formula for the resolution of recognition disputes. It encouraged employers to voluntarily recognize unions, negotiate in good faith, and resolve disputes by means of the conciliation machinery. The government sought to maintain a position on collective bargaining which it alleged to be "neutral." By its statutory silence it implied that the contest between labour and management was essentially a private matter. It ignored the fact that a legal system under which the government played a "neutral" role had the effect of tipping the balance of bargaining power in favour of employers.[18] As J.L. Cohen, a prominent labour lawyer of the day, wrote,

> It [P.C. 2685] ignores the essential fact that in the main, employees are not free either to organize or to negotiate and that no legislative protection, whether the right to organize or to negotiate is furnished by the order in council, by Section 502A of the Criminal Code or by any of the provisions of the IDI Act.[19]

This unenforced "declaration of principles" became the focus of much bitter debate and contributed to labour's disaffection. In contrast to the wage-control policy (P.C. 7440, enacted in December 1940) which was widely publicized and firmly enforced, these labour relations principles were ignored by employers and never followed by the government itself in industries under its own control. While the government was prepared to impose compulsory wage controls, compulsory conciliation, compulsory strike votes, and compulsory reallocation of labour, it continued to maintain that its opposition to "compulsion" precluded the introduction of collective bargaining legislation.[20]

Unions were particularly dissatisfied with the wage-control policies. Early in the war, the labour movement had tentatively supported wage controls. After watching their application in specific situations, this support changed to opposition. In their view, the program was inequitable in its effect on industrial wages as compared to salaries and did not properly account for low wage industries, and was detrimental to collective bargaining. Despite the price controls, it appeared that business was being subsidized for its capital expenditures and was allowed to maintain a comfortable profit. Profits were not strictly controlled. Business had refused to accept a five percent ceiling profit, and the government did not impose one.[21] To many workers, there appeared to be a marked discrepancy between the sacrifices which labour and business were asked to make.[22]

Closely related to these criticisms was the general concern that labour remained unrepresented in the policy-making apparatus of government, although workers were profoundly affected by these policies. Unlike the business community, which was virtually running the war production effort and reaping considerable benefits, the labour movement remained unrepresented and unheard, except when, through the exercise of industrial strength, a government economic objective was jeopardized. Because labour was excluded from the formal decision-making process, its opposition to the government was expressed only on the industrial scene. In order to understand the basis for this opposition, it is necessary to examine the government role in several key strikes. Each involved an important element of the government's labour policy, and each contributed to labour's alienation. Eventually this alienation promoted the two major labour federations to adopt common legislative goals, to forge new political alliances, and to engage in overt political opposition.

The National Steel Car (NASCO) plant in Hamilton was originally organized in late 1940 by the Steelworkers' Organizing Committee (SWOC). When the company refused to meet, the union applied for a conciliation board which eventually was established after a delay of five weeks. The Conciliation Board recommended that a plant-wide, government-supervised representation vote be conducted, and if the union won, the employer should begin negotiations. The union accepted the report but heard nothing further for a month. On 29 April 1941 the membership unanimously voted to strike. Immediately the government became concerned about the possible disruption of war production, since it appeared that the steelworkers in Sault Ste-Marie and Trenton might strike in sympathy with the Hamilton workers. Its response was immediate. Within two days, the government appointed Ernest Brunning controller of the plant, and assured the union that the Conciliation Board Report would be implemented. The representation vote was taken and the union won, but the controller refused to meet. Significantly, he advised the Conciliation Board that he was pursuing this course of action in accordance with instructions that he had received from the government.[23] The absurdity of this situation was noted by the labour nominee on the conciliation board, who wrote to the government:

> There appears to me to be something incongruous in the suggestion that a government appointed Board should be required to inform a government appointed Controller that the principles and policy of an order-in-council (P.C. 2685) enacted at the behest of the government appointing both the Board and the Controller should be observed and lived up to.[24]

When the conciliation board reconvened in June, Brunning advised that, "The matter of union recognition cannot be dealt with at the present time in view of the fact the plant is being operated by a controller appointed by the government."[25] He then called upon the employees to appoint "a representative committee" to meet with him and consider his proposals regarding hours and wages. These proposals were implemented a week later. This procedure was contrary to the principles of collective bargaining embodied in P.C. 2685, but it was obvious that the government was not going to enforce its own order. In July, the union called a second strike. After mediation activities by officials of the Departments of Labour and Munitions and Supply, the strikers returned to work on the understanding that negotiations would finally begin. No negotiations took place, but the controller announced that the workers could be "free" to join any union or employees' association of their choice. He obviously preferred to deal with the association which he himself had established and encouraged in the summer of 1941. Shortly thereafter, the impasse was resolved by the appointment of a new controller who eventually negotiated collective agreements with both the union and the employee association. Despite the representation vote, the union had not achieved official recognition or the status of exclusive bargaining agent. The two organizations in the plant vied with each other until the United Steelworkers of America finally was certified in September 1945. The conduct of the government and its appointee created considerable disillusionment within the trade union movement. Not only was the government unprepared to support union recognition or the principles of P.C. 2685, it also had condoned the establishment of an employer-dominated committee which had been used to undermine the existing union.

Concurrent with the NASCO dispute the first major dispute concerning the application of the government's wage control policy arose at the Peck Rolling Mills plant in Montreal. Peck Rolling Mills was a wholly owned subsidiary of Dominion Steel and Coal Company (DOSCO). The Steelworkers' Organizing Committee had organized 93 percent of the workforce and was granted recognition by the company on the recommendation of a Conciliation Board. The Conciliation Board also found that 50 percent of the workers received less than 30.7 cents an hour. In addition to poor wages, the Peck employees worked long hours (50 to 80 hours per week) in substandard working conditions. The parties fundamentally disagreed on both the level of wages and the proper interpretation of P.C. 7440, the wage-control order. The minority and majority reports of the conciliation board reflected this disagreement.

The employer took a narrow view of the effect of the order. The adequacy of wage rates under the wage order was to be determined in relation to a "norm" which was either the average wage in the 1926–29 period, or such higher rate as might have been attained after 1926. The employer submitted that since Peck wages in 1941 were above the 1926–29 average, they were therefore "fair and reasonable." This was not an exceptional case of depressed or subnormal wage rates. The Peck wages were comparable to other industrial rates in the Montreal area. The majority of the Board concurred with this view, and decided that the most recent wage order freezing wages[26] precluded it from recommending a raise, even though it was recognized that the wages were inadequate. Accordingly, the Board recommended a continuance of the basic wage rate of 30.7 cents an hour and no cost-of-living bonus, except the 15 cents per day which had been paid from September 1940.[27] No national wage level had been established in the steel industry; wage scales were determined locally. Since the Peck rates were not "depressed" by Montreal standards, there was no justification under the order to raise them.[28]

The union supported a broader interpretation of the order and argued that the Peck employees' wages should be compared to wages of other workers across the country engaged in similar work. Since workers in the steel industry were heavily engaged in the national production effort, they should be paid equally for work of equal value. In its view, the Peck wage rate was obviously "depressed and subnormal" and could be adjusted in accordance with the provisions of the order. The Minority Report adopted this argument and contended that the government's wage policy was aimed solely at preventing wages which were already reasonable from rising unduly; wages which were unreasonably low could still be raised. The order was not intended to freeze inadequate wages. There was nothing in the cost of living in Montreal or in the company's ability to pay which justified abnormally low wages in comparison with those paid to other workers in the same industry especially since the majority interpretation would condemn workers to a low wage condition for the duration of the wage policy.[29] The minority recommended an increase of the basic rate to 40 cents an hour. The positions of the parties and the proceedings of the Board were closely monitored, for labour believed that the management interpretation was in conflict with governmental assurances which had been given to organized labour at the time the wage order was proclaimed.[30] Labour feared that the Peck case would become a precedent for other conciliation boards handling wage disputes, as indeed it did. In addition, SWOC was beginning to formulate its demands for a general basic wage increase throughout the steel industry across the country.

In April 1941, after the publication of the two reports and in spite of the wage controls, the Peck workers struck for 40 cents an hour. The government sought to persuade them to return to work without giving in to union demands.[31] Ultimately the Peck employees received an increase in their basic wage rate when the federal government, avoiding any direct reference to the dispute, increased the minimum wage for men to 35 cents an hour and for women to 25 cents an hour.[32] The employees returned to work and the dispute ended with the temporary collapse of the SWOC local.[33]

The inequities of the wage policy, the rigidity with which it was applied in the Peck dispute, and the inconsistencies with which it was applied elsewhere,[34] increased labour alienation. To labour, it appeared that "its only real effect was to provide employers who wished to resist wage demands with an elaborate rationale."[35] Labour dissatisfaction with the wage policy mounted, as did its hostility to the government, which again appeared to be supporting the interests of employers. But it was the defeat of the Kirkland Lake miners in the winter of 1942 which crystallized labour's discontent, unified the movement, and moved the CCL unions into a position of outright opposition to the government.

In Kirkland Lake the issues were very clear. Local 240 of the International Union of Mine Mill and Smelter Workers was seeking recognition from the gold-mining operators. When recognition was refused, the union applied for a conciliation board. In Kirkland Lake, the government decided early not to appoint a controller. It was no more prepared to establish a collective bargaining relationship between a controller and the union than it had been at NASCO, but it was equally reluctant to risk the embarrassment which the NASCO dispute had involved. Instead, the government appointed the Industrial Disputes Inquiry Commission, chaired by Humphrey Mitchell (soon to be the new Minister of Labour) to investigate the dispute before granting a conciliation board. The IDIC was intended only to be a "fact-finding body" and was not supposed to make proposals for settlement. Nevertheless it proposed "the Kirkland Lake Formula" as the basis for a settlement. This formula suggested that the miners should elect "employee" committees in lieu of a "union" committee to negotiate with the mining companies. Management agreed to negotiate with such "internal" bodies while at the same time opposing "unalterably"[36] the recognition of the Mine Mill local. The proposal for new employee committees was a challenge to the legitimacy of the existing union and was bitterly resented. Indeed, the proposal was reminiscent of that of Controller Brunning in the NASCO dispute, except that now it came directly from a senior government official.

The Conciliation Board was finally appointed and unanimously recommended recognition of the union. Its recommendations were ignored by management. Before it could legally strike, the union was obliged by P.C. 7307 to apply for a government-supervised strike vote. Delay followed upon delay, until the strike was fought in the middle of a northern winter, and eventually lost. The union and the CCL recognized that the strike could be won only if the federal government intervened in support of the Conciliation Board Report. The only intervention that took place was by police constables who were ordered by the provincial government to assist the mining companies to operate with strikebreakers.[37] The federal government refused to intervene despite strenuous efforts on the part of the CCL unions and some TLC locals, including public conferences in Kirkland Lake and Ottawa, and the establishment of a network of strike committees across the country. This position was not mere procrastination, but a conscious policy adopted by the Prime Minister and his Minister of Labour.[38] The government was unwilling to endorse the principle of compulsory recognition, even where the trade union enjoyed the support of a majority of the employees, and a conciliation board unanimously recommended recognition as the only way to avoid a strike. Although the government was exercising compulsion every day in order to meet its wartime economic objectives, it continued to oppose compulsory recognition and maintained its belief in the efficacy of employees' committees as an alternative to independent trade unions. In the circumstances, it is difficult to avoid the conclusion that it was not "compulsion" which the government opposed, but, rather, collective bargaining itself. Apparently the government accepted the management view that collective bargaining legislation would encourage union growth and result in more unrest.

Unlike the "New Deal" labour policy of the 1930s, which sought to redress the imbalance of bargaining power and encourage collective bargaining, the Canadian labour policy throughout the war was concerned only with eliminating industrial unrest. The government continued to believe that legislative recognition of collective bargaining would only promote an "adversary relationship," but since there were real differences of interest between labour and management, an adversary relationship and some degree of conflict was inevitable. Labour stressed that the recognition of its status in industry and the introduction of collective bargaining would eliminate recognition strikes, develop negotiating relationships, and thereby improve labour–management relations. The government in 1942 did not agree. For political reasons, the government felt it necessary to conciliate business—its wartime ally in developing the war economy. It was therefore unprepared to establish collective bargaining as a "right" or grant labour an important role in running the war.[39] It was even unprepared to take the lead and set an example as a "good employer" by recognizing existing unions in its own war industries. Although it had a close working relationship with the business community, the government had no close relations with the industrial union movement. When the new union leaders openly questioned the government's good faith and asserted their members' rights even in the critical war situation, King dubbed them "irresponsible." King preferred the leaders of the TLC with whom he had more influence.

Refusal of the government to intervene resulted in the loss of the Kirkland Lake strike. There were several effects of the strike. The local union was temporarily decimated, but in the long run, the labour movement may have benefited. Many younger miners, experienced in trade union organizing, but blacklisted across the north, left to find work in southern Ontario. They invariably became active trade unionists in their new jobs and promoted trade union organization in the expanding war industries. Several rose to leadership positions in the industrial union movement.[40]

H.A. Logan has suggested that the "Kirkland Lake strike marked the low point in industrial relations in the war. But from it began the march toward P.C. 1003."[41] The strike unified the divided labour movement in a common political endeavour. In 1942 the briefs to the government of both the TLC and the CCL favoured positive collective bargaining legislation.[42] The CCL convention soundly condemned Humphrey Mitchell, the new Labour Minister, and demanded his removal from office. Both conventions demanded immediate enforcement of P.C. 2685, particularly in the Crown corporations. King was shaken by his meetings with the delegations from the two Congresses[43] and by the level of opposition at TLC and CCL conventions. In response to labour pressure, he personally intervened[44] to proclaim P.C. 10802. This order authorized Crown companies to bargain collectively with their employees. While it did not clearly make collective bargaining compulsory,[45] it made eventual legislative support of collective bargaining inevitable.[46] However, the delay in its implementation angered organized labour and contributed to its continuing opposition to government policies during 1943.[47] Any hope of accommodation was shattered by the government's handling of the 1943 steel strike.

The steel industry was crucial to war production. It was nationally mobilized and closely controlled, and as such it was an appropriate place to test the government's flexibility in the application of its wage policy. Steelworkers initially proposed wage increases to the Regional War Labour Boards which bore the primary responsibility for implementing the policy. Both the Ontario and the Nova Scotia Regional Boards refused any increase and, as a result, the workers voted overwhelmingly to strike. The threat of a strike by employees of DOSCO and Algoma Steel in the late summer and fall of 1942 represented "the most serious threat to the government's wage policy since its inception,"[48] but the dispute was temporarily postponed by the appointment of a three-man commission of investigation. In January 1943, the Barlow Commission reported. The positions of its members were similar to those taken by the conciliation board in the Peck Rolling Mills dispute. The Majority Report interpreted the most recent wage order in narrow terms. In its view, further adjustment in the basic wage rates was unjustified since there had recently been a cost-of-living bonus and the prevailing rates for unskilled employees were not "substandard." Despite the application of the "national" wage policy, the Board rejected the recommendation that the steel industry be classified a national industry as the union had requested. The Minority Report recommended that the steel industry should be given a special exemption from the wage policy because of the "particular arduousness" of the work, and the "inhumanly long hours." At Algoma more than 40 percent of the steelworkers received less than 55 cents an hour, and in Sydney the proportion in this category was closer to 60 percent. "Testimony ... told a story of hardship and privation, of overcrowding, of financial worry, of acute distress occasioned by illness against which there was no financial protection."[49] Such families did not receive the bare subsistence income set by the Department of Labour, the Dominion Bureau of Statistics, the Toronto Welfare Council, and other welfare agencies. The Majority and Minority Reports also differed on the interpretation of the Commission's terms of reference. The Majority believed its jurisdiction was limited to interpreting and applying the wage order. The Minority member believed the Commission had been appointed because of an acute crisis in the steel industry and its job was not to duplicate the functions of the War Labour Board, but instead to provide the government with a solution to the crisis. He therefore sought to interpret the wage order in light of the situation in the steel industry, the war production effort, the government's labour policy and the public interest.

Following the release of the Commission's Report, 9,000 employees went on strike. Some 2,700 Trenton steelworkers struck in sympathy. Immediately the government called a conference of the interested parties to Ottawa. Negotiations took place directly with the government and senior members of the Cabinet (including King, Howe, and Mitchell) were involved. Despite considerable disagreements in the Cabinet the union secured a number of concessions and a prolonged strike was avoided. In a "Memorandum of Agreement," the government agreed to some recommendations of the Majority Report but steel was to be designated a national industry; the union could present a new case to the National War Labour Board and the steelworkers would be paid a new basic rate of 55 cents an hour.[50]

The strike had a significant impact on the form of future labour legislation, for under pressure, the Prime Minister developed a new policy.[51] During the conference the Prime Minister proposed that the union take its case before a reconstituted "independent" National War Labour Board. His unpopular Labour Minister, Humphrey Mitchell, would resign as Chairman of the NWLB and be replaced by Justice McTague. In this way Mitchell's influence would be limited but his position as Minister of Labour would not be compromised. King "was optimistic that McTague could do what Mitchell failed to do: enforce the government's wage policy without alienating the labour movement completely and without mishandling disputes which would result in national crises and Cabinet intervention."[52] In fact, the NWLB did not succeed in lessening labour opposition. When it reviewed the steel wage case, it lowered the basic wage rate agreed upon in the "Memorandum of Understanding" and withdrew the designation of steel as a national industry. The union had understood that the Board would not be able to change the terms of the Memorandum except to improve on them. Since the Board was now "independent of politics," the Cabinet would not intervene to guarantee its own commitment. There followed a total disillusionment about the worth of any understanding with the government.

By early 1943 the labour movement and the government were completely at odds over the related issues of collective bargaining and wage controls. The government was asking labour to sacrifice wages as part of the war effort, and labour believed that in return there should be a guarantee of collective bargaining rights to protect workers from arbitrary employer action. The lack of collective bargaining legislation and the rigid enforcement of wage controls effectively undermined collective bargaining, and thereby threatened the labour movement itself.

In 1942 the labour movement's bitter experiences caused it to engage in more militant industrial action and also active political support for the CCF, whose labour platform accorded with their own. Throughout 1942, the CCF was attracting members, supporters, and revenue, and was becoming a credible alternative to the two old parties, particularly in the province of Ontario. "The greatest new source from which the CCF was deriving members and revenue was Ontario's mushrooming trade union movement."[53] Three days before the Kirkland Lake Local ended its strike, Joe Noseworthy, the CCF candidate, defeated Arthur Meighen in South York. This campaign, which was actively assisted by organized labour, provided further impetus to CCF organizing. The CCL moved toward a more formal relationship with the CCF, and the CCF-Trade Union Committee in Ontario worked towards this end. Its activities eventually culminated in a labour conference sponsored by the CCF which formally endorsed the party as the "political arm of labour." Only eight months after the CCF victory in South York, the 1942 CCL convention recommended that its constituent unions study the CCF program.[54]

These events did not pass unnoticed. The level of industrial unrest and the surge of support for the CCF motivated Hepburn's previously anti-labour government to do an about-face. At the 1942 CCL convention, Ontario Labour Minister Peter Heenan announced that his government was planning to introduce an Ontario collective bargaining act.[55] This announcement was premature—the Ontario Collective Bargaining Act was not enacted until April 1943—but, against the background of Kirkland Lake and the federal government's continued opposition to collective bargaining, its effect was electrifying. Labour's increasing support of the CCF also influenced the Ontario Conservatives who adopted a Twenty-Two Point Program for the 1943 campaign, which included "comprehensive collective bargaining legislation." The Federal Conservatives chose Progressive Premier John Bracken of Manitoba as its new leader, and drafted a new program designed to combat the CCF. At the end of 1942, King himself expressed "some concern" with the marked rise in CCF support and its developing alliance with organized labour; his main concern was not yet with the CCF.[56] As has already been noted, he responded to labour dissatisfaction directly during the steel strike by reconstituting the NWLB, which became a tripartite body that included J.L. Cohen as the labour representative. The new board was more independent of the Labour Department. It was to meet in public and function as an "industrial court" which would develop a specialized "labour jurisprudence,"[57] and was empowered to inquire and report to the Minister of Labour on labour matters. Thus it would have an indirect role in policy-making.

In April 1943, following a public enquiry by a committee of the Ontario legislature, the Collective Bargaining Act was passed. This legislation represented "the first attempt in Canada to enforce on employers in positive terms a duty to bargain collectively."[58] Like P.C. 10802, it increased the pressure for a comprehensive federal code. The Ontario Liberals had enacted the statute in order to indicate their concern with the state of labour–management relations,[59] but it did not take effect until June, and its passage was too late to prevent the defeat of the Liberals in August. Nevertheless, it was an important influence on the federal government and its provisions were later substantially reproduced in the federal order-in-council P.C. 1003. In addition, the public hearing preceding the bill provided a public forum, which labour used to mobilize support for its position.

At the hearings there was only token opposition from business. The committee canvassed the issue of compulsory collective bargaining and proposed an exclusive bargaining agency for the majority union, legally binding agreements enforceable through arbitration procedures, and the proscription of employer dominated "company unions."[60] Business only tentatively opposed compulsory collective bargaining since it realized that its legislation was now inevitable. However, business groups sought the registration and incorporation of unions so they could be sued for damages, and favoured proportional representation in situations where there existed a union and employee association. Employers proposed that employee committees which were not "unduly influenced" by the employer should be eligible for certification and sought a legislative guarantee of the employer's "right" to state his position on the question of unionization.[61]

The Ontario legislation was a compromise between these two positions. The principle of compulsory collective bargaining was recognized, as was the concept of majority rule and the exclusive bargaining agency. Unions were not incorporated but they did have to file their officers' names and a financial statement with the Registrar of the Labour Court. The wording of the Act was vague about "company unions," but presumably if they were reasonably independent, they could be certified. Labour had advocated a tripartite administrative tribunal to enforce the act, and stressed the importance of industrial relations' experience if the act was to be effectively administered. Business did not express much concern about enforcement. The Ontario Collective Bargaining Act, while modelled in general on the American Wagner Act, established a Labour Court, rather than a labour relations board to administer the statute. The Labour Court was part of the High Court of Ontario and was granted exclusive jurisdiction to handle all questions arising under the Act. Judges rotated and sat for two-week periods in the Labour Court. The Court was empowered to determine the unit of employees appropriate for collective bargaining and certify the trade union which represented the majority of them. It could also order the "decertification" of a union which lost majority support and could refuse to certify an employer dominated organization. In addition, it had broad remedial powers to deal with violations of the act, and could, for example, order the reinstatement of employees unlawfully discharged. The Labour Court mechanism was criticized by labour for its legalism and formality, but organized labour generally supported the act. Despite its imperfections, it was serving a need. It effectively ended the need for recognition strikes. In its first six months of operation, the Labour Court was primarily preoccupied with certification proceedings, and received 130 applications affecting approximately 80,000 persons. While employees' associations continued to be certified as well as unions, certification of unions predominated.[62]

The Labour Court experiment influenced later federal legislation, for, after considering the problems faced by the Court, the federal government rejected this device in favour of a quasi-judicial administrative tribunal. The Labour Court mechanism had been rather cumbersome. The judges had no specific labour relations expertise, and, since they sat in rotation for short periods of time, they did not have the opportunity to develop such expertise. Formal court procedures and rules of evidence were inappropriate and unnecessary. For example, the industrial relations criteria necessary for a sound determination of the appropriate bargaining unit were not necessarily amenable to legal proof.[63] Interestingly, the Court proved less sympathetic to craft unions than the U.S. National Labour Relations Board, and in administering representation votes tended to emphasize the majority principle, and gave relatively less weight to the demands for independent status made by small groups of skilled craftsmen. In this respect, the early reservations of the TLC craft unions concerning the desirability of the Wagner principles turned out to be entirely justified.

In April 1943 the federal government had announced that the NWLB would conduct its own public enquiry into the causes of labour unrest (which in 1943 involved almost a quarter of a million workers and resulted in over a million man-days lost).[64] In February when the NWLB was reconstituted the government had had no intention of introducing a national labour code or of using the Board for this purpose. The change in its attitude was a response to the high level of industrial unrest, and the increasing popularity of the CCF, which was now strongly supported by organized labour.[65] The public hearings of the NWLB gave labour a national platform from which to air its grievances. As in Ontario, there was not a great deal of opposition from business. CCL President A.R. Mosher characterized labour policy to that date as "trying to crowd out the effect rather than eliminate the cause of much of the discontent that prevails among the working people of this country."[66] The UAW brief asserted that in a period of industrial growth, it was unreasonable of the government to attempt to curtail the organizing and bargaining activities of unions,[67] which were intended to modify the old system of managerial paternalism. The labour movement demanded a permanent national labour code which recognized the right of labour to organize, enforced recognition of the majority union, outlawed "company" unions, and established a board to effectively administer the act.

In August 1943 the stunning result of the Ontario election brought the defeat of Nixon's Liberals and the election of George Drew; but more significantly, this month also saw the election of the CCF as Official Opposition. The CCF caucus consisted of 34 members of whom 19 were trade unionists (10 TLC and nine CCL), including Charlie Millard, head of the Steelworkers, and Bob Carlin, head of the Mine, Mill and Smelter Workers.[68] The results of this election finally induced the federal government to alter its labour policy. King recognized that the "CCF had made a telling run in all industrial constituencies, particularly where there had been labour unrest, making clear the combination of the industrial CIO with political CCF."[69] When the Federal Liberals lost four by-elections—two to the CCF—shortly after the Ontario results, King feared that it might even be "the beginning of the end of the Liberal Party federally."[70] He attributed his party's setback to "bad handling of Labour policies," and poor party organization. Pickersgill confirmed that at this point in time King "felt the loss of labour's support was the greatest threat to the chances of the Liberal Party winning the next election."[71]

King immediately acted to forestall "this calamity." In August he made a surprise visit to the TLC convention. At that convention, the TLC finally established a political action committee although it maintained its policy of no affiliation to any political arm of labour. In September the CCL convention endorsed the CCF as the political arm of labour. Also in September King presented a new platform which attacked the CCF and appealed to the labour vote in a speech to the National Liberal Federation. King was, above all, an astute politician. As Daniel Coates has observed:

> The party forming the government between 1935 and 1944 did not accept labour union demands for a change in national labour policy until labour achieved sufficient strength during a war emergency period to join with the CCF party and appear to threaten the survival of the Liberal Party and the government.[72]

In August 1943 both the Majority and the Minority Reports of the NWLB Inquiry were presented to the Minister of Labour. Both recommended a new labour code which would include the principle of compulsory collective bargaining. The government was now committed to legislation, although the Board's reports were not released until January 1944 so that the government could consider its position on both collective bargaining and wage controls. Both issues played a part in the recent labour unrest. In the interim, the government dismissed J.L. Cohen, the labour representative, from the board (in part for his public discussion of the reports prior to their release). The government finally decided to maintain its system of wage controls despite their unpopularity. In these circumstances, legislation on the collective bargaining issue became a political necessity. The political consensus which King was always seeking to preserve had crumbled during the war, as organized workers sought a new status in industry and government.

P.C.1003 was enacted in February 1944. It has been viewed as a turning point in the development of our industrial relations system since it became a model for post-war legislation. It adopted the major points of both NWLB reports. It guaranteed the right to organize and bargain collectively, established a procedure for the certification and compulsory recognition of trade unions with majority support, recognized the exclusive bargaining agency principle, defined unfair labour practices, provided for remedies, and outlawed company unions. It established an administrative tribunal (rather than a court) to enforce the order. It incorporated the basic principles of the American Wagner Act but also continued the distinctly Canadian policy of compulsory conciliation prior to a legal strike. Unlike the American legislation, it contained no preamble or policy statement indicating that collective bargaining was in the public interest or a desirable method of conducting employer-employee relations.[73] Again, in contrast to the American legislation, the parties were not entitled to strike or lockout during the term of the agreement. The collective agreement itself, however, was now legally enforceable. The government's primary concern had been, and continued to be, the elimination of industrial conflict, and the concessions to labour contained in the new legislation were primarily designed to accomplish that purpose. Nevertheless, the legislation was welcomed by labour, since both trade union organizing and collective bargaining were accorded protection and a clear legal status. Recognition strikes were no longer necessary in order to initiate bargaining. The aspirations of employees were sanctioned by law, and could no longer be regarded as illegitimate. Employer opposition to trade unionism was not eliminated but many of its manifestations became illegal.

The immediate political impact of the legislation was to undercut labour's opposition to the government, but because the legislation was implemented in the form of an order-in-council, it would be in effect for the duration of the war only. When it was introduced, the government was responding to an immediate political situation. It was not meant to be a permanent measure. This fact and the increased uncertainty which unions felt at the end of the war concerning the permanence of their organizational and legislative gains, resulted in a new wave of industrial unrest. The emerging issue in this strike wave was union security. These strikes and the decisions taken at a federal-provincial conference immediately following the war ultimately ensured that the wartime advances would be maintained in the post-war era, albeit in a more decentralized industrial relations system than the one developed during the war emergency. In 1948 the Industrial Relations Disputes Investigation Act (IRDI Act) replaced P.C. 1003 and the IDI Act at the federal level. The provinces either entered into this legislation or adopted similar acts of their own.

III.

The war years were crucial for the development of the Canadian labour movement. Union membership grew tremendously. Large industrial unions proved to be permanent. Labour achieved legislative protection as a result of pressure on both the industrial and political fronts. The change in wartime labour relations consisted of a process whereby bargaining relationships were facilitated and thereby stabilized. At the beginning of the war, the government's labour policy had been "non-interventionist"; but despite its alleged "neutrality" it had in practice been restrictive. The old industrial relations system based on little government intervention except through the imposition of conciliation proved inadequate to deal with conflicts over the issue of collective bargaining. The NASCO dispute pointed out these legislative inadequacies. The loss of the Kirkland Lake recognition strike was such a threat to the future of organized labour that thereafter the TLC and the CCL, despite their organizational rivalries, united to demand legislative remedies. The government's refusal to implement collective bargaining legislation and labour's opposition to wage controls impelled the labour movement to take political action.

The year 1943 was a watershed in the development of wartime labour policy as labour's strike activity and political action reached a peak. Such action did not end wage controls but did result in positive legislation in a new system which recognized trade unions, institutionalized collective bargaining, defined unfair labour practices and provided remedies, and legitimized trade union activity through legally binding collective agreements. To regulate industrial relations, the government introduced a new independent mechanism, the specialized administrative tribunal. Henceforth the "rules of the game" would be determined, in part, by a body representative of the parties bound by those rules, and the roles of the judges and courts would be reduced. This mechanism (which was originally merely an extension of wartime political control of the economy) became a permanent part of the policy-making apparatus following the war.

Labour did not gain significant representation in government, but it did gain a limited role on the new tripartite tribunal. These legislative and administrative reforms were not achieved within the context of a socialist society as some labour leaders had hoped. Consequently, the conservative administration of labour legislation would inevitably create tensions between labour, business, and government. Because of their wartime experience, the CCL industrial unions formed a relatively permanent political alliance with the CCF. This factor probably decreased labour's influence as an interest group. The labour movement would never achieve the degree of participation in government which it had sought during the war years.[74]

The impact of trade unionism during the war on the position of employees was significant. Trade union pressure helped to initiate improvements on the job and preserved them at the end of the war. The seniority principle, for example, introduced a new measure of job security. The trade union became a permanent part of the labour relations process at every organized plant, and acted to ensure that the agreement was properly interpreted and administered. The grievance procedure provided a practical method for resolving disputes if an employee believed that he was being treated in an arbitrary or discriminatory manner or had been discharged or disciplined "without just cause." This was perhaps the most important achievement of the period. Mackenzie King could incorporate social welfare measures into the Liberal platform in order to undermine political gains of the CCF (though not its alliance with labour) to ensure his re-election in 1945. But the restrictions on the previously unfettered authority of management and the resulting changes in the status of employees on the shop floor were permanent. To that extent a degree of democracy in industry was achieved.

Endnotes

1. Selig Perlman quoted in E.W. Bakke, C. Kerr and C. Anrod, eds., *Unions, Management and the Public* (New York 1967), p. 47.
2. *Labour Organizations in Canada* (Ottawa 1949), p. 15.
3. Ruth Pierson, "Women's Emancipation and the Recruitment of Women into the Labour Force in World War II," in S.M. Trofimenkoff and A. Prentice, eds., *The Neglected Majority* (Toronto 1977), p. 126.
4. Charles Lipton, *The Trade Union Movement in Canada 1827–1959* (Montreal 1965), p. 267.
5. This was a factor among older workers in the Kirkland Lake strike, *Sudbury Star*, 1 March 1942.
6. In 1946, which is often considered a peak year of industrial unrest in Canada, only one trade union member in six was involved in strike activity. The most recent comparable example of membership participation in strike activity was in 1976 on account of the political "National Day of Protest" against wage controls. See *Strikes and Lockouts in Canada* (Ottawa 1977).
7. For example the Knights of Labor and the One Big Union.
8. Canadian labour historians have emphasized AFL pressure on the TLC expulsion. Certainly this was a factor, but the fundamental disagreements within the TLC prior to 1939 were important. Note Charles Lipton, *Trade Union Movement*, pp. 261–4, and Irving Abella, *Nationalism, Communism and Canadian Labour* (Toronto 1973), ch. 2.
9. William Arnold Martin, "A Study of Legislation Designed to Foster Industrial Peace in the Common Law Jurisdiction of Canada," Ph.D. thesis, University of Toronto, 1954, p. 291.
10. Ibid., pp. 299–302.
11. *TLC Convention Proceedings* (Ottawa 1942).
12. *Labour Gazette* (Ottawa 1943), p. 1613.
13. "The pressures of taxation controls and restrictions were beginning to get ordinary men and women down.... In 1941 for the first time the war began to hit home," in J.L. Granatstein, *Canada's War* (Toronto 1975), p. 159.
14. J.L. Cohen, *Collective Bargaining in Canada* (Toronto 194l), p. 26.
15. The Kirkland Lake strike was an example of a union whose bargaining position was undermined by prolonged delays prior to the walkout.
16. There was a close similarity between management and government views of "irresponsible" union leaders, by whom they usually meant CCL trade unionists.
17. William Arnold Martin, "Industrial Peace," p. 292.
18. Irving Bernstein, *The Turbulent Years* (Boston 1971), p. 78.
19. J.L. Cohen, *Collective Bargaining in Canada* (Toronto 1941), p. 34.
20. This position was clearly stated by the Minister of Labour, Norman McLarty, in a speech on 7 November 1941. See *Ottawa Morning Journal*, 7 November 1941.
21. J.L. Cohen, *Collective Bargaining in Canada*, p. 47. See also J.L. Granatstein, *Canada's War*, pp. 185–186.
22. *Canadian Unionist* (Montreal), September 194l, p. 87.
23. Memo to Prime Minister from SWOC, Local 2352, 3 July 1941, vol. 38, CLC Papers, Public Archives of Canada (PAC).
24. J.L. Cohen to Norman McLarty, 15 May 1941, vol. 38, CLC Papers, PAC.
25. Memo to Prime Minister from SWOC Local 2352, 3 July 1941.
26. P.C. 7440 was interrupted publicly in a narrow way by the Minister of Labour in his "Wartime Wages Policy" speech of 31 March 1941.
27. Conciliation Board Report, vol. 38, CLC Papers, PAC.

28. Ibid.
29. *Minority Report*, Ibid.
30. The government's assurances were to the effect that the wage control policy would be administered flexibly to take account of factors in individual cases. Daniel Coates, "Organized Labor and Politics in Canada: The Development of a National Labor Code," Ph.D. thesis, Cornell University, 1973, p. 84.
31. Memo on Peck Rolling Mills, 21 May 1941, William Lyon Mackenzie King Memoranda, vol. 310, King Papers, PAC.
32. Ibid.
33. Minority Report, vol. 38, CLC Papers, PAC.
34. T. Copp, "The Impact of Wage and Price Controls on Workers in Montreal 1939–47," unpublished paper delivered at CUA Meeting 1976, p. 5.
35. Ibid., p. 6.
36. Conciliation Board Report, in Canadian Unionist, October 1941, pp. 108–109.
37. Private Correspondence, 1942 Strikes—Kirkland Lake, Hepburn Papers, Archives of Ontario.
38. Memo, Norman McLarty to William Lyon Mackenzie, 3 December 194l, King Primary Correspondence, vol. 310, PAC.
39. Ibid.
40. Jim Russell, Joe Rankin Jock Brodie, and Bill Sefton became International Representatives on Staff of the United Steelworkers of America (USWA). Eamon Park, who worked on publicity during the strike, became an International Representative and subsequently Assistant to the National Director in Canada of the USWA. Larry Sefton, the young Recording Secretary of Local 240, went on staff as an International Representative of the Steelworkers and in 1953 was elected as Director of District 6 of that union. He later became a member of the International Executive Board of the Steelworkers' union and a Vice President of the Canadian Labour Congress. Bob Carlin, Local 240's Financial Secretary, became the Canadian Representative for District 8 on the International Board of the International Union of Mine, Mill and Smelter Workers (IUMMSW) in 1942. In 1943 he was elected to the Ontario Legislature as the CCF Member from Sudbury. William Simpson, President, Local 240, became a Staff Representative for the IUMMSW.
41. H.A. Logan, *Trade Unions in Canada* (Toronto 1948), p. 547.
42. Daniel Coates, "Organized Labour," pp.102–106.
43. Ibid., p.106.
44. Ibid., p.105.
45. Bora Laskin, "Recent Labour Legislation in Canada," *Canadian Bar Review*, XXII (November 1944), pp. 776–792.
46. W.A. Martin, "Industrial Peace," p. 346.
47. Daniel Coates, "Organized Labour," p.105.
48. Ibid., p.108.
49. *Labour Gazette* (Ottawa 1943), pp. 61–68.
50. Ibid., p.193.
51. Daniel Coates, "Organized Labour," p.126.
52. Ibid., p.128.
53. G. Caplan, *The Dilemma of Canadian Socialism* (Toronto 1973), p. 95.
54. Ibid.
55. *CCL Convention Proceedings* (Ottawa 1942).
56. Daniel Coates. "Organized Labour," p.138.
57. *Labour Gazette* (Ottawa 1943), p.167.
58. Bora Laskin "Collective Bargaining in Ontario: A New Legislative Approach," *Canadian Bar Review*, XXI (Nov. 1943), p. 684.
59. Daniel Coates, "Organized Labour."
60. Ontario, *Proceedings of Select Committee Re Bargaining between Employers and Employees* (1943), Legislative Library, Toronto.
61. Ibid.
62. "Summary of Activities of the Labour Court, June 14, 1943, to December 31, 1943, Ontario Labour Court, Ontario Department of Labour Papers, Archives of Ontario.

63. Bora Laskin, "Collective Bargaining in Ontario," p. 693.
64. *Strikes and Lockouts in Canada* (Ottawa 1977).
65. Daniel Coates, "Organized Labour," p. 137.
66. Stephen Purdy, "Another Look at Orders-In-Council. P.C. 1003," unpublished graduate paper, York University, 1976, p. 8.
67. Ibid., p. 10.
68. Horowitz, *Canadian Labour in Politics* (Toronto 1968), p. 77.
69. Daniel Coates, "Organized Labour," p.138.
70. Ibid., p.139.
71. Ibid., p. 130.
72. Ibid., p. 225.
73. Such a provision became part of the Ontario legislation in 1970, and the federal legislation in 1972.
74. In its recent opposition to the present wage controls the CLC requested greater consultation in government. When it did not get it, it embarked on its "National Day of Protest." CLC Manifesto (Ottawa, 1976).

Chapter 14

Women and Income Security in the Post-War Period

The Case of Unemployment Insurance, 1945–62

Ann Porter

Federal labour market policies after World War II crucially shaped both the nature of women's labour force participation and their access to the post-war welfare state's social security provisions. This article examines how Canadian federal policy helped shape women's economic status during that period by considering how they fared in the unemployment insurance (UI) scheme from the end of the war until the early 1960s. It is argued that the federal state, in part through the implementing of the UI plan, played a critical role in reinforcing women's marginal economic position. In the case of UI, this occurred by channelling women into low-wage sectors and by limiting women's access to income security benefits. The latter resulted, in particular, from a special UI regulation for married women, which was in effect from 1950 to 1957. The rationale for this regulation, its implications for women, and the factors leading to its eventual revocation, is a major focus of the article.

A second focus concerns the question of the formation and impetus for change in state policies, particularly with regard to women. The literature examining UI's implementation has tended to present state policies as the result of various factors: direct pressure from the business class,[1] state mediation between different classes with the goal of ensuring the long-run stability of the system,[2] or the autonomous decisions made by bureaucrats and other state officials.[3] Such analyses, however, cannot explain adequately either changes in state policies or what the implications of those changes may have been for women. Such an explanation requires greater understanding of the role of gender relations, including not only an examination of changes in the prevailing ideology, but also an assessment of the political organization of women and their relation to other social forces. The 1950s is commonly viewed as a period of retrenchment when the ideology of domesticity prevailed and women were relegated to the home. In fact, however, the position of women changed considerably during this period. Women—especially married women—entered the labour force in growing numbers, while women's organizations and trade unions became increasingly concerned with equality rights for female workers, and attitudes concerning the proper role of women began to evolve. It is these changes which must be examined in order to understand the change in UI policy with regard to married women workers.

The 1940 UI Act was one of the key pieces of legislation to shape Canada's post-war welfare state. It was seen as a way to maintain demand, to bring about greater industrial stability, and to provide workers with some form of income security in times of unemployment. Under the scheme, benefits were calculated as a proportion of earnings, and were to be paid to unemployed workers who had contributed for at least 180 days during the two years immediately preceding the claim, and who showed that they were capable of and available for work but unable to find suitable employment.[4] The plan was to be based on insurance principles and thus to have a sound actuarial basis.

Overarching responsibility for administering the UI program was vested in the Unemployment Insurance Commission, consisting of a chief commissioner, a commissioner representing employees, and one representing employers. An Unemployment Insurance Advisory Committee (UIAC) was established to advise the Commission and to make recommendations regarding the Insurance Fund and the coverage of those not insured under the Act. It was made up of a chairperson and between four and six other members, with an equal number of representatives of employers and employees (appointed by the Governor-in-Council in consultation with their respective organizations). As well, structures were devised to allow for the appeal of decisions made by UI officers. Those whose claim was disallowed had the right to appeal to a tripartite Court of Referees, again made up of representatives of employers, employees, and the government. Under certain conditions the decision of these Courts could, in turn, be appealed to an Umpire chosen from the judges of the Exchequer Court and the Superior Courts of the provinces.[5]

Although the origin of the UI system has been the subject of some debate,[6] until recently little attention has been paid to its implications for gender relations. This question has been addressed by Ruth Roach Pierson, who writes that "gender pervaded the 1934–40 debate on UI, and was inscribed in every clause of the resulting legislation."[7] Specifically, she found that the UI contribution and benefit structure of the 1940 Act reproduced sexually unequal wage hierarchies; women's employment patterns and childcare responsibilities meant they were disadvantaged both in their ability to qualify and in the length of time they were able to draw benefits; women were virtually excluded from the higher levels of the administrative structure; and the prevailing ideology of the "family wage"—which assumed that the male was the head of the household and that married women would be supported by their husbands—led to the inclusion of dependant's allowances in the UI benefit structure. Pierson suggests that, in the framing of the legislation, women's principal access to benefits was to be indirectly through the dependant's allowances.[8]

During World War II, women entered the labour force to an unprecedented degree. Their employment shifted from low-wage jobs in domestic service and unskilled occupations to higher-paid, skilled positions in manufacturing, and their average weekly earnings increased dramatically.[9] For example, women's overall labour force participation increased from 24.4 percent in 1939 to a high of 33.5 percent in 1944,[10] while their average weekly earnings rose from $12.78 to $20.89 in the same period.[11] Given these developments, to what extent did conceptions change concerning women's access to income security benefits?

Despite the upheavals brought about by the war, the federal government documents which helped to shape the post-war period continued to view women's role in much the same way as had been the case prior to 1939: women's place was seen as being primarily in the domestic sphere and the husband was viewed as the chief wage earner.[12] Both Leonard Marsh's *Report on Social Security for Canada* (1943) and the *White Paper on Employment and Income* (1945) expected that a large number of war-time women workers would retire voluntarily from the labour market either to resume or to take up their domestic role.[13] To Marsh, the social security system applied to a woman primarily "in her capacity as housewife."[14] And the 1943 Sub-committee on the Post-war Problems of Women (a subcommittee of the federally appointed Advisory Committee on Reconstruction), even while calling for "equality of remuneration, working conditions and opportunity advancement" for women, believed nonetheless that either marriage or settlement on farms would be the best solution to the problem of large numbers of unemployed single women after the war.[15]

Federal government policy during the post-war reconstruction period reflected these views. Various measures were aimed at reducing women's, especially married women's, attachment to the labour force. These included the closing of daycares,[16] the renewal of civil service regulations barring married women from federal government work,[17] and income tax changes which provided a disincentive to married women to work for pay.[18] Other measures tended to steer women from the relatively well-paid jobs they had occupied during the war to the low-wage service sector—for instance, laid-off women were encouraged to undertake post-war training in such areas as domestic service, household management, waitressing, and hairdressing.[19]

These measures largely were designed to ensure jobs for men at the end of the war. They were introduced amid fears that the high levels of unemployment that had characterized the Depression would recur, as might the unrest that had followed World War I.[20] The result was that women's labour force participation dropped from the 1944 high of 33.5 percent to 25.3 percent in 1946, and remained between 23 percent to 24 percent for the next nine years before increasing once again.[21] What is clear from these measures is that the post-war goal of maintaining a "high and stable level of employment and income"[22] really applied only to men. The notion of full employment was limited not only by the modest goal of a "high and stable" level, but was further restrained through its being applied only to a particular sector of the labour force. As one government document of the period noted, "women are encouraged only to enter the labour market when economic activity is at such a level that their employment will not prevent men from obtaining positions."[23] This meant that for women there was no attempt to ensure either employment or income, and indeed, that such security could be achieved for men only if large numbers of women were encouraged or coerced into leaving the labour force.

Thus, the state was involved in rebuilding a particular type of labour-market structure which involved women moving from relatively highly paid and highly skilled wartime manufacturing jobs into part-time and insecure jobs in the low-paid manufacturing and the growing service sectors. This had the effect of maintaining women in a marginal position within the economy and in a status of economic dependence in the family. This, in turn, ensured the existence of a sizeable labour reserve. That women fulfilled this function was explicitly recognized by, for example, a Department of Labour document from the period which referred to women as the "number one worker reserve" to be "drawn into employment under emergency conditions."[24]

Two particular aspects of the post-war UI scheme contributed fundamentally to women's increased dependence on the male head of the household and their concentration in low-wage job ghettoes. This occurred first through the channelling of women into low-wage sectors; and secondly, through the introduction in 1950 of a regulation imposing additional requirements on married women.

The UI scheme helped channel women into low-wage sectors partly through the way in which it was administered. Records of decisions made by the UI Umpire register numerous cases for the immediate post-war period in which women were disqualified from UI benefits for a specified interval because they had refused to accept work at a fraction of the pay they had been receiving during the war. Often they were expected to accept work in either the service sector or low-wage, female-dominated manufacturing sectors, although they previously had been employed either in the more highly paid manufacturing sectors or by the government. For instance, in 1946 a woman who had been employed as a radio examiner doing war work at 74.58 cents an hour was disqualified for four weeks after refusing general factory work at 45 cents an hour.[25] Another woman, employed as a brewery packer during the war at $33.15 a week, was disqualified for six weeks when she declined a job as a confectionery packer at the industry's prevailing weekly wage of $15.40.[26]

Similarly, a woman employed by the Dominion government from 1940 to 1947 at $152 a month was notified after almost six months of unemployment of a job as a ward aide at a local hospital for $75 a month plus one meal a day for a 48-hour week. When she refused to apply on the basis that she knew nothing of the work and that she had spent time and a considerable amount of money obtaining mechanical drafting training, she was disqualified for six weeks because she had refused to apply for work at a suitable employment.[27] The four- or six-week disqualification in these cases was significant not only for the immediate loss of benefits, but because it indicated the expectations concerning the appropriate work for women even as it held out the threat of further disqualification should similar work be refused in the future.

Some indication of the extent to which women in particular were expected to accept work at reduced wages and in occupations other than those for which they had immediate experience is disclosed by surveying the UI Umpire's decision for 1945–46. Of the 138 appeals heard by the Umpire in this period, 22 were from women who had been disqualified (generally for six weeks) for refusing to accept work at drastically reduced wages and often in a completely different line of work.[28] The Umpire lifted the disqualification in only five of these cases, generally either because the woman had been unemployed for less than a month, or because the wages were considerably less than the prevailing wage in the industry.[29] During the same period, only two men appealed for somewhat similar reasons. In one case, the Umpire ruled that the man was justified in refusing the lower-paid and less-skilled job and the disqualification was lifted.[30] In the other, while the man initially refused the work offered because the wages were too low and the hours of work long, his appeal reveals little about the question of accepting work at lower wages. He appealed on the grounds that the doctor told him not to do strenuous work. In this case, the appeal was rejected because of an inadequate medical certificate.[31]

The issue of women being expected to accept work at low rates of pay was raised in the House of Commons by CCF members Stanley Knowles (Winnipeg North Centre) and Angus MacInnis (Vancouver East). Knowles noted that in Ottawa, married women who took temporary jobs during the war were required to pay UI, even though some asked to be exempted on the grounds that their jobs were only temporary. While women who were laid off from wartime jobs initially were granted UI when they met the usual conditions—that is, they were available for other work similar in character, and work was unavailable for them—women who subsequently applied for UI were offered wholly dissimilar jobs at much lower rates of pay. When they proved unwilling to take such jobs, they were told that they were thereby disqualified from benefits. Knowles referred to stories of:

> married women who had become grade 2 or grade 3 stenographers and who were offered such positions as charwomen, assistants in laundries, ironers, work at slicing bread, icing cakes, baby sitting, housekeeping and so on. When they report that they are unwilling to take positions of this kind and feel that they should not be asked to take them within the meaning of the words "suitable employment," they are simply told by the people in the offices to whom they appeal that nothing can be done in the matter.[32]

MacInnis noted that one directive sent to him from the UI office in 1946 stated that an offer at a wage of 5 cents an hour lower then the former rate might be considered suitable after three weeks of unemployment, and that 10 cents an hour lower might be suitable after four weeks (the equivalent of about $16 a month).[33] It appeared, however, that this directive did not apply to women. MacInnis cited the example of a woman who had been earning $160 a month who was disqualified because she refused to accept a job at $100—a drop of $60 a month. She appealed to the court of Referees. They sustained her disqualification because she had placed a restriction of $125 a month on her services. The employment officer who gave evidence swore that no positions for "girls" that had been listed at the office carried a salary of $125 a month.[34] To some extent private industry clearly played an important role in steering women into low-wage sectors through their reluctance to retain or advertise higher-paid positions for women once the war was over.[35] But, state policy, including the UI system, also had a role to play in this regard.

The policy which most blatantly discriminated against women, however, was the 1950 regulation imposing additional requirements on married women who claimed UI benefits. During the first two-and-a-half months that it was in operation, 10,808 women were disqualified.[36] The regulation remained in effect for seven years, during which time between 12,000 and 14,000 women annually were disqualified at a saving to the UI Fund estimated by the UI Commission at $2,500,000 per year.[37]

Regulation 5A was brought into force by order-in-council P.C. 5090 effective 15 November 1950, following an amendment by the House of Commons to the UI Act (Section 38(1)(d)), empowering the Commission to make regulations with regard to married women. The regulation itself provided that a married woman would be disqualified from UI benefits for a period of two years following her marriage unless she fulfilled certain conditions that would prove her attachment to the labour force. Specifically, beyond the general requirements of being unemployed, capable of and available for work, and unable to find employment, a married woman had to work for at least 90 days (a) after her marriage if she was not employed at the date of her marriage, or (b) after her first separation from work after her marriage if she was working at the time of her marriage. She was exempt from the regulation, however, if her separation from work was due to a shortage of work or an employer's rule against retaining married women, if her husband had died, become incapacitated, had deserted her, or if she had become permanently separated from him. The regulations subsequently were amended somewhat. For instance, the 90-day requirement was reduced to 60, first for those required to work after the first separation after marriage (1951), and later in all cases (1952). The exemptions were also expanded, for instance, to include women who had left employment voluntarily with just cause for reasons solely and directly connected with their employment (1951).

Where did the impetus to enact such a regulation come from? Discussion of Special UI provisions for married women had occurred as early as the 1930s. Pierson noted that it was assumed at the time that married women would be provided for by their husbands. Therefore, for married women to claim UI was "a contradiction in terms or, what was greatly feared, a way to defraud the system." R.B. Bennett's 1935 UI Act (declared *ultra vires* of the federal government and never implemented), empowered the UI Commission to impose additional conditions on "special cases," which included married women. The 1940 Act, however, contained no such provision.[39] The framers of the 1950 married women's regulation cited similar strictures embodied in the British UI Act of 1935 and in a number of U.S. states.[40]

Renewed pressure to enact such a regulation in Canada began as early as 1946 when large numbers of women, especially married women, were being laid off from former war industries or forced to leave full-time work due, for instance, to lack of childcare provisions or the reinstatement of bans on employing married women. Adding insult to injury, it was then suggested that married women were responsible for draining the UI Fund.[41] Pressure to enact such a regulation continued, however, well past the time when women war workers would have been collecting UI, and certainly, by the time it was enacted in 1950, few would have been in this category. Young married women in general, however, became targeted as abusers of the UI Fund.[42]

To some extent, the renewed interest in a regulation for married women can be seen as a continuation of the ideology—never really abandoned—of the family with a male breadwinner and a dependent wife. Pressure to enact such a regulation arose from a context of heightened emphasis on women's domestic role and on the idea that now that the war was over, women should choose once again between employment and marriage, and that it was improper for those who chose the latter to collect UI benefits. This certainly was the view publicized in an Edmonton newspaper in 1946:

> ... it was never intended, surely, that a young woman quitting work in order to get married should thereupon become eligible to draw unemployment benefits. In such a case, the employe [sic] makes her choice between employment and marriage. If she choses [sic] the latter, she can hardly be said to be unemployed, in fact or theory....[43]

In addition, two groups actively called for such a regulation. The first consisted of business associations such as the Canadian Manufacturers Association (CMA) and the Canadian Construction Association (CCA). These two groups submitted briefs in 1949 to the UI Advisory Committee (UIAC) which expressed concern about the large amount of unemployment benefits paid out during 1948–49 and which attributed this partly to the abuse of the UI Fund by married women and pensioners who, they argued, did not really wish to find work.[44] The CCA went so far as to argue that "the vitality of the nation will suffer if people can receive support in this manner."[45]

The second source of pressure came from the UI Commission and the UIAC. Both bodies took up the view that married women were draining the Fund. In its report to the Governor-in-Council for the fiscal years 1946–47 through 1948–49, the UIAC drew attention to the amount of benefit disbursed to recently married women who they suggested were representing themselves as unemployed when in fact they had actually withdrawn from the labour market, had no serious intention of working, and were not obliged by economic circumstances to obtain employment.[46] In July 1949, the Commission proposed a regulation stipulating that married women would be entitled to a benefit only if they contributed to the Fund for an additional period of time following marriage to prove their commitment to the labour force." That same month, the UIAC endorsed this proposal in principle and recommended UI Act amendments empowering the Commission to make such a regulation.[48]

A.D. Watson, the actuarial adviser (responsible for assessing the financial basis of the Fund), also played a role in pointing to married women as the source of a drain on the Fund. The concerns expressed in his December 1949 report virtually mirror those of the two business associations, pointing to the amount paid out in claims in 1947 and 1948, two years with extremely low levels of unemployment, and suggesting that married women and pensioners may have been guilty of drawing on the Fund when they had really left the field of employment. He stated that,

> ... persons who are not available for insurable employment on account of some necessary work about the home ... or on account of illness, personal or in the family, or on account of a birth, marriage or death in the family ... have no right to benefit.[50]

This clearly targeted many women, not just because of their general, everyday domestic responsibilities, but because women have tended to assume a greater share of responsibility in times of illness or death of family members. Watson was concerned, too, about possible abuse because of extending benefits to seasonal workers. Here again women were singled out: "[t]his is an area where married women may prove to be very effective claimants unless controlled by sound regulations."[51] Clearly the "actuarial ideology"[52] included a particular view of women—a view which coincided with that of the business organizations.

The attitude of state officials beyond the Commission and the UIAC was somewhat mixed, but generally supportive of the regulation. While one state official called it an "unjustifiable discrimination,"[53] the Deputy Minister of Labour, A. MacNamara, did not take this view. While stating on one occasion that "personally I am not of the opinion that the skulduggery reported to be going on in regard to married women is as extensive as we have been led to believe,"[54] nevertheless on other occasions stated that the regulations were not unfair and that he recommended them.[55] At yet another time, he adopted a fairly patronizing attitude, and clearly did not view as a cause for concern any harm that the regulation was likely to do to women. In a reply to Fraudena Eaton[56] (one of the few people who might have been considered by the government to be a spokesperson on women's employment issues), who had expressed concern about the regulation, he stated:

> I suppose that there are quite a number of girls who have no intention of working after they get married who will be glad to have Unemployment Insurance Benefits to pay the instalment on the Washing Machine—or is it a new Television set?[57]

The UIAC labour representatives played a somewhat ambiguous role in the implementation of the regulation for married women. The minutes of the July 1949 meeting at which the regulation was approved in principle record no objection from any of the three labour representatives: George Burt (Canadian Congress of Labour), Percy Bengough (President of the Trades and Labour Congress), and Romeo Vallee (Canadian and Catholic Confederation of Labour).[58] At a subsequent meeting in July 1950 when a draft of the regulation was discussed and approved, both Burt and Bengough were absent[59] and thus neither the CCL nor the TLC had any representation.

It is significant that while the committee endorsed a proposal to require additional conditions for married women, it failed to agree on a similar proposal with respect to pensioners and older workers.[60] Clearly, organized labour's strong representation on the latter issue was a critical factor. The UIAC labour members unequivocally opposed this proposal.[61] Also, the Dominion Joint Legislative Committee of the railway transportation brotherhoods presented a brief voicing strong opposition, arguing that it would be unfair to pensioned railroaders to adopt the proposed requirement that they be eligible for benefit following compulsory retirement from the railway only after working an additional 15 weeks to prove their attachment to the labour force. The brief suggested that many would be denied benefits because they would be unable to find work, and thus the principle on which benefits are normally paid would be reversed. The brotherhoods stated that "this obvious violation of the principles of the Act and the destruction of the equity and right of the potential claimant, when in need, must be recognized."[62] Their statement, however, refers only to pensioners and there does not seem to be a similar concern on the part either of the Railway Brotherhoods, or UIAC labour members, about the violation of principles as far as married women were concerned. It is also significant that following the proposal to impose additional conditions on pensioners, the labour bodies were able to secure an amendment to the UI Act to increase the size of the UIAC, so that by July 1950 the railway brotherhoods (along with the railway companies) had direct representation.[63]

Also, there clearly was discussion of the possibility of a trade-off whereby in exchange for regulations regarding married women or pensioners, other workers would be treated more liberally. The UIAC secretary noted that:

> ... the thought has been that if the Fund could be protected against the drain arising from fraudulent claims and claims from groups whose attachment to the labour market is not continuous or genuine, it would probably be possible to meet the demands of organized labour for a reduction of the waiting period and a change in the provisions governing non-compensable days.[64]

It is not clear, however, to what extent the labour unions participated in this discussion.

In the period immediately following the announcement of a possible regulation, the TLC and the CCL took somewhat different positions. Despite the silence or absence of the CCL representative on the UIAC, there were other indications that at least some of the CCL members were opposed to such a regulation, and the CCL as a whole quickly took a position of strong opposition. At its October 1949 convention (following the acceptance in principle of the regulation), the CCL adopted a recommendation (ironically, from the Committee on UI, chaired by Burt) that the "Congress oppose any attempt to impose special qualification [for UI] on pensioners and married women."[65] Individual staff members indicated their opposition to a married women's regulation,[66] while the March 1950 CCL brief to the federal government called the amendment which placed married women in a special category "a retrograde step."[67] At the September 1950 convention, the CCL Committee on UI stated that it viewed the new section of the Act allowing for the married women's regulation as "discrimination and restrictive, calculated to work an injustice on married women who out of economic necessity must remain in the labour market."[68] The Committee "strongly urged that the elimination of this section be sought and that the Congress strongly oppose all further attempts to enact such provisions into the Act."[69]

Two points clearly emerge from the CCL discussion of the issue. First, while there was concern about discrimination against married women, a more fundamental issue—expressed in the statements at the conventions, in the brief to the federal government, and by individual members—was that such a regulation was simply the thin edge of the wedge that would open up the possibility of similar actions being taken against other groups, particularly pensioners, and that the Act as a whole might be undermined.[70] Secondly, it is clear that when the regulation was first proposed in UIAC deliberations, there was neither the interest nor the ability to oppose a regulation for married women in the same way that there was for pensioners.

The TLC took a position that was somewhat more ambiguous. Its September 1950 convention resolved to express concern about the possible restriction of benefits for pensioners and married women and to urge "the Advisory Committee of the UI Commission to allow the payments of benefits to remain as they are at present" (i.e., prior to the enactment of the regulation).[71] Nevertheless, Percy Bengough, a month later, in a memo to Deputy Minister of Labour MacNamara, stated that the married women's regulation was "both necessary and well thought out."[72] It seems that considerable weight was given to this latter position, for MacNamara stated that "in view of his attitude I think there should be no hesitation about putting through the regulations."[73]

In summary, the introduction of the married women's regulation must be seen in the context of a renewed emphasis on the pre-war ideology that married women belong in the domestic sphere. A policy restricting married women's right to UI was in keeping with the notion that they did not belong in the labour force, and that their status as dependents meant that they had more limited need for income security. The enactment of the regulation also reflected in part the overriding concern of both the business associations and the actuarial adviser (and through this person the UI Commission along with several UIAC members) with the scheme's actuarial soundness and the health of the UI Fund, their very limited conception of income security, and their belief that, given any chance, workers will be quick to defraud the system. This led to a somewhat contradictory view of women. On the one hand, the ideology of domesticity presented the image of the housewife content to take care of her family, worrying about their nutritional needs and providing the foundation for "true democracy."[74] On the other hand, the image presented by the promoters of the married women's regulation was that of the conniving married woman, calculating how to abuse the UI Fund to the maximum and who had to be "controlled by sound regulations."

The enactment of the regulation also has to be seen in the context of the constraints of the post-war economy where limited employment opportunity was available, and where the enactment of "high employment" policies required the withdrawal of large numbers of women from the labour force. In the late 1940s for many women it was an economic necessity to work, but unlike during wartime, women, especially married women, had difficulty finding employment. To some extent, in a classic case of blaming the victim, married women were then signalled out as excessive users of the system.

Finally, it is important to assess the nature of the organization and relative strength of the various social forces both inside and outside the state. The fact that the government's final position coincided with the business associations' position, as well as those sections of the state whose views closely mirrored those of business (for example, the actuarial adviser) suggests the strength of the business position. At the same time, an assessment of the relative strength of different sections of the working class is critical in explaining why regulations were enacted against married women, but not other groups of workers. Reflecting no doubt both the attitude and membership of trade unions at the time, the interests of married women workers were not well represented by labour, and opposition equivalent to that concerning pensioners was not mounted. Nor were married working women well represented by women's organizations. Two that were particularly active at the time were the National Council of Women and the Canadian Federation of Business and Professional Women, both of them overwhelmingly middle class in membership. As will be seen below, these groups initially did not speak out in opposition to the regulation. This meant that the interests of women workers were represented neither by the groups pressuring the state to enact particular policies, nor within the institutions of the state itself which were responsible for implementing UI.

It is significant that when the UIAC was established in 1940 there was a "woman's representative."[75] In 1947, however, the position for a woman on the UIAC was dropped.[76] The inability of women to retain representation on this latter body speaks to the relatively weak position of women in this period. As the Conservative MP Ellen Fairclough (Hamilton West) was later to point out, a large percentage of women in the labour force were not organized. Women were working as clerks in stores and in small places which were not unionized. Most had no voice in the administration of the Act, whether through labour unions, management, or as individuals. Thus it was "comparatively easy for the administration to legislate against them for the purpose of disqualification, whether justified or not."[77]

What did these regulations mean for the women concerned? Two sources provide some indication of how the regulation affected individual women. A number of cases were raised in the House of Commons. In addition, further evidence is provided in the decisions of the UI Umpire. A provision to which many objected was the requirement to work 90 days (later 60 days) *after the first job separation* subsequent to marriage. This meant that women who were recently married (and who left or were laid off from their jobs) and did not meet the exemption requirements had to find *another* employment for 90 days before being able to collect their benefits—even if they had been working and paying contributions for many years. CCF member Clarence Gillis (Cape Breton South) provided an example of what this entailed in his region:

> For example, the Maritime Telephone and Telegraph Company put in a dial system. When that happened a lot of women were let out. Many of them were married, and had gone back to work. Some of them had been working for as long as four or five years. But when they registered for unemployment insurance they were told that since this was their first separation after being married, they must go back and take employment for 60 days in order to qualify. That is the way it was administered. For many, many months we wrestled with that particular problem and it was never cleared up.[78]

CCF member Stanley Knowles pointed out that women not only had to be unemployed, but also had to find work in order to be eligible for benefits:

> ... you require of married women ... not only that they be available and not only that they report once a week; you require that they actually be at work. If a married woman needs work, wants it, and tries her best to get it but cannot get it then you deny her unemployment insurance benefits to which she is otherwise entitled because she has not proven her attachment to the labour market by actually being at work.[79]

Although women who became unemployed because of a shortage of work were exempt from the regulation, there were many other situations in which women who were laid off were disqualified for the two-year period following their marriage. For example, one case involved a woman who worked as a folder in a shirt and overall manufacturing company who said she had been laid off for not working overtime (although she had not been told to do so), while the employer claimed that she was dismissed because her work was not satisfactory. She was disqualified for a period of two years from the date of her marriage.[80] Another situation brought forward by two locals of the United Electrical, Radio and Machine Workers of America (UE) involved 80 women who refused to be strikebreakers by returning to work under the employer's terms. The two women who were recently married were disqualified for the two years following their marriage, while the other 78 were able to claim benefits while seeking employment elsewhere.[81] In another case, a woman writing to Stanley Knowles explained that she lost her job at the T. Eaton Co. when she got married because the policy of the department in which she worked was to not employ married women. However, she did not qualify for an exemption to the married women's regulation since Eaton's stated that they had no overall store policy with regard to married women. She was therefore disqualified from receiving UI for two years from the date of her marriage.[82] In her letter to Knowles she noted that:

> The cost of living is so high that my husband and I find it very difficult to get along with only one of us working. For the past three months I have tried to get a job but have been unable to do so. An Insurance Officer told me in an interview that it was almost impossible to place me now that I was married and this same person also told me that I would have to work 90 days before I could claim benefits. When I appealed my case I asked the court how they expected me to work for 90 days if I was unable to find a job and they said "That is the $64.00 question. We can't answer that."[83]

Many cases involved women who had left their employment or been laid off because of pregnancy. The Act had no specific provisions concerning pregnancy (whether in the case of recently married women, or others). By administrative ruling, however, insurance officers generally disqualified women for a six-week period before the expected date of confinement and for six weeks after it, on the grounds that they were not available for work.[84] Under the married women's regulation, however, married women who were left or were laid off (as many were[85]) because of pregnancy were disqualified for a period of two years following marriage.

Clarence Gillis spoke of a case of "rank miscarriage of justice" where a "little girl" in Sydney had paid into the UI fund for five years, had worked for more than 90 days after marriage, but was laid off because she was pregnant and had "slowed up a bit in her work." She was barred from UI benefits for two years.[86] (She would have had to find work for 90 days *after the first separation* subsequent to marriage in order to qualify.) While the regulation was amended in 1955 to allow an exemption if the separation from employment was due to "illness, injury or quarantine," this did not include pregnancy. In the words of the UI Umpire who ruled on the issue, "there can be no question of incapacity for work due to illness in the case of a mere pregnancy."[87] It seems that pregnancy was still considered a voluntary state, and that women who chose to enter that condition were not deserving of an independent source of income security.

One of the exemptions to the regulation was for those who voluntarily left their job for reasons solely and directly connected with their employment, such as a dangerous work situation (1951 revision). A number of cases cited involved women who left their jobs in order to follow their husbands to another city. They were disqualified for a period of two years following marriage, however, because they voluntarily left their jobs for personal rather than employment-related reasons.[88] (Other people who voluntarily left their employment without just cause generally were disqualified for a period of up to six weeks.[89]) This section of the regulation was later amended (1955) so that a woman moving to another city would qualify, but only if there were "reasonable opportunities for her to obtain suitable employment" in that area. The latter phrase meant that many women were still disqualified.[90]

Thus, in all these cases, it can be seen that the consequence of the regulation was to deny an independent source of income security to married women who otherwise were entitled to benefits. Married women were presumed guilty of abuse until they were able to prove otherwise, by finding employment subsequent to marriage.[91] The regulation, which implied that married women did not really need the money and therefore should not be entitled to UI, was contrary to the basis of the scheme, according to which benefits are a right, not something for which a means test should be applied.[92] The overall consequence for women of the measure was to increase their income instability, to increase their dependence on the male head of the household, where they were responsible for meeting the domestic requirements of the family.

What was the reaction of various groups and political actors after the regulation was enacted? Business organizations several times expressed their approval of the regulation.[93] Both the Commission and the actuarial adviser also went to considerable lengths to justify the regulation. For example, Watson, in his report of July 1954, calculated that while the number of married women in insurable employment was about half the number of single women, the number of benefits days paid to them was more than three times as great.[94] While seeming oblivious to the possibility that this might reflect the difficulty married women faced in finding permanent jobs, he argued that the claims of married women on benefit were excessive both as to number and duration.[95] The UI Commission took up this theme and stated that the proportion would be even higher if the regulation were not in force to control unjustified claims.[96] It also suggested that married women were using various tactics when they were sent to jobs to cause employers to reject them, so they could remain on UI. For instance, "trained stenographers who have been taking shorthand for years have suddenly found they have lost their knowledge."[97]

On the other hand, there were numerous protests against the regulation by labour organizations and women's groups, as well as by various members of the House of Commons. Ellen Fairclough, who appears at the time to have been the parliamentary spokesperson for women's organizations, was probably the most persistent of the MPs at calling for its elimination. She also urged on numerous occasions that there be provision for the representation of women on both the UI Commission and the UIAC, and on more than one occasion proposed amendments to that effect.[98] Stanley Knowles and Clarence Gillis of the CCF also, as noted above, played an important role in urging that "this discrimination against married women ... be eliminated."[99]

Of the central labour bodies, the CCL continued to play the most active role in protesting against the married women's regulation and in urging its repeal. Although the regulation did not top its list of concerns about UI in the 1950s (it generally being listed after such issues as the extension of coverage to other occupations, the increase in benefit rates, and so on), the CCL nevertheless had the most visible role (along with MPs) in calling for its repeal. CCL annual conventions consistently passed resolutions reiterating its opposition to the regulation.[100] In its annual brief to the federal government, its submissions to the UIAC and to the UI Commission, the CCL repeatedly expressed its opposition to the discriminatory treatment of married women claimants and called for the elimination, or at least drastic revision, of the married women's regulation and Section 38(1)(d) of the Act allowing the Commission to make regulations regarding married women.[101] Protests against the married women's regulation were also registered at meetings of the labour representatives on the Courts of Referees (attended by the CCL, TLC and CCCL). This was particularly the case for meetings in Quebec, where for example, "the members ... insisted that the regulation be repealed."[102]

One of the major labour initiatives on the issue was a 1951 joint submission to the UI Umpire by the three labour bodies (CCL, TLC, and CCCL), undertaken at the behest of the CCL.[103] The labour representatives argued that Section 38(1)(d) and Benefit Regulation 5A had resulted in "unjustifiably discriminatory action against certain married women"; had introduced an inconsistency in the Act by creating a "class of persons" distinguishable not by the nature of their employment or by their wage arrangement, but merely by marital status; that the blanket disqualification of married women meant that the innocent were being made to suffer; that "this is flagrantly contradictory to our whole concept of justice and to the practice of law in this country" and "is a gross abuse of authority by the Commission and a strengthening of the dead hand of the bureaucracy."[104] The labour submission further objected to the fact that the regulation was applied retroactively and that it was so restrictive that neither the Courts of Referees nor the Umpire had much leeway to modify the insurance officer's decisions. Thus, argued the labour delegation, it curtailed and inhibited the right of appeal provided for in the Act.[105]

The Canadian and Catholic Confederation of Labour also clearly voiced its opposition to the married women's regulation. In addition to participating with the other labour bodies in presentations to the UI Umpire and the UI Commission in which it urged the elimination of the regulation,[106] the CCCL, in its annual brief to Cabinet regularly requested the abolition of the sections of the UI Act and the Regulations which placed married women in a special category.[107] Indeed, in 1951 the CCCL devoted a whole section of their brief (considerably more than the other labour bodies) to the married women's regulation, declaring that it could not agree to "the disqualification in advance of a whole category of insured persons simply because it is more difficult to verify their good faith."[108]

The TLC, on the other hand, was somewhat less active in opposing the regulation. Resolutions continued to be brought forward and passed at TLC conventions expressing opposition to and urging the repeal of the married women's regulation and accompanying statutes.[109] The TLC executive, however, appeared at best lukewarm in its opposition to the regulation. Unlike the CCL, it did not raise the issue in submissions to the UIAC.[110] In a 1951 joint meeting of labour representatives with the UI Commission, the TLC—unlike the other two labour bodies—did not argue that the married women's regulation should be revoked. It simply urged that the words "after her first separation" be dropped so that the additional 90 days that a married women would have to work would simply be after her marriage.[111] The TLC executive council annual convention reports regularly recommended changes to the UI Act, but it was only in 1955 that one urged the removal of the married women's regulation.[112] Similarly, each year in its brief to the federal government, the TLC recommended changes to the UI provisions. But it was not until 1952 that this included changes to the married women's regulation and then it simply was stated that the regulation "should be given more sympathetic consideration" and that the "90 days required to establish benefit rights should be reduced to

60."[113] It is only in 1954 and 1955 that their brief called for abolishing the married women's regulation altogether.[114]

The Canadian Labour Congress, formed with the CCL-TLC merger of 1956, seems to have taken up the former CCL's strong opposition to the married women's regulation. For example, a 1957 brief strongly urged the removal of these regulations, stating that they "perpetuate inequities and discrimination, result in anomalies and undermine confidence in the Act."[115] Individual union locals also played a role in representing their members before the Courts of Referees and the Umpire and urging that the regulation be rescinded.[116]

Women's organizations had a much less institutionalized forum for expressing their views on unemployment insurance than did the labour organizations. Again, this reflected their relative strength and organization at the time. Not only did organized labour have representation on the UIAC and the UIC, but it often made submissions to the UIAC. Women's organizations, on the other hand, had a much less visible presence. It seems they usually were not notified of hearings on the subject of UI or invited to attend.[117] Nevertheless, both individual women and women's organizations as a whole eventually came to play an important role in urging the repeal of the regulation. Two groups which took a stand on the issue were the National Council of Women in Canada (NCW) and the Canadian Federation of Business and Professional Women's Clubs (BPW).

The National Council of Women was an umbrella group to which a range of organizations—church-based, professional, and other—were affiliated.[118] While their meetings to some extent were concerned with arranging social functions, they also discussed and passed resolutions on many important matters of the day, ranging from the guaranteed annual wage to international peace. They supported equal rights and greater opportunities for women in many fields, including the appointment of women to the civil service commission, the Senate and the UI Court of Referees;[119] the right of women to serve on juries; and equal pay legislation.[120] On labour issues, however, their positions often reflected the middle-class bias of their membership. For example, the Economic and Taxation Committee of the NCW suggested that "women of Canada might use their influence to discourage wage demands."[121] On the issue of unemployment, their concern largely took the form of an effort to have their homes redecorated or renovated during the winter months. This was at least in part at the urging of the federal government which had undertaken a campaign to stimulate winter employment.[122]

On the question of the married women's regulation, there was little recorded discussion until the mid-1950s. When a resolution was passed on the issue by the Council of Women of West Algoma in 1951, it was not brought forward to the annual NCW meeting because members of the executive who were in contact with the UI Commission expressed the view that the Commission was dealing with the issue and thus "they did not think anything would be gained by Council action at the present time."[123] In 1953 the issue was discussed in a number of local councils.[124] There is little indication of the content of these discussions, although the Winnipeg Trades and Professions Committee did note that "since recent amendments to this Regulation there appears to be a minimum of hardship imposed on married women ... The benefit fund ... is definitely *not* a subsidy ...."[125]

At the 1954 annual NCW meeting, a resolution was nevertheless brought forward by the Trades and Professions Committee of the Toronto Council of Women that Regulation 5A be rescinded and that the "UI Commission take the same action to protect the Unemployment Insurance Fund against unjust claims from married women as is taken with other categories of claimants."[126] The government's case that married women were claiming a disproportionate amount of benefit was presented by Ruth Hamilton, UIC adviser on women's employment,[127] and after some discussion, the resolution was defeated by 139 to 41 votes.[128] This position was reversed, however, when the same resolution passed at the NCW's 1956 convention.[129] Subsequently, the NCW made representations requesting that the married women's regulation be rescinded both to the labour minister[130] and to Prime Minister Louis St. Laurent.[131]

The BPW brought together women in business and the professions and thus tended to be more focused on the issue of women's employment opportunities. They also passed resolutions on a variety of issues that would improve the position of women. They urged the introduction of equal pay legislation, the removal of discrimination against married women in the federal civil service, the appointment of women to the Senate, the establishment of a women's bureau by the federal government, and so on.[132] On numerous occasions, the BPW passed resolutions urging the federal government to appoint a woman to the UI Commission[133] and that the UI Act be amended to include "sex" as a basis for nondiscrimination in referring applicants to employers (this already was the case with respect to race, creed, colour, ancestry, and origin).[134] Resolutions at both the 1954 and 1956 biennial conventions were passed urging the revocation of the married women's regulation.[135] Representations urging the repeal of the regulation were subsequently made to the federal Minister of Labour, to the Industrial Relations Committee examining the 1955 revisions to the UI Act, and to both Prime Ministers St. Laurent and John Diefenbaker.[136]

The married women's regulation was revoked on 15 November 1957 by PC 1957-1477, shortly after Diefenbaker's Conservative government came to power. Labour Minister Michael Starr, announcing the order in council, cited two reasons for it: a dislike of discrimination, and the continually increasing importance and permanence of married women as working women.[137] In addition, as noted above, both labour and women's groups played a critical role in pushing for the revocation of the regulation. While labour had been more consistently and for a longer period of time urging the abolition of the married women's regulation, the addition in the mid-1950s of the voice of women's organizations was nevertheless crucial.[138] The position of women's groups was given added weight by the fact that Ellen Fairclough, a member of the BPW who for many years had spoken out against the discrimination of women in this regulation, had become a cabinet minister (although not directly responsible for UI) in the new Diefenbaker government.[139]

The question of a special regulation for married women remained a contentious issue into the early 1960s. The issue came up again in the UIAC where, at the request in 1959 of one of the employer representatives, the Commission prepared a memorandum outlining the history of the married women's regulation, providing figures that showed that the proportion of married women claiming benefit had increased since the regulation had been revoked[140] (which is hardly surprising, given the number that had been excluded), and reasserting that "many married women are claiming benefit when they are not really unemployed and available for employment and unable to find work."[141] The Commission also suggested a number of possible solutions, including a return to the old regulation; that a married woman could be excluded from receiving benefit if her husband was employed; that a married women could be disqualified as not available for employment if she had children under school age, and so on.[142] Unlike a decade earlier, however, UIAC members were unable to agree on a recommendation to reinstate some form of regulation for married women. While the employer-members were in favour of such a regulation, the labour representatives were opposed to it. Thus, in the end, no recommendation was forthcoming.[143]

There were also attempts on the part of the Canadian Manufacturer's Association to bring back the regulation. For example, in the CMA's 1959 brief, it was stated strongly that "abuses must be eliminated ... or the Fund will be drained by special minority groups at the expense of the majority of contributors," and that "[a]lthough the Married Women's Regulations were reasonable and designed solely to limit a manifest abuse, they were attacked by women's organizations and labour unions which claimed that married women were being discriminated against."[144] This was followed in 1960 by a virulent letter to the labour minister which argued that UI Act changes had "resulted in dangerous dissipation of the Unemployment Insurance Fund," and identified seasonal workers and "certain types of workers who have left the labour force such as housewives and retired persons" as the source of the drain.[145]

The question of the status of unemployed married women and their use of the UI system also surfaced at the 1960 hearings of a Senate special committee on manpower and employment. Dr. Warren James[146] cited figures to show that a disproportionate number of those registering at UI offices for jobs were married women, particularly under the age of 45, young people, and men over 65.[147] For example, he found that the proportion of women registered for jobs at UI offices who were married (67 percent) was much greater than the proportion of married women in the labour force as a whole (46 percent).[148] He also calculated that two-thirds of married women had a "somewhat tenuous attachment to the labour market,"[149] and concluded that "there are some systematic influences at work which lead many of these people to register for jobs although their membership in the labour force is clearly often marginal."[150]

The economist Sylvia Ostry, appearing before the Committee as an academic expert, similarly drew attention to the phenomenon she referred to as "schizoid respondents"—married women, elderly men, and seasonal workers who classified themselves as "unemployed and seeking work" for the purpose of collecting UI, but not when asked the question by the monthly labour force survey administered by the Dominion Bureau of Statistics.[151] Both of these studies were taken up in the Senate committee's report, which suggested that the high proportion of married women registering for jobs at UI offices "reflects some features of the unemployment insurance system which merit attention."[152]

The actual use that these experts made of the statistics is, it should be noted, highly questionable. It repeatedly was pointed out that the concept of unemployment used in Dominion Bureau of Statistics labour force survey could not be compared to that used for UI purposes.[153] For example, in the labour force survey, if a person had been laid off because of bad weather, or with instructions to return to work within 30 days, he or she was not considered unemployed, yet was entitled to draw UI benefit. Similarly, a person working at all during the survey week, even for part of a day, was not considered as unemployed, but could be drawing UI.

What is lacking in these studies from the period is any analysis of the particular employment situation of married women, or any suggestion that perhaps both the high rate of claims and the high proportion registering for work at UI offices might reflect the difficulty such women had in obtaining jobs, and their concentration in vulnerable employment areas, where they were more likely to be laid off. That such might have been the case was suggested, for instance, in various statements during the early 1950s by the Women's Division of the National Employment Service (the section of the UI Commission that referred people to jobs). For example, the division reported that in 1950 there was a steady increase in the number of female applicants registered at local offices of the Commission for whom it was not possible to find suitable employment. This situation was attributed at least in part to the rising cost of living in Canada and the necessity for married women to find work in order to augment family incomes.[154] In both 1951 and 1952, the division had difficulty filling orders for secretaries, stenographers, and typists although competent women with good qualifications were available:

> ... it was generally the experience of placement officers that most of these applicants were married or in the older age brackets, and thus could not meet requirements of employers' orders in many instances. Despite efforts of

employment officers to persuade employers to consider such applicants, the general trend was for single women well under thirty years of age.[155]

The Women's Division reported in 1954 that the number of unplaced female job applicants had steadily increased, while the number of job vacancies had decreased.[156] Women also appear to have been over-represented among those placed in casual jobs by the U1 employment service, and therefore would be more likely to have renewed claims for benefits. In 1952, women accounted for 36.3 percent of regular placements, but 63 percent of casual placements.[157]

In fact, it appears that women as a whole were not drawing a disproportionate number of claims. Svanhuit Jose, a labour economist appearing at a later round of hearings, pointed out that when account was taken of both single and married women (and many married women had previously contributed as single women), it was evident that a much smaller proportion of women were drawing benefits than were in the insured population and that the proportion of UI money they received was even less. Specifically, she calculated that between 1942 and 1959 women made up from 25 percent to 34 percent of the insured labour force, but accounted for a minimum of 13 percent and a maximum of 26 percent of those drawing benefits, and that the proportion of money paid out that went to women varied from 11 percent to 26 percent.[158] What her figures show is that, far from being a drain on the UI Fund, women as a whole were *subsidizing* it! Nor is there any indication that the UI Fund was actually being drained. The balance in the Fund rose steadily from the time it was started to a peak of $927 million in December 1956.[159] It reached such a high point that the CCL suggested it was over-funded and that the benefit rate consequently should be increased.[160]

The subject of married women's regulation came up a final time during the 1961 hearing of the Committee of Inquiry into UI (the Gill Committee). The committee was set up in part because by the end of the 1950s, unemployment had risen to seven percent and for the first time there was a depletion of the UI Fund. Its terms of reference included determining "the means of correcting any abuses or deficiencies that might be found to exist." A long list of business organizations accused married women (again, along with older workers and seasonal workers) of draining the Fund and urged the reinstatement of married women's regulations.[161] This included the Canadian Manufacturer's Association and the Canadian Construction Association (both of which seemed to have changed their position little in the intervening 10 years) as well as the Canadian Retail Federation, the Canadian Chamber of Commerce, the Canadian Life Insurance Officers' Association, the Canadian Metal Mining Association, the Canadian Lumberman's Association (which claimed that "the greatest abuse is from married women"), and the Canadian Pulp and Paper Association (which argued that "secondary" wage earners should be subjected to more stringent requirements than heads of families). Office Overload, describing itself as giving employment to more than 15,000 mostly married women every year and one of the largest employers of female office workers in Canada, while not calling specifically for regulations for married women, did state that "coming into daily contact as we do with so many temporary workers—as most of these married women are in the labour force for a relatively short period of time ... we are exposed to perhaps more than our share of abuses of the U.I. Fund."[162]

Yet, a number of organizations rejected the reinstatement of regulations for married women. In some respects the tenor of the hearings with respect to women had changed considerably since the time the regulation first was enacted. First, women, both as individuals and as members of organizations, had a more visible presence. Of the two major women's organizations, the NCW in this instance provided the stronger statement with regard to the possibility of a new regulation for married women, declaring that they were "unalterably opposed to any change in regulations which would be prejudicial to the rights and interests of women, whether married or single."[163] The BPW brief contained no specific reference to the question of regulations for married women, but did recommend the inclusion of "sex" in clauses preventing discrimination in employment.[164] A second change was greater support from labour unions on the issue. The National Legislative Committee of the International Railway Brotherhood, which 10 years previously had represented only the interests of pensioners, now stated "its opposition to discrimination against any particular group."[165] A number of other groups and individuals appearing before the committee expressed similarly strong and unequivocal opposition to the reinstatement of regulations restricting benefits to married women. This included the CLC, the Government of Saskatchewan, and Svanhuit Jose, who appeared as an individual before the Committee and expressed concern about "the attacks on working women—most of them unfounded."[166]

Thus, despite the studies of the experts and the requests from business groups, the married women's regulation was not reinstated.[167] This change in state policy reflected a shift in two respects in the position of working women—especially married working women. First, changes were beginning to occur in the prevailing ideology concerning the proper role for women. Between 1951 and 1961, women's overall labour force participation role increased from 24 percent to 29 percent while that of married women doubled from 11 percent to 22 percent and it had increased more than five times (from approximately 4 percent) since 1941.[168] Married women were becoming an increasingly important source of labour both for the growing service sector and the state. This development meant that the idea that women only worked for a short time before marriage and then belonged in the home no longer corresponded to the reality of women's lives. It seemed increasingly anomalous for state policy to be based on such a notion. That changes were beginning to occur in the prevailing ideology is evidenced, for example, in the statement by the Labour Minister, Starr, in announcing the revocation of the regulation, the increased acceptance of the notion that women should be paid equally for work they perform, and so on.[169]

Secondly, the representation of women's interests in the political arena was beginning to change; this would later become more clearly articulated in the "second wave of feminism" of the 1960s. As women began to play an increasingly important role in the paid labour force, their interests came to be better represented both by labour and by women's organizations. While figures on the number of women in unions are not available for this period,[170] increased concern about women workers on the part of labour by the late 1950s can be seen in the growing number of discussions on the role of women in trade unions, the formation of white-collar organizing committees, and the establishment of women's committees in some of the central labour bodies.[171] Women's organizations also had a renewed interest in equality rights for women workers, as evidenced not only by their actions with respect to UI, but also through their efforts to have equal pay legislation introduced, to have a woman's bureau established in the federal Department of Labour, and so on. Particularly important, on certain issues, labour and women's organizations now had a commonality of viewpoint. The result was that whereas in 1950 it was possible to enact a regulation that disqualified a large number of married women from receiving UI benefits, by 1960 this was no longer possible.

Conclusion

It has been seen that the post-war UI scheme contributed in two ways to the tendency to restrict both employment possibilities and income security for women. The first was that in the years immediately following the war, women—unlike men—were disqualified for a period of time from receiving UI unless they accepted work in low-wage sectors, often at a fraction of the pay they had received during the war. The second was the introduction in 1950 of a regulation imposing additional conditions on married women. Combined, these policies had the effect of disqualifying a large number of women from receiving benefits to which they were otherwise entitled, denying many married women an independent source of income security, and contributing to the concentration of women in low-wage job ghettoes. The consequence was to increase women's dependence on the male head of the household and to reinforce the view that women's place was primarily in the domestic sphere.

A second concern of the article has been the question of the formation and dynamic of change in state policies, particularly with regard to women. In this respect, a greater understanding of the role of gender relations, including changes in the prevailing ideology as well as in the relative strength and political representation of women, is important. The married women's regulation was introduced in the context of the economic constraints of the post-war period, where there was a renewed emphasis on the idea that married women belonged in the domestic sphere, but not in the labour force. As the 1950s progressed, however, there was a considerable erosion in this ideology of domesticity. As married women entered the labour force in increasing numbers, the idea that they belonged exclusively in the home no longer corresponded to the reality of their lives. It became more difficult to justify a policy that was based on such an assumption. In addition, in the late 1940s, working women, who constituted a relatively small part of the labour force, were not well represented either by labour or by women's organizations. By the late 1950s, however, both groups began to pursue more actively the issue of equal rights for women workers. The combined opposition of both these groups to a policy that discriminated against certain women was key both in the revocation of the married women's regulation and in ensuring that a similar one was not later reinstated.

Endnotes

1. Alvin Finkel, *Business and Social Reform in the Thirties* (Toronto 1979), ch VI.
2. Carl Cuneo, "State Mediation of Class Contradictions in Canadian Unemployment Insurance, 1930–1935," *Studies in Political Economy*, 3 (1980); Carl Cuneo, "State, Class and Reserve Labour: The Case of the 1941 Canadian Unemployment Insurance Act," *Canadian Review of Sociology and Anthropology*, 16(2)(1979).
3. Leslie A. Pal, "Relative Autonomy Revisited: The Origins of Canadian Unemployment Insurance," *Canadian Journal of Political Science*, XIX:1 (March 1986); Leslie A. Pal, *State, Class and Bureaucracy: Canadian Unemployment Insurance and Public Policy* (Montreal 1988).
4. For an overview of the provisions of the 1940 UI Act see Gary Dingledine, *A Chronology of Response: The Evolution of Unemployment Insurance from 1940 to 1980*, prepared for Employment and Immigration Canada (Ottawa 1981); Leslie Pal, *State, Class and Bureaucracy*; Ray Brown, "Unemployment Insurance and the national Employment Service," *Labour Gazette* (September 1950).
5. Dingledine, *Chronology*, 13.
6. See, for example, Finkel, *Business and Social Reform*, ch VI; Cuneo, "State Mediation"; Cuneo, "State, Class and Reserve Labour"; Leslie A. Pal, "Relative Autonomy Revisited"; Carl Cuneo, "Restoring Class to State Unemployment Insurance," *Canadian Journal of Political Science*, XIX:1 (March 1986); Pal, *State, Class and Bureaucracy*; James Struthers, *"No Fault of Their Own": Unemployment and the Canadian Welfare State, 1914–1941* (Toronto 1983).
7. Ruth Roach Pierson, "Gender and the Unemployment Insurance Debates in Canada, 1934–1940," *Labour/Le Travail*, 25 (1990), 102.
8. Ibid., 93–5.

9. For a discussion of the recruitment of women into the labour force during the war, see Ruth Roach Pierson, *"They're Still Women After All": The Second World War and Canadian Womanhood* (Toronto 1986), ch 1.
10. Labour Canada, Women's Bureau, *Women in the Labour Force: Facts and Figures* (1973 edition) (Ottawa 1974), 227. The proportion of the female labour force in manufacturing increased from 27 percent in 1939 to 37 percent in 1943, while that in domestic service dropped from 18.6 percent to 9.3 percent. Canada, Department of Labour, *Canadian Labour Market* (June 1946), 20.
11. Canada, Department of Labour, *Canadian Labour Market* (December 1946), 16. Before the war, the highest weekly wage paid to women was an average of $15.83 in the fur goods industry. In contrast, during the war, in aircraft manufacturing, shipbuilding and repairs, women received and unprecedented wage of $31.81 per week. Ibid. (June 1946), 20–1.
12. See for example, Leonard Marsh, *Report on Social Security in Canada*, 1943 (Reprinted Toronto 1975), especially the chapter devoted to "women's needs," 209–14.
13. Ibid., 212; Canada, *Department of Reconstruction, Employment and Income with Special Reference to the Initial Period of Reconstruction* (Ottawa 1945), 3.
14. Marsh, *Report on Social Security*, 210. The Marsh Report also discusses the suggestion (present in the Beveridge Report) that women's retirement from the labour force might be encouraged by a general marriage grant or bonus, or allowing previously employed women, on marriage, a commutation of all unemployment insurance contributions paid into the fund. He makes no recommendation on the subject, however. Ibid., 212–3.
15. Gail Cuthbert Brandt, "'Pigeon-Holed and Forgotten': The Work of the Subcommittee on the Post-War Problems of Women, 1943," *Histoire sociale/Social History*, XV, 29 (May 1982), 253, 250.
16. Pierson, *They're Still Women*, 55–60.
17. Ibid., 82.
18. Ibid., 49.
19. Ibid., 83–88.
20. Brandt, "'Pigeon-Holed,'" 239–40.
21. Labour Canada, Women's Bureau, *Women in the Labour Force* (1973 edition), 227.
22. Canada, Department of Reconstruction, *Employment and Income*, 1.
23. Canada, Department of Labour, *Canadian Labour Market* (June 1946), 23.
24. Ibid. (August 1951), 1.
25. Canada, Unemployment Insurance Commission, *Decisions of the Umpire, 1943–1948*, CUB-168, 29 November 1946, 196.
26. Ibid., CUB-122, 6 September 1946, 158.
27. Ibid., CUB-317, 5 February 1948, 327.
28. Ibid. It should be noted that the Umpire's decisions record only those cases which went through to a second level of appeal, and not of all instances of a particular type of disqualification.
29. Significantly, in the 1945–46 period approximately 43 percent of cases coming before the Umpire were brought by women, even though they made up only 34 percent of the insured population (Canada, Dominion Bureau of Statistics, Annual Report on Current Benefit Years Under the Unemployment Insurance Act, 1945, table A, 6). In addition to refusing to accept work at reduced rates of pay, a number of women were disqualified for a certain period of time for such things as wanting to restrict hours of work because of domestic responsibilities, or leaving their job to follow their husbands to another city. In general, it seems that the UI scheme was designed with the male worker as a model, and that in a number of instances the position of women created certain anomalies and meant that they did not fit comfortably within the guidelines laid out by the Act.
30. Canada, Unemployment Insurance Commission, *Decision of the Umpire, 1943–1948* (Ottawa nd), CUB-165, 22 November 1946, 194.
31. Ibid., CUB-113, 25 July 1946, 149.
32. Canada, House of Commons, Debates, 14 July 1947, 5637.
33. Ibid., 5638.
34. Ibid.
35. A government document noted that in 1946 the greatest demand for women was concentrated in the lower-paying occupations such as service work, textile work, and unskilled positions. Canada, Department of Labour, *Canadian Labour Market* (June 1946), 21–2.

36. Canada, House of Commons, Debates, 19 February 1951, 453.
37. Canada, Committee of Inquiry into the Unemployment Insurance Act (Gill Committee) *Report* (Ottawa 1962), 31.
38. Pierson, "Gender," 95.
39. Ibid.
40. See, for example, National Archives of Canada (NAC) Unemploment Insurance Commission (UIC) Records, RG50, vol. 53, 18th meeting UIAC, July 1950, UI Commission to UIAC, 27 June 1950.
41. See, for example, NAC, UIC Records, RG50, vol. 59, file 1, UIAC Correspondence 1946–47, J.G. Bisson, Chief Commissioner to Hon. Humphrey Mitchell, Minister of Labour, 30 August 1947. Bisson noted that several people at the July 1947 meeting of the UIAC argued that the increase in total benefit paid out during the previous year largely reflected the laying off of married women and older persons employed during the war who would not ordinarily have been working or have built up benefits rights.
42. See NAC, UIC Records, RG50, vol. 53, 16th meeting UIAC, July 1949, C.A.L. Murchison, Commissioner UIC to UIAC, 11 July 1949. Murchison suggested that there were two reasons for the drain on the Fund by married women. The first was married women who were laid off after the war, but by 1949 this group had practically ceased to be a problem. The second was the many young women who, on marriage, had no intention of continuing to work, but because job opportunities were not readily available, were able to draw benefits.
43. NAC, UIC Records, RG50, vol. 60, UIAC Reports 1941–1947, "Raiding Jobless Insurance Fund," *Edmonton Journal and Edmonton Bulletin*, 20 December 1946.
44. NAC, UIC Records, RG50, vol. 53, 16th meeting UIAC, July 1949, submission from Canadian Manufacturers Association to UIAC 13 July 1949; submission from Canadian Construction Association to UIAC 16 July 1949.
45. NAC, UIC Records, RG50, vol. 53, 16th meeting UIAC, July 1949, submission from Canadian Construction Association to UIAC 16 July 1949, 2.
46. Canada, Unemployment Insurance Commission, Annual Report (1951), 37.
47. NAC, UIC Records, RG50, vol. 53, 16th meeting UIAC, July 1949, C.A.L. Murchison, Commissioner, UIC to UIAC, 11 July 1949.
48. NAC, UIC Records, RG50, vol. 53, 16th meeting UIAC, July, 1949, "Minutes of the Meeting," 9.
49. NAC, UIC Records, RG50, vol. 53, 17th meeting UIAC, January 1950, "Actuarial Report for the UIAC," 23 December 1949, 24, 28.
50. Ibid., 28.
51. Ibid.
52. Leslie Pal argues that the administrative expertise involved in an insurance scheme took the form of an "actuarial ideology" which was largely removed from class forces. See Pal, "Relative Autonomy Revisited"; Pal, *State, Class and Bureaucracy*.
53. NAC, Department of Labour Records, RG 27, vol. 3458, file 4-11, pt. 5, M.M. Maclean, Director, Industrial Relations Branch to A. MacNamara, 3 October 1950.
54. Ibid., MacNamaara to W.A. Mackintosh, Chairman, UIAC, 4 October 1950.
55. Ibid., MacNamara to N. Robertson, Clerk of the Privy Council, 12 October 1950.
56. During the war Fraudena Eaton was the head of the Women's Division of the National Selective Service agency created to oversee the recruitment and allocation of labour. See Alison Prentice et al., *Canadian Women: A History* (Toronto 1988), 297. In 1956 she became president of the National Council of Women. Rosa L. Shaw, *Proud Heritage: A History of the National Council of Women in Canada* (Toronto 1957).
57. NAC, Department of Labour Records, RG 27, vol. 3458, file 4-11, pt. 5, MacNamara to Mrs. Eaton, 1 April 1950. Another exchange of letters is carried out in a similar vein. In response to a question about the case of "a girl" who married her employer, the UIC legal advisor notes that "of course ... she may obtain relief if her husband becomes incapacitated, dies or is permanently separated from her and I do hope that this provision will not encourage self-imposed widowhood and reveal whatever criminal tendencies a woman may possess." MacNamara take this up and notes that "possibly the best thing for the girl to do would be to send off the attractive male." Ibid., Claude Dubuc to MacNamara, 28 October 1950; MacNamara to Bengough, 30 October 1950.

58. NAC, UIC Records, RG50, vol. 53, 16th meeting UIAC, July 1949, "Minutes of the Meeting." At least one state official expressed surprise at labour's position, noting that it seemed odd that the labour members of the UIAC had approved such a regulation, even in principle. NAC, Department of Labour Records, RG27, vol. 3458, file 4-11, pt. 5, M.M. Maclean, Director, Industrial Relations Branch to MacNamara, 3 October 1950.
59. NAC, UIC Records, RG50, vol. 53, 18th meeting UIAC, July 1950, "Minutes of the Meeting."
60. NAC, Department of Labour Records, RG27, vol. 3458, file 4-11, pt. 5. G.M. Ingersoll to A. MacNamara, 23 November 1949. The issue was also raised at the meeting of the UIAC, January 1950 and the Committee agreed not to recommend amendment of the Act in this regard. NAC, UIC Records, RG50, vol. 53, 17th meeting UIAC, January 1950, "Minutes of the Meeting," 8.
61. NAC, Canadian Labour Congress (CLC) Files, MG28I103, vol. 25, file 2 United Automobile, Aircraft and Agricultural Implement Workers of America, George Burt, 1947–50, Burt to A.R. Mosher, President, CCL, 9 August 1949.
62. NAC, UIC Records, RG50, vol. 53, 17th meeting UIAC, January 1950, "Minutes of the Meeting"; submission, Dominion Joint Legislative Committee, Railway Transporation Brotherhoods.
63. *Labour Gazette* (April 1950), 534; (June 1950), 792.
64. NAC, Department of Labour Records, RG 27, vol. 3458, file 4-11, pt. 5, Ingersoll to MacNamara, 7 October 1950. See also Ibid., Ingersoll to MacNamara, 23 November 1949. A similar point was made at a meeting of the UIAC by the chairperson of the Committee. NAC, UIC Records, RG50, vol. 53, 17th meeting UIAC January 1950, "Minutes of the Meeting."
65. Canadian Congress of Labour, *Proceedings of the Ninth Annual Convention* (October 1949), 96, 98.
66. See, for example, NAC, CLC Files, MG28 I103, vol. 25, file 2, Andy Andras to Pat Conroy, Secretary Treasurer CCL, 7 March 1950; Ibid, vol. 238, file 238-16, Sam Wolstein to Pat Conroy, 4 March 1950.
67. *Canadian Unionist* (April 1950), 80.
68. CCL, *Proceedings of the Tenth Annual Convention* (1950), 76.
69. Ibid., 76–77.
70. For example, the CCL brief to the federal government expressed the concern that such a regulation "is likely to lead to the undermining of the Act by the imposition of restrictions against other classes of workers," *Canadian Unionist* (April 1950), 80. See also NAC, CLC files, MG 28 I103, vol. 25, file 2, Andras to Conroy, 7 March 1950; CCL, *Proceedings of the Tenth Annual Convention* (1950), 76.
71. Trades and Labor Congress of Canada, Report of the Proceedings of the Annual Convention (September 1950), 444. The resolution was brought forward by the New Brunswick Federation of Labour.
72. NAC, Department of Labour Records, RG27, vol. 3458, file 4-11, pt. 5, Bengough to MacNamara, 24 October 1950. He is referring both to the married women's and to another regulation.
73. Ibid., MacNamara to Norman Robertson, Clerk of the Privy Council and Secretary to the Cabinet, 26 October 1950.
74. The term is from the Subcommittee on the Post-war Problems of Women, Brandt, "'Pigeon-Holed,'" 249.
75. NAC, UIC Records, RG50, vol. 59, Ingersoll to A.H. Brown, 30 April 1947. This was Miss Estelle Hewson, from the Border Branch of the Canadian Red Cross Society, Windsor.
76. It is not clearly specified why this change took place. At this time the number of employer and employee representatives was increased from two to three and it was argued that this did not leave room for a women's representative, since the maximum number on the Committee was six plus the chairperson. It appears that the change may have been to ensure regional representation and to allow the addition of a representative from the Quebec labour movement. See Ibid., MacNamara to V.R. Smith, 23 June 1947; Mackintosh to Stangroom 20 August 1946, Ingersoll to Brown, 30 April 1947.
77. Canada, House of Commons, Debates, 10 June 1955, 4625. See also Canada, House of Commons, Standing Committee on Industrial Relations, *Minutes of Proceedings and Evidence*, 26 May 1955, 187–8.

78. Canada, House of Commons, Standing Committee on Industrial Relations, *Minutes of Proceedings and Evidence*, 6 June 1955, 475.
79. Canada, House of commons, Debates, 18 May 1951, 3203.
80. Canada, Unemployment Insurance Commission, *Digest of the Decisions of the Umpire* (Ottawa 1960), CUB 848, 21 August 1952.
81. Canada, House of Commons, Standing Committee on Industrial Relations, *Minutes of Proceedings and Evidence*, 26 May 1955, 262.
82. NAC, Standley Knowles Papers, MG32 C59, file 19-A, UIC cases, correspondence 1942–1952, Mrs. Dora Doersam to Stanley Knowles, 10 May 1951; Milton F. Gregg, Minister of Labour to Stanley Knowles, 11 June 1951. In a subsequent similar case where a woman lost her job at the T. Eaton Co. because of department policy not to keep on married women, the decision to disqualify her was successfully appealed and the woman was therefore able to collect benefits. See Decision of the Umpire CUB 859, 5 September 1952. Quoted in *Labour Gazette* (January, 1953), 118–9.
83. NAC, Stanley Knowles Papers, MG32 C59, file 19-A, UIC cases, correspondence, 1942–1952, Mrs. Dora Doersam to Stanley Knowles, 10 May 1951.
84. See NAC, UIC Records, RG 50, vol. 53, 16th meeting UIAC, July 1949, C.A.L. Murchison, Commissioner, UIC to UIAC 11 July 1949. See also NAC, Department of Labour Records, RG 27, vol. 3458, file 4-11, pt. 7, J.G. Bisson, Chief Commissioner, UIC, to Minister of Labour, 3 September 1954.
85. See for example, Canada, Unemployment Insurance Commission, Digest, CUB 1101, 8 December 1954. In this case an employer laid off a pregnant women six months before her due date and she was disqualified for two years from receiving UI.
86. Canada, House of Commons, Debates, 13 July 1952, 3197–8.
87. CUB 1215, 9 February 1956, reported in *Labour Gazette* (April 1956), 428.
88. Canada, Unemployment Insurance Commission, Digest, CUBS 772 and 773, 6 December, 1951.
89. Dingledine, *Chronology*, 13. Regulation 5A also went much further than the general provision of the Act in recognizing as just cause for leaving employment only those reasons solely and directly connected with employment.
90. See, for instance, Canada, Unemployment Insurance Commission, *Digest*, CUB 1457, 7 February 1958. This issue was also brought up a number of times in the House of Commons. See, for example, Mr. Bryce in Canada, House of Commons, *Debates*, 11 August 1956, 7452.
91. This was later pointed out by the CLC at the 1961 hearing of the Committee of Inquiry into the UI Act. See NAC, Gill Commission Records, RG33/48 vol. 10. Submission to the Committee of Inquiry into the Unemployment Insurance Act by the Canadian Labour Congress, 58.
92. This was pointed out by Svanhuit Jose, NAC, Gill Commission Records, RG33/48 vol 10, Submission to the Committee of Inquiry into Unemployment Insurance, 31.
93. See, for example, NAC, UIC Records, RG50, vol. 54, 24th meeting UIAC, July 1954, "Minutes of the Meeting." The Canadian Manufacturers Association stated that "it would be unsound to consider ... any changes in the Act or Regulations which would have the effect of increasing the drain on the Fund."
94. NAC RG50, vol. 54, 24th meeting UIAC, July 1954, "Actuarial Report," 8–10.
95. Ibid. He also made the suggestion that married women were contributing to the recorded rate of unemployment since they were only registering as unemployed for the purpose of collecting benefits and did not genuinely want employment.
96. Canada, House of Commons, Standing Committee on Industrial Relations, Minutes of Proceedings and Evidence, 6 June 1955, 463–8. Brief from Mr. Barclay, UI Commission. He noted that while married women made up 33.9 percent of the insured labour force in 1954, they accounted for 51.4 percent of all female claimants. Ibid., 468.
97. Ibid., 464. This caused Ellen Fairclough to label Barclay's brief a "slander against women in employment." Ibid., 469. The UI Commission also argued that since in the first month after they came into effect 18 percent of women kept alive their application for employment, 5 percent reported finding work and 77 percent allowed their application to lapse, this proved that they were not really interested in finding employment. Canada, Unemployment Insurance Commission, *Annual Report* (1951), 38.

98. See, for example, Canada, House of Commons, *Debates*, 18 June 1952, 3397. Canada, House of Commons, Standing Committee on Industrial Relations, *Minutes of Proceedings and Evidence*, 26 May 1955, 183–7.
99. Knowles, Canada, House of Commons, *Debates*, 4 June 1952, 2913.
100. In addition to the resolutions passed at the 1949 and 1950 conventions (see notes 65, 68), resolutions on the subject were passed in 1951–1954. See CCL, *Proceedings of the Annual Convention* (1951), 98; (1952), 71; (1953), 87; (1954), 94. In all cases the recommendation to abolish or significantly modify the married women's regulation is part of the Report of the Committee on Unemployment Insurance, which had consolidated the resolutions on the subject. In 1955 the Committee simply expressed surprise that amendments to the regulation recommended by the UIAC and the UI Commission were turned down by Cabinet. Ibid. (1955), 97–8.
101. For the annual briefs, see *Canadian Unionist* (April 1950); (April 1951); (April 1952); (March 1953); (November 1954); (December 1955). On the CCL submissions to the UIAC see NAC, UIC Records, RG50, vol. 53, 19th meeting UIAC, July 1951; 21st meeting UIAC, July 1952; 23rd meeting UIAC July 1953; RG50 vol. 54, 24th meeting UIAC, July 1954. On the submission to the UI Commission see NAC, CLC Files, MG 28 I103, vol. 238, file 238-19; UIC "Minutes of the Meeting with Representatives of Labour Organizations, May 10, 1951."
102. NAC, CLC Files, MG28 I103, vol. 239, file 239-11, "Minutes of a Meeting with Employees' Representatives on the Courts of Reference in the Province of Quebec," 29 March 1952. See also Ibid., file 239-9, "Report on the Conference of Employee Members of the Courts of Referees in the Province of Quebec," 18 February 1951; file 239-12, "Conference of Employee Nominees of the Courts of Referees in Ontario," 19 April 1952. In the latter case only modifications in the regulation were recommended.
103. NAC, CLC Files, MG28 I103 vol. 284, file UI part 5, 19551–1952, J. Marchand, CCCL to A. Andras, CCL, 7 March 1951; A. Andras to P. Conroy, 16 March 1951.
104. NAC, CLC Files, MG28 I103, vol. 238, file 238-20. A. Andras to P. Conroy, 16 March 1951; "Joint Submission to the Umpire Re Appeals Against Disqualification Under Benefit Regulation 5A," 1–6.
105. Ibid.
106. NAC, CLC files, MG28 I103, vol. 284, file UI part 5, 1951–1952, J. Marchand to A. Andras; Ibid., vol. 238, file 238-20, "Joint Submission to the Umpire"; Ibid., vol 238, file 238-19, UIC, "Minutes of the Meeting with Representatives of Labour Organizations," 10 May 1951.
107. *Labour Gazette* (May 1951), 647; (April 1952), 411; (April 1953), 542; (December 1954), 1705; (January 1956), 50; (January 1957), 154.
108. CCCL brief to the federal government. Quoted in *Labour Gazette* (May 1951), 647.
109. Trades and Labor Congress of Canada, *Report of the Proceedings of the Annual Convention* (1951), 196, 276–7; (1952), 173–4; (1954), 475; (1955), 377.
110. See, for example, NAC UIC files, RG50, vol. 53, 19th meeting UIAC, July 1951, TLC submission to the UIAC. The CCL presented submissions to the UIAC far more frequently than did the TLC.
111. NAC, CLC Files, MG28 I103, vol. 238, file 238-19, UIC, "Minutes of Meeting with Labour Organizations," 10 May 1951.
112. Trades and Labor Congress of Canada, *Report of the Proceedings of the Annual Convention, 1949–1955*.
113. *Trades and Labor Congress Journal* (April 1952), 14.
114. Ibid. (November 1954), 8; (January 1956), 9–10.
115. NAC, UIC records, RG 50, vol. 54, 32nd meeting UIAC, July 1957, CLC Submission to the UIAC, 3.
116. The United Electrical, Radio, and Machine Workers of America (UE) appears to have been particularly active in this regard. For example, they appeared, along with the CCL before the Umpire and requested that the Umpire recommend that Regulation 5A and the authoring statute be rescinded. See CUB 655, March 22, 1951, reprinted in full in *Labour Gazette* (May 1951), 711–3. Two locals of UE, as noted earlier, also appeared before the 1955 hearings on the amendments to the UI Act to protest about the case of two married women denied benefits and to urge the elimination of the regulations. Canada, House of Commons, Standing Committee on Industrial Relations, *Minutes of Proceedings and Evidence*, 26 May 1955, 262.

117. It appears, for example, that they were not initially notified of the 1955 hearings on amendments to the UI Act. The issue was raised by Ellen Fairclough, Canada, House of Commons, Standing Committee on Industrial Relations, *Minutes of Proceedings and Evidence*, 17 May 1955, 61.
118. For an analysis of the National Council of Women in an earlier period see Veronica Strong-Boag, *The Parliament of Women: The National Council of Women of Canada, 1893–1929* (Ottawa 1976). See also Rosa L. Shaw, *Proud Heritage*.
119. See, for example, NAC, National Council of Women (NCW) papers, MG28 I25, vol. 97, file 7, Brief to Prime Minister St. Laurent December 1953; vol. 93, file 9, Milton F. Gregg to Mrs. R.J. Marshall, 5 September 1951.
120. See for example, NAC, NCW Papers, MG28 I25, vol. 97, file 11, Resolutions, 1953–54.
121. NAC, NCW Papers, MG28 I25, vol. 99, file 12, Annual Report, *Economics and Taxation Committee*, 1953–54.
122. NAC, NCW Papers, MG28 I25, vol. 99, file 4, Newsletters 1954–55, January–February, 1955, 7; vol. 100, file 16, Newsletters 1955–56, February 1956; vol. 125, file 2, Correspondence 1957–58, Michael Starr to Mrs. Eaton, 9 October 1957; vol. 125, file 3, Correspondence 1958–59, Mrs. Rex Eaton to "Dear President."
123. NAC, NCW Papers, MG28 I25, vol. 92, file 4, Agnes Reau, Chairman, Committee on Resolutions to Mrs. D.F. Duncan, Corresponding Secretary, Fort Williams, 30 April 1951. The view that the UI Commission was dealing with the matter was expressed by Mrs. Finlayson, NCW representative to the National Employment Committee of the UI Commission and Mrs. Turner Bone representative "to the Montreal branch."
124. This was at the request of Isabel Finlayson who suggested that the local Laws and Trades and Professions Committees find out about the application of Regulation 5A in their locality. NAC, NCW Papers, MG28 I25, vol. 96, file 7, I. Finlayson to "Madame Chairman," 6 November 1953.
125. NAC, NCW Papers, MG28 I25, vol. 96, file 10, Local Councils of Women, 1953, 1965, "Report of Trades and Professions Committee presented to Winnipeg Council, 23 April 1954." See also ibid., vol. 97, file 12, Standing Committees, 1953–1954, "Report of the Committee on Laws"; "Report of the Trades and Professions Committee, June 1954."
126. NAC, NCW Papers, MG28 I25, vol. 96, file 1: Annual Meeting, 1954, "Minutes, 61st Annual Meeting June 25–July 1, 1954," 4.
127. Women had somewhat more representation in the employment section of the UI commission than they did with respect to the administration and coverage of the insurance itself. For example, not only was there an adviser on women's employment within the UI commission administrative structure, but women also had representation on the National Employment Committee which oversaw the operations of the employment officers under the jurisdiction of the UI commission. For example, the NCW had a representative on this committee in the 1950s. Rosa L. Shaw, *Proud Heritage*, 199.
128. NAC, NCW Papers, MG28 I25, vol. 96, file 1; Annual Meeting 1954, "Minutes, 61st Annual Meeting June 25–July 1, 1954," 4.
129. The convention proceedings do not reveal the reasons for this abrupt change. See NAC, NCW Papers, MG28 I25, vol. 100, file 1: Annual Meeting, "NCW, Resolutions for Annual Meeting, 1956," vol. 103, file 7: PM and Cabinet: Correspondence, 1956–57, Milton F. Gregg to Mrs. F.F. Worthington, 30 October 1956, acknowledging receipt of recommendation that the married women's regulation be rescinded.
130. NAC, NCW Papers, MG28 I25, vol. 103, file 7, PM and Cabinet: Correspondence, 1956–57, Milton F. Gregg to Mrs. F.F. Worthington, 30 October 1956.
131. *Labour Gazette* (March 1957), 267.
132. See, for example, NAC, Papers of the Candian Federation of Business and Professional Women's Clubs (BPW Papers) MG28 I55, vol. 44, "Minutes of the 13th biennial convention, July, 1952."
133. See, for example, NAC, BPW Papers, MG28 I55, vol. 44, "Minutes of the 10th Convention, July, 1946," 3; vol. 65, Resolutions: 15 June 1948; vol. 45, "Minutes of the Meeting of the Board of Directors 4 June 1955," 6.
134. NAC, BPW Papers, MG28 I55, vol. 12, "Report of Chairman of Standing Committee on Legislation, 1950–52."

135. NAC, BPW Papers, MG28 I55, vol. 44, Minutes of the Biennial Convention July 1956; vol. 45, Reports 1954–56.
136. At Fairclough's request, the Ontario BPW sent a telegram urging the deletion of discriminatory clauses against married women to the labour minister as the 1955 amendments to the UI Act came before the House. See NAC, BPW Papers, MG28 I55, vol. 34, 1955 Correspondence, BPW of Ontario, Ontario Provincial Conference, 30 September–2 October 1955, Report of the Provincial President. The representation to the Industrial Relations Committee took the form of a telegram from the BPW sent to both the labour minister and Fairclough. Canada, Standing Committee on Industrial Relations, *Minutes of Proceedings and Evidence*, 6 June 1955, 472–3. On the meetings with Prime Ministers St. Laurent and Diefenbaker, see NAC, BPW papers, MG28 I55, vol. 81, *The Business and Professional Woman*, XXV (May–June 1957), 6; XXV (January–February 1958), 16.
137. Canada, House of Commons, *Debates*, 15 November 1957, 1171–2.
138. The role of these groups is frequently cited in assessments of why the regulation was eventually revoked. See, for example, Canada, Committee of Inquiry into Unemployment Insurance (Gill Committee), Report, 38, NAC, Gill Commission Records, RG33/48, vol. 10, Svanhuit Jose, Submission to the committee of Inquiry into Unemployment Insurance, 1961, 32; NAC, CLC files, MG28 I103, vol. 285, UI Misc. Inquiries 1959–1960, part 2, Andras to O'Sullivan, 9 February 1960.
139. Fairclough's role was recognized by Fraudene Eaton, President of the NCW, when, in a letter to Fairclough she noted "I recognized that your firm hand on this matter strengthened the hand of the Minister of Labour." NAC, NCW Papers, MG28 I25, vol. 125, file 2: Correspondence 1957–58, Mrs. Rex Eaton to the Honourable Ellen Fairclough, 19 December, 1957.
140. NAC, UIC Records, RG50 vol. 56, 38th meeting UIAC, April 1960; UI Commission to UIAC, 12 July 1960, "Impact of Benefit Regulations to Married Women," 3. The memorandum noted that benefit payments to single women increased by 60 percent between 1957 and 1958, while payment to married women rose by 80 percent.
141. Ibid., 6.
142. Ibid., 6–7.
143. NAC, UIC Records, RG50, vol. 56, 40th meeting UIAC, October 1960, "Special Report of the UIAC resulting from Meeting October 27, 1960,"
144. NAC, Department of Labour Records, RG 27, vol. 3458, file 4-11, pt. 8, Submission to the Standing Committee on Industrial Relation of the House of Commons on Bill C-43, An Act to Amend the Unemployment Insurance Act by the Canadian Manufacturers' Association, 21 May 1959, 13, 16.
145. NAC, Department of Labour Records, RG 27, vol. 3458, file 4-11, pt. 8, J.C. Whitelaw, General Manager, Canadian Manufacturers' Association to Michael Starr, Minister of Labour, 20 December 1960.
146. Dr. James was formerly of the Dominion Bureau of Statistics, then working for the Department of National Defence.
147. Canada, Senate, *Proceedings of the Special Committee of the Senate on Manpower and Employment*, 1960, 217–8.
148. Ibid., 218. The figures on married women registered for jobs is from a survey conducted at the UI offices; those on the proportion in the labour force are from the monthly labour force survey administered by the Dominion Bureau of Statistics.
149. Ibid., 238. This was based on the number indicating that it was not financially necessary to work (and included those indicating that "the extra money is desirable and useful" or that they "like to have something useful to do"), who preferred part time or temporary work, and the proportion whose husbands were working full time. Ibid., 209, 236–8.
150. Ibid., 252.
151. Ibid., 364–6. Such a comparison had also appeared in early reports of the Commission. For example, Barclay, one of the UI Commissioners, noted that in 1946–49 more women were claiming UI benefits than were reported by the labour force survey as without jobs and seeking work. Canada, House of

Commons, Standing Committee on Industrial Relations, *Minutes of Proceedings and Evidence*, 6 June 1955, 464.
152. Canada, Senate, *Report of the Special Committee of the Senate on Manpower and Employment* (Ottawa 1961), 65.
153. This was pointed out, for example, by a staff person at the UI Commission. See NAC, UIC Records, RG50, vol. 53, 18th meeting UIAC, July 1950, W. Thomson, Supervisor of Analysis aand Development Division UI Commission to Chief Commissioner, 20 July 1950. Ostry also notes some of the differences between the two measures, but nevertheless compares the two. Canada, Senate, *Proceedings*, 356–63. The differences are also indicated in Canada, Senate, Report of the Special Committee of the Senate on Manpower and Employment, 14.
154. Canada, Unemployment Insurance Commission, *Annual Report* (1951), 25.
155. Ibid. (1952), 14. See also Ibid. (1951), 25.
156. Ibid. (1954), 14. The division does not distinguish between married and single female applicants.
157. Quoted by Ellen Fairclough. Canada, House of Commons, *Debates*, 18 June 1952, 3396–7.
158. NAC, Gill Commission Records, RG 33/48, vol. 10. Submission to the Committee of Inquiry into the Unemployment Insurance Act by Svanhuit Jose 1961, 34.
159. Canada, Committee of Inquiry into the Unemployment Insurance Act, *Report* (Ottawa 1962), 1.
160. The point was made by Stanley Knowles, quiting a CCL document. Canada, House of Commons, *Debates*, 4 June 1952, 2913.
161. NAC, Gill Commission Records, RG 33/48 vol. 10 for all briefs.
162. NAC, Gill Commission Records, RG 33/48, vol. 10, Submission to the Committee of Inquiry into the Unemployment Insurance Act from Office Overload Co. Ltd., October 1961.
163. NAC, Gill Commission Records, RG 33/48, vol. 10, Submission from the National Committee of Women.
164. NAC, Gill Commission Records, RG 33/48, vol. 10, Submission from the Canadian Federation of Business and Professional Women's Clubs.
165. NAC, Gill Commission Records, RG 33/48, vol. 10, Submission from the National Legislative Committee, International Railway Brotherhood.
166. NAC, Gill Commission Records, RG33/48, vol. 10, Submission from Svanhuit Jose, 11.
167. The Gill Committee recommended that no special regulations be enacted relating to married women, although they did suggest more active claims supervision. Canada, Committee of Inquiry into Unemployment Insurance, *Report*, 12.
168. Sylvia Ostry, *The Female Worker in Canada* (Ottawa 1968), 3–4.
169. By 1961 equal pay laws had been enacted by eight provinces and by the federal government, *Labour Gazette* (June 1965), 518.
170. The Department of Labour in their publication, *Labour Organization in Canada*, did report on the percentage of trade union membership made up of women until the early 1950s. They noted, however, that the figures were unreliable since many of the local labour unions did not differentiate on the basis of sex in their membership records. See, for example, *Labour Organization in Canada* (1948), 19; (1949), 21. In 1953 they discontinued the reports. When the *Labour Gazette* produced a special issue on women in the labour force in 1954, they requested, but were unable to obtain, this information from the central labour bodies. For examples of both the TLC and the CCL inability to provide such figures, see NAC, CLC files, MG28 I103, vol. 269, Dept. of Labour, Misc. part 2, 1952–56. Bengough to H.J. Walker, 19 February 1954; vol. 190, file 6; Federal Dept. of Labour correspondence, Part 1, 1950–54, Burt to Dowd, 3 February, 1954. In 1954 the CCCL estimated that more than a third of its members were women. *Labour Gazette* (March 1954), 389. In 1963 women accounted for 16.3 percent of trade union membership. Canada, Ministry of Trade and Commerce and Dominion Bureau of Statistics, *Annual Report under the Corporations and Labour Unions Return Act, Part II: Labour Unions, 1963* (Ottawa 1966) 37, table 15A.
171. For example, in 1959 a special course on the role of women in trade unions was held for the first time at the CLC Ontario summer school and it was also noted that each year the number of women enrolled in various courses had increased. *Labour Gazette* (September 1950), 910. In 1952 the CCL decided to reserve one of its vice-presidencies for a woman and it also established a women's

committee that was active from 1952–1956 and from 1960–1966. See Lucie Piché, "Entre l'accès à l'égalité et la préservation des modèles: Ambivalence du discours et des revendications du Comité Feminin de la CTCC-CSN, 1952–1966," *Labour/Le Travail*, 29 (Spring 1992); *Labour Gazette* (March 1954), 389. In 1960 a women's committee was also established in the Ontario Federation of Labour, *Labour Gazette* (December 1960), 1290. In 1959 the CLC established a committee to co-ordinate white collar organizing. *Labour Gazette* (August 1959), 797. Individual unions had already established office worker departments. For example, Eileen Tallman was the head of the Office Workers Department of the United Steelworkers of America from 1952 to 1956. It should be noted that while women clearly formed a high proportion of white collar workers, organizing in this area was not necessarily presented as a "women's issue."

Chapter 15

The Red Petticoat Brigade

Mine Mill Women's Auxiliaries and the "Threat from Within," 1940s–70s

Mercedes Steedman

> If you have in any police of a nation, a secret force investigating individuals at all times, including active and true patriots in trade unions and in parliament, then I say that is a gestapo.
>
> Harold Winch, M.P.,
> House of Commons Debates, 25 June 1959.

In 1969 the RCMP filed its last surveillance report on the Ladies' Auxiliary of the Mine, Mill and Smelter Workers union of Sudbury, Ontario.[1] The report closed a file on the local that dated back to the 1940s. Why would the RCMP be interested in this women's organization?

During the post-war period, whenever an auxiliary local in Rossland, British Columbia, or Port Colborne, Ontario, held a tea party, local RCMP officers would report the event to the Security and Intelligence Branch in Ottawa. When the Timmins, Ontario, Local of the Mine Mill Ladies' Auxiliary held a Christmas raffle of Avon cosmetics in fall 1962, the local police dutifully reported the information to the town's RCMP detachment. One typical 1963 report on Sudbury activities noted that the auxiliary locals of the International Union of Mine, Mill and Smelter Workers (IUMM&SW) were "continuing to hold rummage sales, bake sales and draws to raise funds for various charitable organizations," apparently considering this fact to be worthy of the attention of those watching out for the nation's security.[2]

At first glance, perhaps, it may seem ridiculous for the Mounties to be spending their time, year after year, reporting on the success or failure of what often amounted to teas, bazaars, and Tupperware parties; yet for decades the RCMP Special Branch kept files on all the activities of Mine Mill women's auxiliaries across the country. In Northern Ontario it was standard procedure for local Security and Intelligence officers to file the initial report. The information was then processed in North Bay and sent on to the Ottawa headquarters.[3] Each main Local of Mine Mill had a separate file, usually with the caption "Subversive Activities in...." The all-encompassing character of this surveillance is astounding. By the end of the Cold War the Canadian spy machine had a detailed record of these women's activities.

During the Cold War, nearly everyone became a suspect, and women's organizations closely linked to left-led unions such as the

United Electrical Workers (UE) and Mine Mill were obvious targets for surveillance. In a way, the RCMP were reframing apparently harmless tea parties as threats to national security not because of what the women were doing, but because of whom the women had married. Still, the rationale for surveillance involved more than simple guilt by association. If the women were suspect only because they were linked to other Mine Mill activities, then surely reports would have been less frequent. Reports would have focused on Mine Mill women's activities, such as strike support or visits to classified countries, that tied them to left activism. But watching out for rummage sales, bake sales, and draws, often held to support local charities? Tea parties? Was that not extreme? Not according to the RCMP mandate.

The security responsibilities of the RCMP were defined by the 1939 Official Secrets Act. The Force was to discover and prevent espionage and subversion, to screen government employees and to screen applicants for visas and citizenship. By 1953 the RCMP Security and Intelligence division's efforts to carry out this mandate had resulted in 21,000 active files on individuals and 23,000 on organizations.[4] The pursuit of subversive elements in the civil service, the unions, and social groups did not abate. While the Cold War search for "the enemy within" required a broad definition of subversion, the RCMP focus on communists and their so-called front groups predominated in most of the surveillance work. The shifts in Canadian government policy towards the Soviet Union directed some of this work, but by and large the RCMP was left to its own devices. By the 1950s the RCMP focus was on "a Communist Party build up within our borders."[5]

The major counter-subversive action undertaken by the Security Service was the collection and processing of information gathered from informants, secret agents, and public documents. As the RCMP's own analysts Carl Betke and Stan Horrall noted, "The RCMP preferred to employ as far as possible, agents who were not members of the force. Their association with it was temporary, less direct and their employment could be discontinued once their usefulness was over."[6] To supplement its own surveillance reports the RCMP relied on information from local media and sympathetic friends in churches, unions, and cultural associations. The officers did not have to look far afield for their soldiers in the Cold War.

There were no RCMP officers at Ladies' Auxiliary meetings. Surveillance was carried out by concerned citizens who acted as occasional informants. One facet of community surveillance, for instance, was co-operation between the RCMP and the Catholic Church. These extra-state forms of surveillance served to complete the circle of surveillance.

The development of a post-war social consensus that accepted this level of surveillance may seem odd to us now, but to understand why these women's groups were seen as potentially dangerous to the Canadian state, one has to look at the broader Cold War culture. After the Depression of the 1930s and World War II, emotional issues and family relations took on a greater significance in most people's lives. As Mary Louise Adams points out in her study of post-war gender politics:

> In the years following the Second World War, the heterosexual family was valued as the "traditional" foundation of the Canadian social structure. The family was reified as a primary stabilizing influence on both the individual and the nation as a whole.... Mainstream discourses suggested that dissent and difference could weaken the face of democracy in the ideological fight against communism. Canadians were called upon to show an impressive social cohesiveness as evidence of their dedication to the superiority of the Western way of life. A commitment to the family was central to the social homogeneity necessitated by this display.[7]

We are just now beginning to understand the political and cultural ramifications of the Cold War, but it is clear that family life was an ideologically contested site. Putting life back together after the war required a change in gender roles both at home and in the workplace. The war had drawn many working-class women into the waged labour force, and many of them held well-paying jobs for the first time. With the demobilization of soldiers and the dismantling of war production, women were dismissed from most of these jobs. Yet married women continued to enter paid work, and by 1961 they accounted for 22 percent of the female labour force (during the war married women accounted for only 4.5 percent of the female labour force).[8] After the war women moved back into either low-paid work or unpaid work as wives and mothers, but keeping them in the home and keeping them happy represented a real political challenge. Cold War discourse overlaid a changing discourse on gender roles.

The patriotic virtues of a stable family life, with women back in the home as dutiful wives and mothers, were constantly reaffirmed by the state, the media, and the church. Elaine Tyler May points out that women's position in the home is central to the political stability of capitalism. In her study of U.S. families during the Cold War, May outlines the 1959 "kitchen debate" between Nixon and Khrushchev, describing Nixon's response to the communist way of life. Nixon insisted that the superiority of the American way of life "rested not on weapons, but on a secure, abundant family life of modern suburban homes. In these structures, adorned and worshipped by their inhabitants, women would achieve their glory and men would display their success. Consumerism was not an end in itself; it was the means of achieving individuality, leisure and upward mobility."[9] Post-war democratic discourse espoused a more egalitarian civil society in which men and women shared the fruits of the new consumerism, which itself frequently required an extra income. The contradiction between the renewed domesticity and the increase in married women's labour-force participation made it harder to marginalize women's political voice. Post-war popular culture's hierarchical familialism of the 1950s "Father Knows Best" variety co-existed with another increasingly prevalent point of view. While acknowledging the importance of family, this view saw wives and husbands as partners in both the marriage and the community.

While this society still maintained separate domestic and public spheres, the post-war years continued the transformation of earlier forms of domestic ideology. The Cold War message contained a certain ambivalence. When Nixon contrasted the mass dictatorship of communism with the capitalists' rights to free political expression, he was praising individual freedom and familial patriotism as the bulwark of an abundant family life in capitalist societies. If free, individually based political expression was to be one of the defining features of the free world, then the ideology would also reaffirm women's rights as "free" political agents in the post-war gender order. While the post-war domestic feminism was cloaked in Cold War rhetoric, it also opened the political space for women's continued participation in public life.

Indeed, the free-world discourse opened up spaces for political activism, and working-class women made the most of them—even though the Cold War narrative of communist conspiracies attempted to control the meaning of democratic struggle and to challenge the left's attempt to remake life in working-class communities during the 1940s and 1950s. As Dorothy Sue Cobble notes in her re-evaluation of the significance of post-war working-class feminism, "Working class feminists bore the torch of gender equality and justice in the 1940s and 1950s,"[10] and many working-class women, though recognizing their commitment to family life, pushed at the same time for gender equality and social justice in the broader society. For their part, Mine Mill women developed their political and social critique of the post-war economy and social recovery from their standpoint as wives and mothers. Their democratic struggles for post-war reform questioned the normative hold of the Canadian political and social elites on the shape of post-war Canadian life. As "wives and mothers of wage-earners," Mine Mill women frequently sent letters of protest to the Canadian government about rising consumer prices, the lack of available working-class housing, and the need for a national health-care system. On one level the RCMP reports on tea parties may seem a bit ludicrous, then, but on another they were part of a broader national security campaign that viewed all forms of political opposition as a threat to the state.

Cold War Canada: The Sudbury Experience

Support for RCMP surveillance was woven into Sudbury's community. In the 1950s Sudbury was a typical company town. Mining companies employed almost 40 percent of the working population in 1951.[11] The paternalistic control of the two main employers, Inco and Falconbridge, reached far into community life, and the local elite expected loyalty and trust in their ability to lead the community. Post-war labour demands increased the local labour force, housing shortages were common, and the immigrants recruited to assist mining-company production added to the unstable aspects of the community.[12]

In the 1940s and 1950s the Sudbury basin ore deposits accounted for close to 90 percent of all nickel production in the non-communist world.[13] When the local Sudbury union successfully certified in 1944, Local 598 of Mine Mill at Inco became the largest local in the international organization.[14] This left-led union was large enough to pose a threat to the stability of capitalism, and Mine Mill became a central target of Cold War politics. In Sudbury Mine Mill's social unionism challenged the hegemony of a local political and social elite that had long assumed the right to take care of the community. Ruth Reid, an auxiliary activist, long-time volunteer at the Mine Mill summer camp, and widow of Mine Mill's recreational director described the social climate in Sudbury: "This was a Mine Mill town in the 1950s. All the community activities were run by Mine Mill. Everyone from the Mayor and his family to the local doctors' wives and children were at the Mine Mill hall for some activity or another."[15] The centrality of family life to the post-war recovery made it a potential site for subversion, and local elites were quick to recognize the significant influence that Mine Mill men and women were having on local family life. Hence the popularity of Mine Mill's social unionism soon became part of a larger political and cultural struggle for the hearts and minds of Sudbury's working class.

The Organization of Women's Auxiliaries in Northeast Ontario

Sexist assumptions that women, like children, were gullible and susceptible to communist influence meant that women and children were a central site for the battle against communism at home. In the April 1949 issue of *Chatelaine* Ronald Williams warned Canadian women not to be stooges for Communists. He argued, "You have to give the Communists credit for one thing: they have never underestimated the power of women." Williams continued, "The order has gone out here and in all free democracies: *infiltrate into any women's, youth or cultural organization you can find*. . . . This accent on women and youth, this constant drive to tap the tremendous latent power of women in all kinds of activity—churches, homes and school and fraternal clubs, art and culture—is by no means new."[16] These sentiments were echoed by members of the local elite, who believed it was their duty to keep an eye on all of the union's activities. Were women in the Mine Mill auxiliaries dupes of communism or were they communists themselves? Suspicion of even the most innocuous gathering prevailed.

The Mine Mill ladies' auxiliaries had been actively recruiting members since the late 1930s, and by the 1950s they existed in most of the mining centres across Canada. The Mine Mill auxiliaries in both Canada and the United States were part of an international organizational structure under the leadership, by the late 1940s, of Kay Carlin, the Mine Mill auxiliaries' first women's organizer in northeastern Ontario, and the wife of Mine Mill organizer Bob Carlin. Through this organization the auxiliaries pushed for recognition as full partners in the Mine Mill union movement.[17] But most locals were never more than a few hundred strong. While the Sudbury auxiliary signed up several hundred women in the first few years after its charter was granted in 1944, with a union membership of over 14,000 men, the women's group remained small. The main function—according to Agnes Gauthier, president of Sudbury's Local 117 Ladies' Auxiliary in 1950—was to be of assistance to the local wherever and whenever it was needed, to further the cause of labour, and to strive for improved living conditions for miners and their families.[18] The Mine Mill constitution outlined the main purpose of the ladies' auxiliaries as "the education and training of women in the labour movement and to assist their Local Unions in time of need and labour disputes, to support the union in its legislative efforts and to provide educational and cultural activities for our members and their children."[19]

While the male-dominated trade union tried to make a place for its womenfolk in the union, the space the women were able to claim still tied them to conventional gender roles. In the auxiliaries, family loyalty to husbands and children now extended to loyalty to the political aims of the Mine Mill union. Anything else would have been seen as inappropriate and unfeminine.

In her examination of post-war mass culture, Joanne Meyerowitz points out the problematic and contradictory nature of women's political position. She argues:

> Historians sometimes contend that the Cold War mentality encouraged domesticity, that it envisioned family life and especially mothers as buffers against the alleged Communist threat. But Cold war rhetoric had other possible meanings for women. In the *Ladies Home Journal*, authors often used the Cold War to promote women's political participation.... Senator Margaret Chase Smith made the case most strongly: "The way to reverse this socialistic, dictatorial trend and put more *home* in the government is for you women, the traditional homemakers, to become more active in your government." In this line of argument, the Cold War made women's political participation an international obligation.[20]

The contradictory and competing mores of Cold War family values restrained Mine Mill women from stepping outside of those cultural confines at the same time as it extended women's right to political activism. Public service was an important component of auxiliary work. As Ruth Reid puts it, "Someone once referred to the Ladies' Auxiliary as social workers because they supported so many things in the community."[21] The women raised funds for hospitals and schools and worked with the Red Cross. They also organized cultural activities—play schools and movie shows, dance school, drama groups. As Reid says, "At the children's camp the women were there as mothers, cooks, and at the beginning of the summer the parents and Ladies' Auxiliary always helped get the camp cleaned up for the new season."[22]

The women walked a fine line between unfeminine behaviour and pushiness on the one hand, and supportive militancy on the other. Those who chose to become active were usually left-of-centre, working-class women with a strong sense of trade-union consciousness. Many women who became leaders in the auxiliary had previously been political activists. "I think the ones of us who were really prominent, if you want to use that word, were people who had a base in union activity, that knew something about it," observed one auxiliary executive member. "Because it really wasn't a popular thing. The society didn't really accept it. Not at that time."[23]

Given the view of family life as the centre of post-war peace and stability, the church and local business people or elite tended to see women as the gatekeepers of these values, and women's loyalty to the established order was key. Women who joined the union auxiliary were seen as disrupting both the community and the domestic order. As one auxiliary member suggested: "At the time the union was not a socially accepted thing. Not in 1958. I mean, when I was working with the church auxiliary you said that very freely, but you didn't as far as being in the union auxiliary. Because they just, they didn't accept it, society didn't accept it to the extent that they probably would now."[24]

Some of the Mine Mill women understood the political nature of their work in the auxiliaries, but many members were ill-prepared to face the anti-communist backlash and RCMP surveillance that marked their years of activism in the union.

RCMP Reports on Mine Mill Women

RCMP records show continual reporting on all Canadian auxiliaries of Mine Mill. One report from the Timmins detachment provides a glimpse of the RCMP's attitude towards the Mine Mill women:

> It may also be of interest to record that the undermentioned mailing list is maintained by this Ladies Auxiliary and although there is no doubt some innocent trade unionists listed herein, there are a good number who are known to be definitely connected with subversive movements and their correct address may be of interest at Div. H.Q. or for certain individual files.... [three lines deleted].[25]

RCMP security was intent on keeping track of the movements of any Mine Mill women who might at some future time become "subversively inclined."[26] For example, a 22 November 1952 report from the Fort Erie detachment security officers noted, "The writer has endeavored to find out if [deleted] holds any prominence in the Ladies Auxiliary." On 27 February 1956, an officer at the same RCMP detachment observed that the Auxiliary appeared to be "only a social group that do not take an active interest in the affairs of the union." He added, "However, should there be any indication of their interest in that regard in the future, a report will be submitted immediately."[27] Names of conference delegates were routinely submitted to central headquarters so that Special Branch officers could monitor women identified as Communists or seen as being sympathetic to the Communist cause. As a result, all women holding official positions in any Local of the Ladies' Auxiliary came under RCMP scrutiny. Like their male counterparts, national leaders, such as Dorothy McDonald (national co-ordinator of the women's auxiliaries) were detained by U.S. police when they tried to attend international meetings of the union. McDonald's response to her arrest in Chicago in 1949 illustrates her resistance to this infringement of her civil rights. In an open letter to the International board meeting, McDonald outlined her response to the RCMP role in curtailing her travel to the United States. "The mere fact that I am not allowed to enter your country will not stop me from speaking my mind whenever and where ever I see fit and certainly it will not stop me from protesting against tyranny no matter in what form, because I am a firm believer in real democracy."[28]

The Security and Intelligence reports drew information from Mine Mill newspapers, Auxiliary newsletters, and informants who appear to have attended occasional Auxiliary meetings. The RCMP reports frequently included attachments: copies of Mine Mill newspapers, convention reports, and other documents prepared by Mine Mill. Local community members were only too willing to pass along samples of these materials.

While all reports were forwarded to Ottawa, they were also circulated to other units that might be interested in the information. For example, reports on the Timmins and Kirkland Lake locals frequently made their way into the Sudbury detachment files. When co-ordinator Dorothy McDonald announced the call for the Eighth Annual Mine Mill Convention, to be held in Sudbury in February 1956, the South Porcupine RCMP detachment forwarded the information and the accompanying newsletters to the North Bay Security division and on to Ottawa for review. The names of the women attending the convention were duly noted.[29]

RCMP officers also monitored other left-wing newspapers to gain information on

Mine Mill women. For example, when the National Congress of Canadian Women conducted a survey of women's opinions on family allowances, health insurance, and housing, McDonald presented the views of Timmins women. The report, carried in the *Canadian Jewish Weekly*, made its way into RCMP clipping files and more than likely into McDonald's personal file.[30]

While RCMP officers reporting on the Sudbury Ladies' Auxiliary frequently mentioned that the activities of the organization were "*confined* to non-subversive endeavors," the surveillance did not stop.[31] The "rummage sales, bake sales and draws" cited in Constable J. Wiebe's 16 September 1963 report on Sudbury Auxiliary activity are typical of the somewhat less than "subversive" nature of the activities uncovered. These events, Wiebe noted, were in aid of raising funds "for various charitable organizations such as the Canadian National Institute for the Blind, the Children's Aid Society and the Cancer Society."[32] Even such benign reports did not result in an end to the surveillance. What the Mounties wanted was information that would add to the files of "suspected and known Communists" and election to any office in the Auxiliary immediately made one suspect. When the local RCMP detachments tracked the names of all women delegates to the 1956 convention, this information made its way to Ottawa to become part of the growing list of potential subversives.[33]

In May 1962 J.L. Forest, officer in charge of "A" Division of the Security and Intelligence Branch in Ottawa, wrote to the RCMP commissioner suggesting that a file be opened on the Timmins Ladies' Auxiliary. He outlined his reason as follows:

> Local 312 I.U.M.M. & S.W. Ladies Auxiliary in Timmins, Ontario is presently quite active. It is noted in the Mine Mill Ladies Auxiliary Newsletter for April 1962 (forwarded on [deleted] re: Mine Mill Auxiliary Newsletter—General Information) that Local 312 was represented by a delegate at the International Convention of the I.U.M.M. & S.W. held in Toronto, Ontario, March, 1962.[34]

The file was duly opened. A follow-up note on 1 June 1962, directed the records office to create a file entitled "International Mine Mill and Smelter Workers Union, Local 312, Ladies' Auxiliary—Communist Party activities within—Timmins, Ontario." It would seem that attendance at any Mine Mill meeting made a person suspect. A successful recruitment drive by any Local of the women's auxiliaries was sure to draw the interest of the RCMP. By December 1962, Timmins Security and Intelligence officers were dutifully reporting on all the activities of the Local. Clearly, a portion of their reports made use of information from McDonald's Ladies' Auxiliary newsletters.[35] In 1967, after four years of reporting on the Timmins women of Mine Mill, the reporting officer commented, "There has been no activity of importance during the past four years." Still, the surveillance continued.

RCMP reports were not so much interested in the content of the women's political activism as they were in the ever-widening search for potential subversives. The RCMP saw the women as duplicitous stooges for a communist movement, even though, according to the Force's own records, the women were doing nothing that could be remotely construed as a threat to national security. Cold War discourse reframed Mine Mill women's call for peace, justice, and equality for working people as a threat to the patriotic normative culture of the masculine elite. The scope of state surveillance, the criteria of "threat to national security," was wide indeed—extending from anyone who was a communist, to anyone who was friendly with communists, to anyone who could potentially be a stooge for communism.

This wide scope made the RCMP job more difficult, and Security and Intelligence officers learned to be creative. In their review of RCMP activities, internal analysts noted how the RCMP collected information: "From informants and secret agents and from every bit of public information the Section compiled its description of the multi-faceted Communist activity." From the RCMP's point of view this meant:

A knowledge of Communist membership was crucial, in addition, to discovery of Communist activities in organizations not designated Communist: "front groups, labour organizations and mass language groups." The front groups were in the main dedicated to the international "Cominform" strategy of a "peace" campaign launched in the late 1940s. Organizations like the Canadian Peace Congress and various Peace Councils, certain women's and youth groups, and those who advocated "Ban the Bomb" petitions, would appeal to many who were not Communists.... The only way to know the Communist influence in front groups was to keep track of the identities of open and secret Communists who held membership in them.[36]

The Catholic Connection

The fight against communism extended well beyond RCMP record-keeping. The Catholic Church community actively organized against suspected communist infiltration of Mine Mill. Because the communists were able to use unsuspecting citizens to promote their causes, everyone had to be vigilant and everyone was suspect. The local press ran items declaring Mine Mill communist, and by 1959 the recently created Catholic University of Sudbury was offering courses on anti-communism. Professor Alexandre Boudreau warned unsuspecting Sudbury citizens:

Most people distrust the Communist Party and would never *knowingly* have anything to do with it. Since the Communists are relatively few in members, this poses a serious problem for them. Alone and by themselves, they can do practically nothing and you would be surprised to discover how few Communists there are in a city like Sudbury and at the same time what great influence they can exert on the whole population.[37]

In his radio broadcasts and university extension courses Professor Boudreau suggested strategies to Sudburians for "upsetting the communist applecart." He advised, "We can interfere with their recruiting by helping youth work, Scouts, Guides and Church Youth groups and by showing a film on Communism from time to time. We can refuse co-operation or publicity to Communist fronts. We can be sure that no Communist gets elected to office because there is nobody to run against him."[38]

Of course, if you were going to fight communists, you needed to know where they were located. Otherwise the situation could create a climate of fear. This point was made in the House of Commons debates of 28 November 1963. Several members of parliament wanted the government to release a list of subversive organizations. The government refused, arguing that such disclosures would inhibit the RCMP's work. Instead the state practices allowed the climate of suspicion and fear to persist. In Sudbury and many other Mine Mill mining communities the Cold War discourse was sustained by the media, church, and local chamber of commerce attacks on the union.

The local press sent fear into all good Christians, Protestant and Catholic alike, by running stories about the atheism of communism. Popular Cold War discourse produced a steady diet of anti-communist sentiment and rumours about the possibilities of communist infiltration into everyday life. The Cold War propaganda fed on those rumours, as Irene Haluschak, a member of the Ladies' Auxiliary for Local 117, explained:

The women believed that if it was in the *Sudbury Star* then it was true. When the *Sudbury Star* wrote that the Reds had taken over the Mine Mill hall and had put up a communist flag—who had done it was a right-wing group from the Ukrainian community on Frood Road. A lot of women told me, "Well Jesus, Irene, they had put up the communist flag!" I said, "No, they didn't. They [the people who did that] came from Toronto, it said right in the *Sudbury Star*." I said, "You read your paper a little more carefully and you'll see they said alleged." ... The women believed that under communists you would be a slave,

> they would take everything, they would take their house, you wouldn't have anything, you wouldn't be able to go to church. A communist was like a bogeyman, and the women were frightened of them.[39]

The newspaper articles on communism asserted its subversive nature, the way it could spread its tentacles into the family, the school, and the media. Such forms of subversion gave every citizen the responsibility for combating this evil. It placed everyone on guard.

Extending the Scope of Surveillance: Building an Anti-Communist Consensus

The prevailing climate of fear and mistrust provided a compliant populace ready to assist the RCMP in its work. Catholic women, through their Church association, were especially receptive to this propaganda as local priests frequently spoke of the need to combat the spread of communism. At the Fortieth Annual Convention of the Catholic Women's League (CWL), held in Sudbury in 1960, a motion was passed to "recommend that the Justice Department in Ottawa take immediate steps to outlaw the Communist Party of Canada and make known to the public all societies which are communist organized or controlled."[40]

In 1961 the RCMP deputy commissioner publicly identified Mine Mill as one of several unions whose leading executive and policies were associated with the communist movement. He pointed to Sudbury as a community facing bitter strife as a result of the union's presence there. The local Catholic Church papers were quick to pick up on his comments. Reverend R.F. Venti's editorials in the *Catholic Register* focused on the revelations. He noted, "A small group of Communists is trying to take control of the majority. The Sudbury miners need the public support of every citizen in order to win the fight." He continued, "When democracy is attacked, we are attacked. We must speak out; we must protect against any Red force that attempts to take us over; we must show on whose side we are."[41] In the anti-communist discourse, loyalty to the local elite and the church was loosely linked to loyalty to the nation. But Mine Mill women had clearly tied their "loyalties" to the union movement, and this public stance made them immediately suspect.

Irene Haluschak recalled her experience:

> Oh, you could hear some crazy stories! One time somebody said about me, that I was head of the Communist Party in the district and that I had organized cells and I was running this big thing, you know, that was so dangerous. That had come during a local union election. We had won. They said, "Well, why wouldn't they win! Irene's running the whole thing. They have got cells working and Irene's in charge of it." I thought, oh god, to have that power! It was really ridiculous, it was really crazy.[42]

Catholic Church leaders and members fed the fears of communism, encouraging the view that godless elements in the Mine Mill were attempting to subvert the men and women.[43] The anti-communist forces within the Church were able to mobilize lay women in the community through successfully tapping the resources of the CWL.[44] In a community in which about 60 percent of the inhabitants were Catholic, the Church offered an extensive infrastructure to back the forces for the war against communism.[45] Police reports on Mine Mill activities made much use of citizens' observations. Local alderman, priests, and members of the CWL all provided information. An RCMP report of 12 June 1959, advised the central office that "[name deleted] approached the force asking for assistance in 'cleaning up' his local."[46] The state security system could rely on the loyalty of local people for reports on union activities.

The intense anti-communism had the effect of suppressing radical activism in the union and fuelled the internal rivalries in the union and its auxiliaries. During the raids on Mine Mill made by the United Steelworkers of America in the early 1960s, Mine Mill women's auxiliary members were referred to as the "Red petticoat brigade." The prevailing attitude made many people cautious about lending their support to views that would go against the grain of supposed post-war harmony and prosperity. Mine Mill members Stan and Peggy Raciot recalled their experience of red-baiting:

> This onslaught of propaganda that we were communists. What does this horrible communist look like? And it seems nobody can describe them and yet they said it was a horrible thing. To me it is just a word. At the churches they said to get rid of the communists, because there were members [of Mine Mill] that were communist. People didn't say look at all the good things Mine Mill did for us.[47]

As part of their day-to-day surveillance work the RCMP frequently visited the homes of "suspects." While the experienced activists were aware of being targets of RCMP surveillance, others were more easily intimidated. Patricia Chytuk, a founding member of Ladies' Auxiliary Local 117 in Sudbury, recalls receiving a visit:

> I didn't know who they were. They said they were the secret police. If it was now I would have asked them to identify themselves, but then you heard so much. Then they were visiting other people's houses too. A woman phoned me, she was reading an English-language Ukrainian newspaper, she liked it. She was active in our organization. She said, "Oh, what am I going to do? These people came and said I am not supposed to read the paper, it's against the law!" I said, "Come on!" "Well, she said, "these men said they were secret police."
>
> When they came to the house, my goodness, I was frightened. My late husband came in from work as they were leaving. He said, "Who were they?" I said, "They said they were the secret police." He said, "What the heck do they want here?... Just ignore them." Well, I said, "I had two women phone me this week, I didn't tell you because I didn't want to disturb you, but this is what is going on." Finally we had a meeting and they were saying, "Some guy gets paid ten bucks to go and visit you, just ignore them." But it scared a lot of people to leave the paper, not to read the paper.[48]

The RCMP expected compliance among the men and women they threatened and intimidated, and the Force seemed certain that it would not be publicly questioned for such intrusions into the private lives of working-class citizens. It was a no-win situation for those who received a visit from the plain-clothed agents, for if they admitted publicly to having received such a visit, in the eyes of the community they would be as good as guilty. Only an economically and socially secure individual would be able to withstand these paid agents' efforts of intimidation, and many immigrant working-class people were not in that position.

Women's Resistance, and the Refraining of Activism

The Cold War discourse reframed women's socialist and community activism as "communist," and because the state was unwilling to outline exactly what it considered to be subversive, a wide range of activities continued to be suspect. When Doug Fisher, a Co-operative Commonwealth Federation (CCF) Member of Parliament for Port Arthur in the late 1950s, challenged the government to clarify its surveillance practices, he was met with government resistance. Fisher argued, "I am in the liberal tradition and always suspicious of any police activities which are protected from the knowledge of the communality." He warned, "Any time we give an organization authority and work to do that we cannot examine openly and know how they are working, we have to watch very closely; we have to check on it on occasion to make sure it is needed; that the dangers are so severe and terrible that we allow this particular type of police organization to be free from the surveillance of elected representatives."[49] His advice went unheeded, and with no "standard definition of subversive" the RCMP continued to have a free hand to decide who and what was considered subversive. Justice Minister E. Davie Fulton outlined the government's position:

> As to laying down a standard definition alleged to be a Communist front organization. I do not think it is possible to arrive at such definitions. The methods of the Communists are so infinitely various or devious or skillful I should think you would have to have a 100 page book before you could define everyone of the members they might have and therefore every type of organization that could be deemed to be suspect on security grounds.[50]

That the government was unwilling to make public either the organizations it considered subversive or the criteria upon which it made this judgement fuelled public suspicions that anyone who said anything critical of the ruling political party in public was subversive. With no boundaries placed on what constituted "communist activities," there were therefore to be no boundaries on the Mounties' efforts to disclose those activities. RCMP spying merely reflected and monitored the political activities of anyone who was designated by the state and the mainstream political culture as a possible threat to national security.

The post-war conflict between communism and Christian civilization was not actively regulated through state law. In 1950 Prime Minister St. Laurent best expressed the state strategy during the Cold War:

> I firmly believe that some years ago communist leadership was, to a regrettable degree, influential in some labour unions and the question arose as to whether or not some action should be taken by legislative authority in Canada to purge the labour unions. That was not done. We relied on the good sense, good judgement, patriotism and Christian traditions of the labouring people themselves to see that they got rid of these obnoxious influences.[51]

The RCMP surveillance of innocuous social groups was part of a larger social construction of Cold War culture, one that turned neighbour against neighbour and generated a general climate of suspicion. In this way RCMP surveillance served to constrain the character of working-class post-war activism for both men and women. For working-class women activists, these constraints of post-war "normalcy" meant that women who openly advocated women's equality and social justice were immediately suspect, even when they were holding tea parties. Yet Mine Mill women did actively promote a greater voice for women of the day. Through the auxiliary movement, working-class women worked for the cessation of weapons testing, for full disarmament, and for the creation of conditions that, as Dorothy McDonald reported, "would enable women to fulfill their roles in society, as mothers, workers, and citizens which includes the right to work, the protection of motherhood, equal rights with regards to marriage, children and property."[52] The picture of 1950s suburban affluence and family life in the age of *Leave It to Beaver* suggested a cultural ideology in which working-class people fulfilled their consumer dreams and became home owners with stay-at-home moms. Mine Mill women held a different vision of post-war economic and social recovery, and in the immediate post-war years, week after week, year after year, they continued to organize around that vision and build on it, despite constant RCMP intimidation and surveillance.

Endnotes

1. RCMP, Security and Intelligence Branch, "International Union of Mine, Mill and Smelter Workers—Ladies Auxiliary—Local 117, Sudbury, Ontario," report, April 30, 1969, National Archives of Canada (NAC), Ottawa, Record Group (RG) 146.
2. RCMP, Security and Intelligence Branch, "International Union of Mine, Mill and Smelter Workers—Ladies Auxiliary—Local 117, Sudbury, Ontario," report, Sept. 16, 1963, NAC, RG 146.

3. The file system for these reports was multilayered. In addition to the specific local files, the RCMP kept a file entitled Mine Mill, Northern Ontario, and another national-level file system for national convention and general national surveillance on the union. Thus reports at a local level were frequently forwarded to head office to become part of yet another system of files. These files systems are complex, and the maze of evidence can be difficult to decipher. For example, information on Mine Mill women could be located in a file by that name but could also appear as an entry in any of the other file systems. Files on the Labor Progressive Party, ethnic associations, and other union files are all part of the net of information kept by the RCMP on Mine Mill activists.
4. Carl Betke and Stan Horrall, *Canada's Security Service: An Historical Outline, 1864–1966* (Ottawa: RCMP Historical Section, 1978), chap. 6, "From Royal Commission on Espionage to Royal Commission on Security, 1946–1966," Document No. 20, File 117-90-107, obtained through Access to Information Act.
5. Ibid., chap. 4.
6. Ibid.
7. Mary Louise Adams, *The Trouble with Normal: Postwar Youth and the Making of Heterosexuality* (Toronto: University of Toronto Press, 1998), p. 38.
8. Canada Census, as cited in Pat Connelly, *Last Hired, First Fired: Women and the Canadian Work Force* (Toronto: Women's Press, 1978), p. 64.
9. Elaine Tyler May, *Homeward Bound: American Families in the Cold War* (New York: Basic Books, 1988), pp. 17–18.
10. Dorothy Sue Cobble, "Recapturing Working Class Feminism: Union Women in the Postwar Era," in *Not June Cleaver: Women and Gender in Postwar America, 1945–1960*, ed. Joanne Meyerowitz (Philadelphia: Temple University Press, 1994), p. 75.
11. CM. Wallace and A. Thomson, eds., *Sudbury: Rail Town to Regional Capital* (Toronto: Dundurn Press, 1993).
12. Ibid., chaps. 8, 9.
13. John Deverell and the Latin American Working Group, *Falconbridge: Portrait of a Canadian Mining Multinational* (Toronto: James Lorimer and Company, 1975), p. 14. See also Wallace Clement, *Hardrock Mining; Industrial Relations and Technological Changes at INCO* (Toronto: McClelland and Stewart, 1981). Nickel is a key resource, because it is an essential ingredient in making stainless steel, structural steel, and machine parts. The economic prospects for nickel production are closely tied to military and heavy machinery production.
14. Irving Abella, *Nationalism, Communism and Canadian Labour* (Toronto: University of Toronto Press, 1973), p. 90. When a certification vote was held in December 1943 at Inco, 6,913 votes were cast for Mine Mill and 1,187 for the company union; at Falconbridge 765 voted for Mine Mill and 194 voted for the company union. Local 598 was certified as the bargaining agent at Inco on Feb. 4, 1944, and at Falconbridge on March 7, 1944. Jim Tester, "The Shaping of Sudbury: A Labour View," paper presented to the Sudbury Historical Society, April 18, 1979.
15. Interview with Ruth Reid, Sudbury, May 1993.
16. Ronald Williams, "Are You a Stooge for a Communist?" *Chatelaine*, April 1949, pp. 90–94.
17. The Ladies' Auxiliaries of IUMM&SW were, at least technically, autonomous from the main union. They were chartered by the National Executive Board of Mine Mill and awarded their own local numbers and held their own local and national conventions, as well as sending representatives to local, national, and international Mine Mill meetings and conventions.
18. Radio Talk by Agnes Gauthier, Mine Mill Ladies' Auxiliary, April 23, 1950.
19. Bylaws of the Ladies Auxiliaries' of the International Union of Mine Mill and Smelter Workers in Canada, adopted Feb. 27, 1956. Canadian autonomy for Mine Mill was established in 1955. Clement, *Hardrock Mining*, p. 103.
20. Joanne Meyerowitz, "Beyond the Feminine Mystique: A Reassessment of Postwar Mass Culture, 1946–1958," *Journal of American History*, March 1993, p. 1469.
21. "'We're Still Here': A Panel Reviews the Past and Looks to the Future," in *Hard Lessons: The Mine Mill Union in the Canadian Labour Movement*, ed. Mercedes Steedman, Peter Suschnigg, and Dieter K. Buse (Toronto: Dundurn Press, 1995), p. 152.
22. Ibid., p. 151.

23. Interview, Ladies' Auxiliary member (name withheld), Sault Ste. Marie, Ont., March 1992.
24. Ibid.
25. "Subversive Activities in Mine Mill—Local 241," Oct. 10, 1952, RCMP Reports, NAC, RG 146, volume and file number deleted.
26. "Subversive Activities in Mine Mill, Fort Erie Report re National Convention, Feb. 27, 1956, RCMP Reports, NAC, RG 146, volume and file number deleted.
27. "Subversive Activities in Mine Mill—Local 241," Nov. 22, 1952, and Fort Erie RCMP report re National Convention in Sudbury, Feb. 27, 1956, RCMP Reports, NAC, RG 146, volume and file number deleted.
28. Dorothy McDonald, "Talk to Convention," no date, IUMM&SW Archives, University of British Columbia, Vancouver.
29. "Mine Mill Auxiliary Newsletter," Jan. 6, 1956, RCMP Reports, NAC, RG 146, volume and file number deleted.
30. Re: Mine Mill (Women's Auxiliary) Clipping, *Canadian Jewish Weekly*, Ottawa Headquarters, Sept. 18, 1952, RCMP Reports, NAC, RG 146, volume and file number deleted.
31. International Union of Mine Mill and Smelter Workers—Ladies' Auxiliary—Local 117— [deleted]—Sudbury, Ont., Feb. 24, 1964, four pages, RCMP Reports, NAC, RG 146, volume and file number deleted. Emphasis added.
32. International Union of Mine, Mill and Smelter "Workers—Ladies' Auxiliary—Local 117—Sudbury, Ont., Sept. 16, 1963, RCMP Reports, NAC, RG 146.
33. Today, even though delegate names are a matter of public record, the report released under the Access to Information Program (ATIP) still deleted the names of delegates. The RCMP were not always successful in their efforts to regulate the movements of Mine Mill activists crossing the Canada–U.S. border. Timmins Auxiliary members Pat Fournier and Dorothy McDonald, delegates to the 1949 Chicago convention, had been overlooked. "Owing to the fact that it was felt that Local 241 was too impoverished to send a delegate, let alone two. In fact, even now the suspicion is aroused, but it is as yet only a suspicion, that the Labour Progressive Party are footing the bill." Constable G.M. Beaton, Timmins, Security and Intelligence officer, Sept. 15, 1949.
34. J.L. Forest, to the Commissioner, RCMP, May 29, 1962.
35. RCMP Report, "International Mine Mill and Smelter Workers Union, Local 312, Ladies' Auxiliary—Communist Party activities within—Timmins, Ontario," Timmins, S.I.S., Dec. 18, 1962. Most of these investigators' comments are still held as exemptions under the Access to Information Act. Furthermore, most of the information in the file obtained under an access to information request is still exempted. Since the RCMP's bank of suspects was compiled from newspapers and informants who passed on information concerning newly elected officials or on delegates to conventions, most of this information was already in the public domain, yet today the heavy hand of censorship still prevails and in documents released under ATIP much of this public information is still blacked out.
36. Betke and Horrall, *Canada s Security Service*, chap. 6.
37. Prof. Alexandre Boudreau, Program of Courses, 1959–1960, University of Sudbury— Extension Division, Box F43.2, Laurentian University Archives. Boudreau's activities came to the attention of the RCMP. In 1960 the RCMP reported on Boudreau's efforts to extend his anti-communist teachings to the miners. "A steward's school is to be held by Local 598 in Sudbury, on the 15-2-60. . . . Professor Boudreau [deleted] from the University of Sudbury will give four hours of lectures. Boudreau [deleted] is the individual who carried out the intense campaign on behalf of Don Gillis and his slate during the recent Local 598 elections, [deleted] it is the intention of the CPC, Sudbury—to have as many Party members as possible attend the school. Special attention is to be given to [deleted] lectures and attempts are to be made to disrupt these lectures and [deleted] is to be heckled constantly." RCMP Security Service Records, Report on International Union of Mine Mill and Smelter Workers—Local 598—Communist Activities Within, Sudbury, Ont., Feb. 17, 1960, NAC, RG 146.
38. Ibid.
39. Interview with Irene Haluschak, Sudbury, Ont., June 5, 1993.
40. 40th Annual Convention of the Algoma Diocese Catholic Women's League, May 19, 1960, Christ the King Church, Sudbury, Ont., Archives of the Algoma Diocese, North Bay, Ont.
41. Reverent R.F. Venti, "No Place for Neutral," Catholic Register, Oct. 14, 1961.

42. Interview with Irene Haluschak, Sudbury, Ont., May 1993.
43. The strongest anti-communist rhetoric came from within the English Catholic community. The French Catholic Church was less anti-union, as priests in the region supported the Christian labour-movement encyclicals. Interview with Yvonne Obonsawin, Elliot Lake, Ont., April 1995. The French section of the Church, under the direction of Father Albert Regimbal, offered labour studies classes in the parish. Most Reverend Bishop Alexander Carter, circular to the diocese, vol. 2, no. 1, Sept. 15, 1958.
44. The Catholic Women's League dates back to 1932, when the first Church women's organizations were formed in the Algoma diocese. Minutes of the Annual Meetings, Catholic Women's League, May 1932, Archives of the Diocese of Algoma, North Bay, Ont.
45. At the 1960 meeting of the Catholic "Women's League, members were congratulated on the work they had done during the strike. Minutes of the Fortieth Annual Convention, Catholic Women's League, Algoma Diocese, May 16, 1960, p. l 10.
46. RCMP Report, transit slip, June 12, 1959, Constable Northcott to Inspector Parent, NAC, RG 146, access file number 1025-9-91043, part 4, vol. 7. Parent's reply on June 15th stated, "Attached please find subject's personal file. It is noted that extract number 3 and 5 concern very good items of open information but under subjects' alias of [deleted]."
47. Interview with Stan and Peggy Raciot, Mine Mill members, Sudbury, Local 598. Interview conducted by Bea Hart, CBC Radio, no date.
48. Interview with Patricia Chytuk, Sudbury, Ont., May 1997.
49. Quoted in Betke and Horsell, Canada's Security Service, chap. 6.
50. Canada, House of Commons Debates, June 25, 1959, pp. 5149–50.
51. Canada, House of Commons Debates, May 2, 1950, p. 2087.
52. Report by Co-ordinator Dorothy McDonald on Mine Mill Auxiliaries, Eleventh Annual Convention, IUMM&SW, Sept. 14, 1959.

Chapter 16

"The Dresden Story"

Racism, Human Rights, and the Jewish Labour Committee of Canada

Ross Lambertson

Canadian historians have usually ignored the role of organized labour in the post-war struggle for human rights. Bryan Palmer's survey textbook, which refers to most of the current labour historiography, contains no references at all.[1] There do exist a few published articles which link organized labour to the fight for female equality in the workplace,[2] and several other works on human rights touch upon the post-war activities of organized labour.[3] Yet the best sources of information are unpublished theses, primarily in areas other than history, such as political science or social work.[4]

This paper is one attempt to help redress this benign neglect. It demonstrates that organized labour was a central element of the post-war Canadian human-rights policy community.[5] It also shows that one of the key actors in this community was a body called the Canadian Jewish Labour Committee (JLC), the director of which, Kalmen Kaplansky, played a significant part in the struggle against racial and religious discrimination.[6] To illustrate this, the paper includes a case study of one of the major JLC successes—the passage of the Ontario Fair Accommodation Practices Act and the struggle to apply it in the Ontario town of Dresden.[7]

* * * * *

The JLC was founded in 1936, an offshoot of the American Jewish Labor Committee (AJLC)—a trade union umbrella group with roots in the Workmen's Circle, a radical left Jewish fraternal organization that had its origins in Eastern Europe.[8] At its peak it claimed about 50,000 members, coming largely from such Jewish-dominated trade unions as the International Ladies' Garment Workers Union (ILGWU), the Amalgamated Clothing Workers Union (ACWU), and the United Cap, Hat and Millinery Workers Union (UCHMWU).[9]

The JLC was social democratic and anti-communist. In the early part of the century, most socialist Jews in Canada were members of the Workmen's Circle, but in the wake of the Russian Revolution the "left" communists began to move away from the "right" social democrats. By 1926 the two factions had split completely, with the communists leaving to create an organization called the Labour League and the social democrats remaining in the Workman's Circle. The latter continued to be the social and intellectual home of the JLC labour activists, while the former performed the same function for Jewish communists, even after it changed its name in 1945 to the United Jewish People's Order (UJPO). Over the years these two factions remained bitter rivals.[10]

Not surprisingly, the JLC had close ties with the Co-operative Commonwealth Federation (CCF), a party that was social democratic on economic matters and liberal on human-rights.[11] For example, David Lewis, the CCF's first National Secretary, was the son of Morris Lewis, a Workman's Circle socialist, and for many years the Secretary of the JLC. Similarly, Maurice Silcoff, a vice-president of the JLC, was a CCF activist.[12]

During World War II, one of the most pressing issues for the Canadian Jewish community was refugee relief, especially assistance for those few Jews who had managed to escape the Nazi Holocaust. As the war began to draw to a close, however, Jewish activists began to shift from their short-term project of helping victims of foreign anti-Semitism to the longer-term goal of attacking domestic anti-Semitism. At the same time, they broadened their scope, viewing anti-Semitism as simply one part of a larger problem—racial and religious prejudice.[13] In the words of an early JLC report, "Anti-Semitism, anti-Negroism, anti-Catholicism, anti-French or anti-English [sentiments] ... and union-smashing are all part of a single reactionary crusade of hatred and destruction."[14]

Consequently, by 1946 the JLC executive had appointed a national director to combat racial and religious prejudice within the trade union movement in Canada. Their choice, Kalmen Kaplansky, was Polish-born, fluent in Yiddish and English, a war veteran (with the rank of sergeant), a member of the International Typographical Union, Montreal vice-chair of the JLC, and a social democrat with strong ties to the Workmen's Circle and the CCF.[15] He was also, as it turned out, a skilful practitioner of the art of politics—not just the politics of parties and governments, but also that of minority groups and trade unions.

Had Kaplansky attempted to gain trade union support 50 years earlier, no doubt he would have failed. Before the war, organized labour was usually governed by the same racist values as the majority of Canadians.[16] As Canada industrialized, however, the conservative craft unions in Canada, primarily in the Trades and Labor Congress (TLC), came to be augmented by more progressive "industrial" trade unions, represented in Canada by the Canadian Congress of Labour (CCL). Much of Kaplansky's strongest support came from the leaders of major CCL trade unions, such as Charles Millard, Canadian Director of the United Steelworkers of America, and Fred Dowling, Canadian Director of the United Packinghouse Workers.[17]

Kaplansky's work also benefited from recent governmental protection of unions' right to exist and engage in collective bargaining. The trade union movement was strengthened by legal recognition of the workers' right to form unions, go on strike, and bargain collectively, as well as the adoption of the "Rand formula" for union membership. At the same time, unions became more "bureaucratized," and union leaders tried to channel worker energies into the new legally protected structures, as well as devoting more energies to "social unionism"—education courses, social welfare work, and improving the place of trade unions within the larger community.[18]

These developments, moreover, took place within a favourable context of cultural and economic change. Hitler had given racism a bad name, and the entire world was beginning to embrace the new discourse of human rights, exemplified in both the Charter of the United Nations and the 1948 Universal Declaration of Human Rights.[19] At the same time, race relations in the United States provided both negative and positive images. Many Canadians were repelled by segregation in the American Deep South, while at the same time encouraged by the pioneering anti-discrimination legislation of the northern states.[20]

In addition, post-war economic prosperity affected the human rights issues in several ways. It raised the demand for labour, and provided high levels of employment; "white" workers were not as threatened by "foreign" competition as they had been during the Depression, and governments were eager to facilitate their integration into the economy.[21] Meanwhile, economic development created more urbanization and a rising standard of living. As Morton and Granatstein have put it,

> Until the 1940s, Canada had been a poor country, with much of the meanness poverty

> tends to produce. Pre-war Canadians often knew little beyond their own distractions and neighbourhoods, which were small, largely homogeneous, and exclusive. There was usually no room in them for Japanese or Chinese Canadians, and scant tolerance for Jews or blacks or those with "different" attitudes or beliefs.[22]

Finally, Kaplansky also was able to learn from American examples. He began his tenure of JLC Director by taking a three-week trip to New York, where leaders of the American JLC and other national Jewish organizations educated him about a number of their initiatives, including the creation of several local anti-discrimination labour committees, the secretaries of which were JLC representatives.[23]

When he returned to Canada, "determined to fashion a program tailored to Canadian needs and Canadian conditions, while 'borrowing' from the American experience," Kaplansky began to strengthen his position with the two major national trade union organizations. First, he persuaded his friends in the Steelworkers to introduce at the 1947 CCL convention a resolution which called for "vigorous action" on the part of the CCL and its affiliated unions in "the fight for full equality for all peoples, regardless of race, colour, creed, or national origin." The resolution passed, and Kaplansky then began to lobby for the establishment of a "permanent committee on racial tolerance." This was formally constituted in 1948; its members were all Kaplansky allies. [24]

Kaplansky then turned his attention to the TLC. Although this umbrella group still retained a racist exclusionary immigration policy left over from earlier times, it had already begun to change.[25] In 1944 the JLC had persuaded the TLC to set up a permanent National Standing Committee on Racial Discrimination "to promote the unity of Canadians of all racial origins, and to combat and counteract any evidence of racial discrimination in industry in particular and in life in general."[26]

This committee proved to be a useful point of connection for Kaplansky. Its first chair was Claude Jodoin, an officer of the ILGWU and a disciple of Bernard Shane, the Canadian ILGWU manager who was also the JLC treasurer.[27] Jodoin soon became Kaplansky's "closest ally and collaborator." In the fall of 1946, Kaplansky wrote the Racial Discrimination Committee's report, which Jodoin delivered to the TLC annual convention. It was a call to action based on the pragmatic argument that racial antagonism and religious intolerance were "dangerous ideas ... being used by our enemies to divide labor and to distract the attention of the working people of this country from the real issues facing them." In addition, Jodoin spoke in favour of an ILGWU resolution (also written by Kaplansky) condemning discrimination and urging support for "trade unions committees for racial tolerance." The delegates voted overwhelmingly in its favour.[28]

In early 1947 Kaplansky began to lobby for the creation of these committees. By January he had initiated a provisional Labour-Committee to Combat Racial Intolerance in Toronto, by March a Winnipeg committee had been formed, and he also laid the groundwork for the establishment of a Montreal organization.

In April, realizing that the moral legitimacy of these committees would be stronger if trade union rank-and-file members had a chance to participate in their founding, Kaplansky turned his Toronto provisional committee into a standing labour committee at a public meeting open to all interested union members. His proposal encountered significant opposition from Communist unionists who considered Kaplansky, because of his JLC connection, to be a dangerous "red basher." Kaplansky, however, a veteran of political in-fighting in the trade union movement, had arranged that the chairman of the meeting was someone sympathetic to his cause, and he managed to obtain a vote approving the establishment of a new permanent organization dominated by Kaplansky allies—the Toronto Joint Labour Committee to Combat Racial Intolerance.[29]

Meanwhile, Kaplansky had also been struggling with the Canadian Jewish Congress (CJC).[30] Just after the war this organization, the major voice of Canadian Jews, had decided to set up its own "public relations" programme in the field of organized labour. From Kaplansky's perspective, it was abhorrent that a primarily middle-class organization should attempt to "raid" the natural constituency of the JLC. As a result, his initial courting of the TLC and CCL had been in part a campaign against the CJC.[31]

By early 1947 his patient lobbying had paid off. Both the TLC and CCL sent letters to the CJC, suggesting that its nascent attempts to educate workers about human rights were competing against their standing committees on discrimination, and stating that any future co-operation was contingent upon the support of the two committee chairs. Indeed, Aaron Mosher, president of the CCL, ruled that "in view of the circumstances neither my name nor that of the Congress should be used in publishing material except when approved of by our Committee and by the Jewish Labour Committee."[32]

It was clear that Kaplansky had out-manoeuvred the CJC.[33] Their labour program was stalled, while his was fully underway, and in November the CJC agreed to work with the JLC in establishing a "public relations program in the labour field." The national executive director of this program was to be the JLC executive director (Kalmen Kaplansky), responsible to a newly formed Joint Advisory Committee on Labour Relations made up of an equal number of representatives from the JLC and CJC. The annual costs would be split equally between the two organizations, and in return the JLC promised not to seek funds from certain areas of the Jewish community.[34] In the next decade Kaplansky operated with a minimum of interference from the Joint Advisory Committee, consolidating his network of anti-discrimination committees in Montreal, Toronto, Windsor, Winnipeg, and Vancouver. (These will be referred to in this paper as "labour committees.")[35]

Whenever possible, these labour committees bridged the TLC/CCL division.[36] In Toronto, as noted above, the committee was made up of TLC and CCL representatives, and the situation in Windsor was similar. In Winnipeg, the labour committee was tripartite, involving the TLC, the CCL, and the One Big Union (OBU). In Vancouver, only the local TLC unions initially supported the committee, but by 1950 Kaplansky had brought the TLC and CCL organizations together to form a Vancouver joint labour committee. Only in Quebec was he unable to create an all-inclusive committee. The Canadian and Catholic Confederation of Labour (CCCL) was reluctant to become involved with the Montreal group, perhaps because of fears of being submerged in a movement dominated by Anglophone trade unionists.[37]

Each labour committee had a full or part-time paid worker, usually called the "Executive Secretary." All these secretaries were formally hired by, and responsible to, their respective labour committee executives, so that Kaplansky's influence was somewhat constrained. As he wrote of the Toronto group, "the Jewish Labour Committee did not 'own' either the Committee or its Secretary." He was closely involved, however, in the selection of secretaries, and kept a tight rein on their activities. They answered directly to him on a day-to-day basis, and he expected regular written reports. He wrote to each secretary frequently, often several times a week, and on some occasions even twice in one day.[38]

Without Kaplansky's leadership, and the support of the JLC, the labour committees would probably have ceased to exist. Always sensitive to allegations of a "Jewish conspiracy," and knowing that many workers would not be happy to learn that their human rights programs were heavily financed by a body outside the trade union movement, Kaplansky encouraged the committee secretaries to raise money on their own. Nevertheless, the bulk of the funds continued to come from the CJC and JLC.[39]

Over time, Kaplansky gained access to some supplementary funding from a variety of sources: non-Jewish businesses,[40] Jewish-dominated unions, and (beginning in 1952) a number of other labour groups, especially the Steelworkers, the United Packinghouse

"THE REAL TARGET"

Canadian Labour Reports. Credit: Canadian Jewish Archives

Canadian Labour Reports. Credit: National Archives (CLC Papers).

Canadian Labour Reports. Credit: Canadian Jewish Archives

Canadian Labour Reports. Credit: Canadian Jewish Archives

Workers, the United Autoworkers of America, and the Canadian Brotherhood of Railway Employees.[41] Kaplansky also supplemented this income with significant donations from the two TLC and CCL national human rights committees. These cheques were not given directly to the JLC headquarters, but made out to the local labour committees or to Kaplansky's Canadian Labour Reports. In order to maintain centralized control of finances, however, he engaged in a kind of "laundering" of these funds, so that the local committee secretaries endorsed the cheques and sent them on to him.[42]

Trade unions also supported Kaplansky's network in ways other than through donations of money. He later reminisced that he was grateful for "supportive delegations to governmental authorities at every level, free public relations work, free mailing lists, research facilities, purchase of pamphlets, free office and telephone facilities, inclusion in educational undertakings and the free and enthusiastic support of so many staff people and volunteers from both trade union Congresses."[43] The Steelworkers, for example, provided the Toronto committee with free telephone use and office space in their building at 11 1/2 Spadina, and purchased bulk lots of *Canadian Labour Reports*, which they distributed to all their key members.[44] In addition, the Autoworkers created Fair Employment Practices Committees in their locals, members of which often provided volunteer labour for the Kaplansky network in Ontario.[45]

To summarize the activities of the labour committees is no easy task. First of all, this was pioneering work, so that the techniques changed over time as the activists learned their trade. Second, each province consisted of a unique blend of levels of economic development, demographic mix, and politics, so Kaplansky and his secretaries had to adjust their approach to meet local circumstances. Nevertheless, several common patterns emerged. Since prejudice and racism were as common among trade unionists as in the general public, the earliest efforts focused upon extensive programs of public education.[46] This involved the creation and distribution of pamphlets on racism and discrimination, proselytizing at trade union meetings and union labour institutes, holding annual Race Relations Institutes (intensive forums for workers and the general public), and networking with other educational bodies, especially the Canadian Association of Adult Education.[47]

Gradually, however, Kaplansky changed his focus. He saw that it would be difficult (if not impossible) to make Canadians so tolerant as to remove all instances of discrimination. He also realized that in some ways changing attitudes was less important than changing behaviour—people seeking employment do not so much need "tolerance" as they need jobs. The solution, Kaplansky concluded, was to follow the lead already taken by the CJC, which as early as 1946 had been committed to a campaign for a Fair Employment Practices (FEP) Act in Ontario.[48]

Although federal and provincial anti-discrimination statutes are now commonplace, there was little protection for minorities in Canada before the early 1950s. When in 1939, in the case of Christie v. York, the Supreme Court examined the legal status of racial discrimination in the provision of services normally available to the public (such as food and drink or accommodation in a hotel), it ruled in favour of the right to discriminate, basing it upon the legal principle of "complete freedom of commerce."[49] A small breach in this principle appeared in 1944 when, under pressure from both the CCF and the LPP, a minority Conservative government in Ontario created The Racial Discrimination Act, but this legislation only prohibited the posting of signs indicating racial or religious discrimination (e.g. "Whites Only"), and left other forms of discrimination completely legal.[50]

While many Canadians turned a blind eye to racial discrimination, often denying its existence, it was incontrovertibly present in Dresden, a small town in south-western Ontario, not far from the American border.[51] "The Dresden Story" began in the nineteenth century when the town lay at the end of the "underground railroad" for fugitive slaves and a substantial number of blacks settled in the area.[52] Josiah Henson (upon whose life *Uncle Tom's Cabin* was allegedly based), is buried nearby.[53] By the end of World War II blacks constituted close to 20 percent of Dresden's approximately 1,700 inhabitants, but several restaurants and barber shops habitually denied service to them; indeed, even those who did not look like blacks often suffered racial discrimination when members of the community knew their racial heritage. It was, in short, one of the most racially segregated communities in Canada.[54]

One of the Dresden-area blacks who refused to accept this Canadian version of "Jim Crow" was Hugh Burnett, a World War II army veteran who owned his own carpentry business. In 1943 he sent a complaint to the federal Minister of Justice about racial discrimination in Kay's Café, a Dresden restaurant owned by a prominent local citizen named Morley McKay. He was informed that the government could do nothing. Then, about 1948, he launched a lawsuit against McKay, although he did not proceed with it, probably because in the wake of the pre-war Supreme Court decision of Christie v. York the law provided little leverage.[55]

At about this time, Burnett joined with a number of other Dresden-area blacks to form an organization called the National Unity Association (NUA).[56] Just prior to the municipal election of 1948 a delegation from the NUA asked Dresden's town council that a non-discrimination policy be a condition of local business licensing. Although a number of Ontario municipalities had already passed anti-discrimination bylaws, in Dresden the proposal moved forward with glacial slowness.[57]

Meanwhile, the Toronto labour committee joined the Ontario human rights community. While trade unions at the provincial and national level were quite capable of obtaining the ear of government, a local organization such as the Toronto group was less likely to be heard. It needed a public "front" organization, a group that was predominantly middle-class, non-communist, committed to racial equality, and well-connected to the Canadian political elites. The Toronto Association of Civil Liberties (ACL) was an obvious choice. Its president was R.S.K. Seeley, and its board included B.K. Sandwell, Charles Millard, Andrew Brewin, Maude Grant, and Rabbi Abraham Feinberg.[58]

The Association for Civil Liberties, in turn, needed the resources of the Kaplansky network. Drawing its membership from the ranks of the Toronto cultural-intellectual elite, the ACL never generated the membership fees that would have come from a grass-roots mass organization, and it remained a wholly voluntary body, precariously founded on secretary Irving Himel's ability and willingness to run it out of his law office.[59] By contrast, the JLC network had relatively secure funding, widespread membership, access to many volunteers, and permanent paid staff at both the national and local levels.[60]

Close ties between the Association for Civil Liberties and the Toronto labour committee began in early 1949, when the ACL created a Committee on Group Relations. This brought together members of a number of important Toronto-based, human-rights organizations, including Ben Kayfetz of the CJC's Joint Public Relations Committee, William White of the Home Service Association (a Toronto black people's group), and George Tanaka of the Japanese Canadian Citizens' Association. Most importantly, the chair was Vivien Mahood, who had just taken over as the secretary of the Toronto human rights labour committee. A member of Kaplansky's network was now positioned strategically within the Toronto Association for Civil Liberties.[61]

Dresden was one of the first issues facing this new committee. NUA Executive Secretary Hugh Burnett had attended a JLC-sponsored Race Relations Institute as a delegate from his carpenter's union, and deeply moved the others with his stories of discrimination in Dresden. As a result, the Ontario human rights community took the issue to the new Conservative premier, Leslie Frost, on 7 July 1949. Accompanied by about 35 other human-rights activists, Irving Himel presented a brief from the Toronto Association for Civil Liberties on behalf of a "policy network,"[62] of various churches, different ethnic organizations (including Jewish, Polish, Chinese, Japanese, and black), several women's groups, and a number of non-communist trade unions: the International Bookbinders Union, the ILGWU, the Oil Workers Union, the Printing Pressman's Union, the Street Railwaymen's Union, the Textile Workers Union, the United Packinghouse Workers Union, the CCL, and the TLC-affiliated Toronto and District Labour Council.[63]

The main request was passage of a Fair Employment Practices Act prohibiting discrimination in employment, similar to those already existing in several American states. The policy network, however, also asked for action on discriminatory restrictive covenants, and suggested permitting municipalities to cancel the licences of any provider of public services which practised racial or religious discrimination. Although Dresden was not mentioned, it was clearly a part of the brief's subtext.[64]

A few days later, Mahood travelled to Dresden to see the situation first-hand. On the basis of this trip, she began planning a course of action, and her first step was to get in touch with Pierre Berton, the editor of *Maclean's*. The subsequent article by Sidney Katz helped turn the Dresden story into a national issue, and also singled out Morley McKay as one of the main segregationists. Katz quoted the restaurateur as saying, "Do you know that for three days after [each attempt by a black to obtain service] I get raging mad every time I see a Negro. Maybe it's like an animal who's had a smell of blood."[65]

Meanwhile, the issue of non-discriminatory business licensing was finally put to the town voters in a referendum in December 1949. It was defeated by a vote of 517 to 108, and the town became a lightning-rod which attracted a firestorm of attention and criticism. As a Toronto *Globe and Mail* editorial put it, "The decision brings shame to Dresden and to all Ontario."[66]

While the NUA decided to lobby Dresden city council again, the Toronto Association for Civil Liberties asked for another meeting with Premier Frost, arguing that Dresden (along with a number of other incidents) clearly demonstrated the need for both a Fair Accommodation Practices Act and a Fair Employment Practices Act.[67] This time (January 1950) the delegation was even larger than before, consisting of several hundred people and 104 different civil libertarian, church, labour, ethnic, and social welfare organizations, including the NUA.[68]

Frost was initially reluctant to take action. Many of his caucus members were rural Conservatives, as well as members of the Orange Lodge, an organization not known for its commitment to human rights.[69] Moreover, even those who publicly denounced discrimination often denied that it constituted a problem. In 1947, for example, the Conservative Minister of Labour, Charles Daley, told Rabbi Feinberg that "these days, racial discrimination is to a great extent imaginary."[70] Finally, anti-discrimination law could be seen as a deviation from the traditional legal principle of freedom of commerce, a shift away from the broader classical liberal notion of laissez-faire.[71]

On the other hand, there were also compelling reasons to proceed. To begin with, the shift away from classical liberalism had already begun, and Canadians were becoming increasingly comfortable with government's role in creating a welfare state. Moreover, the arguments for minimum wage legislation, family allowances, and so forth, could also be used to justify human rights laws,[72] and as early as 1947 a Gallup Poll had found that 64 percent of Canadians were in favour of a proposal by the Canadian Association of Adult Education to create fair employment practices legislation. Although B.K. Sandwell, the classical liberal editor of *Saturday Night*, and a major player in the Toronto Association for Civil Liberties, initially opposed this proposal, by 1950 even he had shifted his position completely, calling on the Ontario legislature to make "a courageous attempt" and pass such a law.[73]

Premier Frost was genuinely upset about racism and discrimination in his province, partly because he believed that bigotry against Jews and blacks was incompatible with the Christian faith.[74] His attitude, however, can also be explained through class analysis. As Mark Leier has argued, "[w]hatever the dominant sexual and racial ideologies of the day have been, capital has always been quick to jettison them when they no longer served," and race discrimination in the immediate post-war period had far less utility than in earlier times.[75] For Leslie Frost, the world was turning to democracy rather than communism for the protection of human rights, and anti-discrimination legislation in Ontario could therefore combine both practical politics and ideological warfare—stealing some of the thunder of Ontario's communist MPPs as well as demonstrating the virtues of "democratic freedom."[76]

Frost also saw discrimination as threatening the class interests of those who, like himself, were interested in speedy economic development. Knowing that immigration from Britain was drying up, he believed that discrimination against new arrivals from countries such as Italy or Greece might interfere with immigration rates, as well as contribute to domestic social problems. His concern was therefore not entirely with "racial" discrimination against blacks, but rather embraced the broader problem of "ethnic" prejudice.[77]

Moreover, he must have realized that not all business people were racially prejudiced. By passing the Fair Accommodation Practices Act he made it easier for a restaurant or hotel owner to welcome minority group members without the threat of losing "white" clientele to other businesses that openly discriminated. He was not so much undermining property rights as he was eliminating a competitive edge for the minority that insisted on unfair business practices.

As a result of the convergence of these three major sets of interests—human rights lobbyists, the state, and capital[78]—in 1950 Frost took two incremental steps forward.[79] First, he introduced an amendment to the Labour Relations Act which withheld legal protection from any collective agreements discriminating on the basis of race or creed. Then he introduced a bill which prohibited the enforcement of any discriminatory restrictive covenants created in the future. When passed into law, this legislation promoted human rights at the expense of the traditional right of freedom of commerce, but in a limited fashion. It was still legal for both trade unions and employers to discriminate, and the second bill did nothing to strike down restrictive covenants already in existence.[80]

In 1951, however, Frost moved forward with two more steps. To begin with, his government created Canada's first Fair Employment Practices Act.[81] The statute began with a statement that it was now "contrary to public policy" to discriminate on the basis of race, creed, colour, nationality, ancestry or place of origin, and added that this prohibition was in accord with the 1948 Universal Declaration of Human Rights.[82] The legislation then went on to ban any such discrimination in the hiring or employment of workers, balancing this with a prohibition against discrimination in union membership.

No doubt to allay the concerns of those who saw this statute as a violation of freedom of commerce, the law also moved away from the approach taken in 1944 when the Ontario Racial Discrimination Act prohibited discriminatory signs. That statute had made the act of displaying such a sign a quasi-criminal offense. The Ontario FEP Act, however, moved the field of discrimination into the ambit of administrative law, so that to obtain satisfaction a complainant had to overcome a series of bureaucratic obstacles. First, a "conciliation officer" would investigate a complaint. Second, the officer was empowered, providing that he had found evidence of discrimination, to effect an informal settlement. Third, if no such settlement could be reached, the Minister of Labour could appoint a conciliation commission. Fourth, the law also permitted the Labour Minister, at his discretion, to allow a prosecution under the law.

Frost's second pioneering step was the passage, in the same legislative session, of Ontario's first female equal pay legislation, the

Female Employees Fair Remuneration Act.[83] (A number of women's groups, supported by the CCF, but not by organized labour or the other "regular" human rights activists, had lobbied for the passage of a female equal pay law.)[84] This statute contained no reference to public policy or the Universal Declaration, but it did set up the same sort of administrative-prosecutorial model as the earlier FEP Act.

Frost did not, however, move on the issue of discrimination in public accommodation. For a while the NUA hoped that the provincial government might be able to provide some other form of legal redress in Dresden, but in late 1953 the attorney general informed Burnett that the province had no legal power to prohibit racial discrimination in cases where municipalities had refused to pass bylaws.[85] Burnett then approached Donna Hill, recently appointed as secretary of the Toronto labour committee, who began putting together a policy network that would ask for a provincial Fair Accommodation Practices law.[86] Hill and Ben Kayfetz, the Toronto executive director of the CJC's Joint Public Relations Committee, along with JPRC legal advisors such as Bora Laskin and David Lewis, produced another brief. In March 1954 it was presented to Premier Frost by a delegation once again led by the Toronto Association for Civil Liberties.[87]

This time Dresden was a central concern. The ACL brief referred to discrimination against blacks in a number of Ontario communities but noted that, "the height of expression of Jim Crow in Canada is to be found in the town of Dresden, Ontario." In addition, although several people spoke, including the ACL's Himel, a spokesman for the CJC, and representatives of the Ontario branches of the TLC and CCL, Hugh Burnett got the most publicity. He said that he was ashamed to have to plead for his fundamental democratic rights, and shrewdly referred to a possible connection between the rise of communism and dissatisfaction over racial discrimination. "There are no Communists among the coloured people at Dresden," he stated, "but I don't know how long we can assure that if the discrimination practised there is to continue."[88]

Less than a week later the Ontario government introduced Canada's first Fair Accommodation Practices Act, which became law on 6 April 1954.[89] Like the earlier Fair Employment Practices Act, it stated that discrimination on the basis of race, creed, colour, nationality, ancestry, or place of origin was now contrary to public policy, and it also made reference to the Universal Declaration of Human Rights. The enforcement process set out by the law was also similar to that of Frost's two previous anti-discrimination statutes: the laying of a complaint was followed by investigation, informal conciliation, formal conciliation, and (as a last resort) prosecution.[90]

From the perspective of modern anti-discrimination legislation, this process was badly flawed.[91] To begin with, it rested upon an individualistic conception of discrimination; there was no recognition that discrimination was a systemic issue rather than a collection of individual complaints, and there was certainly no process by which the state might provide any assistance to an individual who might lay a complaint.[92] In addition, it was an invitation to political interference; the notion of a human rights commission, acting independently, still lay in the future. Finally, it treated discrimination as simply another issue of labour relations; there was no awareness that conciliating a complaint about a refusal of service might be quite different from conciliating a complaint about factory safety practices, or that it might be necessary to implement the law by means of public servants sensitive to racial issues.[93]

Whatever the defects of the bill, it was not about to change everyone's behaviour immediately. Although a number of Dresden's establishments complied, several restaurants and barber shops continued to flout the law. As a result, Hugh Burnett and other NUA members began to "test" these establishments, relaying information to Sid Blum, who had replaced Donna Hill as secretary of the Toronto labour committee shortly after the passage of the legislation.[94] It was Sid Blum who filed complaints on behalf of the Dresden blacks, and from this point on, although Burnett was more often in the public eye, it was Blum who acted as his behind-the-scenes mentor, with Kalmen Kaplansky standing even further in the shadows behind his labour secretary.[95]

The immediate reaction to the NUA complaints was a decision by Charles Daley, the Ontario Minister of Labour, to send one of his local factory inspectors to begin an investigation. Blum suggested to the government that a factory inspector might not be able to devote enough time to the issue, but then received a letter from Burnett that suggested an even worse scenario—"it comes pretty straight from McKay that when the inspector was down that he stayed with McKay and they had a good time and that he told McKay he had nothing to worry about, he could keep on refusing if he wanted to." Whether or not this was true, the factory inspector reported that there was no evidence of discrimination in the town. J.F. Nutland, the officer in charge of the Fair Accommodation Practices Act in the Department of Labour, then informed Blum that he should not "interfere" with the situation in Dresden, lest he "upset" the community.[96]

It was at this point that tensions in Dresden almost spun out of control. Burnett began receiving anonymous letters threatening his life, and there was talk that the upcoming celebrations for Dresden's centennial might generate mob violence. The NUA therefore wrote the Deputy Attorney General of the province, apprising him of these developments, and complaining about low levels of police protection and co-operation. Meanwhile, Blum issued a press release decrying these threats, and the *Toronto Telegram* published a story entitled "Dresden Negro Warned, Gets Gun for Safety."[97]

Blum had no sympathy for the tender feelings of racists. He believed that "quiet persuasion will usually produce one result: quiet inaction."[98] He was scrupulous, however, about relying upon facts rather than rumours, and therefore on 22 July he went on a two-day, fact-finding trip to Dresden. He found that racial tensions were high, with the locals insisting that either there was no racial problem or that the problem was caused by local blacks who did not "know their place" and who also wanted to marry local, white women. He concluded that the passage of the Fair Accommodation Practices legislation and the subsequent visit of the factory inspector had done little to change the attitudes of the white population. Indeed, there was a widespread misconception that the Fair Accommodation Practices Act did not even exist.[99]

Blum immediately began to orchestrate a large-scale operation which involved both a maximum of publicity and further testing. He lobbied the Ministry of Labour with letters and telephone calls, asking for the appointment of a commission of inquiry.[100] At the same time, he persuaded the two Toronto trade councils to demand that the government take action, and ensured that this was widely reported in the city press.[101] He also provided continual advice and support to Hugh Burnett, sometimes working through the secretary of the Windsor labour committee, and he arranged to have a number of black people visit the offending restaurants so that he could file complaints on their behalf. Just as important, he created an alliance with a *Toronto Telegram* newspaper reporter, who travelled to Dresden to observe the testing process and provided extensive press coverage of the Dresden affair. (One of the reporter's articles, written for the now-defunct magazine *Liberty*, was reprinted with the logo and address of the Toronto labour committee, and widely distributed as an education and lobbying tool.)[102]

In the face of growing public pressure, and a total of eight complaints (including one filed by Burnett on behalf of a travelling black couple from Cincinnati), the Labour Minister finally appointed Judge William F. Schwenger to a one-man commission to determine if the situation warranted prosecution.[103] The hearing took place in Dresden on 27 September, with at least 200 people attending, including newspaper reporters from as far away as Vancouver.[104]

Judge Schwenger held hearings on two separate complaints. First, Hugh Burnett and four other members of the black community claimed that they had been denied service by Morley McKay. Second, a union activist named Lyle Talbot alleged that he and several other blacks had been turned away at Emerson's Soda Bar Restaurant.[105] These complainants were supported by the Toronto and Windsor labour committees, which had filed the complaints on their behalf, and they were represented in court by the former CCF national secretary, David Lewis. As noted earlier, Lewis was a member of the CJC's Joint Public Relations Committee and had close ties with Kaplansky and the JLC. He appeared pro bono, significantly cutting the costs of the two labour committees.[106]

At the hearing the complainants testified about the continuing pattern of racial discrimination. The case against Emerson's restaurant was clouded by the fact that the complainants had arrived shortly before closing time, but there was no doubt that McKay refused to serve blacks. In fact, McKay readily admitted his discrimination, arguing a kind of defence of necessity which stressed property rights, "I have to break the law to protect my business. I have a right to.... My customers have told me if we serve Negroes, they won't come in."[107]

By October the Minister of Labour had received Schwenger's report, but would not make it public, saying that there was no need to take action as long as there was evidence that people were being educated about their legal obligations. In reality, although the report recommended that no further action be taken in the Emersons' case, Schwenger had found that there was sufficient evidence to suggest that McKay was in direct violation of the Fair Accommodation Practices Act, and he unequivocally recommended that he be prosecuted. Labour Minister Daley was obstructing justice and misleading the public as well.[108]

This refusal to release the report precipitated a storm of criticism from the press.[109] Meanwhile, Blum kept up the pressure by arranging another test case about a week later. This time he sent two people, both of them strangers to Dresden. One of them, Bromley Armstrong, was a black trade unionist, the financial secretary of Local 439 of the UAW, and chair of its Fair Employment Practices Committee. The other was Ruth Lor, a Chinese-Canadian who was secretary of the University of Toronto Student Christian Movement.[110] As was expected, when they went to Kay's Café with Hugh Burnett they were refused service. Indeed, Morley McKay appeared to be so upset about the frequent tests that Armstrong was seriously concerned that he might be attacked by the restaurant owner, who was wielding a large meat cleaver and appeared to be having trouble controlling his notorious temper.[111]

This story received prominent coverage in the Toronto newspapers, partly because Blum had been astute enough to invite reporters to witness the test.[112] Although Daley responded angrily, suggesting that the test was the work of "troublemaking Communist groups," Frost did not believe Daley's charge and pressured him to take action. In early November the government announced that it was, for the first time, proceeding with a prosecution under the new Fair Accommodation Practices Act, against Morley McKay, for his refusal to serve Bromley Armstrong. Shortly afterwards, the government announced a second prosecution, this time against the wife of the owner of Emerson's Restaurant, based on complaints by two local blacks, Joseph Hanson and Mrs. Bernard Carter, who had once again tested the establishment on behalf of the NUA.[113]

In January 1955 the restaurateurs were found guilty, but they appealed, and in early September, County Court Judge Henry Grosch overturned the magistrate's decision. He ruled that a restaurant owner could not be held responsible for a refusal of service by his waitress, and added that there had only been evidence of a "postponement" of service rather than a refusal. Moreover, he stated, there was no clear evidence that, even if there had been a refusal, it was racial discrimination.[114]

Human-rights activists reacted angrily, especially when it was pointed out that Grosch had been one of the property owners who, some years earlier, had argued in the *Noble and Wolf* case that a discriminatory restrictive covenant was legal. The Toronto labour committee presented this information to the two Toronto labour councils, which publicly called on the government to appeal the decision and to pass an amendment to the legislation that would make it easier to enforce.[115]

Frost too was angered by the decision. He was quoted as saying, "Surely it isn't necessary that a bank robber must announce that he is going to hold up a bank before he is convicted of bank robbery!" He was unwilling, however, to amend the legislation, maintaining that the error lay with the judge and not the statute.[116]

Although the human rights community (especially its labour component) kept up pressure for a Fair Accommodation Practices Amendment Act that would more clearly define the nature of discrimination, and would also reduce the discretionary power of the Minister of Labour, Blum proceeded to see what he could do with the legislation as it stood.[117] To his delight, Attorney General Kelso Roberts told him privately that he was sympathetic to their cause and that his department would fully co-operate if further tests were held.[118]

Blum and Armstrong, along with some trade unionists from Windsor and London, attempted once more to obtain service from Kay's Café. Each time, however, the restaurant closed shortly after they entered, stayed shut for several hours and then re-opened with a waitress stationed by the window to give warning should the test group return. As a result, McKay began to believe that he had perhaps won—he boasted to one of Blum's white "plants" that he had beaten the previous charges because "they couldn't prove anything."[119]

Due to this impasse, and because the Attorney General's office suggested that it might be better to test the café with someone who was unknown to McKay, Blum changed his tactics and called on two black University of Toronto students, Jake Alleyne and Percy Bruce. By using complete strangers rather than Hugh Burnett or Bromley Armstrong, the Toronto labour committee hoped to get proof of refusal of service rather than simply a pattern of eccentric working hours. In addition, McKay could not claim that he was refusing service for personal reasons rather than reasons of race.[120]

When they went to Dresden in November, the black testers were careful not to provide any reason for dismissing their complaint. They were dressed respectably and were very careful to be polite. In addition, they requested service several times from both the waitress and from McKay, so there could be no doubt about a refusal of service. Moreover, a white student had come down with them from Toronto, entered the café after them, and then asked successfully for service. Finally, Blum had arranged that another student would be in the café simply to observe what had happened.[121]

The test was a success. The two black students were not served, yet the white student "customer" received service quickly. As a result, both Bruce and Alleyne laid complaints, and early the following year McKay was charged a second time for violating the Fair Accommodation Practices law.

At about the same time that the charge was being laid, the Toronto Association for Civil Liberties led yet another delegation to Premier Frost, this time asking for improvements in the Fair Accommodation Practices Act. Once again, the Dresden affair was a primary focus for human rights lobbying, and although Hugh Burnett was not able to join the delegation, it included a number of black activists: Bromley Armstrong (representing the Toronto labour committee), Stanley Grizzle and B.A. Walker (of the Brotherhood of Sleeping Car Porters), and Donald Moore (of the Negro Citizenship Association).[122]

Premier Frost was unwilling either to create an anti-discrimination commission or to amend his Fair Accommodation Practices legislation, but he did mention to Blum that he was optimistic that the law would prove effective. According to Frost, the Crown Attorney prosecuting the first Dresden cases had been ill, and had not handled them very well. In addition, as Blum later wrote to Kaplansky, this time the Attorney-General's Department was "going all out to make this conviction stick," and the case was being directed from Toronto rather than by the Chatham Crown Attorney.[123]

McKay's lawyer argued in court that his client was not responsible for any denial of services on the grounds of race and that the law was in any case unconstitutional criminal law legislation. He also maintained that the testing process was unfair, calling Blum's observer "a plant, a spotter, a spy." The magistrate, however, rejected these arguments, and in late February McKay was found guilty, fined, and assessed court costs. The fines were moderate—$50 on each of two counts—but the costs were over $600, an extremely high figure which reflected the cost of bringing the labour committee witnesses from Toronto to Chatham.[124]

McKay appealed once again, but this time the case went to County Court Justice Lang rather than Grosch. For Lang the case for the complainants was clear—an actual refusal of services had taken place, the owner was responsible, the reason could be nothing other than race, and the legislation was indeed constitutional. He upheld both the conviction and the fine, ruling also that McKay had to bear the costs of both the convictions and the appeal. (The special Crown prosecutor had offered not to press for costs if McKay would undertake to stop discriminating in the future, but McKay's defence lawyer told the court that he wished "to go down with his colors flying.")[125]

McKay decided to appeal to the Ontario Supreme Court, and the court granted leave on the issue of the constitutionality of the Fair Accommodation Practices Act. Yet, in October, he struck his colours, probably realizing that his case was hopeless, and announced that he would not carry through with the appeal. The anti-discrimination forces then waited for a few weeks while government officials informed the Dresden community about their legal obligations and the possibility of future prosecutions. On 16 November 1956, a test group from the NUA asked for service from Kay's Café and the owner complied. Racial segregation in Dresden had come to an end.[126]

* * * * *

The story of Dresden helps illustrate the significant contribution of trade unionists, especially the JLC, to the Canadian post-war human rights struggle.[127] At the same time, it also demonstrates the importance of ethnic/religious co-operation. Jews, blacks, Anglo-Celts, and even Chinese Canadians played leading roles in the fight against racial discrimination in Dresden, and they in turn were supported by groups representing a broad spectrum of Canadians.

Does Dresden, however, tell us much about the inter-relationship of race and class? As David Roediger has noted (American) labour historians in recent years have moved away "from dead end debates about whether to give priority to race or class identity," and have begun to struggle with "the difficult, rewarding task of showing how racial identity and class identity have shaped each other."[128] Yet at the same time, there is today a tendency to avoid overly broad generalizations. As Thomas Sugrue has argued, "... we need to be attentive to the diversity of racial practices, from union to union, from workplace to workplace, and from community to community."[129]

In specific terms, the story of Dresden suggests that the human rights activists' success was the result of a unique concatenation of ideas about race and class—a trans-class consensus that the interests of both workers and employers trumped racial divisions. Kalmen Kaplansky began with the notion that racial (and religious) discrimination hurt the working class (defined primarily as trade unionists), and argued that this split workers, playing into the hands of the "enemy"—the employers. At the same time, Premier Frost not only believed that prejudice violated middle-class ideas about respectability, but also thought that it could threaten the interests of capital; discrimination could undermine his plans for Ontario's economic development.[130]

Moreover, Kaplansky and Frost saw class from a common anti-communist perspective, each believing that his own respective class interest could not be furthered by communism, either at the theoretical or political level.

The Kaplansky view was social-democratic, or what some labour historians have called the "reformist" position—committed to the evolutionary growth of the welfare state while rejecting the radicalism of the communist Labour Progressive Party and its supporters.[131] Frost, for his part, was a reform liberal, believing that capitalism was worth saving by means of astute political tinkering and patching. Human rights legislation, therefore, was intended to help make the world safe for both socialist and liberal democracy.

Of course, Kaplansky and Frost were not the only actors in this story. Since their two viewpoints came to be widely shared, a human rights community made up of diverse class and racial components skilfully lobbied the Ontario government into passing and implementing a Fair Accommodation Practices Act.

Yet, we should be wary of assuming that trade union support for integration in Dresden signalled the arrival of a new age of trade union tolerance for ethnic and religious diversity. American labour historians specializing in race relations have begun to point out the complicated tensions between union leaders and rank-and-file members, as well as the differences between racism on the shop floor, in local communities, and in the voting booth. Progress at one level does not necessarily mean change in another venue.[132]

More work remains to be done about the contribution of labour in general, and the JLC in particular, to Canada's post-war shift into "the age of rights."[133] It is true that at least two articles dealing with the history of anti-discrimination legislation have suggested a less-than-complete commitment to human rights on the part of Canadian trade unions. Both Agnes Calliste (writing on the effect of the federal Fair Employment Practices Act on the railroad porters' struggle against workplace discrimination), and Shirley Tillotson (analyzing the impact of Ontario's Female Employees Fair Remuneration Act on women in trade unions) have demonstrated that certain unions tried to block any movement towards real equality.[134] This suggests that trade union prejudice was much more likely to arise when it came to bread-and-butter issues of hiring and promotion than in situations like Dresden. The new post-war, human-rights discourse and arguments about union solidarity held considerable appeal, but they were never really put to the test in this small Ontario town where the "villains" were small-time capitalists, and for trade unionists the "wages of whiteness" were relatively small or even non-existent.

Nevertheless, the story of Dresden represents an important milestone in the history of organized labour. Without denigrating the role played by the black community in struggling for justice, and admitting also the very significant contribution of groups such as the Canadian Jewish Congress and the Toronto Association for Civil Liberties, this paper has demonstrated that organized labour played a crucial role in the campaign for Canada's first Fair Accommodation Practices Act and the struggle to ensure that it would be effectively applied. While in the past trade unionists had too often opposed racial equality, by the mid-1950s many of them were facilitating Canada's entry into the age of rights.

I thank Ruth Frager and James Walker for their valuable comments and suggestions. I also thank Magda Seydegart, who first told me about Kalmen Kaplansky.

Endnotes

1. *Working-Class Experience: Rethinking the History of Canadian Labour, 1800–1991*, 2nd. ed. (Toronto 1992). In the United States, on the other hand, "the study of race and labor has become an academic growth industry," with numerous historians examining the way organized labour reacted to racism—in some cases contributing to it and in other cases resisting. Eric Arnesen, "Up From Exclusion: Black and White Workers, Race, and the State of Labor History," *Reviews in American History*, 26 (1998), 146–174, at 147. Some American works include: Robert Korstad and Nelson Lichtenstein, "Opportunities Found and Lost: Labor, Radicals, and the Early Civil Rights Movement,"

The Journal of American History, 75, 3 (December 1988); David R. Roediger, *The Wages of Whiteness: Race and the Making of the American Working Class* (New York 1991), and "Race and the Working-Class Past in the United States: Multiple Identities and the Future of Labor History," *International Review of Social History*, 38 (1993), *Supplement*, 127–143; Alan Dawley and Joe William Trotter, Jr., "Race and Class," *Labor History*, 35 (Fall 1994), 486–94; Robert H. Zieger, *The CIO*, 1935–1955 (Chapel Hill and London 1995); Kevin Boyle, *The UAW and the Heyday of American Liberalism, 1945–1968* (Ithaca 1995), and '"There Are No Sorrows That the Union Can't Heal': The Struggle for Racial Equality in the United Automobile Workers, 1940–1960," *Labor History*, 36, 1 (1995), 5–33; Rick Halpern, *Down on the Killing Floor: Black and White Workers in Chicago's Packinghouses, 1904–1954* (Urbana 1997); Thomas J. Sugrue, *The Origins of the Urban Crisis: Race and Inequality in Postwar Detroit* (Princeton 1996); Daniel Letwin, *The Challenge of Interracial Unionism: Alabama Coal Miners, 1878–1921* (Chapel Hill 1998); Calvin Winslow, ed., *Waterfront Workers: New Perspectives on Race and Class* (Urbana and Chicago) 1998. Note also symposia published in *Labor History* on recent works by Zieger, 37 (Spring 1996), Sugrue, 39, 1 (1998), Halpern, 40, 2 (1999), and Letwin, 41, 1 (2000).

2. Gillian Creese, "Sexuality and the Minimum Wage in British Columbia," *Journal of Canadian Studies*, 26,4 (Winter 1991–92), 120–140; Shirley Tillotson, "Human Rights Law as Prism: Women's Organizations, Unions, and Ontario's Female Employees Fair Remuneration Act, 1951," *Canadian Historical Review*, 72, 4 (1991), 532–557; Ann Porter, "Women and Income Security in the Post-War Period: The Case of Unemployment Insurance, 1945–1962," *Labour/Le Travail*, 31 (Spring 1993), 111–44; Gillian Creese, "Power and Pay: The Union and Equal Pay at B.C. Electric/Hydro," *Labour/Le Travail*, 32 (Fall 1993), 225–45.

3. The best and most comprehensive article is by Carmela Patrias and Ruth A. Frager, '"This is our country, these are our rights': Minorities and the Origins of Ontario's Human Rights Campaigns," *Canadian Historical Review*, 82, 1 (2001), 1–35. See also Arnold Bruner, "The Genesis of Ontario's Human Rights Legislation: A Study in Law Reform," *University of Toronto Faculty of Law Review*, 37 (1979), 236–253, and "Citizen Power: The Story of Ontario Human Rights Legislation," *Viewpoints: The Canadian Jewish Quarterly*, 3 (Summer 1981), 4–15; Agnes Calliste, "Sleeping Car Porters in Canada: An Ethnically Submerged Split Labour Market," *Canadian Ethnic Studies* 19, 1 (1987), 1–20; "Blacks on Canadian Railways," *Canadian Ethnic Studies*, 20, 2 (1988), 36–52; Tania Das Gupta, "Anti-Racism and the Organized Labour Movement," in Vic Satzewich, ed., *Racism & Social Inequality in Canada: Concepts, Controversies & Strategies of Resistance* (Toronto 1998); Daniel Hill and Marvin Schiff, *Human Rights in Canada: A Focus on Racism* (Ottawa 1986); R. Brian Howe, "The Evolution of Human Rights Policy in Ontario," *Canadian Journal of Political Science*, 24 (December 1991), 783–802, and "Incrementalism and Human Rights Reform," *Journal of Canadian Studies*, 28 (1993), 29–44; Ronald Manzer, "Human Rights in Domestic Politics and Policy," in Robert O. Matthews and Cranford Pratt, eds., *Human Rights in Canadian Foreign Policy* (Kingston and Montreal 1988), 23–45; James Walker, *"Race," Rights and the Law in the Supreme Court of Canada: Historical Case Studies* (Waterloo 1997). Note also references in Robin Winks, *The Blacks in Canada: A History* (Montreal 1971), 423, 425, 426, 437, 446, 451, 467, 474, as well as two memoirs of black political activists and unionists: Donna Hill, ed., *A Black Man's Toronto 1914–1980: The Reminiscences of Harry Gairey* (Toronto 1981); Stanley G. Grizzle (with John Cooper), *My Name's Not George: The Story of the Brotherhood of Sleeping Car Porters in Canada* (Toronto 1998).

4. Herbert Sohn, "Human Rights Legislation in Ontario: A Case Study," Ph.D. thesis, University of Toronto, 1975; Gordon Mackintosh, "The Development of the Canadian Human Rights Act: A Case Study of The Legislative Process," M.A. thesis, University of Manitoba, 1982; John Bagnall, "The Ontario Conservatives and the Development of Anti-Discrimination Policy," Ph.D. thesis, Queen's University, 1984; Brian Howe, "Human Rights Policy in Ontario: The Tension Between Positive and Negative State Laws," Ph.D. thesis, University of Toronto, 1988; Christopher MacLennan, "Toward the Charter: Canadians and the Demand for a National Bill of Rights, 1929–1960," Ph.D. thesis, University of Western Ontario, 1996; Ross Lambertson, "Activists in the Age of Rights: The Struggle for Human Rights in Canada –1945–1960" Ph.D. thesis (Chapter 6 is the basis for this paper). Note also the video on Kalmen Kaplansky and the JLC, "Working Side By Side: The Struggle for Human Rights" (Ottawa 1985).

5. The concept of "policy community" is taken from political science. It has been defined by Paul Pross as "that part of a political system that—by virtue of its functional responsibilities, its vested interests, and its specialized knowledge—acquires a dominant voice in determining government decisions in a specific field of public activity, and is generally permitted by society at large and the public authorities in particular to determine public policy in that field." Paul A. Pross, *Group Politics and Public Policy* (Toronto 1986), 98; see also William D. Coleman and Grace Skogstad, eds., *Policy Communities and Public Policy in Canada* (Toronto 1990).
6. Most of the papers pertaining to the JLC were donated to the National Archives of Canada (hereafter NAC) by Kalmen Kaplansky, the JLC National Director from 1946 to 1956. Some of the records are in the JLC Papers (hereafter JLCP), some in the Kaplansky Papers (hereafter KKP), and some in the Ontario Labour Committee for Human Rights Papers (hereafter OLCP). The Kaplansky Papers contain a set of his "Reports," at first written for the Joint Advisory Committee on Labour Relations of the Jewish Labour Committee and the Canadian Jewish Congress, and then (from 1956) for the National Standing Committee on Human Rights of the Canadian Labour Congress. His papers also include a set of "Notes" which are comments on these Reports, written while he was Senior Fellow of the Human Rights Research and Education Centre at the University of Ottawa.
7. As James Walker has pointed out, in defending his decision to explain Canadian racism by examining a number of legal decisions, the approach of "newer social history" has revived the "singled-out case" as a method of study, as well as the concept of "thick" narrative. Walker, "*'Race,' Rights and the Law*," 41, 49. Chapter 5 of his book is a case study about how the Toronto JLC labour committee helped to challenge immigration law discriminating against people from the Caribbean.
8. Menahem Kaufman, *An Ambiguous Partnership: Non-Zionists and Zionists in America 1939–1948* (Detroit 1991), 12–16, 46.
9. NAC, KKP, MG30, A 53, "Notes," 1946–7, vol. 20, file 3,3-21; Stuart E. Rosenberg, "The Jewish Community in Canada," *A History* vol. 1 (Toronto 1970), 172; Ruth A. *Frager, Sweatshop Strife: Class, Ethnicity, and Gender in the Jewish Labour Movement of Toronto, 1900–1939* (Toronto 1992), 53–4.
10. Frager, *Sweatshop Strife,* especially Chapter 8; Erna Paris, *Jews: An Account of Their Experience in Canada* (Toronto 1980), 134–5, 147.
11. "Their liberalism kept them from being communists while their socialism prevented them from becoming liberals." Walter Young, *The Anatomy of a Party: The National CCF 1932–61* (Toronto 1969), 137.
12. Cameron Smith, *The Unfinished Journey* (Toronto 1989), Chapters 10 and 11; David Lewis, *The Good Fight: Political Memoirs 1909–1958* (Toronto 1981), 22, 135. Lewis refers (at 225) to his 1943 CCF federal election nomination meeting where Maurice Silcoff was co-chair and the future JLC Executive Director (Kalmen Kaplansky) was secretary.
13. As Kaplansky noted, Jewish workers had far less union and political power than in the United States, and "... we had to reach out beyond the Jewish labour sector and make it a part of the overall involvement of the trade union movement. Otherwise, we would have remained a small, relatively insignificant group." NAC, KKP, MG30, A 53, vol. 20, file 3, "Notes," 1946–7, 17.
14. NAC, KKP, MG30, A 53, vol. 20, file 4, "Report of Activities for Improved Human Relations of the Jewish Labor [sic] Committee of Canada for the Year Ending July 31, 1947," 2.
15. Kaplansky was a member of the CCF National Council, and ran as a candidate in a federal by-election in 1950. NAC, KKP, MG30, A 53, vol. 20, file 4, "Report" July 31, 1947, 1; vol. 20, file 3, "Notes," 1946–7, 1–3, 37–45, 150; "Notes," 1950, 58–9, 88; interview with Kalmen Kaplansky, 12 June 1996.
16. The literature on pre-war union opposition to "foreign" labour has usually focused upon the exclusion of Asians, especially in British Columbia. See, for example, Gillian Creese, "Exclusion or Solidarity? Vancouver Workers Confront the 'Oriental Problem,'" B.C. *Studies*, 86 (Winter 1988–89), 24–49; Jin Tan, "Chinese Labour and the Reconstituted Social Order of British Columbia," *Canadian Ethnic Studies*, 19, 3 (1987), 68–88; Palmer, *Working Class Experience*, 123–4, 212–3, 266.
17. NAC, KKP, MG30, A 53, vol. 20, file 3, "Notes," 1946–7, 104. Charles Millard was one of the most powerful members of the provincial CCF. He served as a CCF vice-president (and Ontario CCF President) throughout the 1940s, and was an Ontario MPP from 1943 to 1945 and again

from 1948 to 1951. See Morden Lazarus, *Years of Hard Labour: An Account of the Canadian workingman, his organizations and tribulations, over a period of more than a hundred years* (Don Mills 1974), 54; J.T. Morley, *Secular Socialists: The CCF/NDP In Ontario: A Biography* (Montreal 1984), 177–8; Laurel Sefton MacDowell, "The Career of a Canadian Trade Union Leader: C.H. Millard, 1937–1946," *Relations industrielles/Industrial Relations*, 43 (1988), 609–32. For Fred Dowling, see Lazarus, *Years of Hard Labour*, 74.

18. For a discussion of union educational programs in the early 1950s, see David Smith, "A Survey Report on Labour Education in Canada," 15 March 1951, *Canadian Labour Congress Papers* (hereafter *CLCP*), vol. 204, file 9; Gerald Friesen, "Adult Education and Union Education: Aspects of English Canadian Culture History in the Twentieth Century," *Labour/Le Travail*, 34 (Fall 1994), 163–88. For critical overviews of social unionism, see Bryan Palmer, *Working-Class Experience*, 280–4, 337, 371; Leo Panitch and Donald Swartz, "Towards Permanent Exceptionalism: Coercion and Consent in Canadian Industrial Relations," *Labour/Le Travail*, 13 (Spring 1984): 133–157, at 145. By contrast, see Shirley Tillotson's examination of one aspect of post-war social unionism—welfare work—in "'When our membership awakens': Welfare work and union activism, 1950–1965," *Labour/Le Travail*, 40 (Fall 1997), 137–69.
19. For a quick overview of racist ideas in Canada as well as a discussion of the emergence of a "war conscience," see Chapter 1 of Walker, *"Race," Rights and the Law*.
20. For a discussion of how the United States was responding to post-war racial tensions, and how Harry Truman was "twisting liberalism in new [reform liberal] directions," see John Frederick Martin, *Civil Rights and the Crisis of Liberalism: The Democratic Party 1945–1976* (Boulder 1979), 69–76.
21. Some of the reasons why Ontario Premier Leslie Frost supported the passage of anti-discrimination legislation are discussed below.
22. Desmond Morton and J.L. Granatstein, *Victory 1945: Canadians from War to Peace* (Calgary 1984), 253. According to political scientist Brian Howe, "Historical evidence in Canada does suggest that human rights do suffer in hard times." R. Brian Howe, "Human Rights in hard times: the post-war Canadian experience," *Canadian Public Administration/Administration Publique du Canada*, 35, 1 (Winter 1992), 461–84, at 465.
23. NAC, KKP, MG30, A 53, vol. 20, file 3, "Notes," 1946–7, 1–2; Canadian Jewish Congress Archives (hereafter CJCA), CD Box 2, file 28z, "Voice of the Unconquered; Monthly Newsletter of the [American] Jewish Labor Committee" (January–February 1946).
24. NAC, KKP, MG30, A 53, vol. 20, file 3, "Notes," 1946–7, 72, 106, 108–110; vol. 24, file 3, "Report," 11 October 1948. Andras was also a brother-in-law of David Lewis. NAC, KKP, MG30 A 53, vol. 20, file 3, "Notes," 1946–7, 104–5. The chair was R.J. Lamoureux, Montreal Sub-director of the United Steelworkers of America (and a CCF activist), while its two other members were Eamon Park, Publicity Director of the Steelworkers (as well as a CCF member of the Ontario legislature), and Andy Andras, Assistant Director of the CCL (and close friend).
25. The TLC Platform demanded "exclusion of all races that cannot be properly assimilated into the national life of Canada." NAC, KKP, MG30, A 53, vol. 20, file 3, "Notes," 1946–7, 85, 90; Freda Hawkins, Canada and Immigration: Public Policy and Public Concern (Montreal and London 1972), 85. The TLC deleted this platform plank in 1948, approving a Cloak and Dressmaker's Union resolution drafted by Kaplansky. NAC, KKP, MG30, A 53, vol. 20, file 5, "Notes," 1948, 90–2.
26. NAC, KKP, MG30, A 53, vol. 20, file 3, "Notes," 1946–7, 91–2 and file 5, "Notes," 1948, 22–8. The committee only became "activated" in 1946, after Kaplansky became the Director of the JLC. It was later renamed the National Standing Committee against Racial Intolerance.
27. According to a CJC report, Shane admitted in confidence that he was willing to dictate Jodoin's activities regarding the JLC's anti-discrimination programme. CJCA, CD Box 2, file 28z, "Organized Labour in Canada."
28. NAC, KKP, MG30, A 53, vol. 20, file 3, "Notes," 1946–7, 94–8. The Kaplansky network constantly emphasized that prejudice endangered labour solidarity. See, for example, its *Canadian Labour Reports* pamphlet, "You Belong to a Minority," issued about 1949, which states that, "Unionists know that race hatred and discrimination is used as a weapon to smash unions. Those who promote race hatred are invariably the loudest opponents of unionism. Divide and rule is their method in destroying unions by setting one racial group against the other." Angus MacInnis Memorial Collection, University of British Columbia Special Collections, vol. 39A, file 11.

29. While it was not immediately clear that the committee chair (Ford Brand, Secretary-Treasurer of the TLC-affiliated Toronto District Labour Council, and a member of the Orange Lodge), would be very supportive, Kaplansky had strong allies in the form of the vice-chair (CCL representative Eamon Park) and the secretary-treasurer (Abraham Kirzner of the ILGWU, a vice-president of the JLC). In time, however, even Brand became a strong supporter. "Charge Labor Group Aim Is Largely 'Soviet Baiting,'" *Toronto Star*, 11 February 1947; Kaplansky interview, 12 June 1996; NAC, KKP, MG30, A 53, vol. 20, file 3, "Notes," 1946–7, 174–181, 210–11; file 13, "Notes," 1952, 62; vol. 21, file 2, "Notes," 1954, 70; NAC, JLCP, MG28, V 75, vol. 41, file 4, Toronto Provisional Committee "Minutes," 15 April 1947. Note that in 1954 the formal name of the Toronto committee became the "Toronto Joint Labour Committee for Human Rights."
30. The CJC was an umbrella group for a large number of Jewish organizations. In the 1930s it had formed an alliance with the Jewish rights group, B'nai B'rith, creating a Joint Public Relations Committee (JPRC) for the purpose of combatting anti-Semitism. The JPRC had equal representation from the two constituent groups, but all public statements were to be made by the CJC, as the official voice of Jews in Canada. Ontario Jewish Archives (hereafter OJA), B.G. Kayfetz, introduction to the "Finding Aid of the Joint Community Relations Committee 1938–78"; Rosenberg, *In the Midst of Freedom*, 46.
31. Interview with Kalmen Kaplansky, 12 June 1996. Kaplansky has also noted that some CJC "supporters were engaged in union-busting activities and most of them did not share our faith in social democracy." NAC, KKP, MG30, A 53, vol. 20, file 3, "Notes," 1946–7, 47. In addition, the CJC at that time also included a traditional antagonist of the JLC, the communist-oriented United Jewish People's Order (UJPO).
32. CJCA, ZA 1947, vol. 10, file 127, Percy Bengough [TLC President] to [A.H.J.] Zaitlin [CJC "public relations" worker], 11 March 1947, and Mosher to Zaitlin, 12 March 1947. See also Zaitlin's memorandum to Hayes, 15 July 1947, CJCA, ZA 1947, vol. 11, file 127a.
33. CJCA, CD vol. 2, file 28z, Zaitlin to Hayes, 5 May 1947, and ZA 1947, vol. 11, file 127a, Zaitlin to Hayes, 15 July 1947. Note that the JPRC was also committed to human rights work outside the ranks of organized labour. Ben Kayfetz, executive director of the Toronto JPRC, recalls that when he was hired in 1947 he was told that his main focus should be lobbying for anti-discrimination legislation, and this led to an intensive campaign of moulding public opinion. Interview, 7 June, 1996; letter from Ben Kayfetz to Ross Lambertson, 27 April 2000.
34. NAC, KKP, MG30, A 53, vol. 20, file 3, "Notes," 1946–7, 129–143; CJCA.Z A 1947, vol. 11, file 127a, "Labour Committee Minutes," 10 December 1947. The CJC donated, at first, about $12,000 a year. NAC, KKP, MG30, A 53, vol. 20, file 3, "Notes," 1946–7, 130.
35. NAC, KKP, MG30, A 53, vol. 20, file 3, "Notes," 1946–7, 55–6. Kaplansky also managed to create a Hamilton committee in 1948, but it did not last for very long. He was also unable to set up permanent groups in Victoria and Calgary. In the late 1950s Kaplansky's successor, Sid Blum, organized a Halifax committee, as well as subsidiary bodies in Amherst and Sydney.
36. According to Kaplansky, "Ours was the only major continuous effort in which the two organizations participated jointly prior to the merger of the two in 1956." NAC, KKP, MG30, A 53, vol. 20, file 3, "Notes," 1946–7, 60.
37. NAC, KKP, MG30, A 53, vol. 20, file 3, "Notes," 1946–7, 57, 155–71, 211, 250–1; file 5, "Notes," 1948, 36–7, 74–5, 79; file 7, "Notes," 1949, 120.
38. NAC, KKP, MG30, A 53, vol. 20, file 3, "Notes," 1946–7, 165.
39. Interview with Kalmen Kaplansky, 12 June 1996; NAC, KKP, MG30, A 53, vol. 20, file 3, "Notes," 1946–7, 130; NAC, JLCP, MG28, V 75, vol. 41, file 6, Kaplansky to Gordon Milling [the third Toronto committee secretary], 15 May 1952.
40. Kaplansky insisted that no firms with Jewish owners be approached, since this would upset the CJC, but several non-Jewish companies donated money to the Toronto group, often over a number of years: Loblaw's, Canadian Breweries, Robert Simpson Co., Ontario Automobile Co., and O'Keefe's. NAC, JLCP, MG28, V 75, vol. 41, file 14, Donna Hill to Kaplansky, 16 November 1953; NAC, OLCP, MG28, 1 173, vol. 2, file 1 ("Donations, 1948–1955").
41. NAC, KKP, MG30, A 53, vol. 20, file 3, "Notes," 1946–7, 188–192; file 5, "Notes," 1948, 56; file 13, "Notes," 1952, 77; "Notes," 1954, 3; JLCP, MG28, V 75, vol. 41, files 16, 18, and

20—Toronto committee's "Financial Statement," April 1954, November 1954, April 1955, May 1955. Note also that Charles Millard made personal donations. Interview with Kalmen Kaplansky, 12 June 1996.

42. By the early 1950s the TLC and CCL human rights committees were contributing $1,000.00 each to the JLC human rights program; see NAC, KKP, MG30, A 53, vol. 20, file 13, "Notes," 1952, 76–7; vol. 20, file 14, "Notes," 1953, 119–20; NAC, JLCP, MG28, V 75, vol. 13, file 20, Andras to Kaplansky, 18 June 1953, and vol. 41, file 11, Kaplansky to Gordon Milling [second Toronto committee secretary], 25 June 1953. Canadian Labour Reports, a source of information about human rights issues in Canada, was formally a TLC publication but came under Kaplansky's direct editorial control.
43. NAC, KKP, MG30, A 53, vol. 21, file 2, "Notes," 1954, 3–4.
44. NAC, JLCP, MG28, V 75, vol. 41, file 4, "Report of Progress, 1951"; file 5, Milling to Kaplansky, 11 February 1952; vol. 13, file 8, Kaplansky to Gower Markle [Steelworkers' Director of Education], 23 August 1956; file 9, Markle to Sid Blum [Fifth Toronto Committee Secretary], 9 September 1959; interview with Kaplansky, 12 June 1996. Note also the Autoworkers' offer to pay the costs of reprinting an article on Dresden which Blum intended to use for publicity purposes. NAC, KKP, MG30, A 53, vol. 21, file 4, "Notes," 1955, 121–125.
45. There are numerous references in Kaplansky's papers to support from the UAW and its fair employment practices committees, including the efforts of future CLC President Dennis McDermott, who served for a while as chair of the Local 439 FEP committee. By 1953 McDermott was also an active member of the Toronto labour committee. NAC, SLCP, MG28 V 75, vol. 20, file 8, "Report," December 1949; vol. 41, file 9, "Report," 26 February 1953; vol. 41, file 14, "Report," 4 November 1953.
46. NAC, KKP, MG30, A 53, vol. 20, file 3, "Notes," 1946–7,160. See the debate "Education v. Laws—Which Way to Tolerance," in *Canadian Labour Reports* (September 1949), partly reproduced in Kaplansky's "Notes" for 1949, at 113–5. NAC, KKP, MG30, A 53, vol. 20, file 7. See also Sid Blum's summary, "Human Rights in the Labour Movement," reproduced in Kaplansky's "Notes" for 1956, at 128–9. NAC, KKP, MG30, A 53, vol. 21, file 6.
47. NAC, KKP, MG30, A 53, vol. 20, file 3, "Notes," 1946–7,59,79,187,199; file 5, "Notes," 1948, 5, 66–72, 132–3; file 7, "Notes," 1949, 129–133; NAC, JLCP, MG28, V 75, vol. 13, file 15, Kaplansky to Mosher, 29 August 1947.
48. NAC, KKP, MG30, A 53, vol. 20, file 3, "Notes," 1946–7, 58, 184; vol. 21, file 4, "Notes," 1955, 52–5. For a reference to the CJC approaching the Toronto labour committee with its plans for an Ontario Fair Employment Act, see "Notes," 1946–7, 190. One of the first steps in the CJC campaign to achieve a Fair Employment Law came with the funding of a Gallup poll to test public opinion (mentioned below). OJA, Joint Community Relations Committee Collection, MG8 S, Joint Community Relations Committee Papers (hereafter JCRCP), JPRC Correspondence 1946, Box 3, file 1, "Minutes," 17 June 1946, and JPRC Correspondence 1947, Reel 3, file 23, "Activities Report," 28 May 1947; J.H. Fine, "Public Relations," [CJC] *Congress Bulletin*, 30 May 1947.
49. For a discussion of this case, see Chapter 3 of Walker, *"Race," Rights and the Law*.
50. An Act to Prevent the Publication of Discriminatory Matter Referring to Race or Creed, SO 1944, c. 51. Despite the limitations of the new statute, the classical liberal Toronto *Globe and Mail* castigated the government for entering a field that it had no business attempting to regulate. "Racial Bill Not the Cure," and "Racial Bill Safeguarded," 10, 13 March 1944.
51. There were many well-publicized incidents of racial discrimination in post-war Ontario. For a first-hand account of some of them, see Hill, *A Black Man's Toronto*.
52. "The Dresden Story" is the title of a once widely distributed 1954 National Film Board production dealing with racial prejudice and discrimination in Dresden. It was made before the issue was resolved, and contains interviews with many of the townspeople, both black and white.
53. For an overview of contemporary Dresden, as well as a summary of the events surrounding the struggle to eliminate "Jim Crow" during the late 1940s and the 1950s, see Stuart McLean, *Welcome Home: Travels in Smalltown Canada* (Toronto 1992).
54. Sidney Katz, "Jim Crow Lives in Dresden," *Maclean's Magazine*, 1 November 1949; NAC, KKP, MG30, A 53, vol. 20, file 7, "Report," July–August 1949; NAC, OLCP, MG28, I 173, vol. 12, file

2, "Hugh Burnette's remarks on Dresden," 18 January 1954, and Sid Blum, "Report on Visit to Dresden," 22, 23 July 1954; *The Dresden Story*. However, the town was not entirely segregated. The children went to school together and mixed in the Boy Scouts and Girl Guides, while both blacks and whites were welcome at the Legion. Yet except for the Catholic Church, blacks were not welcome at any of the "white" churches.

55. The author is indebted to James Walker for background information about Burnett; the two became good friends as a result of Walker's historical research. In the documents examined for this chapter, Burnett signed his name "Burnette." According to Walker (personal communication to the author, 30 July 1998), he sometimes spelled it "Burnett," and later in life found that this was the spelling on the tomb of his grandfather or great-grandfather; from that time on he used only that spelling and asked that Walker also use it. This is the spelling that Walker used in *"Race," Rights and the Law* and Stuart McLean followed Walker's advice in *Welcome Home*. Information about Burnett's complaint in 1943 comes from Walker (at 176). Information about the lawsuit is contained in the 1955 decision by Justice Grosch (discussed below); Burnett refers to it having taken place "a little more than six" years previously. A copy of the Grosch decision is in the OJA, JPRC Collection, vol. 6, file 13.
56. NAC, OLCP, MG28, 1 173, vol. 12, file 2, "Hugh Burnette's remarks on Dresden," 18 January 1954.
57. Katz, "Jim Crow," 51–2; testimony of Lyle E. Talbot of the Windsor Council on Group Relations in *Minutes of Proceedings and Evidence of the Special Committee on Human Rights and Fundamental Freedoms* (Ottawa 1960), 256; Katz, "Jim Crow"; OJA, Joint Community Relations Committee Collection, MG8 S, JCRCP, JPRC Correspondence 1947, Reel 6, file 12, Burnett to Ben Kayfetz, 9 April 1949; "Dresden Puts Off Race Referendum on Technicality," *Globe* 19 April 1949.
58. Most of these ACL board members were what might be called "nodal actors" in the Ontario human rights community, linking together different organizations and elements of society. Sandwell was editor of *Saturday Night* magazine and formerly Rector of Queen's University. As already noted, Millard was national director of the Steelworkers, and Brewin was one of his associates in the provincial CCF elite. Feinberg was Rabbi of Holy Blossom Temple in Toronto, and chair of the JPRC. Seeley, as Provost of Trinity College, had close ties to academia, while Maude Grant, formerly dean of women at Royal Victoria College at McGill (and incidentally, the mother of philosopher George Grant) was part of Canada's intellectual-social elite. In addition, the Japanese Canadian Citizen's Association was affiliated with the ACL, and supported its campaigns for anti-discrimination legislation. NAC, *Japanese Canadian Citizen's Association Papers* (hereafter *JCCAP*), MG28, V 7, vol. 14, file 17, [George] Tanaka [JCCA President] to [Ontario Premier Leslie] Frost, 6 January 1950, and Tanaka to [ACL Secretary Irving] Himel, 24 February 1950.
59. Himel was another nodal actor in the human rights community. He worked with the Workers' Education Association and the CJC in the Drummond Wren case against restrictive covenants, served as lobbyist and legal counsel for the Committee for the Repeal of the Chinese Immigration Act, and helped to run the ACL-affiliated Committee for a Bill of Rights. He remained with the ACL from its conception until the early 1960s, when he assisted in its reincarnation as the Canadian Civil Liberties Association. He was also, during the Dresden affair, a member of the JPRC.
60. Donna Hill, the paid secretary of the Toronto labour committee from 1953–4, remembers that she and Ben Kayfetz, the paid secretary of the JPRC in Toronto, did most of the work in cobbling together ad hoc coalitions. Interview, 8 June 1996. Ben Kayfetz also recalls that the ACL was a useful non-sectarian cover for the activities of the JPRC. Interview, 7 June, 1996.
61. NAC, KKP, MG30, A 53, vol. 20, file 7, "Notes," 1949, 39; NAC, OLCP, MG28,1173, vol. 9, file 1, "Committee on Group Relations of the Association For Civil Liberties." Note that Eamon Park of the Toronto labour committee was also a member of the ACL Council. NAC, JCCAP, MG28, V 7, vol. 15, file 23, Irving Himel to George Tanaka [ACL list attached], 9 May 1949.
62. A policy community can form different policy networks. William Coleman and Grace Skogstad have defined a policy network as "the properties that characterize the relationships among the particular set of actors that forms around an issue of importance to the policy community"; see their "Policy Communities and Policy Networks: A Structural Approach" in *Policy Communities and Public*

Policy in Canada (Toronto 1990), 14–33 at 26. See also, Chapter 6 ("Policy Communities and Networks") of Leslie A. Pal, *Beyond Policy Analysis: Public Issue Management in Turbulent Times* (Scarborough 1997).

63. NAC, Mrs. W.L. [Maude] Grant Papers, MG30, D 59, vol. 47, file "Notes and Memoranda: Civil Liberties Association," "Brief in Respect to Legislation Dealing with Expressions of Racial and Religious Discrimination in Ontario"; "Delegation Impresses Frost: Says He'll Act on Race Discrimination," *Star*, 8 June 1949; "Demand New Law to Guard Rights of Racial Groups," *Globe*, 8 June 1949; NAC, KKP, MG30, A 53, vol. 20, file 8, "Report," June 1949. A list of the groups and individuals in the many delegations led by the ACL in the late 1940s and the 1950s can be found in the appendices of Sohn, "Human Rights Legislation."
64. NAC, KKP, MG30, A 53, vol. 20, file 5, "Notes," 1948,44; Katz, "Jim Crow."
65. Katz, "Jim Crow."
66. "Dresden Voters Reject Equality for Negroes," Globe, 6 December 1949; "Wide Criticism Follows Plebiscite in Dresden," *Globe*, 7 December 1949; "Dresden Draws the Color Line" [editorial], *Globe*, 8 December 1949; "Dresden Is Sensitive," *Saturday Night*, 21 February 1950.
67. Ontario Archives (hereafter OA), Premier Leslie Frost Papers (hereafter LFP), General Correspondence, vol. 48, file 87-G, "To Mayor Walter S. Weese and Council" [NUA brief], 5 February 1951.
68. "Brief from 70 Groups Asks Wider Legislation to Fight Discrimination," *Globe*, 25 January 1950; NAC, CLCP, MG28, 1103, vol. 335, file "Civil Rights—Association for Civil Liberties," "A Brief to the Premier of Ontario (24 January 1950)."
69. John Bagnall, "The Ontario Conservatives," 200. Bagnall notes that, according to the Conservative MPP Allan Grossman, Frost often said that his job was like feeding a young child—he could no more obtain immediate acceptance of minority rights than a parent could cajole a child into eating a large meal. Bagnall, "The Ontario Conservatives," 200, 338 (note 114).
70. Patrias and Frager, "'This is our Country,'" 31 (draft copy, kindly lent by the authors). Such denial was common. As Kaplansky's successor as JLC director (Sid Blum) wrote to his Toronto labour committee secretary, "Canada isn't the U.S.—where problems are obvious, ever-present and serious. In Canada, at least one or two or even three of these conditions are usually missing. We have to dig for both the victims of discrimination and some of the problems." NAC, JLCP, MG28, V 75, vol. 42, file 19, Blum to Maxwell, 13 May 1958. Note also the comment of Constance Backhouse: "The pattern of 'racelessness' that pervades Canadian legal history encouraged Canadian citizens to maintain a 'stupefying innocence,' in the words of Dionne Brand, about the enormity of racial oppression." Constance Backhouse, *Colour-Coded: A Legal History of Racism in Canada, 1900–1950* (Toronto 1999), 278.
71. As the Mayor of Dresden argued, "[t]his is a democratic country.... You can't force anyone to serve Negroes." Katz, "Jim Crow," 9. For a discussion of how the emergence of Ontario human rights legislation reflected a shift to reform liberal values, see Howe, "The Evolution of Human Rights Policy"; R. Brian Howe and David Johnson, *Restraining Equality: Human Rights Commissions in Canada* (Toronto 1999), chapter 1.
72. For writings on welfare state development which touch upon anti-discrimination law, see: Donald Bellamy, "Social Policy in Ontario," in Bessie Touzel, ed., *The Province of Ontario: Its Social Services*, 11th edn (Toronto 1983); Leslie A. Pal, "Federalism, Social Policy, and the Constitution," in Jacqueline S. Ismail, ed., *Canadian Social Welfare Policy: Federal and Provincial Dimensions* (Montreal 1985). For writings on anti-discrimination law which link it to the growth of the "ethical" or "positive" state, see: Ronald Manzer, *Public Policies and Political Development in Canada* (Toronto 1985); Anderson, "The Development of Human Rights Protection"; Howe, "Human Rights Policy."
73. "Employment Problem," and "Discrimination Problem," *Saturday Night*, 4 July 1947, and 7 February 1950. Sandwell asked in the former article, "How can any law be enforced that will prohibit the discrimination on race or religion and leave unimpaired the rights of discrimination on ability and honesty?" He added, in a question that indicates the staying power of post-war racism, "What would be their [i.e. the supporters of the law] reaction if they found a Negro waiting to shave them in a barber shop, or to give them a permanent wage in a coiffeur's?"
74. Roger Graham, *Old Man Ontario*, 177.

75. Mark Leier, "Forum: W[h]ither Labour History: Regionalism, Class, and the Writing of B.C. History," *B.C. Studies*, 111 (Autumn 1996), 61–98, at 97 of Leier's "Response."
76. Bagnall, "The Ontario Conservatives," Chapter 4; Kayfetz to Lambertson, 27 April 2000. Note that the LPP (Communist) member of the Ontario legislature, J.B. Salsberg, visited Dresden in 1949, and was later accused by another parliamentarian of having caused "dissension and trouble," an allegation which Salsberg denied. Ontario Legislative Assembly, Debates, 1 April 1954, 1085–6.
77. Bagnall, "The Ontario Conservatives," Chapter 4. Some of the above probably applies to Frost's attitude towards gender discrimination. Shirley Tillotson also suggests that Frost may have agreed to the 1951 gender equality act in part because of a fear that the Korean War might create a labour shortage in "defence" industries. Tillotson, "Human Rights Law as Prism," 544.
78. Howe and Johnson argue that the period of immediate post-war human rights legislation supports "the pluralist version of society-centred theory." By this they mean that it was society (rather than the state) that drove events, and within society the pressure for change came from individuals and interest groups rather than the capitalist class. The evidence presented in this paper suggests that Howe and Johnson are fundamentally correct, although this quotation glosses over some important nuances (some of which they refer to in their book), such as the reasons why the state and capital were willing to accede to political pressure. *Restraining Equality*, 26.
79. Most students of this period have concluded that human rights activists adopted an "incremental" approach to human rights legislation, which fitted nicely with Frost's approach to legal change. See Herbert Sohn, "Human Rights Legislation," 278–281; R. Brian Howe: "The Evolution of Human Rights Policy in Ontario," 791, "Incrementalism and Human Rights Reform," and "Human Rights Policy in Ontario," 122; John Bagnall, "The Ontario Conservatives," note 52, at 99 and note 114, at 338.
80. *The Labour Relations Act*, 1950, c. 34 (b); *The Conveyancing and Law of Property Amendment Act*, SO 1950, c. 11.
81. *An Act to Promote Fair Employment Practices in Ontario*, SO 1951, c. 24.
82. The issue of discrimination and "public policy" had recently been raised in two important legal cases involving discriminatory restrictive covenants. For a discussion, see Walker, *"Race," Rights and the Law*, Chapter 4.
83. *An Act to Ensure Fair Remuneration to Female Employees*, SO 1951, c. 26. For a discussion of the struggle for this statute, and an explanation of its weaknesses, see Shirley Tillotson, "Human Rights Law as Prism."
84. Tillotson points out that, in the late 1940s the Steelworkers and the United Electrical Workers were the strongest labour supporters of gender pay equality, but the concerns of the former dwindled, and the latter was marginalised by anti-communist policies (53 8–541). Kaplansky's papers reveal some, but not very much, concern for this issue (e.g. "Notes," 1950, 108; 1952, 24). Patrias and Frager have asserted that most rights activists "reflected the sexism that was so widespread in Canadian society at that time." Patrias and Frager, "'This is our country,'" 5.
85. NAC, JLCP, MG28, V 75, vol. 42, file 15, Hill to Kaplansky, 5 January 1954.
86. An American sociologist by training, Hill had been active in the NAACP; she had also helped lobby for fair employment practices legislation in Ohio, both as a volunteer and as a paid activist for a citizen's group. She was married to Dan Hill, the black American sociologist who later became the first director of the Ontario Human Rights Commission. "Notes," 1953, 79, NAC, KKP, MG30, A 53, vol. 20, file 15; interview with Donna Hill, 8 June 1996. Donna Hill later edited *A Black Man's Toronto* and served as an editorial consultant and researcher for her husband's pamphlet, *Human Rights in Canada*.
87. OA, LFP, General Correspondence, vol. 48, file 87–G, "To Mayor Walter S. Weese and Council," 5 February 1951; NAC, OLCP, MG28,1 173, vol. 12, file 1, Hill to Burnett, 16 December 1953; Burnett to Hill, 24 December 1953; "Discrimination 'Not Illegal' in Ontario," and "No Ontario Law Against 'Jim Crow' Negro Group Told," *Toronto Telegram*, 10 and 11 December 1953; NAC, KKP, MG30, A 53, vol. 21, file 3, "Report," January 1954, and February 1954, and vol. 21, file 2, "Notes," 1954, 6–7; NAC, OLCP, MG28, 1173, vol. 12, file 1, Hill to Burnett and Kayfetz, 2 February 1954; OJA, JCRCP, JPRC Correspondence 1947, vol. 5, file 3.
88. "Discrimination Protest Heard By Frost, Cabinet," *Star*, 24 March 1954; NAC, JLCP, MG28, V 75, vol. 19, file 6, Himel to "Dear Friends," 5 February 1954.

89. *An Act to Promote Fair Accommodation Practices in Ontario*, SO 1954, c. 28. In the debates on the bill, Frost referred to the pressure of lobbyists such as the Civil Liberties Association, but according to comments by J.B. Salsberg, a Communist member of the legislature who had supported the notion for some time, Frost was probably thinking about introducing such a bill before the delegation reached him. Ontario Legislative Assembly, *Debates*, 29 March 1954, 974; 1 April 1954, 1087, 1080.
90. The law also repealed the 1944 Racial Discrimination Act.
91. For a discussion of the shift from quasi-criminal human rights legislation to this early form of anti-discrimination law, and then to modern human rights codes, see Walter S. Tarnopolsky, *Discrimination and the Law* (Toronto 1982), Chapter 2. Some of the problems of the legislation were immediately clear to the Toronto labour committee. See, for example, NAC, JLCP, MG28, V 75, vol. 41, file 16, Hill to Kaplansky, 5 April and 4 May, 1954.
92. Tillotson has commented on the "individualistic orientation of the human rights discourse." "Human Rights Law as Prism," 534.
93. Tillotson has pointed out the reluctance of bureaucrats to interpret Ontario's gender equality statute in a generous fashion. "Human Rights Law as Prism," 546–8.
94. Blum at this time was 28 years old, a war veteran, and an American citizen. He had attended the University of Toronto and had received not only a B.A. but also an M.A. (in Sociology and Economics). He had previously been employed in the Education and Welfare Department of the CCL. NAC, JLCP, MG28, V 75, vol. 41, file 16, Blum to Hill, 23 April 1954.
95. NAC, OLCP, MG28,1173, vol. 12, file 2, "Leaflet for NUA Sixth Annual Banquet"; file 1, notarized statement by Hugh Burnett, 17 June 1954, and Blum to Burnett, 21 June 1954. The OLCP contain a number of complaints filed by Blum on behalf of NUA members from June to September 1954. By August, Blum calculated that the number of FAP complaints from Dresden was at least four times that of complaints from the rest of the province. NAC, OLCP, MG28, 1173, vol. 12, file 1, Blum to Toronto labour committee members, 1 August 1954.
96. "Official Sent to Dresden in Racial Fuss," *Telegram*, 25 June 1954; NAC, OLCP, MG28, 1173, vol. 12, file 2, Blum to Rev. Grant L. Mills [Dresden United Church], 11 August 1954; vol. 12, file 1, Burnett to Blum, n.d. [1954]; NAC, OLCP, MG28, 1 173, vol. 12, file 22, Blum's report of "telephone conversation with Mr. Nutland," 13 July 1954.
97. *Telegram*, 19 June 1954. As noted in McLean, *Welcome Home* (82–3), Burnett had been threatened on several earlier occasions, beginning about 1948. NAC, OLCP, MG28,1 173, vol. 12, file 1, Burnett to Magone [Deputy Attorney General], 28 June 1954 (ex. to Blum); NAC, OLCP, MG28,1173, vol. 12, file 2, Blum's press release [sent to both the Globe and the Telegram], 30 June 1954, and Blum to Nutland, 29 June 1954. The NUA agreed to refrain from activity during the week of the centennial celebrations, but only as a temporary concession.
98. From the dedication of Alan Borovoy's *Uncivil Obedience: The Tactics and Tales of a Democratic Agitator* (Toronto 1991). Borovoy, who is best known as the General Counsel for the Canadian Civil Liberties Association, became secretary of the Toronto labour committee about two years after Blum replaced Kaplansky as JLC executive director in 1957.
99. NAC, OLCP, MG28,1173, vol. 12, file 2, "Report on Visit to Dresden," 22, 23 July 1954; NAC, JLCP, MG28, V 75, vol. 41, file 17, "Dresden, The Fair Accommodation Practices Act, and the Frost Government," 26 July 1954.
100. NAC, OLCP, MG28, 1 173, vol. 12, file 2, Blum to Daley, 3 September 1954.
101. "Ontario Govt. Ignores Own Law, Labor Charges," *Star*, 6 August 1954; "Dresden—Labour Jim Crow Still Stalks," *Telegram*, 6 August 1954; NAC, OLCP, MG28,1 173, vol. 12, file 1, Blum to Toronto labour committee members, 1 August 1954, and vol. 6, file 10, Blum to Burnett, 5 January 1955.
102. NAC, OLCP, MG28,1 173, vol. 12, file 2, Blum to Burnett, 14 October 1954; NAC, KKP, MG30, A 53, vol. 21, file 2, "Notes," 1954, 76, and file 4, "Notes," 1955, 122; Gordon Donaldson, "Race Law Fails, Negroes Insulted," *Telegram*, 2 September 1954, and "Fear 'Martyr' Atmosphere if Prosecutions in Dresden," 3 September 1954; Gordon Donaldson, "I Saw Race Hatred in a Canadian Town," *Liberty*, December 1955. The black Secretary of the Windsor Labour Committee, Harold Johnson, was also working hard behind the scenes, meeting frequently with members of the NUA to discuss strategy, and attempting to dramatize the Dresden story for the public. NAC, KKP, MG30, A 53, vol. 43, file 23, "Report" for August 1954.

103. "Negro Tourists Refused Meal, Is Dresden Charge," *Star*, 28 August 1954; "Commissioner to Probe Cases of Discrimination," *Globe*, 31 August 1954. No other inquiries under the FAP Act were held until the courts had settled the Dresden issues. NAC, JLCP, MG28, V 75, vol. 42, file 5, "Report," June 1956.
104. Bagnall, "The Ontario Conservatives," 299–302; NAC, KKP, MG30, A 53, vol. 21, file 3, "Report," July, August, and September 1954; "Admit Refusing Food To Colored Customers to 'Protect Business,'" *Star*, 28 September 1954; "Racial Bar Test Could Set Canadian Precedent," and "Negroes Barred to Protect Business," *Vancouver Sun*, 27 and 28 September 1954.
105. NAC, OLCP, MG28,1 173, vol. 12, file 2, Blum to Daley, 3 September 1954; OA, RG 76-3-0-2, "Legal Rulings 1954–1958 FAPA," "Report of His Honour Judge W.F. Schwenger In the Matter of the Fair Accommodation Practices Act, 1954, and in the Matter of a complaint of Hugh R. Burnette," and "Report of His Honour Judge W.F. Schwenger In the Matter of the Fair Accommodation Practices Act, 1954, Re: Complaint of Lyle Emerson Talbot." (Henceforth both of these documents will be referred to simply as the "Schwenger Report.") Lyle Talbot was a member of Ford Motor Co. Local 200 UAW, and volunteered in the Windsor Interracial Council (later the Windsor Council on Group Relations), from which position he had been in contact with the Toronto labour committee concerning Dresden since 1948.
106. NAC, KKP, MG30, A 53, vol. 21, file 3, "Report," September 1954.
107. Schwenger Report; "Admit Refusing Food."
108. "Decide Against Prosecution," *Globe*, 21 October 1954; Schwenger Report. The report is dated 13 October 1954; evidently Daley had it for a week before making his decision public.
109. "Slap on the Wrist" [editorial], *Globe*, 21 October 1954; "Fetters on Law" [editorial], *Telegram*, 22 October 1954; Frank Tumpane, "Daley's Cream Puff," *Globe*, 23 October 1954.
110. Armstrong had been involved with the Toronto labour committee in some earlier discrimination cases (concerning the Ontario Liquor Board) before he began testing the restaurants in Dresden. In 1955 he became a member of the Toronto labour committee, and years later he was given the Order of Ontario for his human rights work. In the 1990's he worked for the Ontario Labour Relations Board, but still identified himself as a trade unionist. Interview with Armstrong, 26 July 1994; NAC, JLCP, MG28, V 75, vol. 41, file 11, Toronto labour committee "Report," 29 June 1953; file 14, report on Mercury Club hearing, 26 November 1953; transcript of remarks by Armstrong, "Racial Equality in the Workplace: Retrospect and Prospect," in Harish Jain, Barbara M. Pitts, and Gloria DeSantis, eds., *Equality for All* (Hamilton 1991).
111. NAC, OLCP, MG28, 1 173, vol. 6, file 10, Blum to Burnett [including a summary of Armstrong's complaint], 6 December 1954; interview with Bromley Armstrong, 26 July 1994.
112. Gordon Donaldson, "Daley Backs Faith," Telegram, 30 October 1954; "Dresden's Color Bar," *Star*, 30 October 1954; "How Armstrong Challenged Dresden," *The Canadian Negro*, January 1955.
113. "Action on Race Issue Possible, Daley Says," *Globe*, 2 November 1954; "Daley Consents to Charge Dresden Restaurant Man," *Star*, 3 November 1954; "Contend Café in Dresden Refused to Serve Negroes," *Globe*, 8 November 1954; Regina v. Emerson [1955], 113 CCC 69; NAC, JLCP, MG28, V 75, vol. 42, file 1, Blum to Kaplansky, 10 February 1956, and vol. 21, file 3, "Report," October 1954 and November 1954; OA, LFP, General Correspondence, vol. 61, file Code 119, "Hara-Hars 1950–1961," Frost to Harshaw, 10 November 1954.
114. *Regina v. Emerson; Regina v. McKay* [1955], 113 CCC 56.
115. NAC, KKP, MG30, A 53, vol. 21, file 5, "Report," September 1955, and file 4, "Notes," 1955, 92. The 1955 records of the Ontario CJC indicate a strong interest in the Dresden case, and its Joint Public Relations Committee played an important advisory role. For example, Blum was invited to attend a meeting of the JPRC, in order to discuss how to respond to Grosch's decision. This meeting included a wealth of legal talent: Bora Laskin, Jacob Finkelman, Irving Himel, Sidney Midanik, Hal Linden, and Ben Kayfetz as secretary. OJA, JPRC, JPRC Minutes, 19 September 1955, vol. 6, file 2.
116. NAC, KKP, MG30, A 53, vol. 21, file 4, "Notes," 1955, 99. By this time a number of other complaints had been laid under the FAP Act. In March 1956 a bureaucrat reported that 33 complaints had been laid, but that so far only the Dresden cases had gone to court. NAC, KKP, MG30, A 53, vol. 21, file 7, "Report," March 1954.

117. The brief pointed out that in New York the power to prosecute had been taken out of the hands of elected politicians and given to a specialized administrative board. OA, Attorney General's Records, RG 4-02, vol. 86, file 15, Burnett to [Attorney General] Roberts, 12 September 1955; Grizzle [Brotherhood of Sleeping Car Porters] to Roberts, 15 September 1955; Kearns [Toronto District Trades and Labor Council] to Roberts, 21 September 1955; Young [Essex & Kent Counties Trades and Labor Council] to Roberts, 3 October 1955; Montgomery [The Toronto and Lakeshore Labour Council] to Roberts, 12 October 1955; Irving Himel, "Dresden," Canadian Forum, October 1955.
118. NAC, KKP, MG30, A 53, vol. 21, file 4, "Notes," 1955, 99. Earlier, Roberts had been approached by Ben Kayfetz of the CJC's Joint Public Relations Committee and become converted to the merits of a Fair Accommodation Practices law; he had also studied the issue for Premier Frost. Sohn, "Human Rights Legislation," 137; OA, LFP, vol. 162, file: "Racial Discrimination, Letters re," Roberts to Frost, 5 March 1954.
119. NAC, KKP, MG30, A 53, vol. 21, file 4, "Notes," 1955, 89–97, 114; OJA, JCRCP, JPRC Correspondence, vol. 6, file 2, JPRC "Minutes," 19 September 1955; NAC, KKP, MG30, A 53, vol. 21, file 5, "Report," September 1955 and October 1955; "Café Man Fined; Denied Service to Two Negroes," *Globe*, 29 February 1956.
120. NAC, KKP, MG30, A 53, vol. 21, file 4, "Notes," 1955, 113–5; NAC, OLCP, MG28, 1 173, vol. 6, file 10, Blum to Burnett, 3 November 1955.
121. "The Apple Pie Case Starts Color Row," *Telegram*, 18 January 1956; "Draw Blind, Lock Door McKay's System of No Service'—Crown," *Star*, 18 January 1956; "Café Man Fined; Denied Service to Two Negroes," *Globe*, 29 February 1956; NAC, OLCP, MG28,1 173, vol. 12, file 2, "Summary of Evidence re: Complaints of Denial of Service"; Regina Ex Rel. Nutland v. McKay [1956], 115 CCC 104. Blum also advised Burnett to meet with the "leading citizens of the town" to defuse racial tensions. NAC, OLCP, MG28, 1 173, vol. 6, file 10, Blum to Burnett, 21 December 1955.
122. "Fair Practices New Deal Sought by 11 Groups," *Globe*, 10 February 1956; NAC, JLCP, MG28, V 75, vol. 42, file 1, Blum to Kaplansky, 5 January, 1955 [sic; obviously Blum meant to write 1956], and Blum to Kaplansky, 10 February 1956; OA, LFP, RG3, vol. 26, file "Civil Liberties; Fair Accommodation Practices Act 1953," "To the Prime Minister of the Province of Ontario" [copy of the brief]. See also the slightly inaccurate but useful discussion in Peter Oliver, *Unlikely Tory: The Life and Politics of Allan Grossman* (Toronto 1985), 108–9.
123. NAQ JLCP, MG28, V 75, vol. 42, file 1, Blum to Kaplansky, 10 February 1956.
124. Draw Blind, Lock Door McKay's System of 'No Service'—Crown," *Star*, 18 January 1956; "Café Man Fined; Denied Service to Two Negroes," *Globe*, 29 February 1956; NAC, KKP, MG30, A 53, vol. 21, file 7, "Report," January 1956, February 1956.
125. *R. ex rel. Nutland v. McKay* [1956], 5 DLR (2d) 403, 105 CCC 56; NAC, KKP, MG30, A 53, vol. 21, file 7, "Report," May 1956; vol. 21, file 6, "Notes," 1956, 26, 71; Ronald Collister, "Guilty in Color Case—Won't Change Stand," *Telegram*, 23 May 1956; "Dresden Verdict in Race Bias Case Upheld in Court," *Globe*, 24 May 1956.
126. NAC, JLCP, MG28, V 75, vol. 42, file 4, "Report," November 1956; NAC, KKP, MG30, A 53, vol. 21, file 6, "Notes," 1956, 119; file 7, "Report," June 1956 and November 1956.
127. As Kaplansky has noted, the role of the JLC in the Dresden issue was ignored by the press at the time. NAC, KKP, MG30, A 53, vol. 21, file 4, "Notes," 1955, 121–4.
128. David Roediger, "Race and the Working-Class Past in the United States: Multiple Identities and the Future of Labor History," *International Review of Social History*, 38 (1993), Supplement, 127–143, at 131. See also Dawley and Trotter, "Race and Class," 491–2. This challenge has recently been taken up by Ruth A. Frager, "Labour History and the Interlocking Hierarchies of Class, Ethnicity, and Gender: A Canadian Perspective," *International Review of Social History*, 44 (1999), 217–47.
129. Thomas J. Sugrue, "Segmented Work, Race-Conscious Workers: Structure, Agency and Division in the CIO Era," *International Review of Social History*, 41 (December 1996), 389–406 at 393. See also the remark by Ruth Frager that "[l]abour historians need to analyze the different ways in which class, ethnic, and gender hierarchies have interlocked in specific historical circumstances." Frager, "Labour History," 245 (italics added).
130. It perhaps goes without saying that both Kaplansky and Frost saw racial inequality as a more serious threat than gender inequality—the conventional wisdom of the period. Moreover, neither of them

bought into the belief, often stated by "segregationists" in Dresden, that the demand by blacks for racial equality was rooted in a desire for miscegenation.

131. Bryan Palmer has referred disparagingly to "trade union leaders in Canada [who] are overwhelmingly committed to the principles of reformist politics, a basic tenet of which is the divide that dichotomizes class struggle, relegating the economic battle at the point of production to trade unionism and the parliamentary contest over the direction of the state to the New Democratic Party.... Labour's leaders stand fast, not for the interests of workers as a whole, as a *class*, but for *their* union's rights over particular workers and their dues." Palmer, *Working Class Experience*, 370–1 (italics in original).
132. For an overview, see Bruce Nelson, "Class, Race and Democracy in the CIO." Typical of these historians is the remark by Sugrue that "The myriad ways that working-class culture, on the shop floor and at home, limited the social democratic agenda of the CIO and of post-New Deal liberalism is a topic well worth greater research." Thomas J. Sugrue, "Segmented Work, Race-Conscious Workers," 391.
133. This phrase comes from Louis Henkin, *The Age of Rights* (New York 1990).
134. Tillotson, "Human Rights Law as Prism"; Calliste, "Sleeping Car Porters." Note also the references to trade union recalcitrance on human rights issues in Patrias and Frager," This Is Our Country," 38–40.

Chapter 17

Defending Honour, Demanding Respect

Manly Discourse and Gendered Practice in Two Construction Strikes, Toronto, 1960–61

Franca Iacovetta

Neither historians of masculinity nor their subjects—men—are monolithic groups. The emerging field of gender history, though sometimes considered a site reserved for reified postmodern exercises in literary deconstruction, already has produced a literature marked by various approaches and topics.[1] Earlier polarized debates over the role of "representation" versus "structure" in shaping history—debates that saw discourse analysts and historical materialists locked in battle—have given way to sophisticated efforts by scholars, including both class-oriented feminists and Marxists, to consider ways of integrating key insights from both approaches.[2] The willingness of some "social determinists" to entertain post-structuralist insights regarding, for instance, the power of linguistic symbols and discourse is not so surprising given that, as Neville Kirk has astutely observed, these historians have been far more attuned to such complicating issues than their detractors have admitted.[3]

More specifically, historians of masculinity have begun demonstrating that masculinity, like femininity, is neither a biological state of being nor a fixed and unitary set of practices and identities. As a relational construct, masculinity, like femininity, is forged in particular contexts and by the critical forces, including class, race-ethnicity, state power, patriarchy, and ideology, that shape such contexts. Sympathetic accounts of male cultures, whether the gentlemanly ambience of the men's club or the class-conscious camaraderie of the union hall, are not sufficient. Nor are studies intended solely to map the diversity of masculine identities. Just as women's history has shown that femininity cannot be grasped without a consideration of women's oppression, studies of masculinity must seriously dissect men's privilege and power, especially in relation to "the other," whether women, gay men, or racial-ethnic minorities.[4]

But if the critical aim of the history of masculinity is the excavation of male power and privilege, how, then, do we write about men who belonged to a marginal male group? What happens when we shift the lens to male subjects who were themselves "othered"—in this case, as exploited immigrants who escaped a hostile homeland only to occupy, in their adopted home, the unenviable position of pick-and-shovel man, racially inferior newcomer, and dangerous foreigner? This paper revisits two strikes that rocked the Toronto construction trades in the early 1960s. My 1992 study, *Such Hardworking People*, analyzed the class and ethnic dimensions of those conflicts; this study uses recent scholarship in gender history to focus more closely on the male images and, immigrant (and racial) discourses that helped give shape to the campaigns.[5] The strikes were triggered by Italian immigrants, mostly former peasants and rural artisans from southern Italy, and they featured mass rallies, brutal class exploitation, charismatic labour leaders, and violence. The essay argues that the workers' grievances became forcefully articulated within an immigrant discourse that coalesced around the image of the honourable family man whose proven capacity for hard work, "nation-building," and self-sacrifice entitled him to respect and better treatment. Such discontents and demands were encapsulated in a striker's rallying cry: "End immigrant slavery—Think of your families."

In highlighting the masculine discourses of the strikes, this chapter in no way suggests that symbols, rhetoric, and ritual alone propelled Italian workers to strike. The discourse of the honourable immigrant took shape in the real and overlapping contexts of workplace, household, neighbourhood, and community, and drew on a combination of Old World and New World patterns and beliefs, both mixing and colliding. But while language and ritual may not have created the harsh class conditions of Toronto's post-war construction trades, they were the means by which Italian immigrant workers gave meaning to events and experiences. Such men were negotiating their gender identities, like their class, racial-ethnic, and newcomer status, amid the challenges occasioned by their transition from peasants in a marginal and inhospitable rural economy to urban, industrial waged workers in a booming but hostile New World metropolis.

Workplace experiences interacted with and were filtered through the men's perceptions of themselves as honourable workers. That image was based on their capacity to endure tough and dangerous work, and in their (shifting) capacity to act as the family's chief provider and protector, especially amid the new uncertainties engendered by immigration. It was also rooted in their privileges as the acknowledged head of the household, even while they negotiated with wives who might challenge that status. Indeed, though the strikes were male dramas, women and the gender dynamics of immigrant households played decisive roles. Once articulated and transformed into a strike platform, manly discourse helped to crystallize a defining moment for the strikers: their transition from foreign greenhorns tolerating slaughterhouse conditions to skilled tradesmen and experienced labourers demanding humane treatment. Militancy was fuelled by masculinist ideology that, as men, strikers had the prerogative and obligation to fight injustice, but manly militance also threatened to represent strikers as hooligans and bullies when picket-line violence erupted. Contrasting racial images of "slave" versus "free" labour and a desire to improve their racial status as Toronto's "almost black" newcomers also infused this discourse, suggesting that the strikes illuminate as well how Italian immigrant workers came to define themselves as White Canadians. In short, a discourse of "defending honour" and "demanding respect" became an effective tool for mobilizing Italian workers precisely because it resonated so deeply with the men's real lives and aspirations.

Greenhorns Enter "the Jungle"

The construction industry is a deeply gendered, intensely male work world, one associated with risky jobs, dangerous worksites, and rough men. Historically, images of construction workers have ranged widely: accomplished craftsmen carrying on established traditions, exploited immigrants performing brute labour on the resource frontier, tough-talking, cigar-chomping union bosses, and uncouth louts who harass women walking past building sites. In recent years, the industry's tough, machismo image derives from a notoriety fuelled by countless court inquiries, royal commissions, and media exposés investigating charges of fraudulent business practices, employer abuses, and union corruption.[6]

The association of Italian immigrant men with construction jobs has been a strong and enduring one. The predominant image is of wage-hungry, dark-skinned, and ever-mobile peasants transformed into "human steam shovels" who, by brute force and sheer doggedness, built the infrastructure of the world capitalist economy—railroads, tunnels, sewers, houses, subways, factories, highways, and skyscrapers.[7] To that, we could add the racist metaphors that offered cruel caricature of their marginal class position and "in-between" racial status as undesirable southern Europeans: "sweatback," "the Chinese of Europe," "Australia's olive peril," "pick-and-shovel men," and, from the men's own mouths, *lavoratori de diavuli* ("the devil's workers"). All are subhuman metaphors that help capture the brutal exploitation and racial derision to which millions of Italian migrant and immigrant men, particularly southerners, have been subjected.[8] This image dominates despite the presence of skilled craftsmen and the diverse work patterns actually exhibited by Italian immigrants throughout the nineteenth and twentieth centuries.[9]

In Toronto, the association of Italian men with construction work, though evident earlier, was solidified in the two decades after World War II. So strong did their identification with construction become that some observers virtually ascribed to Italian men an innate, racial affinity for mortar, bricks, and wheelbarrow. Such equations overlapped with racist depictions of culturally backward and, in the words of one Torontonian, "ignorant, almost black"[10] men. In an era before significant migration of immigrants of colour from Asia, the Caribbean, and elsewhere, southern Italians in early post-war Toronto occupied a vulnerable racial status. Italian men were acutely aware of this fact; for some, the 1960 and 1961 union drives would mark their refusal to continue to accept anything less than the rights enjoyed by White, unionized Canadian workers.

The Italian influx of Toronto's construction trades was part of the so-called Italian "invasion" of post-war Toronto, which saw well over 100,000 Italians arrive in the city by 1965. Post-1945 boom conditions and a rapidly expanding metropolis created a huge demand for construction workers. By 1961, more than 15,000 Italians, or fully one-third of Toronto's working Italian men, were employed in construction, and they represented one-third of the city's total construction workforce.

As developers and builders eagerly exploited the seemingly insatiable demand for post-war housing and services, new roads, sewers, and houses and apartments were extended into the city's sprawling suburbs. Whether single, recently married, or fathers of young children, men in their twenties and thirties from the agro-villages of the impoverished Italian south dominated the ranks of greenhorns who took on risky and dangerous outdoor jobs. They infiltrated the entire industry, working on building sites erecting residential, industrial, and commercial structures and on engineering projects building roads, bridges, and sewage systems. Their daily work life was daunting. "Sandhogs" (tunnellers) on sewage and hydro sites worked deep underground. Others quickly earned the scars, sore backs, and gnarled hands of ditchdiggers, digging trenches for the installation of gas mains or sewers. Braced against early winter winds or the soaring heat of summer, workers faced daily the risk of injury, including death by cave-ins. Men on road-building and paving sites were exposed to gas leaks and explosions that could maim or kill. The oral testimonies of Italian construction workers unleash painful memories of injuries experienced or witnessed: men's limbs impaled on pipes; backs broken from falls from poorly assembled scaffolds, skyscraper beams, or elevator shafts; hands and feet cracked and frozen from exposure; and faces cut from shattered glass.[11]

By far the largest Italian concentration developed in the house and apartment sector: approximately 65 percent for the field, and 85 percent for certain trades, such as bricklaying and carpentry. Unlike large sections of the non-residential field, where craft unions affiliated with the American Federation of Labor (AFL) maintained closed shops and safeguarded apprenticeship programs, the housing field was unorganized, permitting informal methods of recruitment and training to flourish. Many Italians who became tradesmen, for example, actually performed semi-skilled work learned "on the job," mostly in the non-certified trades such as carpentry, bricklaying, and cement finishing— a situation that reinforced demeaning stereotypes of Italians as inferior pick-and-shovel men masquerading as craftsmen.[12] Italians also became employers, but at the lowest levels, running small trade-specific subcontracting firms and assembling work crews from among former co-workers, kin, and *paesani*. The profusion of firms best served the interests of the developers and builders who engaged in bid-peddling that left many subcontractors to run their businesses on a shoestring.[13] The latter had little legal recourse if builders declared their work substandard and withheld payment.

Most victimized of all, however, were the workers. The AFL unions (also called "commercial" or "old-line" unions) had failed to organize the residential field, where the features that generally hampered union drives in construction—volatile markets, numerous small employers, scattered work crews, large supplies of newcomers, and intense job competition—found extreme expression by the recession years of the late 1950s. Hard times made Canadian unionists even less inclined to organize immigrants, especially those whom they considered to be "inferior craftsmen," whose presence might undercut union wages. Italian residential workers were thus especially vulnerable to employer cost-cutting techniques. In an effort to cover their losses on tenders for which they had underbid, and under pressure from their own "bosses"—builders and developers—to complete projects on time, subcontractors subjected their workers to speed-ups and long workdays, ignored costly and time-consuming safety regulations, and withheld wages. With growing regularity, Italian workers complained of hours inexplicably "docked" from their paycheques. Fly-by-night contractors (both Italian and non-Italian) also arrived, ruthlessly exploiting their work crews in order to finish projects for which they had grossly underbid—and then disappeared before paycheques bounced at the bank. To compete amid this cut-throat competition, legitimate small contractors resorted to similar tactics, including kickback schemes wherein a worker returned a portion of his wages to the employer as a condition of his employment. As employers ignored safety codes, accidents and injuries continued. Already trailing behind the commercial trades, residential wages plummeted.[14] Employer violations of the Vacations with Pay Act, Workmen's Compensation Act, Unemployment Insurance, and other protective legislation increased.

Fighting Back: Men without Women?

In recalling these events, immigrant bricklayer Marco Abate observed that such crippling conditions threatened to dehumanize the men who worked daily in a context that exploited and demeaned them. "The residential field," he said, "was a jungle, a no man's land.... It was like our life was so cheap, not worth anything. Like we could hear a builder saying, 'Some Italians die today, got injured. Oh well, send us another load.'" In describing a brutal regime, Abate used a popular, racial image of the jungle as a remote place where lawlessness and subhuman or primitive conditions prevailed. As Mediterraneans acutely aware of their "undesirable" racial status among White Canadians, Italian workers probably would have agreed with Abate's efforts to distinguish themselves as White ethnics far removed from the jungles of faraway worlds. They likely would have agreed with the rest of Abate's comments—that reforming Toronto's residential sector would also serve to rehabilitate themselves from popular images of southern Italians as a culturally backward people accustomed to substandard treatment and subhuman conditions. Unless Italian workers "fought back," Abate declared in the tough words of a blue-collar worker, "we were doomed" to a brutal life.[15]

The event that prompted men to fight back occurred on 17 March 1960, when five Italian workers installing an underground water main beneath the Don River at Hogg's Hollow, on Toronto's northern limits, were killed. A fire had swept through the tunnel's main shaft, leaving the men to suffocate under an avalanche of mud. A subsequent inquiry revealed that the project had violated numerous safety standards and inspection had been inadequate. The rescue mission had been sabotaged by faulty equipment.[16]

The Hogg's Hollow disaster highlighted features central to Italian immigrant men's lives, including their vulnerability in the face of dangerous work. It also vividly captured their status as gendered subjects: whether husbands, fathers, or sons, these men occupied a critical link in their family's transition from peasants or artisans in a marginal rural economy to urban wage-earners in an industrial city. At the time of the disaster, one of the victims, John Fusile, 27, had been boarding with his four brothers while sending money overseas to his elderly parents and his wife, and awaiting the arrival of wife and baby. Alexandra and Guido Mantella, both in their early twenties, and another brother also working in construction, had been supporting a family still residing in Italy. So had 27-year-old Pasquale Allegrezza. John Corrigle, 46, was the eldest victim and the only one who had been reunited with his family. He had also met another goal for which thousands of immigrant couples would endure years of indebtedness, thrift, and financial sacrifice to attain—home-ownership.[17]

Of course, not all men, once abroad, fulfilled their obligations to family and kin. Some squandered their paycheques, whether out of willful abandon, resentment, or despair. Others "opted out" of family networks, deserting elderly parents or abandoning wives and children back home. (The "bigamist" and his "American" wife are recurring images in migrant folktales and songs.) Even men who fulfilled most family-designated expectations were not necessarily beyond reproach in their personal treatment—or mistreatment—of women and children. Still, most of Toronto's Italian men closely resembled the Hogg's Hollow victims in their apparent willingness to carry out family-defined goals. That so many did so was not solely a reflection of men's emotional commitment to wife, parents, and children, though the ties of sentiment that bound immigrant families could be very intense indeed. It also attests to the crucial importance that allegiance to the family and a family-defined code of honour played in Italian men's self-identity and self-respect as honourable men. The activities that shaped their lives in Toronto—earning wages, sending home remittances, living as "bachelors" on an impossible budget until the others arrived, filling out sponsorship papers to secure the entry of kin, and making preparations to purchase a modest house—were simultaneously strategies of economic survival long familiar to immigrants and critical markers of Italian men's trustworthiness as family providers and protectors.

The published biographies of the Hogg's Hollow victims helped rescue them as hard-working members of struggling Italian families. Moreover, many Italian workers saw in Hogg's Hollow their own stories of pain and the varied sources of their masculine self-identity: fathers, sons, and brothers with familial obligations, working-class foreigners relegated to unsafe jobs, and immigrants determined to improve their lives and demand respect. The tragedy, of course, also exposed their vulnerability and graphically displayed how unsafe and risky jobs could sabotage dreams and destroy families. If Italian men derived considerable *onore* (honour) from their capacity to act as family protectors and providers, the reverse engendered *vergogna* (shame) and an acute sense of failure. As one man put it, "you came here to make a better life, when you can't you feel ashamed, you want to do for your family." Such transplanted notions of manly honour informed and reinforced the strong class discontent that Italian workers had developed over the brutal conditions of their work.[18]

Although the fatalities had occurred outside the housing field, Hogg's Hollow triggered a massive union campaign among Italian residential workers. For some observers, Hogg's Hollow was yet one more indication of the industry's brutal regime. As one journalist quipped, "For years, they've been dying in ones and twos in Don Mills and Scarborough. Falling off rickety scaffolds with no safety hats, no work boots, not even gloves.... The only thing different about ... Hogg's Hollow is that five guys died in a hellhole underground."[19] But for the workers inside "the jungle," most of them immigrants whose experience with unions in Italy had been confined to fascist-imposed organizations, the event marked a political awakening and a profound shift in vantage point—from that of unskilled foreign greenhorn prepared to endure a brutal regime to established tradesman and experienced labourer declaring entitlement to decent working wages and safe jobs.

At the time of the disaster, the two men who would dominate the leadership of the immigrant organizing campaigns, Bruno Zanini and Charles Irvine, had already scored some union gains among several trades. Now, Italian workers flooded the new residential unions that collectively became known as the Brandon Union Group.[20] The Brandon Group was composed of five trades (each with its own AFL charter)—the bricklayers, cement masons, plasterers, carpenters, and labourers—and an executive consisting of immigrant organizers and seasoned unionists.[21] But real power resided with Irvine, an old-line unionist and an international vice-president with the AFL's Plasterers and Cement Masons, and Zanini, a union novice but a quick study. Brashness characterized their style. A member of Toronto's small prewar Italian community and the city's interwar youth gang culture, the stocky Zanini was a bricklayer and frustrated opera singer now bent on securing fame as champion of underdogs. Equally tough and authoritarian was the tall and rangy Scottish-born Charles Irvine. While Irvine knew that his own membership would be more secure if the Italians were organized, he was an opportunist as well as a maverick who had initiated the early immigrant drives without notifying his superiors in Washington.

Irvine and Zanini called an (illegal) organizational walkout for 1 August 1960; it turned into a fierce, three-week struggle that involved an estimated 6,000 Italian workers.[22] Despite numerous obstacles,[23] the Brandon Group workers, supported by Teamsters and some commercial locals,[24] won a union contract. They had sabotaged the residential field, forcing numerous contractors to form associations, strike negotiating committees, and hammer out contracts,[25] while inaugurating a working relationship with old-line unionists and the labour movement.[26] Still, the campaign had unionized less than half of the residential firms, and before long it was clear that many employers were resorting to familiar cost-cutting tactics. By spring 1961, more than 1,000 union grievances had been filed with the Ontario Labour Relations Board.

Determined to organize a greater portion of the field, Brandon leaders called a second strike. Though reeling from winter lay-offs, Italian men responded enthusiastically. The 1961 strike, from 29 May to 15 July, involved far greater numbers and the support of the old-line unions, whose sympathy strikes shut down subway, road-paving, and other projects. In the fourth week, more than 15,000 men were out and some 12,000 public utilities employees looked perched to follow. A solidarity rally held at the Canadian National Exhibition grandstand drew some 17,000 supporters.[27] The state took the strike seriously, as evidenced by Premier Leslie Frost's "peace plan" proposal providing for more safety inspectors, a royal commission to investigate labour relations, and a special arbitration board to adjudicate alleged contract violations. These measures brought the 1961 dispute to an end, although subsequent inquiries and strikes made clear that basic conflicts were never fully resolved. That local leaders had sought help from the controversial U.S. Teamster leader, Jimmy Hoffa, ensured that the 1961 strike even contributed to the industry's notoriety.

The issue of notoriety begs the question: were Italians tricked by the charismatic personalities who led the strikes? Did the image of adoring crowds of Italian men huddled around Irvine and Zanini conjure up fascist-era stereotypes of Italians as "sheep" (rather than "men") easily misled by orators? These issues worried some men yet did not deter thousands from walking off the job. Workers recognized the leaders' talents and hoped to benefit from them. Both men were effective grassroots organizers, especially Zanini, who spent hours talking with men at job sites and in the street corners, billiard halls, and other male gathering places of Toronto's Little Italies. In the ongoing exchanges of stories about unpaid wages, on-site injuries, and family tragedies, Zanini tapped into the men's deep-seated sense of workplace injustice. He also drew effectively on the vocabulary that resonated deeply with the men's self-identity as hard-working, self-respecting, and honourable family men. Irvine especially met the men's evident desire for dynamic leadership. "Charlie had such a way," recalled one worker. "Nobody knew English, but the way he talked, it made sense to everyone. He inspired so much confidence, a born leader."[28]

The Italian men who joined the campaign did so in defiance of powerful building interests and Italian community elites, most of them Italo-Canadian professionals and businessmen fearful that the strike would generate negative publicity and that the union bosses might displace their own dominance. Also opposed was the Catholic Church, whose Italian-speaking parish priests defended the integrity of the hard-pressed Italian subcontractors, whom they depicted as equally hard-working family men making ends meet. Defence of manly honour, then, was not confined to strikers. Critics invoked similar images when trying to discredit the workers' actions. Gianni Grohovaz, editor of the mainstream Italo-Canadian newspaper, the *Corriere Canadese*, claimed sympathy for the workers yet denounced Zanini's "selfish desire to be *il capo* (the head) of all the Italian workers." Grohovaz also partly blamed the workers for the crisis, writing that "the immigrants, by accepting work that was unsafe or paid less than the legal rate, were letting themselves be treated as if they were second-class citizens." His accusation that at union meetings "gossip, profane language and political speeches had taken the place of a proper program" inferred that strikers were behaving as less than honourable men. In 1960, Italian residential workers received no support from the old-line unions, save for Teamsters truck drivers who refused to deliver supplies to housing sites. Indeed, a rivalry developed in this strike between the Brandon campaign and an AFL-Building Trades Council certification campaign.[29]

Just as family and community intersected with daily workplace life, a worker's decision to strike was not made exclusively on the building site but, rather, within the overlapping arenas of work, union hall, family, household, and community. It was influenced by transplanted familial strategies and traditions and by the networks of reciprocity that characterized relations among kin and co-villagers in the households and neighbourhoods of the immigrant wards. Here it is worth considering the basis of decision-making within Italian households. Many of Toronto's Italians brought with them a family-centred culture of work characteristic of peasant family economies, one in which household members sacrificed individual pursuits to contribute (through labour and/or earning power) to the financial well-being of the family unit. Artisanal families, though organized around a different type of work, had a similar family-oriented work ethos. It combined an assumption of patriarchal authority with a commitment to economic co-operation. As heads of the households, married men in particular enjoyed power and prestige over wives, children, and even elderly parents. Of course, some men abused their power, although, unfortunately, my evidence is silent on this issue. The immigrants described here, however, clearly felt the pressures attached to their status and derived pride from their capacity to meet their duties. As one construction worker put it: "You make sacrifices, get up at 5 o'clock in the morning and wait for the truck to take you to sometimes you don't know where. And for what? To clean out the mud and mix cement for hours so the family can make a better life."[30]

On both sides of the ocean, Italian men enjoyed greater freedoms, especially sexual liberties, than women, and southern European cultures are replete with double standards or codes of honour denying women the opportunities and choices permitted men. Moreover, women's sexual infractions, including adultery, were treated as dangerous transgressions that undermined the moral authority of cuckolded husbands and brought shame to the entire family. Still, Italian families, like most families, though patriarchal in organization, were social arenas of negotiation, even if among members with unequal status, power, and resources. Within pre-migration and immigrant households, women were essential to family survival—a reality that men recognized—and many did lay claim to certain rights and privileges. An Italian woman's public acknowledgement of her husband's "superior" status did not deter her from placing herself at the centre of wide networks of family, kin, and *paesani*. Nor did it prevent her from negotiating aggressively with her husband, working around and behind him, hiding information from him, or seeking help from allies if he placed unreasonable barriers in her way. By the same token, men who might publicly boast about their authority could act differently once beyond the purview of fellow men and willingly share decision-making with their wives.[31]

In immigrant families across the diaspora, Italian peasant women appear to have maintained their customary "power of the purse," making front-line decisions about the family budget.[32] This pattern prevailed in post-war Toronto. But Toronto's post-war Italian women differed from their counterparts in earlier and other immigrant contexts in their propensity for waged work. In Toronto, many assumed timely roles as critical wage-earners. By 1961, more than 40 percent of adult Italian women in Toronto, mostly immigrants, were registered in the city's female labour force, mainly in low- and semiskilled factory jobs. Thousands more worked in the informal economy, making money "under the table" as babysitters and cleaning ladies. This pattern reflected, of course, the gap between the male breadwinner ideology and the reality of insufficient and inconsistent male wages. On average, Italian women earned half the wages of Italian men,[33] yet their income was so indispensable that it calls into question the definition of women as secondary wage-earners. Wives earned year-round wages while husbands faced seasonal or regular unemployment, and women's wages were a main source of income when men were sidelined by injury, illness, or strikes.

It is therefore not surprising that while Italian workers envisioned the strike as a battle of honour among men, they had made the decision to join, or not, in consultation with wives (and, in some cases, parents) and by weighing several factors. The reluctance of some couples to participate reflected a deep desire to secure work, at virtually any cost, out of sheer economic need. This was especially true of recent arrivals, but could also prompt those who had overextended themselves by buying a house or starting up a subcontracting firm. Uncertain of their legal rights as immigrants, some genuinely feared that the government might deport strikers. Most fearful were those immigrants who had quietly greased the palms of semi-legitimate middlemen to secure exit visas, the families of contract workers who had prematurely jumped jobs or been unceremoniously released before their one-year labour contract had officially expired, and others who for various reasons had "fudged the facts" on their immigration papers. Some employers exploited such fears, threatening job dismissal and deportation. But in other cases workers felt loyal to the employer, frequently a relative, who had sponsored and hired them, especially when work bonds reinforced the ties of kin, village, and community. Given these conflicting demands, men's use of breadwinner rhetoric—that as male heads of household they were striking to ensure their families' survival—may have served to soften any sense of disloyalty to family or friends and resolve any sense of guilt that they were imperilling their family's status in Canada.

Indeed, consultation with wives is a recurring theme in the recollections of married strikers. According to a Brandon agent, Frank Colantonio, a peasant-turned-carpenter and immigrant organizer, negotiations with wives involved endless talk about whether the couple or family could weather the storm financially. Were their modest savings sufficient? Could a wife's earnings cover necessary costs for the duration? Could they borrow money? For some families, this meant cultivating a credit rating with local Italian store owners; for others, it meant turning to a relative who might be modestly better off. Given the youthfulness of Toronto's Italian families, many couples could not turn to older children as additional or substitute wage-earners. Those with children over 16 had to decide whether to take the child out of school to earn money. Where a son or daughter was already working, detailed calculations were made about how far such incomes could be stretched. And it was the women, of course, who found ways to feed and clothe the family and pay bills on a much reduced income. The wife of a Brandon organizer, who at the time had two toddlers, recalled that "it was a hard time, thinking for the children, worrying about the money. But I supported my husband, he was doing good things to help Italian workers, to help ourselves."[34] For people accustomed to making sacrifices with long-term goals in mind, the decision to endure short-term pain for the prospect of greater security and safety was a difficult but not unfamiliar one.

Still, Italian women played no public role in the 1960 or 1961 strikes and their conspicuous absence from the streets and community halls deserves more explanation. As labour historians have documented, women's strike support activities, including crowd protests, picketing, and morale-building events, have featured prominently in strikes involving considerable community mobilization. Mining and textile towns "on strike," for example, revealed women's strong ties to their community and their capacity for being "radicals of the worst sort"—troublemakers, street fighters, and boycotters, rather than orthodox unionists.[35] While Toronto was hardly a single-industry town, the construction drives did require effective mobilization within the Italian community and beyond. Women's absence from the public events can best be explained by several related factors. First, it was partially linked to the logistics involved in waging a construction strike, where pickets were scattered across a large region—in this case, a vast territory encompassing the city's neighbouring and distant suburban and ex-urban areas of development. For many Italian women, whose daily lives were rooted in the neighbourhoods and workshops of the city, especially in the west-end wards, the work sites were largely out of their frame of reference. As one woman put it, the suburbs "for us then, was still farm country."[36] Also, few women would have obtained a driver's licence, making them dependent on public transportation (which could be infrequent in barely developed ex-urban areas) or men with available cars and pick-up trucks. Also important was the high ratio of women with small children, which limited women's capacity for public action. But answers related to logistics alone will not suffice. After all, car and truck pools could have been organized, had organizers considered it important. It also cannot entirely explain why women did not attend the morning rallies and solidarity events, which took place in local venues. Furthermore, Italian mothers with young children could usually find the resources for child care within their own neighbourhood and community.

Second, cultural and ideological factors were also at play. Doubtless, women's public absence reflected in part the prevailing cultural and patriarchal norms among Italian men regarding female honour and women's proper place—which, at least ideally, did not include the aggressively male sphere of a muddy, unsafe, and even violent building site. That Italian men did not envision a public role for women in these union drives is borne out in the campaign rallies, slogans, and even recollections of strikers, all of which invoked the exclusively male image of men acting on the family's behalf. Nor did Italian women (like other women) find welcoming the masculine culture of union hall or construction site. Too much, however, should not be made of cultural explanations of immigrant women's behaviour, as they invariably draw on and confirm misleading racial-ethnic stereotypes. Historians have largely exploded the myth of the "cowering" Italian woman by documenting instances of their militancy, both as strike supporters and strikers.[37] Like other women from rural or working-class backgrounds, Italian women were not necessarily constrained by a North American code of femininity that associated respectability with demure, ladylike behaviour. When they did strike, they became enthusiastic participants in shouting matches, aggressive picket-line duty, and other defiant actions.[38]

Probably the most important factor accounting for women's public absence from the construction campaigns resulted from their critical position as family wage-earners. We must return to their remarkably high rate of labour force participation in Toronto's post-war economy. The importance of their wage-earning capacity during these strikes cannot be exaggerated. In a mixed industrial economy that did offer women jobs, Italian women with construction worker husbands on strike were not confined to supporting roles. Those who had been employed continued to work, often taking on longer workdays for modest but critical pay increases. Others landed their first Canadian jobs during these campaigns, though their inexperience meant their relegation to low-skilled and low-paid work. Women's full-time and part-time jobs took on enormous importance among striking families at the same time as they imposed huge pressures on women, who faced the strains of the double day and the added pressures of stretching even more from even less.

Women's contribution to household budgets did receive public recognition during the 1961 strike when the press began probing the price being paid by strikers and their families. As in the past, strikers did not enjoy regular strike pay, and as the campaign moved into its fourth, fifth, and sixth weeks, families suffered. Some couples lost homes by defaulting on mortgages, while others could not pay the rent. In requesting financial aid from the internationals in Washington, immigrant organizer Marino Toppan noted: "We are going to win but meantime we have hundreds of people begging for their children."[39] But neither the occasional donations from unions nor the aid of kin and neighbours could replace the efforts of wives, who again stretched dwindling resources and toiled in shops and factories. The press highlighted Italian women's shift into the role of family breadwinner. In her profiles of striking wives, reporter Rosemary Boxer noted a depressingly familiar irony: the situation had forced many women, including the steam press operators and garment workers she interviewed, to tolerate substandard conditions, poor wages, and kickback schemes. Even at that, these women were earning the family's sole wages. Women's absence from public rallies and pickets was more than matched by their wage-earning efforts.[40]

"End Immigrant Slavery—Think of Your Families!"

The morning rally that kicked off the 1960 campaign became a recurring public spectacle in both strikes. Taking place in the smoke-filled and overcrowded rooms of an Italian movie theatre in the west end, the morning rallies began on a ceremonial note, as Irvine and Zanini led the men in silent prayer. They then quickly transformed into highly boisterous events, complete with fiery speeches and spontaneous outbursts from the floor. The costumes and artefacts of the construction worker, objects characterized by manliness, were everywhere in evidence: young men in workpants and heavy construction boots (but dressed up with inexpensive suit jackets); hundreds of small pick-up trucks parked outside the theatre; and the carpenter's two-by-four "plank," which was waved about at meetings. The strike leaders cultivated such manly symbols as a sign of the workers' aggressive determination to win. Irvine brandished his own two-by-four, this one with a spike driven through it, calling it a workingman's "plank of action."

Strike leaders and organizers appealed to various themes close to workers' hearts. In speeches Irvine and Zanini stressed the integrity of the immigrants' struggle and denounced the developers and builders who opposed them. They appealed to the seriousness that men attached to their self-definition as the family's breadwinner and the fears or shame unleashed by their inability to perform it. During one meeting, Zanini dramatically took the stage with his pockets stuffed with cheques stamped NSF. Waving them furiously about, he shouted: "This is the sort of exploitation that should be stopped. Canada is a free country and immigrants should be treated the same as Canadians!" As the crowd roared its approval, more men jumped onto the platform to produce their NSF paycheques. Organizer Marino Toppan shouted: "An end to immigrant slavery—think of your families!" In response, men chanted, "Canadian wages, Canadian hours!"[41]

Aggressive rhetoric and symbols were obvious appeals to the strikers' masculinity. Refusing to be treated like second-class citizens, Italian workers loudly defended the honour of their work and boldly asserted their right to be accorded the same respect as Canadian workers. The campaigns, recalled Abate, were "an Italian uprising.... We were saying 'Enough to this kind of exploitation.'"[42] In articulating a masculine discourse of immigrant honour, Italian workers also drew on contrasting images of manly versus unmanly behaviour and human versus subhuman treatment. This included compelling racial metaphors, especially that of "free" worker versus unfree "slave." Such distinctions, as recent scholarship reveals, have long informed the public discourse of White workers in North American labour movements. It has also shaped the discourse of marginal "White ethnic" workers keen to dissociate themselves from the most despised racial minorities, namely Blacks and Asians, and link themselves more closely with the dominant majority.[43] Toronto's Italian workers drew a link between eliminating the "jungle" status of the industry and gaining greater respectability within the wider society. Similar conclusions might be drawn about the recurring metaphor of the construction industry as a "slaughterhouse." By fighting back, it was argued, men could humanize the industry and themselves. These themes converge in Colantonio's recent memoir, in which he recalls what he said when delivering his first speech at a morning rally:

> I talked about the years of broken laws and low wages, the cutthroat competition that forced so many contractors to take advantage of Italians desperate for work, the crooked contractors who didn't hesitate to treat us like slaves and then cheat us on our wages. "'Low wages and phoney cheques are bad enough,' I said.... 'Even worse is the complete disregard for safety. Just take a trip out to the WCB [Workmen's Compensation Board] Rehab Centre.... My dear countrymen, this is not an industry. This is a slaughterhouse....' I tried to appeal to the pride that I knew so many of us felt as men who worked so hard for such long hours to provide for our families, only to be treated like farm animals on the job and dangerous foreigners on the street. 'Show the world you are human beings and not the bunch of jackasses some people think you are. Show them you want a union. Show them you want a contract!'"[44]

Strikers defined their actions as the angry but reasonable responses of hard-working men who had been shabbily treated, which became abundantly clear in an incident during the 1960 drive involving Johnny Lombardi, an Italian-Canadian entertainment promoter and self-proclaimed "mayor" of "Little Italy." Insisting that most immigrants are "very very happy," Lombardi blamed "the recent noise" on a few "young rabblerousers" and "poolroom, coffee-counter hangers-on" who "have no right to speak for the Italian community." "The statements they are making about exploitation," he added, "is hurting the well-meaning immigrants—the one who needs a job and will work at anything to provide for his family." Once again, a critic had invoked the image of the honourable immigrant family man to denounce the strikers. The strikers responded with a rash of angry pickets around Lombardi's grocery store. An organizer for the Laborers, Nick Gileno, told reporters: "We are hard-working people. Lombardi lives with us and should tell the truth." Toppan added, "I am a good bricklayer and have worked myself up. I want Lombardi to know that I haven't time for poolrooms—I have worked every day since coming to Canada." The strikers won this battle: Lombardi apologized and subsequently supported the 1961 strike.[45]

Convincing the wider community was a more difficult task. Italian strikers had to defend themselves against a competing, anti-immigrant discourse in which contradictory but consistently negative images of them as selfish and calculating schemers, easily manipulated dupes, and violence-prone minorities dominated. Dozens of Torontonians wrote to the city's English-language newspapers expressing disapproval, even contempt, for the strikers. The violence that marked each campaign fuelled the ire of bigots who dubbed Italians as "hot-blooded" and incapable of respecting the law or dismissed them as a mob-like "gang of union men."[46]

The issue of male violence deserves scrutiny. Although strikers saw builders and developers as the villains, much of the actual conflict occurred at the job sites, where Italian picketers confronted hostile Italian and other workers whom they hoped to recruit into their union movement. Emotions ran high at the sites and assaults inevitably occurred. During the 1961 strike, for example, a housing site in Markham saw 150 strikers and workers engaged in a brick-throwing exchange, which resulted in several serious injuries and put some of the duelling men in hospital. The Toronto Builders Exchange took advantage of the situation, portraying picketers as "goon squads" and "ruffians" savagely destroying property and machinery.[47]

When violence did erupt, union leaders blamed employers and police. Police arrests of contractors for intimidating strikers and, in one case, waving a gun at pickets, gave some credence to union charges.[48] When, for instance, strikers in North York were arrested in 1961 after allegedly trying to prevent a police officer on a motorcycle from driving through the crowd of picketers in an effort to disperse them, the Brandon executive charged police with arbitrarily confiscating picket signs from workers, rough-handling them, and calling them "wops," "DPs," and other derogatory names.[49] Strike organizers downplayed the violence. While admitting that men sometimes got "carried away" during the face-to-face heckling at the sites, they insisted that order, not chaos, characterized these encounters. Their presence, insisted union organizers, gave many of the working men the encouragement they needed to join the campaign. According to Colantonio, organizers stayed calm, reminding strikers: "We're here to communicate, to behave like gentlemen."[50]

The question of responding with violence was a delicate one for leaders to navigate. To maintain the public claims that strikers were honourable men, defending their families and trying to win justice, union leaders had to insist that strikers were not hooligans or gangsters, but responsible and legitimate members of Canadian society. But to maintain solidarity among the striking men, leaders needed to reinforce men's claims to masculinity, among which was a sense that as men they were obliged to take action when threatened, to respond with force when necessary. Irvine's "plank of action" was not just words—it was a board with a nail, a symbol of the workers' trades but also a potential weapon. The potential for physical force and for violence, which in part defined men's social role, had to be symbolically deployed, even as real acts of violence had to be contained.

Defending their manly honour against charges of picket-line harassment and vigilante violence became crucial, particularly during the 1961 strike when police and the courts intensified their efforts to demonize the strikers. "Arrests will be made," promised Toronto's deputy police chief in 1961, "as long as groups of men roam the city and terrorize other workers, contractors, and citizens." The police tried to intimidate strikers into submission by increasing surveillance, ordering "special details" to watch over larger sites, and arresting hundreds of strikers. Etobicoke's chief of police put it bluntly: "We're going to take them up by the truckload and dump strikers in the Don [jail]."[51] Since few strikers could afford bail, arrested men inevitably spent some time in jail. In an incident that caused police authorities some embarrassment, police patrols rounded up strikers in Etobicoke and then, during questioning, hinted at the possibility of deportation. According to strikers' recollections, police also used other intimidation techniques, "manhandling" the men during arrest and sometimes beating them.[52]

The courts seemed equally bent on achieving submission, but by making an example of some men. In 1961, they chose 20-year-old Giancarlo (John) Stefanini, an organizer with the Common Laborers arrested on obstruction charges. Police testified that Stefanini had incited strikers to harass working men and then refused to disperse the group when ordered to do so. Since Stefanini had spoken in Italian, the police probably had not understood him. But he was convicted and the judge endorsed Crown counsel's proposal for a stiff jail sentence: six months.[53]

But the most heavy-handed tactics of all were those of the builders and critics who raised the bogeyman of deportation. In so doing, they transformed a whispering campaign of rumour and innuendo into a public debate over the rights of Italian men to defend their honour and demand respect in a context in which they were "othered," as foreign workers and non-citizens. The deportation question revealed the competing discourses of critics determined to undermine the strikers' legitimacy by conjuring up lurid images of hooligans disrespectful of the law and demagogue-led ruffians bent on destruction. The strikes were indeed contested terrain. Contrasting images of the honourable immigrant versus dangerous foreigner, like the contrasting explanations of the recurring violence, were more than merely linguistic symbols and rhetorical flourishes unleashed by the strike. Once articulated and effectively manipulated, they helped shape the contours of the conflict, including its escalation into a deportation affair.

H.P. Hyatt, president of the Metropolitan Toronto House and Building Association, triggered the deportation debate in June 1961 when he requested the Minister of Immigration, Ellen Fairclough, to deport immigrants convicted of strike-related violence.[54] Fairclough refused, but the request provoked critics and supporters to respond. The discourse deployed by both groups drew on contrasting images of honourable and dishonourable men. Critics included unionists and staunch conservatives. The former revealed their distrust of Italians as unionists, usually by dubbing them the authors of their own misfortune. As one Canadian worker put it, Italians were "willing to accept lower wages than the standard" but "now faced with the problem of a strike, they want people to feel sorry for them." Other unionists blamed immigrant selfishness, claiming that Italian workers had placed their desires for houses, cars, and other luxuries before the greater cause of working men. In short, Italians had failed to measure up to the honourable traditions of the labour movement.[55] Ironically, conservative anti-labour critics, keen on deportation and quick to attribute the strikes to demagogues and "hot-blooded" Italians, also invoked images of the Italian strikers as dishonourable, untrustworthy, and even dangerous men. In a letter to the *Globe and Mail*, one writer said the strike had "shattered" her "confidence in Canadian democracy" because it had permitted "a gang of union men to converge upon a construction development and intimidate the workers until naked fear makes them rush to protect their families." Others argued that as strikers kept others from exercising their right to work, all of them should be deported. Perhaps the most unequivocal of all was the critic who described the strikers as "nothing but a howling, screaming pack of unruly hooligans."[56]

The strikers countered with familiar claims about peaceful information pickets and controlled crowds. Yet the debate clearly exposed their vulnerability as non-citizens and unleashed deep-seated fears. For men who brought with them well-aged suspicions of the state, as well as recent experiences with fascism and a war fought in their own backyards, the idea that governments might run roughshod over people's rights was not an entirely foreign one—the assurances of the Immigration Minister notwithstanding.

What Italian strikers could not have predicted, however, was that the deportation affair would mobilize enormous support for their campaign from within the immigrant and wider communities. Initially, Toronto's daily newspapers welcomed the strikes as a chance to eliminate immigrant exploitation in construction, though *Globe and Mail* editorials expressed concern over union rivalries and the illegality issue. The support was linked at first to the Hogg's Hollow revelations, which had graphically revealed exploitative conditions and abusive employers. A *Telegram* editorial that captured media outrage over Hogg's Hollow also mirrored the Italian workers' own claims as nation-builders: "Men who labor beneath the surface of a city provide physical comforts and civic security to hundreds of thousands. What a lavish expenditure of energy and sacrifice to give city dwellers the most commonplace conveniences of modern life."[57] Indeed, the conservative *Telegram* remained surprisingly sympathetic during both strikes, in part because of its labour columnist, Frank Drea, a young muckraking, crusading reporter. His columns offered "human portraits" of beleaguered strikers and chronicled the demanding daily routines of men that, as in the case of labourer Dominic Moscone, involved "rising at 4 am to walk fifteen miles to his pick-up depot and not returning home until after dark—all for the princely sum of $1.00 an hour." Drea reported on injuries and woefully inadequate compensation awards, and his columns also reinforced the workers' projected image, calling them upstanding immigrants—not radicals or Communists—entitled to better protections.[58]

The greater public support was engendered in 1961. Convinced that nativists were running a smear campaign against all Italians, previously unsympathetic elites in the immigrant community came on side, including Grohovaz, who declared: "The battle of the Italian workers has now become our battle.... [it] is not only about a labour dispute but involves us all in the inalienable rights of the Italian immigrants."[59] In the face of growing violence, the English-language dailies (as in 1960) had begun to waver in their support of the strikers, but they now switched gears, condemning the builders and deportation advocates. In defending Italian men's honour, Rosemary Boxer drew on romantic stereotypes of "sunny Italy," declaring that "violence is not their normal way. Italians are gay and fun loving, sentimental and emotional." But she also blamed matters on Canadian failure to "understand" or "help" immigrants, saying "this whole situation is an open sore on our community and society." A *Star* editorial expressed astonishment at such "unwarranted intimidation" of immigrants addressing legitimate grievances. "Canadian law," another warned, "should not be used as a club to scare men into docile acceptance of bad working conditions." The *Globe and Mail* agreed: "the deportation request," it declared, "is so contrary to the principles of democracy that one is left wondering if the builders are aware that they live in a democracy."[60]

Sympathetic Torontonians also condemned the deportation request and defended the strikers as hard-working immigrants and family men. A Canadian woman living in an Italian neighbourhood wrote: "I have watched the men go out with their lunch boxes in the morning [and] come home at dark, bone tired and weary but always with a smile and a laugh to quiet their children. I have talked to shopkeepers who marvel they don't starve." Another writer, H. Dust, defended the Italians against charges of staging an illegal strike with claims that it was "[e]qually abhorant [sic] for some contractors to take unfair advantage of immigrants." And if unionists were among the strike's opponents, they also numbered among its strong supporters, applauding the Italians for their courage and welcoming the opportunity to create a more unified labour movement. As one Canadian worker put it: "the immigrants are fighting our fight, along with their own." Finally, the city's labour leaders endorsed a resolution condemning the Home Builders Association. Significantly, its wording echoed the strikers' discourse of the manly, honourable immigrant. "What should be deported," it read, "is long hours, low pay, deplorable and dangerous working conditions and the exploitation and cheating of immigrants who wish only to build for themselves and their families a better life in Canada."[61]

The debate over deportation suggests the ways that claims to honourable masculinity could support broader claims to citizenship. Just as their claims to familial leadership justified their participation in union action, Italian working-men's claims to honourable masculinity underscored their rights as members of a democratic society. Others claimed status as nation-builders. "Italians," P. Palozzi declared in a letter to the press, "did not come to Canada to steal jobs or to work at low rates, but to build a better, stronger Canada. We don't know where the race track is, or where Florida and California are in winter—but we know where our job is."[62] If designed and maintained properly, the gendered norms of masculinity, forged out of particular class and ethnic context, held the power to signify citizenship and nation-building, even for the least powerful groups of immigrant working people.

Masculinity—Some Theoretical and Political Issues

For labour scholars, unionists, and Italian workers, the impact of the immigrant union drives on industrial relations in the construction industry remains open for debate.[63] But the strikes offer an opportunity to explore the dynamic processes involved in the formation of the gender identities of immigrant male workers, to probe the shifting boundaries, transitions, and transformative moments, the configurations of work, household, and community, and the interplay of transplanted and emergent strategies, customs, and gender relations as they unfolded in an immigrant context.

A central question has framed this particular rendering of the strikes: how did men who otherwise felt disadvantaged, marginal, and exploited derive a sense of manly honour? In seeking to address that question, this chapter draws some larger conclusions. It argues against a static, snapshot view of masculinity (and, indeed, femininity) or idealist constructions of manhood. It speaks in favour of studies of masculinity that both acknowledge the active role that language, symbols, and discourse can play in the construction of class, gender, and racial-ethnic identities *and* seek to integrate a sensitivity to discursive practices into, as Kirk suggests, a "wider framework of analysis which embraces agency and structure, saying and doing, the conscious and unconscious, and the willed and intended consequences of individual and social action and thought."[64] Gender, like class or ethnicity, is neither a static structure nor a neatly packaged set of prescribed practices and identities. It is an evolving, relational process. The gender identity of Italian immigrant construction workers did not arrive fully formed upon their arrival in post-war Toronto but was negotiated and remade in changing and challenging contexts. Men articulated and projected their masculine image and manly discourse amid the transitional contexts occasioned by their migration experience and the class exploitation, gendered practices, immigrant households, racial derision, and material sacrifice that helped define that experience. The dominant masculine discourse of the honourable immigrant that emerged within the overlapping contexts of rickety scaffolds, crowded flats, multi-family households, neighbourhood parks, and union halls both articulated and reinforced Italian men's determination to earn public respect for labours performed and rehabilitate their customary status and privilege as family breadwinner and protector.

Second, an explicit assumption underlying this paper, namely, that historians seriously take up the challenge of scrutinizing men as gendered subjects, is intended as more than an elitist exercise in deconstructing the multiple meanings embedded in the metaphors, "Italian human steam shovel," "wetback," or "almost black" pick-and-shovel man. As an exercise in politically engaged scholarship, this study reminds us of the crucial role that women and the politics of gender play in the political mobilization of male workers and working-class communities. On the surface, the construction strikes appeared to be exclusively male dramas orchestrated by Italian men (and their male allies). Yet, the men's decision to "fight back" and their capacity to endure two long and bitter struggles without benefit of strike pay were contingent in large part on women's wage-earning and other forms of support and, to a lesser degree, on the support mobilized within the immigrant and wider communities. The union drives were limited in scope, aiming at concrete bread-and-butter issues, yet they hint at the wisdom of labour strategies aimed at cultivating cross-gender, community, and broad-based alliances.

Finally, this chapter suggests that we think carefully about a hierarchy of masculinities.[65] Even a study aimed at retrieving the dignity of men treated abysmally by more powerful men and vested capitalist interests cannot ignore title patriarchal privileges and advantages that even marginal immigrant men enjoyed compared to their wives and other women in their community. Nor can we continue to celebrate naively the violent actions of men on strike.[66] Yet we need also to acknowledge that masculinities, like real men, do not enjoy equal status, power, and influence. In the same spirit in which feminist labour historians have argued against monolithic, essentialist models of patriarchy,[67] this essay suggests the need to discern between the masculinities of powerful men and those of homosexuals, racial-ethnic minorities, workers, and the poor.

Endnotes

1. Consider, for example, this small sample: Leonore Davidoff and Catherine Hall, *Family Fortunes: Men and Women of the English Middle Class, 1780–1850* (Chicago, 1987); Joy Parr, *The Gender of Breadwinners: Women, Men and Change in Two Industrial Towns* (Toronto, 1990); Michael Roper and John Tosh, eds, *Manful Assertions: Masculinities in Britain Since 1800* (London and New York, 1991); Ava Baron, ed., *Work Engendered: Toward a New History of American Labor History* (Ithaca, NY, 1991); George Chauncey, *Gay New York: Gender, Urban Culture and the Gay Male World, 1890–1940* (New York, 1994); Keith Jenkins, ed., *The Postmodern History Reader* (New York, 1997).
2. For example, the essays in *Signs* 19, 2 (Summer 1994); Regina Kunzel, "Pulp Fiction and Problem Girls: Reading and Rewriting Single Pregnancy in the Postwar United States," *American Historical Review* 100 (Dec. 1995); Franca Iacovetta and Wendy Mitchinson, eds, *On the Case: Explorations in Social History* (Toronto, 1998).
3. Neville Kirk, "History, Language, Ideas and Post-Modernism: A Materialist View," in Jenkins, ed., *The Postmodern History Reader*. See also Christine Stansell, "Response to Joan Scott," *International and Labor Working Class History* 31 (Spring 1987).
4. See Michael Roper and John Tosh, "Introduction," in Roper and Tosh, eds, *Manful Assertions*.
5. Franca Iacovetta, *Such Hardworking People: Italian Immigrants in Post-war Toronto* (Montreal and Kingston, 1992). While I remain committed to the materialist focus of my original portrayal (ch. 5), this version highlights the varied gender dynamics involved, incorporates some post-structuralist insights regarding the role of language in giving shape to experience, discontents, and demands, and adds some new material.
6. See, for example, *The Goldenberg Report* (Ottawa, 1962); Catherine Wismer, *Sweethearts: The Builders, the Mob, and the Men* (Toronto, 1968); H.C. Goldenberg and J.H. Crispo, eds, *Construction Labour Relations* (Toronto, 1968).
7. A fuller discussion is in Donna Gabaccia and Franca Iacovetta, "Women, Work, and Protest in the Italian Diaspora: An International Research Agenda," *Labour/Le Travail* 42 (Fall 1998).
8. See, for example, Michael La Sorte, *La Merica: Images of Italian Greenhorn Experience* (Philadelphia, 1985); Donna Gabaccia and Fraser Ottanelli, "Diaspora or International Proletariate?," *Diasporas* 6 (Spring 1997); James R. Barrett and David Roediger, "The In Between Peoples: Race,

Nationality, and the "New Immigrant" Working Class," *Journal of American Ethnic History* 16 (Spring 1997).

9. On the image and reality of the "pick-and-shovel" metaphor in its many national and continental contexts, see George E. Pozzetta and Bruno Ramirez, eds, *The Italian Diaspora Across the Globe* (Toronto, 1992).
10. Archives of Ontario, Department of Planning and Development, Immigration Branch Files, F.J. Love to Premier Leslie Frost, 1 Sept. 1954. See also Iacovetta, *Such Hardworking People*, ch. 5.
11. Interviews with author.
12. *Toronto Telegram*, letter to editor, A.E Chapman et al., 5 Apr. 1960; interviews with author.
13. Bid-peddling refers to the practice whereby builders pressured a contractor into lowering his price below his competitor's by revealing the latter's bid. Such practices violated the principle of competitive tendering of contracts.
14. In bricklaying and carpentry, hourly rates dropped by half, from $2.50 to between $1.00–$1.50. Labourers earned as low as 80 cents an hour.
15. Interview with author (pseudonym).
16. Iacovetta, *Such Hardworking People*, ch. 2.
17. By 1971, approximately 77 percent of Canada's Italians owned their homes, compared with 55 percent of the general population. For Toronto, Italians recorded the highest proportion, with over 83 percent of Italians owning their own homes. Anthony Richmond and Warren Kalback, *Factors in the Adjustment of Immigrants and Their Descendants* (Ottawa, 1980), 404–7.
18. Interview with author.
19. Reporter Frank Drea, cited in Frank Colantonio, *From the Ground Up: An Italian Immigrant's Story* (Toronto, 1997). I gratefully acknowledge the generosity of Frank Colantonio, who sadly passed away before his memoir was published, for sharing his manuscript with me.
20. The union met in a hall in an Italian neighbourhood of west-end Toronto, on Brandon Ave.
21. The Brandon locals were: Bricklayers, Masons, and Plasterers' International Union of America, Local 40; International Hod Carriers, Building and Common Laborers' Union of America, Local 811; United Brotherhood of Carpenters and Joiners of America, Local 1190; Operative Plasterers and Cement Masons' International Association of the United States and Canada, Local 117 (Plasterers) and Local 117-C (Cement Masons).
22. The 1960 strike was illegal because it was a recognition strike. Under the Ontario Labour Relations Act, strikes are prohibited until a union has been certified or voluntarily recognized by the employer and until conciliation procedures have been completed. The 1961 strike was a recognition strike for some and hence illegal; for those under contract, the strike was illegal because the Labour Relations Act prohibited strikes during the life of a collective agreement.
23. This included the rival AFL union campaign, which was launched with the official support of mainstream labour organizations such as the Canadian Labour Congress.
24. Local 211 (Teamsters) voted in favour of a sympathy strike, interrupting truck deliveries of ready-mix cement and other materials to non-union projects. So did the Commercial Bricklayers' Union, Local 183, which had a large Italian membership, and the Plasterers.
25. The final contracts, covering over 200 firms and some 7,000 workers, set a 40-hour week (for labourers, 45 hours), general increases of 40–50 cents, 4 percent vacation pay, and some safety provisions. This raised the official hourly rate of the highest paid trade, bricklayers, from $2.60 to $3.05, and the lowest paid, labourers, from $1.55 to $2.00.
26. *Toronto Star*, 8 Aug. 1960; *Labour Gazette*, Aug. 1960.
27. *Toronto Telegram*, 26 June 1961.
28. Interview with author. An unflattering portrait of Zanini is in Colantonio, *From the Ground Up*.
29. Irvine and Zanini had jumped the gun on the AFL's plan to lead a union drive among immigrants on the grounds, they claimed, that the old-line unions could not be trusted.
30. Cited in Frank Drea, *Telegram* column, 31 Mar. 1960.
31. See, for example, Charlotte Gower Chapman, *Milocca: A Sicilian Village* (Cambridge, Mass., 1971); Ann Cornelisen, *Women of the Shadows: A Study of the Wives and Mothers of Southern Italy* (New York, 1977); Constance Cronin, *The Sting of Change: Sicilians in Sicily and Australia* (Chicago, 1970); Donna Gabbaccia, *From Sicily to Elizabeth Street: Housing and Social Change*

among Italian Immigrants (Albany, NY, 1984); Judith E. Smith, *Family Connections: A History of Italian and Jewish Immigrant Lives in Providence, Rhode Island 1900–1940* (Albany, NY, 1985); Iacovetta, *Such Hardworking People*.
32. Gabaccia and Iacovetta, "Women, Work, and Protest in the Italian Diaspora."
33. In 1961, Italian-speaking men in Toronto earned on average $3,016; Italian-speaking women earned on average $1,456. Anthony Richmond, *Immigrants and Ethnic Groups in Metropolitan Toronto* (Toronto, 1967), 22.
34. Interviews with author.
35. Ardis Cameron, *Radicals of the Worst Sort: Laboring Women in Lawrence, Massachusetts, 1860–1912* (Chicago, 1993). See also Steven Penfold, "'Have You No Manhood In You?': Gender and Class in the Cape Breton Coal Towns," *Acadiensis* 23, 2 (Spring 1994): 21–44; Priscilla Long, "The Women of the Colorado Iron and Fuel Strike, 1913–14," in Ruth Milkman, ed., *Women, Work and Protest: A Century of U.S. Women's Labor History* (Boston, 1985).
36. Interview with author.
37. Robert Ventresca, "'Cowering Women, Combative Men?': Femininity, Masculinity and Ethnicity on Strike in Two Southern Ontario Towns, Italians on Strike in Postwar Ontario, 1960–1980," *Labour/Le Travail* 39 (Spring 1997): 125–58.
38. For example, Columba Furio, "The Cultural Background of the Italian Immigrant Woman and Its Impact on Her Unionization in the New York Garment Industry, 1880–1919," in George Pozzetta, ed., *Pane e Lavoro: The Italian-American Working Class* (Toronto, 1980); Cameron, Radicals; Ventresca, "'Cowering Women, Combative Men?'"; Gabaccia and Iacovetta, "Women, Work, and Protest in the Italian Diaspora"; Carina Silberstein, "Becoming Visible: Italian Immigrant Women in the Garment and Textile Industries in Argentina, 1890–1930," and Jennifer Guglielmo, "What Have We Got to Lose? Italian American Women's Workplace Organizing Strategies, East Harlem, New York, 1930–1940," both papers presented to the Berkshire Conference on the History of Women, June 1996.
39. National Archives of Canada, MG 31, vol. 1, Marino Toppan Papers, File on Correspondence and Memoirs, 1961–8, Toppan to Thomas Murphy, Washington, 7 July 1961.
40. Rosemary Boxer, *Toronto Telegram*, 24 June, 9 July 1961; interviews with author.
41. Cited in *Toronto Telegram*, 2 Aug. 1960.
42. Interview with author.
43. On this theme, see David Roediger, *The Wages of Whiteness: Race and the Making of the American Working-class* (London, 1991); Barrett and Roediger, "In Between Peoples"; Franca Iacovetta, "Manly Militants, Cohesive Communities, and Defiant Domestics: Writing about Immigrants in Canadian History," *Labour/Le Travail* 36 (Fall 1995): 217–52.
44. Colantonio, *From the Ground Up*, ch. 5, 100–1.
45. *Toronto Star*, 29 Mar., 4, 7 Apr. 1960; *Toronto Telegram*, 30, 31 Mar. 1960.
46. *Globe and Mail*, 12 June 1961 (D.Allen).
47. *Toronto Telegram*, 2, 3 Aug. 1960; *Toronto Star*, 2, 3 Aug. 1960; *Globe and Mail*, 2, 3 Aug. 1960.
48. *Toronto Telegram*, 2, 3 Aug. 1960; *Toronto Star*, 2, 3 Aug. 1960.
49. *Toronto Telegram*, 3, 4 Aug. 1960; *Toronto Star*, 4 Aug. 1960; *Globe and Mail*, 4, 6 Aug 1960.
50. Colantonio, *From the Ground Up*, ch. 4, 24; interviews with author; *Toronto Telegram*, letter to editor, 2 June 1960.
51. *Toronto Telegram*, 20, 22 June 1961.
52. Interviews with author.
53. *Globe and Mail*, 22, 23 June 1961; *Toronto Telegram*, 22 June 1961; *Toronto Star*, 22 June 1961; Kenneth Bagnell, *Canadese: A Portrait of the Italian Canadians* (Toronto, 1989), 159–60.
54. *Toronto Star*, 3 June 1961; *Toronto Telegram*, 3, 6 June 1961; editorial, *Canadian Labour* 6 (Sept. 1961): 4.
55. *Globe and Mail*, 17 June 1961 (A.E. Burt); *Toronto Star*, 6, 7, 16 June 1961.
56. *Globe and Mail*, 12 June 1961 (D. Allen), 7 June 1961 (R.A. Meagan).
57. *Toronto Telegram*, 19 Mar. 1960.

58. For example, ibid., 31 Mar., 3, 5, 8, 11 Apr. 1960.
59. Cited ibid., 23 July 1961.
60. Boxer cited in Colantonio, From the Ground Up, ch. 6, 136–7; *Toronto Star*, 3, 7 June 1961; *Globe and Mail*, 7 June 1961.
61. *Toronto Star*, 8 July 1961; *Globe and Mail*, 16 June 1961 (H. Dust); *Toronto Telegram*, 5 July 1961 (D. Braithwaite); *Toronto Star*, 24 June 1961 (sheet metal worker). See also *Star*, 3, 10 June 1961; *Telegram*, 3, 6, 7, 27 June 1961.
62. *Toronto Star*, 29 Mar., 4, 7 Apr. 1960; *Toronto Telegram*, 30, 31 Mar. 1960.
63. For some differing perspectives, see references in note 2.
64. Kirk, "History, Language, Ideas and Post-modernism," 239.
65. See, for example, Roper and Tosh, "Introduction"; Joy Parr, "Gender and Historical Practice," in Joy Parr and Mark Rosenfeld, eds, *Gender and History in Canada* (Toronto, 1996); R.W. Connell, "The Big Picture: Masculinities in Recent World History," *Theory and Society* 22 (1993); Madge Pon, "Like a Chinese Puzzle: The Construction of Chinese Masculinity in Jack Canuck," in Parr and Rosenfeld, eds, *Gender and History in Canada*.
66. An insightful look at this complex issue is Nancy Forestell, "Historians and the Politics of Masculinity," paper presented to the Canadian Historical Association, June 1996.
67. For example, Ava Baron, "Gender and Labour History: Learning from the Past, Looking to the Future," in Baron, ed., *Work Engendered*; Alice Kessler-Harris, *Out to Work: A History of Wage-Earning Women in the United States* (New York, 1982); Bettina Bradbury, "Women's History and Working-Class History," *Labour/Le Travail* 19 (Spring 1987); Linda Kealey, *Enlisting Women for the Cause: Women, Labour and the Left in Canada, 1890–1920* (Toronto, 1998).

Critical-Thinking Questions

1. What issues created conflict between organized labour and the federal government during World War II? What outcomes partially resolved their differences?
2. How did women's expectations about employment change as a result of their wartime employment? To what extent did the administration of the Unemployment Insurance Act reflect older views of female employment, and how did the changes to the regulations reflect updated ideas about women's work in the labour force?
3. What role did women's auxiliaries play in many unions? Why were some a target of RCMP surveillance during the Cold War?
4. How did unions' views on immigration change after World War II? What role did the Jewish Labour Committee play in the emergence of policies on human rights in Canadian society?
5. What conditions in the booming post-war construction industry led to strikes? What were the outcomes of the two strikes in Toronto and how were they linked to changing identities concerning masculinity?

Further Readings

Blake, Raymond B. and Jeff Keshen (eds.). *Social Welfare Policy in Canada* (Toronto: Copp Clark, 1995). This collection of essays examines the coming of the welfare state in Canada in piecemeal form through the passage of various pieces of legislation.

Iacovetta, Franca. *Such Hardworking People: Italian Immigrants in Postwar Toronto* (Montreal and Kingston: McGill-Queen's University Press, 1992). An examination of post-World War II Toronto, this monograph discusses how Italian immigrants made the transition from being peasants in Italy to becoming industrial workers in Canada.

Kaplan, William. *Everything That Floats: Pat Sullivan, Hal Banks, and the Seamen's Unions of Canada* (Toronto: University of Toronto Press, 1987). This analysis of unions on the Canadian waterfront concludes that neither the Communist-influenced Canadian Seamen's Union nor the gangster-run Seafarers' International Union had their members' interests at heart.

Lambertson, Ross. *Repression and Resistance: Canadian Human Rights Activists, 1930–1960* (Toronto: University of Toronto Press, 2005). This is a study of activists, including trade unionists, who fought for human rights and a Bill of Rights in twentieth-century Canada and who opposed discrimination and civil liberties violations in the wartime and Cold War periods.

MacDowell, Laurel Sefton. *"Remember Kirkland Lake": The Gold Miners' Strike of 1941–1942* (Toronto: University of Toronto Press, 1983; Canadian Scholars' Press, 2001) Set during World War II, MacDowell's study examines this important gold miners' strike, which, though lost, united the labour movement behind the demand for collective bargaining legislation in Canada.

MacDowell, Laurel Sefton. *Renegade Lawyer: The Life of J.L. Cohen* (Toronto: University of Toronto Press and The Osgoode Society, 2001). As the first influential labour lawyer in Canada, Cohen was an effective advocate for working people in the years of the Great Depression and World War II. He rose to the top of his field, contributed to the legislation underpinning the modern industrial relations system, but his tragic personal life undermined his health and reputation.

Radforth, Ian. *Bushworkers and Bosses: Logging in Northern Ontario, 1900–1980* (Toronto: University of Toronto Press, 1987). This monograph examines the nature of work, changing technology, and the efforts of loggers in northern Ontario, most of whom were immigrants, to become unionized in the face of strong employer opposition.

Sangster, Joan. *Earning Respect: The Lives of Working Women in Small-Town Ontario, 1920–1960* (Toronto: University of Toronto Press, 1995). This study examines the lives of working women in Peterborough, as they struggled with changing employment conditions during the Great Depression and World War II.

Sugiman, Pamela. *Labour's Dilemma: the Gender Politics of Auto Workers in Canada, 1937–1979* (Toronto: University of Toronto Press, 1994). Though the UAW was a democratic and socially progressive union, its overwhelmingly male leadership and membership discriminated against the small groups of women auto workers in their midst. From the 1960s, in the context of the modern women's movement, these women gained confidence in their identity and fought for gender equality.

Sufrin, Eileen Tallman. *The Eaton Drive: The Campaign to Organize Canada's Largest Department Store, 1948–1952* (Toronto: Fitzhenry and Whiteside, 1982). Eileen Tallman was an important organizer in the drive to unionize employees of Eaton's, and she later wrote a book about the experience. The effort failed by a small margin, but was significant, as the labour movement did not try again to unionize in the private retail sector for many years.

PART IV

From Stagflation to Globalization (1974–2000)

In Quebec, post-war prosperity and the creation of the welfare state helped spawn the Quiet Revolution after the death in 1959 of Maurice Duplessis, the conservative, anti-labour premier of many years. Duplessis had articulated an older, increasingly outmoded kind of nationalism, which romanticized a French-speaking, rural, Catholic culture in Quebec, even as the province continued to industrialize. This had the effect of preserving that province as a low-wage region in Canada. The Quiet Revolution involved demands for more and better jobs, and catch-up in labour standards for Quebec workers with other Canadian workers. But it also led to self-confidence and a new nationalism, focused on the French language, which accommodated the reality of a growing urban industrial society, which was becoming increasingly secular. Thus the Quiet Revolution eventually went beyond the liberal federalism of Premier Jean Lesage to the creation of the separatist Parti Québecois (PQ) in 1968, led by René Levesque, which formed the government in Quebec in 1976. Quebec labour had supported the Quiet Revolution and the Liberals, but moved towards greater militancy, organized large numbers of workers including public sector employees into the CNTU, and supported the PQ and sovereignty association as that movement grew. Ralph Peter Guntzel traces labour's political path in the context of growing Quebec nationalism, even though for class and collective bargaining reasons, labour and the PQ did not always agree. The PQ was led by some of the new francophone, middle-class professionals, who in collective bargaining situations sat across the table from the trade unionists.

A very important theme in post-war Canada was the rapid growth of public-sector unions, which departed from a consultation model with employers in labour relations and adopted collective bargaining. The range of employees represented by these new unions broadened to include professionals, such as teachers and nurses, whose numbers expanded with the growth of larger public health and educational sectors. Increasingly such groups demanded the right to strike and converted their organizations into real unions for collective bargaining purposes, usually changing their leadership in the process. Many provincial jurisdictions at first did not allow either civil servants or professionals (or both) to strike. Rebecca Coulter describes the situation for nurses in Alberta, who, like many other such groups, had to strike illegally. Public-sector unionism increased the proportion of organized women in the labour movement, as female employment in the expanding service sector of the economy increased steadily. Thus, the collective bargaining system for mostly male, blue-collar employees in the private sector, which emerged from the war, broadened and adapted to include growing numbers of public-sector and professional workers—many of whom were female.

After the 1970s, workplaces in Canada were changing quickly. As the industrial manufacturing sector of the economy gradually shrank, the service sector expanded rapidly. While public-sector service employees gained collective-bargaining rights, service workers in the private sector often were unable to organize, either because they were part-time or transient, which made such workforces difficult to unionize—as in the case of the fast food industry which Ester Reiter describes—or because employers were adamantly opposed to unions and fought all organizing efforts, as in the case of banks and insurance companies. Increasingly, jobs were transformed by technology, sometimes as a result of wartime discoveries converted to peacetime uses (for example, the chemical industry), or because changes stimulated by the computer revolution totally transformed workplaces (such as offices and car plants). The changing nature of work resulted in increased occupational health cases, which in turn resulted in new occupational health-and-safety acts all across the country. Laurel Sefton MacDowell discusses how unions' participation in actions involving occupational health educated workers about healthy work environments, which in turn caused the labour movement to formulate environmental policy relating to society as a whole. In doing so, labour worked out a complicated relationship with the growing Canadian environmental movement. Sometimes there was conflict: for example when trying to save jobs in the B.C. lumber industry. But often labour and the environmental lobby could work together on issues of water pollution, acid rain, and later in an international reform movement, to put social and environmental issues on the table in the restructured, international free-trade regime.

Technology led to globalization of the economy because it helped many companies to become mobile. It led to the development of a new trend: instead of seeing people moving to jobs (as in the case of generations of immigrants), companies frequently threatened or did shut down and move to other countries where workers were paid poor wages and were not unionized. Globalization of the economy gave companies more power over workers, threatened labour standards on jobs, resulted in companies' contracting out jobs to non-union employees, decreased the level of unionization in Canada, and made organizing the unorganized more difficult. Sam Gindon discusses some of these trends in the Canadian auto industry, where globalization pressures for free trade eventually ended the auto pact from which Canada had benefited, and created conflict between American and Canadian leaders over using tactics of concession bargaining or militancy in collective bargaining. The result was the breakaway of the Canadian autoworkers from the UAW, the creation of a new national union—the Canadian Auto Workers—with leadership intent on pursuing hard bargaining and supporting the growing anti-free-trade forces in Canada. Free trade became the policy of the country as a result of several agreements in the 1980s, but the CAW survived and pursued an aggressive organizing policy in a more general union of diverse workers, a strategy pursued by other unions in Canada, too. As in the past, Canadian workers had to fight hard for any rights on the job, and were most successful if they were part of the labour movement, which successive generations organized and reorganized in response to changing economic and political conditions.

Chapter 18

The Confédération des syndicats nationaux (CSN), the Idea of Independence, and the Sovereigntist Movement, 1960–1980

Ralph Peter Güntzel

In early June 1979, the CSN, Quebec's second-largest labour union central, held a special convention on the national question. The 1,000 delegates were to discuss a variety of issues related to Quebec's constitutional status and the socio-economic condition of francophones in Quebec. On the third day of the convention several high-ranking CSN officers led by the central's vice-president, André L'Heureux, proposed a resolution in support of independence for Quebec. A long and intense debate ensued. In the end, only one quarter of the delegates rallied behind the pro-independence proposal.[1] This vote did not mean, however, that the CSN endorsed federalism. Quite the opposite: in early April 1980, the CSN recommended to its members to vote "yes" in the referendum in order to permit the Parti québécois government to negotiate sovereignty-association. On the eve of the Quebec referendum, the CSN position on the issue of separation was ambiguous. To explain this ambiguity we must consider CSN history at the time of the Quiet Revolution.

The evolution of the CSN position on the independence question during the 1960s and 1970s can be divided into three phases. From 1960 to 1966, the CSN opted for federalism and provincial autonomy and rejected separation. From 1966 to 1972, most CSN leaders, and many rank-and-file members, came to favour independence. As a result, the CSN gradually moved away from its federalist stand and became increasingly sympathetic toward independence. In 1972, though, this process came to a halt. For the remainder of the decade the union central avoided any clear-cut stand. This paper seeks to cast light on the rise of separatism within the CSN after 1966, as well as its hesitation waltz during the 1970s. Both phenomena can only be understood with a prior knowledge of the ideological radicalization which the union central underwent between 1960 and 1980. Hence, I will first give an account of the CSN's socio-economic outlook, and then discuss its stance on constitutional questions. Although this study does not pretend to be a comparative analysis, the experiences of Quebec's other union centrals are considered briefly as well.

I.

The Confédération des travailleurs catholiques du Canada (CTCC) was founded in 1921 under the influence of the Roman Catholic Church. For a long time it adhered to Catholic social doctrine and defined as its goal the defense of traditional French-Canadian values, particularly against such adversaries as the international, religiously neutral unions. In pursuit of this goal, the CTCC opposed state intervention in the social and educational fields, and advocated collaboration with the business community.[2] It was only in the 1940s and 1950s that the CTCC leadership's socio-economic outlook began to change. Gradually the idea of preserving traditional French-Canadian society was supplanted by the ideology of "catching-up." The central now wanted Quebec to copy the institutions and standards of other Western societies. CTCC demands aimed at parity with Ontario in terms of salaries, work-conditions, labour relations, health services, and the education system.[3]

Many of the proposals aired by the CTCC-CSN were to be taken up during Quebec's Quiet Revolution. Between 1960 and 1966, Premier Jean Lesage and his Liberal government implemented the ambitious reform program that was at the heart of the Quiet Revolution. The team around Lesage advocated planning the economy to avoid such disturbances as those Canada had experienced during the first post-war depression, 1957 to 1961. It wanted to render the workplace more humane, and to make systematic provisions for the aged, the unemployed, and the sick as well as for an efficient, highly skilled, and professional labour force. Inspired by institutions and standards in other Western societies, the Quiet Revolution's reforms vastly expanded state intervention in the economy, in social, health, and welfare services, and in the educational system. An economic planning council was created, and various provincial capital pools, such as the Société générale de financement and the Caisse de dépôt et placement, were set up. All private hydroelectric companies were nationalized. New hospital insurance benefits gave Quebec residents free access to hospital and diagnostic services. The health-care and educational systems, formerly largely administered by the Church and private organizations, now became subject to state control.

The CSN was important in the coalition supporting the Liberal reform drive.[4] The union central also benefited from many Quiet Revolution measures, most particularly the reform of Quebec labour relations. With the new labour code of July 1964, Bill 5 in June 1965, and the Civil Servants' Act in August 1965, the right to strike—except where essential services were in jeopardy—was given to workers employed by hospitals, school commissions, and municipalities, to teachers, and to civil servants. It should be noted, however, that extending the right to strike to the public sector had not been among the Liberal Party's original intentions. Rather, it was the demands and pressure of organized labour which led to the new legislation. According to labour historian Jacques Rouillard, these laws placed Quebec in the vanguard of North American labour legislation. "Pour la premiere fois, l'enthousiasme issu de la Révolution tranquille porte les conquêtes sociales au-delà du modèle proposé par les autres sociétés nord-américaines."[5]

All the aforementioned reforms and others, such as the replacement of the spoils system by the merit system, and Bill 16 including the equalization of spouses in marriage, were introduced within a short time. While the reforms of the Quiet Revolution rapidly followed each other, they gave the population the impression of witnessing not only radical change but even the dawn of a new era. Since all those reforms had a distinctly progressive character, they helped heighten expectations. Many intellectuals, students, and labour-union militants expected the reforms to herald a more just and egalitarian society in which wealth would be distributed more equally.[6] Some of them joined radical political movements such as Parti pris, Révolution québécoise, and the Parti socialiste du Québec (PSQ). They could do so without being marginalized because the Quiet Revolution had created a new openness in intellectual life and thereby laid the basis for the free expression of radical ideas. It was in the last phase of the Quiet Revolution, during 1965–66 that radical political movements became increasingly prolific. At the same time disappointment with the achievements of the Quiet Revolution started to set in. Unemployment rates remained higher and average incomes lower in Quebec than in Ontario. Moreover, the instability and insecurity of the economic situation did not change in the least. During the late 1960s and early 1970s, the economic situation deteriorated and unemployment rates began to rise dramatically.[7] At the same time, government debts accumulated. The expansion of the public sector had led to an increase in costs and taxes. Yet while taxes went up the standard of living did not rise.[8]

The disappointment about the results of the Quiet Revolution was particularly pronounced within the CSN. This was largely due to the evolution of public-sector negotiations from 1965 onwards. The rapid rise of unionization in this sector created a situation in which the state and the CSN found themselves to be opponents at the bargaining table and in industrial conflicts. Unlike other employers, the state disposed of legislative powers which it used to enact special back-to-work legislation. Moreover, numerous court injunctions prevented or ended public-sector negotiations on the ground that essential services were in jeopardy. Under those circumstances, striking—the classical weapon of unionism—proved to be no longer effective.[9] The multiplication and aggravation of these conflicts during the second half of the 1960s increasingly frustrated and radicalized the CSN. Disappointed with the results of the Quiet Revolution, and more particularly its newly established system of industrial relations, more and more rank-and-file activists and union leaders—particularly in the public sector—started to reassess the power structures of existing society and redefine the character and the form of union activities. They soon concluded that the Quebec state was inherently hostile to working-class interests, no matter which party held power.[10] For them the obvious explanation of this hostility was the state's dependence on the business community.[11] In addition they considered it necessary to create new forms of unionism, since the traditional ones had become insufficient.[12] Towards the end of the decade, they came to analyze the market economy from a Marxist viewpoint without, however, employing Marxist terminology. From there they went on to advocate a socialist society and to politicize union activities accordingly.

In the early 1970s, a variety of events reinforced this ideological radicalization. In April 1970, the Parti libéral du Québec came to power. Led by Robert Bourassa, the new government embarked on a pro-business course of which the most prominent features were a disregard for state interventionism and support for private enterprise.[13] Half a year after the provincial elections, the October Crisis and the invocation of the War Measures Act took place. About one quarter of the people arrested during the crisis were labour-union activists. This infringement on citizens' civil liberties evoked the wrath of many CSN leaders and rank-and-file members. In the wake of the October Crisis, the CSN became more hostile towards the state apparatus. According to historian Jean-François Cardin, "[la CSN] ne craint plus d'attaquer directement l'Etat et son rôle d'appui à la bourgeoisie dans l'exploitation des travailleurs."[14] The early 1970s also witnessed several dramatic industrial conflicts, such as the strike at *La Presse* in 1971. This dispute crested on 29 October of that year, when police violently broke up a demonstration supporting the strikers, leaving behind one dead and several wounded. Thirty-seven militants were arrested on this occasion. Seven months later, CSN president Marcel Pépin and the presidents of Quebec's two other labour union centrals, were sentenced to jail for one year on the grounds that they had encouraged the illegal public-sector strike of April 1972.[15]

In the aftermath of the Quiet Revolution, the left within the union central underwent both a considerable radicalization and an increase in numerical strength. As a result, the left was able to exercise an ever-growing influence on the CSN's general orientation. In its quest to dominate the central, the left was pitted against a group of more moderate or conservative activists, the most of whom belonged to private-sector unions. It would be simplistic, however, to equate the left with the public sector and the right with the private sector. In fact, most public-sector union members were no more radical than their peers in private-sector unions. Most professionals adhered to elitist attitudes and held the average worker in disregard.[16] A 1970 poll of CSN-organized teachers showed that most of them did not think that unions should get involved in political activities.[17] The poll confirmed the findings of the CSN political action committee report presented at the 1968 confederal convention. The report stated that most CSN members were neither politicized nor willing to join the political activities of the labour movement. Quite similarly, in its report to the 1972 confederal convention, the Committee of the Twelve, an *ad hoc* committee on ideological issues, pointed out that Quebec's political parties and their ideas exercised a dominant influence among the CSN membership.[18]

While the CSN general membership was unwilling to fundamentally change the socio-economic system, the central's active membership became increasingly radical between the mid-1960s and the early 1970s.[19] The rise of the left was greatly helped by the dynamic personality of Marcel Pépin, president of the CSN from 1965 to 1976. Pépin's determination and leadership qualities were unmatched by those heading the right wing of the central.[20] He was surrounded by a group of intellectuals to which belonged Richard Daigneault, Pierre Vadeboncoeur, André L'Heureux, and Michel Rioux. This "think tank" was sensitive to the wave of protest sweeping through Quebec in the wake of the Quiet Revolution, and favoured the radicalization of the union central. Due to its close relationship with the president, the group wielded enormous informal power within the CSN. Its influence on decision-making processes paralleled that of the elected officers. Thus its opponents on the right referred to the group as "*le pouvoir parallèle*."[21] Pépin and his collaborators were pushed forward not only by the general atmosphere of post-Quiet Revolution Quebec, by public-sector militants, and union councillors emerg-ing from the student movement and socialist organizations, but also by a radical faction within the CSN's own left wing. Led by Michel Chartrand, the radical left in 1969 conquered the Conseil central des syndicats nationaux de Montréal (CCSNM), a CSN suborganization which represents all unions in the Montreal region. Under Chartrand's presidency, the CCSNM made ideological commitments which were path-breaking for the CSN as a whole. In 1970, the CCSNM proposed the CSN should officially reject capitalism and endorse socialism.[22]

Since Pépin and his followers were afraid to jeopardize the unity of the central, relations between the radical faction and the more moderate faction within the left were often characterized by tension and mutual suspicion.[23] Relations between both factions were rendered even more difficult by the personal animosity between Pépin and Chartrand. In 1971, however, all elements of the left joined forces in order to give the CSN the socialist orientation advocated by the CCSNM. The debate on the official ideology of the union central finally erupted in open conflict between the left and right.[24] Aggravated by dissent over which strategy to adopt in the 1972 public-sector negotiations, this conflict split the movement. Being in a minority situation, the right wing decided to leave the union central. The CSN lost about 70,000 members, which equalled one-third of its membership. Many of those who left the CSN went on to found a new, non-political union central, the Centrale des syndicats démocratiques (CSD).[25]

After the departure of the dissenters, almost all leaders of the CSN were partisans of socialism. They agreed on the need for fundamental socio-economic change. They thought the economic activities of society should be planned, and should aim at fulfilling the needs of the population. Furthermore, they endorsed the principle of collective ownership of the means of production, and of workers' participation in the economic decision-making process. Yet within the framework of these principles, they had different visions of socialism. Some CSN socialists wanted the collective ownership of the means of production to be comprehensive, while others wanted to limit it to certain key sectors such as natural resources. For the latter group, the expansion of the co-operative sector and workers' co-ownership were preferable to the nationalization of the entire economy.[26] CSN socialists took positions somewhere between those of social democracy and communism. In some instances their positions bordered on those of classical social democracy committed to minimize differences of wealth and to nationalize some sectors of the economy. Unlike social democrats, however, CSN socialists were prepared to go much further to eliminate private ownership of the means of production and principle of profit. What made CSN socialists different from communists was their insistence on democratic planning and decision-making. CSN socialists did not envisage a leading role for the Communist Party, nor a proletarian revolution. CSN socialists agreed that socialism should be attained peacefully, but remained unclear on how it should be brought about.

In October 1972, the confederal council—the CSN's highest decision-making body between its confederal conventions—adopted almost unanimously a declaration rejecting capitalism and endorsing socialism.[27] The resolution, though, failed to define socialism and instead called for "la poursuite d'une étude dans tout le mouvement visant à définir le contenu d'un socialisme québécois et les étapes de sa réalisation."[28] This hesitance to take a definite stand not only reflected the varying interpretations of socialism among CSN radicals, but also the insecurity these radicals felt toward the rank-and-file majority of their organization. The fact that the central's leadership was left-leaning did not mean that the right was now absent from the ranks of the CSN. A large number of militants, and a majority of the rank-and-file membership were opposed to any fundamental socio-economic change, but they remained faithful to the CSN despite its socialist orientation. They found its services satisfactory and distrusted the risk of joining a small, newborn central. Although the members of the confederal council appeared courageous in October 1972, the CSN leadership was deeply affected by the defections. The socialist CSN leaders were well aware that they had to anticipate the reactions of their largely anti-socialist constituency if future disaffiliations were to be avoided. Therefore they decided not to pursue elaborations on official CSN ideology. All plans to discuss the definition of the CSN version of socialism, and the steps required to attain a socialist society, were postponed. Instead, priority was given to the political education of the membership.[29]

In the end, very little energy was devoted to political education since the CSN underwent yet another crisis from 1973 to 1976. The enormous rise of the cost of living led many unions to try to force employers to reopen collective agreements in order to increase salaries. Walkouts and illegal strikes multiplied. The CSN strike fund rapidly became exhausted. This period was characterized by internal struggles about moves to raise per capita contributions to the strike fund. In the public sector unions were resentful of fee increases. In this sector, strikes were normally ended by special laws and court injunctions after only a few days. However, strike-fund benefits were disbursed only after two weeks of striking. About 20,000 members, mostly nurses and professionals, refused to pay the increases and consequently were forced to leave the CSN.[30]

While the union central was recuperating from its most recent losses over the fee-increase issue, several factions of Marxist-Leninist militants started to make their presence felt. They belonged to a variety of political organizations, the most important of which were En Lutte! and the Parti communiste ouvrier (PCO). They all agreed on the need for a revolutionary overthrow of capitalist society, but were fiercely opposed to each other on various theoretical issues. Although their organizations were tiny, due to their devotion, training, and discipline, the Marxist-Leninists began to exert considerable influence within the CSN. They were most successful in public-sector unions and regional CSN sub-organizations such as the CCSNM.[31] With the rise of the communist far left, ideological division within the union central became even more pronounced. In the latter 1970s, despite having lost a large number of members due to ideological differences, the CSN was ideologically less homogenous than ever. In these circumstances, the CSN leadership found its margin of manoeuverability extremely limited. It was constantly faced with the threat of internal divisions and renewed disaffiliations. Norbert Rodrigue, who succeeded Marcel Pépin as CSN president in 1976, was highly sensitive to this problem.[32] His leadership aimed at consolidating the movement, while cautiously pursuing the socialist education of its membership. Rodrigue avoided new disaffiliations, but made little or no headway regarding the spread of socialist thinking.[33] When he stepped down in 1982, the internal debate on socialism had not taken place. His successors discontinued the socialist discourse without any hesitation.[34]

As is suggested by the example of the Centrale d'enseignement du Québec (CEQ), Quebec's third-largest labour union central, the CSN was not the only union central to experience ideological radicalization and factional strife. Originally called Corporation des Instituteurs et Institutrices catholiques, the CEQ was renamed Corporation des Enseignants du Québec in 1967 before it received its present name in 1974. It was only in the late 1960s and early 1970s that the CEQ transformed itself from a professional association into a labour-union central. Teachers continued to dominate the central's membership, although the CEQ began to organize non-teachers in 1971. Like the CSN, the CEQ adopted a radical discourse in the early 1970s. Propagating a Marxist analysis of Quebec society, the central continuously attacked the state as the defender of the capitalist class. Yet the CEQ did not propose any alternative to the capitalist system. Unlike that of the CSN, the discourse of the CEQ was void of any reference to socialism. The CEQ leadership intended to elaborate upon a vision of society after an internal debate among the rank-and-file membership. Since a large part of the rank-and-file membership did not share the leadership's radicalism, the debate was continuously postponed and eventually dropped. Many CEQ members were sympathetic to social democracy and to the idea of gradual change within the parameters of the market economy. Toward the end of the 1970s the moderates made their presence more strongly felt, and in the early 1980s CEQ radicalism came to an end. The central dropped its Marxist analysis and the language of class struggle.[35]

Unlike the CSN and the CEQ, the Fédération des Travailleurs du Québec (FTQ), Quebec's largest union central did not experience any significant ideological radicalization. Dominated by such social-democratic leaders as Louis Laberge, Fernand Daoust, and Jean Gérin-Lajoie, the FTQ showed remarkable ideological consistency during the 1960s and 1970s. Apart from a brief period of more-radical discourse in the early 1970s, the FTQ was content to criticize the market economy, but not to fundamentally oppose it. Advocating state interventionism, economic planning, and the nationalization of certain sectors of the economy, the FTQ favoured a reformist course of gradual change. The central's leadership had little regard for Marxist analysis. As Jean Gérin-Lajoie put it:

> Ce qu'on défend, c'est une action sociale-démocrate.... L'analyse de classe n'a rien à voir avec la réalité sociale; c'est un concept livresque qu'on n'a pas adapté des endroits d'où elle provient. C'est un outil d'analyse qui n'a aucune valeur sur le plan de l'action.[36]

During the 1960s and the 1970s, organized labour in Quebec spoke with a social-democratic and a socialist voice. More than anything else it was the following three phenomena that forged its ideological outlook: first, the experience of the Quiet Revolution which had brought with it high expectations and bitter disappointments; second, the constraints of public-sector negotiations where employers could frustrate strikes by back-to-work legislation; and third, the climate of protest and criticism that swept through Quebec and other Western societies in the late 1960s. Whether more moderate social democrats or more radical socialists provided the leadership for the various union bodies, was to some extent a personality question. More important, however, were the experiences in industrial conflicts and the disposition of rank-and-file activists. A social-democratic leadership prevailed in the FTQ, which represented mostly private-sector workers. The CSN and the CEQ, on the other hand, recruited most of their members from the public sector. Frustrated by the course of the disputes in the public sector, many CSN and CEQ rank-and-file activists had become increasingly radical. By the early 1970s, both centrals had a socialist leadership.

The CSN and the CEQ were most comprehensive in their critique of the market economy. Yet they were hesitant to elaborate upon any alternative vision of society. This reluctance resulted not from any lack of zeal on the part of the leadership, but from the ideological heterogeneity of the rank-and-file membership. While many of the most active rank-and-filers were sympathetic to radical socio-economic change, the majority of them, including in particular the more passive members, opposed any such notion. CSN leaders, such as Pépin and Rodrigue, were aware of this gap between the leadership and a large part of the rank-and-file membership. In the 1970s, the CSN presidents hoped to close this gap by adjusting the outlook of the rank-and-filers to their own. Having witnessed the schism of 1972, they were very cautious, however, in their attempts to bring about this adjustment.

II.

From its foundation up to the 1950s, the CTCC adhered to a double nationalism which was both French-Canadian and pan-Canadian. The linking idea which enabled the central to combine, two seemingly contradictory national allegiances was that of "the pact between two races." Canada was perceived as a country made up of French Canadians and English Canadians, both of whom were separated by language and religion as well as by legal arrangements necessary for the preservation of their respective traditions. In order to preserve French Canada's heritage the CTCC advocated a high degree of provincial autonomy. Regarding Canada as a shelter for traditional French-Canadian culture, the CTCC continuously demanded full equality between French Canadians and English Canadians, bilingualism and biculturalism, and—since the 1940s—the repatriation of the constitution and the transformation of Canada into a republic.[37]

On the eve of the Quiet Revolution, however, the CTCC's constitutional outlook became more ambiguous. On the one hand, the central continued to defend provincial autonomy, since it exercised more influence on the provincial than on the federal government.[38] Yet on the other hand, the rise of intellectuals such as Jean Marchand, Gérard Pelletier, Marcel Pépin, and Pierre Vadeboncoeur made the CTCC increasingly critical of French-Canadian nationalism. For this group of union leaders and councillors, French-Canadian nationalism was responsible for the backwardness of Quebec's socio-economic institutions.[39] They led the CTCC to reject the idea of conserving all traits of traditional French-Canadian culture. Instead, the central came to advocate the modernization of the province of Quebec along the lines of other Western societies.

As has been seen, in 1960 the Lesage government set out to modernize Quebec institutions. Yet unlike the CSN, which merely wanted to reform the socio-economic system, the Liberal government also pursued a nationalist agenda. Lesage's "équipe de tonnerre" aimed at ending the economic inferiority of Quebec's francophone population. Its goal was economic and social equality between the province's francophone majority and anglophone minority. To do so, the Lesage team sought to transfer economic decision-making processes into francophone hands. The provincial government intervened in the economy in order to help expand the tiny francophone business community. It hoped that the existence of a strong francophone business community would ultimately make French-speaking Quebecers "maîtres chez eux." Lesage's neo-nationalist programme stimulated French-speaking Quebecers' national pride.

Unlike traditional French-Canadian nationalism, the neo-nationalism of the Quiet Revolution had nothing static and submissive about it. It challenged existing power structures in a province where social-class divisions coincided almost identically with divisions between ethnic groups.[40]

Quiet Revolution neo-nationalism also constituted a conscious break with French Canada's past. Francophones in Quebec no longer perceived their collectivity as "la nation canadienne francaise" but as "la nation québécoise." French-Canadian identity turned into Quebecois identity. At the same time, an increasing number of francophones questioned the status of Quebec within Confederation. Among the numerous separatist organizations created in the early 1960s the Rassemblement pour l'indépendance nationale (RIN) was by far the largest one. Like various other separatist parties and movements, the RIN perceived French-speaking Quebecers as a colonized people. As Marcel Chaput, co-founder and second president of the RIN wrote, French Canada "a été conquis par les armes, occupé, dominé, exploité, et ... encore aujourd'hui son destin repose, dans une très large mesure, entre les mains d'une autre nation qui lui est étrangère."[41] Chaput and the RIN wanted to end Confederation, because for them it meant both the political and economic domination of Quebec.[42]

Headed by Jean Marchand, CSN president from 1961 to 1965, the union central rejected the idea of separation. CSN leaders saw no need for such a change. More importantly, like their FTQ peers, they feared the possible economic repercussions of independence, including a decline of the living standards and increased unemployment.[43] In addition, Marchand, Pelletier, and many others were unwilling to distinguish between traditional nationalism and neo-nationalism. They regarded separatism as just another facet of reactionary French-Canadian nationalism.[44]

In 1964, the CSN leadership created a special committee to study of biculturalism, joint programs, self-determination, and separatism. In early 1965, the committee asked Pierre Elliot Trudeau to draft a memorandum on Quebec's constitutional status. Trudeau accepted and produced a document in which separatism was entirely discarded. According to Pierre Vadeboncoeur, Trudeau's text was nothing less than "un pamphlet virulent contre l'indépendance du Québec."[45] The memorandum was favourably received by the leaders of the CSN, the FTQ, and the Union des cultivateurs catholiques (UCC), who intended to present it to the Constitutional Committee of Quebec's National Assembly. Vadeboncoeur and André L'Heureux, who had become separatists in 1963 and 1962 respectively,[46] were shocked. They approached Pépin arguing that it would be premature to take a definitive stand on the issue, since public opinion was still evolving. Only after long and difficult discussions—involving Vadeboncoeur, L'Heureux, constitutional expert Jacques-Yvan Morin, and Marcel Pépin—was Pépin finally convinced that Trudeau's text should be revised.[47]

In September 1966, the CSN, the FTQ, and the UCC jointly submitted the memorandum to the Constitutional Committee of the Quebec National Assembly in 1966. The memorandum came out in favour of "[un] fédéralisme adapté à la réalité actuelle." The most important of its numerous suggestions to reform the federalist system were: a charter of rights and liberties to be included in the constitution; a supreme court to interpret the constitution; the equality of the two languages on the federal level; bilingualism in those provinces where there was a linguistic minority exceeding 15 percent of the population or half a million people. The memorandum also wanted the provinces to acquire full responsibility in the cultural, educational, and welfare sectors. In addition, it called for a mechanism to harmonize provincial welfare policies. The document rejected a greater centralization of powers in Ottawa as detrimental to the interests of Quebec. It also opposed the concept of associated states as well as the independence option. Any radical change of the constitution was to be avoided. In addition, the memorandum considered

Quebec sovereignty to be "une hypothèse et non une thèse; une hypothèse insuffisante pour permettre non seulement l'adhésion mais une discussion objective de quelque importance."[48]

Although the CSN membership had no say in composing the memorandum, the CSN 1966 confederal convention did not hesitate to endorse the document retrospectively. It was not long thereafter, though, that the constitutional vision of the CSN leadership was challenged from within the union central.

III.

In the 1966 provincial elections, the Lesage Liberals were defeated and Quebec separatists gained about nine percent of the public vote. In the provincial elections four years later, the separatists would win one quarter of the public vote. The significant increase of support for the sovereignty option was largely due to the general disappointment with the immediate results of the Lesage government's economic nationalism. As has been said, the neo-nationalism of the Quiet Revolution was dynamic and expansionist, establishing the economic reconquest of Quebec as its ultimate goal. Creating high expectations among French-speaking Quebecers, its immediate results were meagre. Throughout the 1960s, the expansion of the francophone business community made little headway. As anglophone control of the private sector remained largely unchanged, francophone mobility in the private sector continued to be limited. The francophone community did not significantly improve its socio-economic status relative to other ethnic groups.[49] The ensuing disenchantment with the continued socio-economic inferiority of francophones directly benefited the separatist movement. Towards the end of the 1960s, more and more francophone Quebecers became convinced that the well-being of the francophone collectivity could only be brought about with the help of an independent Quebec state.

The rise of separatism in post-Quiet Revolution Quebec also affected the CSN. During the period 1966 to 1972, sympathies for independence within the CSN were most pronounced among the professionals, teachers, provincial and municipal civil servants, and public-sector workers in general.[50] Regardless of which sector they belonged to, separatists within the union central were divided into two factions: first, the moderates who wanted to attain independence to end the minority situation of Quebec within the Confederation, and to allow francophones to be economically successful; second, the radicals who saw independence as a precondition for the creation of a socialist society in Quebec. It was the latter group of socialist separatists who became dominant in the CSN during the 1970s. Originally, this group was formed by union militants and councillors, who previously had been members of the PSQ that was dissolved in 1966. In 1963 the PSQ had been founded by disenchanted New Democratic Party members from Quebec. They opposed the centralism of the NDP which, according to them, disregarded the fact that Quebec was a nation of its own.[51] Former PSQ members, such as Michel Chartrand and André L'Heureux, no longer saw any viable prospects for co-operation between the left in Quebec and the left in Canada. This attitude was most clearly expressed in the following 1972 statement by the Chartrand-led CCSNM:

> Il n'y a plus à espérer, comme le démontre abondamment l'histoire, qu'un mouvement politique populaire né dans l'ouest du Canada puisse gagner efficacement les provinces de l'Est, et inversement.... Dans un pays comme le Canada, l'impérialisme et le capitalisme n'ont pas à diviser pour régner, vu que les divisions sont déjà profondément inscrites dans la géographie, les cultures, l'histoire, les traditions, les mentalités et les intérêts particuliers entre le Québec d'une part et les provinces anglophones d'autre part.[52]

Under these circumstances, the installation of a socialist government in Ottawa appeared to be only a remote possibility. The creation of a socialist Quebec therefore, necessitated the separation of Quebec from Canada. Chartrand, L'Heureux, and other militants on the left of the CSN, knew that independence would not automatically lead to socialism. They thought, though, that only independence could make socialism possible.

While forming only a tiny group at the end of the Quiet Revolution, by 1972 the number of separatists among the CSN membership had increased enormously. The growing popularity of separatism was greatly helped by four phenomena: the failure of all CSN efforts to expand into other provinces and into sectors under the jurisdiction of the Canadian labour code in the mid-1960s; the appeal and credibility of the independence option due to René Lévesque's personality and the progressive image of the Parti québécois (PQ); the language debate beginning in 1969; and the invocation of the War Measures Act in October 1970.

During the mid-1960s, all CSN efforts to expand into areas under the jurisdiction of the Canadian Labour Code failed. All international and interprovincial companies in areas such as communications, including radio, TV, telephone, and transportation, fell under the jurisdiction of this code. Negotiating units in these sectors were Canada-wide. In 1965–66, the CSN tried to win over railway workers in East Angus and Pointe St-Charles, as well as the francophone employees of Radio Canada. In all cases, the workers in question belonged to unions affiliated with the Canadian Labour Congress (CLC). Although enjoying the support of the workers concerned, the CSN was unable to form new unions. This was due to the veto of the Canadian Labour Relations Board, on which the CLC held three seats and the CSN only one. Having met with such disappointments associated with the federalist system of labour relations, many CSN activists and officers began to see federalism more critically.[53] Not long afterwards, the CSN initiative to expand beyond the province of Quebec came to nothing.[54]

With the founding of the Mouvement Souveraineté Association (MSA) in November 1967, public debate about Quebec's constitutional status intensified significantly. The new importance of the independance option was reflected in the CSN monthly *Le Travail*. Having ignored the issue in previous years, in early 1968 *Le Travail* started to discuss the national question.[55] The fact that this discussion could now take place in the CSN mouthpiece was partly due to René Lévesque's tremendous personal popularity among workers and trade unionists."[56] As a minister in the Lesage cabinet, he had won the sympathy of organized labour with social-democratic proposals such as complete unionization, free education, and economic planning.[57] In addition to Lévesque's personal prestige, the PQ's social-democratic program created sympathy for the new party among CSN members and officers. Moreover in its early years, the PQ appeared to be open to progressive proposals, and even courted workers to join its ranks. Not surprisingly the PQ came to be seen as the party of political and social change.[58] Lévesque's takeover of the leadership of the independence movement and the founding of the MSA-PQ made the sovereignty option more attractive and more credible. Unlike other separatist leaders, such as Marcel Chaput and Pierre Bourgault (Chaput's successors president of the RIN), Lévesque had experience in holding political power. The addition of new, distinguished members to the PQ also increased the party's credibility. In autumn 1969, Cadres, the journal of the professionals organized within the CSN, commented on Jacques Parizeau's arrival in the ranks of the PQ.

> Personne ne peut [...] contester la compétence économique de Parizeau [...] Avec l'entrée en scène de Parizeau, la notion d'un Québec séparé prend une dimension nouvelle. L'indépendance devient une option politique valable, qui se discute au mérite. Lévesque lui avait donné son caractère sérieux qu'elle n'avait jamais eu. Avec Parizeau, elle cesse d'être une aventure.[59]

The fierce debates on the language issue late in the decade were another reason for the rise of separatism within the CSN. By the end of the 1960s, Quebec nationalists demanded government action to make French the language of work in order to ensure greater social mobility for Quebec francophones. In addition, they wanted the government to reform the educational system so that immigrants would be forced to integrate into the French-speaking community. They hoped thereby to ward off the perceived threat of the assimilation of francophones. The CSN quickly became involved in the language debate. In January 1969, the Central came out in favour of French as the language of the workplace. At the same time the CSN adopted a declaration of principles regarding instruction and culture, which stipulated that the Quebec educational system should be founded on language.[60]

During the October Crisis, the CSN again joined the camp of Quebec nationalists. As previously mentioned, many of those arrested were labour union militants, the most prominent being Michel Chartrand. In a Common Front with René Lévesque and the PQ, the CSN denounced the invocation of the War Measures Act for its infringement on citizens' civil liberties. An improved relationship between the CSN and the PQ was not the only result of the October Crisis. Equally important was the fact that a significant number of Quebecers, within or outside the labour union movement, came to resent the federal intervention. This resentment in many cases led to a questioning of the federal system as such.[61]

Ever since the end of the Quiet Revolution, CSN militants had become involved in a highly animated and controversial debate on independence. In 1967 the Syndicat professionnel des enseignants criticized the CSN leadership for the 1966 memorandum, and took a clear stand in favour of independence.[62] The teachers' union was supported by the Syndicat des fonctionnaires municipaux de Montréal which demanded that the CSN hold an internal referendum on the independence question.[63] The CSN leadership, however, tried to avoid any formal discussion of the issue, and especially any internal referendum. CSN president Pépin was a diehard federalist who believed Quebec could become socialist without having to leave Confederation and who cherished the ideal of anticapitalist solidarity from coast to coast.[64] In addition, he and other CSN leaders did not want any internal divisions about this issue to become evident. In April 1968, the CSN executive committee proposed to conduct an opinion poll instead of an internal referendum. In January 1969, when called to decide on the issue, the confederal council could not come to an agreement and dropped the proposal despite dissent.[65] Yet, the separatists within the central continued to pressure the leadership to hold an internal referendum and to change the CSN position on the national question. Slowly, the power relations within the CSN changed in favour of the separatists. Even before the departure of the right in 1972, various CSN bodies, particularly in the public sector, had taken a pro-separatist stand.[66] With the departure of the largely federalist right, the CSN separatists finally found themselves in a position of strength among CSN leaders and militants alike. The union central, with the votes of the separatists, decided in October 1972 that a formal debate and referendum on the independence issue was to be launched among the membership in order to establish a new CSN position.[67]

The experiences of both the FTQ and the CEQ during the late 1960s and the early 1970s resembled that of the CSN. In both organizations, an increasing number of members came to support separation. As in the case of the CSN membership, this increase was largely caused by the new credibility that separatism enjoyed after the arrival of René Lévesque and the creation of the PQ, by the debates of the language issue, and by the ramifications of the October Crisis. The official discourse of the FTQ and the CEQ reflected the new popularity of the idea of independence. The 1969 FTQ convention discontinued the practice of denouncing separation which dated back to 1963. The 1972 CEQ convention even took a stand in favour of independence. The convention resolved, however, that this endorsement was not to be regarded as the CEQ's official position and that an internal referendum ought to take place in order to establish such a stance.[68] As will be seen, several years were to pass before either CEQ or CSN followed through on their 1972 decisions.

IV.

Until 1976 (for the remainder of Marcel Pépin's presidency), no internal debate of the national question took place. The leadership shelved the national question since it wanted to consolidate the membership, and avoid the risk of internal division over the independence issue. In addition, continued financial problems and the debates on fee increases absorbed all energies. Despite the absence of dramatic events, the number of adherents to the idea of sovereignty continued to increase. Separatism now gained popularity among members of private-sector unions. At the same time, on the far left, a group of determined federalists emerged. The Marxist-Leninist militants opposed separation which they thought would alienate Quebec workers from the Canadian working class, and thereby benefit their common class enemy, the Canadian bourgeoisie.[69]

In July 1976 Norbert Rodrigue succeeded Pépin as CSN president. For the first time in CSN history, its six-member executive committee had strong separatist leanings. The new CSN president was known to favour the idea of independence Furthermore, vice-presidents André L'Heureux and Francine Lalonde had been very vocal supporters of separation since the early 1960s. (The latter even became a minister in René Lévesque's second cabinet.) Only five months after the CSN leadership change, the PQ came to power on the promise of holding a referendum within four years. Rodrigue concluded that the union central could no longer avoid an internal debate and referendum concerning the CSN stand on the Quebec national question.[70] In September 1977, an orientation committee headed by Rodrigue, and including 20 of the central's most influential leaders, was formed. Its function was to conduct and analyze the internal debate on the national question. Most of the committee members were sympathetic to independence.[71] Yet only a minority of committee members, such as Francine Lalonde, André L'Heureux, Michel Bourdon, and Robert Tremblay, wanted to make the propagation of independence the committee's priority. Led by Norbert Rodrigue, the majority of committee members had two other goals in mind: to avoid internal divisions and renewed disaffiliations over the independence issue, and to instill carefully a socialist spirit into the movement.

The committee's preliminary report to the 1978 confederal convention bore witness to this dual aim. The document stated that the CSN "comprend dans ses rangs des travailleurs de différents niveaux de conscience, de différentes sensibilités et allégeances idéologiques et politiques." Inspired by Rodrigue's goal of consolidating the membership, the report proclaimed the necessity of establishing a lowest common denominator position that could be shared by the entire membership. Since the CSN enjoyed no consensus on the issue of separation, the committee considered it premature "de chercher à répondre par un oui ou un non à l'indépendance du Québec."[72] The report also declared openly the committee's second priority:

> Le débat sur la question nationale ... doit être pour nous l'occasion de poursuivre ... le débat plus global que nous menons sur notre projet de société.... Cette démarche de réflexion sur la question nationale pourra ... exercer une capacité d'attraction afin que plus de travailleurs se retrouvent dans les positions de la CSN.[73]

The document stated that Quebec francophones had far less access to better-paid jobs than anglophones. Unlike the neo-nationalists and the advocates of independence, the CSN orientation committee did not propose to remedy this situation by the expanding francophone businesses under the guidance of the Quebec state. Instead, the CSN leaders maintained that there was an economic system in existence which provided a structural base on which exploitation might take the form of national oppression. The committee did not yearn for change merely of the character and composition of the business community. Its aim was to end an economic system based on the antagonism of employer and employees. Hence, the committee report urged Quebec workers to combine the struggle against national oppression with the struggle against capitalism.[74]

In winter 1978–79, the CSN finally embarked upon its vast internal debate and referendum on the national question. The tone of the debate and the outcome of the referendum were significantly influenced by the deterioration in CSN–PQ relations which the 1970s had witnessed. These relations had become visibly strained after the PQ had attained power in 1976. The earliest tensions, however, had appeared in the early 1970s. Unlike the CSN, the PQ never had envisaged any fundamental change in the socio-economic system. Thus the PQ leadership had little sympathy for the ideological orientation the CSN had adopted in 1972. René Lévesque had never hidden his disregard for radicals on the left, whom he denounced as "les missionnaires de la table rase qui grenouillent dans les chapelles marginales de la révolution miracle et de l'ultra-gauchisme doctrinaire des anarcho-patriotes."[75] At a meeting with CSN militants in 1973, Jacques Parizeau criticized the CSN for having chosen "une option politique qui n'est pas la nôtre." He then went on to reject "une transformation totale de la société et des choses comme la nationalisation des terres qui a un sens à Cuba mais pas ici et dont personne ne voudrait ici."[76] Since 1971–72, the PQ leaders took care to distance their party from the CSN so that the public would not associate the PQ with the labour central's radicalism.[77]

Despite the growing gap between the CSN and the PQ, the PQ continued to claim numerous supporters among the CSN membership. Many union members appreciated the PQ's commitments to bring about sovereignty and to implement various social-democratic reforms.[78] Rank-and-file support for the PQ was so noticeable that the CSN executive committee became concerned about it. On the eve of the 1976 provincial election, the CSN executive declared:

> Il importe de mettre nos membres en garde contre l'illusion que le PQ pourrait changer fondamentalement la condition des travailleurs.... S'il est important de donner une leçon au Parti libéral, il faut être bien conscient qu'au lendemain de l'élection, même si le PQ prenait le pouvoir, nous serions placés devant une autre gouvernment qui, de gré ou de force, serait asservi à la classe dominante.[79]

Once in power, Lévesque's PQ government chose to ignore many aspects of its social-democratic platform in an attempt to gain support from the business community and more conservative voters.[80] The Lévesque administration, however, did implement several significant social reforms. It raised the minimum wage to the highest level in North America and, until 1979, indexed this to the cost of living. Moreover, it introduced free dental care for children under age 16 years, and set up a public system of automobile insurance against personal injury.[81] Other noteworthy social legislation included Bill 45 which revised the Quebec labour code. The bill permitted a unionization vote if more than 35 percent of the employees had signed union cards, and obliged an employer to rehire a striker after the end of a strike. In principle, the bill prohibited the employment of scabs, but permitted an employer to hire workers during a strike in order to safeguard essential services and protect his or her property.[82] Although the bill was "more progressive than anything existing in any other North-American jurisdiction,"[83] the CSN executive severely criticized the bill for enabling the employer to hire scabs under the aforementioned conditions. To the CSN leadership, Bill 45 proved that the PQ government was by no means favourably disposed towards the workers.[84]

Bill 45 was not the only piece of PQ governmental policy that met with CSN criticism. Cuts in social services and education budgets cost the PQ government much sympathy within the CSN.[85] At the central's confederal convention in June of 1978 its leadership launched a general attack on the Lévesque government. It criticized the government for having restricted the budget for social affairs; for having failed to introduce legislation regarding maternal leave, abortion, and the application of the principle equal pay for equal work; for having failed to introduce legislation to promote health and security in the workplace; for not having fought against inflation, unemployment, the closing of enterprises, and poverty in general; and for having displayed anti-labour attitudes in the field of industrial relations.[86] The harsh criticisms were only partly inspired by the PQ government's failure to live up to the expectations of CSN socialists. The CSN leadership also wanted to mobilize the rank-and-file membership for the public-sector negotiations which were to be held in 1979.

The 1978 convention took an emotional turn after violence erupted between convention delegates and the provincial police. The clash occurred when about 200 delegates demonstrated at Sainte-Thérèse to express their solidarity with the strikers at the Commonwealth Plywood factory. Several CSN militants were injured on the occasion the most well-known of them being vice-president L'Heureux. Some militants were arrested; others fled. Those who evaded arrest returned to the convention floor. Many wore bandages, and all had horrifying stories to tell. Feelings ran high, and CSN delegates were quick to denounce the PQ government which they held responsible for the actions of the police. Several CSN delegates ostentatiously destroyed their PQ membership cards on the floor of the convention room, receiving applause from those who had always mistrusted the PQ government.[87] After the incident at Sainte-Thérèse, PQ supporters within the CSN became even more marginalized.[88]

The CSN referendum held in the winter 1978–79 had several noteworthy results. About 4,380 members—2.8 percent of all 155,704 CSN members—participated in the internal debate and referendum.[89] Only half the participants wanted the CSN to take a stand on the independence issue.[90] There were four reasons why so many opposed such a stand. First, some did not want the CSN involved in political activities at all. These members advocated a purely economic unionism limiting CSN activities to collective bargaining.[91] Second, many were opposed to separation. Fearing the potential economic repercussions of separation most of these federalists were particularly concerned with the prospect of job losses and a decline in the standard of living.[92] Less numerous, but very vocal, were those federalists who defended the thesis that separation would divide workers in Quebec and Canada to the class enemy's benefit. Third, a large group did not want the CSN to endorse independence because they considered this to constitute an automatic endorsement of the PQ. They either regarded the PQ as a party defending the interests of the business community or did not want to diminish the bargaining power of public and para-public sector unions.[93] Fourth, a good number of militants were afraid of internal divisions and renewed disaffiliations which might be the result of a CSN stand in favour of independence.[94]

Faced with the ambiguity of its membership and unwilling to take a stand that could be interpreted as an endorsement of the PQ, the majority of the CSN leadership decided to drop the issue of an official stand on the independence question. Led by André L'Heureux and Michel Bourdon, a minority of CSN leaders maintained that the CSN should endorse independence since it was a precondition for ending the national oppression of French-speaking Quebecers and for creating a socialist society. Yet, their recommendations were defeated by the orientation committee, the confederal council, and the special confederal convention on the national question of June 1979.[95] Instead, the special convention resolved in favour of "une démarche d'appropriation par le peuple québécois des pouvoirs et des institutions politiques, économiques et culturels."[96] Failing to specify the number and exact nature of the powers and institutions mentioned, the resolution perfectly reflected the varying opinions of the CSN membership.

The orientation committee report presented at the 1979 convention amounted to a full-fledged attack on the PQ government. The document argued that Quebec needed to curb foreign control of the Quebec economy and develop its weak secondary sector on the basis of advanced technologies.[97] Having established these parameters, the CSN leaders severely criticized the PQ government for its incoherent development strategy and its unwillingness to challenge the hold of American capital on the Quebec economy.[98] Despite its wordy condemnation of the separatist leaders, the orientation committee report did display an inherent separatist logic. Under the federalist system only the federal government possessed the powers to restructure the Quebec economy. As the CSN leaders well knew, the federal government always had been tied intimately to the Ontario business community, and therefore could not be depended upon where Quebec economic development was at issue.[99] The provincial government, however, would be overburdened with such a task since its powers were too limited. Hence, to develop Quebec's secondary sector and to attack the foreign domination of the Quebec economy would necessitate a massive transfer of powers from Ottawa to Quebec. If anything, the CSN project was even more comprehensive than René Lévesque's sovereignty-association.

Since the 1979 special convention on the national question had neither rejected nor endorsed independence, the issue remained far from settled. With the referendum of 20 May 1980 approaching, internal debate intensified. On 11 April 1980, the confederal convention held a special meeting to discuss the CSN's stand on the referendum. While many militants did not want the organization to adopt an official position, both the executive and the orientation committee were determined to endorse a "yes" in the referendum. As Norbert Rodrigue pointed out, during the previous years the CSN had managed to establish a critical distance from the PQ and its vision of society. Consequently, nobody could mistake a CSN stand in favour of the "yes" side as an unqualified endorsement of the PQ. Rodrigue also pointed out that Quebec needed to appropriate political institutions and powers since this would create better conditions in the workers' struggle for a socialist society.[100] Following Rodrigue's recommendations, the confederal council with an overwhelming majority, came out in favour of a "yes" in the referendum.[101]

Like the CSN, the FTQ did not formally endorse independence but took a stand assenting to the negotiation of sovereignty-association. Unlike the CSN, FTQ support for a "yes" in the referendum failed to ignite protracted discussion. Since the early 1970s, relations between the FTQ and the PQ had been cordial. Their respective visions of society were not as far apart as those of the CSN and the PQ. In the provincial election of 1976, the FTQ had endorsed the PQ. After the PQ had come to power, relations between the FTQ and the PQ government were harmonious. The FTQ leadership was pleased with the PQ governmental record (including Bill 45). Meanwhile, the CEQ was unable to take a stand either on Quebec's constitutional status or on the referendum question. The CEQ's ability to make political commitments had become a casualty in the struggle that deadlocked CEQ moderates and radicals. After the PQ had taken power, the moderates were no longer willing to denounce the Quebec government as an agent of capitalist interests. When the central's radicals proposed a resolution that supported independence and rejected the PQ's vision of society, the moderates refused to fall in line. The resolution fell through. Furthermore, since the moderates expected the radicals to use the referendum campaign as an occasion to launch an all-out attack on the PQ government, they opted against CEQ participation in the referendum campaign.[102]

As this brief look at the FTQ and the CEQ shows, on the eve of the referendum, none of

Quebec's three large labour union centrals took a stand in favour of independence. In the CSN and the FTQ, too many rank-and-file members remained partisans of federalism. Furthermore, many CSN members, and most of the central's leaders, wanted to avoid a gesture that could be interpreted as support for the PQ government. This consideration also played a role in the debates within the CEQ. Since its membership consisted almost entirely of teachers who enjoy a high degree of job security, the CEQ was the only union central that potentially could have mustered overwhelming support for independence. Yet the CEQ radicals were determined to link a resolution in favour of independence to a condemnation of the PQ, while the moderates were equally determined to prevent any such condemnation. The same mechanism also made it impossible for the CEQ to take a stand on the referendum question. For the FTQ and the CSN it was less problematical to take such a stand. Dominated by social democrats, the FTQ simply followed up its earlier policies of support for the PQ government. The CSN, on the other hand, was dominated by radicals who faced no significant opposition from moderate social democrats. Thus they could combine a ringing denunciation of the PQ with a recommendation to vote "yes" in the referendum.

V.

Quebec sovereigntism and the radicalism of the CSN shared the same roots. Both phenomena were products of the enthusiasm that accompanied the Quiet Revolution and the disenchantment that followed it. Although both concepts challenged the status quo, their ultimate goals were different. CSN radicalism aimed at fundamental change in the socio-economic system and the replacement of the market economy by a socialist economy. Sovereigntism, by contrast, sought fundamental change in Quebec's constitutional status and the transformation of the province into a sovereign nation-state. As abstractions, sovereigntism and socialism are not inherently incompatible. It fell to those propagating the two concepts to decide on the degree of compatibility they would have in real life. In the event, the Lévesque-led sovereigntist movement opted for a market economy, while the majority of CSN radicals favoured independence. The CSN radicals did so for two reasons: first, they felt that co-operation between the left in English Canada and the left in Quebec was impossible; second, they perceived Quebec society at that time as more progressive. PQ sovereigntists and CSN socialists shared the idea of Quebec independence. They disagreed in their visions of society: one group advocated the market economy, the other one socialism. Thus their relationship was bound to be discordant.

Ideological dispositions were not the only determinants of the relationship between sovereigntism and socialism in Quebec during the 1970s. To a large extent, this relationship was determined by the relative popularity both options enjoyed. In the wake of the Quiet Revolution, sovereigntism flourished much more rapidly than did socialism. Sovereigntist parties had already been in existence when the PQ was founded in 1968. The CSN embraced socialism only five years later. Both sovereigntism and socialism had a high profile in Quebec political culture during the 1970s. Neither of them, though, was a complete success by the end of the decade. Although it may have been less attractive than the status quo in 1980, the sovereigntist option certainly was more popular than the socialist one. The defense of French Canada and Quebec's autonomy were issues deeply rooted in Quebec. The sovereigntist movement could benefit from those traditions, while the socialist movement did not have any such base in the Quebecers' collective mentality.

The popularity of sovereigntism was felt even within the ranks of the CSN. Among many rank-and-file members, René Lévesque was more popular than the CSN leaders, and the PQ enjoyed a degree of credibility that surpassed that of the CSN. Many CSN members subscribed to the PQ's vision of society rather than that of the CSN socialists. Consequently, the socialist option lost potential sympathizers and activists. Many of those who had the idealism to invest their time and energy to challenge existing socio-political structures were drawn to the sovereigntist movement rather than the socialist one. By comparison, the group of socialists was small. Since the sovereigntist movement recruited its followers from the pool of potential socialist activists, the CSN socialists saw Lévesque's PQ as a dangerous competitor. The only way to stand up to this competitor was to denounce it continuously and vociferously.

The coexistence of sovereigntism and socialism was tainted by the continuous attacks from the socialists. This type of coexistence could have improved had the PQ made an effort to reach conciliation. Representing only a small constituency, the CSN socialists were only minor players in Quebec politics. The fact that the CSN carried little political weight did not endear its CSN socialism to the PQ. Instead of conciliation, the PQ put demarcation on the agenda. With pride, René Lévesque stated:

> Our hands are not in any way tied as far as the unions are concerned.... We owe not a cent, not a dollar, to the employers, or to the unions.... We have no organic ties, which means that we can be the government of all the people without being a puppet to any one sector.[103]

The relationship between the PQ and the CSN was characterized by ideological differences, denunciations, and neglect. It is hardly surprising that sovereigntists and socialists rarely joined forces.

Despite ideological differences and mutual disregard, a sovereigntist triumph was in the best interest of the CSN socialists. Once they had come to the conclusion that co-operation with the left in English Canada either was impossible or undesirable, the CSN socialists automatically narrowed their framework to Quebec. In order to implement radical socio-economic change within that framework, they needed to patriate all major decision-making processes to Quebec. This reasoning would have been invalid only if Quebec society had been considerably more conservative than English Canadian society. This clearly was not the case. Furthermore, as long as the majority of progressives in the province were preoccupied with the cause of sovereignty, socialism was condemned to take a back seat. Only after independence would those idealistic energies be available to take on other struggles. Of course, sovereigntist triumph would not have guaranteed the subsequent triumph of socialism, but only independence could have made a socialist society possible. The CSN socialists could only arrive in the cockboat in the wake of the sovereigntist man-of-war.

The thought of endorsing an idea identified with the much-criticized Lévesque government certainly made many CSN socialists ill at ease. This uneasiness, though, did not prevent the socialist CSN leaders grouped around Norbert Rodrigue from realizing that the success of socialism depended on the success of sovereigntism. Yet the CSN socialists could not impose their will on the entire CSN membership. The CSN was not a political party; its members shared economic concerns, not political ideologies. As the internal debate of 1978–79 revealed, a large group—possibly one half—of the rank-and-file membership was opposed to a formal endorsement of independence because they were federalists, or because they did not think it proper for the CSN to concern itself with political issues. The long list of disaffiliations during the 1970s had made the CSN leadership very sensitive to rank-and-file opinions. Thus, more than anything else, it was opposition emanating from the rank-and-file membership that prevented an official CSN endorsement of independence in 1979–80.

I would like to acknowledge with thanks the financial assistance of the Faculty of Graduate Studies and Research, McGill University. I would also like to thank Andrée Lévesque and Auroshakti Jeyachandran who read earlier versions of this article. Finally I would like to express my gratitude to Normand Ouellet, Mario Robert, and Lucie Courtemanche of the CSN documentation service.

Endnotes

1. CSN, Procès-verbal, congrès confédéral 1979, 131–2; Louis-Gilles Francoeur. "Indépendance: La CSN ne s'avance pas." *Le Devoir*, 4 juin 1979, 3; Laval LeBorgne, "Une résolution pronant l'indépendance est défaite: La CSN refuse tout appui au PQ," *La Presse*, 4 juin 1979, Al2.
2. Louis-Marie Tremblay, *Le syndicalisme Québécois: Idéologies de la CSN et de la FTQ, 1940–1970* (Montreal 1972), 30; Bernard Solasse, "Les idéologies de la FTQ et de la CSN, 1960–1978." *Idéologies au Canada français*, ed. par F. Dumont et al (Quebec 1981), tome 1, 223; Leo Roback et Louis-Marie Tremblay, "Le nationalisme au sein des syndicats Québécois," *Canadian Review of Studies in Nationalism*, 5 (1978), 239. Older accounts often associate the CTCC with timid unionism avoiding confrontation. See for instance Harold A. Logan, *Trade Unions in Canada: Their Development and Functioning* (Toronto 1948), 579–603; Charles Lipton, *The Trade Union Movement of Canada, 1827–1959*, 4th ed. (Toronto 1978), 224–5. Jacques Rouillard, however, has shown that the practice of the CTCC was more militant than its ideology and that the relatively low strike-rate of the CTCC in the 1920s was not so much the result of its ideology as of its incohesiveness and the large proportion of non-specialized workers affiliated with the CTCC. See Jacques Rouillard, *Histoire de la CSN 1921–1981* (Montreal 1981), 83–6, 94–5.
3. Roback et Tremblay, "Le nationalisme au sein des syndicats Québécois," 239–42, 245. The ideological evolution of the CTCC found its symbolic expression in a change of name: in 1960 the CTCC became the Confédération des syndicats nationaux (CSN).
4. Carla Lipsig-Mummé, "The Web of Dependence: Quebec Labour Unions in Politics Before 1976," in Alain Gagnon, ed., *Quebec: State and Society* (Toronto 1984), 297, 300; Henry Milner, *Politics in the New Quebec* (Toronto 1978), 178; Raymond Hudon, *Syndicalisme d'opposition en société liberale: la culture politique de la CSN* (Quebec 1974), 81.
5. Jacques Rouillard, *Histoire du syndicalisme au Québec: des origines à nos jours* (Montreal 1989), 301.
6. Ibid., 409–10.
7. Gerald Bernier et Robert Boily, *Le Québec en chiffres de 1850 à nos jours* (Montreal 1986), 238.
8. Michael Smith, "The Transformation of Labour Relations in Quebec: An Analysis," in Katherina Lundy and Barbara Warme, eds., *Work in the Canadian Context: Continuity despite Change* (Toronto 1981), 369.
9. This became apparent in the hospital strike of 1966, the teachers' strike and the strike at Hydro-Quebec in 1967, and the conflict at the Régie des alcools in 1968–1969. See also Claude Lemelin, "Les deux prochaines années seront loin d'être facile pour la CSN," *Le Devoir*, 17 octobre 1968, 18; Rouillard, *Histoire du syndicalisme Québécois*, 408.
10. Solasse, "Les idéologies de la FTQ et de la CSN," 227.
11. For example, see Marcel Pépin, "Une société bâtie pour l'homme," CSN, Procès-verbal, congrès confédéral 1966, 15, 20–1.
12. For example, see also Marcel Pépin, "Le deuxième front," CSN, Procès-verbal, congrès confédéral 1968, 12–42.
13. Rouillard, *Histoire du syndicalisme au Québec*, 410–1.
14. Jean-Frangois Cardin, *La crise d'octobre 1970 et le mouvement syndical* (Montreal 1988), 261.
15. On the strike at *La Presse* see Marc Raboy, *Movements and Messages: Media and Radical Politics in Quebec* (Toronto 1984), 81–4. On the public sector negotiations and strike in 1972, see Diane Ethier, Jean-Marc Piotte et Jean Reynolds, *Les travailleurs contre l'Etat bourgeois, avril et mai 1972* (Montreal 1975).
16. Claude Lemelin, "Les deux prochaines années seront loin d'être façiles pour les dirigeants de la CSN," *Le Devoir*," 17 octobre 1968, 18; Michel Sabourin, "Congrès de la Fédération des ingénieurs et cadres: 'Nous sommes bien payés, petits-bourgeois, mais des travailleurs quand même'—Jean-Guy Rodrigue," *Québec-Presse*, 3 juin 1973, 8.
17. Bernard Chaput, "Faudra-t-il s'en mêler un jour?" *Nouveau Pouvoir*, 1 mai 1970, 2.
18. CSN, Procès-verbal, congrès confédéral 1968, 272–3; CSN, Procès-verbal, congrès confédéral 1972, 93.

19. "Active members" are those who participate in the activities of their union body on a regular basis. In the case of the CSN, this group was only a minority. On the problem of rank-and-file passivity in the CSN, see Jean-Luc Duguay, "La CSN instituerait une enquête sur la désaffection des conseils centraux," *Le Devoir*, 9 décembre 1970; CSN, Procès-verbal, conseil confédéral, 17–20 novembre 1976, 27; André Lauzon, Serge Deniers, Pierre Martin, "Nos pratiques syndicales," *Unité ouvrière*, avril 1979, 9–12; Hudon, *Syndicalisme d'opposition en société libérale*, 354–7.
20. Pierre Vadeboncoeur, "Marcel Pépin: Un nouveau départ," *Nouvelles CSN* (30 mars 1990), 11–2; Evelyn Dumas-Gagnon, "Que se passe-t-il à la CSN? 2: Au delà d'un conflict de personnalité," *Le Devoir*, 28 décembre 1967, 1, 24.
21. Evelyn Dumas-Gagnon, "Le départ de Sauvé provoque un débat d'une rare violence," *Le Devoir*, 2 décembre 1967, 5; "'Une clique d'intellectuels anarchiques,'" *Québec-Presse*, 4 juin 1972, 9.
22. "Le conseil central de Montréal (CSN) propose une déclaration de principe," *Québec-Presse*, 1 février 1970, 9a.
23. For example, see Jacques Lafrenière, "Chartrand: une 'philosophic politique': La CSN veut canaliser la contestation de ses membres," *La Presse*, 25 janvier 1969, 10; "L'affrontement Pépin-Chartrand a eu lieu dans un climat de liberté d'expression," *Québec-Presse*, 18 janvier 1970, 5; Jean-Luc Duguay, "Marcel Pépin a l'ouverture du congrès: La CSN éclatera si elle se lance dans Faction politique partisane," *Le Devoir*, 7 décembre 1970, 1.
24. Jacques Kaeble, '"Ne comptons que sur nos propres moyens': Marcel Pépin: 'L'état d'insecurité des travailleurs est très grand,'" *Québec-Presse*, 24 octobre 1971, 15; "Yvon Valcin critique la direction de la CSN," *Le Devoir*, 4 décembre 1971, 2; "L'exécutif du Conseil central de Québec est contre le manifeste de la CSN," *Québec-Presse*, 16 janvier 1972, 18; CSN, Procès-verbal, conseil confédéral, 23–25 février 1972, 12–5.
25. Gabriel Gaudette, "La culture politique de la CSD," *Recherches sociographiques*, 17, 1 (1976), 35–72. See also Pierre Richard, "La CSN perdra 27,000 membres: les fonctionnaires: La désaffiliation acquise de justesse," *Le Devoir*, 26 septembre 1972, 1, 6.
26. The different visions of socialism are discussed in Comité des Douze, CSN, Procès-verbal, congrès confédéral 1972, 81–7. See also the internal working paper "Ne comptons que sur nos propres moyens" (Montreal 1971) and Marcel Pépin's reaction to the working paper in Jacques Kaeble, '"Ne comptons que sur nos propres moyens': Marcel Pépin: "L'état d'insecurité' des travailleurs est très grand,'" *Québec-Presse*, 24 octobre 1971, 15.
27. CSN, Procès-verbal, congrès confédéral 1972, 101,176.
28. Ibid., 176.
29. CSN, Procès-verbal, congrès confédéral 1974, 101–3.
30. Louis Favreau et Pierre L'Heureux avec la collaboration de Paul Michel, *Le projet de société de la CSN de 1966 à aujourd'hui: Crise et avenir du syndicalisme au Québec* (Montréal 1984), 112–3; Rouillard, *Histoire du syndicalisme québécois*, 331, 415.
31. Interview with union councillor Peter Bakvis, Montreal, 29 May 1990; Interview with ex-CSN vice-président Francine Lalonde, Montreal, 19 June 1990; Interview with union councillor Marc Lesage, Montreal, 5 July 1990; Jacques Benoît, *L'extrême gauche* (Montréal 1977); Irène Ellenberger, "L'action politique syndicale dans les années 1970: Témoinage de Irène Ellenberger, ex-présidente du Conseil central de Montréal (CSN)," RCHTQ, *Bulletin*, 40 (Hiver 1988), 23–43.
32. Pierre Dupont et Gisèle Tremblay, *Les syndicats en crise* (Montréal 1976), 101–2.
33. In many unions the CSN's socialist discourse met with disinterest or opposition. See for instance: [Paul Cliché, Ginette Galarneau, Fiore Fionda,] "Rapport préliminaire concernant la campagne de consultation sur la question nationale en vue de congrès des 1er, 2 et 3 juin 1979." 17 mai 1979, 4. Archives de la CSN, Dossier "Question nationale 1976–1980," 370 (2-2-2-3); "Les travailleurs face à la question nationale: Quelles questions devons nous nous poser?," *Le Travail*, avril–mai 1979, 9.
34. This rupture with 10 years of CSN radicalism has not yet been the topic of systematic analysis. The best account to date has been provided by a group of CSN socialists: Favreau et l'Heureux, *Le projet de société de la CSN*, 167–81.
35. Rouillard, *Histoire du syndicalisme au Québec*, 362–70.

36. Jean Gérin-Lajoie in an interview with Gisèle Tremblay, Dupont, et Tremblay, *Les syndicats en crise*, 120. See also Rouillard, *Histoire du syndicalisme au Québec*, 318–22; Solasse, "Les idéologies de la FTQ et de la CSN," 228–48.
37. Louis-Marie Tremblay, *Le syndicalisme québécois: Les idéologies de la CSN et de la FTQ, 1940–1970*, 30–2, 41.
38. Ibid.
39. "La CSN et le séparatisme," *Le Travail*, décembre 1961, 5.
40. Kenneth McRoberts, *Quebec: Social Change and Political Crisis*, 3rd ed. (Toronto 1988), 132; William Coleman, *The Independence Movement in Quebec, 1945–1980* (Toronto 1984), 92, 99; P.-A. Linteau et al, *Histoire du Québec contemporain: tome 2: Le Québec depuis 1930* (Montréal 1986), 394; Rouillard, *Histoire du syndicalisme au Québec*, 294; Alain Gagnon and Mary B. Montcalm, *Quebec beyond the Quiet Revolution* (Scarborough, Ontario 1990), 9, 18, 25, 45.
41. Marcel Chaput, *Pourquoi je suis séparatiste* (Montréal 1969), 19.
42. Ibid, 27, 33.
43. "La CSN et le séparatisme," *Le Travail*, décembre 1961, 5; Gabriel Gagnon, "Pour un socialisme décolonisateur," *Parti pris*, septembre/octobre 1966,49. For the FTQ see, Rouillard, *Histoire du syndicalisme au Québec*, 323; François Cyr et Rémi Roy, *Eléments d'histoire de la FTQ: La FTQ et la question nationale* (Montréal 1981), 67–9.
44. In June 1964, the CSN monthly *Le Travail* published a manifesto by Pierre Elliott Trudeau, Marc Lalonde, and others which clearly stated: "Nous croyons au fédéralisme comme régime politique au Canada ... le séparatisme québécois nous apparaît non seulement comme une perte de temps, mais comme un recul." "Pour une politique fonctionnelle," *Le Travail*, juin 1964, Appendix, 5–6.
45. Pierre Vadeboncoeur, "Geoffrey: Une conscience," *Nouvelles CSN*, 2 mars 1990,11.
46. Ibid.; André L'Heureux, *Sécrétariat d'action politique*, Montreal, janvier 1976, 45. Archives de la CSN, Dossier "Question nationale" 430 (1-9-1-3).
47. "Une grosse vulgarité," *Parti Pris*, février 1965, 18; Vadeboncoeur, "Geoffrey: Une conscience," 9–11.
48. "Mémoire sur les problèmes constitutionels présenté conjointement par la CSN, le FTQ et l'UCC," CSN, Procès-verbal, congrès confédéral 1966, 459–64.
49. This situation was highlighted by the *Report of Royal Commission on Bilingualism and Biculturalism*, published in 1969, which stated francophone Quebecers ranked 12th among 14 ethnic groups with respect to average income. *Report of the Royal Commission on Bilingualism and Biculturalism*, Volume 3a (Ottawa 1969), 23.
50. Ralph Guntzel, "La FPPSCQ, la CSN et la question nationale depuis 1964," *Le Travail, Profession et Société*, 1:1 (printemps 1990), 4; "La CSN refuse d'enquêter sur l'opinion constitutionelle de ses 225,000 membres," *La Presse*, 27 janvier 1969, 10; "Les dirigeants montréalais de la CSN appuient le PQ," *Québec-Presse*, 22 mars 1970, 3; FNEQ, Procès-verbal, congrès fédéral, 27–29 novembre 1970, 39–40.
51. André L'Heureux, Secrétariat d'action politique, Montréal, janvier 1976, 45. Archives de la CSN, Dossier "Question nationale" 430 (1-9-1-3).
52. "Construire par la base une démocratie socialiste au Québec," *Le Travail*, mai 1972, 3; CCSNM, "Résolution pour l'indépendance du Québec, 14e congrès du CCSNM, avril 1972"; Louis LeBorgne, *La CSN et la question nationale depuis 1960* (Montréal 1975), 196–8.
53. Claude Larivière, "Les libertés syndicales et le pancanadianisme," *L'Action nationale*, LV, 9–10 (1966), 1125–8.
54. CSN, Procès-verbal, congrès confédéral 1966, 368–9; CSN, Procès-verbal, congrès confédéral 1968, 64–5.
55. See, "L'avenir du Québec, c'est surtout l'affaire des salariés," *Le Travail*, janvier 1968, 18–9; "Un statut particulier dans un fédéralisme nouveau," *Le Travail*, mai 1968, 18–9.
56. Leo Roback, "Quebec Workers in the Twentieth Century," in W.J.C. Cherwinski and Gregory S. Kealey, eds., *Lectures in Canadian Labour and Working Class History* (St. John's 1985), 179–80.
57. Vera Murray, *Le Parti québécois: de la fondation à la prise du pouvoir* (Montréal 1976), 217.
58. Favreau et L'Heureux, *Le Projet de société de la CSN*, 102.

59. Mario Cardinal, "Enfin un débat des adultes," *Cadres*, septembre/octobre 1969, 12.
60. CSN, Procès-verbal, congrès confédéral 1968, 517; "La CSN adopte un programme d'action axée sur la nécessité d'un 2e front," *Le Devoir*, 27 janvier 1969, 3.
61. Jean-François Cardin, *La Crise d'octobre 1970 et le mouvement syndical* (Montréal 1988).
62. CSN, Procès-verbal, congrès confédéral 1968, 535.
63. Ibid, 521.
64. Jacques Keable, "'Ne comptons que sur nos propres moyens': Marcel Pépin: 'L'état d'insécurité des travailleurs est très grand'," *Québec-Presse*, 24 octobre 1971, 15; Marcel Pépin, "Un camp de la liberté." CSN, Procès-verbal, congrès confédéral 1970, 26.
65. CSN, Procès-verbal, conseil confédéral, 16 et 17 avril 1968, 4–5; CSN, Procès-verbal, congrès confédéral 1968, 335, 513, 515, 521.
66. See for instance, FPSCQ, Procès-verbal, conseil fédéral, 1971, 13; FNEQ, Procès-verbal, conseil fédéral, 27–29 novembre 1970, 39–40; CSN, Procès-verbal, conseil confédéral, 1968, 535; "Construire par la base une démocratic socialiste au Québec," *Le Travail*, mai 1972, 3.
67. CSN, Procès-verbal, congrès confédéral, 1972, 173–7; Pierre Richard, "Optant pour le socialisme: La CSN organisera un référendum sur l'indépendance," *Le Devoir*, 5 octobre 1972, 1.
68. On the FTQ, Rouillard, *Histoire du syndicalisme au Québec*, 324–5; Cyr et Roy, *Elements d'histoire de la FTQ*, 95–140. On the CEQ, Rouillard, *Histoire du syndicalisme au Québec*, 369; Louise Clermont-Laliberté, *Dix ans de pratiques syndicates: La CEQ 1970–1980* (Quebec [1980]), 85.
69. Yves Taschereau, "Ils sont fous," *L'Actualité*, novembre 1976, 50; Benoit, *L'extrême gauche*, 102, 114.
70. CSN, Procès-verbal, congrès confédéral, 17–20 novembre 1976,26.
71. Interview with Peter Bakvis, Montreal, 29 May 1990; Interview with Francine Lalonde, Montreal, 19 June 1990; Interview with Marc Lesage, Montreal, 5 July 1990.
72. CSN, Procès-verbal, congrès confédéral, 1978, 185.
73. Ibid, 150–1; see also, "Eléments pour une discussion de masse: Document de travail," présenté au Comité d'orientation CSN, le 21 décembre 1978, 6–7. Archives de la CSN, Dossier "Question nationale 1976–1980," 370 (2-2-2-3).
74. CSN, Procès-verbal, congrès confédéral, 1978,181.
75. "La peur de faire peur," *Le Devoir*, 20 mai 1980,9.
76. "Les travailleurs sont toujours seuls: Marion et Forget vs. Parizeau," *Le Travail*, octobre/novembre 1974, 19.
77. Claude Masson, "Pépin joue le tout pour le tout: Face aux dissensions internes à la CSN, il engage une lutte à finir avec Bourassa," *La Presse*, 14 juin 1972, A5; Lipsig-Mummé, "The Web of Dependence," 305.
78. *Québec-Presse*, 29 avril 1973, Supplément 1er mai, 28; "Un million de québécois," *Le Travail*, janvier 1974, 26–31 ; "C'est comme ça qu'on est," *Le Travail*, 27 juin 1974, 6; CSN, Procès-verbal, congrès confédéral, 1978, 163.
79. Comité exécutif de la CSN, "Votons pour renforcer notre capacité de lutter." Document soumis au bureau confédéral de la CSN le 31 octobre 1976. CSN, Procès-verbal, bureau confédéral, terme 1976–1978, 34.
80. Don and Vera Murray, "The Parti québécois: From Opposition to Power," in Hugh G. Thorburn, ed., *Party Politics in Canada*, 4th éd. (Scarborough, Ontario 1979), 245, 251; John Fitzmaurice, *Quebec and Canada: Past, Présent, and Future* (London 1985), 198–9; Favreau et L'Heureux, *Le projet de société de la CSN*, 132; François Demers, *Chroniques impertinentes du troisième Front commun syndical, 1979–1980* (Montréal 1982), 97.
81. McRoberts, *Quebec: Social Change and Political Crisis*, 267–8; Linteau et al, *Histoire du Québec contemporain: tome 2: Le Québec depuis 1930*, 658.
82. Rouillard, *Histoire du syndicalisme au Québec*, 424.
83. Reginald A. Whitaker, "The Quebec Chauldron: A Recent Account," in Gagnon, ed., *Quebec: State and Society*, 83.
84. CSN, Procès-verbal, congrès confédéral 1978, 6, 47–60.
85. Interview with Peter Bakvis, Montreal, 29 May 1990.
86. CSN, Procès-verbal, congrès confédéral 1978, 156–66.

87. Pierre Vennat, "La CSN de retour devant la Commonwealth avec 'son' système d'ordre: 'Cette attaque sauvage est un coup monté,'" *La Presse*, 8 juin 1978, A3; Interview with Peter Bakvis, Montreal, 29 May 1990.
88. Interview with Francine Lalonde, Montreal, 19 June 1990.
89. CSN, *Rapport sur la consultation sur la question nationale* (Montreal 1979), 4; Bernier et Boily, *Le Québec en chiffres*, 316.
90. *Rapport sur la consultation sur la question nationale*, 4.
91. For example, see Response of the *Syndicat des travailleurs de Roberval*. Archives de la CSN, Dossier "Question nationale," 1696 (23-3-4-3) and response of the *Syndicat des employés des Aciers Atlas*. Archives de la CSN, Dossier "Question nationale," 370 (2-2-2-3). The orientation committee did not ask the participants to explain their stand. Yet some of the ballots returned to the committee did give reasons under the heading "other remarks."
92. Interview with Peter Bakvis, Montréal, 29 May 1990; Marcel Pépin, "Pourquoi les travailleurs hésitent devant la thèse péquiste," *Le Devoir*, 19 juillet 1980, 2.
93. Rapport sur la consultation sur la question nationale, 5; FNEQ, Procès-verbal, conseil fédéral, 24–27 mai 1979, 10.
94. For example, see Response of the *Syndicat national des employés de soutien de la commission scolaire du Cap-de-la-Madelaine*, Archives de la CSN, Dossier "Question nationale," 370 (2-2-2-3) and Response of the *Syndicat national des employés de Garage de Rimouski*. Archives de la CSN, Dossier "Question nationale," 370 (2-2-2-3).
95. CSN, Procès-verbal, conseil confédéral, 3–5 mai 1979, 398–9; CSN, Procès-verbal, congrès confédéral 1979, 131–2.
96. CSN, Procès-verbal, conseil confédéral, 1979, 147.
97. Ibid., 74–5.
98. Ibid., 61–7.
99. Ibid., 37–51.
100. ICSN, Procès-verbal, conseil confédéral, 11 avril 1980, 927–8
101. "La CSN décide de rallier le camp du OUI," *Le Devoir*, 12 avril 1980, 7; Laval LeBorgne, "Le conseil confédéral de la CSN vote Oui," *La Presse*, 12 avril 1980, A2.
102. On the FTQ see, Rouillard, *Histoire du syndicalisme au Québec*, 325–7; Cyr et Roy, *Éléments d'histoire de la FTQ*, 155–98. On the CEQ see, Rouillard, *Histoire du syndicalisme au Québec*, 369–70; Clermont-Laliberté, *Dix ans de pratiques syndicales*, 86.
103. René Lévesque, *My Quebec* (Toronto 1979), 45.

Chapter 19

Alberta Nurses and the "Illegal" Strike of 1988

Rebecca Priegert Coulter

On 25 January 1988, more than 11,000 staff nurses who were members of the United Nurses of Alberta (UNA) directly challenged the province's *Labour Relations Act*, which prohibits strikes by hospital workers, and began an illegal strike that was to last for 19 days. Because the willingness of union members to strike is an important measure of worker militancy, the ability of the UNA to call an illegal strike and sustain it in the face of extremely punitive retaliatory measures by employers and the state is compelling evidence that Alberta nurses are the most militant members of an occupational group of women that has become increasingly militant over the past few years.[1] Indeed, for UNA, the 1988 strike was the seventh one, and the fourth involving hospital nurses, since the union's founding in 1977.[2]

The 1988 strike provides a key entry point for understanding the organization and politics of the United Nurses of Alberta and opens up questions about how a professional women's union[3] positions itself with respect to both the male-dominated union movement and the women's movement in Canada. What is it that explains the solidarity and militancy of Alberta's unionized nurses? To explore this question this chapter begins by looking at UNA's formative experiences with collective bargaining and government intervention and then discusses the conditions which contributed to the nurses' ability to call and maintain the illegal strike of 1988. It then outlines the events leading up to the strike and provides a brief history of the strike itself. Finally, the strike and its aftermath are examined in the context of a discussion of UNA's relations with the labour movement and women's organizing.

Unionizing Alberta Nurses

Prior to 1977, the Alberta Association of Registered Nurses (AARN) was the only organization which gave nurses a province-wide collective voice. Established in 1916, the AARN, like contemporary nurses' organizations elsewhere, used occupational closure strategies in an effort to attain professional status for nursing. That is, by attempting to control standards of nursing practice and the education of nurses, the AARN hoped to establish nursing as an independent profession which could lay claim to acceptable levels of remuneration for its members as well as allow nurses control over their own work.[4] However, by the mid-1960s the salaries and conditions of work in the province compared unfavourably with many other provincial jurisdictions, and Alberta nurses began to organize bargaining units at the hospital level to seek redress. Between 1964 and 1966, 12 Staff Nurse Associations were certified by the Board of Industrial Relations and 38 were recognized voluntarily by hospital boards. This grass-roots and locally initiated approach to organizing undoubtedly contributed to nurses' sense of ownership of "their" union. Within the AARN, a Provincial Staff Nurse Committee (PSNC), which excluded management nurses, was created to handle collective-bargaining activities.

In the late 1960s and early 1970s disputes between nurses and their employers intensified as the nature of the nursing work changed and hospitals became larger and more bureaucratized. In 1972, the growing militancy of rank-and-file nurses was demonstrated by the decision of the AARN to remove its ban on strike action by nurses. Finally, as a result of a growing division within AARN between the management nurses who controlled the Provincial Council and the PSNC, the PSNC broke away on 6 May 1977 to establish an independent union, the United Nurses of Alberta.[5]

The timing of and the context for the creation of a separate union for staff nurses was significant. In 1975, the federal Liberal government began the process of reducing funding for health care. Increases in funding were tied to the GNP rather than to the real costs of health care. Block funding replaced cost-sharing and transfer payments from the federal government to provincial governments were reduced. During this period (1975–8) the federal government also instituted its program of wage and price controls. Both cutbacks in funding for health care and wage controls were used by employers to argue against wage increases and improved working conditions for Alberta nurses. The inability or unwillingness of the AARN to respond forcefully to the employers, and the nature of the conflict between management and staff nurses within the professional association, further distanced staff nurses from the cautious approach to collective bargaining favoured by the AARN and enhanced the solidarity of staff nurses.

When the UNA moved into its new office in June 1977, province-wide negotiations were in progress and had reached the conciliation stage. Few in the new union felt that conciliation would result in significant gains for hospital nurses. On 4 July 1977, the union began a legal strike at seven Alberta hospitals. Within four days the provincial government intervened by declaring a public emergency and ordering the nurses back to work. With no strike fund and only two months' worth of dues in the bank, the nurses could not afford to defy the government order and returned to work. The government set up an emergency tribunal to award a settlement binding on both parties and appointed Mr Justice Bowen as the arbitrator. This first strike established a pattern of UNA militancy and government intervention that led directly to the 1988 strike.

Nurses benefited financially from the Bowen award. Given a nine percent wage increase at a time when the province, following the federal government's lead on wage controls, had legislated a six percent ceiling, UNA became one of the few unions to gain exemption. The provincial cabinet had to issue a special Order-in-Council allowing employers to pay the full nine percent increase. At the same time, Mr Justice Bowen rejected UNA's demand for an automatic dues-collection clause. He said that because nurses were professionals "they would not require any coercion of any kind to own up to their obligations and pay their required dues, and therefore the clause was unnecessary."[6] Ironically, this decision increased the union's visibility in its formative year. Union leaders had to campaign actively for members and nurses had to make a conscious decision to join the union by signing a release allowing employers to deduct union dues from their paycheques.

UNA, then, was born under circumstances which quickly focused attention on a number of key elements including the presumed split between professional and union activities, the question of striking, and the role of the government in settling disputes. The union's first foray into strike action did not lead to a negotiated settlement but did produce a substantial wage increase. This outcome can only have solidified support for the union. Within the context of cutbacks to health-care funding, the high visibility of the union movement's opposition to wage controls, and the increased militancy of other professionals (such as teachers in the 1970s), nurses received validation for their decision to unionize.

The 10 years following the founding of UNA were marked by a number of negotiated settlements and a several strikes during which the provincial government exercised increasingly repressive measures against the union. A collective agreement which included provisions for the application of the Rand formula was reached through negotiations in 1978–9. The next round of negotiations did not go as well, and in April 1980 UNA began a legal strike at 79 hospitals. After three days members were ordered back to work. This time they refused the order and challenged its validity in the courts. While the case was being argued, negotiations resumed and a settlement was reached.

A central issue in the 1980 negotiations was the professional-responsibility clause. Alberta's *Nursing Profession Act* makes it clear that nurses have a professional responsibility for the quality of patient care. Nurses can lose their licences to practise if it can be shown that they did not provide appropriate care. Originally part of a strategy that sought dignity and decent wages through professionalization, the concept of professional responsibility is now a means through which nurses attempt to exercise some real control in their workplace. Arguing that a professional-responsibility clause is necessary because it relates directly to their legal liability for patient care and their ability to protect their licences to nurse and hence their livelihood, nurses can use such a clause to demand better standards of care and increased staffing on hospital wards. In fact, professional-responsibility clauses represent a melding of the organizational strategies of professionalization and unionization for control in the workplace. It is no surprise that hospital employers have opposed such clauses as a direct attack on management rights. As a result of the 1980 strike, however, Alberta nurses won a professional-responsibility clause along with a 39.8 percent wage increase over two years, improved work scheduling, and 50 other contract improvements.[7] Union activity and the willingness to strike had paid off for nurses, but the provincial government again had shown its proclivity to interfere with the bargaining process.

In 1981 a new round of bargaining began. Indicative of a new confidence in their worth and power, the nurses demanded a 40–52 percent wage increase over two years, voluntary overtime and improved scheduling provisions, new health and safety measures, and 229 other changes or new items. In the absence of a settlement by December 1981, the union held a strike vote among its 8,300 hospital nurses and, although some locals voted not to strike, the overall results gave UNA a strike mandate. At this point, Alberta's minister of labour intervened and using provisions of the *Labour Relations Act* ordered a Disputes Inquiry Board. This board was to hold hearings into the outstanding items and make recommendations for a settlement. Both parties, UNA and the Alberta Hospitals' Association (AHA), were ordered to attend the hearings of the Disputes Inquiry Board.

When the board brought down its recommendations, the minister of labour ordered a government-supervised vote among UNA members. However, UNA, in keeping with its constitution, had already decided on its own vote and directed its members to boycott the government vote even though the government threatened to impose the results of its own vote, regardless of how few nurses actually participated. Ultimately, the government backed down and the results of the UNA vote were accepted.[8] This vote rejected the recommendations of the Disputes Inquiry Board. A few days later the Labour Relations Board refused UNA's request to conduct a second strike vote in those locals which had previously voted against the strike but wanted a chance to reconsider. On 16 February 1982, 6,000 nurses at 69 Alberta hospitals went on strike.

On 10 March the government acted to stop the strike. Bill 11, which was an order to force nurses back to work immediately, was introduced and passed on the same day. The bill included severe anti-union sanctions including large fines, the threat of decertification, and restrictions on individuals with respect to working for or holding office in a trade union. The legislation also ordered both parties to appear at a tribunal which would issue a binding settlement. The nurses decided to return to work and in July the tribunal awarded a 29 percent wage increase over two years, improved scheduling, a safety clause which stipulated that nurses should not have to work alone, and access for nurses to hospital boards. No gains were made on the question of voluntary overtime.

The following spring Bill 44 was passed by the Alberta legislature. The bill amended the *Labour Relations Act* to remove the legal right to strike from all hospital workers including nurses. The legislation provided for compulsory arbitration as a settlement mechanism and specified that awards had to reflect government fiscal policy. The legislation included stiff monetary penalties for unions and union members who decided to defy its conditions and a provision which allowed an employer to apply to the Labour Relations Board for a six-month cessation of dues collection. Nurses believed that the legislation was aimed directly at them and while the next two rounds of bargaining resulted in negotiated settlements between UNA and the AHA, it was only a matter of time before the union would confront the punitive conditions of the new legislation directly.

Baptized in a strike and growing through the experiences of two other hospital strikes, members of UNA developed a strong sense of solidarity. Heavy-handed government intervention only succeeded in building a strong oppositional culture within UNA, for nurses grew increasingly angry about any interference with their right to free and unfettered collective bargaining. Since nurses always seemed to be the first occupational group subjected to a range of fines and sanctions, UNA's membership developed a strong sense of its own power. Government sanctions also contributed to a process in which nurses began to reflect on the gender specificity of their work and their union practices. Margaret Ethier, president of UNA from 1980–88, put this understanding bluntly. Commenting on Bill 11 she said, "I believe it was pure and simple revenge, and I can understand that. After all, [Premier] Lougheed's boys don't take kindly to being out-smarted by a bunch of women."[9] Becoming "bad girls" was increasingly less threatening to nurses and, indeed, was fast becoming part of the union culture.[10]

The union leadership has worked very hard at fostering grass-roots development and involvement. UNA's demand-setting process is open and democratized, with the result that nurses understand and become committed to the union's bargaining position. A bargaining year starts with meetings in each of the hospital locals in which members go over the current agreement and come up with a list of changes and additions that they want. By June each local has sent a list of its demands in to the elected negotiating committee. This committee compiles the demands from all the locals, considers them, and makes recommendations about the demands. The demands from all locals along with the committee's recommendations are then sent back to each of the locals for discussion and consideration. The locals then send delegates to a provincial demand-setting meeting where the negotiating committee presents its set of proposed demands for that round of bargaining. Approximately 400 delegates meet over three days to consider the negotiating committee's recommendations. Delegates may make changes to the committee's recommendations, but all changes must be based on demands which originated with the locals in the first place. No new demands can be introduced. Each proposal is thoroughly debated and requires a two-thirds approval in order to be included in the final list of demands. The final set of demands coming out of this delegate meeting is then sent back to the locals for ratification, and once it has been approved by at least 50 percent of the locals and 50 percent of the members, the package becomes UNA's opening position at the bargaining table.

After negotiations with the AHA begin, UNA members are informed about developments quickly through phone fan-outs, meetings, mailings, electronic mail, and articles in the union's *News Bulletin*. During the course of negotiations, at least one reporting meeting is held. Elected delegates from the locals meet with the negotiating committee to receive information and to give advice and direction.

During negotiations, if the employers make an acceptable offer of settlement, the negotiating committee may sign a Memorandum of Settlement. The committee then calls a reporting meeting to present the memorandum and recommend its ratification. If the delegates at the meeting agree with the recommendation, the memorandum is sent out to the locals for a ratification vote. If the employers refuse to table an acceptable offer, the negotiating committee calls a reporting meeting, presents the details of the stalemate or impasse, provides an assessment of the bargaining that has occurred to date, and recommends that a strike vote be held in all affected locals. Because UNA categorically refuses to recognize any third-party intervention in negotiations, the only choice before members is to accept the employers' last offer or to go on strike for an improved offer. If the vote supports strike action, the negotiating committee sets the strike and all affected locals are called out. If strike action is rejected by the members, the negotiating committee goes back to the table and accepts the employers' last offer. The memorandum is then sent out to the locals for ratification.[11]

Two principles govern UNA's approach to collective bargaining. The first is that no roll-backs or concessions will ever be considered by the union. The second is that the union rejects all government interference in the form of arbitration, conciliation, or mediation and claims its right to strike as though no legislation to the contrary existed. Clearly UNA has a powerful commitment to free collective bargaining and to a process which "allows members of UNA to make decisions at every point ... about what they will work for and what they will not." The union leadership recognizes that it is the open and democratic process of demand setting and reporting back which "inspires and motivates the members."[12] Hibberd, noting that the union has utilized the work skills of its members (especially their communication links) to build solidarity and collective commitment to negotiating packages, agrees that the demand-setting process allows "maximum involvement in the generation of demands, and in the ratification of the final negotiating package," and it is the process which generates widespread support among members.[13] Put another way, the members experience a strong sense of ownership with respect to bargaining demands because they have been actively involved at each stage.

During the 1980s other events served to increase nurses' solidarity. The much-publicized case of child deaths in Toronto's Hospital for Sick Children, the scapegoating of one nurse, Susan Nelles, and the lack of respect and consideration accorded nurses during the hearings of the Grange Royal Commission confirmed for nurses that their expertise and work were unrecognized and undervalued.[14] As Growe puts it, the Grange Commission marked "the point in history when the largest organized group of women in Canada lost their innocence"[15] and began to see the realities of their gender and work locations with more clarity.

While nurses are increasingly educated to value holistic, individualized care, hospital work systems are bureaucratically organized with an emphasis on rapid task completion and compliance with established policies and procedures.[16] Like many women workers, nurses have been left with many responsibilities but little authority, and they work within a hierarchical structure that vests most power in the hands of the doctors and administrators who are removed from the day-to-day realities of patient care. As Wilma Scott Heide points out, "health policy decisions and funding are made in the context of a value system that is white, patriarchal, and capitalist."[17] As a result, few resources have been directed towards those areas that nurses feel need attention. This helps account for the fact that nurses in the 1970s and 1980s turned to the potential of collective bargaining to effect change in their workplace and work lives. They were fed up with under-staffing and over-work, with inadequate supplies and equipment, with threats to their health and safety, and with the emphasis on business efficiency rather than patient care.

In many ways, the 1988 strike ended up being about all those things. After the strike was over, the president of UNA, Margaret Ethier, stated that nurses had gone on strike for better wages and working conditions "including the important working condition of being treated with respect." However, she also observed,

> We did not go on strike to protest the health care cutbacks; to show the public that the taxes they pay for proper health care are often spent on anything but patient care; to show that it is becoming more difficult, if not impossible, for nurses to provide quality care, or even safe care for our patients.
>
> We did not go on strike to change the law; to expose to the public the unfairness of current labour laws....
>
> We didn't go on strike to inspire other nurses and other trade unionists and individual members of the public; to set an example of what can and should be done when people believe enough is enough; to make people realize that sometimes it is necessary to face and deal with conflict and confrontation ... to show the strength that can be derived from a group that is fully committed to common goals—in spite of their personal, political and social differences.
>
> These were not the reasons we went on strike, but the effect of our strike was that we achieved all of the above.[18]

The "Illegal" Strike of 1988

While the union's history, the collective memory of the nurses, the material circumstances of nursing, and the specific social and economic climate all made the 1988 strike possible, it was the union's democratic processes which provided the flashpoint for the nurses' militancy. Negotiations began in the fall of 1987 for a new collective agreement. Among the items taken to the table by UNA were ones concerning nurse safety, patient care, and the professional-responsibility article. The employers came to the table proposing many take-aways. In January 1988 the UNA negotiating team received a final offer from the employers, an offer which demonstrated that the proposed roll-backs would not be withdrawn. A reporting meeting was called for 5 January 1988 in Calgary. During discussions of the employers' offer, delegates at the meeting came to the conclusion that their negotiating team had agreed to a provision dealing with short- and long-term disability and Workers' Compensation that amounted to a take-away. Reiterating the cardinal rule that the union would never accept roll-backs, take-aways, regressions, or concessions, delegates at the reporting meeting sent the negotiating team back to the table to tell the employers that the disability provision was not acceptable and that no memorandum of settlement would ever be ratified if it contained that clause. At the same time, a vote on the employers' last offer was set for 22 January with a ballot reading "Are you willing to go on strike for an improved offer?"

The negotiating team returned to the table and informed the employers of UNA's decision. As a result the employers went to the Labour Relations Board and charged UNA with negotiating in bad faith. At the same time, the AHA asked the LRB to find the union in breach of the legislation which outlawed strikes in the hospitals. The employers took the position that the wording on the ballot constituted a threat to strike, an act which was prohibited by law. On 22 January at 3 a.m., the LRB handed down a ruling; this ruling stated that the wording on the ballot did indeed constitute a threat to strike and hence the vote would be illegal. The LRB issued a cease-and-desist order prohibiting the strike vote scheduled to begin that morning.

Between 3 a.m. and 7 a.m. UNA utilized its phone fan-out system to inform members of the LRB ruling, and at 7 a.m. voting started in defiance of that ruling. Nurses were outraged that they could so easily lose the democratic right to vote. As one veteran nurse put it, nurses "are women with a lot of resolve. We're not putting up with this."[19] In fact, all 104 eligible hospital locals held the vote with a large voter turn-out. Of the 11,436 nurses eligible to vote, 8,688 defied the ban. Heather Smith, a UNA negotiator in 1988 and now UNA president, observed, "It's not that we don't take the threats seriously, it's just this time we feel we have to be firm and stand our ground."[20] In essence, the nurses began engaging in an illegal act the moment they cast ballots. Of those voting, 76 percent voted to go on strike. On this basis, the negotiating committee called for a strike to commence at all hospitals at 7:30 a.m. on 25 January 1988.

From the first day of the strike, nurses faced punitive retaliatory actions and these actions quickly escalated. For example, some employers immediately applied to the LRB for permission to cease collecting union dues for six months. At the same time, unions from across Canada began sending telegrams and letters of support, and Dave Werlin, president of the Alberta Federation of Labour, promised that Alberta workers would support UNA financially. On the second day of the strike the courts granted an injunction against picketing at three Calgary hospitals and 1,000 nurses responded by turning up at those hospitals to walk the line. On the third day some individual nurses were served with civil contempt-of-court charges and by the end of the strike over 75 individual charges were laid and heard. On the same day, the Alberta government, through the acting attorney-general, charged UNA with criminal contempt. The Minister of Labour also named a mediator, but because of UNA's opposition on principle to third-party intervention, the union rejected the mediator. Instead, the union asked for an "independent facilitator" who would have some real power to influence the government with respect to monetary issues and increased funding. A facilitator, Chip Collins, was appointed on 31 January.

On 1 February UNA appeared in court on criminal contempt charges. The government requested a $1 million fine and sequestration of the union's bank accounts and assets. According to UNA, sequestration had never been used in North America. On 4 February UNA was fined $250,000, which sum was to be paid within five days on threat of sequestration. The magnitude of this sum was symbolized by the inability of the cash register to produce one receipt for UNA's secretary-treasurer when she went to pay the fine on 9 February. Instead, she got two receipts for $90,000 and one for $70,000. By the end of the strike the union had paid a total of $400,000 in fines for criminal contempt and $26,750 for civil contempt.[21]

While UNA was making court appearances, so, too, were locals and individual nurses. On 10 February, for example, 10 locals and individual members of varying numbers from most of the locals were found in civil contempt and fined. On the same day, employers, who had been keeping up a steady barrage of disciplinary letters to members of small locals, stepped up their action and began to terminate nurses' employment. Three nurses in Fort Vermilion-High Level were told that termination notices were in the mail; Barrhead terminated 13 nurses; 4 nurses in Rocky Mountain House and 75 in Lethbridge were told they would be fired if they did not report for work within 48 hours. In Lac La Biche a black van actually drove all over the town to deliver termination notices.[22] Punishment and fear-mongering were being employed as strategies to break the union and the nurses' solidarity.

These strategies were unsuccessful; despite a bitterly cold winter, nurses remained on the picket lines across the province. David Harrigan, vice-president of UNA, estimated that only about 10 percent of the nurses were scabbing.[23] As one nurse with 18 years' experience said, "We really hate being out here. But we have no choice. What do we do?" Another nurse with 14 years of service spoke of her stomach being in knots when she had to do picket duty, and said she was pessimistic about how successful the strike might be. Nonetheless, she backed the strike because "I'm supporting my fellow workers right now. The other girls I work with, this is their work, their life, their only means of money."[24] A much younger nurse said, "I'm angry. It is not right. We were pushed into a comer.... We didn't have a choice."[25]

An editorial in the *Calgary Herald* concurred. Nurses "have not received a square deal from their employers, who have given the impression that one class of essential worker can be treated as indentured servants with impunity."[26] Another commentator noted that "the nurses won the battle for public opinion hands down."[27] The most tangible evidence of wide support was the more than $500,000 raised from donations both big and small. Pensioners donated the dollar or two they could afford, a group of employees at a McDonald's in California passed the hat at work and sent the money to the strike fund. Other individuals, groups, and unions sent money to the Friends of Alberta Nurses Society (FANS), set up by the AFL to ensure that donations would not be sequestered.

By 10 February UNA and the AHA had all but reached a settlement. The only sticking point was the employers' insistence on retaining the right to stop collecting union dues. UNA members report hearing the president of the AHA say to reporters as he left the hotel, "They have to be punished somehow." On 11 February an improved offer was tabled by the AHA and employers withdrew their applications to suspend dues collection. On 12 February UNA members voted to accept that offer and a negotiated settlement was reached. The nurses returned to work the following day.

Conclusion

The union now terms the 1988 settlement a "tread water" one. Over a 27-month contract, wage raises of 8 to 10.9 percent, depending on seniority, were won, but vacation entitlements remained unchanged.

For UNA "the most important victory was forcing the employer to remove the takeaways from the table." At the same time, the union leadership believes that the benefits of the 1988 strike were reflected in the gains made during the 1990 round of negotiations.[28]

The 1988 "illegal" strike was significant, too, because it captured the imagination and support of a wide range of people and highlighted UNA's relationships with other unions and with the women's movement. Women's groups and unions rallied to the cause, literally and figuratively, and put pressure on the provincial government to provide funds for a settlement. The National Action Committee on the Status of Women (NAC) and its member groups sent telegrams and letters to the premier urging a rapid settlement. As Edmonton Working Women put it, "the country's attention was captured by the courage, strength and unity of the members of the United Nurses of Alberta who went on an illegal strike. They defied the law to defend their own democratic rights, and to oppose the erosion of workers' rights on all fronts ... [and to] fight for the patients' rights to quality, publicly funded health care."[29]

While the union and women's movements rallied to the cause during the 1988 strike, UNA has consistently eschewed formal affiliation with either. UNA co-operates with the Alberta Federation of Labour on many projects but co-exists with, rather than joins, the federation. Affiliations with the CLC, the CCU, and the CFL have all been discussed and rejected, ostensibly because of the monetary costs of membership. The decision not to affiliate with the CLC was reinforced when observers sent to the CLC convention in Montreal were troubled by the actions of several large unions on the floor and in the backrooms, especially with respect to the treatment accorded the Edmonton Firefighters who were attempting to break away from their international union. The UNA observers came away convinced that the trade-union movement in Canada was male-dominated and not democratic enough. UNA's position that "nurses will speak for nurses" and its reluctance to affiliate officially with the CLC suggest a consciousness and practice developed out of a workplace where for too long nurses have had to take orders from (male) doctors and have occupied a place in a patriarchal institution which is low in power, prestige, and status.[30] In the end, Alberta nurses are not prepared to trade the benefits of separate organizing and independent decision-making for membership in a trade-union organization where nurses would likely face gender struggles comparable to those that confront them in the workplace.[31]

While nurses have begun to develop some consciousness of themselves as women workers and have used some of the conceptual tools of feminism to understand and explain their lives, UNA has not been identified, nor has it identified itself, as a feminist union. The first executive director of the UNA, Bob Donahue, was Metis and senior nurses recall him talking about the similarities between the oppression of aboriginal peoples and the oppression of nurses because they were women.[32] Although nurses may have agreed with this analysis, UNA has not become an active participant in the women's movement in the way that the Federation of Women Teachers' Associations of Ontario has. For example, UNA has not joined NAC, at least partly because the union does not wish to risk an internal split on the abortion issue.[33] But the failure of nurses to identify with the women's movement might also be explained partly by the fact that socialist feminists have tended to overlook the work of women employed in traditional professions or have regarded such women as privileged, while liberal feminists have inadvertently downgraded the importance of nursing through programmatic demands which focus on women's entry to non-traditional (that is, male) professions such as medicine and law.

During the 1988 strike women's groups "discovered" nurses and provided considerable support for them. Nonetheless, striking nurses primarily identified as workers and unionists and were not inclined to see their experiences in the context of any larger women's struggle. For example, Barb Strange, president of the Local at the Calgary General Hospital said, "This dispute has become a power struggle.... They're not just worried about keeping costs down. They have the mentality that they are the masters and we're the servants and how dare we step out of line."[34] While we could read gender into her observations, it is not explicitly stated; on the other hand, the use of the master/servant analogy recognizes class and traditional boss/worker dimensions.

It is clear, however, that striking nurses benefited from the gains of the women's movement. Although the relationship between feminism and nursing remains "uneasy,"[35] public discussion which focused on how women's caring and nurturing work was devalued and on critiques of the organizational and power structure of hospitals were based in feminist analysis and on the gender-specificity of nursing work. Further use of feminist analysis would allow nurses to develop expanded understandings about attitudes towards them and about their work as *women*'s work. If nurses, as women workers and women unionists, want to move forward with a broad social agenda for health care, they will have to "harness their visions of a preferred future to a larger understanding of power relations in health care, including *the interaction of the sexual division of labour* with bureaucratic methods of organizing work"[36] (my emphasis).

Indeed, shortly after the strike, some nurses began to question whether collective bargaining provided all the tools necessary to take care of their workplace concerns. Irene Gouin, vice-president of UNA Local 79 in 1988, reflected on the gains and losses associated with the strike. "We're going to have to take much more initiative in between strike action. This is the fourth time we've gone to bargaining and very few health-care, patient-care, and employee-safety concerns have ever been achieved at the table. We're going to have to try and find some other avenues to do that."[37] Indeed, since the 1988 strike, UNA's leadership has begun to assess what strategies in addition to collective bargaining will aid nurses in achieving their goals.[38]

Lessons from women's-movement organizing might suggest ways in which nurses could reconsider their relationship with other women workers in the hospital setting in order to make significant changes in patient care. As White has pointed out, women hospital workers (as opposed to men) have an "attachment to healing."[39] However, the hierarchical structure of hospitals separates nurses from nursing assistants and other health-care workers, and nurses have not been active in breaking the divisions down. In fact, nurses use, rather than challenge, demarcationary practices of occupational closure or exclusion to separate themselves from other health-care workers below them in the hierarchy.[40] As Allen has argued, this approach is "masculinist" and "professionalist" in orientation and can actually be "viewed as in *opposition* to collective bargaining or unionism."[41] Organizing with other women in the workplace might prove a beneficial strategy for nurses seeking fundamental changes in health care, for this strategy would enhance the collective power of all hospital workers. Put another way, perhaps nurses should organize not only within their profession but across their sector, much as the Ontario Secondary School Teachers' Federation has begun to organize not just teachers but all workers in secondary schools.

In Alberta, the wages and working conditions of nurses have been improved through the astute use of traditional collective-bargaining strategies and the willingness of UNA members to directly challenge government intervention in negotiations between employees and employers. The solidarity of nurses and their union consciousness were strengthened further through the shared experience of an "illegal" strike. And bridges, some shakier than others, were built among UNA, other unions, and the women's movement in 1988. To what extent the lessons of the strike will shape nurses' efforts to control their work, improve patient care, and transform the health-care system remains to be seen.

Endnotes

1. See, for example, Larry Haiven, "The State and Nursing Industrial Relations: The Case of Four Western Canadian Nurses' Strikes," unpublished paper presented jointly to the Canadian Sociology and Anthropology Association and the Society for Socialist Studies annual meetings, Kingston, June 1991; Sarah Jane Growe, *Who Cares? The Crisis in Canadian Nursing* (Toronto: McClelland and Stewart 1991); Judith M. Hibberd, "Organized Political Action: The Labor Struggle in Alberta," in Alice J. Baumgart and Jenniece Larsen, eds, *Canadian Nursing Faces the Future: Development and Change* (St Louis: C.V. Mosby Company 1988), 489-99. On Australian nurses see Liz Ross, "Sisters Are Doing It for Themselves ... And Us," *Hecate* 13, no. 1 (1987): 83–99.
2. The other three strikes involved nurses at the Hardisty Nursing Home (1981), the Parklands Nursing Home (1982), and in eight health units across the province (1985). Nurses in eight health units were locked out in 1982. See Trudy Richardson, "United Nurses of Alberta History" (Edmonton: United Nurses of Alberta 1992).
3. The membership of the UNA is 97 percent female. Although the 3 percent male membership may exercise "more influence than their numbers would indicate," there is no doubt that the UNA is a union of women. Interview with Trudy Richardson, UNA education officer, 9 March 1992.
4. For a discussion of nurses' strategies of professionalization or occupational closure, see Anne Witz, *Professions and Patriarchy* (London and New York: Routledge 1992) and David G. Allen, "Professionalism, Occupational Segregation by Gender and Control of Nursing," *Women and Politics* 6, no. 3 (Fall 1986): 1–24.
5. See Richardson, "UNA History," for events leading up to the formation of UNA; see Growe for events leading up to the formation of nurses' unions as distinct from professional associations.
6. Quoted in United Nurses of Alberta, "Brief on Collective Bargaining," February 1992.
7. Richardson, "UNA History," 8.
8. As a result of this conflict, the law was later changed. The new law made it illegal for unions to refuse to take part in a government-supervised vote. The government also was given the power to impose its vote results as a way to settle disputes.
9. Quoted in Don Braid, "Strike Has Tories in Tight Corner," *Calgary Herald*, 26 Jan. 1988, A8.
10. Growe 134.
11. This description of the bargaining process is based on UNA "Brief on Collective Bargaining," and an interview with Richardson, 9 March 1992.

12. UNA, "Brief on Collective Bargaining," 12.
13. Hibberd 494.
14. Elaine Buckley Day, "A Twentieth-Century Witch Hunt: A Feminist Critique of the Grange Royal Commission into Deaths at the Hospital for Sick Children," *Studies in Political Economy* 24 (Autumn 1987): 13–39; Dorothy E. Smith, *The Conceptual Practices of Power: A Feminist Sociology of Knowledge* (Toronto: University of Toronto Press 1990), 101–3; Growe 26–43.
15. Growe 39.
16. Alice J. Baumgart and Jenniece Larsen, "Introduction to Nursing in Canada," in Baumgart and Larsen 8; M. Louise Fitzgerald, "Nursing," *Signs: Journal of Women in Culture and Society* 2, no. 4 (Summer 1977): 818–34; Pat Armstrong, "Where Have All the Nurses Gone?" *Healthsharing*, Summer 1988, 17–19; Marie Campbell, "Management as 'Ruling': A Class Phenomenon in Nursing," *Studies in Political Economy* 27 (Autumn 1988): 29–51.
17. Wilma Scott Heide, "Feminist Activism in Nursing and Health Care," in Janet Muff, ed., *Socialization, Sexism, and Stereotyping: Women's Issues in Nursing* (St Louis: C.V. Mosby Company 1982), 256. See also Ann Game and Rosemary Pringle, *Gender at Work* (Sydney: George Allen and Unwin 1983), 94–118; Eva Gamarnikow, "Sexual Division of Labour: The Case of Nursing," in Annette Kuhn and AnnMarie Wolpe, eds, *Feminism and Materialism: Women and Modes of Production* (London: Routledge 1978), 96–123.
18. Quoted in Rebecca Coulter and Trudy Richardson, "Militancy and Alberta Nurses," *The Year Left*, forthcoming.
19. "Nurses to Walk Out," *Sunday Herald*, 24 Jan. 1988, A1–A2.
20. "Nurses Defy Law," *Calgary Herald*, 23 Jan. 1988, A1–A2.
21. The UNA appealed the fines for criminal contempt, but in 1992 the Supreme Court of Canada, in a 4–3 ruling, let the fines stand.
22. Details of the strike are drawn from Coulter and Richardson.
23. "Emergency Problem," *Calgary Herald*, 1 Feb. 1988, Al.
24. "Nurses Plan Mass Rally," *Calgary Herald*, 31 Jan. 1988, A1–A2.
25. "Nurses Insist They'll Walk the Line Despite the Fine," *Calgary Herald*, 6 Feb. 1988, B1.
26. "Strike Is Unnecessary," *Calgary Herald*, 26 Jan. 1988, A4.
27. Jack Spearman, "Arrogance Trips Conservatives," *Calgary Herald*, 16 Feb. 1988, A4.
28. Richardson, "UNA History," 15.
29. Interview with Irene Gouin in "Alberta Nurses Victorious in 'Illegal Strike,' Challenging the Barriers," *Edmonton Working Women Newsletter*, Spring/Summer 1988, 4.
30. Interview with Trudy Richardson, 9 March 1992.
31. For discussions of the problems confronting women who work in mixed-sex unions, see several other chapters in this book. Also, see Cynthia Cockburn, *In the Way of Women: Men's Resistance to Sex Equality in Organizations* (Ithaca, NY: ILR Press 1991).
32. Interview with Trudy Richardson, 9 March 1992.
33. Ibid., 15 May 1992.
34. "Moore Suggests Pact Way To Go," *Calgary Herald*, 6 Feb. 1988, A1–A2.
35. Janet Kerr and Jannetta MacPhail, *Canadian Nursing: Issues and Perspectives* (Toronto: McGraw-Hill Ryerson 1988), 60; William K. Carroll and Rennie Warburton, "Feminism, Class Consciousness and Household-Work Linkages among Registered Nurses in Victoria," *Labour/Le Travail* 24 (Fall 1989): 131–45.
36. Baumgart and Larsen 10.
37. "Alberta Nurses Victorious," 5–6.
38. Interview with Trudy Richardson, 15 May 1992.
39. Jerry P. White, *Hospital Strike: Women, Unions, and Public Sector Conflict* (Toronto: Thompson Educational Publishing 1990).
40. Witz 44–8.
41. Allen 12.

Chapter 20

Greening the Canadian Workplace

Unions and the Environment

Laurel Sefton MacDowell

Over the last two decades, it has been common for the media to focus on the conflict between workers and environmentalists. The "war in the woods" in British Columbia over the future of old growth forests, and the confrontations in the Temagami forest in Ontario, made national and international news. Typically, the media has portrayed land-use issues as a choice between jobs or the environment, conveying the tension between the social equity objectives of trade unionists and environmentalists' ecological goals.[1] In this chapter, I will argue that this picture is too simple. Workers are not only interested in jobs and job security. They also share a common experience with environmental groups of being pressure groups, sometimes marginalized, in a society which historically and currently has placed priority on development and often ignored both workers' needs for a secure, healthy workplace and environmental issues like biodiversity and a clean atmosphere.[2] The media stories, in focusing on workers' interest in job security, have thus ignored the labour movement's environmental policies, its experience with environmental problems in the workplace, and its occasional co-operation with community groups concerning broader environmental issues. It is these environmental struggles that I document here. I conclude, however, that while substantial gains have been made, Canadian workers face formidable obstacles in a resource-dependent economy, where jobs and revenue are tied closely to resource-extractive and polluting industries.

Linking Occupational Health and Safety with Broader Environmental Concerns

The Canadian labour movement has long been concerned about environmental hazards on the job which threaten the health and safety of workers. Since the 1960s, unions have called for improvements in occupational health and safety legislation, and their experience in trying to achieve a cleaner and safer work environment has led the labour movement at all levels to broaden its concern, develop policies for a healthier environment, and work with community groups to achieve such ends. Throughout the 1970s and 1980s, as unions increasingly brought occupational health and safety matters to the bargaining table, the number of strikes over such issues increased, and unions allocated more staff, time, and money to reducing workplace hazards and disease.[3]

There are many examples of union action regarding occupational health and safety. One of the more significant was a strike in June 1971 by the International Chemical Workers

Union against the Canadian Johns-Manville Co. Ltd. in east Toronto. It was unique in that the main issue was unsafe plant air. Several workers had developed asbestosis, and provincial safety inspectors ordered the company to install a new ventilation system to exhaust asbestos-soaked air.[4] In 1973 the Energy and Chemical Workers Union (ECWU) struck Shell Chemical in Sarnia and won recognition of joint health and safety committees and full disclosure of the chemicals used in the workplace.[5] In September 1981, the United Steel Workers of America (USWA) negotiated a contract provision with Denison Mines Ltd. and Rio Algom Ltd. to allow inspectors access to company health and safety records and the authority to shut down workplaces they deemed unsafe. The union pushed for this breakthrough on health and safety issues as uranium mine workers were exposed "to significantly higher amounts of silica dust than in other mines, as well as several types of radiation and potentially cancer-causing uranium dust."[6]

Union action has often resulted from exploitive employers who have ignored both workers' health and the environment. One spectacular case was the Robson-Lang tannery, operating for 50 years in Barrie, Ontario, before closing in 1986. There, half the workforce (87 of 165 people), all members of the United Food and Chemical Workers' Union, had died of lung or throat cancer by 1990 from exposure to lethal substances like chromium dust. While working at the plant, the workers were unaware and the union apparently uninformed of the dangers. At the same time, the company discharged waste in excess of the legal limit into Kempenfelt Bay, on which it was located. This was in spite of municipal and provincial environment ministry officials frequently warning and threatening to lay charges against the company between 1969 and 1977. After the plant closed, and a condominium was to be built on the site, the soil proved so contaminated with chromium that it had to be removed to a landfill site before the construction could proceed. It was at this stage that the Simcoe County Injured Workers' Association finally took up the employees' cause at the Workers' Compensation Board and the case became public.[7] Through such events, unions have learned of employers' past abuse of their employees' health and their similar neglect of the natural environment.

Unions have also expanded their lobbying activities for better protective legislation, tougher regulations, more information about toxic substances in the workplace and financial aid to train their members about workplace hazards to improve work environments.[8] Governments have responded by setting up inquiries like the Ontario Royal Commission on Matters of Health and Safety to which, for example, the Ontario Federation of Labour (OFL) and the ECWU have presented briefs advocating an immediate reduced exposure to asbestos, a ban on its future use and rapid action to regulate new hazardous chemicals in the workplace.[9] As such, occupational health and safety issues have gained publicity and government attention, new legislation has been introduced which recognizes the worker's right to refuse unsafe work without reprisal, the right to information about work hazards, and the right to participate through joint worksite health and safety committees in resolving problems. The 1972 Saskatchewan legislation set the precedent and by the end of the 1970s, Ontario, Quebec, Alberta, Manitoba, New Brunswick, and Newfoundland had passed similar legislation. In 1978, for example, Ontario amended its Occupational Health and Safety Act, and workers won the right to refuse unsafe work and to be part of mandatory joint health and safety committees. In the following three years, 435 workers exercised their rights to refuse dangerous work.[10]

In 1988, Ontario adopted the Workplace Hazardous Materials Information System agreement, a national standard for testing and labelling substances, and disclosing information and educating workers about them.[11] In 1989–90, Bill 208 introduced closer scrutiny of workplaces by the joint committees. It placed the onus for responsible occupational health and safety decisions on workers and their employers and strengthened the requirement that workers or unions select their own representatives. Joint workplace committees became mandatory in more places of work and were given new powers "to obtain information about tests of any equipment, biological, chemical or physical agents in the workplace," to consult with the employer concerning tests and testing procedures, and the controversial right to "bilaterally shut down operations under dangerous circumstances."[12] Monthly inspections of the workplace were required by the joint committees and employers had to respond promptly in writing to joint committee recommendations and provide a timetable for implementing recommendations to which it agreed. Employers in specified industries "wherever workers could be exposed to hazardous biological, chemical or physical agents" were required to establish workplace medical surveillance programs with medical examinations and tests. The bill increased the powers of government inspectors; employers were required to share more information with workers and to pay for more occupational health and safety related services. Enacted in January 1991 after intense debate inside and outside the legislature over issues like the right of certified joint committee members to stop work, expanded grounds for work refusals, and mandatory pay for workers investigating work refusals, the legislation meant that virtually all Ontario employers were required to implement and enforce an open occupational health and safety policy for their particular businesses. It ensured adequate training and better informed worker representatives and allowed "workers to act meaningfully in the workplace to protect their own health and safety."[13]

Despite improved legislation, more empowered government inspectors and joint health and safety committees in workplaces across the country, the Canadian labour movement has continued to view collective bargaining as its preferred route to achieve ongoing, lasting occupational health and safety improvements. Once a law is established, labour has used it as a basis for further negotiation because "what has been achieved in health and safety laws has resulted from breakthroughs by strong unions and sometimes by strike action," as in the 1980s when there were many walkouts and wildcat strikes over issues of occupational disease and safety.[14] The reason for Canadian unions resorting to the collective bargaining approach is not only because it works at the local level of the job. It also protects unions from the effects of negative changes in legislation or loss of rights enacted by newly elected provincial governments. When, for example, workers became discouraged that the Ontario government might weaken Bill 208 and drop the work-stoppage provision, Local 1000 Canadian Union of Public Employees (CUPE) negotiated and won a stoppage provision in its contract, and this strategy was adopted in many steelworkers' bargaining sessions as well.[15] Joint occupational health and safety committees can range from small local groups without any authority to make policy or spending decisions, to larger committees with real clout. In the former case, collective bargaining supplements their work. In cases where the law is broken, and inspectors are slow or negligent, workers fall back on union negotiations.

Some unions have also gone beyond legislative lobbying by establishing their own health and occupational centres. In 1984, the Manitoba Federation of Labour established and ran an Occupational Health Centre in Winnipeg. In Hamilton, unions set up a Workers' Occupational Health Clinic for both union and non-union workers.[16] In 1993 the OFL began to broaden its focus when it pushed for protection of workers who refused to perform work that would damage the environment and the Ontario NDP government responded with an Environmental Bill of Rights which protected workers who blew the whistle on polluting employers.[17] Thus the experience gained by unions fighting occupational health and safety issues in work environments in the 1970s and 1980s, broadened to include community health and safety issues in the environment as a whole in the 1990s.

As workers linked environmental problems on the job to broader community issues, union conventions in the late 1980s adopted new policy positions. In 1988 the Canadian Labour Congress (CLC) established an Environmental Committee to educate trade unionists and forge links with environmental groups.[18] In 1989, the USWA National Policy Conference adopted a comprehensive environmental policy called "the Steelworkers' Environmental Action Plan." In 1990, the CLC convention passed a statement entitled "A New Decade: Our Future." It contained a section on "sustainable prosperity" which stated that Canadian workers were no strangers to environmental problems as "in our workplaces, the health and safety problems our members face are on the front lines of the fight for a cleaner environment" and workers in their communities have joined other Canadians in reacting to problems of air pollution, waste disposal, and degradation of public recreational resources. It recommended tougher environmental standards and penalties for their violation, as well as protection and compensation for workers whose jobs were affected by environmental reforms.[19]

In 1991, the first Canadian Auto Workers (CAW) conference on the environment[20] established an Environment Fund, and Local 636 in Woodstock Ontario negotiated a contract clause whereby the company paid an amount into the fund equal to pay for a minute per month per employee, and this agreement also resulted in the establishment of a joint union–management environment committee to discuss issues and develop educational materials. Another CAW Local in Coquitlam B.C. extended its health and safety committee at Co-Van International to include the environment. It was mandated to eliminate or reduce pollutants, promote recycling, and employees were given "whistleblower protection" if they reported releases of hazardous materials into the air, earth, or water systems, to the authorities.[21]

In 1991, the Pulp, Paper and Woodworkers of Canada demanded laws to eliminate chlorine-based products in Canada by 1995 as "chlorine dioxide is harmful to workers and the environment, and organochlorines threaten the fisheries and public health."[22] In June 1991, Local 6500 USWA and Inco created an Environmental Awareness Committee to review environmental issues and enlarge the focus of the existing safety and health committee. A joint press release stated that "for the first time in Canadian industrial labour relations," concern about the environment has led to the establishment of a senior level union-management committee "whose purpose is to identify environmental problems in the workplace and recommend solutions."[23] In 1989, Inco committed $500 million to contain 90 percent of its sulphur dioxide emissions by 1994. The company also increased its efforts to clean up conditions both inside and outside the workplace, after being "hounded" by the union to "clean up its act" and attacked by environmentalists as a major producer of pollutants which caused acid rain.[24] In Manitoba, the Government Employees Association developed an environmental strategy to evaluate the health and safety of government offices but also provided its members with information to improve the environmental standards in their homes.[25]

At the national level in 1993, the CLC (with government, company, and environmental representatives) participated in the Accelerated Reduction and Elimination of Toxic Substances program, which aimed to establish a national standard for pollution prevention. The labour congress explicitly linked the use of toxic substances in the workplace to the destruction of the community environment and stated that it was concerned for "the health and safety of workers who must use pollutants on the job. Its other [concern] was to secure income and job protection for anyone displaced from work as a result of pollution elimination programs."[26]

Union/Community Co-operation

In the 1990s, the connection between occupational health and safety issues on the job and broader environmental concerns in the community was made more frequently in labour circles. Some examples of union/community co-operation have emerged but not as many as might be expected, given the labour movement's record of working to improve health and safety standards. In the early 1980s, unions like the steelworkers and paperworkers worked with grassroots organizations such as Great Lakes United and Acid Rain Coalition to fight toxic pollutants in the air and water systems in eastern Canada.[27] The Green Work Alliance (GWA) in Toronto led by Nick de Carlo of Brampton Local 1967 CAW and Stan Gray of Greenpeace, worked towards a green future by promoting environmentally friendly industries. Formed as traditional manufacturing plants in Toronto and Mississauga closed, the GWA worked under the banner "Green Jobs not Pink Slips" and sought to retrain workers for jobs in green industries organized to conserve energy and water supplies. In 1993, however, Greenpeace management left GWA after the unions attempted unsuccessfully to organize its office staff, an episode which reflected the class tensions which sometimes prevent greater union/environmentalist co-operation.[28]

A more successful example of co-operation is the non-profit Suzuki Environmental Foundation, created in 1981 by the United Fishermen and Allied Workers' Union, named after an early trade unionist and environmentalist. Most of its initial funding came from the sale of herring, caught and donated by members. In the 1990s, as the B.C. fishery was threatened with pollution, the Suzuki Foundation fought back by organizing campaigns to stop pulp mill pollution, the destruction of estuaries, dam projects, fish farms, poor logging practices, and other actions that endangered fish stocks and habitat. It also planned to "conduct workshops that teach loggers about the biology of the salmon stream, which logging practices are a violation of the Federal Fisheries Act and how we can work together to stop the damage."[29] Rank and file union members with the help of federal government money cleaned up the marshlands around the Fraser River which provide oxygen and resting spots for salmon as they go down the river to the ocean.

In its work, Foundation members have sat on government advisory committees and joined forces with First Nations councils, community organizations, environmental groups, as well as other unions. One such coalition—the Georgia Strait Alliance—took the Greater Vancouver Regional District to court for several pollution infractions under the Federal Fisheries Act to prevent water from a sewage overflow pipe, which was lethal to fish, from being spewed into the waterfront.[30]

The Suzuki Foundation represents people whose jobs depend on a healthy environment, and who do not approach environmental issues simply as preservationists. Through coalitions of groups, activists like Miranda Holmes learned that "it's really important for unions and environmental groups to join forces" and stress their mutual interests but it is made more difficult when business and the mainstream media perpetuate a jobs-versus-environment approach.[31]

Conclusion

Labour has a vested interest in resolving health and safety problems in the workplace as many of today's most pressing environmental issues like exposure to toxic substances such as asbestos and PCBs began as on-the-job health and safety issues. The advantage to environmentalists of having unions engaged in cleaning up the environment is that often they can work on preventing problems at the source—on job sites. As a CLC policy statement put it, "as trade unionists we understand instinctively the conflicts between the corporate bottom line and the public interest that underlie much of the environmental debate." From the environmentalist side, Paul Muldoon of Pollution Probe has acknowledged the need for labour's expertise in workplace safety and trade issues in relation to toxic substances.[32] "Often," as Reg Basken of the ECWU has noted, "trade unionist action to protect their members from ... industry-based hazards is the first and most essential step towards ensuring public safety," as they contribute their organizing skills to assist community-based initiatives to confront broader environmental issues.

Co-operation between workers and environmentalists, however, remains difficult and the gulf partly reflects class tension, cultural differences, and a different perspective of the work process.[33] Workers (it is often assumed by middle-class environmentalists) are only interested in keeping their jobs at any cost, while some workers (who feel frustrated at environmentalists' apparent lack of concern about disappearing employment) stereotype environmentalists as hopeless romantics bent on preserving wilderness for the sake of a few owls.[34] Greater dialogue and co-operation between the two groups might lead to workable policies including short-term "workers' environmental compensation funds" and the longer term development and promotion of green industries.

There is thus a link between social equity and ecology, as the power imbalance in society has created both socio-economic injustices and environmental damage,[35] but groups concerned about the environment often have different priorities depending on their vulnerability in a rapidly changing economy. In its Statement on the Environment 1990, the CAW recognized that the battle for a healthier environment must be fought on several fronts, that "the interests of the union and the environmental movements largely coincide," and that they must work together.[36] But the issues remain complex. The CAW appeared to be protecting jobs over the environment when it complained about the Ontario NDP government's proposed tax on "gas guzzling" cars; however, the union has also developed pro-environment policies, recognized the damage of cars' emissions to the environment, and supported more public transit, tighter emission controls for cars, and the manufacturing of vehicles which run on alternative fuels.[37] In 1991, Keith Newman of the Canadian Paperworkers' Union expressed the belief that regulations in the pulp and paper industry need not harm employment security and environmental protection, but added that there may be instances of "job blackmail" whereby workers might be convinced by employers that their support of pollution controls could lead to layoffs. David Bennett of the CLC believes that strategies to improve on ecology can succeed if they are combined with an industrial strategy, which must involve "transition measures for workers caught up in environmental change."[38]

Both labour and environmental groups consist of citizens who reside in communities where cleaning up pollution and maintaining biodiversity is essential to future public health.[39] Clearly, in the context of the global environmental issues looming in the twenty-first century, current class divisions between workers and environmentalists must be overcome for "the pollution that poisons workers also ruins communities and leads us to demand that the clean-up be both inside and outside the workplace at the same time."[40] Better communication can be facilitated by a more tolerant appreciation of the complexity of the issues, by environmentalists becoming more sensitized to how class relates to ecological issues, and by workers developing more consciousness of the environmental and social consequences of their actions. Such an approach will hopefully transcend the polarized slogan "Jobs or the Environment" so often used in the mainstream media.

The greatest problem confronting both workers and environmentalists, however, is the strength of the industrial community and its pursuit of growth at the expense of the environment.[41] This challenge is reflected in labour's many efforts to rely on direct action and collective bargaining rather than safety legislation and government enforcement of regulations. This is no doubt a global trend as governments are cutting spending and services by relaxing work safety legislation or making safety regulations meaningless as monies for enforcement are cut. This may be particularly acute in Canada, where the dominant resource industries have been destructive to the environment, and where "job-blackmail" of workers and governments by resource corporations figure prominently. In Ontario, the internationally renowned

Occupational Disease Panel, an independent agency providing objective information on workers' compensation claims, was closed by the Harris government in Ontario after intense lobbying by the provincial mining industry.[42] In Nova Scotia, 26 coal miners lost their lives in the Westray coal mine explosion in 1992 because of the province's blinkered pursuit of resource revenue at the expense of workers' safety.[43] And in Quebec, which harbours the world's second-largest chrysolite asbestos industry, "the danger of asbestos is almost a forbidden subject" as the government focuses on job creation.[44]

Endnotes

1. Elaine Bernard, "Labour and the Environment: A Look at B.C.'s 'War in the Woods,'" in *Getting on Track: Social Democratic Strategies for Ontario*, ed. Daniel Drache (Montreal and Kingston: McGill-Queen's University Press, 1992), 202; Robert Paehlke and Pauline Vaillancourt Roseneau, "Environment/Equity Tensions in North American Politics," *Policy Studies Journal* 21, No. 4 (1993), 672.
2. H.V. Nelles, *The Politics of Development: Forests, Mines, and Hydro-Electric Power in Ontario 1849–1941* (Toronto: Macmillan, 1974); Eric Tucker, *Administering Danger in the Workplace: The Law and Politics of Occupational Health and Safety Regulation in Ontario 1850–1914* (Toronto: University of Toronto Press, 1990).
3. *The Facts February* (1985), 40; this trend was also true of the United States. Daniel Faber and James O'Connor, "The Struggle for Nature: Environmental Crises and the Crisis of Environmentalism in the United States," *Capitalism, Nature, Socialism* 2 (1989), 12–21.
4. *Toronto Telegram* June 30, 1971.
5. *At the Source* 14, No. 1 (1993), 6.
6. *Globe and Mail* September 7, 1981.
7. Julian Zuckerbrot, "A Tale from the Dark Side: What Went Wrong at Robson-Lang," *Occupational Health and Safety Canada* 6, No. 5 (1990), 70–76.
8. *The Facts* February (1988), 40.
9. *Globe and Mail* February 6, 1978.
10. Stan Gray, "The Squeaky Wheel," *Occupational Health and Safety Canada* 6, No. 4 (1991), 114; "Workers have more and more used their right to refuse unsafe work. At times they have also engaged in massive shop action—exacting an economic penalty in order to force employers to clean-up." The vast majority—97 percent in Quebec between 1981 and 1988—of right-to-refuse cases have been carried out by unionized workers, as non-union workers either did not know their rights or were afraid of employer reprisals. Scott Williams, "The Right to Refuse Unsafe Work," *Occupational Health and Safety Canada* 4, No. 1 (1988), 25. By the time this legislation was introduced, 48 percent of unionized workplaces already had such committees in place and the right to refuse dangerous work had also been won by many union negotiators before it was entrenched in law. Thus such legislation was often based on concessions already won in union contracts. Peter Renter, "Paradise Lost," *Occupational Health and Safety Canada* 4, No. 5 (1988).
11. David Bennett, "Environmental Contaminants: Legal Protection," *Canadian Labour* (February 1987), 13.
12. Lee-Anne Jack, "Behind the Headlines," *Occupational Health and Safety Canada* 6, No. 5 (1990), 79–80.
13. William R. Watson, "Ontario's Bill 208: What You May Have Missed," *Occupational Health and Safety Canada*, 7, No. 2 (1991), 108.
14. Renter, op. cit.
15. *At the Source* 11, No. 1 (1990).
16. *Steel Shots* November 29, 1984.
17. CAIM/CLC(1993), 2; Glen William, "Legislating Rights and Responsibilities," *Occupational Health and Safety Canada* (Sept/Oct 1992), 37–39; see also OPSEU's Proposal for An Environmental Bill of Rights, March 1, 1991, file-Pollution and the Environment 1991, Centre for Industrial Relations Library, University of Toronto.

18. In 1993 the CLC collaborated with the National Round Table on the Environment and the Economy to publish a handbook for union environment committees and joint labour–management environment committees. Ted Schrecker, *Sustainable Development: Getting There From Here* (Ottawa: CLC and the National Roundtable on the Environment and Economy, 1993)
19. CLC Convention 1990, Document #14, "A New Decade: Our Future," Pollution file, Centre for Industrial Relations Library, University of Toronto; Michelle Walsh, "Safety and Health: Cleaning Up Our Act," *Canadian Labour* (Spring 1988), 29.
20. CAW Memo, 21, No. 9 (March 15, 1991).
21. *CAW Health and Safety Newsletter* (August 1993), 7.
22. *CCU Bulletin* (May 1991).
23. *Steel* Labor 54, No. 2 (1991)
24. *Globe and Mail* January 5, 1989
25. Contact 21, No. 3 (1991).
26. *CALM/CLC Today* (1993).
27. *Labour Times* (April 1994), 8.
28. *Labour Times* (June 1993); Stan Gray, "Labour's Environmental Challenge," *Canadian Dimension* 28, No. 4 (1994); Roger Keil, "Green Work Alliance: The Political Economy of Social Ecology," *Studies in Political Economy* 44 (1994), 36.
29. *Our Times* 13, No. 1 (1994).
30. The Canadian Paperworkers Union and PPWC also participated with environmental organizations in the Save the Georgia Strait coalition.
31. *Our Times* 13, No. 1 (1994)
32. "A New Decade: Our Future," op. cit.; *Our Times* (April 1994).
33. Bill Megalli, "Jobs Versus the Environment: Difficult Decisions Ahead," *Labour Gazette* (June 1978), 228–32. The cultural gulf between environmentalists and loggers has been analyzed as a distinction between "clearcut culture" and "cathedral culture" by Michael M'Gonigle, "The Stein River: Wilderness, Culture and Human Survival," *Alternatives* 5, No. 3 (1988), 12–21.
34. *Daily Labour Report* (The Bureau of National Affairs, Washington D.C.), 62 (April 2, 1993). The natural resource conflict in the western United States over the fate of old-growth forests became a lightning rod of the Endangered Species Act (ESA) as environmentalists argued in court that the northern spotted owl was threatened. They won several injunctions from 1989 to cease logging on federal lands and challenged federal timber sales and management plans. Nine million acres of federal timberland in Oregon, Washington and California were closed to logging resulting in the loss of 150 lumber and plywood mills and the layoff of 15,000 workers, which the Sierra Club argued were a small fraction of jobs in the regional economy of the States affected by the issue. The owl became a symbol of balancing species preservation with economic considerations.
35. Stan Gray, "Double Exposure: The Environment as a Worker's Issue," *Our Times* (June 1992), 28–29; Stan Gray, "Democracy, Jobs and the Environment," *Canadian Dimension* 26, No. 8 (1992), 17.
36. *CAW Contact* 20, No. 33 (1990).
37. *Labour Times* (April 1994).
38. *Labour Research Exchange* (April 1992), 8.
39. Stan Gray, "Labour's Environmental Challenge," *Canadian Dimension* 28, No. 4 (1994). He advocates that unions bring more environmental issues to the bargaining table, even as they deal with the effects of recession and global economic restructuring because of the alarming 1994 report of the IJC which showed ecological damage harming fish, plants, water, and people.
40. David Bennet, "How Will Labour Handle Environmental Issues," *Our Times* (November 1990), 11.
41. Glen Williams, "Greening the Canadian Political Economy," *Studies in Political Economy* 37 (Spring 1992): 5–30.
42. Canadian Broadcasting Corporation Radio 740 AM. April 13, 1997.
43. *Globe and Mail* December 2, 1997. The report of the disaster is entitled "The Westray Story: A Predictable Path to Disaster."
44. *Globe and Mail* November 25, 1997.

Chapter 21

Life in a Fast-Food Factory

Ester Reiter

The growth of large multinational corporations in the service industries in the post-World War II years has transformed our lives. The needs and tastes of the public are shaped by the huge advertising budgets of a few large corporations. The development of new industries has transformed work, as well as social life. This paper focuses on the technology and the labour process in the fast-food sector of the restaurant industry. Using Marx's description of the transitions from craft to manufacture to large-scale industry, it considers the changes in the restaurant industry brought about by the development of fast-food chains. The description of life in a fast-food factory is based on my experience working in a Burger King outlet in 1980/1.

The Rise of the Fast-Food Industry

Eating out is big business. The restaurant industry in Canada has grown from some 14,000 establishments in 1951 to nearly 30,000 in 1978.[1] Sales in 1982 were 9.6 billion dollars nationally, which, even taking into account the declining value of the dollar, is still a six-fold increase over the past thirty years.[2] Although people with higher incomes dine out more frequently, all Canadians are spending money on food away from home. In 1978, over 32 cents of every food dollar was spent on food outside the home.[3]

Since the late 1960s, fast-food restaurants have been growing at a much higher rate than independent restaurants, virtually colonizing the suburbs.[4] Local differences in taste and style are obliterated as each town offers the familiar array of trademarked foods: neat, clean, and orderly, the chains serve up the same goods from Nova Scotia to Vancouver Island. The casualties of this phenomenal growth are the small "mom and pop" establishments, rather than the higher-priced, full-service restaurants. Fast-food outlets all conform to a general pattern. Each has a limited menu, usually featuring hamburger, chicken, or fried fish. Most are part of a chain, and most require customers to pick up their own food at a counter.[5] The common elements are minimum delay in getting the food to the customer (hence "fast food") and prices that are relatively low compared to those at full-service restaurants.

The fast-food industry is an example of what Harry Braverman called the extension of the universal market.[6] That is, the family moves into the sphere of the market. The effect of this "extension" on the family has been varied. Often, new technology applied to some household task at first removes the activity from the home; later, still newer technologies return the activity to the home in an altered form. By the late 1930s, for example, many families had come to send a good part of their laundry to power laundries; later when washing machines were widely available, the laundry was returned to the home—to be washed most often, by women.[7] Similarly, the development of the movie industry during the first half of the twentieth century drew people out of their homes. After television was developed, however, the market at home proved more lucrative, and now virtually every Canadian family has at least one television set, while the movie industry has been declining since the 1950s.[8]

The entry of capital into the food production and consumption process has had several different effects. In the 1930s, for instance, techniques were developed for the quick freezing of foods. The perfection of these techniques made it possible to purchase increasingly diverse arrays of foods that need only be "heated and served." By the 1950s, the growth of large shopping-plaza supermarkets overwhelmed grocery stores, putting the small, independent corner grocer out of business. Shopping trips can be less frequent when large amounts of frozen and packaged foods are purchased, and the huge increase in families owning automobiles made possible visits to the more distant, large shopping plazas.

Seeking to supplement their sales to the supermarkets, large food processors like Kraft began to market their products to the restaurant industry in the late 1960s. Food production has been largely taken over by large corporations, but now different capital interests wrestle with each other to determine whether food consumption is going to take place in public businesses or in the home. Restaurant officials welcomed the new products (such as preportioned jellies, frozen entrees, canned soups) enthusiastically. In 1967, one restaurant official predicted that "custom-made food will soon be as luxurious as custom-made automobiles or shirts."[10] As these new processed, preportioned foods were introduced into public eating places, franchised restaurants began to appear in Canada. These were usually connected to larger parent companies that had started a few years earlier in the United States. "Franchising" confers the right, on payment of an agreed fee, to sell certain products under a recognized trade name; the items are backed by national advertisements and on-the-spot promotions. The products offered are limited in number and are produced in prescribed ways, using machinery specified by and purchased from the franchisor.[11]

During the early years, fast-food franchising seemed like a bottomless gold mine, and indeed a few western operators became millionaires when Colonel Sanders' Kentucky Fried Chicken was first franchised in Canada. The franchise system seemed to offer the small businessman the opportunity of a lifetime: permitting a big corporation to dictate how a business should be run promised to minimize risks in this very risky business. By 1970, *Canadian Hotel and Restaurant* magazine estimated that about 75 percent of all fast-food outlets were controlled by franchising companies. Three companies, Kentucky Fried Chicken, A&W, and Chicken Delight—all affiliates of United States corporations—together controlled 60 percent of the 1,457 franchised outlets in Canada. The large multinational corporations that produced grocery products extended their interest in the restaurant industry by entering it directly in the late 1960s with the purchase of restaurant chains. For example, Lever Brothers Ltd, a wholly owned subsidiary of Unilever, acquired A&W Food Services of Canada and Shopsy's Foods Ltd. General Foods acquired the White Spots restaurant chain in western Canada, as well as two other chains: Canterbury Foods (which ran the Crock 'n Block restaurants) and the "1867" restaurants. General Foods is one of the largest processors of packaged groceries, with products ranging from coffee (Maxwell House, Yuban, Sanka, Brim) to breakfast cereals and dessert foods under the "Jell-O," "Bird's Eye," and "Minute Brand" names.[12]

The largest of the fast-food restaurants—McDonald's—entered the Canadian market in 1968. Since May 1983, over 450 of its outlets were operating in Canada, posting $636.5 million in gross annual sales—part of an empire of 6,800 stores in 27 countries with more than $25 billion in sales in 1983. The second-largest fast-food chain is Burger King. Founded in 1954 by James McLamore and David Edgerton, Burger King became a wholly owned subsidiary of Pillsbury in 1967, during the first wave of mergers between packaged-food and restaurant chains. The company grew from 257 restaurants at the time of the merger to 3,022 by May 1981. About 130,000 people are employed in Burger Kings all over the world. By November 1982, there were 87 Burger King stores in Canada, 40 of them company-owned.[13] The Canadian-owned company stores operated at an average gross profit of 60 percent in 1980/81.

Transforming the Operations of a Kitchen

Until approximately 25 years ago, all restaurant work involved an extensive division of labour: a complex hierarchy within the kitchen required workers with varying levels of skill and training. For a restaurant to be successful, all workers had to co-ordinate their efforts. A supervisor's function was not only to ensure that the work was done, but to see that the various parts of the operation were synchronized. William Whyte, who studied the restaurant industry in the United States, described the production process:

> Timing and co-ordination are the keynotes of the operation. If the customer does not get his food when he wants it, he is upset. If the waitress cannot get it from the service pantry, she chafes at the delay. And so on down into the kitchen. A breakdown anywhere in the chain of production, transfer and service sends repercussions through the entire organization. No one can fail to feel its effects, for the restaurant is an organization made up of highly interdependent parts. If one part fails to function, the organization can no longer operate.
>
> The parts are the people who handle the food and adjust their work to each other. But cooks, pantry girls, waitresses, and other workers are not the only important parts. To keep this delicately adjusted machine functioning requires supervision of a high order. At each important point there must be a supervisor helping to organize the work of the employees and to organize their relations with each other to eliminate the friction and build up the co-operation essential to efficiency.[14]

This production arrangement resembles what Marx called "manufacture." In the restaurant described by William Whyte, the skill of the worker remains central to the production process. The commodity created (the meal served to the customer) is the social product of many workers' efforts. Human beings, using tools to assist them in their work, remain the organs of the productive mechanism.

In the fast-food industry, the machines, or the instruments of labour, assume a central place. Instead of assisting workers in the production of the meal, the machines tended by workers are dominant; we now have an objective organization of machines confronting the worker. Marx described this as the transition from "manufacture" to "large-scale industry."[15] Since the motion of the factory proceeds from the machinery and not from the worker, working personnel can continually be replaced. Frequent change in workers will not disrupt the labour process—a shift in organization applauded by *Harvard Business Review* contributor, Theodore Levitt.[16] According to Levitt, this new model is intended to replace the "humanistic concept of service" with the kind of technocratic thinking that in other fields has replaced "the high cost and erratic elegance of the artisan with the low-cost munificence of the manufacturer." McDonald's is a "supreme" example of this kind of thinking.

> The systematic substitution of equipment for people, combined with the carefully planned use and positioning of technology, enables McDonald's to attract and hold patronage in proportions no predecessor or imitator has managed to duplicate.... If machinery is

> to be viewed as a piece of equipment with the capability of producing a predictably standardized customer-satisfying output while minimizing the operating discretion of its attendant, that is what a McDonald's outlet is. It is a machine that produces with the help of totally unskilled machine tenders, a highly polished product. Through painstaking attention to total design and facilities planning, everything is built integrally into the machine itself, into the technology of the system. The only choice available to the attendant is to operate it exactly as the designers intended.

The labour process so admired by Levitt has been adopted by many of the large fast-food companies. In the case of Burger King, the adoption has been a literal one: Donald Smith, the operations executive at McDonald's who developed this system, was hired away in January 1977 to become president of Burger King. There, he initiated a number of projects under the heading "Operation Grand Slam," which changed the system of menu and food preparation in an effort to duplicate McDonald's success.[17]

Managing a Store

The brain centre of all Burger King outlets, company-owned or franchised, lies in Burger King headquarters in Miami, Florida. It is there that the Burger King bible, the *Manual of Operating Data*, is prepared. The procedures laid down in the manual must be followed to the letter by all Burger King stores. To ensure that procedures are indeed followed, each outlet is investigated and graded twice yearly by a team from regional headquarters. Termed a "Restaurant Operations Consultation," the assessment administered by the investigators gives each store a numerical grade according to a detailed 43-page list of what to look for and how many points each particular aspect is worth. When a store is being investigated, both managers and workers clean frenetically and work as hard as possible. A great deal depends on these investigations, as a manager could be transferred or demoted, or a franchisee's license withdrawn, if the showing is poor.

The criteria for grading a store give heavy weighting to those items that are crucial to a store's profitability. Profitability rests primarily on the volume of a store's sales and the cost of those sales. Therefore, cleanliness, not only in the food-production area, but also in the toilets and the surrounding parking area is stressed so that customers will be attracted to the store. In order to maximize volume and minimize labour costs, there is tremendous emphasis on what Burger King management calls SOS or speed of service. The demand on an individual unit's production capacity can fluctuate as much as 1,000 percent over an hour in the period before a lunch or dinner to the height of the meal rush. Demand is at its peak during the lunch hour, which accounts for about 20 percent of sales for the day; the more people served during the hours of 12 p.m. to 1 p.m., the higher the sales volume in the store.

Up Front, the Burger King publication for store managers, reminds them that "an aware manager understands that maintaining speed of service is like putting money in the bank."[18] The publication refers to Miami studies that show customers will wait patiently for only three minutes from the moment of entering the store; after that, they will walk away. Ideally, then, service time should never exceed three minutes.[19] Labour costs are also kept down by minimizing the use of full-time workers and by hiring minimum-wage part-time workers. Workers are asked to fill out an availability sheet when they are hired, indicating the hours they can work. Particularly when students are involved, management pressures them to make themselves as available as possible, though no guarantees are provided for how many hours a week of work they will be given, or on which days they will be asked to work.

Burger King pushed the common restaurant industry practice of using part-time workers one step further in 1978 with the development of a new labour-scheduling method called the "people game." Under this new system, hourly sales projections are recorded, based upon the previous three weeks' sales. Hourly manning guides are then used to allot labour for each hour's projected sales. Scheduling is done each week for the coming week and workers are expected to come to the store and check the labour schedule each week to see when they are supposed to show up. The *Manual of Operating Data* recommends that as many short shifts as possible be assigned, so that few breaks will be required. This rule, the manual notes, is especially important in areas where labour laws require paid breaks.

Food and paper costs make up about 40 percent of the cost of sales in Burger King outlets. These costs are essentially fixed, owing to company requirements that all Burger King outlets buy their stock from approved distributors. While such a policy offers the advantages of bulk purchasing, it also ties each outlet to costs set by head-office negotiations, leaving little room for purchase–cost reductions. In effect, individual stores have control over food costs in only two areas—"waste" of food and meals provided to employees. Both together make up less than 4 percent of the cost of sales. "Waste" consists of food pre-prepared for lunch and dinner shifts that is not sold in the time limit set for each food (10 minutes for sandwiches, 5 minutes for fries). The discarded food is carefully counted and recorded after each meal rush. Employees are under pressure to have enough food ready so that customers can be served quickly, but are held responsible for any "waste" that results. A chart on the kitchen wall graphs the waste percentage each day. Employee meals are also monitored, and limits on food items available to workers are imposed. For example, while workers were formerly allowed any sandwich, fries or dessert, and a drink, they are now allowed a meal costing not more than $2.50 in menu prices. A manager must inspect all choices, and initial the meal selection listed by workers on their time cards.

Store operations are designed from head office in Miami. In 1980, this office commissioned a study to find ways of lowering labour costs, increasing workers' productivity, and maintaining the most efficient inventories. The various components of a restaurant's operations were defined: customer-arrival patterns, manning or positioning strategies, customer/cashier interactions, order characteristics, production-time standards, stocking rules, and inventory. Time-motion reports for making the various menu items, as well as corporate standards for service were also included in the calculation, and the data were all entered into a computer. By late 1981, it was possible to provide store managers not only with a staffing chart for hourly sales—indicating how many people should be on the floor given the predicted volume of business for that hour—but also where they should be positioned, based on the type of kitchen design. Thus, although staffing had been regulated since the late 1970s, what discretion managers formerly had in assigning and utilizing workers has been eliminated. The use of labour is now calculated precisely, as is any other objectively defined component of the system, such as store design, packaging, and inventory.[20]

Having determined precisely what workers are supposed to be doing and how quickly they should be doing it, the only remaining issue is that of getting them to perform to specifications. "Burger King University," located at headquarters in Miami was set up to achieve this goal. Housed in a remodelled art gallery, the multimillion-dollar facility is staffed by a group of "professors" who have worked their way up in the Burger King system to the rank of district manager. Burger King trains its staff to do things "not well, but right," the Burger King way.[21] Tight control over Burger King restaurants throughout the world rests on standardizing operations—doing things the "right" way—so that outcomes are predictable. The manager of a Burger King outlet does not necessarily need any knowledge of restaurant operations because the company provides it. What Burger King calls "people skills" are required; thus a job description for a manager indicated that he/she

- Must have good verbal communication skills
- Must have patience, tact, fairness, and social sensitivity in dealing with customers and hourly employees

- Must be able to supervise and motivate team of youthful employees and conduct himself/herself in a professional manner
- Must present a neat, well-groomed image
- Must be willing to work nights, weekends, and holidays.[22]

In 1981, a new crew-training program, designed as an outcome of the computer-simulation study was developed. The training program is called "The Basics of Our Business" and is meant to "thoroughly train crew members in all areas of operations and to educate them on how Burger King and the restaurant where they work ... fit into the American free-enterprise system." In addition, the training program involves supervised work at each station, and a new feature that requires every employee to pass a standardized test on appropriate procedures for each station in the store.

Burger King thus operates with a combination of control techniques: technology is used to simplify the work and facilitate centralization, while direct control or coercion is exercised on the floor to make sure the pace of the work remains swift. "If there's time to lean, there's time to clean," is a favourite saying among managers. In fact, workers are expected to be very busy all the time they are on shifts, whether or not there are customers in the store. Sitting down is never permissible; in fact, the only chair in the entire kitchen is in the manager's office in a glassed-in cubicle at the rear of the kitchen. From there, the manager can observe the workers at their jobs. The application of these techniques is supported by a legitimizing ideology that calls for "patience, fairness, and social sensitivity" in dealing with customers in order to increase sales and profits "for the betterment of Burger King corporation and its employees."[23]

Working at Burger King

I did fieldwork on the fast-food industry by working at a Burger King outlet in suburban Toronto in 1980/1. The Burger King at which I worked was opened in 1979, and by 1981 was the highest volume store in Canada with annual sales of over one million dollars. Everything in the customers' part of the store was new, shiny, and spotlessly clean. Live plants lent a touch of class to the seating area. Muzak wafted through the air, but customers sat on chairs designed to be sufficiently uncomfortable to achieve the desired customer turnover rate of one every 20 minutes. Outside the store, customers could eat at concrete picnic tables and benches in a professionally landscaped setting, weather permitting. Lunches, particularly Thursdays, Fridays, and Saturdays, were the busiest times, and during those periods, customers were lined up at all the registers waiting to be served. During the evenings, particularly on Friday nights, families with young children were very much in evidence. Young children, kept amused by the plastic giveaway toys provided by the restaurant and sporting Burger King crowns, sat contentedly munching their fries and sipping their carbonated drinks.

Workers use the back entrance at Burger King when reporting for work. Once inside, they go to a small room (about seven by twelve feet), which is almost completely occupied by an oblong table where crew members have their meals. Built-in benches stretch along both sides of the wall, with hooks above for coats. Homemade signs, put up by management, decorate the walls. One printed, framed, sign read,

WHY CUSTOMERS QUIT

1% die
2% move away
5% develop other friendships
9% competitive reasons
14% product dissatisfactions
68% quit because of ATTITUDE OF INDIFFERENCE TOWARDS CUSTOMER BY RESTAURANT MANAGER OR SERVICE PERSONNEL

Another sign reminded employees that only 1/3 ounce of ketchup and 1/9 ounce of mustard is supposed to go on the hamburgers; a crew member using more is cheating the store, while one using less is not giving customers "value" for their dollar.

The crew room is usually a lively place. An AM/FM radio is tuned to a rock station while the teenage workers coming off or on shift talk about school and weekend activities or flirt with each other. Children and weddings are favourite topics of conversation for the older workers. In the evenings, the talk and horsing around among the younger workers gets quite spirited, and now and then a manager appears to quieten things down. Management initiatives are not all geared to control through discipline; social activities such as skating parties, baseball games, and dances are organized by "production leaders" with the encouragement of the managers—an indication that the potentially beneficial effects for management of channelling the informal social relationships at the workplace are understood. Each worker must punch a time card at the start of a shift. The management urges people to come upstairs five minutes before starting time. The time card, however, is not to be punched until its time for the scheduled shift to actually begin. A positioning chart, posted near the time clock, lists the crew members who are to work each meal, and indicates where in the kitchen they are to be stationed.

There are no pots and pans in the Burger King kitchen. As almost all foods enter the store ready for the final cooking process, pots and pans are not necessary. Hamburgers arrive in the form of patties; french fries are pre-cut and partially pre-cooked; so are the chicken, fish, and veal to be used in sandwiches. Buns are pre-cut and ready to be toasted, while condiments like pickles and onions arrive in the store pre-sliced. Lettuce comes pre-shredded; only the tomatoes are sliced on the premises. The major kitchen equipment consists of the broiler/toaster, the fry vats, the milkshake and coke machines, and the microwave ovens. In the near future, new drink machines will be installed in all Burger King outlets that will automatically portion the drinks; the hot-cocoa machine already operates in this way. Even when made from scratch, hamburgers do not require particularly elaborate preparation, and whatever minimal decision-making might once have been necessary is now completely eliminated by machines. At Burger King, hamburgers are cooked as they pass through the broiler on a conveyor belt at a rate of 835 patties per hour. Furnished with a pair of tongs, the worker picks up the burgers as they drop off the conveyor belt, puts each on a toasted bun, and places the hamburgers and buns in a steamer. The jobs may be hot and boring, but they can be learned in a matter of minutes.

The more interesting part of the procedure lies in applying condiments and microwaving the hamburgers. The popularity of this task among Burger King employees rests on the fact that it is unmechanized and allows some discretion to the worker. As the instructions for preparing a "Whopper" (the Burger King name for a large hamburger) indicates, however, management is aware of this area of worker freedom and makes strenuous efforts to eliminate it by outlining exactly how this job is to be performed:

- remove preassembled sandwich from steamer
- sandwiches in the steamer are good for 10 minutes maximum
- do not take more than 2 sandwiches at one time
- the HEEL which is the lower part of the sandwich is composed of bun heel and meat patty goes in whopper carton
- on the mat we place 4 pickle slices evenly over the meat on each corner
- then we add 1/2 oz. ketchup evenly in a spiral circular motion, over the pickles, starting from the outside edges of the meat and work your way to centre
- then place 1/2 oz. of onions evenly over the ketchup in such a way that there will be a bit of onion in every bite of the sandwich....

Despite such directives, the "Burger and Whopper Board" positions continue to hold their attraction for the workers, for this station requires two people to work side by side, and thus allows the opportunity for conversation. During busy times, as well, employees at this station also derive some work satisfaction from their ability to "keep up." At peak times, a supply of ready-made sandwiches is placed in chutes ready for the cashiers to pick up; the manager decides how many sandwiches should be in the chutes according to a formula involving sales predictions for that time period. At such times, the challenge is to keep pace with the demand and not leave the cashiers waiting for their orders. The managers will sometimes spur the "Whopper-makers" on with cries of "Come on guys, let's get with it," or "Let's go, team."

As with the production of hamburgers, the cooking of french fries involves virtually no worker discretion. The worker, following directions laid out in the *Manual of Operating Data*, empties the frozen, pre-cut, bagged fries into fry baskets about two hours before they will be needed. When cooked fries are needed, the worker takes a fry basket from the rack and places it on a raised arm above the hot oil, and presses the "on" button. The arm holding the fry basket descends into the oil, and emerges two minutes and twenty seconds later; a buzzer goes off and the worker dumps the fries into the fry station tray where they are kept warm by an overhead light. To ensure that the proper portions are placed into bags, a specially designed tool is used to scoop the fries up from the warming table. Jobs at this station are generally reserved for boys, as the work goes more quickly with a strong wrist. The job can get quite hectic when only one worker is at the station because cooked fries must be on hand when needed. The fry-tender must put new baskets down, take the cooked fries out and bag them, and all the while make certain there are enough partially cooked onion rings ready. At peak periods, the worker seems to be running constantly to keep up with the buzzers. Working near the oil makes one feel slimy; teenagers working at this station commonly complain that they tend to develop pimples.

Even at this station, though, management is concerned about limiting what little worker discretion is possible. Despite the use of a specially designed scoop to control the portions each customer is given, a sign placed in the crew room for a few weeks admonished crew about being too generous with fry portions.

> FRY YIELD Fry yield is the amount of regular portions you get from the total amount of fries used. The ideal amount is 410 portions from each 100 lb. of fries used.
>
> At the moment our fry yield is in the unacceptable range of 365–395 portions of fries for each 100 lb. of fries which is below Burger King standards.

At the cash register, the "counter hostess" takes the order and rings it up on the computerized register. The "documentor" contains 88 colour-coded items, ensuring that all variations of an order are automatically priced. For example, a hamburger with extra tomatoes can be punched in, and the 10-cent charge for the extra tomatoes will appear on the printout. As a menu item is punched in at the counter, it will appear on printers in the appropriate location in the kitchen. In this manner, the worker at sandwiches, for example, can look up at the printer and check what kind of sandwich is required. When the customer hands over the money, the cashier rings in "amount tendered" and the correct amount of change to be returned to the customer is rung up. Thus, cashiers need only remember to smile and ask customers to come again. Although it takes a few days working at the cash register to build up speed, the basics can be learned in a few hours.

The computerized cash register not only simplifies ordering and payment, but is used to monitor sales and thus assist in staffing. If sales are running lower than expected, some workers will be asked to leave early. It is difficult for workers to turn down the managers' request: "Wouldn't you like to go home early today?" But on more than one occasion, workers complained that the cost of bus fare ate up almost their entire earning for that shift. Output at each station is also monitored through the cash register. Finally, the computer at all company stores is linked through a modem to the head office in Miami. Top management has access to information on the performance of each store on a daily basis, and this information is routed back to the Canadian division headquarters in Mississauga.

Unlike the tremendous variation in skills in running the restaurant of the 1940s, skill levels required in a Burger King have been reduced to a common denominator. In a traditional restaurant of the 1940s, there was a wide variation in the levels of skills needed to do each necessary job: a trained chef would have spent many years developing his or her craft, while the dishwasher would have learned the necessary skills in a few days. At Burger King, the goal is to reduce all skills to a common, easily learned level and to provide for cross-training. At the completion of the 10-hour training program, each worker is able to work at a few stations. Skills for any of the stations can be learned in a matter of hours; the simplest jobs, such as filling cups with drinks, or placing the hamburgers and buns on the conveyor belt, can be learned in minutes. As a result, although labour turnover cuts into the pace of making hamburgers, adequate functioning of the restaurant is never threatened by people leaving. However, if workers are to be as replaceable as possible, they must be taught not only to perform their jobs in the same way, but also to resemble each other in attitudes, disposition, and appearance. Thus, workers are taught not only to perform according to company rules, but also are drilled on personal hygiene, dress (shoes should be brown leather or vinyl, not suede), coiffure (hair tied up for girls and not too long for boys), and personality. Rule 17 of the handout to new employees underlines the importance of smiling: "Smile at all times, your smile is the key to our success."

While management seeks to make workers into interchangeable tools, workers themselves are expected to make a strong commitment to the store. If they wish to keep jobs at Burger King, they must abide by the labour schedule:

> You must be able to close two times a week, that is be available from four o'clock till midnight on weekdays, or 1 AM on Friday or Saturday nights. The schedules you fill in apply for the school semester. In the summer we know everybody can work all hours. All part timers (those who work after school) must indicate availability for weekends.[24]

Workers (especially teenagers) are, then, expected to adjust their activities to the requirements of Burger King. For example, workers must apply to their manager two weeks in advance to get time off to study for exams or attend family functions. Parents are seen by management as creating problems for the store, as they do not always appreciate Burger King's demand for priority in their children's schedules. Thus, the manager warns new trainees to "remember, your parents don't work here and don't understand the situation. If you're old enough to ask for a job, you're old enough to be responsible for coming."[25]

The Workers

One of the results of the transformation of the labour process from one of "manufacture" to that of "large-scale industry" is the emerging market importance of the young worker. While artisans require long training to achieve their skills, machine-tenders' primary characteristics are swiftness and endurance. Thus, young workers become ideal commodities: they are cheap, energetic, and in plentiful supply. As well, they can be used as a marketing tool for the industry: the mass-produced, smiling teenager, serving up the symbols of the good life in North America—hamburgers, cokes, and fries.

Making up about 75 percent of the Burger King workforce, the youngsters who worked after school, on weekends, and on holidays were called "part-timers." The teenage workers (about half of them boys, half girls) seemed to vary considerably in background. Some were college-bound youngsters who discussed their latest physics exam while piling on the pickles. Others were marking time until they reached the age of 16 and could leave school. One brother and sister had a father who was unemployed and ill; they were helping to pay the family's rent and food. Some of the teenagers spent all the money they earned on clothes, food, and entertainment, while others saved a portion of their earnings. Given the low pay, and the erratic scheduling, none of the Burger King workers could depend on their jobs for their total financial support.

The daytime workers—the remaining 25 percent of the workforce—were primarily married women of mixed economic backgrounds. Consistent with a recent study of part-time workers in Canada, most of these women contributed their wages to the family budget.[26] Although they were all working primarily because their families needed the money, a few women expressed their relief at getting out of the house, even to come to Burger King. One woman said: "At least when I come here, I'm appreciated. If I do a good job, a manager will say something to me. Here, I feel like a person. I'm sociable and I like being amongst people. At home, I'm always cleaning up after everybody and nobody ever notices!"[27] Many of these women would arrive at work early in order to have a coffee and talk with one another—an interaction denied them in the isolation of their homes, where they are still responsible for all of the domestic labour.

Common to both the teenagers and the housewives was the view that working at Burger King was peripheral to their major commitments and responsibilities; the part-time nature of the work contributed to this attitude. Workers saw the alternative available to them as putting up with the demands of Burger King or leaving; in fact, leaving seemed to be the dominant form of protest. During my period in the store, on average, 11 people out of 94 hourly employees quit at each two-week pay period. While a few workers had stayed at Burger King for periods as long as a few years, many did not last through the first two weeks. The need for workers is constant; occasionally even the paper place-mats on the customers' trays invited people to work in the "Burger King family." "If you're enthusiastic and like to learn, this is the opportunity for you. Just complete the application and return it to the counter." At other times, bounties were offered for live workers. A sign that hung in the crew room for a few weeks read:

> Wanna make $10?
>
> It's easy! All you have to do is refer a friend to me for employment. Your friend must be able to work over lunch (Monday–Friday). If your friend works here for at least one month, you get $20. (And I'm not talking Burger Bucks either.)

Burger King's ability to cope with high staff turnover means that virtually no concessions in pay or working conditions are offered to workers to entice them to remain at Burger King. In fact, more attention is paid to the maintenance of the machinery than to "maintaining" the workers; time is regularly scheduled for cleaning and servicing the equipment, but workers may not leave the kitchen to take a drink or use the bathroom during the lunch and dinner rushes.

The dominant form—in the circumstances, the only easily accessible form—of opposition to the Burger King labour process is, then, the act of quitting. Management attempts to head off any other form of protest by insisting on an appropriate "attitude" on the part of the workers. Crew members must constantly demonstrate their satisfaction with working at Burger King by smiling at all times. However, as one worker remarked, "Why should I smile? There's nothing funny around here. I do my job and that should be good enough for them." It was not, however, and this worker soon quit. Another woman who had worked in the store for over a year also left. A crew member informed me that she had been fired for having a "poor attitude." The same crew member commented: "It's a wonder she wasn't fired a long time ago. She didn't enjoy the work and everybody knew it." I myself was threatened with expulsion from the store for having a "poor attitude" when I obeyed, without sufficient enthusiasm, an order to move from the front counter station to the broiler/steamer station.

Several other incidents underlined the extent to which Burger King could impose its will on workers. One involved the new plan—developed in Miami and introduced into the Toronto outlet in February 1982 at a crew meeting—to cut down labour costs by intensifying work. The new training program made conditions especially difficult for production leaders, who were now expected to give workers tests to make sure they knew their stations (exactly how to make "Whoppers," how long to put them in the microwave oven, etc.) without taking time off from their normal duties. Workers experienced great difficulty in following through on this training scheme because under the new guidelines, fewer people were available to serve the same number of customers; however, there was no organized opposition to the scheme. Nor was there organized opposition when meal allotments were reduced to a $2.50 limit. Although workers grumbled about the change, no one challenged the decision. The one instance in which staff objections forced the outlet to back down involved the right to work: all workers had been told that they were expected to attend the Burger King picnic, and that those normally scheduled to work at that time would have to lose a day's pay. (Crews from another store were to be sent over to keep the outlet running.) Four crew members objected, stating that they could not afford to lose pay by going to the picnic, and management allowed them to work. Such instances were few and far between, however. As one manager informed me, Burger King was careful to dismiss any crew person who was dissatisfied: "One bad apple could ruin the whole barrel."

Management control and lack of worker opposition is further explained by the fact that other jobs open to teenagers are no better, and in some cases are worse, than the jobs at Burger King. The workers at Burger King all agreed that any job that paid the full rather than the student minimum wage would be preferable to a job at Burger King; but they also recognized that their real alternatives would often be worse. Work at a donut shop, for example, also paid student minimum wage, under conditions of greater social isolation; baby-sitting was paid poorly; and the hours for a paper route were terrible. Work at Burger King was a first job for many of the teenagers, and they enjoyed their first experience of earning their own money. And at Burger King, these young men and women were in the position of meeting the public, even if the forms of contact were limited by a vocabulary developed in Burger King headquarters: "Hello. Welcome to Burger King. May I take your order?" Interaction with customers, who came in all shapes, sizes, and ages, had some intrinsic interest.

In sum, workers at Burger King are confronted with a labour process that puts management in complete control. Furnished with state-of-the-art restaurant technology, Burger King outlets employ vast numbers of teenagers and married women—a population with few skills and little commitment to working at Burger King. In part, this lack of commitment is understood through reference to a labour process that offers little or no room for work satisfaction. Most jobs can be learned in a very short time (a matter of minutes for some) and workers are required to learn every job, a fact that underlines the interchangeable nature of the jobs and the workers who do them. The work is most interesting when the store is busy; sweeping and mopping already clean floors, or wiping counters that do not really require wiping is not anyone's idea of necessary or interesting work. If the alternative to "leaning" is "cleaning," then it is far preferable to really be busy. Paradoxically, work intensity—Burger King's main form of assault on labour costs—remains the only aspect of the job that can provide any challenge for the worker. Workers would remark with pride how they "didn't fall behind at all," despite a busy lunch or dinner hour.

My findings in the fast-food industry are not very encouraging. In contrast to Michael Burawoy,[28] for example, who found that male workers in a unionized machine shop were able to set quotas and thereby establish some control over the labour process, I found that the women and teenagers at Burger King are under the sway of a labour process that eliminates almost completely the possibility of forming a workplace culture independent of, and in opposition to, management.

It would be reassuring to dismiss the fast-food industry as representing something of an anomaly in the workplace; teenagers will eventually finish school and become "real workers," while housewives with families are actually domestic workers, also not to be compared with adult males in more skilled jobs. Unfortunately, there are indications that the teenagers and women who work in this type of job represent not an anomalous but an increasingly typical kind of worker, in the one area of the economy that continues to grow—the service sector. The fast-food industry represents a model for other industries in which the introduction of technology will permit the employment of low-skilled, cheap, and plentiful workers. In this sense, it is easy to be pessimistic and find agreement with Andre Gorz's depressing formulation of the idea of work:

> The terms "work" and "job" have become interchangeable: work is no longer something that one *does* but something that one *has*.
>
> Workers no longer "produce" society through the mediation of the relations of production; instead the machinery of social production as a whole produces "work" and imposes it in a random way upon random, interchangeable individuals.[29]

The Burger King system represents a major triumph for capital: it has established a production unit with constant and variable components that are almost immediately replaceable. However, the reduction of the worker to a simple component of capital requires more than the introduction of a technology; workers' autonomous culture must be eliminated as well, including the relationships among workers, their skills, and their loyalties to one another. The smiling, willing, homogeneous worker must be produced and placed on the Burger King assembly line.

While working at Burger King, I saw for myself the extent to which Burger King has succeeded in reducing its workforce to a set of interchangeable pieces. However, I also saw how insistently the liveliness and decency of the workers emerged in the informal interaction that occurred. Open resistance is made virtually impossible by the difficulty of identifying who is responsible for the rules that govern the workplace: the workers know that managers follow orders coming from higher up. The very high turnover of employees indicates that workers come to understand that their interests and Burger King's are not one and the same. As young people and women begin to realize that their jobs in the fast-food industry are not waystations en route to more promising and fulfilling work, they will perhaps be moved to blow the whistle on the Burger King "team." The mould for the creation of the homogeneous worker assembling the standardized meal for the homogeneous consumer is not quite perfected.

Endnotes

1. Dominion Bureau of Statistics [hereafter DBS], *1951 Census* (Ottawa 1954), VII, table 6; Statistics Canada, Restaurants, *Caterers and Taverns Industry* (Ottawa 1978), cat. 65-535, table 1, 14.
2. Statistics Canada, *Market Research Handbook* (Ottawa 1983), cat. 63-224, tables 3—11, 169.
3. Statistics Canada, *Urban Family Food Expenditure* (Ottawa 1978), cat. 62-548; Dominion Bureau of Statistics, *Urban Family Food Expenditure* (Ottawa 1953), cat. 62-511.
4. Foodservice and Hospitality Magazine, *Fact File—Canada's Hospitality Business*, 4th ed. (Toronto n.d.).
5. This definition comes from the National Restaurant Association and is reprinted in Marc Leepson, "Fast Food, U.S. Growth Industry," *Editorial Research Reports* 7 (1978): 907.
6. See Harry Braverman, *Labor and Monopoly Capital* (New York 1954), 13.

7. Bonnie Fox, "Women's Domestic Labour and Their Involvement in Wage Work" (Ph.D. dissertation, University of Alberta 1980), table 15-A, 427.
8. M.C. Urquhart and K.H.A. Buckley, *Historical Statistics of Canada*, 2nd edition (Ottawa 1983), V410-416.
9. An example of this struggle is in a *Toronto Star* article called "Fast Foods—It's Giving the Supermarkets Indigestion," 25 April 1977, 1. Both fast-food and supermarket entrepreneurs state that they are competing for the same food dollar.
10. *Foodservice and Hospitality*, 23 October 1967, 5.
11. *Foodservice and Hospitality*, February 1981, 38.
12. Moody's *Industrial Manual* (New York 1981); J.M. Stopard, *World Directory of Multinational Enterprises* (Detroit 1981–2); and *Who Owns Whom: North America* (London 1982).
13. Promotional material from Burger King Canada head office in Mississauga, Ontario.
14. William Foote Whyte, *Human Relations in the Restaurant Industry* (New York 1948), 3.
15. Karl Marx, *Capital, vol. I* ([1867]; New York 1977), ch. xv.
16. Theodore Levitt, "Production Line Approach to Service," *Harvard Business Review* 50, no. I (Sept.–Oct. 1972): 51–2.
17. Robert L. Emerson, *Fast Food, the Endless Shakeout* (New York 1979), 291.
18. *Up Front* 2, no. 6 (Miami n.d.): 2.
19. A "Shape Up" campaign instituted at the beginning of 1982 attempted to set a new goal of a 2 1/2-minute service time.
20. "Kitchen design—the drive for efficiency," insert in *Nation's Restaurant News*, 31 August 1981.
21. Personal communication, Burger King "professor," 4 January 1982.
22. Job description handout for Burger King managers, 1981.
23. Handouts to Burger King crew members, 1981.
24. Burger King training session in local outlet, July 1981.
25. Ibid.
26. Labour Canada, *Commission of Inquiry into Part-Time Work* (Ottawa 1983) [Wallace commission].
27. Personal communication, Burger King worker, 8 August 1981.
28. Michael Burawoy, *Manufacturing Consent* (Chicago 1979).
29. Andre Gorz, *Farewell to the Working Class* (Boston 1982), 71.

Chapter 22

Globalization, Nationalism, and Internationalism

Sam Gindin

In Canada's case, globalization was hardly new; it essentially meant "continentalism"—further integration into the U.S. economy and, courtesy of American interests, an eventual move towards also bringing Mexico into that relationship. Despite the apparent inevitability of this trend, Canadians put up resistance well into the eighties. Even the federal Liberals had included nationalist elements in their policies during the early eighties (the National Energy Policy and the Foreign Investment Review Agency), and, of course, there was the massive mobilization against free trade in the mid-to-late eighties.

In contrast to the popular resistance to globalization and continentalism, a unique, favourable consensus had emerged within business. In the past, those in the business world in Canada had always been divided on the issues of free trade and nationalism, depending on whether they were concerned with protecting domestic markets or searching for foreign markets. However, by the eighties, no significant division remained. Big business was united on the free trade issue and small business fell into step behind that leadership. In spite of the feelings of some individual capitalists, not one section of business was part of the anti-free-trade alliance. In fact, it was becoming very difficult to define the term *Canadian* as it applied to business.

The Mulroney Tories became the vehicle through which big business defeated nationalist-leaning policies and, by way of the FTA, essentially achieved the constitutionalized economic integration into the United States. But even the Tories recognized the antagonism across the country; in the campaign that preceded the move towards the FTA, they knew enough to keep a safe distance from continentalism.

This popular opposition wasn't based solely on abstract nationalism: it was a result of the fact that the United States, once a model of the good life, no longer held much appeal. Further economic integration with the U.S. might be viewed as unavoidable from the perspective of uncertainty and fear, but it hardly had the power to move people with its promises and vision. The role of autoworkers in the economy placed the union at the centre of the debate on globalization and further integration into the United States; the response of the union placed it at the centre of the oppositional movement.

By the mid-seventies, the integration of the Canadians into the UAW and the American economy seemed complete: wages were virtually equal, the industry was more integrated than any other cross-border industry in the world, and the opposition to this integration had apparently collapsed. But during this period, Canadian workers began to shift the focus of their bargaining from the United States to Canada. Having achieved wage parity with the Americans, Canadians lost interest in catching up with the Americans.

In the past, Canadian UAW members, attempting to steadily improve their living standards, turned first to bargaining and then to national political action. The promise of the good life through collective bargaining was the ultimate lure of ties to the American union. But the situation had changed in two ways. First, as the post-war period of relative security and sharing in steady growth ended, the importance of bargaining seemed to diminish in relation to political events. Recession and restraint shifted union attention towards job policies and industrial strategies, legislated wage controls, labour laws as they affected organizing, and employment standards as they influenced health and safety and plant closures. To deal with such issues required addressing domestic politics; Canadians had to adopt a national perspective. For the Canadian UAW, building new ties with Canadian workers became more important than reinforcing the ties to American labour.

Second, even in bargaining itself—which remains a crucial element even as the significance of the political climate grows—the American leadership role was waylaid. The relative weakness of American labour, compared to the general militancy of the Canadian movement in this period, led to the greater attraction of wage comparisons within Canada over those in the U.S. It was in the process of bargaining, the *raison d'être* of unions, that the issues of Canadian autonomy and union direction came to a head.

The corporations had responded to the intensified competition they faced (and encouraged via free trade and capital mobility) with a new belligerence towards their workers. The companies, with auto in the lead, had made the transformation of collective bargaining relationships a crucial part of their overall strategy. The general disenchantment amongst Canadians with the American model was matched within the Canadian UAW by a growing disillusionment with the American union's response to this attack. The difference in the response of the Canadian UAW to the same corporate assault led to the split inside the UAW.

This conflict between the union and its parent organization reflected national differences, but more important, it stemmed from divergent strategies and notions of the role of unions. The Canadians were challenging the logic of globalization in a way that was both nationalist and concerned with the purpose of nationalism. Had the Canadian UAW even reluctantly adopted the American response, the union would have become just another vehicle for bringing American ideology and directions into Canada. Alternatively, since these differences over direction also existed to some extent within Canada, the UAW would have become a mechanism for reinforcing the weakest tendencies within Canadian labour. Instead, the Canadian UAW was able to retain its leading role in the labour movement and in broader struggles such as the fight against free trade.

The direction of the Canadian UAW seemed, however, to undermine the historic internationalism of progressive unionism. According to internationalists, corporate internationalism was based on competitiveness, while worker internationalism was based on solidarity. This definition was true, yet it skirted key problems. The international labour movement was too diverse to effectively co-ordinate activities. Each national labour movement was rooted in its distinct stage of development. Each movement faced a different context, and each was separated by cultural and ideological differences. These variations became most obvious in the difficulties encountered by Canada and the United States in their attempts to develop practical cross-border strategies. These problems arose in spite of the countries' relatively similar language and culture.

But more important, international solidarity couldn't work unless each of the labour movements became stronger. New kinds of international solidarity are not compatible with a reality that includes an American labour movement that has been unable to organize its own "South"; a Mexican labour movement in which workers at different auto plants within the same company can't even communicate with each other; and a Canadian movement that can't organize the fastest-growing sectors (private service).

Under these circumstances, if labour wants to challenge the internationalism of the corporations, it must first be strong nationally. However, national strength does not simply mean strong national governments. Such governments legislated wage controls, imposed the FTA, skewed taxes against working people, and forced cut-backs in the social wage on the general population ("for its own good"). Similarly, national strength means more than allegedly strong unions. Unions that are strong enough to sell wage concessions and false partnerships will reinforce rather than challenge the view that there is no alternative.

Rather, national strength requires local and national institutions—unions, community organizations, political parties, and the service and administrative bodies within the various levels of the state—that are accessible to working people, and that are democratic and effective. These institutions must be able to articulate working-class needs and fight on behalf of and alongside workers in their struggles. Only on such a national base can internationalism be meaningfully achieved.

While the Canadians were breaking away from the international union (which was really an American-based union with a Canadian section) and concentrating on building a strong national union and national movement, the CAW also increased its commitment to internationalism. After the split, the CAW channelled more resources into international education and the enforcement of solidarity, especially through its ties to the South African labour movement, South and Central America, and (later) Mexico. In bargaining, the union negotiated a company-paid Social Justice Fund which financed important international projects. These international ties included some awareness of long-term self-interest but they could not be, and generally were not, justified in terms of developing goals such as "international bargaining" or "joint efforts to affect corporate decisions." They reflected cultural solidarity, and a direct identification with workers in struggle.

The struggles in other countries would be fought on a national basis, and the role of internationalism was both modest and indirect: to attract national and international attention to issues, to provide financial assistance and technical and moral support, and to act nationally to limit the power and ideology of capital. If Canadians and American autoworkers could resist their employers' attempts to speed up the line, Volkswagen workers in Mexico would face less pressure to work at a pace that forced 40-year-olds into involuntary retirement. If Canadians could challenge the logic of competitiveness (rather than try to compete with fellow workers in other countries), then workers in South Africa would feel less isolated when they also resisted that logic. In essence, progressive internationalism can only be built on a strong and progressive nationalism.

Confidence and Independence

Given the pressures of globalization and the dependent relationship that had existed within the union and Canada for so long, how did the Canadian UAW develop the self-confidence to attempt a split from its parent organization?

Unions do not set out explicitly to develop confidence. On the contrary, concrete issues and struggles absorb their time and energy. And while educational campaigns and policies can help, it is the struggles themselves, rather than any prearranged plan, that build collective confidence. Yet building confidence contributes to no less than building the potential of the union to survive attacks and initiate progress. In a sense, the entire history of the Canadian UAW centres on the development of that potential amongst its activists and members.

As Big Three bargaining developed in the early eighties, each step further escalated the stakes and each success seemed to build the Canadian UAW's ability and confidence to act independently.... Struggles outside the Big

Three—against wage controls, with antiunion employers, over plant closures and wage concessions—set the stage for the Canadian UAW's decision in early spring of 1982 to reject the American proposal of opening the Ford and GM collective agreements. In a sense, once the actual decision was made, rejection of the American direction was relatively easy to uphold, since it didn't require the Canadians to go on strike or risk immediate retaliation. The real test was to come when the agreements expired and the alternative was a strike; would the companies let them get away with trying to achieve more than the Americans?

The mood within the labour movement was sombre and even sympathetic; reporters were writing articles on the defeat of labour. An editorial in the *Financial Times* in April, 1980, warned against any economic stimulus. The economic establishment was determined to let the 1979 recession continue as a crucial part of the fight against inflation and to break the resistance of the stubborn labour movement. In the early eighties, unemployment was higher in Canada than in any other developed capitalist country.

And in the auto industry, a report by Ross Perry, *The Future of Canada's Auto Industry*, summarized the prevailing pessimism: "Two recent studies predicted a reduction [in jobs] in the range of 30 and 50 percent from the peak employment year 1978 to the mid-1980s. This amounts to a loss of between 29,000 and 41,000 direct wage-earning jobs. These forecasts are based on conservative assumptions...." In this context, unions were wondering if they could resist the concessionary patterns being set in the U.S., especially after the once powerful and still respected American UAW felt compelled to move in that direction.

GM was the target in the fall of 1982. As the negotiations began, the new GM president calmly made the same threats that had, in the United States, led to the rally of public support for the company. He declared publicly in September 1982, that a refusal by the Canadians to fall in line with the Americans could lead to the full-scale closure of facilities and plant relocation. It was, however, one thing to ask workers to "do their part" and another to threaten entire communities with devastation if they didn't comply. Rather than mobilizing public support, the comments sparked a public backlash (in future, GM and other companies laid the groundwork for their demands with slightly more sophistication).

The lay-offs in the industry, especially the scheduled weeks of downtime, were so pervasive during the 1982 negotiations that the union had difficulty finding a strike deadline during which even half the workers would be working. On the dates that would have been the normal deadline at Ford, for example, no assembly plant was scheduled to work. The union took a cautious position: it recognized not only that times were difficult, but also that it faced an environment that differed from the American one (e.g. Canadian inflation was higher). The union had done its homework; it publicly took advantage of GM's vulnerable position as a foreign multinational. It also sent the clear message to the company that it would settle if the company made a reasonable offer, but that it was ready to fight if GM forced it to the wall.

General Motors decided that a war would be too costly and settled without a strike. It succeeded in removing the PPH program from the agreement though the Canadian agreements retained it slightly longer than those of the Americans. The company did not ask the Canadians to repay the COLA that workers had retained by not reopening, and the Canadians won a small wage increase, over and above COLA. The Canadians breathed a sigh of relief. Their gains were modest, but they had challenged the Big Three collective bargaining system—including both the companies and their own union—and survived.

Unfortunately, the feelings of relief were short-lived. A dispute at Chrysler followed, and the Chrysler workers stated their demands in absolute terms. They had lost $1.15 per hour when the concessions agreement removed COLA. Other catch-up demands could wait; the workers wanted first and foremost to reinstate COLA. Chrysler had offered the American workers a continuation of the agreement with future COLA but without the restoration of the lost COLA and other wage increases. The workers rejected the agreement by a vote of two to one but the union leadership convinced them that a strike would be suicidal. They therefore ended up in limbo, with no agreement and no strike.

In Canada, the company, newspaper editorials, and every consultant on the continent were joined by the international union itself in warning workers that the cupboard was bare. With the added authority of President Doug Fraser's vantage point on Chrysler's board of directors, the UAW was telling the Canadians that their demands were unreasonable. An increase as small as 25 cents per hour would push Chrysler into bankruptcy and cause the loss of hundreds of thousands of jobs. If the Canadians demanded more, Chrysler might actually do what GM had only threatened—leave Canada.

The Canadian UAW's analysis concluded that the wage issue had little or nothing to do with Chrysler's survival. The key was economic recovery and Chrysler's ability to return to full-capacity utilization. Nor did it make sense for Chrysler to move out of Canada. Relocation would be extremely costly, and the company could make substantial profits in Canada even at the wages the workers insisted on. Nevertheless, Chrysler did have the power to carry out any decision it made, and the Canadians had no guarantees.

The leadership decided the risk was necessary, and the membership simultaneously made it clear—by way of wildcats, at membership meetings, and through their bargaining committees—that it wouldn't accept any other decision. The strike began on 5 November 1982. During the Chrysler strike, newspaper reporters had been told by their editors to balance the stories by finding breaks in solidarity. But the reporters were themselves surprised at the degree of support for the strike on the picket lines and at the workers' ability to argue against concessions and justify demands. The solidarity of the workers was overwhelming across all the Canadian units.

Chrysler's expectation that pressure on the workers would weaken the union did not come true; in fact community support from other unions, many local businesses, and sections of the church was growing. Nor did the company's hope—that, one way or another, the Canadians would be influenced by their parent organization in Detroit—materialize.

Chrysler's top negotiators arrived from the U.S. The head of finance came. UAW president Doug Fraser came. And Iacocca himself slipped quietly into Toronto to meet with White. After a five-week strike, it was Chrysler that made the concessions. The company agreed to the opening day economic demands of the workers, and the Canadians even won an acceptable increase for the Americans (75 cents per hour plus future COLA). By 1985, Chrysler was recording the highest profits in its 60-year history while paying wages that were higher than those it had earlier warned would result in bankruptcy.

The Chrysler strike had "really done it." The Canadians had achieved something that the American union was not only unable to do, but had in fact relinquished. They had also shown that they could generate the pressure necessary to force the Americans to come to Canada and negotiate on the basis of Canadian demands. Along the way, they proved that their analysis and intuition were correct, while the experts (including the union leadership in the U.S.) were wrong. The Canadian David had been smarter and tougher than the American Goliath, and even non-union Canadians expressed admiration.

Then came the 1984 bargaining round. General Motors had settled in the U.S. with no real wage increases built into the agreement (the ratification vote was only 57 percent). The Canadians decided to target GM again. Chrysler had not yet been brought back to pattern (i.e., parity with GM and Ford) so it wasn't an option. Since Ford hadn't yet settled in the U.S., targeting Ford risked entanglement in the American strategy. If, for example, the U.S. went on strike while Canada was already on strike, the Canadians could be left hanging until the Americans had settled. This vulnerability was the last thing the Canadian union needed.

This time, the confrontation dealt with who had ultimate authority over the bargaining program in Canada—the Canadian director or the UAW president. The 1982 GM settlement in Canada had been reached without a strike, and the American leadership had rationalized the differences in terms of higher Canadian inflation and the profit-sharing plans, negotiated by the Americans and rejected by the Canadians. At Chrysler later that year, the Americans disagreed with the timing of the Canadian demands (i.e., immediate restoration of the COLA float) but they couldn't criticize the Canadians' ultimate goal: bringing Chrysler back to parity with GM and Ford. Now, however, the union was involved in pattern bargaining for the entire Canadian auto industry. The Canadians were asserting independence and, by their actions, essentially saying to American workers, who were themselves questioning the leadership of their union, "Hey! You don't have to go down that road!"

It is possible to imagine the two sections of the union simply deciding to follow their own agendas within the same international union. Other unions seemed to have managed this arrangement. However, this plan was not an option given the specific nature of the UAW as an organization, and the lack of consensus within the American section on its own direction. There is no other example in the history of bargaining of a relationship that is as integrated as that between Canada and the U.S. in the Big Three negotiations. In fact, there are very few domestic industries with such integrated bargaining. Workers doing the same job have generally earned the same wage, whether they worked for GM, Ford, or Chrysler and whether they worked in Canada or the United States. In the past, rigid wage parity was a source of strength for the workers on both sides of the border; at a time of strain, it became an inflexibility that the structure couldn't handle.

To be more accurate, the structure invited comparisons. It was those comparisons that the American leadership, rather than the union structure, couldn't handle. The American leadership, in its attempt to sell the new direction, was meeting stiff resistance from American workers; the last thing it wanted was a Canadian presence that highlighted this resistance at conventions and intercorporate conferences, and most of all by their bargaining directions and outcomes.

The bargaining with GM Canada was unsuccessful, in part because the American UAW leadership warned GM to limit what it gave to the Canadians. The Canadians went on strike—nervous and very apprehensive about the high stakes, and with the knowledge that the company and the American leadership of their own union were talking to each other. But by this time, the Canadian union had defined its course, and it understood that it had substantial bargaining clout. Although the common perception of globalization was that it represented a shift in power to the corporations, leaving workers relatively defenceless, the Canadians knew better. Corporations were indeed more powerful, but the internationalization of production also left companies more vulnerable at any particular point in time.

In the past, the corporations usually retained excess capacity to meet sudden increases in demand, and they often had the luxury of double-sourcing: if one plant shut down, another could pick up some of the slack. But as the companies cut overhead to save costs, this flexibility also disappeared. And as they reduced duplication, increased specialization, and moved to just-in-time production, many groups of workers were left with the power to affect a disproportionately wide range of a company's operations. The Canadian strike made this power especially clear, as 50,000 American workers were soon laid off, with more to follow.

The catch was that the companies retained the power to move those crucial parts of their operations, though at some cost, to locations where the workers were under "better control." As a result, the Canadians had both the power to win and, as one worker put it, the power to hang themselves. The union had to balance its demands, taking corporate warnings of competitive limits with a grain of salt, but also aware that the threats were not just propaganda.

In the long term, that balance could be shifted in the workers' favour only if national and international legislation limited corporate mobility, and if workers' militancy became more generalized on a global basis. International ad hoc militancy—with or without formal international links—would at least leave the corporations nervous about the expense of relocation with the possible rise of militancy at the new site.

The Canadian leadership made it clear that whether or not its strike was approved by the parent organization, it would strike for the right to share in the industry's growth in productivity. The solidarity of the workers was strong, and after a 13-day strike, GM conceded annual improvements for each year of the agreement. This increase wasn't labelled the traditional AIF, but was renamed "special Canadian adjustment" (SCA) and added to COLA rather than the base rate; like COLA and the base rate, the SCA was included in calculating overtime, premiums, vacation pay, etc. The reason for this creative introduction of yet another initialism into the agreement was to obscure the visibility of the Canadian gains and limit the antagonism of the American UAW. The workers ratified the agreement by a vote of almost six to one.

The GM strike confirmed the ability of the Canadian UAW to act independently in the most difficult of circumstances. The union had taken on the largest manufacturing company in the world and shown that, in spite of globalization, workers had a measure of power. The workers had confronted their own union and established their own Canadian pattern. The face of the union now wore a giddy smile. That smile mixed pride, surprise at the union's progress, growing self-confidence, and nervousness about the ultimate step of permanently separating from the international union and past dependency.

The Split

Detroit's interference in the Canadian negotiations made future change in the bargaining relationship inevitable. The bargaining successes were obviously crucial in allaying the apprehension that remained, but also critical was the role played by the Canadian director, Bob White.

White had many of the attributes of other leaders: he was clever and bright, articulate, astute in sizing up both people and situations, and he revelled in responsibility and tough decisions. Like all leaders in the UAW, he had been significantly influenced by the social unionism of Walter Reuther. Although originally opposed to Dennis McDermott's appointment as director of the Canadian region, White worked closely with McDermott and credited him with influencing White's own social perspectives.

White's greatest attribute was that he clearly understood who he represented. Electoral politics was very important, but always secondary to the impact of any policy or event on working people and the union. The workers and their union were the foundation of both bargaining and future political strength. His personal ties to the international leadership were painful to break, but he would never let those ties stand in the way of his representing Canadian workers.

Robert White was the first (and only) Canadian labour leader to become a media star; he was a nationalist speaking for the underdog, youthful and open. He respected the media, understood it, and used it, but he never overestimated it or became overly dependent on its judgements. He spoke to the members through the media, and the status the media conferred on White was shared by the membership. Through the news clips of White speaking to and often even on behalf of Canadians, UAW activists and members began to see themselves as leading a fight that extended beyond their interests to a broader national arena. White had not intended to make history by leading a breakaway from the international union. His great contribution as a leader was that when the historic opportunity did arise, he didn't try to escape from it.

White had decided to go to the Canadian Council in early December to garner support for autonomy demands from the international union. (White wanted to ensure that the Canadian bargaining conference would set Canadian goals, and that the control over the right to strike, over access to the strike fund, and over Canadian staff would rest with the Canadian director.) Just before the council meeting, White called a meeting to inform the staff of his intentions and to test the waters. The six-hour session included arguments for and against taking the steps that would very likely lead to the split. The impressive overall commitment of the staff members to press ahead in spite of any risks to themselves—their paycheques came from Detroit—reinforced White's determination and strengthened the resolution he took to the council. As was happening in the union overall, the struggle over the future of the Canadian UAW had unified the staff and brought out the best in them.

The debate at the council was equally impressive. Some delegates made passionate appeals for international solidarity and historic ties, and a few questioned whether the union could survive on its own. But the delegates had been through enough over the past few years to clearly understand that they had to assert their autonomy. No one really expected Detroit's reaction to lead to anything but a split. The only questions for most delegates were when the split would occur and under what conditions.

When, as expected, the international executive board rejected those conditions, White returned to the council on 11 December 1984. The Canadian union's "parliament" decided that day, virtually unanimously, to establish a new Canadian union. Of 350 delegates, only four voted against the decision. In his own comments to the council, White emphasized that, with the formation of their own union, Canadians could no longer blame the Americans for any failures. The point of full autonomy was full responsibility.

The new union would obviously need a governing structure between conventions that was broader than its current single elected officer (the director). White proposed the formation of a 12-member national executive board (NEB), which would (in line with caucus sensitivities) be representative of all sections of the union. Eventually, affirmative action positions were included for two women and one person of colour. To limit potential bureaucratization, only three officers would hold full-time positions: the president, the secretary-treasurer, and the Quebec director. Since the remaining officers would retain their current union functions, officers would, in some cases, continue to work on a part-time or full-time basis in the workplace.

Because the two large locals in Quebec themselves could dominate any vote in Quebec and thereby choose one of the NEB members, the overall convention formally elected the Quebec director. In fact, this "safety valve" was never used; the elected Quebec caucus member was rubber-stamped by the delegates in recognition of Quebec's unique status. This procedure was later modified so that Quebec's candidate for the board did not need the ratification of the convention.

The three full-time officers, plus two others, would be elected at the convention. The remaining seven would include those elected as executive officers of the Canadian Council (six), plus the elected president of the Quebec Council. This method allowed for a partial integration of the council and NEB structures but also assured some stability in the case of a radical electoral change in the union. A complete change would have to occur over two elections at least a year apart (i.e., at the convention and the Council meeting).

Within the union, the remaining controversy over the split was as much about the process as about the decision. This controversy was especially heated at the crucial and politically divided Oshawa Local (Local 222). Some members argued that the Canadian Council had no constitutional authority to make such a decision and that, considering the fundamental nature of the decision, the council should have called for a referendum vote. They were right about the council not having the constitutional blessing to make the decision, but a referendum in Canada also held no "constitutional authority." The central issue was not constitutional authority; it was the democratic legitimacy of the split in Canada.

The option of a referendum was discussed in some depth at the national office. The reason for its ultimate rejection was that, while adding little, it created substantial risk. There was no question that the members overwhelmingly supported the split. The staff, local activists, and the delegates elected to council were in regular contact with members and readily confirmed this support, as did the meetings and newspapers of the local unions. Even former UAW president Doug Fraser, who was critical of the Canadians for leaving, laughed when asked about a referendum vote; according to Fraser, "White would easily get 85 percent." The concern about a referendum was less about letting the members decide—they had made their feelings known through other forums—than about creating an opening for others outside the Canadian UAW to intervene, even at the last moment.

The companies had already mentioned that they were rethinking future investments. If the Council announced a vote, the companies could have escalated such warnings in order to influence the debate. The American UAW knew that White had the full support of the leadership. If there was an in-plant vote, however, the UAW could certainly release rumours about a refusal to transfer any monies to the new union, leaving it without a strike fund and reinforcing concerns about staff salaries and services. Since the collective agreements were legally with the parent union, not the Canadian UAW, it could be argued that once the Canadian office led a breakaway, that office was no longer the bargaining agent for any of the units in Canada.

An elected union official in Local 222, the largest Local in the union, actually raised this issue with the Ontario Labour Relations Board to give the government an excuse to step in and challenge the council decision. If the Oshawa Local had subsequently decided to stay in the international organization, the resolution to split might have quickly unravelled. Other GM units would not have wanted to be separated from Oshawa, and other Big Three workers would be worried about bargaining without GM. As it turned out, while the membership meetings eventually held in Oshawa were rambunctious, workers still voted overwhelmingly to support the council decision.

Once the Canadian Council made its decision and exhibited the solidarity that would discourage the companies, the government, or the UAW from trying to intimidate Canadian workers, it asked each Local to hold meetings to ratify the decision. Any Local that chose to reject the decision and form a new union could stay with the international union. At the meeting of Local 251 in Wallaceburg, 58 percent of the membership of about 1,500 decided to stay with the UAW.

Over the nine months following the council decision, financial and legal matters were settled. The UAW agreed to transfer $36 million to the Canadians; this amount was less than their fair share but it was sufficient to equip the new union with an adequate strike fund and some cash for administrative purposes. At the founding convention in early September, 1985, the Canadian UAW formally established the new union, and in the summer of 1986, the union was renamed the Canadian Auto Workers.

A Culture of Resistance

The massive disinvestments in auto and the dissolution of the Autopact predicted by the experts in the event of a Canadian split didn't materialize. Yet economic restructuring both within the workplace and through plant closures was taking its toll. The new Mulroney government had made clear—after the election, of course—that it would shift power to the corporations by way of a greater reliance on markets and competitiveness. The test of any policy or activity would be whether or not it increased Canada's competitiveness in business terms.

In the mid-eighties, the CAW suffered casualties in terms of plant closures, especially in the auto parts sector, and any gains that were made were generally limited and vulnerable to future changes. But the union continued to fight back. This stubborn resistance was central to the CAW's survival and strength as a social force in the country. One measure of the strength of the new union was that, after the split, it did not withdraw into a shell to consolidate, rebuild, and establish some breathing room. Its activism at all levels increased with barely a missed beat. Expectations were raised, Detroit's valuable services were more than adequately replaced, and rather than having to cope with the loss of financial subsidies from the UAW, the CAW found itself with additional resources for its own priorities. The split didn't drain or divert the CAW; it energized the union.

The attitude of the new union was that it could and should participate in all relevant struggles. It supported other workers on strike, made organizing even more of a priority, invested a sizable portion of its strike fund in modernizing and expanding the education centre, assisted locals in developing their own newspapers, introduced innovations in bargaining, and played a vital national role in the crucial debate over free trade and the future of the country.

The first act of the new union involved a group of young women who had, with the support of the CLC and its affiliates, taken on one of the most powerful institutions in the country—the Canadian Bank of Commerce. Along with other unions, the Canadian UAW contributed money for strike pay, and it also provided staff. The minute the formation of the CAW was officially declared, the bank workers marched into the convention in Toronto.

After giving the workers a boisterous feet-stomping ovation, the CAW delegates followed the strikers, many single mothers and immigrant women, out of the hotel and down Bay Street to the bank's headquarters. For the CAW, this support indicated recognition of the changing nature of the workforce and made a statement about solidarity with low-paid workers.

The union's first two financial decisions were also significant. They involved organizing and education; that is, expanding the union's membership base and deepening its commitment. The responsible Canadian section of the union had, since the sixties, led all regions within the UAW in organizing. With its new independence, it decided to hire 10 additional organizers for a year to protect existing standards in the union and accelerate the recruitment of new workers. The decision was in part related to the opportunities created by the wave of media attention surrounding the split. The CAW had been receiving increasing numbers of calls from groups of workers attracted by both the union's well-publicized successes and the fact that it was becoming Canadian (which, to these workers, meant that decisions were made in Canada, not in a foreign country, and that money collected in Canada stayed in the country).

The decision regarding education was much more costly and risky. It involved the rebuilding and expansion of the union's education centre in Port Elgin. That expenditure reflected the priority the union placed on education and was indicative of the permanence of the CAW. It announced that the union was here to stay and that it was building for the future. This education centre belonged to the workers. At Port Elgin, workers exchanged information about the latest management strategies in the workplace, tried to get a handle on the deficit, and learned about a history they had previously been denied—their own. It was a place where they studied the role of workers in the scheme of things. Port Elgin was also the home of the CAW's unique Family Education Program. Run in the summer as two weeks of vacation and education for the families of CAW members, the program symbolized the union's commitment to integrating the family and union culture. And, as the home of the Canadian Council, Port Elgin was the place where activists renewed contacts with old friends and later met in crowded rooms to share rumours and complaints or out-yell each other in debates. Paintings, photographs, and posters reflected everyday lives and paid tribute to past struggles. At Port Elgin, working people were more than "just workers."

In collective bargaining, the union consolidated its separation from the U.S. and tried to restore the notion that bargaining was not about corporate demands (concessions) but about workers' demands (sharing in progress, improving the workplace). The union lobbied for legislated changes, and when Parliament wavered under corporate pressure, as it did with indexed pensions and advanced lay-off notice in Ontario, the union confronted it in bargaining—both to win gains and to demonstrate that the change in legislation was in fact practical. And with its new control over its finances, the CAW was able to provide financial support for the struggles of other unions when they came for help: woodworkers on the West Coast, telephone workers in Newfoundland, food-processing workers in Alberta, public sector workers in Ottawa.

The "culture of resistance" that had developed in the union was rooted in a historical legacy and recent involvement in struggles. The role of education was to reinforce and consolidate that culture ("education" also included films, pamphlets, union newspapers, music, and even writing classes that encouraged workers to resist the dominant culture and tell their own stories). As a culture that permeated the union, it did not depend on or wait for leadership from "the top." Local activists and members proved themselves quite capable of leading on their own. The best example of this autonomy was in aerospace, where the local leadership at de Havilland Aircraft and then McDonnell-Douglas took on the issue of health and safety and led the largest collective refusals Canada had ever seen.

When Mulroney announced his intention to move towards the FTA with the United States in 1986, the CAW was there in opposition with its credibility and organizational/financial clout. Leadership meetings and forums were held in every community with a CAW base across the country. Bob White, as leader of the CAW, was generally viewed as a central leader and spokesperson for the anti-free trade coalition. Over one million pamphlets were distributed in the plants, to homes, at schools, and in malls. Full-page ads appeared in newspapers across the country when opposition to the agreement was flagging and in need of revitalization. And CAW activists across the country brought the issue into the plants and worked with others to introduce more Canadians to politics by way of the anti-FTA fight.

In spite of the subsequent close defeat, the fight against free trade proved the potential of the Canadian labour movement and highlighted its importance as a relevant and democratic social force. Without the intervention of the labour movement, the crucial debate over the future direction of the country would have been a brief and hardly noticeable interruption in Canadian life. In the past, the economic and political elite of the country had always been divided on free trade. Now, however, business was united in its favour; the media, with a few exceptions, endorsed that support; and opposition from the NDP had no fire. Canadian labour, along with its resource-poor but commitment-rich coalition partners, forced a national discussion which, at least for a brief moment, had the establishment nervously making accommodating promises.

After the 1988 federal election, Bob White of the CAW and Leo Gerrard of the steelworkers' union each wrote scathing public criticisms of the NDP's belated and tepid handling of the free trade issue. The tone of the criticisms didn't suggest any break with support for the party, but it highlighted an emerging change in labour's attitude to the party.

The labour movement seemed to be rebelling against past notions that the NDP had all the political savvy and labour's role was to provide the bodies and money. The movement was asserting that it had fully understood the significance and potential of the free trade issue while the party caucus had not; that it had broadened the notion of politics and mobilized public opinion in a way their the party had not; and that even in terms of narrow electoral strategies, it was right and the party was wrong. While these events were encouraging in terms of labour's development, they reflected the NDP's inability to deal with the new economic times. That failure would reveal itself even more painfully in the 1990s. The comment made by Charlotte Yates in *From Plant to Politics* on the relationship between the CCF/NDP and the UAW/CAW in the early eighties seemed to be confirmed: "The party moved away from its social democratic principles towards a more conservative political image at the same time that the UAW was becoming more politically militant in its own action.... As had happened so many times in the past, the UAW and the NDP were marching to the beat of two different drummers."

The UAW made its breakthrough in Oshawa in 1937, after a 15-day strike against GM. That strike was dragged out and given national significance by the interference of the premier of Ontario. In 1984, another strike at GM of similar duration was catapulted into national prominence by an external player. This time, the interference came from the source that had inspired the Canadians to establish their own branch of the UAW in the thirties, but whose own spirit had since been sapped—the American UAW. The internal UAW conflict that was the inevitable result led to the formation of a new Canadian union. The breakthrough of 1937 had developed into the breakaway of 1984.

This event had a current context and immediate causes, but it cannot be fully understood without reaching back to the past. The autoworkers were not the first to break away from an American-based union. Other unions in telecommunications, paper, and chemical had made this move in the seventies. What gave the split of the Canadian UAW such importance was not only the union's prominence in Canada, but its past role as a leading defender of international unionism and the issues and timing surrounding the break with the Americans.

The Canadian move to independence was a statement about coming of age that contrasted with the country's own increasing economic dependence on the United States. The split was therefore also one step in the building of a Canadian working class. The significance of this step is not that Canadians are inherently superior, but that the struggle to improve workers' lives and communities can only be won if it is fought on the basis of a national project linked to a national labour movement. History isn't made in the abstract, but in specific spaces with specific cultural, economic, administrative, and political histories.

The years just before and after the split were probably the most exciting in the history of the Canadian UAW. This excitement had less to do with good times (old problems persisted and new ones arrived) than with the union remaining a place where it was still possible to fight for, and hang on to, alternative ideals. The issue the union now faced was whether, in these most difficult of times, it could maintain that twin sense of resistance and possibilities.

Critical-Thinking Questions

1. How did the CSN (CNTU) grow as a union movement after 1960? How did its ideas about Quebec society and its role in it change with the emergence of several types of separatism?
2. Why did professionals, such as nurses, seek collective bargaining and the right to strike after 1960? What barriers did they face that made the 1988 Alberta nurses' strike illegal?
3. What changes in the workplace contributed to new health-and-safety laws in Canada in the 1970s? How did unions' experience with occupational health-and-safety situations cause them to relate to environmental issues?
4. What changes in the Canadian economy and society contributed to the emergence of the fast-food industry? What was the nature of work and the quality of working conditions for employees in such jobs, and why were they non-union?
5. How did globalization affect the Canadian economy of unionized workers? What repercussions did these changes have on the auto industry, auto unions, and autoworkers?

Further Readings

Crean, Susan. *Grace Hartman: A Woman For Her Time* (Toronto, New Star Books, 1995). Crean's biography of Grace Hartman, the first female leader of the Canadian Union of Public Employees, discusses the post-war period of rapid membership growth amongst public-sector workers during her tenure and the resulting challenges.

Duffy, Ann, Daniel Glenday, and Norene Pupo. *Good Jobs, Bad Jobs, No Jobs: The Transformation of Work in the Twenty-First Century* (Toronto: Harcourt Brace, 1997). Written by sociologists, these essays seek to examine the changing job market in the late twentieth century with its insecurities, and often, poor work standards, sporadic layoffs, long hours, and no unions.

Rapaport, David. *No Justice, No Peace: the 1996 OPSEU Strike against the Harris Government in Ontario* (Montreal and Kingston: McGill-Queen's University Press, 1999). Depicting the conflict between the Canadian labour movement and the anti-labour, neo-conservative Harris government in Ontario, Rapaport analyzes how OPSEU managed to survive a strike, which it considered a win and which many pundits had predicted would collapse.

Reiter, Ester. *Making Fast Food* (Montreal and Kingston: McGill-Queens' University Press, 1996). With the rise of the fast-food industry in Canada, Reiter investigates working conditions among its employees, particularly the young and seniors who often work part-time. She herself gained first-hand experience working for a major employer, while conducting research interviews.

Roberts, Wayne. *"Don't Call Me Servant": Government Work and Unions in Ontario, 1911–1984* (Toronto: Ontario Public Service Employees Union, 1994). This historical monograph discusses the jobs and status of Ontario civil servants, who made a transition from being members of an association to forming a new union and seeking collective bargaining rights.

White, Bob. *Hard Bargains: My Life on the Line* (Toronto: McClelland and Stewart, 1987). In his autobiography, Bob White writes about his rapid rise during his career in the Canadian labour movement, first as an auto worker, then as head of the UAW, and finally as the President of the Canadian Labour Congress.

White, Julie. *Sisters and Solidarity: Women and Unions in Canada* (Toronto: Thompson Educational, 1993). White discusses the increase in women union members in Canada, which accompanied the rise in female employment generally after World War II. She investigates their issues, demonstrates their activism and their struggle to win leadership positions in the labour movement, and points out that to grow organized labour needs to organize the private-service sector where many poorly paid women work.